International Children's Rights Instruments

International Children's Rights Instruments

Edited by

Karl Hanson, Ton Liefaard, Roberta Ruggiero,
Elena Patrizi, Katrien Klep, and Lucy Opoka

BRILL | NIJHOFF

LEIDEN | BOSTON

The open access publication of this book has been published with the support of Centre for Children's Rights Studies, University of Geneva; Department of Child Law, Leiden University; and Children's Rights European Academic Network (CREAN)

Library of Congress Cataloging-in-Publication Data

Title: International children's rights instruments: spectacle and affect of monument removal / edited by Karl Hanson, Ton Liefaard, Roberta Ruggiero, Elena Patrizi, Katrien Klep, and Lucy Opoka.
Description: Leiden ; Boston : Brill/Nijhoff, 2025. |
Identifiers: LCCN 2024048387 (print) | LCCN 2024048388 (ebook) | ISBN 9789004681217 (hardback) | ISBN 9789004681224 (ebook)
Subjects: LCSH: Children (International law) | Children's rights. | Children–Legal status, laws, etc.
Classification: LCC K639 .I565 2025 (print) | LCC K639 (ebook) | DDC 341.4/8572–dc23/eng/20241017
LC record available at https://lccn.loc.gov/2024048387
LC ebook record available at https://lccn.loc.gov/2024048388

Typeface for the Latin, Greek, and Cyrillic scripts: "Brill". See and download: brill.com/brill-typeface.

ISBN 978-90-04-68121-7 (hardback)
ISBN 978-90-04-68122-4 (e-book)
DOI 10.1163/9789004681224

This book is printed on acid-free paper and produced in a sustainable manner.

Contents

Notes on Editors

Karl Hanson
is the Director of the Centre for Children's Rights Studies and a Professor at the Faculty of Law, University of Geneva, Switzerland. He teaches primarily in the *Master interdisciplinaire en droits de l'enfant* and the *Master of Advanced Studies in Children's Rights*. Additionally, he lectures on children's rights at the Faculties of Law of both the University of Geneva and the University of Zurich. His research and publications focus on interdisciplinary children's rights theories, working children and child labour norms and policies, international children's rights law, and juvenile justice. Karl Hanson serves as Chair of the Children's Rights European Academic Network (CREAN) and is a co-editor of the journal *Childhood*.

Ton Liefaard
is Professor of Children's Rights and holds the UNICEF Chair in Children's Rights at the Department of Child Law and Health Law of Leiden University, The Netherlands. He has founded the Master of Laws: Advanced Studies in International Children's Rights and initiated the Leiden Children's Rights Observatory, an open access platform on children's rights jurisprudence. He teaches and publishes widely on issues related to international children's rights, including the UN Convention on the Rights of the Child, juvenile justice, child friendly justice, deprivation of liberty of children, violence against children and access to justice for children.

Roberta Ruggiero
is Director of the Children's Rights Academy at the Centre for Children's Rights Studies of the University of Geneva, Switzerland. Her publications and primary research interests lie in interdisciplinary Children's Rights Studies, including critical analysis of States' compliance with international legal children's rights obligations, impact assessments of public policies and actors, and the role of knowledge brokering between academia and policymakers. She is the author and co-editor of several books, including *Monitoring State Compliance with the UN Convention on the Rights of the Child*.

Elena Patrizi
is Ph.D. Candidate at the Faculty of Law and Research Assistant at the Centre for Children's Rights Studies of the University of Geneva, Switzerland. She holds a Master's Degree in Law from the University of Urbino (2013) and an

LLM in International Humanitarian Law and Human Rights from the Geneva Academy (2016).

Katrien Klep
is Assistant Professor in Child Law at Leiden University, The Netherlands. She teaches and publishes on issues related to international children's rights, especially access to justice for children and Independent Children's Rights Institutions.

Lucy Opoka
is Ph.D. Candidate at the Department of Child Law and Health Law of Leiden University, The Netherlands. She holds a Bachelor's Degree in Law from the Catholic University of Eastern Africa (2013) and an Advanced LLM in International Children's Rights from Leiden University (2019).

Introduction

International Children's Rights, a Complex Field of Law

This comprehensive collection of international children's rights instruments is an essential and fully accessible resource for students, researchers and professionals in the field of children's human rights. The collection supplements the several academic handbooks on children's rights studies and on international children's rights law that have been published during the recent years (see below for a selection of some of the most important handbooks and reference works). Over the years, the international legal framework of children's rights has developed into a complex set of different legal sources that regulate the protection of the human rights and fundamental freedoms of children. The complexity of the framework results from the co-existence of and interaction between United Nations treaties and resolutions, regional human rights instruments, including treaties, recommendations, resolutions and guidelines, and legal instruments in adjacent fields of international law, including private and public international law. For students, researchers, and professionals, it is critical to have a comprehensive overview of these sources of law relevant to children's rights and to have easy access to them. This collection, which is the result of a collaboration between two well-established Master's programmes in children's rights, aims to provide for this.

University of Geneva – Master of Advanced Studies in Children's Rights

The Master of Advanced Studies in Children's Rights (MCR) is a part-time international and interdisciplinary postgraduate programme on children's rights. The programme is designed for professionals who work within the children's rights field, and it offers an advanced interdisciplinary approach to the study of children's rights. The MCR takes advantage of its geographical location and academic context, by including customized visits to Geneva-based international organizations and through the active participation of international rewarded scholars and experts coming from all over the world.

 | DOI:10.1163/9789004681224_002

Leiden University – Master of Laws: Advanced Studies in International Children's Rights

The Leiden Advanced LL.M. programme is a small-scale, highly advanced study programme for (post)graduate students from all over the world. Students participate in an international classroom, and are offered in-depth specialization in the rights and interests of children from a legal perspective. Students learn what children's rights mean and how to promote and protect the rights of children around the world, in light of the global challenges of today and tomorrow. Moreover, students will actively engage with the many networks Leiden Law School and Leiden University have to offer.

Content of the Collection

The collection consists of seven sections organised thematically. Each section includes international and/or regional legal documents, both hard and soft law instruments. The themes as well as the instruments were carefully selected by the editorial team and include two sections with general children's rights and human rights instruments respectively, followed by international and regional instruments on the issues of asylum, migration and trafficking, violence and exploitation, child labour, children in the justice system and private international law.

It was unavoidable to be selective and to make choices, some of which were difficult. Consequently, the collection does not provide an exhaustive collection of instruments. Certain areas could not be covered entirely or not at all, which explains why, for example, there are no special sections on international humanitarian law or legal instruments in relation to digital technologies. As far as the regional instruments are concerned, the collection's primary focus is on the Inter-American, European and African regional human rights systems. Other regions were not included, at the cost of, for example, the Southeast Asian region, where children's rights standard-setting has taken place under the auspice of the Association of Southeast Asian Nations (ASEAN). Moreover, General Comments were not included because these can easily be found on the website of the UN Committee on the Rights of the Child and the African Committee of Experts on the Rights and Welfare of the Child.

Diverse Nature of International Children's Rights

The collection reveals the rich nature and diverse range of topics governed by international children's rights law. The effective protection of children's rights will benefit from the acknowledgement that matters of children's rights are increasingly regulated at the international and regional levels. The complex nature of international children's rights law requires the use of various legal sources in close connection with each other. The editors hope that this collection will assist students, researchers and professionals in studying and using international children's rights in a comprehensive and effective manner, which, mindful of Article 41 of the United Nations Convention on the Rights of the Child, will ultimately be conducive to the realisation of the rights of the child.

Acknowledgements

The editors express their gratitude to Brill | Nijhoff publishers for its willingness to publish this collection and for supporting the publishing process. In addition, the editors would like to thank Mike Sikkink, student-assistant at the Department of Child Law of Leiden University, for his support in preparing the manuscript.

Selection of Recently Published Handbooks and Commentaries on Children's Rights

Kilkelly, U., & Liefaard, T. (2020). *International Human Rights of Children*. Springer Nature.

Ruck, M. D., Peterson-Badali, M., & Freeman, M. (2016). *Handbook of Children's Rights: Global and Multidisciplinary Perspectives*. Taylor & Francis.

Tobin, J. (2019). *The UN Convention on the Rights of the Child: A commentary*. Oxford University Press.

Todres, J., & King, S. M. (2020). *The Oxford Handbook of Children's Rights Law*. Oxford University Press.

Vaghri, Z., Zermatten, J., Lansdown, G., & Ruggiero, R. (2022). *Monitoring State Compliance with the UN Convention on the Rights of the Child: An Analysis of Attributes*. Springer Nature.

Vandenhole, W., Desmet, E., Reynaert, D., & Lembrechts, S. (2015). *Routledge International Handbook of Children's Rights Studies.* Routledge.

Vandenhole, W., Türkelli, G. E., & Lembrechts, S. (2019). *Children's Rights: A Commentary on the Convention on the Rights of the Child and Its Protocols.* Edward Elgar Publishing.

PART I

Children's Rights Instruments

CHAPTER 1

Geneva Declaration of the Rights of the Child

Adopted 26 September 1924, League of Nations

By the present Declaration of the Rights of the Child, commonly known as the Declaration of Geneva, men and women of all nations, recognising that mankind owes to the child the best that it has to give, declare and accept it as their duty that, beyond and above all considerations of race, nationality or creed:

I. The child must be given the means requisite for its normal development, both materially and spiritually;

II. The child that is hungry must be fed; the child that is sick must be nursed; the child that is backward must be helped; the delinquent child must be reclaimed; and the orphan and the waif must be sheltered and succoured;

III. The child must be the first to receive relief in times of distress;

IV. The child must be put in a position to earn a livelihood and must be protected against every form of exploitation;

V. The child must be brought up in the consciousness that its talents must be devoted to the service of its fellow men.

CHAPTER 2

Declaration of the Rights of the Child

Proclaimed by General Assembly resolution 1386(XIV) of 20 November 1959

Preamble

Whereas the peoples of the United Nations have, in the Charter, reaffirmed their faith in fundamental human rights and in the dignity and worth of the human person, and have determined to promote social progress and better standards of life in larger freedom,

Whereas the United Nations has, in the Universal Declaration of Human Rights, proclaimed that everyone is entitled to all the rights and freedoms set forth therein, without distinction of any kind, such as race, colour, sex, language, religion, political or other opinion, national or social origin, property, birth or other status,

Whereas the child, by reason of his physical and mental immaturity, needs special safeguards and care, including appropriate legal protection, before as well as after birth,

Whereas the need for such special safeguards has been stated in the Geneva Declaration of the Rights of the Child of 1924, and recognized in the Universal Declaration of Human Rights and in the statutes of specialized agencies and international organizations concerned with the welfare of children,

Whereas mankind owes to the child the best it has to give,

Now therefore,

The General Assembly

Proclaims this Declaration of the Rights of the Child to the end that he may have a happy childhood and enjoy for his own good and for the good of society the rights and freedoms herein set forth, and calls upon parents, upon men and women as individuals, and upon voluntary organizations, local authorities and national Governments to recognize these rights and strive for their observance by legislative and other measures progressively taken in accordance with the following principles:

Principle 1

The child shall enjoy all the rights set forth in this Declaration. Every child, without any exception whatsoever, shall be entitled to these rights, without distinction or discrimination on account of race, colour, sex, language, religion, political or other opinion, national or social origin, property, birth or other status, whether of himself or of his family.

Principle 2

The child shall enjoy special protection, and shall be given opportunities and facilities, by law and by other means, to enable him to develop physically, mentally, morally, spiritually and socially in a healthy and normal manner and in conditions of freedom and dignity. In the enactment of laws for this purpose, the best interests of the child shall be the paramount consideration.

Principle 3

The child shall be entitled from his birth to a name and a nationality.

Principle 4

The child shall enjoy the benefits of social security. He shall be entitled to grow and develop in health; to this end, special care and protection shall be provided both to him and to his mother, including adequate pre-natal and post-natal care. The child shall have the right to adequate nutrition, housing, recreation and medical services.

Principle 5

The child who is physically, mentally or socially handicapped shall be given the special treatment, education and care required by his particular condition.

Principle 6

The child, for the full and harmonious development of his personality, needs love and understanding. He shall, wherever possible, grow up in the care and under the responsibility of his parents, and, in any case, in an atmosphere of affection and of moral and material security; a child of tender years shall not, save in exceptional circumstances, be separated from his mother. Society and the public authorities shall have the duty to extend particular care to children without a family and to those without adequate means of support. Payment of State and other assistance towards the maintenance of children of large families is desirable.

Principle 7

The child is entitled to receive education, which shall be free and compulsory, at least in the elementary stages. He shall be given an education which will promote his general culture, and enable him, on a basis of equal opportunity, to develop his abilities, his individual judgement, and his sense of moral and social responsibility, and to become a useful member of society.

The best interests of the child shall be the guiding principle of those responsible for his education and guidance; that responsibility lies in the first place with his parents.

The child shall have full opportunity for play and recreation, which should be directed to the same purposes as education; society and the public authorities shall endeavour to promote the enjoyment of this right.

Principle 8

The child shall in all circumstances be among the first to receive protection and relief.

Principle 9

The child shall be protected against all forms of neglect, cruelty and exploitation. He shall not be the subject of traffic, in any form.

The child shall not be admitted to employment before an appropriate minimum age; he shall in no case be caused or permitted to engage in any occupation or employment which would prejudice his health or education, or interfere with his physical, mental or moral development.

Principle 10

The child shall be protected from practices which may foster racial, religious and any other form of discrimination. He shall be brought up in a spirit of understanding, tolerance, friendship among peoples, peace and universal brotherhood, and in full consciousness that his energy and talents should be devoted to the service of his fellow men.

CHAPTER 3

Convention on the Rights of the Child

Adopted and opened for signature, ratification and accession by General Assembly resolution 44/25 of 20 November 1989Entry into force 2 September 1990, in accordance with article 49(1)[1]

Preamble

The States Parties to the present Convention,

Considering that, in accordance with the principles proclaimed in the Charter of the United Nations, recognition of the inherent dignity and of the equal and inalienable rights of all members of the human family is the foundation of freedom, justice and peace in the world,

Bearing in mind that the peoples of the United Nations have, in the Charter, reaffirmed their faith in fundamental human rights and in the dignity and worth of the human person, and have determined to promote social progress and better standards of life in larger freedom,

Recognizing that the United Nations has, in the Universal Declaration of Human Rights and in the International Covenants on Human Rights, proclaimed and agreed that everyone is entitled to all the rights and freedoms set forth therein, without distinction of any kind, such as race, colour, sex, language, religion, political or other opinion, national or social origin, property, birth or other status,

Recalling that, in the Universal Declaration of Human Rights, the United Nations has proclaimed that childhood is entitled to special care and assistance,

Convinced that the family, as the fundamental group of society and the natural environment for the growth and well-being of all its members and particularly children, should be afforded the necessary protection and assistance so that it can fully assume its responsibilities within the community,

Recognizing that the child, for the full and harmonious development of his or her personality, should grow up in a family environment, in an atmosphere of happiness, love and understanding,

Considering that the child should be fully prepared to live an individual life in society, and brought up in the spirit of the ideals proclaimed in the Charter

1 The chart of signatures and ratifications as well as the text of declarations and reservations made by States parties can be consulted at https://treaties.un.org.

of the United Nations, and in particular in the spirit of peace, dignity, tolerance, freedom, equality and solidarity,

Bearing in mind that the need to extend particular care to the child has been stated in the Geneva Declaration of the Rights of the Child of 1924 and in the Declaration of the Rights of the Child adopted by the General Assembly on 20 November 1959 and recognized in the Universal Declaration of Human Rights, in the International Covenant on Civil and Political Rights (in particular in articles 23 and 24), in the International Covenant on Economic, Social and Cultural Rights (in particular in article 10) and in the statutes and relevant instruments of specialized agencies and international organizations concerned with the welfare of children,

Bearing in mind that, as indicated in the Declaration of the Rights of the Child, "the child, by reason of his physical and mental immaturity, needs special safeguards and care, including appropriate legal protection, before as well as after birth",

Recalling the provisions of the Declaration on Social and Legal Principles relating to the Protection and Welfare of Children, with Special Reference to Foster Placement and Adoption Nationally and Internationally; the United Nations Standard Minimum Rules for the Administration of Juvenile Justice (The Beijing Rules); and the Declaration on the Protection of Women and Children in Emergency and Armed Conflict,

Recognizing that, in all countries in the world, there are children living in exceptionally difficult conditions, and that such children need special consideration,

Taking due account of the importance of the traditions and cultural values of each people for the protection and harmonious development of the child,

Recognizing the importance of international co-operation for improving the living conditions of children in every country, in particular in the developing countries,

Have agreed as follows:

Part I

Art. 1 For the purposes of the present Convention, a child means every human being below the age of eighteen years unless, under the law applicable to the child, majority is attained earlier.

Art. 2 1. States Parties shall respect and ensure the rights set forth in the present Convention to each child within their jurisdiction without discrimination

of any kind, irrespective of the child's or his or her parent's or legal guardian's race, colour, sex, language, religion, political or other opinion, national, ethnic or social origin, property, disability, birth or other status.
2. States Parties shall take all appropriate measures to ensure that the child is protected against all forms of discrimination or punishment on the basis of the status, activities, expressed opinions, or beliefs of the child's parents, legal guardians, or family members.
Art. 3 1. In all actions concerning children, whether undertaken by public or private social welfare institutions, courts of law, administrative authorities or legislative bodies, the best interests of the child shall be a primary consideration.
2. States Parties undertake to ensure the child such protection and care as is necessary for his or her well-being, taking into account the rights and duties of his or her parents, legal guardians, or other individuals legally responsible for him or her, and, to this end, shall take all appropriate legislative and administrative measures.
3. States Parties shall ensure that the institutions, services and facilities responsible for the care or protection of children shall conform with the standards established by competent authorities, particularly in the areas of safety, health, in the number and suitability of their staff, as well as competent supervision.
Art. 4 States Parties shall undertake all appropriate legislative, administrative, and other measures for the implementation of the rights recognized in the present Convention. With regard to economic, social and cultural rights, States Parties shall undertake such measures to the maximum extent of their available resources and, where needed, within the framework of international co-operation.
Art. 5 States Parties shall respect the responsibilities, rights and duties of parents or, where applicable, the members of the extended family or community as provided for by local custom, legal guardians or other persons legally responsible for the child, to provide, in a manner consistent with the evolving capacities of the child, appropriate direction and guidance in the exercise by the child of the rights recognized in the present Convention.
Art. 6 1. States Parties recognize that every child has the inherent right to life.
2. States Parties shall ensure to the maximum extent possible the survival and development of the child.
Art. 7 1. The child shall be registered immediately after birth and shall have the right from birth to a name, the right to acquire a nationality and, as far as possible, the right to know and be cared for by his or her parents.
2. States Parties shall ensure the implementation of these rights in accordance with their national law and their obligations under the relevant international

instruments in this field, in particular where the child would otherwise be stateless.

Art. 8 1. States Parties undertake to respect the right of the child to preserve his or her identity, including nationality, name and family relations as recognized by law without unlawful interference.

2. Where a child is illegally deprived of some or all of the elements of his or her identity, States Parties shall provide appropriate assistance and protection, with a view to speedily re-establishing his or her identity.

Art. 9 1. States Parties shall ensure that a child shall not be separated from his or her parents against their will, except when competent authorities subject to judicial review determine, in accordance with applicable law and procedures, that such separation is necessary for the best interests of the child. Such determination may be necessary in a particular case such as one involving abuse or neglect of the child by the parents, or one where the parents are living separately and a decision must be made as to the child's place of residence.

2. In any proceedings pursuant to paragraph 1 of the present article, all interested parties shall be given an opportunity to participate in the proceedings and make their views known.

3. States Parties shall respect the right of the child who is separated from one or both parents to maintain personal relations and direct contact with both parents on a regular basis, except if it is contrary to the child's best interests.

4. Where such separation results from any action initiated by a State Party, such as the detention, imprisonment, exile, deportation or death (including death arising from any cause while the person is in the custody of the State) of one or both parents or of the child, that State Party shall, upon request, provide the parents, the child or, if appropriate, another member of the family with the essential information concerning the whereabouts of the absent member(s) of the family unless the provision of the information would be detrimental to the well-being of the child. States Parties shall further ensure that the submission of such a request shall of itself entail no adverse consequences for the person(s) concerned.

Art. 10 1. In accordance with the obligation of States Parties under article 9, paragraph 1, applications by a child or his or her parents to enter or leave a State Party for the purpose of family reunification shall be dealt with by States Parties in a positive, humane and expeditious manner. States Parties shall further ensure that the submission of such a request shall entail no adverse consequences for the applicants and for the members of their family.

2. A child whose parents reside in different States shall have the right to maintain on a regular basis, save in exceptional circumstances personal relations and direct contacts with both parents. Towards that end and in accordance

with the obligation of States Parties under article 9, paragraph 1, States Parties shall respect the right of the child and his or her parents to leave any country, including their own, and to enter their own country. The right to leave any country shall be subject only to such restrictions as are prescribed by law and which are necessary to protect the national security, public order (ordre public), public health or morals or the rights and freedoms of others and are consistent with the other rights recognized in the present Convention.

Art. 11 1. States Parties shall take measures to combat the illicit transfer and non-return of children abroad.

2. To this end, States Parties shall promote the conclusion of bilateral or multilateral agreements or accession to existing agreements.

Art. 12 1. States Parties shall assure to the child who is capable of forming his or her own views the right to express those views freely in all matters affecting the child, the views of the child being given due weight in accordance with the age and maturity of the child.

2. For this purpose, the child shall in particular be provided the opportunity to be heard in any judicial and administrative proceedings affecting the child, either directly, or through a representative or an appropriate body, in a manner consistent with the procedural rules of national law.

Art. 13 1. The child shall have the right to freedom of expression; this right shall include freedom to seek, receive and impart information and ideas of all kinds, regardless of frontiers, either orally, in writing or in print, in the form of art, or through any other media of the child's choice.

2. The exercise of this right may be subject to certain restrictions, but these shall only be such as are provided by law and are necessary:

(a) For respect of the rights or reputations of others; or

(b) For the protection of national security or of public order (ordre public), or of public health or morals.

Art. 14 1. States Parties shall respect the right of the child to freedom of thought, conscience and religion.

2. States Parties shall respect the rights and duties of the parents and, when applicable, legal guardians, to provide direction to the child in the exercise of his or her right in a manner consistent with the evolving capacities of the child.

3. Freedom to manifest one's religion or beliefs may be subject only to such limitations as are prescribed by law and are necessary to protect public safety, order, health or morals, or the fundamental rights and freedoms of others.

Art. 15 1. States Parties recognize the rights of the child to freedom of association and to freedom of peaceful assembly.

2. No restrictions may be placed on the exercise of these rights other than those imposed in conformity with the law and which are necessary in a democratic

society in the interests of national security or public safety, public order (ordre public), the protection of public health or morals or the protection of the rights and freedoms of others.

Art. 16 1. No child shall be subjected to arbitrary or unlawful interference with his or her privacy, family, home or correspondence, nor to unlawful attacks on his or her honour and reputation.

2. The child has the right to the protection of the law against such interference or attacks.

Art. 17 States Parties recognize the important function performed by the mass media and shall ensure that the child has access to information and material from a diversity of national and international sources, especially those aimed at the promotion of his or her social, spiritual and moral well-being and physical and mental health.

To this end, States Parties shall:

(a) Encourage the mass media to disseminate information and material of social and cultural benefit to the child and in accordance with the spirit of article 29;

(b) Encourage international co-operation in the production, exchange and dissemination of such information and material from a diversity of cultural, national and international sources;

(c) Encourage the production and dissemination of children's books;

(d) Encourage the mass media to have particular regard to the linguistic needs of the child who belongs to a minority group or who is indigenous;

(e) Encourage the development of appropriate guidelines for the protection of the child from information and material injurious to his or her well-being, bearing in mind the provisions of articles 13 and 18.

Art. 18 1. States Parties shall use their best efforts to ensure recognition of the principle that both parents have common responsibilities for the upbringing and development of the child. Parents or, as the case may be, legal guardians, have the primary responsibility for the upbringing and development of the child. The best interests of the child will be their basic concern.

2. For the purpose of guaranteeing and promoting the rights set forth in the present Convention, States Parties shall render appropriate assistance to parents and legal guardians in the performance of their child-rearing responsibilities and shall ensure the development of institutions, facilities and services for the care of children.

3. States Parties shall take all appropriate measures to ensure that children of working parents have the right to benefit from child-care services and facilities for which they are eligible.

Art. 19 1. States Parties shall take all appropriate legislative, administrative, social and educational measures to protect the child from all forms of physical or mental violence, injury or abuse, neglect or negligent treatment, maltreatment or exploitation, including sexual abuse, while in the care of parent(s), legal guardian(s) or any other person who has the care of the child.
2. Such protective measures should, as appropriate, include effective procedures for the establishment of social programmes to provide necessary support for the child and for those who have the care of the child, as well as for other forms of prevention and for identification, reporting, referral, investigation, treatment and follow-up of instances of child maltreatment described heretofore, and, as appropriate, for judicial involvement.
Art. 20 1. A child temporarily or permanently deprived of his or her family environment, or in whose own best interests cannot be allowed to remain in that environment, shall be entitled to special protection and assistance provided by the State.
2. States Parties shall in accordance with their national laws ensure alternative care for such a child.
3. Such care could include, inter alia, foster placement, kafalah of Islamic law, adoption or if necessary placement in suitable institutions for the care of children. When considering solutions, due regard shall be paid to the desirability of continuity in a child's upbringing and to the child's ethnic, religious, cultural and linguistic background.
Art. 21 States Parties that recognize and/or permit the system of adoption shall ensure that the best interests of the child shall be the paramount consideration and they shall:

(a) Ensure that the adoption of a child is authorized only by competent authorities who determine, in accordance with applicable law and procedures and on the basis of all pertinent and reliable information, that the adoption is permissible in view of the child's status concerning parents, relatives and legal guardians and that, if required, the persons concerned have given their informed consent to the adoption on the basis of such counselling as may be necessary;

(b) Recognize that inter-country adoption may be considered as an alternative means of child's care, if the child cannot be placed in a foster or an adoptive family or cannot in any suitable manner be cared for in the child's country of origin;

(c) Ensure that the child concerned by inter-country adoption enjoys safeguards and standards equivalent to those existing in the case of national adoption;

(d) Take all appropriate measures to ensure that, in inter-country adoption, the placement does not result in improper financial gain for those involved in it;

(e) Promote, where appropriate, the objectives of the present article by concluding bilateral or multilateral arrangements or agreements, and endeavour, within this framework, to ensure that the placement of the child in another country is carried out by competent authorities or organs.

Art. 22 1. States Parties shall take appropriate measures to ensure that a child who is seeking refugee status or who is considered a refugee in accordance with applicable international or domestic law and procedures shall, whether unaccompanied or accompanied by his or her parents or by any other person, receive appropriate protection and humanitarian assistance in the enjoyment of applicable rights set forth in the present Convention and in other international human rights or humanitarian instruments to which the said States are Parties.

2. For this purpose, States Parties shall provide, as they consider appropriate, co-operation in any efforts by the United Nations and other competent intergovernmental organizations or non-governmental organizations co-operating with the United Nations to protect and assist such a child and to trace the parents or other members of the family of any refugee child in order to obtain information necessary for reunification with his or her family. In cases where no parents or other members of the family can be found, the child shall be accorded the same protection as any other child permanently or temporarily deprived of his or her family environment for any reason, as set forth in the present Convention.

Art. 23 1. States Parties recognize that a mentally or physically disabled child should enjoy a full and decent life, in conditions which ensure dignity, promote self-reliance and facilitate the child's active participation in the community.

2. States Parties recognize the right of the disabled child to special care and shall encourage and ensure the extension, subject to available resources, to the eligible child and those responsible for his or her care, of assistance for which application is made and which is appropriate to the child's condition and to the circumstances of the parents or others caring for the child.

3. Recognizing the special needs of a disabled child, assistance extended in accordance with paragraph 2 of the present article shall be provided free of charge, whenever possible, taking into account the financial resources of the parents or others caring for the child, and shall be designed to ensure that the disabled child has effective access to and receives education, training, health care services, rehabilitation services, preparation for employment and

recreation opportunities in a manner conducive to the child's achieving the fullest possible social integration and individual development, including his or her cultural and spiritual development

4. States Parties shall promote, in the spirit of international co-operation, the exchange of appropriate information in the field of preventive health care and of medical, psychological and functional treatment of disabled children, including dissemination of and access to information concerning methods of rehabilitation, education and vocational services, with the aim of enabling States Parties to improve their capabilities and skills and to widen their experience in these areas. In this regard, particular account shall be taken of the needs of developing countries.

Art. 24 1. States Parties recognize the right of the child to the enjoyment of the highest attainable standard of health and to facilities for the treatment of illness and rehabilitation of health. States Parties shall strive to ensure that no child is deprived of his or her right of access to such health care services.

2. States Parties shall pursue full implementation of this right and, in particular, shall take appropriate measures:

(a) To diminish infant and child mortality;

(b) To ensure the provision of necessary medical assistance and health care to all children with emphasis on the development of primary health care;

(c) To combat disease and malnutrition, including within the framework of primary health care, through, inter alia, the application of readily available technology and through the provision of adequate nutritious foods and clean drinking-water, taking into consideration the dangers and risks of environmental pollution;

(d) To ensure appropriate pre-natal and post-natal health care for mothers;

(e) To ensure that all segments of society, in particular parents and children, are informed, have access to education and are supported in the use of basic knowledge of child health and nutrition, the advantages of breast-feeding, hygiene and environmental sanitation and the prevention of accidents;

(f) To develop preventive health care, guidance for parents and family planning education and services.

3. States Parties shall take all effective and appropriate measures with a view to abolishing traditional practices prejudicial to the health of children.

4. States Parties undertake to promote and encourage international cooperation with a view to achieving progressively the full realization of the right recognized in the present article. In this regard, particular account shall be taken of the needs of developing countries.

Art. 25 States Parties recognize the right of a child who has been placed by the competent authorities for the purposes of care, protection or treatment of his or her physical or mental health, to a periodic review of the treatment provided to the child and all other circumstances relevant to his or her placement.
Art. 26 1. States Parties shall recognize for every child the right to benefit from social security, including social insurance, and shall take the necessary measures to achieve the full realization of this right in accordance with their national law.
2. The benefits should, where appropriate, be granted, taking into account the resources and the circumstances of the child and persons having responsibility for the maintenance of the child, as well as any other consideration relevant to an application for benefits made by or on behalf of the child.
Art. 27 1. States Parties recognize the right of every child to a standard of living adequate for the child's physical, mental, spiritual, moral and social development.
2. The parent(s) or others responsible for the child have the primary responsibility to secure, within their abilities and financial capacities, the conditions of living necessary for the child's development.
3. States Parties, in accordance with national conditions and within their means, shall take appropriate measures to assist parents and others responsible for the child to implement this right and shall in case of need provide material assistance and support programmes, particularly with regard to nutrition, clothing and housing.
4. States Parties shall take all appropriate measures to secure the recovery of maintenance for the child from the parents or other persons having financial responsibility for the child, both within the State Party and from abroad. In particular, where the person having financial responsibility for the child lives in a State different from that of the child, States Parties shall promote the accession to international agreements or the conclusion of such agreements, as well as the making of other appropriate arrangements.
Art. 28 1. States Parties recognize the right of the child to education, and with a view to achieving this right progressively and on the basis of equal opportunity, they shall, in particular:
(a) Make primary education compulsory and available free to all;
(b) Encourage the development of different forms of secondary education, including general and vocational education, make them available and accessible to every child, and take appropriate measures such as the introduction of free education and offering financial assistance in case of need;

(c) Make higher education accessible to all on the basis of capacity by every appropriate means;
(d) Make educational and vocational information and guidance available and accessible to all children;
(e) Take measures to encourage regular attendance at schools and the reduction of drop-out rates.

2. States Parties shall take all appropriate measures to ensure that school discipline is administered in a manner consistent with the child's human dignity and in conformity with the present Convention.

3. States Parties shall promote and encourage international co-operation in matters relating to education, in particular with a view to contributing to the elimination of ignorance and illiteracy throughout the world and facilitating access to scientific and technical knowledge and modern teaching methods. In this regard, particular account shall be taken of the needs of developing countries.

Art. 29 1. States Parties agree that the education of the child shall be directed to:
(a) The development of the child's personality, talents and mental and physical abilities to their fullest potential;
(b) The development of respect for human rights and fundamental freedoms, and for the principles enshrined in the Charter of the United Nations;
(c) The development of respect for the child's parents, his or her own cultural identity, language and values, for the national values of the country in which the child is living, the country from which he or she may originate, and for civilizations different from his or her own;
(d) The preparation of the child for responsible life in a free society, in the spirit of understanding, peace, tolerance, equality of sexes, and friendship among all peoples, ethnic, national and religious groups and persons of indigenous origin;
(e) The development of respect for the natural environment.

2. No part of the present article or article 28 shall be construed so as to interfere with the liberty of individuals and bodies to establish and direct educational institutions, subject always to the observance of the principle set forth in paragraph 1 of the present article and to the requirements that the education given in such institutions shall conform to such minimum standards as may be laid down by the State.

Art. 30 In those States in which ethnic, religious or linguistic minorities or persons of indigenous origin exist, a child belonging to such a minority or who is indigenous shall not be denied the right, in community with other members of his or her group, to enjoy his or her own culture, to profess and practise his or her own religion, or to use his or her own language.

Art. 31 1. States Parties recognize the right of the child to rest and leisure, to engage in play and recreational activities appropriate to the age of the child and to participate freely in cultural life and the arts.

2. States Parties shall respect and promote the right of the child to participate fully in cultural and artistic life and shall encourage the provision of appropriate and equal opportunities for cultural, artistic, recreational and leisure activity.

Art. 32 1. States Parties recognize the right of the child to be protected from economic exploitation and from performing any work that is likely to be hazardous or to interfere with the child's education, or to be harmful to the child's health or physical, mental, spiritual, moral or social development.

2. States Parties shall take legislative, administrative, social and educational measures to ensure the implementation of the present article. To this end, and having regard to the relevant provisions of other international instruments, States Parties shall in particular:

(a) Provide for a minimum age or minimum ages for admission to employment;

(b) Provide for appropriate regulation of the hours and conditions of employment;

(c) Provide for appropriate penalties or other sanctions to ensure the effective enforcement of the present article.

Art. 33 States Parties shall take all appropriate measures, including legislative, administrative, social and educational measures, to protect children from the illicit use of narcotic drugs and psychotropic substances as defined in the relevant international treaties, and to prevent the use of children in the illicit production and trafficking of such substances.

Art. 34 States Parties undertake to protect the child from all forms of sexual exploitation and sexual abuse. For these purposes, States Parties shall in particular take all appropriate national, bilateral and multilateral measures to prevent:

(a) The inducement or coercion of a child to engage in any unlawful sexual activity;

(b) The exploitative use of children in prostitution or other unlawful sexual practices;

(c) The exploitative use of children in pornographic performances and materials.

Art. 35 States Parties shall take all appropriate national, bilateral and multilateral measures to prevent the abduction of, the sale of or traffic in children for any purpose or in any form.

Art. 36 States Parties shall protect the child against all other forms of exploitation prejudicial to any aspects of the child's welfare.

Art. 37 States Parties shall ensure that:

(a) No child shall be subjected to torture or other cruel, inhuman or degrading treatment or punishment. Neither capital punishment nor life imprisonment without possibility of release shall be imposed for offences committed by persons below eighteen years of age;

(b) No child shall be deprived of his or her liberty unlawfully or arbitrarily. The arrest, detention or imprisonment of a child shall be in conformity with the law and shall be used only as a measure of last resort and for the shortest appropriate period of time;

(c) Every child deprived of liberty shall be treated with humanity and respect for the inherent dignity of the human person, and in a manner which takes into account the needs of persons of his or her age. In particular, every child deprived of liberty shall be separated from adults unless it is considered in the child's best interest not to do so and shall have the right to maintain contact with his or her family through correspondence and visits, save in exceptional circumstances;

(d) Every child deprived of his or her liberty shall have the right to prompt access to legal and other appropriate assistance, as well as the right to challenge the legality of the deprivation of his or her liberty before a court or other competent, independent and impartial authority, and to a prompt decision on any such action.

Art. 38 1. States Parties undertake to respect and to ensure respect for rules of international humanitarian law applicable to them in armed conflicts which are relevant to the child.

2. States Parties shall take all feasible measures to ensure that persons who have not attained the age of fifteen years do not take a direct part in hostilities.

3. States Parties shall refrain from recruiting any person who has not attained the age of fifteen years into their armed forces. In recruiting among those persons who have attained the age of fifteen years but who have not attained the age of eighteen years, States Parties shall endeavour to give priority to those who are oldest.

4. In accordance with their obligations under international humanitarian law to protect the civilian population in armed conflicts, States Parties shall take all feasible measures to ensure protection and care of children who are affected by an armed conflict.

Art. 39 States Parties shall take all appropriate measures to promote physical and psychological recovery and social reintegration of a child victim of: any form of neglect, exploitation, or abuse; torture or any other form of cruel, inhuman or degrading treatment or punishment; or armed conflicts. Such recovery and reintegration shall take place in an environment which fosters the health, self-respect and dignity of the child.

Art. 40 1. States Parties recognize the right of every child alleged as, accused of, or recognized as having infringed the penal law to be treated in a manner consistent with the promotion of the child's sense of dignity and worth, which reinforces the child's respect for the human rights and fundamental freedoms of others and which takes into account the child's age and the desirability of promoting the child's reintegration and the child's assuming a constructive role in society.

2. To this end, and having regard to the relevant provisions of international instruments, States Parties shall, in particular, ensure that:

(a) No child shall be alleged as, be accused of, or recognized as having infringed the penal law by reason of acts or omissions that were not prohibited by national or international law at the time they were committed;

(b) Every child alleged as or accused of having infringed the penal law has at least the following guarantees:

  (i) To be presumed innocent until proven guilty according to law;

  (ii) To be informed promptly and directly of the charges against him or her, and, if appropriate, through his or her parents or legal guardians, and to have legal or other appropriate assistance in the preparation and presentation of his or her defence;

  (iii) To have the matter determined without delay by a competent, independent and impartial authority or judicial body in a fair hearing according to law, in the presence of legal or other appropriate assistance and, unless it is considered not to be in the best interest of the child, in particular, taking into account his or her age or situation, his or her parents or legal guardians;

  (iv) Not to be compelled to give testimony or to confess guilt; to examine or have examined adverse witnesses and to obtain the participation and examination of witnesses on his or her behalf under conditions of equality;

  (v) If considered to have infringed the penal law, to have this decision and any measures imposed in consequence thereof reviewed by a higher competent, independent and impartial authority or judicial body according to law;

(vi) To have the free assistance of an interpreter if the child cannot understand or speak the language used;

(vii) To have his or her privacy fully respected at all stages of the proceedings.

3. States Parties shall seek to promote the establishment of laws, procedures, authorities and institutions specifically applicable to children alleged as, accused of, or recognized as having infringed the penal law, and, in particular:

(a) The establishment of a minimum age below which children shall be presumed not to have the capacity to infringe the penal law;

(b) Whenever appropriate and desirable, measures for dealing with such children without resorting to judicial proceedings, providing that human rights and legal safeguards are fully respected.

4. A variety of dispositions, such as care, guidance and supervision orders; counselling; probation; foster care; education and vocational training programmes and other alternatives to institutional care shall be available to ensure that children are dealt with in a manner appropriate to their well-being and proportionate both to their circumstances and the offence.

Art. 41 Nothing in the present Convention shall affect any provisions which are more conducive to the realization of the rights of the child and which may be contained in:

(a) The law of a State Party; or

(b) International law in force for that State.

Part II

Art. 42 States Parties undertake to make the principles and provisions of the Convention widely known, by appropriate and active means, to adults and children alike.

Art. 43 1. For the purpose of examining the progress made by States Parties in achieving the realization of the obligations undertaken in the present Convention, there shall be established a Committee on the Rights of the Child, which shall carry out the functions hereinafter provided.

2. The Committee shall consist of ten experts of high moral standing and recognized competence in the field covered by this Convention. The members of the Committee shall be elected by States Parties from among their nationals and shall serve in their personal capacity, consideration being given to equitable geographical distribution, as well as to the principal legal systems.

3. The members of the Committee shall be elected by secret ballot from a list of persons nominated by States Parties. Each State Party may nominate one person from among its own nationals.
4. The initial election to the Committee shall be held no later than six months after the date of the entry into force of the present Convention and thereafter every second year. At least four months before the date of each election, the Secretary-General of the United Nations shall address a letter to States Parties inviting them to submit their nominations within two months. The Secretary-General shall subsequently prepare a list in alphabetical order of all persons thus nominated, indicating States Parties which have nominated them, and shall submit it to the States Parties to the present Convention.
5. The elections shall be held at meetings of States Parties convened by the Secretary-General at United Nations Headquarters. At those meetings, for which two thirds of States Parties shall constitute a quorum, the persons elected to the Committee shall be those who obtain the largest number of votes and an absolute majority of the votes of the representatives of States Parties present and voting.
6. The members of the Committee shall be elected for a term of four years. They shall be eligible for re-election if renominated. The term of five of the members elected at the first election shall expire at the end of two years; immediately after the first election, the names of these five members shall be chosen by lot by the Chairman of the meeting.
7. If a member of the Committee dies or resigns or declares that for any other cause he or she can no longer perform the duties of the Committee, the State Party which nominated the member shall appoint another expert from among its nationals to serve for the remainder of the term, subject to the approval of the Committee.
8. The Committee shall establish its own rules of procedure.
9. The Committee shall elect its officers for a period of two years.
10. The meetings of the Committee shall normally be held at United Nations Headquarters or at any other convenient place as determined by the Committee. The Committee shall normally meet annually. The duration of the meetings of the Committee shall be determined, and reviewed, if necessary, by a meeting of the States Parties to the present Convention, subject to the approval of the General Assembly.
11. The Secretary-General of the United Nations shall provide the necessary staff and facilities for the effective performance of the functions of the Committee under the present Convention.
12. With the approval of the General Assembly, the members of the Committee established under the present Convention shall receive emoluments from

United Nations resources on such terms and conditions as the Assembly may decide.

Art. 44 1. States Parties undertake to submit to the Committee, through the Secretary-General of the United Nations, reports on the measures they have adopted which give effect to the rights recognized herein and on the progress made on the enjoyment of those rights:

(a) Within two years of the entry into force of the Convention for the State Party concerned;

(b) Thereafter every five years.

2. Reports made under the present article shall indicate factors and difficulties, if any, affecting the degree of fulfilment of the obligations under the present Convention. Reports shall also contain sufficient information to provide the Committee with a comprehensive understanding of the implementation of the Convention in the country concerned.

3. A State Party which has submitted a comprehensive initial report to the Committee need not, in its subsequent reports submitted in accordance with paragraph 1 (b) of the present article, repeat basic information previously provided.

4. The Committee may request from States Parties further information relevant to the implementation of the Convention.

5. The Committee shall submit to the General Assembly, through the Economic and Social Council, every two years, reports on its activities.

6. States Parties shall make their reports widely available to the public in their own countries.

Art. 45 In order to foster the effective implementation of the Convention and to encourage international co-operation in the field covered by the Convention:

(a) The specialized agencies, the United Nations Children's Fund, and other United Nations organs shall be entitled to be represented at the consideration of the implementation of such provisions of the present Convention as fall within the scope of their mandate. The Committee may invite the specialized agencies, the United Nations Children's Fund and other competent bodies as it may consider appropriate to provide expert advice on the implementation of the Convention in areas falling within the scope of their respective mandates. The Committee may invite the specialized agencies, the United Nations Children's Fund, and other United Nations organs to submit reports on the implementation of the Convention in areas falling within the scope of their activities;

(b) The Committee shall transmit, as it may consider appropriate, to the specialized agencies, the United Nations Children's Fund and other competent bodies, any reports from States Parties that contain a request, or indicate a need, for technical advice or assistance, along with the Committee's observations and suggestions, if any, on these requests or indications;

(c) The Committee may recommend to the General Assembly to request the Secretary-General to undertake on its behalf studies on specific issues relating to the rights of the child;

(d) The Committee may make suggestions and general recommendations based on information received pursuant to articles 44 and 45 of the present Convention. Such suggestions and general recommendations shall be transmitted to any State Party concerned and reported to the General Assembly, together with comments, if any, from States Parties.

Part III

Art. 46 The present Convention shall be open for signature by all States.

Art. 47 The present Convention is subject to ratification. Instruments of ratification shall be deposited with the Secretary-General of the United Nations.

Art. 48 The present Convention shall remain open for accession by any State. The instruments of accession shall be deposited with the Secretary-General of the United Nations.

Art. 49 1. The present Convention shall enter into force on the thirtieth day following the date of deposit with the Secretary-General of the United Nations of the twentieth instrument of ratification or accession.

2. For each State ratifying or acceding to the Convention after the deposit of the twentieth instrument of ratification or accession, the Convention shall enter into force on the thirtieth day after the deposit by such State of its instrument of ratification or accession.

Art. 50 1. Any State Party may propose an amendment and file it with the Secretary-General of the United Nations. The Secretary-General shall thereupon communicate the proposed amendment to States Parties, with a request that they indicate whether they favour a conference of States Parties for the purpose of considering and voting upon the proposals. In the event that, within four months from the date of such communication, at least one third of the States Parties favour such a conference, the Secretary-General shall convene the conference under the auspices of the United Nations. Any amendment adopted by a majority of States Parties present and voting at the conference shall be submitted to the General Assembly for approval.

2. An amendment adopted in accordance with paragraph 1 of the present article shall enter into force when it has been approved by the General Assembly of the United Nations and accepted by a two-thirds majority of States Parties.
3. When an amendment enters into force, it shall be binding on those States Parties which have accepted it, other States Parties still being bound by the provisions of the present Convention and any earlier amendments which they have accepted.
Art. 51 1. The Secretary-General of the United Nations shall receive and circulate to all States the text of reservations made by States at the time of ratification or accession.
2. A reservation incompatible with the object and purpose of the present Convention shall not be permitted.
3. Reservations may be withdrawn at any time by notification to that effect addressed to the Secretary-General of the United Nations, who shall then inform all States. Such notification shall take effect on the date on which it is received by the Secretary-General.
Art. 52 A State Party may denounce the present Convention by written notification to the Secretary-General of the United Nations.
Denunciation becomes effective one year after the date of receipt of the notification by the Secretary-General.
Art. 53 The Secretary-General of the United Nations is designated as the depositary of the present Convention.
Art. 54 The original of the present Convention, of which the Arabic, Chinese, English, French, Russian and Spanish texts are equally authentic, shall be deposited with the Secretary-General of the United Nations.

In witness thereof the undersigned plenipotentiaries, being duly authorized thereto by their respective Governments, have signed the present Convention.

CHAPTER 3.A

Optional Protocol to the Convention on the Rights of the Child on the Involvement of Children in Armed Conflict

Adopted and opened for signature, ratification and accession by General Assembly resolution 54/263 of 25 May 2000
Entry into force 12 February 2002, in accordance with article 10(1)

The States Parties to the present Protocol,

Encouraged by the overwhelming support for the Convention on the Rights of the Child, demonstrating the widespread commitment that exists to strive for the promotion and protection of the rights of the child,

Reaffirming that the rights of children require special protection, and calling for continuous improvement of the situation of children without distinction, as well as for their development and education in conditions of peace and security,

Disturbed by the harmful and widespread impact of armed conflict on children and the long-term consequences this has for durable peace, security and development,

Condemning the targeting of children in situations of armed conflict and direct attacks on objects protected under international law, including places generally having a significant presence of children, such as schools and hospitals,

Noting the adoption of the Statute of the International Criminal Court and, in particular, its inclusion as a war crime of conscripting or enlisting children under the age of 15 years or using them to participate actively in hostilities in both international and non-international armed conflicts,

Considering, therefore, that to strengthen further the implementation of rights recognized in the Convention on the Rights of the Child there is a need to increase the protection of children from involvement in armed conflict,

Noting that article 1 of the Convention on the Rights of the Child specifies that, for the purposes of that Convention, a child means every human being below the age of 18 years unless, under the law applicable to the child, majority is attained earlier,

Convinced that an optional protocol to the Convention raising the age of possible recruitment of persons into armed forces and their participation in hostilities will contribute effectively to the implementation of the principle that the best interests of the child are to be a primary consideration in all actions concerning children,

Noting that the twenty-sixth international Conference of the Red Cross and Red Crescent in December 1995 recommended, inter alia, that parties to conflict take every feasible step to ensure that children under the age of 18 years do not take part in hostilities,

Welcoming the unanimous adoption, in June 1999, of International Labour Organization Convention No. 182 on the Prohibition and Immediate Action for the Elimination of the Worst Forms of Child Labour, which prohibits, inter alia, forced or compulsory recruitment of children for use in armed conflict,

Condemning with the gravest concern the recruitment, training and use within and across national borders of children in hostilities by armed groups distinct from the armed forces of a State, and recognizing the responsibility of those who recruit, train and use children in this regard,

Recalling the obligation of each party to an armed conflict to abide by the provisions of international humanitarian law,

Stressing that this Protocol is without prejudice to the purposes and principles contained in the Charter of the United Nations, including Article 51, and relevant norms of humanitarian law,

Bearing in mind that conditions of peace and security based on full respect of the purposes and principles contained in the Charter and observance of applicable human rights instruments are indispensable for the full protection of children, in particular during armed conflicts and foreign occupation,

Recognizing the special needs of those children who are particularly vulnerable to recruitment or use in hostilities contrary to this Protocol owing to their economic or social status or gender,

Mindful of the necessity of taking into consideration the economic, social and political root causes of the involvement of children in armed conflicts,

Convinced of the need to strengthen international cooperation in the implementation of this Protocol, as well as the physical and psychosocial rehabilitation and social reintegration of children who are victims of armed conflict,

Encouraging the participation of the community and, in particular, children and child victims in the dissemination of informational and educational programmes concerning the implementation of the Protocol,

Have agreed as follows:

Art. 1 States Parties shall take all feasible measures to ensure that members of their armed forces who have not attained the age of 18 years do not take a direct part in hostilities.

Art. 2 States Parties shall ensure that persons who have not attained the age of 18 years are not compulsorily recruited into their armed forces.

Art. 3 1. States Parties shall raise the minimum age for the voluntary recruitment of persons into their national armed forces from that set out in article 38, paragraph 3, of the Convention on the Rights of the Child, taking account of the principles contained in that article and recognizing that under the Convention persons under 18 are entitled to special protection.

2. Each State Party shall deposit a binding declaration upon ratification of or accession to this Protocol that sets forth the minimum age at which it will permit voluntary recruitment into its national armed forces and a description of the safeguards that it has adopted to ensure that such recruitment is not forced or coerced.

3. States Parties that permit voluntary recruitment into their national armed forces under the age of 18 shall maintain safeguards to ensure, as a minimum, that:

(a) Such recruitment is genuinely voluntary;

(b) Such recruitment is done with the informed consent of the person's parents or legal guardians;

(c) Such persons are fully informed of the duties involved in such military service;

(d) Such persons provide reliable proof of age prior to acceptance into national military service.

4. Each State Party may strengthen its declaration at any time by notification to that effect addressed to the Secretary-General of the United Nations, who shall inform all States Parties. Such notification shall take effect on the date on which it is received by the Secretary-General.

5. The requirement to raise the age in paragraph 1 of the present article does not apply to schools operated by or under the control of the armed forces of the States Parties, in keeping with articles 28 and 29 of the Convention on the Rights of the Child.

Art. 4 1. Armed groups that are distinct from the armed forces of a State should not, under any circumstances, recruit or use in hostilities persons under the age of 18 years.

2. States Parties shall take all feasible measures to prevent such recruitment and use, including the adoption of legal measures necessary to prohibit and criminalize such practices.

3. The application of the present article under this Protocol shall not affect the legal status of any party to an armed conflict.

Art. 5 Nothing in the present Protocol shall be construed as precluding provisions in the law of a State Party or in international instruments and international humanitarian law that are more conducive to the realization of the rights of the child.

Art. 6 1. Each State Party shall take all necessary legal, administrative and other measures to ensure the effective implementation and enforcement of the provisions of this Protocol within its jurisdiction.

2. States Parties undertake to make the principles and provisions of the present Protocol widely known and promoted by appropriate means, to adults and children alike.

3. States Parties shall take all feasible measures to ensure that persons within their jurisdiction recruited or used in hostilities contrary to this Protocol are demobilized or otherwise released from service. States Parties shall, when necessary, accord to these persons all appropriate assistance for their physical and psychological recovery and their social reintegration.

Art. 7 1. States Parties shall cooperate in the implementation of the present Protocol, including in the prevention of any activity contrary to the Protocol and in the rehabilitation and social reintegration of persons who are victims of acts contrary to this Protocol, including through technical cooperation and financial assistance. Such assistance and cooperation will be undertaken in consultation with concerned States Parties and relevant international organizations.

2. States Parties in a position to do so shall provide such assistance through existing multilateral, bilateral or other programmes, or, inter alia, through a voluntary fund established in accordance with the rules of the General Assembly.

Art. 8 1. Each State Party shall submit, within two years following the entry into force of the Protocol for that State Party, a report to the Committee on the Rights of the Child providing comprehensive information on the measures it has taken to implement the provisions of the Protocol, including the measures taken to implement the provisions on participation and recruitment.

2. Following the submission of the comprehensive report, each State Party shall include in the reports they submit to the Committee on the Rights of the Child, in accordance with article 44 of the Convention, any further information with respect to the implementation of the Protocol. Other States Parties to the Protocol shall submit a report every five years.

3. The Committee on the Rights of the Child may request from States Parties further information relevant to the implementation of this Protocol.

Art. 9 1. The present Protocol is open for signature by any State that is a party to the Convention or has signed it.

2. The present Protocol is subject to ratification and is open to accession by any State. Instruments of ratification or accession shall be deposited with the Secretary-General of the United Nations.

3. The Secretary-General, in his capacity as depositary of the Convention and the Protocol, shall inform all States Parties to the Convention and all States that have signed the Convention of each instrument of declaration pursuant to article 13.

Art. 10 1. The present Protocol shall enter into force three months after the deposit of the tenth instrument of ratification or accession.

2. For each State ratifying the present Protocol or acceding to it after its entry into force, the present Protocol shall enter into force one month after the date of the deposit of its own instrument of ratification or accession.

Art. 11 1. Any State Party may denounce the present Protocol at any time by written notification to the Secretary-General of the United Nations, who shall thereafter inform the other States Parties to the Convention and all States that have signed the Convention. The denunciation shall take effect one year after the date of receipt of the notification by the Secretary-General. If, however, on the expiry of that year the denouncing State Party is engaged in armed conflict, the denunciation shall not take effect before the end of the armed conflict.

2. Such a denunciation shall not have the effect of releasing the State Party from its obligations under the present Protocol in regard to any act that occurs prior to the date on which the denunciation becomes effective. Nor shall such a denunciation prejudice in any way the continued consideration of any matter that is already under consideration by the Committee prior to the date on which the denunciation becomes effective.

Art. 12 1. Any State Party may propose an amendment and file it with the Secretary-General of the United Nations. The Secretary-General shall thereupon communicate the proposed amendment to States Parties, with a request that they indicate whether they favour a conference of States Parties for the purpose of considering and voting upon the proposals. In the event that, within four months from the date of such communication, at least one third of the States Parties favour such a conference, the Secretary-General shall convene the conference under the auspices of the United Nations. Any amendment adopted by a majority of States Parties present and voting at the conference shall be submitted to the General Assembly for approval.

2. An amendment adopted in accordance with paragraph 1 of the present article shall enter into force when it has been approved by the General Assembly of the United Nations and accepted by a two-thirds majority of States Parties.

3. When an amendment enters into force, it shall be binding on those States Parties that have accepted it, other States Parties still being bound by the provisions of the present Protocol and any earlier amendments that they have accepted.

Art. 13 1. The present Protocol, of which the Arabic, Chinese, English, French, Russian and Spanish texts are equally authentic, shall be deposited in the archives of the United Nations.
2. The Secretary-General of the United Nations shall transmit certified copies of the present Protocol to all States Parties to the Convention and all States that have signed the Convention.

CHAPTER 3.B

Optional Protocol to the Convention on the Rights of the Child on the Sale of Children, Child Prostitution and Child Pornography

Adopted and opened for signature, ratification and accession by General Assembly resolution 54/263 of 25 May 2000
Entry into force 18 January 2002, in accordance with article 14(1)

The States Parties to the present Protocol,

Considering that, in order further to achieve the purposes of the Convention on the Rights of the Child and the implementation of its provisions, especially articles 1, 11, 21, 32, 33, 34, 35 and 36, it would be appropriate to extend the measures that States Parties should undertake in order to guarantee the protection of the child from the sale of children, child prostitution and child pornography,

Considering also that the Convention on the Rights of the Child recognizes the right of the child to be protected from economic exploitation and from performing any work that is likely to be hazardous or to interfere with the child's education, or to be harmful to the child's health or physical, mental, spiritual, moral or social development,

Gravely concerned at the significant and increasing international traffic of children for the purpose of the sale of children, child prostitution and child pornography,

Deeply concerned at the widespread and continuing practice of sex tourism, to which children are especially vulnerable, as it directly promotes the sale of children, child prostitution and child pornography,

Recognizing that a number of particularly vulnerable groups, including girl children, are at greater risk of sexual exploitation, and that girl children are disproportionately represented among the sexually exploited,

Concerned about the growing availability of child pornography on the Internet and other evolving technologies, and recalling the International Conference on Combating Child Pornography on the Internet (Vienna, 1999) and, in particular, its conclusion calling for the worldwide criminalization of the production, distribution, exportation, transmission, importation, intentional possession and advertising of child pornography, and stressing the importance of closer cooperation and partnership between Governments and the Internet industry,

 | DOI:10.1163/9789004681224_007

Believing that the elimination of the sale of children, child prostitution and child pornography will be facilitated by adopting a holistic approach, addressing the contributing factors, including underdevelopment, poverty, economic disparities, inequitable socio-economic structure, dysfunctioning families, lack of education, urban-rural migration, gender discrimination, irresponsible adult sexual behaviour, harmful traditional practices, armed conflicts and trafficking of children,

Believing that efforts to raise public awareness are needed to reduce consumer demand for the sale of children, child prostitution and child pornography, and also believing in the importance of strengthening global partnership among all actors and of improving law enforcement at the national level,

Noting the provisions of international legal instruments relevant to the protection of children, including the Hague Convention on the Protection of Children and Cooperation with Respect to Inter-Country Adoption, the Hague Convention on the Civil Aspects of International Child Abduction, the Hague Convention on Jurisdiction, Applicable Law, Recognition, Enforcement and Cooperation in Respect of Parental Responsibility and Measures for the Protection of Children, and International Labour Organization Convention No. 182 on the Prohibition and Immediate Action for the Elimination of the Worst Forms of Child Labour,

Encouraged by the overwhelming support for the Convention on the Rights of the Child, demonstrating the widespread commitment that exists for the promotion and protection of the rights of the child,

Recognizing the importance of the implementation of the provisions of the Programme of Action for the Prevention of the Sale of Children, Child Prostitution and Child Pornography and the Declaration and Agenda for Action adopted at the World Congress against Commercial Sexual Exploitation of Children, held at Stockholm from 27 to 31 August 1996, and the other relevant decisions and recommendations of pertinent international bodies,

Taking due account of the importance of the traditions and cultural values of each people for the protection and harmonious development of the child,

Have agreed as follows:

Art. 1 States Parties shall prohibit the sale of children, child prostitution and child pornography as provided for by the present Protocol.

Art. 2 For the purpose of the present Protocol:

(a) Sale of children means any act or transaction whereby a child is transferred by any person or group of persons to another for remuneration or any other consideration;

(b) Child prostitution means the use of a child in sexual activities for remuneration or any other form of consideration;

(c) Child pornography means any representation, by whatever means, of a child engaged in real or simulated explicit sexual activities or any representation of the sexual parts of a child for primarily sexual purposes.

Art. 3 1. Each State Party shall ensure that, as a minimum, the following acts and activities are fully covered under its criminal or penal law, whether these offences are committed domestically or transnationally or on an individual or organized basis:

(a) In the context of sale of children as defined in article 2:
   (i) The offering, delivering or accepting, by whatever means, a child for the purpose of:
      a. Sexual exploitation of the child;
      b. Transfer of organs of the child for profit;
      c. Engagement of the child in forced labour;
   (ii) Improperly inducing consent, as an intermediary, for the adoption of a child in violation of applicable international legal instruments on adoption;

(b) Offering, obtaining, procuring or providing a child for child prostitution, as defined in article 2;

(c) Producing, distributing, disseminating, importing, exporting, offering, selling or possessing for the above purposes child pornography as defined in article 2.

2. Subject to the provisions of a State Party's national law, the same shall apply to an attempt to commit any of these acts and to complicity or participation in any of these acts.

3. Each State Party shall make these offences punishable by appropriate penalties that take into account their grave nature.

4. Subject to the provisions of its national law, each State Party shall take measures, where appropriate, to establish the liability of legal persons for offences established in paragraph 1 of the present article. Subject to the legal principles of the State Party, this liability of legal persons may be criminal, civil or administrative.

5. States Parties shall take all appropriate legal and administrative measures to ensure that all persons involved in the adoption of a child act in conformity with applicable international legal instruments.

Art. 4 1. Each State Party shall take such measures as may be necessary to establish its jurisdiction over the offences referred to in article 3, paragraph 1, when the offences are committed in its territory or on board a ship or aircraft registered in that State.

2. Each State Party may take such measures as may be necessary to establish its jurisdiction over the offences referred to in article 3, paragraph 1, in the following cases:

(a) When the alleged offender is a national of that State or a person who has his habitual residence in its territory;

(b) When the victim is a national of that State.

3. Each State Party shall also take such measures as may be necessary to establish its jurisdiction over the above-mentioned offences when the alleged offender is present in its territory and it does not extradite him or her to another State Party on the ground that the offence has been committed by one of its nationals.

4. This Protocol does not exclude any criminal jurisdiction exercised in accordance with internal law.

Art. 5 1. The offences referred to in article 3, paragraph 1, shall be deemed to be included as extraditable offences in any extradition treaty existing between States Parties and shall be included as extraditable offences in every extradition treaty subsequently concluded between them, in accordance with the conditions set forth in those treaties.

2. If a State Party that makes extradition conditional on the existence of a treaty receives a request for extradition from another State Party with which it has no extradition treaty, it may consider this Protocol as a legal basis for extradition in respect of such offences. Extradition shall be subject to the conditions provided by the law of the requested State.

3. States Parties that do not make extradition conditional on the existence of a treaty shall recognize such offences as extraditable offences between themselves subject to the conditions provided by the law of the requested State.

4. Such offences shall be treated, for the purpose of extradition between States Parties, as if they had been committed not only in the place in which they occurred but also in the territories of the States required to establish their jurisdiction in accordance with article 4.

5. If an extradition request is made with respect to an offence described in article 3, paragraph 1, and if the requested State Party does not or will not extradite on the basis of the nationality of the offender, that State shall take suitable measures to submit the case to its competent authorities for the purpose of prosecution.

Art. 6 1. States Parties shall afford one another the greatest measure of assistance in connection with investigations or criminal or extradition proceedings brought in respect of the offences set forth in article 3, paragraph 1, including assistance in obtaining evidence at their disposal necessary for the proceedings.

2. States Parties shall carry out their obligations under paragraph 1 of the present article in conformity with any treaties or other arrangements on mutual legal assistance that may exist between them. In the absence of such treaties or arrangements, States Parties shall afford one another assistance in accordance with their domestic law.

Art. 7 States Parties shall, subject to the provisions of their national law:

(a) Take measures to provide for the seizure and confiscation, as appropriate, of:

  (i) Goods such as materials, assets and other instrumentalities used to commit or facilitate offences under the present Protocol;

  (ii) Proceeds derived from such offences;

(b) Execute requests from another State Party for seizure or confiscation of goods or proceeds referred to in subparagraph (a) (i);

(c) Take measures aimed at closing, on a temporary or definitive basis, premises used to commit such offences.

Art. 8 1. States Parties shall adopt appropriate measures to protect the rights and interests of child victims of the practices prohibited under the present Protocol at all stages of the criminal justice process, in particular by:

(a) Recognizing the vulnerability of child victims and adapting procedures to recognize their special needs, including their special needs as witnesses;

(b) Informing child victims of their rights, their role and the scope, timing and progress of the proceedings and of the disposition of their cases;

(c) Allowing the views, needs and concerns of child victims to be presented and considered in proceedings where their personal interests are affected, in a mariner consistent with the procedural rules of national law;

(d) Providing appropriate support services to child victims throughout the legal process;

(e) Protecting, as appropriate, the privacy and identity of child victims and taking measures in accordance with national law to avoid the inappropriate dissemination of information that could lead to the identification of child victims;

(f) Providing, in appropriate cases, for the safety of child victims, as well as that of their families and witnesses on their behalf, from intimidation and retaliation;

(g) Avoiding unnecessary delay in the disposition of cases and the execution of orders or decrees granting compensation to child victims.

2. States Parties shall ensure that uncertainty as to the actual age of the victim shall not prevent the initiation of criminal investigations, including investigations aimed at establishing the age of the victim.
3. States Parties shall ensure that, in the treatment by the criminal justice system of children who are victims of the offences described in the present Protocol, the best interest of the child shall be a primary consideration.
4. States Parties shall take measures to ensure appropriate training, in particular legal and psychological training, for the persons who work with victims of the offences prohibited under the present Protocol.
5. States Parties shall, in appropriate cases, adopt measures in order to protect the safety and integrity of those persons and/or organizations involved in the prevention and/or protection and rehabilitation of victims of such offences.
6. Nothing in the present article shall be construed as prejudicial to or inconsistent with the rights of the accused to a fair and impartial trial.
Art. 9 1. States Parties shall adopt or strengthen, implement and disseminate laws, administrative measures, social policies and programmes to prevent the offences referred to in the present Protocol. Particular attention shall be given to protect children who are especially vulnerable to these practices.
2. States Parties shall promote awareness in the public at large, including children, through information by all appropriate means, education and training, about the preventive measures and harmful effects of the offences referred to in the present Protocol. In fulfilling their obligations under this article, States Parties shall encourage the participation of the community and, in particular, children and child victims, in such information and education and training programmes, including at the international level.
3. States Parties shall take all feasible measures with the aim of ensuring all appropriate assistance to victims of such offences, including their full social reintegration and their full physical and psychological recovery.
4. States Parties shall ensure that all child victims of the offences described in the present Protocol have access to adequate procedures to seek, without discrimination, compensation for damages from those legally responsible.
5. States Parties shall take appropriate measures aimed at effectively prohibiting the production and dissemination of material advertising the offences described in the present Protocol.
Art. 10 1. States Parties shall take all necessary steps to strengthen international cooperation by multilateral, regional and bilateral arrangements for the prevention, detection, investigation, prosecution and punishment of those responsible for acts involving the sale of children, child prostitution, child pornography and child sex tourism. States Parties shall also promote international

cooperation and coordination between their authorities, national and international non-governmental organizations and international organizations.
2. States Parties shall promote international cooperation to assist child victims in their physical and psychological recovery, social reintegration and repatriation.
3. States Parties shall promote the strengthening of international cooperation in order to address the root causes, such as poverty and underdevelopment, contributing to the vulnerability of children to the sale of children, child prostitution, child pornography and child sex tourism.
4. States Parties in a position to do so shall provide financial, technical or other assistance through existing multilateral, regional, bilateral or other programmes.
Art. 11 Nothing in the present Protocol shall affect any provisions that are more conducive to the realization of the rights of the child and that may be contained in:
(a) The law of a State Party;
(b) International law in force for that State.
Art. 12 1. Each State Party shall submit, within two years following the entry into force of the Protocol for that State Party, a report to the Committee on the Rights of the Child providing comprehensive information on the measures it has taken to implement the provisions of the Protocol.
2. Following the submission of the comprehensive report, each State Party shall include in the reports they submit to the Committee on the Rights of the Child, in accordance with article 44 of the Convention, any further information with respect to the implementation of the Protocol. Other States Parties to the Protocol shall submit a report every five years.
3. The Committee on the Rights of the Child may request from States Parties further information relevant to the implementation of this Protocol.
Art. 13 1. The present Protocol is open for signature by any State that is a party to the Convention or has signed it.
2. The present Protocol is subject to ratification and is open to accession by any State that is a party to the Convention or has signed it. Instruments of ratification or accession shall be deposited with the Secretary-General of the United Nations.
Art. 14 1. The present Protocol shall enter into force three months after the deposit of the tenth instrument of ratification or accession.
2. For each State ratifying the present Protocol or acceding to it after its entry into force, the present Protocol shall enter into force one month after the date of the deposit of its own instrument of ratification or accession.

Art. 15 1. Any State Party may denounce the present Protocol at any time by written notification to the Secretary-General of the United Nations, who shall thereafter inform the other States Parties to the Convention and all States that have signed the Convention. The denunciation shall take effect one year after the date of receipt of the notification by the Secretary-General of the United Nations.

2. Such a denunciation shall not have the effect of releasing the State Party from its obligations under this Protocol in regard to any offense that occurs prior to the date on which the denunciation becomes effective. Nor shall such a denunciation prejudice in any way the continued consideration of any matter that is already under consideration by the Committee prior to the date on which the denunciation becomes effective.

Art. 16 1. Any State Party may propose an amendment and file it with the Secretary-General of the United Nations. The Secretary-General shall thereupon communicate the proposed amendment to States Parties, with a request that they indicate whether they favor a conference of States Parties for the purpose of considering and voting upon the proposals. In the event that, within four months from the date of such communication, at least one third of the States Parties favor such a conference, the Secretary-General shall convene the conference under the auspices of the United Nations. Any amendment adopted by a majority of States Parties present and voting at the conference shall be submitted to the General Assembly for approval.

2. An amendment adopted in accordance with paragraph 1 of the present article shall enter into force when it has been approved by the General Assembly of the United Nations and accepted by a two-thirds majority of States Parties.

3. When an amendment enters into force, it shall be binding on those States Parties that have accepted it, other States Parties still being bound by the provisions of the present Protocol and any earlier amendments that they have accepted.

Art. 17 1. The present Protocol, of which the Arabic, Chinese, English, French, Russian and Spanish texts are equally authentic, shall be deposited in the archives of the United Nations.

2. The Secretary-General of the United Nations shall transmit certified copies of the present Protocol to all States Parties to the Convention and all States that have signed the Convention.

CHAPTER 3.C

Optional Protocol to the Convention on the Rights of the Child on a Communications Procedure

Adopted and opened for signature, ratification and accession by General Assembly resolution 66/138 of 19 December 2011
Entry into force 14 April 2014, in accordance with article 19(1)

The States parties to the present Protocol,

Considering that, in accordance with the principles proclaimed in the Charter of the United Nations, the recognition of the inherent dignity and the equal and inalienable rights of all members of the human family is the foundation of freedom, justice and peace in the world,

Noting that the States parties to the Convention on the Rights of the Child (hereinafter referred to as "the Convention") recognize the rights set forth in it to each child within their jurisdiction without discrimination of any kind, irrespective of the child's or his or her parent's or legal guardian's race, colour, sex, language, religion, political or other opinion, national, ethnic or social origin, property, disability, birth or other status,

Reaffirming the universality, indivisibility, interdependence and interrelatedness of all human rights and fundamental freedoms,

Reaffirming also the status of the child as a subject of rights and as a human being with dignity and with evolving capacities,

Recognizing that children's special and dependent status may create real difficulties for them in pursuing remedies for violations of their rights,

Considering that the present Protocol will reinforce and complement national and regional mechanisms allowing children to submit complaints for violations of their rights,

Recognizing that the best interests of the child should be a primary consideration to be respected in pursuing remedies for violations of the rights of the child, and that such remedies should take into account the need for child-sensitive procedures at all levels,

Encouraging States parties to develop appropriate national mechanisms to enable a child whose rights have been violated to have access to effective remedies at the domestic level,

 | DOI:10.1163/9789004681224_008

Recalling the important role that national human rights institutions and other relevant specialized institutions, mandated to promote and protect the rights of the child, can play in this regard,

Considering that, in order to reinforce and complement such national mechanisms and to further enhance the implementation of the Convention and, where applicable, the Optional Protocols thereto on the sale of children, child prostitution and child pornography and on the involvement of children in armed conflict, it would be appropriate to enable the Committee on the Rights of the Child (hereinafter referred to as "the Committee") to carry out the functions provided for in the present Protocol,

Have agreed as follows:

Part 1: General Provisions

Article 1 – Competence of the Committee on the Rights of the Child

1. A State party to the present Protocol recognizes the competence of the Committee as provided for by the present Protocol.
2. The Committee shall not exercise its competence regarding a State party to the present Protocol on matters concerning violations of rights set forth in an instrument to which that State is not a party.
3. No communication shall be received by the Committee if it concerns a State that is not a party to the present Protocol.

Article 2 – General Principles Guiding the Functions of the Committee

In fulfilling the functions conferred on it by the present Protocol, the Committee shall be guided by the principle of the best interests of the child. It shall also have regard for the rights and views of the child, the views of the child being given due weight in accordance with the age and maturity of the child.

Article 3 – Rules of Procedure

1. The Committee shall adopt rules of procedure to be followed when exercising the functions conferred on it by the present Protocol. In doing so, it shall have regard, in particular, for article 2 of the present Protocol in order to guarantee child-sensitive procedures.
2. The Committee shall include in its rules of procedure safeguards to prevent the manipulation of the child by those acting on his or her behalf and may decline to examine any communication that it considers not to be in the child's best interests.

Article 4 – Protection Measures

1. A State party shall take all appropriate steps to ensure that individuals under its jurisdiction are not subjected to any human rights violation, illtreatment or intimidation as a consequence of communications or cooperation with the Committee pursuant to the present Protocol.
2. The identity of any individual or group of individuals concerned shall not be revealed publicly without their express consent.

Part II: Communications Procedure

Article 5 – Individual Communications

1. Communications may be submitted by or on behalf of an individual or group of individuals, within the jurisdiction of a State party, claiming to be victims of a violation by that State party of any of the rights set forth in any of the following instruments to which that State is a party:
(a) The Convention;
(b) The Optional Protocol to the Convention on the sale of children, child prostitution and child pornography;
(c) The Optional Protocol to the Convention on the involvement of children in armed conflict.
2. Where a communication is submitted on behalf of an individual or group of individuals, this shall be with their consent unless the author can justify acting on their behalf without such consent.

Article 6 – Interim Measures

1. At any time after the receipt of a communication and before a determination on the merits has been reached, the Committee may transmit to the State party concerned for its urgent consideration a request that the State party take such interim measures as may be necessary in exceptional circumstances to avoid possible irreparable damage to the victim or victims of the alleged violations.
2. Where the Committee exercises its discretion under paragraph 1 of the present article, this does not imply a determination on admissibility or on the merits of the communication.

Article 7 – Admissibility

The Committee shall consider a communication inadmissible when:
(a) The communication is anonymous;
(b) The communication is not in writing;

(c) The communication constitutes an abuse of the right of submission of such communications or is incompatible with the provisions of the Convention and/or the Optional Protocols thereto;
(d) The same matter has already been examined by the Committee or has been or is being examined under another procedure of international investigation or settlement;
(e) All available domestic remedies have not been exhausted. This shall not be the rule where the application of the remedies is unreasonably prolonged or unlikely to bring effective relief;
(f) The communication is manifestly ill-founded or not sufficiently substantiated;
(g) The facts that are the subject of the communication occurred prior to the entry into force of the present Protocol for the State party concerned, unless those facts continued after that date;
(h) The communication is not submitted within one year after the exhaustion of domestic remedies, except in cases where the author can demonstrate that it had not been possible to submit the communication within that time limit.

Article 8 – Transmission of the Communication

1. Unless the Committee considers a communication inadmissible without reference to the State party concerned, the Committee shall bring any communication submitted to it under the present Protocol confidentially to the attention of the State party concerned as soon as possible.
2. The State party shall submit to the Committee written explanations or statements clarifying the matter and the remedy, if any, that it may have provided. The State party shall submit its response as soon as possible and within six months.

Article 9 – Friendly Settlement

1. The Committee shall make available its good offices to the parties concerned with a view to reaching a friendly settlement of the matter on the basis of respect for the obligations set forth in the Convention and/or the Optional Protocols thereto.
2. An agreement on a friendly settlement reached under the auspices of the Committee closes consideration of the communication under the present Protocol.

Article 10 – Consideration of Communications

1. The Committee shall consider communications received under the present Protocol as quickly as possible, in the light of all documentation submitted to it, provided that this documentation is transmitted to the parties concerned.
2. The Committee shall hold closed meetings when examining communications received under the present Protocol.
3. Where the Committee has requested interim measures, it shall expedite the consideration of the communication.
4. When examining communications alleging violations of economic, social or cultural rights, the Committee shall consider the reasonableness of the steps taken by the State party in accordance with article 4 of the Convention. In doing so, the Committee shall bear in mind that the State party may adopt a range of possible policy measures for the implementation of the economic, social and cultural rights in the Convention.
5. After examining a communication, the Committee shall, without delay, transmit its views on the communication, together with its recommendations, if any, to the parties concerned.

Article 11 – Follow-Up

1. The State party shall give due consideration to the views of the Committee, together with its recommendations, if any, and shall submit to the Committee a written response, including information on any action taken and envisaged in the light of the views and recommendations of the Committee. The State party shall submit its response as soon as possible and within six months.
2. The Committee may invite the State party to submit further information about any measures the State party has taken in response to its views or recommendations or implementation of a friendly settlement agreement, if any, including as deemed appropriate by the Committee, in the State party's subsequent reports under article 44 of the Convention, article 12 of the Optional Protocol to the Convention on the sale of children, child prostitution and child pornography or article 8 of the Optional Protocol to the Convention on the involvement of children in armed conflict, where applicable.

Article 12 – Inter-State Communications

1. A State party to the present Protocol may, at any time, declare that it recognizes the competence of the Committee to receive and consider communications in which a State party claims that another State party is not fulfilling its obligations under any of the following instruments to which the State is a party:

(a) The Convention;

(b) The Optional Protocol to the Convention on the sale of children, child prostitution and child pornography;
(c) The Optional Protocol to the Convention on the involvement of children in armed conflict.

2. The Committee shall not receive communications concerning a State party that has not made such a declaration or communications from a State party that has not made such a declaration.
3. The Committee shall make available its good offices to the States parties concerned with a view to a friendly solution of the matter on the basis of the respect for the obligations set forth in the Convention and the Optional Protocols thereto.
4. A declaration under paragraph 1 of the present article shall be deposited by the States parties with the Secretary-General of the United Nations, who shall transmit copies thereof to the other States parties. A declaration may be withdrawn at any time by notification to the Secretary-General. Such a withdrawal shall not prejudice the consideration of any matter that is the subject of a communication already transmitted under the present article; no further communications by any State party shall be received under the present article after the notification of withdrawal of the declaration has been received by the Secretary-General, unless the State party concerned has made a new declaration.

Part III: Inquiry Procedure

Article 13 – Inquiry Procedure for Grave or Systematic Violations

1. If the Committee receives reliable information indicating grave or systematic violations by a State party of rights set forth in the Convention or in the Optional Protocols thereto on the sale of children, child prostitution and child pornography or on the involvement of children in armed conflict, the Committee shall invite the State party to cooperate in the examination of the information and, to this end, to submit observations without delay with regard to the information concerned.
2. Taking into account any observations that may have been submitted by the State party concerned, as well as any other reliable information available to it, the Committee may designate one or more of its members to conduct an inquiry and to report urgently to the Committee. Where warranted and with the consent of the State party, the inquiry may include a visit to its territory.
3. Such an inquiry shall be conducted confidentially, and the cooperation of the State party shall be sought at all stages of the proceedings.

4. After examining the findings of such an inquiry, the Committee shall transmit without delay these findings to the State party concerned, together with any comments and recommendations.
5. The State party concerned shall, as soon as possible and within six months of receiving the findings, comments and recommendations transmitted by the Committee, submit its observations to the Committee.
6. After such proceedings have been completed with regard to an inquiry made in accordance with paragraph 2 of the present article, the Committee may, after consultation with the State party concerned, decide to include a summary account of the results of the proceedings in its report provided for in article 16 of the present Protocol.
7. Each State party may, at the time of signature or ratification of the present Protocol or accession thereto, declare that it does not recognize the competence of the Committee provided for in the present article in respect of the rights set forth in some or all of the instruments listed in paragraph 1.
8. Any State party having made a declaration in accordance with paragraph 7 of the present article may, at any time, withdraw this declaration by notification to the Secretary-General of the United Nations.

Article 14 – Follow-Up to the Inquiry Procedure

1. The Committee may, if necessary, after the end of the period of six months referred to in article 13, paragraph 5, invite the State party concerned to inform it of the measures taken and envisaged in response to an inquiry conducted under article 13 of the present Protocol.
2. The Committee may invite the State party to submit further information about any measures that the State party has taken in response to an inquiry conducted under article 13, including as deemed appropriate by the Committee, in the State party's subsequent reports under article 44 of the Convention, article 12 of the Optional Protocol to the Convention on the sale of children, child prostitution and child pornography or article 8 of the Optional Protocol to the Convention on the involvement of children in armed conflict, where applicable.

Part IV: Final Provisions

Article 15 – International Assistance and Cooperation

1. The Committee may transmit, with the consent of the State party concerned, to United Nations specialized agencies, funds and programmes and other competent bodies its views or recommendations concerning communications

and inquiries that indicate a need for technical advice or assistance, together with the State party's observations and suggestions, if any, on these views or recommendations.
2. The Committee may also bring to the attention of such bodies, with the consent of the State party concerned, any matter arising out of communications considered under the present Protocol that may assist them in deciding, each within its field of competence, on the advisability of international measures likely to contribute to assisting States parties in achieving progress in the implementation of the rights recognized in the Convention and/or the Optional Protocols thereto.

Article 16 – Report to the General Assembly
The Committee shall include in its report submitted every two years to the General Assembly in accordance with article 44, paragraph 5, of the Convention a summary of its activities under the present Protocol.

Article 17 – Dissemination of and Information on the Optional Protocol
Each State party undertakes to make widely known and to disseminate the present Protocol and to facilitate access to information about the views and recommendations of the Committee, in particular with regard to matters involving the State party, by appropriate and active means and in accessible formats to adults and children alike, including those with disabilities.

Article 18 – Signature, Ratification and Accession
1. The present Protocol is open for signature to any State that has signed, ratified or acceded to the Convention or either of the first two Optional Protocols thereto.
2. The present Protocol is subject to ratification by any State that has ratified or acceded to the Convention or either of the first two Optional Protocols thereto. Instruments of ratification shall be deposited with the Secretary-General of the United Nations.
3. The present Protocol shall be open to accession by any State that has ratified or acceded to the Convention or either of the first two Optional Protocols thereto.
4. Accession shall be effected by the deposit of an instrument of accession with the Secretary-General.

Article 19 – Entry into Force

1. The present Protocol shall enter into force three months after the deposit of the tenth instrument of ratification or accession.

2. For each State ratifying the present Protocol or acceding to it after the deposit of the tenth instrument of ratification or instrument of accession, the present Protocol shall enter into force three months after the date of the deposit of its own instrument of ratification or accession.

Article 20 – Violations occurring after the Entry into Force

1. The Committee shall have competence solely in respect of violations by the State party of any of the rights set forth in the Convention and/or the first two Optional Protocols thereto occurring after the entry into force of the present Protocol.

2. If a State becomes a party to the present Protocol after its entry into force, the obligations of that State vis-à-vis the Committee shall relate only to violations of the rights set forth in the Convention and/or the first two Optional Protocols thereto occurring after the entry into force of the present Protocol for the State concerned.

Article 21 – Amendments

1. Any State party may. propose an amendment to the present Protocol and submit it to the Secretary-General of the United Nations. The Secretary-General shall communicate any proposed amendments to States parties with a request to be notified whether they favour a meeting of States parties for the purpose of considering and deciding upon the proposals. In the event that, within four months of the date of such communication, at least one third of the States parties favour such a meeting, the Secretary-General shall convene the meeting under the auspices of the United Nations. Any amendment adopted by a majority of two thirds of the States parties present and voting shall be submitted by the Secretary-General to the General Assembly for approval and, thereafter, to all States parties for acceptance.

2. An amendment adopted and approved in accordance with paragraph 1 of the present article shall enter into force on the thirtieth day after the number of instruments of acceptance deposited reaches two thirds of the number of States parties at the date of adoption of the amendment. Thereafter, the amendment shall enter into force for any State party on the thirtieth day following the deposit of its own instrument of acceptance. An amendment shall be binding only on those States parties that have accepted it.

Article 22 – Denunciation

1. Any State party may denounce the present Protocol at any time by written notification to the Secretary-General of the United Nations. The denunciation shall take effect one year after the date of receipt of the notification by the Secretary-General.

2. Denunciation shall be without prejudice to the continued application of the provisions of the present Protocol to any communication submitted under articles 5 or 12 or any inquiry initiated under article 13 before the effective date of denunciation.

Article 23 – Depositary and Notification by the Secretary-General

1. The Secretary-General of the United Nations shall be the depositary of the present Protocol.

2. The Secretary-General shall inform all States of:

(a) Signatures, ratifications and accessions under the present Protocol;

(b) The date of entry into force of the present Protocol and of any amendment thereto under article 21;

(c) Any denunciation under article 22 of the present Protocol.

Article 24 – Languages

1. The present Protocol, of which the Arabic, Chinese, English, French, Russian and Spanish texts are equally authentic, shall be deposited in the archives of the United Nations.

2. The Secretary-General of the United Nations shall transmit certified copies of the present Protocol to all States.

PART II

General Human Rights Instruments

CHAPTER 4

Universal Declaration of Human Rights

Adopted and proclaimed by General Assembly resolution 217 A (III) of 10 December 1948

Preamble

Whereas recognition of the inherent dignity and of the equal and inalienable rights of all members of the human family is the foundation of freedom, justice and peace in the world,

Whereas disregard and contempt for human rights have resulted in barbarous acts which have outraged the conscience of mankind, and the advent of a world in which human beings shall enjoy freedom of speech and belief and freedom from fear and want has been proclaimed as the highest aspiration of the common people,

Whereas it is essential, if man is not to be compelled to have recourse, as a last resort, to rebellion against tyranny and oppression, that human rights should be protected by the rule of law,

Whereas it is essential to promote the development of friendly relations between nations,

Whereas the peoples of the United Nations have in the Charter reaffirmed their faith in fundamental human rights, in the dignity and worth of the human person and in the equal rights of men and women and have determined to promote social progress and better standards of life in larger freedom,

Whereas Member States have pledged themselves to achieve, in co-operation with the United Nations, the promotion of universal respect for and observance of human rights and fundamental freedoms,

Whereas a common understanding of these rights and freedoms is of the greatest importance for the full realization of this pledge,

Now, therefore,

The General Assembly,

Proclaims this Universal Declaration of Human Rights as a common standard of achievement for all peoples and all nations, to the end that every individual and every organ of society, keeping this Declaration constantly in mind, shall strive by teaching and education to promote respect for these rights and freedoms and by progressive measures, national and international, to secure their universal and effective recognition and observance, both among the peoples of Member States themselves and among the peoples of territories under their jurisdiction.

Art. 1 All human beings are born free and equal in dignity and rights. They are endowed with reason and conscience and should act towards one another in a spirit of brotherhood.

Art. 2 Everyone is entitled to all the rights and freedoms set forth in this Declaration, without distinction of any kind, such as race, colour, sex, language, religion, political or other opinion, national or social origin, property, birth or other status.

Furthermore, no distinction shall be made on the basis of the political, jurisdictional or international status of the country or territory to which a person belongs, whether it be independent, trust, non-self-governing or under any other limitation of sovereignty.

Art. 3 Everyone has the right to life, liberty and the security of person.

Art. 4 No one shall be held in slavery or servitude; slavery and the slave trade shall be prohibited in all their forms.

Art. 5 No one shall be subjected to torture or to cruel, inhuman or degrading treatment or punishment.

Art. 6 Everyone has the right to recognition everywhere as a person before the law.

Art. 7 All are equal before the law and are entitled without any discrimination to equal protection of the law. All are entitled to equal protection against any discrimination in violation of this Declaration and against any incitement to such discrimination.

Art. 8 Everyone has the right to an effective remedy by the competent national tribunals for acts violating the fundamental rights granted him by the constitution or by law.

Art. 9 No one shall be subjected to arbitrary arrest, detention or exile.

Art. 10 Everyone is entitled in full equality to a fair and public hearing by an independent and impartial tribunal, in the determination of his rights and obligations and of any criminal charge against him.

Art. 11 1. Everyone charged with a penal offence has the right to be presumed innocent until proved guilty according to law in a public trial at which he has had all the guarantees necessary for his defence.

2. No one shall be held guilty of any penal offence on account of any act or omission which did not constitute a penal offence, under national or international law, at the time when it was committed. Nor shall a heavier penalty be imposed than the one that was applicable at the time the penal offence was committed.

Art. 12 No one shall be subjected to arbitrary interference with his privacy, family, home or correspondence, nor to attacks upon his honour and reputation. Everyone has the right to the protection of the law against such interference or attacks.

Art. 13 1. Everyone has the right to freedom of movement and residence within the borders of each State.

2. Everyone has the right to leave any country, including his own, and to return to his country.

Art. 14 1. Everyone has the right to seek and to enjoy in other countries asylum from persecution.

2. This right may not be invoked in the case of prosecutions genuinely arising from non-political crimes or from acts contrary to the purposes and principles of the United Nations.

Art. 15 1. Everyone has the right to a nationality.

2. No one shall be arbitrarily deprived of his nationality nor denied the right to change his nationality.

Art. 16 1. Men and women of full age, without any limitation due to race, nationality or religion, have the right to marry and to found a family. They are entitled to equal rights as to marriage, during marriage and at its dissolution.

2. Marriage shall be entered into only with the free and full consent of the intending spouses.

3. The family is the natural and fundamental group unit of society and is entitled to protection by society and the State.

Art. 17 1. Everyone has the right to own property alone as well as in association with others.

2. No one shall be arbitrarily deprived of his property.

Art. 18 Everyone has the right to freedom of thought, conscience and religion; this right includes freedom to change his religion or belief, and freedom, either alone or in community with others and in public or private, to manifest his religion or belief in teaching, practice, worship and observance.

Art. 19 Everyone has the right to freedom of opinion and expression; this right includes freedom to hold opinions without interference and to seek, receive and impart information and ideas through any media and regardless of frontiers.

Art. 20 1. Everyone has the right to freedom of peaceful assembly and association.

2. No one may be compelled to belong to an association.

Art. 21 1. Everyone has the right to take part in the government of his country, directly or through freely chosen representatives.

2. Everyone has the right of equal access to public service in his country.

3. The will of the people shall be the basis of the authority of government; this will shall be expressed in periodic and genuine elections which shall be by universal and equal suffrage and shall be held by secret vote or by equivalent free voting procedures.

Art. 22 Everyone, as a member of society, has the right to social security and is entitled to realization, through national effort and international co-operation and in accordance with the organization and resources of each State, of the economic, social and cultural rights indispensable for his dignity and the free development of his personality.

Art. 23 1. Everyone has the right to work, to free choice of employment, to just and favourable conditions of work and to protection against unemployment.

2. Everyone, without any discrimination, has the right to equal pay for equal work.

3. Everyone who works has the right to just and favourable remuneration ensuring for himself and his family an existence worthy of human dignity, and supplemented, if necessary, by other means of social protection.

4. Everyone has the right to form and to join trade unions for the protection of his interests.

Art. 24 Everyone has the right to rest and leisure, including reasonable limitation of working hours and periodic holidays with pay.

Art. 25 1. Everyone has the right to a standard of living adequate for the health and well-being of himself and of his family, including food, clothing, housing and medical care and necessary social services, and the right to security in the event of unemployment, sickness, disability, widowhood, old age or other lack of livelihood in circumstances beyond his control.

2. Motherhood and childhood are entitled to special care and assistance. All children, whether born in or out of wedlock, shall enjoy the same social protection.

Art. 26 1. Everyone has the right to education. Education shall be free, at least in the elementary and fundamental stages. Elementary education shall be compulsory. Technical and professional education shall be made generally available and higher education shall be equally accessible to all on the basis of merit.

2. Education shall be directed to the full development of the human personality and to the strengthening of respect for human rights and fundamental freedoms. It shall promote understanding, tolerance and friendship among all nations, racial or religious groups, and shall further the activities of the United Nations for the maintenance of peace.

3. Parents have a prior right to choose the kind of education that shall be given to their children.

Art. 27 1. Everyone has the right freely to participate in the cultural life of the community, to enjoy the arts and to share in scientific advancement and its benefits.
2. Everyone has the right to the protection of the moral and material interests resulting from any scientific, literary or artistic production of which he is the author.
Art. 28 Everyone is entitled to a social and international order in which the rights and freedoms set forth in this Declaration can be fully realized.
Art. 29 1. Everyone has duties to the community in which alone the free and full development of his personality is possible.
2. In the exercise of his rights and freedoms, everyone shall be subject only to such limitations as are determined by law solely for the purpose of securing due recognition and respect for the rights and freedoms of others and of meeting the just requirements of morality, public order and the general welfare in a democratic society.
3. These rights and freedoms may in no case be exercised contrary to the purposes and principles of the United Nations.
Art. 30 Nothing in this Declaration may be interpreted as implying for any State, group or person any right to engage in any activity or to perform any act aimed at the destruction of any of the rights and freedoms set forth herein.

CHAPTER 5

International Convention on the Elimination of All Forms of Racial Discrimination

Adopted and opened for signature, ratification and accession by General Assembly resolution 2106 A (XX) of 21 December 1965
Entry into force on 4 January 1969, in accordance with article 19

The States Parties to this Convention,

Considering that the Charter of the United Nations is based on the principles of the dignity and equality inherent in all human beings, and that all Member States have pledged themselves to take joint and separate action, in co-operation with the Organization, for the achievement of one of the purposes of the United Nations which is to promote and encourage universal respect for and observance of human rights and fundamental freedoms for all, without distinction as to race, sex, language or religion,

Considering that the Universal Declaration of Human Rights proclaims that all human beings are born free and equal in dignity and rights and that everyone is entitled to all the rights and freedoms set out therein, without distinction of any kind, in particular as to race, colour or national origin,

Considering that all human beings are equal before the law and are entitled to equal protection of the law against any discrimination and against any incitement to discrimination,

Considering that the United Nations has condemned colonialism and all practices of segregation and discrimination associated therewith, in whatever form and wherever they exist, and that the Declaration on the Granting of Independence to Colonial Countries and Peoples of 14 December 1960 (General Assembly resolution 1514 (XV)) has affirmed and solemnly proclaimed the necessity of bringing them to a speedy and unconditional end,

Considering that the United Nations Declaration on the Elimination of All Forms of Racial Discrimination of 20 November 1963 (General Assembly resolution 1904 (XVIII)) solemnly affirms the necessity of speedily eliminating racial discrimination throughout the world in all its forms and manifestations and of securing understanding of and respect for the dignity of the human person,

Convinced that any doctrine of superiority based on racial differentiation is scientifically false, morally condemnable, socially unjust and dangerous, and

DOI:10.1163/9789004681224_010

that there is no justification for racial discrimination, in theory or in practice, anywhere,

Reaffirming that discrimination between human beings on the grounds of race, colour or ethnic origin is an obstacle to friendly and peaceful relations among nations and is capable of disturbing peace and security among peoples and the harmony of persons living side by side even within one and the same State,

Convinced that the existence of racial barriers is repugnant to the ideals of any human society,

Alarmed by manifestations of racial discrimination still in evidence in some areas of the world and by governmental policies based on racial superiority or hatred, such as policies of apartheid, segregation or separation,

Resolved to adopt all necessary measures for speedily eliminating racial discrimination in all its forms and manifestations, and to prevent and combat racist doctrines and practices in order to promote understanding between races and to build an international community free from all forms of racial segregation and racial discrimination,

Bearing in mind the Convention concerning Discrimination in respect of Employment and Occupation adopted by the International Labour Organisation in 1958, and the Convention against Discrimination in Education adopted by the United Nations Educational, Scientific and Cultural Organization in 1960,

Desiring to implement the principles embodied in the United Nations Declaration on the Elimination of All Forms of Racial Discrimination and to secure the earliest adoption of practical measures to that end,

Have agreed as follows:

Part I

Art. 1 1. In this Convention, the term "racial discrimination" shall mean any distinction, exclusion, restriction or preference based on race, colour, descent, or national or ethnic origin which has the purpose or effect of nullifying or impairing the recognition, enjoyment or exercise, on an equal footing, of human rights and fundamental freedoms in the political, economic, social, cultural or any other field of public life.

2. This Convention shall not apply to distinctions, exclusions, restrictions or preferences made by a State Party to this Convention between citizens and non-citizens.

3. Nothing in this Convention may be interpreted as affecting in any way the legal provisions of States Parties concerning nationality, citizenship or

naturalization, provided that such provisions do not discriminate against any particular nationality.

4. Special measures taken for the sole purpose of securing adequate advancement of certain racial or ethnic groups or individuals requiring such protection as may be necessary in order to ensure such groups or individuals equal enjoyment or exercise of human rights and fundamental freedoms shall not be deemed racial discrimination, provided, however, that such measures do not, as a consequence, lead to the maintenance of separate rights for different racial groups and that they shall not be continued after the objectives for which they were taken have been achieved.

Art. 2 1. States Parties condemn racial discrimination and undertake to pursue by all appropriate means and without delay a policy of eliminating racial discrimination in all its forms and promoting understanding among all races, and, to this end:

(a) Each State Party undertakes to engage in no act or practice of racial discrimination against persons, groups of persons or institutions and to ensure that all public authorities and public institutions, national and local, shall act in conformity with this obligation;

(b) Each State Party undertakes not to sponsor, defend or support racial discrimination by any persons or organizations;

(c) Each State Party shall take effective measures to review governmental, national and local policies, and to amend, rescind or nullify any laws and regulations which have the effect of creating or perpetuating racial discrimination wherever it exists;

(d) Each State Party shall prohibit and bring to an end, by all appropriate means, including legislation as required by circumstances, racial discrimination by any persons, group or organization;

(e) Each State Party undertakes to encourage, where appropriate, integrationist multiracial organizations and movements and other means of eliminating barriers between races, and to discourage anything which tends to strengthen racial division.

2. States Parties shall, when the circumstances so warrant, take, in the social, economic, cultural and other fields, special and concrete measures to ensure the adequate development and protection of certain racial groups or individuals belonging to them, for the purpose of guaranteeing them the full and equal enjoyment of human rights and fundamental freedoms. These measures shall in no case entail as a con sequence the maintenance of unequal or separate rights for different racial groups after the objectives for which they were taken have been achieved.

Art. 3 States Parties particularly condemn racial segregation and apartheid and undertake to prevent, prohibit and eradicate all practices of this nature in territories under their jurisdiction.

Art. 4 States Parties condemn all propaganda and all organizations which are based on ideas or theories of superiority of one race or group of persons of one colour or ethnic origin, or which attempt to justify or promote racial hatred and discrimination in any form, and undertake to adopt immediate and positive measures designed to eradicate all incitement to, or acts of, such discrimination and, to this end, with due regard to the principles embodied in the Universal Declaration of Human Rights and the rights expressly set forth in article 5 of this Convention, inter alia:

(a) Shall declare an offence punishable by law all dissemination of ideas based on racial superiority or hatred, incitement to racial discrimination, as well as all acts of violence or incitement to such acts against any race or group of persons of another colour or ethnic origin, and also the provision of any assistance to racist activities, including the financing thereof;

(b) Shall declare illegal and prohibit organizations, and also organized and all other propaganda activities, which promote and incite racial discrimination, and shall recognize participation in such organizations or activities as an offence punishable by law;

(c) Shall not permit public authorities or public institutions, national or local, to promote or incite racial discrimination.

Art. 5 In compliance with the fundamental obligations laid down in article 2 of this Convention, States Parties undertake to prohibit and to eliminate racial discrimination in all its forms and to guarantee the right of everyone, without distinction as to race, colour, or national or ethnic origin, to equality before the law, notably in the enjoyment of the following rights:

(a) The right to equal treatment before the tribunals and all other organs administering justice;

(b) The right to security of person and protection by the State against violence or bodily harm, whether inflicted by government officials or by any individual group or institution;

(c) Political rights, in particular the right to participate in elections – to vote and to stand for election – on the basis of universal and equal suffrage, to take part in the Government as well as in the conduct of public affairs at any level and to have equal access to public service;

(d) Other civil rights, in particular:

    (i) The right to freedom of movement and residence within the border of the State;

- (ii) The right to leave any country, including one's own, and to return to one's country;
- (iii) The right to nationality;
- (iv) The right to marriage and choice of spouse;
- (v) The right to own property alone as well as in association with others;
- (vi) The right to inherit;
- (vii) The right to freedom of thought, conscience and religion;
- (viii) The right to freedom of opinion and expression;
- (ix) The right to freedom of peaceful assembly and association;

(e) Economic, social and cultural rights, in particular:

- (i) The rights to work, to free choice of employment, to just and favourable conditions of work, to protection against unemployment, to equal pay for equal work, to just and favourable remuneration;
- (ii) The right to form and join trade unions;
- (iii) The right to housing;
- (iv) The right to public health, medical care, social security and social services;
- (v) The right to education and training;
- (vi) The right to equal participation in cultural activities;

(f) The right of access to any place or service intended for use by the general public, such as transport hotels, restaurants, cafes, theatres and parks.

Art. 6 States Parties shall assure to everyone within their jurisdiction effective protection and remedies, through the competent national tribunals and other State institutions, against any acts of racial discrimination which violate his human rights and fundamental freedoms contrary to this Convention, as well as the right to seek from such tribunals just and adequate reparation or satisfaction for any damage suffered as a result of such discrimination.

Art. 7 States Parties undertake to adopt immediate and effective measures, particularly in the fields of teaching, education, culture and information, with a view to combating prejudices which lead to racial discrimination and to promoting understanding, tolerance and friendship among nations and racial or ethnical groups, as well as to propagating the purposes and principles of the Charter of the United Nations, the Universal Declaration of Human Rights, the United Nations Declaration on the Elimination of All Forms of Racial Discrimination, and this Convention.

Part II

Art. 8 1. There shall be established a Committee on the Elimination of Racial Discrimination (hereinafter referred to as the Committee) consisting of eighteen experts of high moral standing and acknowledged impartiality elected by States Parties from among their nationals, who shall serve in their personal capacity, consideration being given to equitable geographical distribution and to the representation of the different forms of civilization as well as of the principal legal systems.
2. The members of the Committee shall be elected by secret ballot from a list of persons nominated by the States Parties. Each State Party may nominate one person from among its own nationals.
3. The initial election shall be held six months after the date of the entry into force of this Convention. At least three months before the date of each election the Secretary-General of the United Nations shall address a letter to the States Parties inviting them to submit their nominations within two months. The Secretary-General shall prepare a list in alphabetical order of all persons thus nominated, indicating the States Parties which have nominated them, and shall submit it to the States Parties.
4. Elections of the members of the Committee shall be held at a meeting of States Parties convened by the Secretary-General at United Nations Headquarters. At that meeting, for which two thirds of the States Parties shall constitute a quorum, the persons elected to the Committee shall be nominees who obtain the largest number of votes and an absolute majority of the votes of the representatives of States Parties present and voting.
5.
(a) The members of the Committee shall be elected for a term of four years. However, the terms of nine of the members elected at the first election shall expire at the end of two years; immediately after the first election the names of these nine members shall be chosen by lot by the Chairman of the Committee.
(b) For the filling of casual vacancies, the State Party whose expert has ceased to function as a member of the Committee shall appoint another expert from among its nationals, subject to the approval of the Committee.
6. States Parties shall be responsible for the expenses of the members of the Committee while they are in performance of Committee duties.
Art. 9 1. States Parties undertake to submit to the Secretary-General of the United Nations, for consideration by the Committee, a report on the legislative,

judicial, administrative or other measures which they have adopted and which give effect to the provisions of this Convention:

(a) within one year after the entry into force of the Convention for the State concerned; and
(b) thereafter every two years and whenever the Committee so requests. The Committee may request further information from the States Parties.

2. The Committee shall report annually, through the Secretary General, to the General Assembly of the United Nations on its activities and may make suggestions and general recommendations based on the examination of the reports and information received from the States Parties. Such suggestions and general recommendations shall be reported to the General Assembly together with comments, if any, from States Parties.

Art. 10 1. The Committee shall adopt its own rules of procedure.

2. The Committee shall elect its officers for a term of two years.

3. The secretariat of the Committee shall be provided by the Secretary General of the United Nations.

4. The meetings of the Committee shall normally be held at United Nations Headquarters.

Art. 11 1. If a State Party considers that another State Party is not giving effect to the provisions of this Convention, it may bring the matter to the attention of the Committee. The Committee shall then transmit the communication to the State Party concerned. Within three months, the receiving State shall submit to the Committee written explanations or statements clarifying the matter and the remedy, if any, that may have been taken by that State.

2. If the matter is not adjusted to the satisfaction of both parties, either by bilateral negotiations or by any other procedure open to them, within six months after the receipt by the receiving State of the initial communication, either State shall have the right to refer the matter again to the Committee by notifying the Committee and also the other State.

3. The Committee shall deal with a matter referred to it in accordance with paragraph 2 of this article after it has ascertained that all available domestic remedies have been invoked and exhausted in the case, in conformity with the generally recognized principles of international law. This shall not be the rule where the application of the remedies is unreasonably prolonged.

4. In any matter referred to it, the Committee may call upon the States Parties concerned to supply any other relevant information.

5. When any matter arising out of this article is being considered by the Committee, the States Parties concerned shall be entitled to send a representative to take part in the proceedings of the Committee, without voting rights, while the matter is under consideration.

Art. 12 1.

(a) After the Committee has obtained and collated all the information it deems necessary, the Chairman shall appoint an ad hoc Conciliation Commission (hereinafter referred to as the Commission) comprising five persons who may or may not be members of the Committee. The members of the Commission shall be appointed with the unanimous consent of the parties to the dispute, and its good offices shall be made available to the States concerned with a view to an amicable solution of the matter on the basis of respect for this Convention.

(b) If the States parties to the dispute fail to reach agreement within three months on all or part of the composition of the Commission, the members of the Commission not agreed upon by the States parties to the dispute shall be elected by secret ballot by a two-thirds majority vote of the Committee from among its own members.

2. The members of the Commission shall serve in their personal capacity. They shall not be nationals of the States parties to the dispute or of a State not Party to this Convention.

3. The Commission shall elect its own Chairman and adopt its own rules of procedure.

4. The meetings of the Commission shall normally be held at United Nations Headquarters or at any other convenient place as determined by the Commission.

5. The secretariat provided in accordance with article 10, paragraph 3, of this Convention shall also service the Commission whenever a dispute among States Parties brings the Commission into being.

6. The States parties to the dispute shall share equally all the expenses of the members of the Commission in accordance with estimates to be provided by the Secretary-General of the United Nations.

7. The Secretary-General shall be empowered to pay the expenses of the members of the Commission, if necessary, before reimbursement by the States parties to the dispute in accordance with paragraph 6 of this article.

8. The information obtained and collated by the Committee shall be made available to the Commission, and the Commission may call upon the States concerned to supply any other relevant information.

Art. 13 1. When the Commission has fully considered the matter, it shall prepare and submit to the Chairman of the Committee a report embodying its findings on all questions of fact relevant to the issue between the parties and containing such recommendations as it may think proper for the amicable solution of the dispute.

2. The Chairman of the Committee shall communicate the report of the Commission to each of the States parties to the dispute. These States shall, within three months, inform the Chairman of the Committee whether or not they accept the recommendations contained in the report of the Commission.
3. After the period provided for in paragraph 2 of this article, the Chairman of the Committee shall communicate the report of the Commission and the declarations of the States Parties concerned to the other States Parties to this Convention.
Art. 14 1. A State Party may at any time declare that it recognizes the competence of the Committee to receive and consider communications from individuals or groups of individuals within its jurisdiction claiming to be victims of a violation by that State Party of any of the rights set forth in this Convention. No communication shall be received by the Committee if it concerns a State Party which has not made such a declaration.
2. Any State Party which makes a declaration as provided for in paragraph 1 of this article may establish or indicate a body within its national legal order which shall be competent to receive and consider petitions from individuals and groups of individuals within its jurisdiction who claim to be victims of a violation of any of the rights set forth in this Convention and who have exhausted other available local remedies.
3. A declaration made in accordance with paragraph 1 of this article and the name of any body established or indicated in accordance with paragraph 2 of this article shall be deposited by the State Party concerned with the Secretary-General of the United Nations, who shall transmit copies thereof to the other States Parties. A declaration may be withdrawn at any time by notification to the Secretary-General, but such a withdrawal shall not affect communications pending before the Committee.
4. A register of petitions shall be kept by the body established or indicated in accordance with paragraph 2 of this article, and certified copies of the register shall be filed annually through appropriate channels with the Secretary-General on the understanding that the contents shall not be publicly disclosed.
5. In the event of failure to obtain satisfaction from the body established or indicated in accordance with paragraph 2 of this article, the petitioner shall have the right to communicate the matter to the Committee within six months.
6.
(a) The Committee shall confidentially bring any communication referred to it to the attention of the State Party alleged to be violating any provision of this Convention, but the identity of the individual or groups of individuals concerned shall not be revealed without his or their express consent. The Committee shall not receive anonymous communications;

(b) Within three months, the receiving State shall submit to the Committee written explanations or statements clarifying the matter and the remedy, if any, that may have been taken by that State.

7.

(a) The Committee shall consider communications in the light of all information made available to it by the State Party concerned and by the petitioner. The Committee shall not consider any communication from a petitioner unless it has ascertained that the petitioner has exhausted all available domestic remedies. However, this shall not be the rule where the application of the remedies is unreasonably prolonged;

(b) The Committee shall forward its suggestions and recommendations, if any, to the State Party concerned and to the petitioner.

8. The Committee shall include in its annual report a summary of such communications and, where appropriate, a summary of the explanations and statements of the States Parties concerned and of its own suggestions and recommendations.

9. The Committee shall be competent to exercise the functions provided for in this article only when at least ten States Parties to this Convention are bound by declarations in accordance with paragraph 1 of this article.

Art. 15 1. Pending the achievement of the objectives of the Declaration on the Granting of Independence to Colonial Countries and Peoples, contained in General Assembly resolution 1514 (XV) of 14 December 1960, the provisions of this Convention shall in no way limit the right of petition granted to these peoples by other international instruments or by the United Nations and its specialized agencies.

2.

(a) The Committee established under article 8, paragraph 1, of this Convention shall receive copies of the petitions from, and submit expressions of opinion and recommendations on these petitions to, the bodies of the United Nations which deal with matters directly related to the principles and objectives of this Convention in their consideration of petitions from the inhabitants of Trust and Non-Self-Governing Territories and all other territories to which General Assembly resolution 1514 (XV) applies, relating to matters covered by this Convention which are before these bodies;

(b) The Committee shall receive from the competent bodies of the United Nations copies of the reports concerning the legislative, judicial, administrative or other measures directly related to the principles and objectives of this Convention applied by the administering Powers within the

Territories mentioned in subparagraph (a) of this paragraph, and shall express opinions and make recommendations to these bodies.

3. The Committee shall include in its report to the General Assembly a summary of the petitions and reports it has received from United Nations bodies, and the expressions of opinion and recommendations of the Committee relating to the said petitions and reports.

4. The Committee shall request from the Secretary-General of the United Nations all information relevant to the objectives of this Convention and available to him regarding the Territories mentioned in paragraph 2 (a) of this article.

Art. 16 The provisions of this Convention concerning the settlement of disputes or complaints shall be applied without prejudice to other procedures for settling disputes or complaints in the field of discrimination laid down in the constituent instruments of, or conventions adopted by, the United Nations and its specialized agencies, and shall not prevent the States Parties from having recourse to other procedures for settling a dispute in accordance with general or special international agreements in force between them.

Part III

Art. 17 1. This Convention is open for signature by any State Member of the United Nations or member of any of its specialized agencies, by any State Party to the Statute of the International Court of Justice, and by any other State which has been invited by the General Assembly of the United Nations to become a Party to this Convention.

2. This Convention is subject to ratification. Instruments of ratification shall be deposited with the Secretary-General of the United Nations.

Art. 18 1. This Convention shall be open to accession by any State referred to in article 17, paragraph 1, of the Convention.

2. Accession shall be effected by the deposit of an instrument of accession with the Secretary-General of the United Nations.

Art. 19 1. This Convention shall enter into force on the thirtieth day after the date of the deposit with the Secretary-General of the United Nations of the twenty-seventh instrument of ratification or instrument of accession.

2. For each State ratifying this Convention or acceding to it after the deposit of the twenty-seventh instrument of ratification or instrument of accession, the Convention shall enter into force on the thirtieth day after the date of the deposit of its own instrument of ratification or instrument of accession.

Art. 20 1. The Secretary-General of the United Nations shall receive and circulate to all States which are or may become Parties to this Convention reservations made by States at the time of ratification or accession. Any State which objects to the reservation shall, within a period of ninety days from the date of the said communication, notify the Secretary-General that it does not accept it.
2. A reservation incompatible with the object and purpose of this Convention shall not be permitted, nor shall a reservation the effect of which would inhibit the operation of any of the bodies established by this Convention be allowed. A reservation shall be considered incompatible or inhibitive if at least two thirds of the States Parties to this Convention object to it.
3. Reservations may be withdrawn at any time by notification to this effect addressed to the Secretary-General. Such notification shall take effect on the date on which it is received.
Art. 21 A State Party may denounce this Convention by written notification to the Secretary-General of the United Nations. Denunciation shall take effect one year after the date of receipt of the notification by the Secretary-General.
Art. 22 Any dispute between two or more States Parties with respect to the interpretation or application of this Convention, which is not settled by negotiation or by the procedures expressly provided for in this Convention, shall, at the request of any of the parties to the dispute, be referred to the International Court of Justice for decision, unless the disputants agree to another mode of settlement.
Art. 23 1. A request for the revision of this Convention may be made at any time by any State Party by means of a notification in writing addressed to the Secretary-General of the United Nations.
2. The General Assembly of the United Nations shall decide upon the steps, if any, to be taken in respect of such a request.
Art. 24 The Secretary-General of the United Nations shall inform all States referred to in article 17, paragraph 1, of this Convention of the following particulars:
(a) Signatures, ratifications and accessions under articles 17 and 18;
(b) The date of entry into force of this Convention under article 19;
(c) Communications and declarations received under articles 14, 20 and 23;
(d) Denunciations under article 21.
Art. 25 1. This Convention, of which the Chinese, English, French, Russian and Spanish texts are equally authentic, shall be deposited in the archives of the United Nations.
2. The Secretary-General of the United Nations shall transmit certified copies of this Convention to all States belonging to any of the categories mentioned in article 17, paragraph 1, of the Convention.

IN FAITH WHEREOF the undersigned, being duly authorized by their respective Governments, have signed the present Convention, opened for signature at New York, on the seventh day of March, one thousand nine hundred and sixty-six.

CHAPTER 6

International Convenant on Civil and Political Rights

Adopted and opened for signature, ratification and accessionby General Assembly resolution 2200A (XXI) of 16 December 1966
Entry into force 23 March 1976, in accordance with article 49

The States Parties to the present Covenant,

Considering that, in accordance with the principles proclaimed in the Charter of the United Nations, recognition of the inherent dignity and of the equal and inalienable rights of all members of the human family is the foundation of freedom, justice and peace in the world,

Recognizing that these rights derive from the inherent dignity of the human person,

Recognizing that, in accordance with the Universal Declaration of Human Rights, the ideal of free human beings enjoying civil and political freedom and freedom from fear and want can only be achieved if conditions are created whereby everyone may enjoy his civil and political rights, as well as his economic, social and cultural rights,

Considering the obligation of States under the Charter of the United Nations to promote universal respect for, and observance of, human rights and freedoms,

Realizing that the individual, having duties to other individuals and to the community to which he belongs, is under a responsibility to strive for the promotion and observance of the rights recognized in the present Covenant,

Agree upon the following articles:

Part I

Art. 1 1. All peoples have the right of self-determination. By virtue of that right they freely determine their political status and freely pursue their economic, social and cultural development.
2. All peoples may, for their own ends, freely dispose of their natural wealth and resources without prejudice to any obligations arising out of international economic co-operation, based upon the principle of mutual benefit, and

international law. In no case may a people be deprived of its own means of subsistence.
2. The States Parties to the present Covenant, including those having responsibility for the administration of Non-Self-Governing and Trust Territories, shall promote the realization of the right of self-determination, and shall respect that right, in conformity with the provisions of the Charter of the United Nations.

Part II

Art. 2 1. Each State Party to the present Covenant undertakes to respect and to ensure to all individuals within its territory and subject to its jurisdiction the rights recognized in the present Covenant, without distinction of any kind, such as race, colour, sex, language, religion, political or other opinion, national or social origin, property, birth or other status.
2. Where not already provided for by existing legislative or other measures, each State Party to the present Covenant undertakes to take the necessary steps, in accordance with its constitutional processes and with the provisions of the present Covenant, to adopt such legislative or other measures as may be necessary to give effect to the rights recognized in the present Covenant.
3. Each State Party to the present Covenant undertakes:
(a) To ensure that any person whose rights or freedoms as herein recognized are violated shall have an effective remedy, notwithstanding that the violation has been committed by persons acting in an official capacity;
(b) To ensure that any person claiming such a remedy shall have his right thereto determined by competent judicial, administrative or legislative authorities, or by any other competent authority provided for by the legal system of the State, and to develop the possibilities of judicial remedy;
(c) To ensure that the competent authorities shall enforce such remedies when granted.

Art. 3 The States Parties to the present Covenant undertake to ensure the equal right of men and women to the enjoyment of all civil and political rights set forth in the present Covenant.

Art. 4 1. In time of public emergency which threatens the life of the nation and the existence of which is officially proclaimed, the States Parties to the present Covenant may take measures derogating from their obligations under the present Covenant to the extent strictly required by the exigencies of the

situation, provided that such measures are not inconsistent with their other obligations under international law and do not involve discrimination solely on the ground of race, colour, sex, language, religion or social origin.
2. No derogation from articles 6, 7, 8 (paragraphs 1 and 2), 11, 15, 16 and 18 may be made under this provision.
3. Any State Party to the present Covenant availing itself of the right of derogation shall immediately inform the other States Parties to the present Covenant, through the intermediary of the Secretary-General of the United Nations, of the provisions from which it has derogated and of the reasons by which it was actuated. A further communication shall be made, through the same intermediary, on the date on which it terminates such derogation.
Art. 5 1. Nothing in the present Covenant may be interpreted as implying for any State, group or person any right to engage in any activity or perform any act aimed at the destruction of any of the rights and freedoms recognized herein or at their limitation to a greater extent than is provided for in the present Covenant.
2. There shall be no restriction upon or derogation from any of the fundamental human rights recognized or existing in any State Party to the present Covenant pursuant to law, conventions, regulations or custom on the pretext that the present Covenant does not recognize such rights or that it recognizes them to a lesser extent.

Part III

Art. 6 1. Every human being has the inherent right to life. This right shall be protected by law. No one shall be arbitrarily deprived of his life.
2. In countries which have not abolished the death penalty, sentence of death may be imposed only for the most serious crimes in accordance with the law in force at the time of the commission of the crime and not contrary to the provisions of the present Covenant and to the Convention on the Prevention and Punishment of the Crime of Genocide. This penalty can only be carried out pursuant to a final judgement rendered by a competent court.
3. When deprivation of life constitutes the crime of genocide, it is understood that nothing in this article shall authorize any State Party to the present Covenant to derogate in any way from any obligation assumed under the provisions of the Convention on the Prevention and Punishment of the Crime of Genocide.

4. Anyone sentenced to death shall have the right to seek pardon or commutation of the sentence. Amnesty, pardon or commutation of the sentence of death may be granted in all cases.
5. Sentence of death shall not be imposed for crimes committed by persons below eighteen years of age and shall not be carried out on pregnant women.
6. Nothing in this article shall be invoked to delay or to prevent the abolition of capital punishment by any State Party to the present Covenant.
Art. 7 No one shall be subjected to torture or to cruel, inhuman or degrading treatment or punishment. In particular, no one shall be subjected without his free consent to medical or scientific experimentation.
Art. 8 1. No one shall be held in slavery; slavery and the slave-trade in all their forms shall be prohibited.
2. No one shall be held in servitude.
3.
(a) No one shall be required to perform forced or compulsory labour;
(b) Paragraph 3 (a) shall not be held to preclude, in countries where imprisonment with hard labour may be imposed as a punishment for a crime, the performance of hard labour in pursuance of a sentence to such punishment by a competent court;
(c) For the purpose of this paragraph the term "forced or compulsory labour" shall not include:
  (i) Any work or service, not referred to in sub-paragraph (b), normally required of a person who is under detention in consequence of a lawful order of a court, or of a person during conditional release from such detention;
  (ii) Any service of a military character and, in countries where conscientious objection is recognized, any national service required by law of conscientious objectors;
  (iii) Any service exacted in cases of emergency or calamity threatening the life or well-being of the community;
  (iv) Any work or service which forms part of normal civil obligations.

Art. 9 1. Everyone has the right to liberty and security of person. No one shall be subjected to arbitrary arrest or detention. No one shall be deprived of his liberty except on such grounds and in accordance with such procedure as are established by law.
2. Anyone who is arrested shall be informed, at the time of arrest, of the reasons for his arrest and shall be promptly informed of any charges against him.
3. Anyone arrested or detained on a criminal charge shall be brought promptly before a judge or other officer authorized by law to exercise judicial power and shall be entitled to trial within a reasonable time or to release. It shall not

be the general rule that persons awaiting trial shall be detained in custody, but release may be subject to guarantees to appear for trial, at any other stage of the judicial proceedings, and, should occasion arise, for execution of the judgement.
4. Anyone who is deprived of his liberty by arrest or detention shall be entitled to take proceedings before a court, in order that that court may decide without delay on the lawfulness of his detention and order his release if the detention is not lawful.
5. Anyone who has been the victim of unlawful arrest or detention shall have an enforceable right to compensation.
Art. 10 1. All persons deprived of their liberty shall be treated with humanity and with respect for the inherent dignity of the human person.
2.
(a) Accused persons shall, save in exceptional circumstances, be segregated from convicted persons and shall be subject to separate treatment appropriate to their status as unconvicted persons;
(b) Accused juvenile persons shall be separated from adults and brought as speedily as possible for adjudication.
3. The penitentiary system shall comprise treatment of prisoners the essential aim of which shall be their reformation and social rehabilitation. Juvenile offenders shall be segregated from adults and be accorded treatment appropriate to their age and legal status.
Art. 11 No one shall be imprisoned merely on the ground of inability to fulfil a contractual obligation.
Art. 12 1. Everyone lawfully within the territory of a State shall, within that territory, have the right to liberty of movement and freedom to choose his residence.
2. Everyone shall be free to leave any country, including his own.
3. The above-mentioned rights shall not be subject to any restrictions except those which are provided by law, are necessary to protect national security, public order (ordre public), public health or morals or the rights and freedoms of others, and are consistent with the other rights recognized in the present Covenant.
4. No one shall be arbitrarily deprived of the right to enter his own country.
Art. 13 An alien lawfully in the territory of a State Party to the present Covenant may be expelled therefrom only in pursuance of a decision reached in accordance with law and shall, except where compelling reasons of national security otherwise require, be allowed to submit the reasons against his expulsion and to have his case reviewed by, and be represented for the purpose before, the

competent authority or a person or persons especially designated by the competent authority.

Art. 14 1. All persons shall be equal before the courts and tribunals. In the determination of any criminal charge against him, or of his rights and obligations in a suit at law, everyone shall be entitled to a fair and public hearing by a competent, independent and impartial tribunal established by law. The Press and the public may be excluded from all or part of a trial for reasons of morals, public order (ordre public) or national security in a democratic society, or when the interest of the private lives of the parties so requires, or to the extent strictly necessary in the opinion of the court in special circumstances where publicity would prejudice the interests of justice; but any judgement rendered in a criminal case or in a suit at law shall be made public except where the interest of juvenile persons otherwise requires or the proceedings concern matrimonial disputes or the guardianship of children.

2. Everyone charged with a criminal offence shall have the right to be presumed innocent until proved guilty according to law.

3. In the determination of any criminal charge against him, everyone shall be entitled to the following minimum guarantees, in full equality:

(a) To be informed promptly and in detail in a language which he understands of the nature and cause of the charge against him;

(b) To have adequate time and facilities for the preparation of his defence and to communicate with counsel of his own choosing;

(c) To be tried without undue delay;

(d) To be tried in his presence, and to defend himself in person or through legal assistance of his own choosing; to be informed, if he does not have legal assistance, of this right; and to have legal assistance assigned to him, in any case where the interests of justice so require, and without payment by him in any such case if he does not have sufficient means to pay for it;

(e) To examine, or have examined, the witnesses against him and to obtain the attendance and examination of witnesses on his behalf under the same conditions as witnesses against him;

(f) To have the free assistance of an interpreter if he cannot understand or speak the language used in court;

(g) Not to be compelled to testify against himself or to confess guilt.

4. In the case of juvenile persons, the procedure shall be such as will take account of their age and the desirability of promoting their rehabilitation.

5. Everyone convicted of a crime shall have the right to his conviction and sentence being reviewed by a higher tribunal according to law.

6. When a person has by a final decision been convicted of a criminal offence and when subsequently his conviction has been reversed or he has been pardoned on the ground that a new or newly discovered fact shows conclusively that there has been a miscarriage of justice, the person who has suffered punishment as a result of such conviction shall be compensated according to law, unless it is proved that the non-disclosure of the unknown fact in time is wholly or partly attributable to him.
7. No one shall be liable to be tried or punished again for an offence for which he has already been finally convicted or acquitted in accordance with the law and penal procedure of each country.
Art. 15 1. No one shall be held guilty of any criminal offence on account of any act or omission which did not constitute a criminal offence, under national or international law, at the time when it was committed. Nor shall a heavier penalty be imposed than the one that was applicable at the time when the criminal offence was committed. If, subsequent to the commission of the offence, provision is made by law for the imposition of the lighter penalty, the offender shall benefit thereby.
2. Nothing in this article shall prejudice the trial and punishment of any person for any act or omission which, at the time when it was committed, was criminal according to the general principles of law recognized by the community of nations.
Art. 16 Everyone shall have the right to recognition everywhere as a person before the law.
Art. 17 1. No one shall be subjected to arbitrary or unlawful interference with his privacy, family, home or correspondence, nor to unlawful attacks on his honour and reputation.
2. Everyone has the right to the protection of the law against such interference or attacks.
Art. 18 1. Everyone shall have the right to freedom of thought, conscience and religion. This right shall include freedom to have or to adopt a religion or belief of his choice, and freedom, either individually or in community with others and in public or private, to manifest his religion or belief in worship, observance, practice and teaching.
2. No one shall be subject to coercion which would impair his freedom to have or to adopt a religion or belief of his choice.
3. Freedom to manifest one's religion or beliefs may be subject only to such limitations as are prescribed by law and are necessary to protect public safety, order, health, or morals or the fundamental rights and freedoms of others.
4. The States Parties to the present Covenant undertake to have respect for the liberty of parents and, when applicable, legal guardians to ensure the

religious and moral education of their children in conformity with their own convictions.

Art. 19 1. Everyone shall have the right to hold opinions without interference.

2. Everyone shall have the right to freedom of expression; this right shall include freedom to seek, receive and impart information and ideas of all kinds, regardless of frontiers, either orally, in writing or in print, in the form of art, or through any other media of his choice.

3. The exercise of the rights provided for in paragraph 2 of this article carries with it special duties and responsibilities. It may therefore be subject to certain restrictions, but these shall only be such as are provided by law and are necessary:

(a) For respect of the rights or reputations of others;

(b) For the protection of national security or of public order (ordre public), or of public health or morals.

Art. 20 1. Any propaganda for war shall be prohibited by law.

2. Any advocacy of national, racial or religious hatred that constitutes incitement to discrimination, hostility or violence shall be prohibited by law.

Art. 21 The right of peaceful assembly shall be recognized. No restrictions may be placed on the exercise of this right other than those imposed in conformity with the law and which are necessary in a democratic society in the interests of national security or public safety, public order (ordre public), the protection of public health or morals or the protection of the rights and freedoms of others.

Art. 22 1. Everyone shall have the right to freedom of association with others, including the right to form and join trade unions for the protection of his interests.

2. No restrictions may be placed on the exercise of this right other than those which are prescribed by law and which are necessary in a democratic society in the interests of national security or public safety, public order (ordre public), the protection of public health or morals or the protection of the rights and freedoms of others. This article shall not prevent the imposition of lawful restrictions on members of the armed forces and of the police in their exercise of this right.

3. Nothing in this article shall authorize States Parties to the International Labour Organisation Convention of 1948 concerning Freedom of Association and Protection of the Right to Organize to take legislative measures which would prejudice, or to apply the law in such a manner as to prejudice, the guarantees provided for in that Convention.

Art. 23 1. The family is the natural and fundamental group unit of society and is entitled to protection by society and the State.

2. The right of men and women of marriageable age to marry and to found a family shall be recognized.
3. No marriage shall be entered into without the free and full consent of the intending spouses.
4. States Parties to the present Covenant shall take appropriate steps to ensure equality of rights and responsibilities of spouses as to marriage, during marriage and at its dissolution. In the case of dissolution, provision shall be made for the necessary protection of any children.
Art. 24 1. Every child shall have, without any discrimination as to race, colour, sex, language, religion, national or social origin, property or birth, the right to such measures of protection as are required by his status as a minor, on the part of his family, society and the State.
2. Every child shall be registered immediately after birth and shall have a name.
3. Every child has the right to acquire a nationality.
Art. 25 Every citizen shall have the right and the opportunity, without any of the distinctions mentioned in article 2 and without unreasonable restrictions:
(a) To take part in the conduct of public affairs, directly or through freely chosen representatives;
(b) To vote and to be elected at genuine periodic elections which shall be by universal and equal suffrage and shall be held by secret ballot, guaranteeing the free expression of the will of the electors;
(c) To have access, on general terms of equality, to public service in his country.
Art. 26 All persons are equal before the law and are entitled without any discrimination to the equal protection of the law. In this respect, the law shall prohibit any discrimination and guarantee to all persons equal and effective protection against discrimination on any ground such as race, colour, sex, language, religion, political or other opinion, national or social origin, property, birth or other status.
Art. 27 In those States in which ethnic, religious or linguistic minorities exist, persons belonging to such minorities shall not be denied the right, in community with the other members of their group, to enjoy their own culture, to profess and practise their own religion, or to use their own language.

Part IV

Art. 28 1. There shall be established a Human Rights Committee (hereafter referred to in the present Covenant as the Committee). It shall consist of eighteen members and shall carry out the functions hereinafter provided.

2. The Committee shall be composed of nationals of the States Parties to the present Covenant who shall be persons of high moral character and recognized competence in the field of human rights, consideration being given to the usefulness of the participation of some persons having legal experience.
3. The members of the Committee shall be elected and shall serve in their personal capacity.
Art. 29 1. The members of the Committee shall be elected by secret ballot from a list of persons possessing the qualifications prescribed in article 28 and nominated for the purpose by the States Parties to the present Covenant.
2. Each State Party to the present Covenant may nominate not more than two persons. These persons shall be nationals of the nominating State.
3. A person shall be eligible for renomination.
Art. 30 1. The initial election shall be held no later than six months after the date of the entry into force of the present Covenant.
2. At least four months before the date of each election to the Committee, other than an election to fill a vacancy declared in accordance with article 34, the Secretary-General of the United Nations shall address a written invitation to the States Parties to the present Covenant to submit their nominations for membership of the Committee within three months.
3. The Secretary-General of the United Nations shall prepare a list in alphabetical order of all the persons thus nominated, with an indication of the States Parties which have nominated them, and shall submit it to the States Parties to the present Covenant no later than one month before the date of each election.
4. Elections of the members of the Committee shall be held at a meeting of the States Parties to the present Covenant convened by the Secretary General of the United Nations at the Headquarters of the United Nations. At that meeting, for which two thirds of the States Parties to the present Covenant shall constitute a quorum, the persons elected to the Committee shall be those nominees who obtain the largest number of votes and an absolute majority of the votes of the representatives of States Parties present and voting.
Art. 31 1. The Committee may not include more than one national of the same State.
2. In the election of the Committee, consideration shall be given to equitable geographical distribution of membership and to the representation of the different forms of civilization and of the principal legal systems.
Art. 32 1. The members of the Committee shall be elected for a term of four years. They shall be eligible for re-election if renominated. However, the terms of nine of the members elected at the first election shall expire at the end of two years; immediately after the first election, the names of these nine

members shall be chosen by lot by the Chairman of the meeting referred to in article 30, paragraph 4.
2. Elections at the expiry of office shall be held in accordance with the preceding articles of this part of the present Covenant.
Art. 33 1. If, in the unanimous opinion of the other members, a member of the Committee has ceased to carry out his functions for any cause other than absence of a temporary character, the Chairman of the Committee shall notify the Secretary-General of the United Nations, who shall then declare the seat of that member to be vacant.
2. In the event of the death or the resignation of a member of the Committee, the Chairman shall immediately notify the Secretary-General of the United Nations, who shall declare the seat vacant from the date of death or the date on which the resignation takes effect.
Art. 34 1. When a vacancy is declared in accordance with article 33 and if the term of office of the member to be replaced does not expire within six months of the declaration of the vacancy, the Secretary-General of the United Nations shall notify each of the States Parties to the present Covenant, which may within two months submit nominations in accordance with article 29 for the purpose of filling the vacancy.
2. The Secretary-General of the United Nations shall prepare a list in alphabetical order of the persons thus nominated and shall submit it to the States Parties to the present Covenant. The election to fill the vacancy shall then take place in accordance with the relevant provisions of this part of the present Covenant.
3. A member of the Committee elected to fill a vacancy declared in accordance with article 33 shall hold office for the remainder of the term of the member who vacated the seat on the Committee under the provisions of that article.
Art. 35 The members of the Committee shall, with the approval of the General Assembly of the United Nations, receive emoluments from United Nations resources on such terms and conditions as the General Assembly may decide, having regard to the importance of the Committee's responsibilities.
Art. 36 The Secretary-General of the United Nations shall provide the necessary staff and facilities for the effective performance of the functions of the Committee under the present Covenant.
Art. 37 1. The Secretary-General of the United Nations shall convene the initial meeting of the Committee at the Headquarters of the United Nations.
2. After its initial meeting, the Committee shall meet at such times as shall be provided in its rules of procedure.
3. The Committee shall normally meet at the Headquarters of the United Nations or at the United Nations Office at Geneva.

Art. 38 Every member of the Committee shall, before taking up his duties, make a solemn declaration in open committee that he will perform his functions impartially and conscientiously.

Art. 39 1. The Committee shall elect its officers for a term of two years. They may be re-elected.

2. The Committee shall establish its own rules of procedure, but these rules shall provide, inter alia, that:

(a) Twelve members shall constitute a quorum;

(b) Decisions of the Committee shall be made by a majority vote of the members present.

Art. 40 1. The States Parties to the present Covenant undertake to submit reports on the measures they have adopted which give effect to the rights recognized herein and on the progress made in the enjoyment of those rights:

(a) Within one year of the entry into force of the present Covenant for the States Parties concerned;

(b) Thereafter whenever the Committee so requests.

2. All reports shall be submitted to the Secretary-General of the United Nations, who shall transmit them to the Committee for consideration. Reports shall indicate the factors and difficulties, if any, affecting the implementation of the present Covenant.

3. The Secretary-General of the United Nations may, after consultation with the Committee, transmit to the specialized agencies concerned copies of such parts of the reports as may fall within their field of competence.

4. The Committee shall study the reports submitted by the States Parties to the present Covenant. It shall transmit its reports, and such general comments as it may consider appropriate, to the States Parties. The Committee may also transmit to the Economic and Social Council these comments along with the copies of the reports it has received from States Parties to the present Covenant.

5. The States Parties to the present Covenant may submit to the Committee observations on any comments that may be made in accordance with paragraph 4 of this article.

Art. 41 1. A State Party to the present Covenant may at any time declare under this article that it recognizes the competence of the Committee to receive and consider communications to the effect that a State Party claims that another State Party is not fulfilling its obligations under the present Covenant. Communications under this article may be received and considered only if submitted by a State Party which has made a declaration recognizing in regard to itself the competence of the Committee. No communication shall be received by the Committee if it concerns a State Party which has not made such a declaration. Communications received under this article shall be dealt with in accordance with the following procedure:

(a) If a State Party to the present Covenant considers that another State Party is not giving effect to the provisions of the present Covenant, it may, by written communication, bring the matter to the attention of that State Party. Within three months after the receipt of the communication the receiving State shall afford the State which sent the communication an explanation or any other statement in writing clarifying the matter, which should include, to the extent possible and pertinent, reference to domestic procedures and remedies taken, pending, or available in the matter.

(b) If the matter is not adjusted to the satisfaction of both States Parties concerned within six months after the receipt by the receiving State of the initial communication, either State shall have the right to refer the matter to the Committee, by notice given to the Committee and to the other State.

(c) The Committee shall deal with a matter referred to it only after it has ascertained that all available domestic remedies have been invoked and exhausted in the matter, in conformity with the generally recognized principles of international law. This shall not be the rule where the application of the remedies is unreasonably prolonged.

(d) The Committee shall hold closed meetings when examining communications under this article.

(e) Subject to the provisions of sub-paragraph (c), the Committee shall make available its good offices to the States Parties concerned with a view to a friendly solution of the matter on the basis of respect for human rights and fundamental freedoms as recognized in the present Covenant.

(f) In any matter referred to it, the Committee may call upon the States Parties concerned, referred to in sub-paragraph (b), to supply any relevant information.

(g) The States Parties concerned, referred to in sub-paragraph (b), shall have the right to be represented when the matter is being considered in the Committee and to make submissions orally and/or in writing.

(h) The Committee shall, within twelve months after the date of receipt of notice under sub-paragraph (b), submit a report:

    (i) If a solution within the terms of sub-paragraph (e) is reached, the Committee shall confine its report to a brief statement of the facts and of the solution reached;

(ii) If a solution within the terms of sub-paragraph (e) is not reached, the Committee shall confine its report to a brief statement of the facts; the written submissions and record of the oral submissions made by the States Parties concerned shall be attached to the report. In every matter, the report shall be communicated to the States Parties concerned.

2. The provisions of this article shall come into force when ten States Parties to the present Covenant have made declarations under paragraph 1 of this article. Such declarations shall be deposited by the States Parties with the Secretary-General of the United Nations, who shall transmit copies thereof to the other States Parties. A declaration may be withdrawn at any time by notification to the Secretary-General. Such a withdrawal shall not prejudice the consideration of any matter which is the subject of a communication already transmitted under this article; no further communication by any State Party shall be received after the notification of withdrawal of the declaration has been received by the Secretary-General, unless the State Party concerned has made a new declaration.

Art. 42 1.

(a) If a matter referred to the Committee in accordance with article 41 is not resolved to the satisfaction of the States Parties concerned, the Committee may, with the prior consent of the States Parties concerned, appoint an ad hoc Conciliation Commission (hereinafter referred to as the Commission). The good offices of the Commission shall be made available to the States Parties concerned with a view to an amicable solution of the matter on the basis of respect for the present Covenant;

(b) The Commission shall consist of five persons acceptable to the States Parties concerned. If the States Parties concerned fail to reach agreement within three months on all or part of the composition of the Commission the members of the Commission concerning whom no agreement has been reached shall be elected by secret ballot by a two-thirds majority vote of the Committee from among its members.

2. The members of the Commission shall serve in their personal capacity. They shall not be nationals of the States Parties concerned, or of a State not Party to the present Covenant, or of a State Party which has not made a declaration under article 41.

3. The Commission shall elect its own Chairman and adopt its own rules of procedure.

4. The meetings of the Commission shall normally be held at the Headquarters of the United Nations or at the United Nations Office at Geneva. However, they may be held at such other convenient places as the Commission may

determine in consultation with the Secretary-General of the United Nations and the States Parties concerned.

5. The secretariat provided in accordance with article 36 shall also service the commissions appointed under this article.

6. The information received and collated by the Committee shall be made available to the Commission and the Commission may call upon the States Parties concerned to supply any other relevant information.

7. When the Commission has fully considered the matter, but in any event not later than twelve months after having been seized of the matter, it shall submit to the Chairman of the Committee a report for communication to the States Parties concerned.

(a) If the Commission is unable to complete its consideration of the matter within twelve months, it shall confine its report to a brief statement of the status of its consideration of the matter;

(b) If an amicable solution to the matter on the basis of respect for human rights as recognized in the present Covenant is reached, the Commission shall confine its report to a brief statement of the facts and of the solution reached.

(c) If a solution within the terms of sub-paragraph (b) is not reached, the Commission's report shall embody its findings on all questions of fact relevant to the issues between the States Parties concerned, and its views on the possibilities of an amicable solution of the matter. This report shall also contain the written submissions and a record of the oral submissions made by the States Parties concerned.

(d) If the Commission's report is submitted under sub-paragraph (c), the States Parties concerned shall, within three months of the receipt of the report, notify the Chairman of the Committee whether or not they accept the contents of the report of the Commission.

8. The provisions of this article are without prejudice to the responsibilities of the Committee under article 41.

9. The States Parties concerned shall share equally all the expenses of the members of the Commission in accordance with estimates to be provided by the Secretary-General of the United Nations.

10. The Secretary-General of the United Nations shall be empowered to pay the expenses of the members of the Commission, if necessary, before reimbursement by the States Parties concerned, in accordance with paragraph 9 of this article.

Art. 43 The members of the Committee, and of the ad hoc conciliation commissions which may be appointed under article 42, shall be entitled to the facilities, privileges and immunities of experts on mission for the United Nations as laid down in the relevant sections of the Convention on the Privileges and Immunities of the United Nations.

Art. 44 The provisions for the implementation of the present Covenant shall apply without prejudice to the procedures prescribed in the field of human rights by or under the constituent instruments and the conventions of the United Nations and of the specialized agencies and shall not prevent the States Parties to the present Covenant from having recourse to other procedures for settling a dispute in accordance with general or special international agreements in force between them.

Art. 45 The Committee shall submit to the General Assembly of the United Nations through the Economic and Social Council, an annual report on its activities.

Part V

Art. 46 Nothing in the present Covenant shall be interpreted as impairing the provisions of the Charter of the United Nations and of the constitutions of the specialized agencies which define the respective responsibilities of the various organs of the United Nations and of the specialized agencies in regard to the matters dealt with in the present Covenant.

Art. 47 Nothing in the present Covenant shall be interpreted as impairing the inherent right of all peoples to enjoy and utilize fully and freely their natural wealth and resources.

Part VI

Art. 48 1. The present Covenant is open for signature by any State Member of the United Nations or member of any of its specialized agencies, by any State Party to the Statute of the International Court of Justice, and by any other State which has been invited by the General Assembly of the United Nations to become a Party to the present Covenant.

2. The present Covenant is subject to ratification. Instruments of ratification shall be deposited with the Secretary-General of the United Nations.

3. The present Covenant shall be open to accession by any State referred to in paragraph 1 of this article.

4. Accession shall be effected by the deposit of an instrument of accession with the Secretary-General of the United Nations.

5. The Secretary-General of the United Nations shall inform all States which have signed this Covenant or acceded to it of the deposit of each instrument of ratification or accession.

Art. 49 1. The present Covenant shall enter into force three months after the date of the deposit with the Secretary-General of the United Nations of the thirty-fifth instrument of ratification or instrument of accession.

2. For each State ratifying the present Covenant or acceding to it after the deposit of the thirty-fifth instrument of ratification or instrument of accession, the present Covenant shall enter into force three months after the date of the deposit of its own instrument of ratification or instrument of accession.

Art. 50 The provisions of the present Covenant shall extend to all parts of federal States without any limitations or exceptions.

Art. 51 1. Any State Party to the present Covenant may propose an amendment and file it with the Secretary-General of the United Nations. The Secretary-General of the United Nations shall thereupon communicate any proposed amendments to the States Parties to the present Covenant with a request that they notify him whether they favour a conference of States Parties for the purpose of considering and voting upon the proposals. In the event that at least one third of the States Parties favours such a conference, the Secretary-General shall convene the conference under the auspices of the United Nations. Any amendment adopted by a majority of the States Parties present and voting at the conference shall be submitted to the General Assembly of the United Nations for approval.

2. Amendments shall come into force when they have been approved by the General Assembly of the United Nations and accepted by a two-thirds majority of the States Parties to the present Covenant in accordance with their respective constitutional processes.

3. When amendments come into force, they shall be binding on those States Parties which have accepted them, other States Parties still being bound by the provisions of the present Covenant and any earlier amendment which they have accepted.

Art. 52 Irrespective of the notifications made under article 48, paragraph 5, the Secretary-General of the United Nations shall inform all States referred to in paragraph 1 of the same article of the following particulars:

(a) Signatures, ratifications and accessions under article 48;

(b) The date of the entry into force of the present Covenant under article 49 and the date of the entry into force of any amendments under article 51.

Art. 53 1. The present Covenant, of which the Chinese, English, French, Russian and Spanish texts are equally authentic, shall be deposited in the archives of the United Nations.
2. The Secretary-General of the United Nations shall transmit certified copies of the present Covenant to all States referred to in article 48.
IN FAITH WHEREOF the undersigned, being duly authorized thereto by their respective Governments, have signed the present Covenant, opened for signature at New York, on the nineteeth day of December, one thousand nine hundred and sixty-six.

CHAPTER 6.A

Optional Protocol to the International Covenant on Civil and Political Rights

Adopted and opened for signatures, ratification and accession by the General Assembly resolution 2200 A (XXI) of 16 December 1966
Entry into force 23 March 1976, in accordance with article 9

The States Parties to the present Protocol,

Considering that in order further to achieve the purposes of the International Covenant on Civil and Political Rights (hereinafter referred to as the Covenant) and the implementation of its provisions it would be appropriate to enable the Human Rights Committee set up in part IV of the Covenant (hereinafter referred to as the Committee) to receive and consider, as provided in the present Protocol, communications from individuals claiming to be victims of violations of any of the rights set forth in the Covenant.

Have agreed as follows:

Art. 1 A State Party to the Covenant that becomes a party to the present Protocol recognizes the competence of the Committee to receive and consider communications from individuals subject to its jurisdiction who claim to be victims of a violation by that State Party of any of the rights set forth in the Covenant. No communication shall be received by the Committee if it concerns a State Party to the Covenant which is not a party to the present Protocol.

Art. 2 Subject to the provisions of article 1, individuals who claim that any of their rights enumerated in the Covenant have been violated and who have exhausted all available domestic remedies may submit a written communication to the Committee for consideration.

Art. 3 The Committee shall consider inadmissible any communication under the present Protocol which is anonymous, or which it considers to be an abuse of the right of submission of such communications or to be incompatible with the provisions of the Covenant.

Art. 4 1. Subject to the provisions of article 3, the Committee shall bring any communications submitted to it under the present Protocol to the attention of the State Party to the present Protocol alleged to be violating any provision of the Covenant.

 DOI:10.1163/9789004681224_012

2. Within six months, the receiving State shall submit to the Committee written explanations or statements clarifying the matter and the remedy, if any, that may have been taken by that State.

Art. 5 1. The Committee shall consider communications received under the present Protocol in the light of all written information made available to it by the individual and by the State Party concerned.

2. The Committee shall not consider any communication from an individual unless it has ascertained that:

(a) The same matter is not being examined under another procedure of international investigation or settlement;

(b) The individual has exhausted all available domestic remedies. This shall not be the rule where the application of the remedies is unreasonably prolonged.

3. The Committee shall hold closed meetings when examining communications under the present Protocol.

4. The Committee shall forward its views to the State Party concerned and to the individual.

Art. 6 The Committee shall include in its annual report under article 45 of the Covenant a summary of its activities under the present Protocol.

Art. 7 Pending the achievement of the objectives of resolution 1514 (XV) adopted by the General Assembly of the United Nations on 14 December 1960 concerning the Declaration on the Granting of Independence to Colonial Countries and Peoples, the provisions of the present Protocol shall in no way limit the right of petition granted to these peoples by the Charter of the United Nations and other international conventions and instruments under the United Nations and its specialized agencies.

Art. 8 1. The present Protocol is open for signature by any State which has signed the Covenant.

2. The present Protocol is subject to ratification by any State which has ratified or acceded to the Covenant. Instruments of ratification shall be deposited with the Secretary-General of the United Nations.

3. The present Protocol shall be open to accession by any State which has ratified or acceded to the Covenant.

4. Accession shall be effected by the deposit of an instrument of accession with the Secretary General of the United Nations.

5. The Secretary-General of the United Nations shall inform all States which have signed the present Protocol or acceded to it of the deposit of each instrument of ratification or accession.

Art. 9 1. Subject to the entry into force of the Covenant, the present Protocol shall enter into force three months after the date of the deposit with the

Secretary-General of the United Nations of the tenth instrument of ratification or instrument of accession.
2. For each State ratifying the present Protocol or acceding to it after the deposit of the tenth instrument of ratification or instrument of accession, the present Protocol shall enter into force three months after the date of the deposit of its own instrument of ratification or instrument of accession.
Art. 10 The provisions of the present Protocol shall extend to all parts of federal States without any limitations or exceptions.
Art. 11 1. Any State Party to the present Protocol may propose an amendment and file it with the Secretary-General of the United Nations. The Secretary-General shall thereupon communicate any proposed amendments to the States Parties to the present Protocol with a request that they notify him whether they favour a conference of States Parties for the purpose of considering and voting upon the proposal. In the event that at least one third of the States Parties favours such a conference, the Secretary-General shall convene the conference under the auspices of the United Nations. Any amendment adopted by a majority of the States Parties present and voting at the conference shall be submitted to the General Assembly of the United Nations for approval.
2. Amendments shall come into force when they have been approved by the General Assembly of the United Nations and accepted by a two-thirds majority of the States Parties to the present Protocol in accordance with their respective constitutional processes.
3. When amendments come into force, they shall be binding on those States Parties which have accepted them, other States Parties still being bound by the provisions of the present Protocol and any earlier amendment which they have accepted.
Art. 12 1. Any State Party may denounce the present Protocol at any time by written notification addressed to the Secretary-General of the United Nations. Denunciation shall take effect three months after the date of receipt of the notification by the Secretary-General.
2. Denunciation shall be without prejudice to the continued application of the provisions of the present Protocol to any communication submitted under article 2 before the effective date of denunciation.
Art. 13 Irrespective of the notifications made under article 8, paragraph 5, of the present Protocol, the Secretary-General of the United Nations shall inform all States referred to in article 48, paragraph 1, of the Covenant of the following particulars:
(a) Signatures, ratifications and accessions under article 8;
(b) The date of the entry into force of the present Protocol under article 9 and the date of the entry into force of any amendments under article 11;

(c) Denunciations under article 12.

Art. 14 1. The present Protocol, of which the Chinese, English, French, Russian and Spanish texts are equally authentic, shall be deposited in the archives of the United Nations.

2. The Secretary-General of the United Nations shall transmit certified copies of the present Protocol to all States referred to in article 48 of the Covenant.

IN FAITH WHEREOF the undersigned, being duly authorized thereto by their respective Governments, have signed the present Protocol, opened for signature at New York, on the nineteenth day of December, one thousand nine hundred and sixty-six

CHAPTER 6.B

Second Optional Protocol to the International Covenant on Civil and Political Rights Aiming at the Abolition of the Death Penalty

Adopted and opened for signature, ratification and accession by the General Assembly resolution 44/128 of 15 December 1989
Entry into force 11 July 1991, in accordance with article 8(1)

The States Parties to the present Protocol,

Believing that abolition of the death penalty contributes to enhancement of human dignity and progressive development of human rights,

Recalling article 3 of the Universal Declaration of Human Rights, adopted on 10 December 1948, and article 6 of the International Covenant on Civil and Political Rights, adopted on 16 December 1966,

Noting that article 6 of the International Covenant on Civil and Political Rights refers to abolition of the death penalty in terms that strongly suggest that abolition is desirable,

Convinced that all measures of abolition of the death penalty should be considered as progress in the enjoyment of the right to life,

Desirous to undertake hereby an international commitment to abolish the death penalty,

Have agreed as follows:

Art. 1 1. No one within the jurisdiction of a State Party to the present Protocol shall be executed.

2. Each State Party shall take all necessary measures to abolish the death penalty within its jurisdiction.

Art. 2 1. No reservation is admissible to the present Protocol, except for a reservation made at the time of ratification or accession that provides for the application of the death penalty in time of war pursuant to a conviction for a most serious crime of a military nature committed during wartime.

2. The State Party making such a reservation shall at the time of ratification or accession communicate to the Secretary-General of the United Nations the relevant provisions of its national legislation applicable during wartime.

3. The State Party having made such a reservation shall notify the Secretary-General of the United Nations of any beginning or ending of a state of war applicable to its territory.

Art. 3 The States Parties to the present Protocol shall include in the reports they submit to the Human Rights Committee, in accordance with article 40 of the Covenant, information on the measures that they have adopted to give effect to the present Protocol.

Art. 4 With respect to the States Parties to the Covenant that have made a declaration under article 41, the competence of the Human Rights Committee to receive and consider communications when a State Party claims that another State Party is not fulfilling its obligations shall extend to the provisions of the present Protocol, unless the State Party concerned has made a statement to the contrary at the moment of ratification or accession.

Art. 5 With respect to the States Parties to the first Optional Protocol to the International Covenant on Civil and Political Rights adopted on 16 December 1966, the competence of the Human Rights Committee to receive and consider communications from individuals subject to its jurisdiction shall extend to the provisions of the present Protocol, unless the State Party concerned has made a statement to the contrary at the moment of ratification or accession.

Art. 6 1. The provisions of the present Protocol shall apply as additional provisions to the Covenant.

2. Without prejudice to the possibility of a reservation under article 2 of the present Protocol, the right guaranteed in article 1, paragraph 1, of the present Protocol shall not be subject to any derogation under article 4 of the Covenant.

Art. 7 1. The present Protocol is open for signature by any State that has signed the Covenant.

2. The present Protocol is subject to ratification by any State that has ratified the Covenant or acceded to it. Instruments of ratification shall be deposited with the Secretary-General of the United Nations.

3. The present Protocol shall be open to accession by any State that has ratified the Covenant or acceded to it.

4. Accession shall be effected by the deposit of an instrument of accession with the Secretary-General of the United Nations.

5. The Secretary-General of the United Nations shall inform all States that have signed the present Protocol or acceded to it of the deposit of each instrument of ratification or accession.

Art. 8 1. The present Protocol shall enter into force three months after the date of the deposit with the Secretary-General of the United Nations of the tenth instrument of ratification or accession.

2. For each State ratifying the present Protocol or acceding to it after the deposit of the tenth instrument of ratification or accession, the present Protocol shall enter into force three months after the date of the deposit of its own instrument of ratification or accession.

Art. 9 The provisions of the present Protocol shall extend to all parts of federal States without any limitations or exceptions.

Art. 10 The Secretary-General of the United Nations shall inform all States referred to in article 48, paragraph 1, of the Covenant of the following particulars:

(a) Reservations, communications and notifications under article 2 of the present Protocol;

(b) Statements made under articles 4 or 5 of the present Protocol;

(c) Signatures, ratifications and accessions under article 7 of the present Protocol;

(d) The date of the entry into force of the present Protocol under article 8 thereof.

Art. 11 1. The present Protocol, of which the Arabic, Chinese, English, French, Russian and Spanish texts are equally authentic, shall be deposited in the archives of the United Nations.

2. The Secretary-General of the United Nations shall transmit certified copies of the present Protocol to all States referred to in article 48 of the Covenant.

CHAPTER 7

International Covenant on Economic, Social and Cultural Rights

Adopted and opened for signatures, ratification and accession by General Assembly resolution 2200A (XXI) of 16 December 1966
Entry into force 3 January 1976, in accordance with article 27

Preamble

The States Parties to the present Covenant,

Considering that, in accordance with the principles proclaimed in the Charter of the United Nations, recognition of the inherent dignity and of the equal and inalienable rights of all members of the human family is the foundation of freedom, justice and peace in the world,

Recognizing that these rights derive from the inherent dignity of the human person,

Recognizing that, in accordance with the Universal Declaration of Human Rights, the ideal of free human beings enjoying freedom from fear and want can only be achieved if conditions are created whereby everyone may enjoy his economic, social and cultural rights, as well as his civil and political rights,

Considering the obligation of States under the Charter of the United Nations to promote universal respect for, and observance of, human rights and freedoms,

Realizing that the individual, having duties to other individuals and to the community to which he belongs, is under a responsibility to strive for the promotion and observance of the rights recognized in the present Covenant,

Agree upon the following articles:

Part I

Art. 1 1. All peoples have the right of self-determination. By virtue of that right they freely determine their political status and freely pursue their economic, social and cultural development.

2. All peoples may, for their own ends, freely dispose of their natural wealth and resources without prejudice to any obligations arising out of international economic co-operation, based upon the principle of mutual benefit, and

© KARL HANSON ET AL., 2025 | DOI:10.1163/9789004681224_014

international law. In no case may a people be deprived of its own means of subsistence.
3. The States Parties to the present Covenant, including those having responsibility for the administration of Non-Self-Governing and Trust Territories, shall promote the realization of the right of self-determination, and shall respect that right, in conformity with the provisions of the Charter of the United Nations.

Part II

Art. 2 1. Each State Party to the present Covenant undertakes to take steps, individually and through international assistance and co-operation, especially economic and technical, to the maximum of its available resources, with a view to achieving progressively the full realization of the rights recognized in the present Covenant by all appropriate means, including particularly the adoption of legislative measures.
2. The States Parties to the present Covenant undertake to guarantee that the rights enunciated in the present Covenant will be exercised without discrimination of any kind as to race, colour, sex, language, religion, political or other opinion, national or social origin, property, birth or other status.
3. Developing countries, with due regard to human rights and their national economy, may determine to what extent they would guarantee the economic rights recognized in the present Covenant to non-nationals.
Art. 3 The States Parties to the present Covenant undertake to ensure the equal right of men and women to the enjoyment of all economic, social and cultural rights set forth in the present Covenant.
Art. 4 The States Parties to the present Covenant recognize that, in the enjoyment of those rights provided by the State in conformity with the present Covenant, the State may subject such rights only to such limitations as are determined by law only in so far as this may be compatible with the nature of these rights and solely for the purpose of promoting the general welfare in a democratic society.
Art. 5 1. Nothing in the present Covenant may be interpreted as implying for any State, group or person any right to engage in any activity or to perform any act aimed at the destruction of any of the rights or freedoms recognized herein, or at their limitation to a greater extent than is provided for in the present Covenant.
2. No restriction upon or derogation from any of the fundamental human rights recognized or existing in any country in virtue of law, conventions, regulations

or custom shall be admitted on the pretext that the present Covenant does not recognize such rights or that it recognizes them to a lesser extent.

Part III

Art. 6 1. The States Parties to the present Covenant recognize the right to work, which includes the right of everyone to the opportunity to gain his living by work which he freely chooses or accepts, and will take appropriate steps to safeguard this right.

2. The steps to be taken by a State Party to the present Covenant to achieve the full realization of this right shall include technical and vocational guidance and training programmes, policies and techniques to achieve steady economic, social and cultural development and full and productive employment under conditions safeguarding fundamental political and economic freedoms to the individual.

Art. 7 The States Parties to the present Covenant recognize the right of everyone to the enjoyment of just and favourable conditions of work which ensure, in particular:

(a) Remuneration which provides all workers, as a minimum, with:

(i) Fair wages and equal remuneration for work of equal value without distinction of any kind, in particular women being guaranteed conditions of work not inferior to those enjoyed by men, with equal pay for equal work;

(ii) A decent living for themselves and their families in accordance with the provisions of the present Covenant;

(b) Safe and healthy working conditions;

(c) Equal opportunity for everyone to be promoted in his employment to an appropriate higher level, subject to no considerations other than those of seniority and competence;

(d) Rest, leisure and reasonable limitation of working hours and periodic holidays with pay, as well as remuneration for public holidays.

Art. 8 1. The States Parties to the present Covenant undertake to ensure:

(a) The right of everyone to form trade unions and join the trade union of his choice, subject only to the rules of the organization concerned, for the promotion and protection of his economic and social interests. No restrictions may be placed on the exercise of this right other than those prescribed by law and which are necessary in a democratic society in the interests of national security or public order or for the protection of the rights and freedoms of others;

(b) The right of trade unions to establish national federations or confederations and the right of the latter to form or join international trade-union organizations;
(c) The right of trade unions to function freely subject to no limitations other than those prescribed by law and which are necessary in a democratic society in the interests of national security or public order or for the protection of the rights and freedoms of others;
(d) The right to strike, provided that it is exercised in conformity with the laws of the particular country.

2. This article shall not prevent the imposition of lawful restrictions on the exercise of these rights by members of the armed forces or of the police or of the administration of the State.

3. Nothing in this article shall authorize States Parties to the International Labour Organisation Convention of 1948 concerning Freedom of Association and Protection of the Right to Organize to take legislative measures which would prejudice, or apply the law in such a manner as would prejudice, the guarantees provided for in that Convention.

Art. 9 The States Parties to the present Covenant recognize the right of everyone to social security, including social insurance.

Art. 10 The States Parties to the present Covenant recognize that:

1. The widest possible protection and assistance should be accorded to the family, which is the natural and fundamental group unit of society, particularly for its establishment and while it is responsible for the care and education of dependent children. Marriage must be entered into with the free consent of the intending spouses.

2. Special protection should be accorded to mothers during a reasonable period before and after childbirth. During such period working mothers should be accorded paid leave or leave with adequate social security benefits.

3. Special measures of protection and assistance should be taken on behalf of all children and young persons without any discrimination for reasons of parentage or other conditions. Children and young persons should be protected from economic and social exploitation. Their employment in work harmful to their morals or health or dangerous to life or likely to hamper their normal development should be punishable by law. States should also set age limits below which the paid employment of child labour should be prohibited and punishable by law.

Art. 11 1. The States Parties to the present Covenant recognize the right of everyone to an adequate standard of living for himself and his family, including adequate food, clothing and housing, and to the continuous improvement of living conditions. The States Parties will take appropriate steps to ensure the

realization of this right, recognizing to this effect the essential importance of international co-operation based on free consent.
2. The States Parties to the present Covenant, recognizing the fundamental right of everyone to be free from hunger, shall take, individually and through international co-operation, the measures, including specific programmes, which are needed:
(a) To improve methods of production, conservation and distribution of food by making full use of technical and scientific knowledge, by disseminating knowledge of the principles of nutrition and by developing or reforming agrarian systems in such a way as to achieve the most efficient development and utilization of natural resources;
(b) Taking into account the problems of both food-importing and food-exporting countries, to ensure an equitable distribution of world food supplies in relation to need.

Art. 12 1. The States Parties to the present Covenant recognize the right of everyone to the enjoyment of the highest attainable standard of physical and mental health.
2. The steps to be taken by the States Parties to the present Covenant to achieve the full realization of this right shall include those necessary for:
(a) The provision for the reduction of the stillbirth-rate and of infant mortality and for the healthy development of the child;
(b) The improvement of all aspects of environmental and industrial hygiene;
(c) The prevention, treatment and control of epidemic, endemic, occupational and other diseases;
(d) The creation of conditions which would assure to all medical service and medical attention in the event of sickness.

Art. 13 1. The States Parties to the present Covenant recognize the right of everyone to education. They agree that education shall be directed to the full development of the human personality and the sense of its dignity, and shall strengthen the respect for human rights and fundamental freedoms. They further agree that education shall enable all persons to participate effectively in a free society, promote understanding, tolerance and friendship among all nations and all racial, ethnic or religious groups, and further the activities of the United Nations for the maintenance of peace.
2. The States Parties to the present Covenant recognize that, with a view to achieving the full realization of this right:
(a) Primary education shall be compulsory and available free to all;
(b) Secondary education in its different forms, including technical and vocational secondary education, shall be made generally available and

accessible to all by every appropriate means, and in particular by the progressive introduction of free education;

(c) Higher education shall be made equally accessible to all, on the basis of capacity, by every appropriate means, and in particular by the progressive introduction of free education;

(d) Fundamental education shall be encouraged or intensified as far as possible for those persons who have not received or completed the whole period of their primary education;

(e) The development of a system of schools at all levels shall be actively pursued, an adequate fellowship system shall be established, and the material conditions of teaching staff shall be continuously improved.

3. The States Parties to the present Covenant undertake to have respect for the liberty of parents and, when applicable, legal guardians to choose for their children schools, other than those established by the public authorities, which conform to such minimum educational standards as may be laid down or approved by the State and to ensure the religious and moral education of their children in conformity with their own convictions.

4. No part of this article shall be construed so as to interfere with the liberty of individuals and bodies to establish and direct educational institutions, subject always to the observance of the principles set forth in paragraph 1 of this article and to the requirement that the education given in such institutions shall conform to such minimum standards as may be laid down by the State.

Art. 14 Each State Party to the present Covenant which, at the time of becoming a Party, has not been able to secure in its metropolitan territory or other territories under its jurisdiction compulsory primary education, free of charge, undertakes, within two years, to work out and adopt a detailed plan of action for the progressive implementation, within a reasonable number of years, to be fixed in the plan, of the principle of compulsory education free of charge for all.

Art. 15 1. The States Parties to the present Covenant recognize the right of everyone:

(a) To take part in cultural life;

(b) To enjoy the benefits of scientific progress and its applications;

(c) To benefit from the protection of the moral and material interests resulting from any scientific, literary or artistic production of which he is the author.

2. The steps to be taken by the States Parties to the present Covenant to achieve the full realization of this right shall include those necessary for the conservation, the development and the diffusion of science and culture.

3. The States Parties to the present Covenant undertake to respect the freedom indispensable for scientific research and creative activity.
4. The States Parties to the present Covenant recognize the benefits to be derived from the encouragement and development of international contacts and co-operation in the scientific and cultural fields.

Part IV

Art. 16 1. The States Parties to the present Covenant undertake to submit in conformity with this part of the Covenant reports on the measures which they have adopted and the progress made in achieving the observance of the rights recognized herein.
2.
(a) All reports shall be submitted to the Secretary-General of the United Nations, who shall transmit copies to the Economic and Social Council for consideration in accordance with the provisions of the present Covenant.
(b) The Secretary-General of the United Nations shall also transmit to the specialized agencies copies of the reports, or any relevant parts therefrom, from States Parties to the present Covenant which are also members of these specialized agencies in so far as these reports, or parts therefrom, relate to any matters which fall within the responsibilities of the said agencies in accordance with their constitutional instruments.

Art. 17 1. The States Parties to the present Covenant shall furnish their reports in stages, in accordance with a programme to be established by the Economic and Social Council within one year of the entry into force of the present Covenant after consultation with the States Parties and the specialized agencies concerned.
2. Reports may indicate factors and difficulties affecting the degree of fulfilment of obligations under the present Covenant.
3. Where relevant information has previously been furnished to the United Nations or to any specialized agency by any State Party to the present Covenant, it will not be necessary to reproduce that information, but a precise reference to the information so furnished will suffice.

Art. 18 Pursuant to its responsibilities under the Charter of the United Nations in the field of human rights and fundamental freedoms, the Economic and Social Council may make arrangements with the specialized agencies in respect of their reporting to it on the progress made in achieving the observance of the provisions of the present Covenant falling within the scope of their activities.

These reports may include particulars of decisions and recommendations on such implementation adopted by their competent organs.

Art. 19 The Economic and Social Council may transmit to the Commission on Human Rights for study and general recommendation or, as appropriate, for information the reports concerning human rights submitted by States in accordance with articles 16 and 17, and those concerning human rights submitted by the specialized agencies in accordance with article 18.

Art. 20 The States Parties to the present Covenant and the specialized agencies concerned may submit comments to the Economic and Social Council on any general recommendation under article 19 or reference to such general recommendation in any report of the Commission on Human Rights or any documentation referred to therein.

Art. 21 The Economic and Social Council may submit from time to time to the General Assembly reports with recommendations of a general nature and a summary of the information received from the States Parties to the present Covenant and the specialized agencies on the measures taken and the progress made in achieving general observance of the rights recognized in the present Covenant.

Art. 22 The Economic and Social Council may bring to the attention of other organs of the United Nations, their subsidiary organs and specialized agencies concerned with furnishing technical assistance any matters arising out of the reports referred to in this part of the present Covenant which may assist such bodies in deciding, each within its field of competence, on the advisability of international measures likely to contribute to the effective progressive implementation of the present Covenant.

Art. 23 The States Parties to the present Covenant agree that international action for the achievement of the rights recognized in the present Covenant includes such methods as the conclusion of conventions, the adoption of recommendations, the furnishing of technical assistance and the holding of regional meetings and technical meetings for the purpose of consultation and study organized in conjunction with the Governments concerned.

Art. 24 Nothing in the present Covenant shall be interpreted as impairing the provisions of the Charter of the United Nations and of the constitutions of the specialized agencies which define the respective responsibilities of the various organs of the United Nations and of the specialized agencies in regard to the matters dealt with in the present Covenant.

Art. 25 Nothing in the present Covenant shall be interpreted as impairing the inherent right of all peoples to enjoy and utilize fully and freely their natural wealth and resources.

Part v

Art. 26 1. The present Covenant is open for signature by any State Member of the United Nations or member of any of its specialized agencies, by any State Party to the Statute of the International Court of Justice, and by any other State which has been invited by the General Assembly of the United Nations to become a party to the present Covenant.
2. The present Covenant is subject to ratification. Instruments of ratification shall be deposited with the Secretary-General of the United Nations.
3. The present Covenant shall be open to accession by any State referred to in paragraph 1 of this article.
4. Accession shall be effected by the deposit of an instrument of accession with the Secretary-General of the United Nations.
5. The Secretary-General of the United Nations shall inform all States which have signed the present Covenant or acceded to it of the deposit of each instrument of ratification or accession.
Art. 27 1. The present Covenant shall enter into force three months after the date of the deposit with the Secretary-General of the United Nations of the thirty-fifth instrument of ratification or instrument of accession.
2. For each State ratifying the present Covenant or acceding to it after the deposit of the thirty-fifth instrument of ratification or instrument of accession, the present Covenant shall enter into force three months after the date of the deposit of its own instrument of ratification or instrument of accession.
Art. 28 The provisions of the present Covenant shall extend to all parts of federal States without any limitations or exceptions.
Art. 29 1. Any State Party to the present Covenant may propose an amendment and file it with the Secretary-General of the United Nations. The Secretary-General shall thereupon communicate any proposed amendments to the States Parties to the present Covenant with a request that they notify him whether they favour a conference of States Parties for the purpose of considering and voting upon the proposals. In the event that at least one third of the States Parties favours such a conference, the Secretary-General shall convene the conference under the auspices of the United Nations. Any amendment adopted by a majority of the States Parties present and voting at the conference shall be submitted to the General Assembly of the United Nations for approval.
2. Amendments shall come into force when they have been approved by the General Assembly of the United Nations and accepted by a two-thirds majority of the States Parties to the present Covenant in accordance with their respective constitutional processes.

3. When amendments come into force they shall be binding on those States Parties which have accepted them, other States Parties still being bound by the provisions of the present Covenant and any earlier amendment which they have accepted.

Art. 30 Irrespective of the notifications made under article 26, paragraph 5, the Secretary-General of the United Nations shall inform all States referred to in paragraph 1 of the same article of the following particulars:

(a) Signatures, ratifications and accessions under article 26;

(b) The date of the entry into force of the present Covenant under article 27 and the date of the entry into force of any amendments under article 29.

Art. 31 1. The present Covenant, of which the Chinese, English, French, Russian and Spanish texts are equally authentic, shall be deposited in the archives of the United Nations.

2. The Secretary-General of the United Nations shall transmit certified copies of the present Covenant to all States referred to in article 26.

IN FAITH WHEREOF the undersigned, being duly authorized thereto by their respective Governments, have signed the present Covenant, opened for signature at New York, on the nineteenth day of December, one thousand nine hundred and sixty-six.

CHAPTER 7.A

Optional Protocol to the International Covenant on Economic, Social and Cultural Rights

Adopted and opened for signature, ratification and accession by General Assembly resolution 63/117 of 10 December 2008
Entry into force 5 May 2013, in accordance with article 18(1)

Preamble

The States Parties to the present Protocol,

Considering that, in accordance with the principles proclaimed in the Charter of the United Nations, recognition of the inherent dignity and of the equal and inalienable rights of all members of the human family is the foundation of freedom, justice and peace in the world,

Noting that the Universal Declaration of Human Rights proclaims that all human beings are born free and equal in dignity and rights and that everyone is entitled to all the rights and freedoms set forth therein, without distinction of any kind, such as race, colour, sex, language, religion, political or other opinion, national or social origin, property, birth or other status,

Recalling that the Universal Declaration of Human Rights and the International Covenants on Human Rights recognize that the ideal of free human beings enjoying freedom from fear and want can only be achieved if conditions are created whereby everyone may enjoy civil, cultural, economic, political and social rights,

Reaffirming the universality, indivisibility, interdependence and interrelatedness of all human rights and fundamental freedoms,

Recalling that each State Party to the International Covenant on Economic, Social and Cultural Rights (hereinafter referred to as the Covenant) undertakes to take steps, individually and through international assistance and cooperation, especially economic and technical, to the maximum of its available resources, with a view to achieving progressively the full realization of the rights recognized in the Covenant by all appropriate means, including particularly the adoption of legislative measures,

Considering that, in order further to achieve the purposes of the Covenant and the implementation of its provisions, it would be appropriate to enable the Committee on Economic, Social and Cultural Rights (hereinafter referred

 | DOI:10.1163/9789004681224_015

to as the Committee) to carry out the functions provided for in the present Protocol,

Have agreed as follows:

Article 1 – Competence of the Committee to Receive and Consider Communications

1. A State Party to the Covenant that becomes a Party to the present Protocol recognizes the competence of the Committee to receive and consider communications as provided for by the provisions of the present Protocol.
2. No communication shall be received by the Committee if it concerns a State Party to the Covenant which is not a Party to the present Protocol.

Article 2 – Communications

Communications may be submitted by or on behalf of individuals or groups of individuals, under the jurisdiction of a State Party, claiming to be victims of a violation of any of the economic, social and cultural rights set forth in the Covenant by that State Party. Where a communication is submitted on behalf of individuals or groups of individuals, this shall be with their consent unless the author can justify acting on their behalf without such consent.

Article 3 – Admissibility

1. The Committee shall not consider a communication unless it has ascertained that all available domestic remedies have been exhausted. This shall not be the rule where the application of such remedies is unreasonably prolonged.
2. The Committee shall declare a communication inadmissible when:
(a) It is not submitted within one year after the exhaustion of domestic remedies, except in cases where the author can demonstrate that it had not been possible to submit the communication within that time limit;
(b) The facts that are the subject of the communication occurred prior to the entry into force of the present Protocol for the State Party concerned unless those facts continued after that date;
(c) The same matter has already been examined by the Committee or has been or is being examined under another procedure of international investigation or settlement;
(d) It is incompatible with the provisions of the Covenant;
(e) It is manifestly ill-founded, not sufficiently substantiated or exclusively based on reports disseminated by mass media;

(f) It is an abuse of the right to submit a communication; or when
(g) It is anonymous or not in writing.

Article 4 – Communications Not Revealing a Clear Disadvantage

The Committee may, if necessary, decline to consider a communication where it does not reveal that the author has suffered a clear disadvantage, unless the Committee considers that the communication raises a serious issue of general importance.

Article 5 – Interim Measures

1. At any time after the receipt of a communication and before a determination on the merits has been reached, the Committee may transmit to the State Party concerned for its urgent consideration a request that the State Party take such interim measures as may be necessary in exceptional circumstances to avoid possible irreparable damage to the victim or victims of the alleged violations.
2. Where the Committee exercises its discretion under paragraph 1 of the present article, this does not imply a determination on admissibility or on the merits of the communication.

Article 6 – Transmission of the Communication

1. Unless the Committee considers a communication inadmissible without reference to the State Party concerned, the Committee shall bring any communication submitted to it under the present Protocol confidentially to the attention of the State Party concerned.
2. Within six months, the receiving State Party shall submit to the Committee written explanations or statements clarifying the matter and the remedy, if any, that may have been provided by that State Party.

Article 7 – Friendly Settlement

1. The Committee shall make available its good offices to the parties concerned with a view to reaching a friendly settlement of the matter on the basis of the respect for the obligations set forth in the Covenant.
2. An agreement on a friendly settlement closes consideration of the communication under the present Protocol.

Article 8 – Examination of Communications

1. The Committee shall examine communications received under article 2 of the present Protocol in the light of all documentation submitted to it, provided that this documentation is transmitted to the parties concerned.

2. The Committee shall hold closed meetings when examining communications under the present Protocol.
3. When examining a communication under the present Protocol, the Committee may consult, as appropriate, relevant documentation emanating from other United Nations bodies, specialized agencies, funds, programmes and mechanisms, and other international organizations, including from regional human rights systems, and any observations or comments by the State Party concerned.
4. When examining communications under the present Protocol, the Committee shall consider the reasonableness of the steps taken by the State Party in accordance with part II of the Covenant. In doing so, the Committee shall bear in mind that the State Party may adopt a range of possible policy measures for the implementation of the rights set forth in the Covenant.

Article 9 – Follow-Up to the Views of the Committee

1. After examining a communication, the Committee shall transmit its views on the communication, together with its recommendations, if any, to the parties concerned.
2. The State Party shall give due consideration to the views of the Committee, together with its recommendations, if any, and shall submit to the Committee, within six months, a written response, including information on any action taken in the light of the views and recommendations of the Committee.
3. The Committee may invite the State Party to submit further information about any measures the State Party has taken in response to its views or recommendations, if any, including as deemed appropriate by the Committee, in the State Party's subsequent reports under articles 16 and 17 of the Covenant.

Article 10 – Inter-State Communications

1. A State Party to the present Protocol may at any time declare under the present article that it recognizes the competence of the Committee to receive and consider communications to the effect that a State Party claims that another State Party is not fulfilling its obligations under the Covenant. Communications under the present article may be received and considered only if submitted by a State Party that has made a declaration recognizing in regard to itself the competence of the Committee. No communication shall be received by the Committee if it concerns a State Party which has not made such a declaration. Communications received under the present article shall be dealt with in accordance with the following procedure:
(a) If a State Party to the present Protocol considers that another State Party is not fulfilling its obligations under the Covenant, it may, by

written communication, bring the matter to the attention of that State Party. The State Party may also inform the Committee of the matter. Within three months after the receipt of the communication the receiving State shall afford the State that sent the communication an explanation, or any other statement in writing clarifying the matter, which should include, to the extent possible and pertinent, reference to domestic procedures and remedies taken, pending or available in the matter;

(b) If the matter is not settled to the satisfaction of both States Parties concerned within six months after the receipt by the receiving State of the initial communication, either State shall have the right to refer the matter to the Committee, by notice given to the Committee and to the other State;

(c) The Committee shall deal with a matter referred to it only after it has ascertained that all available domestic remedies have been invoked and exhausted in the matter. This shall not be the rule where the application of the remedies is unreasonably prolonged;

(d) Subject to the provisions of subparagraph (c) of the present paragraph the Committee shall make available its good offices to the States Parties concerned with a view to a friendly solution of the matter on the basis of the respect for the obligations set forth in the Covenant;

(e) The Committee shall hold closed meetings when examining communications under the present article;

(f) In any matter referred to it in accordance with subparagraph (b) of the present paragraph, the Committee may call upon the States Parties concerned, referred to in subparagraph (b), to supply any relevant information;

(g) The States Parties concerned, referred to in subparagraph (b) of the present paragraph, shall have the right to be represented when the matter is being considered by the Committee and to make submissions orally and/or in writing;

(h) The Committee shall, with all due expediency after the date of receipt of notice under subparagraph (b) of the present paragraph, submit a report, as follows:

  (i) If a solution within the terms of subparagraph (d) of the present paragraph is reached, the Committee shall confine its report to a brief statement of the facts and of the solution reached;

(ii) If a solution within the terms of subparagraph (d) is not reached, the Committee shall, in its report, set forth the relevant facts concerning the issue between the States Parties concerned. The written submissions and record of the oral submissions made by the States Parties concerned shall be attached to the report. The Committee may also communicate only to the States Parties concerned any views that it may consider relevant to the issue between them.

In every matter, the report shall be communicated to the States Parties concerned.

2. A declaration under paragraph 1 of the present article shall be deposited by the States Parties with the Secretary-General of the United Nations, who shall transmit copies thereof to the other States Parties. A declaration may be withdrawn at any time by notification to the Secretary-General. Such a withdrawal shall not prejudice the consideration of any matter that is the subject of a communication already transmitted under the present article; no further communication by any State Party shall be received under the present article after the notification of withdrawal of the declaration has been received by the Secretary-General, unless the State Party concerned has made a new declaration.

Article 11 – Inquiry Procedure

1. A State Party to the present Protocol may at any time declare that it recognizes the competence of the Committee provided for under the present article.
2. If the Committee receives reliable information indicating grave or systematic violations by a State Party of any of the economic, social and cultural rights set forth in the Covenant, the Committee shall invite that State Party to cooperate in the examination of the information and to this end to submit observations with regard to the information concerned.
3. Taking into account any observations that may have been submitted by the State Party concerned as well as any other reliable information available to it, the Committee may designate one or more of its members to conduct an inquiry and to report urgently to the Committee. Where warranted and with the consent of the State Party, the inquiry may include a visit to its territory.
4. Such an inquiry shall be conducted confidentially and the cooperation of the State Party shall be sought at all stages of the proceedings.
5. After examining the findings of such an inquiry, the Committee shall transmit these findings to the State Party concerned together with any comments and recommendations.

6. The State Party concerned shall, within six months of receiving the findings, comments and recommendations transmitted by the Committee, submit its observations to the Committee.
7. After such proceedings have been completed with regard to an inquiry made in accordance with paragraph 2 of the present article, the Committee may, after consultations with the State Party concerned, decide to include a summary account of the results of the proceedings in its annual report provided for in article 15 of the present Protocol.
8. Any State Party having made a declaration in accordance with paragraph 1 of the present article may, at any time, withdraw this declaration by notification to the Secretary-General.

Article 12 – Follow-Up to the Inquiry Procedure

1. The Committee may invite the State Party concerned to include in its report under articles 16 and 17 of the Covenant details of any measures taken in response to an inquiry conducted under article 11 of the present Protocol.
2. The Committee may, if necessary, after the end of the period of six months referred to in article 11, paragraph 6, invite the State Party concerned to inform it of the measures taken in response to such an inquiry.

Article 13 – Protection Measures

A State Party shall take all appropriate measures to ensure that individuals under its jurisdiction are not subjected to any form of ill-treatment or intimidation as a consequence of communicating with the Committee pursuant to the present Protocol.

Article 14 – International Assistance and Cooperation

1. The Committee shall transmit, as it may consider appropriate, and with the consent of the State Party concerned, to United Nations specialized agencies, funds and programmes and other competent bodies, its views or recommendations concerning communications and inquiries that indicate a need for technical advice or assistance, along with the State Party's observations and suggestions, if any, on these views or recommendations.
2. The Committee may also bring to the attention of such bodies, with the consent of the State Party concerned, any matter arising out of communications considered under the present Protocol which may assist them in deciding, each within its field of competence, on the advisability of international measures likely to contribute to assisting States Parties in achieving progress in implementation of the rights recognized in the Covenant.

3. A trust fund shall be established in accordance with the relevant procedures of the General Assembly, to be administered in accordance with the financial regulations and rules of the United Nations, with a view to providing expert and technical assistance to States Parties, with the consent of the State Party concerned, for the enhanced implementation of the rights contained in the Covenant, thus contributing to building national capacities in the area of economic, social and cultural rights in the context of the present Protocol.
4. The provisions of the present article are without prejudice to the obligations of each State Party to fulfil its obligations under the Covenant.

Article 15 – Annual Report

The Committee shall include in its annual report a summary of its activities under the present Protocol.

Article 16 – Dissemination and Information

Each State Party undertakes to make widely known and to disseminate the Covenant and the present Protocol and to facilitate access to information about the views and recommendations of the Committee, in particular, on matters involving that State Party, and to do so in accessible formats for persons with disabilities.

Article 17 – Signature, Ratification and Accession

1. The present Protocol is open for signature by any State that has signed, ratified or acceded to the Covenant.
2. The present Protocol is subject to ratification by any State that has ratified or acceded to the Covenant. Instruments of ratification shall be deposited with the Secretary-General of the United Nations.
3. The present Protocol shall be open to accession by any State that has ratified or acceded to the Covenant.
4. Accession shall be effected by the deposit of an instrument of accession with the Secretary-General of the United Nations.

Article 18 – Entry into Force

1. The present Protocol shall enter into force three months after the date of the deposit with the Secretary-General of the United Nations of the tenth instrument of ratification or accession.
2. For each State ratifying or acceding to the present Protocol, after the deposit of the tenth instrument of ratification or accession, the Protocol shall enter into force three months after the date of the deposit of its instrument of ratification or accession.

Article 19 – Amendments

1. Any State Party may propose an amendment to the present Protocol and submit it to the Secretary-General of the United Nations. The Secretary-General shall communicate any proposed amendments to States Parties, with a request to be notified whether they favour a meeting of States Parties for the purpose of considering and deciding upon the proposals. In the event that, within four months from the date of such communication, at least one third of the States Parties favour such a meeting, the Secretary-General shall convene the meeting under the auspices of the United Nations. Any amendment adopted by a majority of two thirds of the States Parties present and voting shall be submitted by the Secretary-General to the General Assembly for approval and thereafter to all States Parties for acceptance.

2. An amendment adopted and approved in accordance with paragraph 1 of the present article shall enter into force on the thirtieth day after the number of instruments of acceptance deposited reaches two thirds of the number of States Parties at the date of adoption of the amendment. Thereafter, the amendment shall enter into force for any State Party on the thirtieth day following the deposit of its own instrument of acceptance. An amendment shall be binding only on those States Parties which have accepted it.

Article 20 – Denunciation

1. Any State Party may denounce the present Protocol at any time by written notification addressed to the Secretary-General of the United Nations. Denunciation shall take effect six months after the date of receipt of the notification by the Secretary-General.

2. Denunciation shall be without prejudice to the continued application of the provisions of the present Protocol to any communication submitted under articles 2 and 10 or to any procedure initiated under article 11 before the effective date of denunciation.

Article 21 – Notification by the Secretary-General

The Secretary-General of the United Nations shall notify all States referred to in article 26, paragraph 1, of the Covenant of the following particulars:

(a) Signatures, ratifications and accessions under the present Protocol;

(b) The date of entry into force of the present Protocol and of any amendment under article 19;

(c) Any denunciation under article 20.

Article 22 – Official Languages

1. The present Protocol, of which the Arabic, Chinese, English, French, Russian and Spanish texts are equally authentic, shall be deposited in the archives of the United Nations.

2. The Secretary-General of the United Nations shall transmit certified copies of the present Protocol to all States referred to in article 26 of the Covenant.

CHAPTER 8

Convention on the Elimination of All Forms of Discrimination against Women

Adopted and opened for signature, ratification and accession by General Assembly resolution 34/180 of 18 December 1979
entry into force 3 September 1981, in accordance with article 27(1)

The States Parties to the present Convention,

Noting that the Charter of the United Nations reaffirms faith in fundamental human rights, in the dignity and worth of the human person and in the equal rights of men and women,

Noting that the Universal Declaration of Human Rights affirms the principle of the inadmissibility of discrimination and proclaims that all human beings are born free and equal in dignity and rights and that everyone is entitled to all the rights and freedoms set forth therein, without distinction of any kind, including distinction based on sex,

Noting that the States Parties to the International Covenants on Human Rights have the obligation to ensure the equal right of men and women to enjoy all economic, social, cultural, civil and political rights,

Considering the international conventions concluded under the auspices of the United Nations and the specialised agencies promoting equality of rights of men and women,

Noting also the resolutions, declarations and recommendations adopted by the United Nations and the specialised agencies promoting equality of rights of men and women,

Concerned, however, that despite these various instruments extensive discrimination against women continues to exist,

Recalling that discrimination against women violates the principles of equality of rights and respect for human dignity, is an obstacle to the participation of women, on equal terms with men, in the political, social, economic and cultural life of their countries, hampers the growth of the prosperity of society and the family and makes more difficult the full development of the potentialities of women in the service of their countries and of humanity,

Concerned that in situations of poverty women have the least access to food, health, education, training and opportunities for employment and other needs,

 | DOI:10.1163/9789004681224_016

Convinced that the establishment of the new international economic order based on equity and justice will contribute significantly towards the promotion of equality between men and women,

Emphasizing that the eradication of apartheid, all forms of racism, racial discrimination, colonialism, neo-colonialism, aggression, foreign occupation and domination and interference in the internal affairs of States is essential to the full enjoyment of the rights of men and women,

Affirming that the strengthening of international peace and security, the relaxation of international tension, mutual co-operation among all States irrespective of their social and economic systems, general and complete disarmament, in particular nuclear disarmament under strict and effective international control, the affirmation of the principles of justice, equality and mutual benefit in relations among countries and the realization of the right of peoples under alien and colonial domination and foreign occupation to self-determination and independence, as well as respect for national sovereignty and territorial integrity, will promote social progress and development and as a consequence will contribute to the attainment of full equality between men and women,

Convinced that the full and complete development of a country, the welfare of the world and the cause of peace require the maximum participation of women on equal terms with men in all fields,

Bearing in mind the great contribution of women to the welfare of the family and to the development of society, so far not fully recognized, the social significance of maternity and the role of both parents in the family and in the upbringing of children, and aware that the role of women in procreation should not be a basis for discrimination but that the upbringing of children requires a sharing of responsibility between men and women and society as a whole,

Aware that a change in the traditional role of men as well as the role of women in society and in the family is needed to achieve full equality between men and women,

Determined to implement the principles set forth in the Declaration on the Elimination of Discrimination against Women and, for that purpose, to adopt the measures required for the elimination of such discrimination in all its forms and manifestations,

Have agreed on the following:

Part I

Art. 1 For the purposes of the present Convention, the term "discrimination against women" shall mean any distinction, exclusion or restriction made on the basis of sex which has the effect or purpose of impairing or nullifying the recognition, enjoyment or exercise by women, irrespective of their marital status, on a basis of equality of men and women, of human rights and fundamental freedoms in the political, economic, social, cultural, civil or any other field.
Art. 2 States Parties condemn discrimination against women in all its forms, agree to pursue by all appropriate means and without delay a policy of eliminating discrimination against women and, to this end, undertake:

(a) To embody the principle of the equality of men and women in their national constitutions or other appropriate legislation if not yet incorporated therein and to ensure, through law and other appropriate means, the practical realization of this principle;
(b) To adopt appropriate legislative and other measures, including sanctions where appropriate, prohibiting all discrimination against women;
(c) To establish legal protection of the rights of women on an equal basis with men and to ensure through competent national tribunals and other public institutions the effective protection of women against any act of discrimination;
(d) To refrain from engaging in any act or practice of discrimination against women and to ensure that public authorities and institutions shall act in conformity with this obligation;
(e) To take all appropriate measures to eliminate discrimination against women by any person, organization or enterprise;
(f) To take all appropriate measures, including legislation, to modify or abolish existing laws, regulations, customs and practices which constitute discrimination against women;
(g) To repeal all national penal provisions which constitute discrimination against women.

Art. 3 States Parties shall take in all fields, in particular in the political, social, economic and cultural fields, all appropriate measures, including legislation, to ensure the full development and advancement of women, for the purpose of guaranteeing them the exercise and enjoyment of human rights and fundamental freedoms on a basis of equality with men.
Art. 4 1. Adoption by States Parties of temporary special measures aimed at accelerating de facto equality between men and women shall not be considered discrimination as defined in the present Convention, but shall in no way entail as a consequence the maintenance of unequal or separate standards;

these measures shall be discontinued when the objectives of equality of opportunity and treatment have been achieved.

2. Adoption by States Parties of special measures, including those measures contained in the present Convention, aimed at protecting maternity shall not be considered discriminatory.

Art. 5 States Parties shall take all appropriate measures:

(a) To modify the social and cultural patterns of conduct of men and women, with a view to achieving the elimination of prejudices and customary and all other practices which are based on the idea of the inferiority or the superiority of either of the sexes or on stereotyped roles for men and women;

(b) To ensure that family education includes a proper understanding of maternity as a social function and the recognition of the common responsibility of men and women in the upbringing and development of their children, it being understood that the interest of the children is the primordial consideration in all cases.

Art. 6 States Parties shall take all appropriate measures, including legislation, to suppress all forms of traffic in women and exploitation of prostitution of women.

Part II

Art. 7 States Parties shall take all appropriate measures to eliminate discrimination against women in the political and public life of the country and, in particular, shall ensure to women, on equal terms with men, the right:

(a) To vote in all elections and public referenda and to be eligible for election to all publicly elected bodies;

(b) To participate in the formulation of government policy and the implementation thereof and to hold public office and perform all public functions at all levels of government;

(c) To participate in non-governmental organizations and associations concerned with the public and political life of the country.

Art. 8 States Parties shall take all appropriate measures to ensure to women, on equal terms with men and without any discrimination, the opportunity to represent their Governments at the international level and to participate in the work of international organizations.

Art. 9 1. States Parties shall grant women equal rights with men to acquire, change or retain their nationality. They shall ensure in particular that neither marriage to an alien nor change of nationality by the husband during marriage

shall automatically change the nationality of the wife, render her stateless or force upon her the nationality of the husband.
2. States Parties shall grant women equal rights with men with respect to the nationality of their children.

Part III

Art. 10 States Parties shall take all appropriate measures to eliminate discrimination against women in order to ensure to them equal rights with men in the field of education and in particular to ensure, on a basis of equality of men and women:

(a) The same conditions for career and vocational guidance, for access to studies and for the achievement of diplomas in educational establishments of all categories in rural as well as in urban areas; this equality shall be ensured in pre-school, general, technical, professional and higher technical education, as well as in all types of vocational training;

(b) Access to the same curricula, the same examinations, teaching staff with qualifications of the same standard and school premises and equipment of the same quality;

(c) The elimination of any stereotyped concept of the roles of men and women at all levels and in all forms of education by encouraging coeducation and other types of education which will help to achieve this aim and, in particular, by the revision of textbooks and school programmes and the adaptation of teaching methods;

(d) The same opportunities to benefit from scholarships and other study grants;

(e) The same opportunities for access to programmes of continuing education, including adult and functional literacy programmes, particularly those aimed at reducing, at the earliest possible time, any gap in education existing between men and women;

(f) The reduction of female student drop-out rates and the organization of programmes for girls and women who have left school prematurely;

(g) The same Opportunities to participate actively in sports and physical education;

(h) Access to specific educational information to help to ensure the health and well-being of families, including information and advice on family planning.

Art. 11 1. States Parties shall take all appropriate measures to eliminate discrimination against women in the field of employment in order to ensure, on a basis of equality of men and women, the same rights, in particular:

(a) The right to work as an inalienable right of all human beings;

(b) The right to the same employment opportunities, including the application of the same criteria for selection in matters of employment;

(c) The right to free choice of profession and employment, the right to promotion, job security and all benefits and conditions of service and the right to receive vocational training and retraining, including apprenticeships, advanced vocational training and recurrent training;

(d) The right to equal remuneration, including benefits, and to equal treatment in respect of work of equal value, as well as equality of treatment in the evaluation of the quality of work;

(e) The right to social security, particularly in cases of retirement, unemployment, sickness, invalidity and old age and other incapacity to work, as well as the right to paid leave;

(f) The right to protection of health and to safety in working conditions, including the safeguarding of the function of reproduction.

2. In order to prevent discrimination against women on the grounds of marriage or maternity and to ensure their effective right to work, States Parties shall take appropriate measures:

(a) To prohibit, subject to the imposition of sanctions, dismissal on the grounds of pregnancy or of maternity leave and discrimination in dismissals on the basis of marital status;

(b) To introduce maternity leave with pay or with comparable social benefits without loss of former employment, seniority or social allowances;

(c) To encourage the provision of the necessary supporting social services to enable parents to combine family obligations with work responsibilities and participation in public life, in particular through promoting the establishment and development of a network of child-care facilities;

(d) To provide special protection to women during pregnancy in types of work proved to be harmful to them.

3. Protective legislation relating to matters covered in this article shall be reviewed periodically in the light of scientific and technological knowledge and shall be revised, repealed or extended as necessary.

Art. 12 1. States Parties shall take all appropriate measures to eliminate discrimination against women in the field of health care in order to ensure, on a basis of equality of men and women, access to health care services, including those related to family planning.

2. Notwithstanding the provisions of paragraph 1 of this article, States Parties shall ensure to women appropriate services in connection with pregnancy, confinement and the post-natal period, granting free services where necessary, as well as adequate nutrition during pregnancy and lactation.

Art. 13 States Parties shall take all appropriate measures to eliminate discrimination against women in other areas of economic and social life in order to ensure, on a basis of equality of men and women, the same rights, in particular:

(a) The right to family benefits;

(b) The right to bank loans, mortgages and other forms of financial credit;

(c) The right to participate in recreational activities, sports and all aspects of cultural life.

Art. 14 1. States Parties shall take into account the particular problems faced by rural women and the significant roles which rural women play in the economic survival of their families, including their work in the non-monetized sectors of the economy, and shall take all appropriate measures to ensure the application of the provisions of the present Convention to women in rural areas.

2. States Parties shall take all appropriate measures to eliminate discrimination against women in rural areas in order to ensure, on a basis of equality of men and women, that they participate in and benefit from rural development and, in particular, shall ensure to such women the right:

(a) To participate in the elaboration and implementation of development planning at all levels;

(b) To have access to adequate health care facilities, including information, counselling and services in family planning;

(c) To benefit directly from social security programmes;

(d) To obtain all types of training and education, formal and non-formal, including that relating to functional literacy, as well as, inter alia, the benefit of all community and extension services, in order to increase their technical proficiency;

(e) To organize self-help groups and co-operatives in order to obtain equal access to economic opportunities through employment or self-employment;

(f) To participate in all community activities;

(g) To have access to agricultural credit and loans, marketing facilities, appropriate technology and equal treatment in land and agrarian reform as well as in land resettlement schemes;

(h) To enjoy adequate living conditions, particularly in relation to housing, sanitation, electricity and water supply, transport and communications.

Part IV

Art. 15 1. States Parties shall accord to women equality with men before the law.
2. States Parties shall accord to women, in civil matters, a legal capacity identical to that of men and the same opportunities to exercise that capacity. In particular, they shall give women equal rights to conclude contracts and to administer property and shall treat them equally in all stages of procedure in courts and tribunals.
3. States Parties agree that all contracts and all other private instruments of any kind with a legal effect which is directed at restricting the legal capacity of women shall be deemed null and void.
4. States Parties shall accord to men and women the same rights with regard to the law relating to the movement of persons and the freedom to choose their residence and domicile.
Art. 16 1. States Parties shall take all appropriate measures to eliminate discrimination against women in all matters relating to marriage and family relations and in particular shall ensure, on a basis of equality of men and women:
(a) The same right to enter into marriage;
(b) The same right freely to choose a spouse and to enter into marriage only with their free and full consent;
(c) The same rights and responsibilities during marriage and at its dissolution;
(d) The same rights and responsibilities as parents, irrespective of their marital status, in matters relating to their children; in all cases the interests of the children shall be paramount;
(e) The same rights to decide freely and responsibly on the number and spacing of their children and to have access to the information, education and means to enable them to exercise these rights;
(f) The same rights and responsibilities with regard to guardianship, wardship, trusteeship and adoption of children, or similar institutions where these concepts exist in national legislation; in all cases the interests of the children shall be paramount;
(g) The same personal rights as husband and wife, including the right to choose a family name, a profession and an occupation;
(h) The same rights for both spouses in respect of the ownership, acquisition, management, administration, enjoyment and disposition of property, whether free of charge or for a valuable consideration.
2. The betrothal and the marriage of a child shall have no legal effect, and all necessary action, including legislation, shall be taken to specify a minimum

age for marriage and to make the registration of marriages in an official registry compulsory.

Part v

Art. 17 1. For the purpose of considering the progress made in the implementation of the present Convention, there shall be established a Committee on the Elimination of Discrimination against Women (hereinafter referred to as the Committee) consisting, at the time of entry into force of the Convention, of eighteen and, after ratification of or accession to the Convention by the thirty-fifth State Party, of twenty-three experts of high moral standing and competence in the field covered by the Convention. The experts shall be elected by States Parties from among their nationals and shall serve in their personal capacity, consideration being given to equitable geographical distribution and to the representation of the different forms of civilization as well as the principal legal systems.
2. The members of the Committee shall be elected by secret ballot from a list of persons nominated by States Parties. Each State Party may nominate one person from among its own nationals.
3. The initial election shall be held six months after the date of the entry into force of the present
Convention. At least three months before the date of each election the Secretary-General of the United Nations shall address a letter to the States Parties inviting them to submit their nominations within two months. The Secretary-General shall prepare a list in alphabetical order of all persons thus nominated, indicating the States Parties which have nominated them, and shall submit it to the States Parties.
4. Elections of the members of the Committee shall be held at a meeting of States Parties convened by the Secretary-General at United Nations Headquarters. At that meeting, for which two thirds of the States Parties shall constitute a quorum, the persons elected to the Committee shall be those nominees who obtain the largest number of votes and an absolute majority of the votes of the representatives of States Parties present and voting.
5. The members of the Committee shall be elected for a term of four years. However, the terms of nine of the members elected at the first election shall expire at the end of two years; immediately after the first election the names of these nine members shall be chosen by lot by the Chairman of the Committee.
6. The election of the five additional members of the Committee shall be held in accordance with the provisions of paragraphs 2, 3 and 4 of this article,

following the thirty-fifth ratification or accession. The terms of two of the additional members elected on this occasion shall expire at the end of two years, the names of these two members having been chosen by lot by the Chairman of the Committee.
7. For the filling of casual vacancies, the State Party whose expert has ceased to function as a member of the Committee shall appoint another expert from among its nationals, subject to the approval of the Committee.
8. The members of the Committee shall, with the approval of the General Assembly, receive emoluments from United Nations resources on such terms and conditions as the Assembly may decide, having regard to the importance of the Committee's responsibilities.
9. The Secretary-General of the United Nations shall provide the necessary staff and facilities for the effective performance of the functions of the Committee under the present Convention.
Art. 18 1. States Parties undertake to submit to the Secretary-General of the United Nations, for consideration by the Committee, a report on the legislative, judicial, administrative or other measures which they have adopted to give effect to the provisions of the present Convention and on the progress made in this respect:
(a) Within one year after the entry into force for the State concerned; and
(b) Thereafter at least every four years and further whenever the Committee so requests.
2. Reports may indicate factors and difficulties affecting the degree of fulfilment of obligations under the present Convention.
Art. 19 1. The Committee shall adopt its own rules of procedure.
2. The Committee shall elect its officers for a term of two years.
Art. 20 1. The Committee shall normally meet for a period of not more than two weeks annually in order to consider the reports submitted in accordance with article 18 of the present Convention.
2. The meetings of the Committee shall normally be held at United Nations Headquarters or at any other convenient place as determined by the Committee.
Art. 21 1. The Committee shall, through the Economic and Social Council, report annually to the General Assembly of the United Nations on its activities and may make suggestions and general recommendations based on the examination of reports and information received from the States Parties. Such suggestions and general recommendations shall be included in the report of the Committee together with comments, if any, from States Parties.
2. The Secretary-General of the United Nations shall transmit the reports of the Committee to the Commission on the Status of Women for its information.

Art. 22 The specialized agencies shall be entitled to be represented at the consideration of the implementation of such provisions of the present Convention as fall within the scope of their activities. The Committee may invite the specialized agencies to submit reports on the implementation of the Convention in areas falling within the scope of their activities.

Part VI

Art. 23 Nothing in the present Convention shall affect any provisions that are more conducive to the achievement of equality between men and women which may be contained:
(a) In the legislation of a State Party; or
(b) In any other international convention, treaty or agreement in force for that State.

Art. 24 States Parties undertake to adopt all necessary measures at the national level aimed at achieving the full realization of the rights recognized in the present Convention.

Art. 25 1. The present Convention shall be open for signature by all States.
2. The Secretary-General of the United Nations is designated as the depositary of the present Convention.
3. The present Convention is subject to ratification. Instruments of ratification shall be deposited with the Secretary-General of the United Nations.
4. The present Convention shall be open to accession by all States. Accession shall be effected by the deposit of an instrument of accession with the Secretary-General of the United Nations.

Art. 26 1. A request for the revision of the present Convention may be made at any time by any State Party by means of a notification in writing addressed to the Secretary-General of the United Nations.
2. The General Assembly of the United Nations shall decide upon the steps, if any, to be taken in respect of such a request.

Art. 27 1. The present Convention shall enter into force on the thirtieth day after the date of deposit with the Secretary-General of the United Nations of the twentieth instrument of ratification or accession.
2. For each State ratifying the present Convention or acceding to it after the deposit of the twentieth instrument of ratification or accession, the Convention shall enter into force on the thirtieth day after the date of the deposit of its own instrument of ratification or accession.

Art. 28 1. The Secretary-General of the United Nations shall receive and circulate to all States the text of reservations made by States at the time of ratification or accession.

2. A reservation incompatible with the object and purpose of the present Convention shall not be permitted.

3. Reservations may be withdrawn at any time by notification to this effect addressed to the Secretary-General of the United Nations, who shall then inform all States thereof. Such notification shall take effect on the date on which it is received.

Art. 29 1. Any dispute between two or more States Parties concerning the interpretation or application of the present Convention which is not settled by negotiation shall, at the request of one of them, be submitted to arbitration. If within six months from the date of the request for arbitration the parties are unable to agree on the organization of the arbitration, any one of those parties may refer the dispute to the International Court of Justice by request in conformity with the Statute of the Court.

2. Each State Party may at the time of signature or ratification of the present Convention or accession thereto declare that it does not consider itself bound by paragraph 1 of this article. The other States Parties shall not be bound by that paragraph with respect to any State Party which has made such a reservation.

3. Any State Party which has made a reservation in accordance with paragraph 2 of this article may at any time withdraw that reservation by notification to the Secretary-General of the United Nations.

Art. 30 The present Convention, the Arabic, Chinese, English, French, Russian and Spanish texts of which are equally authentic, shall be deposited with the Secretary-General of the United Nations.

IN WITNESS WHEREOF the undersigned, duly authorized, have signed the present Convention.

CHAPTER 9

Convention against Torture and Other Cruel, Inhuman or Degrading Treatment or Punishment

Adopted and opened for signature, ratification and accession by General Assembly resolution 39/46 of 10 December 1984
Entry into force 26 June 1987, in accordance with article 27(1)

The States Parties to this Convention,

Considering that, in accordance with the principles proclaimed in the Charter of the United Nations, recognition of the equal and inalienable rights of all members of the human family is the foundation of freedom, justice and peace in the world,

Recognizing that those rights derive from the inherent dignity of the human person,

Considering the obligation of States under the Charter, in particular Article 55, to promote universal respect for, and observance of, human rights and fundamental freedoms,

Having regard to article 5 of the Universal Declaration of Human Rights and article 7 of the International Covenant on Civil and Political Rights, both of which provide that no one shall be subjected to torture or to cruel, inhuman or degrading treatment or punishment,

Having regard also to the Declaration on the Protection of All Persons from Being Subjected to Torture and Other Cruel, Inhuman or Degrading Treatment or Punishment, adopted by the General Assembly on 9 December 1975,

Desiring to make more effective the struggle against torture and other cruel, inhuman or degrading treatment or punishment throughout the world,

Have agreed as follows:

Part I

Art. 1 1. For the purposes of this Convention, the term "torture" means any act by which severe pain or suffering, whether physical or mental, is intentionally inflicted on a person for such purposes as obtaining from him or a third person information or a confession, punishing him for an act he or a third person has committed or is suspected of having committed, or intimidating or coercing

© KARL HANSON ET AL., 2025 | DOI:10.1163/9789004681224_017

him or a third person, or for any reason based on discrimination of any kind, when such pain or suffering is inflicted by or at the instigation of or with the consent or acquiescence of a public official or other person acting in an official capacity. It does not include pain or suffering arising only from, inherent in or incidental to lawful sanctions.

2. This article is without prejudice to any international instrument or national legislation which does or may contain provisions of wider application.

Art. 2 1. Each State Party shall take effective legislative, administrative, judicial or other measures to prevent acts of torture in any territory under its jurisdiction.

2. No exceptional circumstances whatsoever, whether a state of war or a threat of war, internal political instability or any other public emergency, may be invoked as a justification of torture.

3. An order from a superior officer or a public authority may not be invoked as a justification of torture.

Art. 3 1. No State Party shall expel, return ("refouler") or extradite a person to another State where there are substantial grounds for believing that he would be in danger of being subjected to torture.

2. For the purpose of determining whether there are such grounds, the competent authorities shall take into account all relevant considerations including, where applicable, the existence in the State concerned of a consistent pattern of gross, flagrant or mass violations of human rights.

Art. 4 1. Each State Party shall ensure that all acts of torture are offences under its criminal law. The same shall apply to an attempt to commit torture and to an act by any person which constitutes complicity or participation in torture.

2. Each State Party shall make these offences punishable by appropriate penalties which take into account their grave nature.

Art. 5 1. Each State Party shall take such measures as may be necessary to establish its jurisdiction over the offences referred to in article 4 in the following cases:

(a) When the offences are committed in any territory under its jurisdiction or on board a ship or aircraft registered in that State;

(b) When the alleged offender is a national of that State;

(c) When the victim is a national of that State if that State considers it appropriate.

2. Each State Party shall likewise take such measures as may be necessary to establish its jurisdiction over such offences in cases where the alleged offender is present in any territory under its jurisdiction and it does not extradite him pursuant to article 8 to any of the States mentioned in paragraph 1 of this article.

3. This Convention does not exclude any criminal jurisdiction exercised in accordance with internal law.

Art. 6 1. Upon being satisfied, after an examination of information available to it, that the circumstances so warrant, any State Party in whose territory a person alleged to have committed any offence referred to in article 4 is present shall take him into custody or take other legal measures to ensure his presence. The custody and other legal measures shall be as provided in the law of that State but may be continued only for such time as is necessary to enable any criminal or extradition proceedings to be instituted.

2. Such State shall immediately make a preliminary inquiry into the facts.

3. Any person in custody pursuant to paragraph 1 of this article shall be assisted in communicating immediately with the nearest appropriate representative of the State of which he is a national, or, if he is a stateless person, with the representative of the State where he usually resides.

4. When a State, pursuant to this article, has taken a person into custody, it shall immediately notify the States referred to in article 5, paragraph 1, of the fact that such person is in custody and of the circumstances which warrant his detention. The State which makes the preliminary inquiry contemplated in paragraph 2 of this article shall promptly report its findings to the said States and shall indicate whether it intends to exercise jurisdiction.

Art. 7 1. The State Party in the territory under whose jurisdiction a person alleged to have committed any offence referred to in article 4 is found shall in the cases contemplated in article 5, if it does not extradite him, submit the case to its competent authorities for the purpose of prosecution.

2. These authorities shall take their decision in the same manner as in the case of any ordinary offence of a serious nature under the law of that State. In the cases referred to in article 5, paragraph 2, the standards of evidence required for prosecution and conviction shall in no way be less stringent than those which apply in the cases referred to in article 5, paragraph 1.

3. Any person regarding whom proceedings are brought in connection with any of the offences referred to in article 4 shall be guaranteed fair treatment at all stages of the proceedings.

Art. 8 1. The offences referred to in article 4 shall be deemed to be included as extraditable offences in any extradition treaty existing between States Parties. States Parties undertake to include such offences as extraditable offences in every extradition treaty to be concluded between them.

2. If a State Party which makes extradition conditional on the existence of a treaty receives a request for extradition from another State Party with which it has no extradition treaty, it may consider this Convention as the legal basis for

extradition in respect of such offences. Extradition shall be subject to the other conditions provided by the law of the requested State.
3. States Parties which do not make extradition conditional on the existence of a treaty shall recognize such offences as extraditable offences between themselves subject to the conditions provided by the law of the requested State.
4. Such offences shall be treated, for the purpose of extradition between States Parties, as if they had been committed not only in the place in which they occurred but also in the territories of the States required to establish their jurisdiction in accordance with article 5, paragraph 1.
Art. 9 1. States Parties shall afford one another the greatest measure of assistance in connection with criminal proceedings brought in respect of any of the offences referred to in article 4, including the supply of all evidence at their disposal necessary for the proceedings.
2. States Parties shall carry out their obligations under paragraph 1 of this article in conformity with any treaties on mutual judicial assistance that may exist between them.
Art. 10 1. Each State Party shall ensure that education and information regarding the prohibition against torture are fully included in the training of law enforcement personnel, civil or military, medical personnel, public officials and other persons who may be involved in the custody, interrogation or treatment of any individual subjected to any form of arrest, detention or imprisonment.
2. Each State Party shall include this prohibition in the rules or instructions issued in regard to the duties and functions of any such persons.
Art. 11 Each State Party shall keep under systematic review interrogation rules, instructions, methods and practices as well as arrangements for the custody and treatment of persons subjected to any form of arrest, detention or imprisonment in any territory under its jurisdiction, with a view to preventing any cases of torture.
Art. 12 Each State Party shall ensure that its competent authorities proceed to a prompt and impartial investigation, wherever there is reasonable ground to believe that an act of torture has been committed in any territory under its jurisdiction.
Art. 13 Each State Party shall ensure that any individual who alleges he has been subjected to torture in any territory under its jurisdiction has the right to complain to, and to have his case promptly and impartially examined by, its competent authorities. Steps shall be taken to ensure that the complainant and witnesses are protected against all ill-treatment or intimidation as a consequence of his complaint or any evidence given.
Art. 14 1. Each State Party shall ensure in its legal system that the victim of an act of torture obtains redress and has an enforceable right to fair and adequate

compensation, including the means for as full rehabilitation as possible. In the event of the death of the victim as a result of an act of torture, his dependants shall be entitled to compensation.
2. Nothing in this article shall affect any right of the victim or other persons to compensation which may exist under national law.
Art. 15 Each State Party shall ensure that any statement which is established to have been made as a result of torture shall not be invoked as evidence in any proceedings, except against a person accused of torture as evidence that the statement was made.
Art. 16 1. Each State Party shall undertake to prevent in any territory under its jurisdiction other acts of cruel, inhuman or degrading treatment or punishment which do not amount to torture as defined in article 1, when such acts are committed by or at the instigation of or with the consent or acquiescence of a public official or other person acting in an official capacity. In particular, the obligations contained in articles 10, 11, 12 and 13 shall apply with the substitution for references to torture of references to other forms of cruel, inhuman or degrading treatment or punishment.
2. The provisions of this Convention are without prejudice to the provisions of any other international instrument or national law which prohibits cruel, inhuman or degrading treatment or punishment or which relates to extradition or expulsion.

Part II

Art. 17 1. There shall be established a Committee against Torture (hereinafter referred to as the Committee) which shall carry out the functions hereinafter provided. The Committee shall consist of ten experts of high moral standing and recognized competence in the field of human rights, who shall serve in their personal capacity. The experts shall be elected by the States Parties, consideration being given to equitable geographical distribution and to the usefulness of the participation of some persons having legal experience.
2. The members of the Committee shall be elected by secret ballot from a list of persons nominated by States Parties. Each State Party may nominate one person from among its own nationals. States Parties shall bear in mind the usefulness of nominating persons who are also members of the Human Rights Committee established under the International Covenant on Civil and Political Rights and who are willing to serve on the Committee against Torture.
3. Elections of the members of the Committee shall be held at biennial meetings of States Parties convened by the Secretary-General of the United Nations.

At those meetings, for which two thirds of the States Parties shall constitute a quorum, the persons elected to the Committee shall be those who obtain the largest number of votes and an absolute majority of the votes of the representatives of States Parties present and voting.

4. The initial election shall be held no later than six months after the date of the entry into force of this Convention. At least four months before the date of each election, the Secretary-General of the United Nations shall address a letter to the States Parties inviting them to submit their nominations within three months. The Secretary-General shall prepare a list in alphabetical order of all persons thus nominated, indicating the States Parties which have nominated them, and shall submit it to the States Parties.

5. The members of the Committee shall be elected for a term of four years. They shall be eligible for re-election if renominated. However, the term of five of the members elected at the first election shall expire at the end of two years; immediately after the first election the names of these five members shall be chosen by lot by the chairman of the meeting referred to in paragraph 3 of this article.

6. If a member of the Committee dies or resigns or for any other cause can no longer perform his Committee duties, the State Party which nominated him shall appoint another expert from among its nationals to serve for the remainder of his term, subject to the approval of the majority of the States Parties. The approval shall be considered given unless half or more of the States Parties respond negatively within six weeks after having been informed by the Secretary-General of the United Nations of the proposed appointment.

7. States Parties shall be responsible for the expenses of the members of the Committee while they are in performance of Committee duties.

Art. 18 1. The Committee shall elect its officers for a term of two years. They may be re-elected.

2. The Committee shall establish its own rules of procedure, but these rules shall provide, inter alia, that:

(a) Six members shall constitute a quorum;

(b) Decisions of the Committee shall be made by a majority vote of the members present.

3. The Secretary-General of the United Nations shall provide the necessary staff and facilities for the effective performance of the functions of the Committee under this Convention.

4. The Secretary-General of the United Nations shall convene the initial meeting of the Committee. After its initial meeting, the Committee shall meet at such times as shall be provided in its rules of procedure.

5. The States Parties shall be responsible for expenses incurred in connection with the holding of meetings of the States Parties and of the Committee, including reimbursement to the United Nations for any expenses, such as the cost of staff and facilities, incurred by the United Nations pursuant to paragraph 3 of this article.

Art. 19 1. The States Parties shall submit to the Committee, through the Secretary-General of the United Nations, reports on the measures they have taken to give effect to their undertakings under this Convention, within one year after the entry into force of the Convention for the State Party concerned. Thereafter the States Parties shall submit supplementary reports every four years on any new measures taken and such other reports as the Committee may request.

2. The Secretary-General of the United Nations shall transmit the reports to all States Parties.

3. Each report shall be considered by the Committee which may make such general comments on the report as it may consider appropriate and shall forward these to the State Party concerned. That State Party may respond with any observations it chooses to the Committee.

4. The Committee may, at its discretion, decide to include any comments made by it in accordance with paragraph 3 of this article, together with the observations thereon received from the State Party concerned, in its annual report made in accordance with article 24. If so requested by the State Party concerned, the Committee may also include a copy of the report submitted under paragraph 1 of this article.

Art. 20 1. If the Committee receives reliable information which appears to it to contain well-founded indications that torture is being systematically practised in the territory of a State Party, the Committee shall invite that State Party to co-operate in the examination of the information and to this end to submit observations with regard to the information concerned.

2. Taking into account any observations which may have been submitted by the State Party concerned, as well as any other relevant information available to it, the Committee may, if it decides that this is warranted, designate one or more of its members to make a confidential inquiry and to report to the Committee urgently.

3. If an inquiry is made in accordance with paragraph 2 of this article, the Committee shall seek the co-operation of the State Party concerned. In agreement with that State Party, such an inquiry may include a visit to its territory.

4. After examining the findings of its member or members submitted in accordance with paragraph 2 of this article, the Commission shall transmit

these findings to the State Party concerned together with any comments or suggestions which seem appropriate in view of the situation.

5. All the proceedings of the Committee referred to in paragraphs 1 to 4 of this article s hall be confidential, and at all stages of the proceedings the co-operation of the State Party shall be sought. After such proceedings have been completed with regard to an inquiry made in accordance with paragraph 2, the Committee may, after consultations with the State Party concerned, decide to include a summary account of the results of the proceedings in its annual report made in accordance with article 24.

Art. 21 1. A State Party to this Convention may at any time declare under this article that it recognizes the competence of the Committee to receive and consider communications to the effect that a State Party claims that another State Party is not fulfilling its obligations under this Convention. Such communications may be received and considered according to the procedures laid down in this article only if submitted by a State Party which has made a declaration recognizing in regard to itself the competence of the Committee. No communication shall be dealt with by the Committee under this article if it concerns a State Party which has not made such a declaration. Communications received under this article shall be dealt with in accordance with the following procedure;

(a) If a State Party considers that another State Party is not giving effect to the provisions of this Convention, it may, by written communication, bring the matter to the attention of that State Party. Within three months after the receipt of the communication the receiving State shall afford the State which sent the communication an explanation or any other statement in writing clarifying the matter, which should include, to the extent possible and pertinent, reference to domestic procedures and remedies taken, pending or available in the matter;

(b) If the matter is not adjusted to the satisfaction of both States Parties concerned within six months after the receipt by the receiving State of the initial communication, either State shall have the right to refer the matter to the Committee, by notice given to the Committee and to the other State;

(c) The Committee shall deal with a matter referred to it under this article only after it has ascertained that all domestic remedies have been invoked and exhausted in the matter, in conformity with the generally recognized principles of international law. This shall not be the rule where the application of the remedies is unreasonably prolonged or is unlikely to bring effective relief to the person who is the victim of the violation of this Convention;

(d) The Committee shall hold closed meetings when examining communications under this article;
(e) Subject to the provisions of subparagraph (c), the Committee shall make available its good offices to the States Parties concerned with a view to a friendly solution of the matter on the basis of respect for the obligations provided for in this Convention. For this purpose, the Committee may, when appropriate, set up an ad hoc conciliation commission;
(f) In any matter referred to it under this article, the Committee may call upon the States Parties concerned, referred to in subparagraph (b), to supply any relevant information;
(g) The States Parties concerned, referred to in subparagraph (b), shall have the right to be represented when the matter is being considered by the Committee and to make submissions orally and/or in writing;
(h) The Committee shall, within twelve months after the date of receipt of notice under subparagraph (b), submit a report:
    (i) If a solution within the terms of subparagraph (e) is reached, the Committee shall confine its report to a brief statement of the facts and of the solution reached;
    (ii) If a solution within the terms of subparagraph (e) is not reached, the Committee shall confine its report to a brief statement of the facts; the written submissions and record of the oral submissions made by the States Parties concerned shall be attached to the report.

In every matter, the report shall be communicated to the States Parties concerned.

2. The provisions of this article shall come into force when five States Parties to this Convention have made declarations under paragraph 1 of this article. Such declarations shall be deposited by the States Parties with the Secretary-General of the United Nations, who shall transmit copies thereof to the other States Parties. A declaration may be withdrawn at any time by notification to the Secretary-General. Such a withdrawal shall not prejudice the consideration of any matter which is the subject of a communication already transmitted under this article; no further communication by any State Party shall be received under this article after the notification of withdrawal of the declaration has been received by the Secretary-General, unless the State Party concerned has made a new declaration.

Art. 22 1. A State Party to this Convention may at any time declare under this article that it recognizes the competence of the Committee to receive and consider communications from or on behalf of individuals subject to its jurisdiction who claim to be victims of a violation by a State Party of the provisions of the Convention. No communication shall be received by the Committee if it concerns a State Party which has not made such a declaration.

2. The Committee shall consider inadmissible any communication under this article which is anonymous or which it considers to be an abuse of the right of submission of such communications or to be incompatible with the provisions of this Convention.

3. Subject to the provisions of paragraph 2, the Committee shall bring any communications submitted to it under this article to the attention of the State Party to this Convention which has made a declaration under paragraph 1 and is alleged to be violating any provisions of the Convention. Within six months, the receiving State shall submit to the Committee written explanations or statements clarifying the matter and the remedy, if any, that may have been taken by that State.

4. The Committee shall consider communications received under this article in the light of all information made available to it by or on behalf of the individual and by the State Party concerned.

5. The Committee shall not consider any communications from an individual under this article unless it has ascertained that:

(a) The same matter has not been, and is not being, examined under another procedure of international investigation or settlement;

(b) The individual has exhausted all available domestic remedies; this shall not be the rule where the application of the remedies is unreasonably prolonged or is unlikely to bring effective relief to the person who is the victim of the violation of this Convention.

6. The Committee shall hold closed meetings when examining communications under this article.

7. The Committee shall forward its views to the State Party concerned and to the individual.

8. The provisions of this article shall come into force when five States Parties to this Convention have made declarations under paragraph 1 of this article. Such declarations shall be deposited by the States Parties with the Secretary-General of the United Nations, who shall transmit copies thereof to the other States Parties. A declaration may be withdrawn at any time by notification to the Secretary-General. Such a withdrawal shall not prejudice the consideration of any matter which is the subject of a communication already transmitted under this article; no further communication by or on behalf of an individual shall be received under this article after the notification of withdrawal of the declaration has been received by the Secretary-General, unless the State Party has made a new declaration.

Art. 23 The members of the Committee and of the ad hoc conciliation commissions which may be appointed under article 21, paragraph 1 (e), shall be entitled to the facilities, privileges and immunities of experts on mission for the United Nations as laid down in the relevant sections of the Convention on the Privileges and Immunities of the United Nations.
Art. 24 The Committee shall submit an annual report on its activities under this Convention to the States Parties and to the General Assembly of the United Nations.

Part III

Art. 25 1. This Convention is open for signature by all States.
2. This Convention is subject to ratification. Instruments of ratification shall be deposited with the Secretary-General of the United Nations.
Art. 26 This Convention is open to accession by all States. Accession shall be effected by the deposit of an instrument of accession with the Secretary-General of the United Nations.
Art. 27 1. This Convention shall enter into force on the thirtieth day after the date of the deposit with the Secretary-General of the United Nations of the twentieth instrument of ratification or accession.
2. For each State ratifying this Convention or acceding to it after the deposit of the twentieth instrument of ratification or accession, the Convention shall enter into force on the thirtieth day after the date of the deposit of its own instrument of ratification or accession.
Art. 28 1. Each State may, at the time of signature or ratification of this Convention or accession thereto, declare that it does not recognize the competence of the Committee provided for in article 20.
2. Any State Party having made a reservation in accordance with paragraph 1 of this article may, at any time, withdraw this reservation by notification to the Secretary-General of the United Nations.
Art. 29 1. Any State Party to this Convention may propose an amendment and file it with the Secretary-General of the United Nations. The Secretary-General shall thereupon communicate the proposed amendment to the States Parties with a request that they notify him whether they favour a conference of States Parties for the purpose of considering and voting upon the proposal. In the event that within four months from the date of such communication at least one third of the States Parties favours such a conference, the Secretary-General shall convene the conference under the auspices of the United Nations. Any amendment adopted by a majority of the States Parties present and voting at

the conference shall be submitted by the Secretary-General to all the States Parties for acceptance.
2. An amendment adopted in accordance with paragraph 1 of this article shall enter into force when two thirds of the States Parties to this Convention have notified the Secretary-General of the United Nations that they have accepted it in accordance with their respective constitutional processes.
3. When amendments enter into force, they shall be binding on those States Parties which have accepted them, other States Parties still being bound by the provisions of this Convention and any earlier amendments which they have accepted.
Art. 30 1. Any dispute between two or more States Parties concerning the interpretation or application of this Convention which cannot be settled through negotiation shall, at the request of one of them, be submitted to arbitration. If within six months from the date of the request for arbitration the Parties are unable to agree on the organization of the arbitration, any one of those Parties may refer the dispute to the International Court of Justice by request in conformity with the Statute of the Court.
2. Each State may, at the time of signature or ratification of this Convention or accession thereto, declare that it does not consider itself bound by paragraph 1 of this article. The other States Parties shall not be bound by paragraph 1 of this article with respect to any State Party having made such a reservation.
3. Any State Party having made a reservation in accordance with paragraph 2 of this article may at any time withdraw this reservation by notification to the Secretary-General of the United Nations.
Art. 31 1. A State Party may denounce this Convention by written notification to the Secretary-General of the United Nations. Denunciation becomes effective one year after the date of receipt of the notification by the Secretary-General.
2. Such a denunciation shall not have the effect of releasing the State Party from its obligations under this Convention in regard to any act or omission which occurs prior to the date at which the denunciation becomes effective, nor shall denunciation prejudice in any way the continued consideration of any matter which is already under consideration by the Committee prior to the date at which the denunciation becomes effective.
3. Following the date at which the denunciation of a State Party becomes effective, the Committee shall not commence consideration of any new matter regarding that State.
Art. 32 The Secretary-General of the United Nations shall inform all States Members of the United Nations and all States which have signed this Convention or acceded to it of the following:
(a) Signatures, ratifications and accessions under articles 25 and 26;

(b) The date of entry into force of this Convention under article 27 and the date of the entry into force of any amendments under article 29;
(c) Denunciations under article 31.

Art. 33 1. This Convention, of which the Arabic, Chinese, English, French, Russian and Spanish texts are equally authentic, shall be deposited with the Secretary-General of the United Nations.

2. The Secretary-General of the United Nations shall transmit certified copies of this Convention to all States.

CHAPTER 9.A

Optional Protocol to the Convention against Torture and Other Cruel, Inhuman or Degrading Treatment or Punishment

Adopted and opened for signature, ratification and accession by General Assembly resolution 57/199 of 18 December 2002
Entry into force 22 June 2006, in accordance with article 28(1)

Preamble

The States Parties to the present Protocol,

Reaffirming that torture and other cruel, inhuman or degrading treatment or punishment are prohibited and constitute serious violations of human rights,

Convinced that further measures are necessary to achieve the purposes of the Convention against Tortureand Other Cruel, Inhuman or Degrading Treatment or Punishment (hereinafter referred to as the Convention) and to strengthen the protection of persons deprived of their liberty against torture and other cruel, inhuman or degrading treatment or punishment,

Recalling that articles 2 and 16 of the Convention oblige each State Party to take effective measures to prevent acts of torture and other cruel, inhuman or degrading treatment or punishment in any territory under its jurisdiction,

Recognizing that States have the primary responsibility for implementing those articles, that strengthening the protection of people deprived of their liberty and the full respect for their human rights is a common responsibility shared by all and that international implementing bodies complement and strengthen national measures,

Recalling that the effective prevention of torture and other cruel, inhuman or degrading treatment or punishment requires education and a combination of various legislative, administrative, judicial and other measures,

Recalling also that the World Conference on Human Rights firmly declared that efforts to eradicate torture should first and foremost be concentrated on prevention and called for the adoption of an optional protocol to the Convention, intended to establish a preventive system of regular visits to places of detention,

Convinced that the protection of persons deprived of their liberty against torture and other cruel, inhuman or degrading treatment or punishment can be strengthened by non-judicial means of a preventive nature, based on regular visits to places of detention,

Have agreed as follows:

Part 1: General Principles

Art. 1 The objective of the present Protocol is to establish a system of regular visits undertaken by independent international and national bodies to places where people are deprived of their liberty, in order to prevent torture and other cruel, inhuman or degrading treatment or punishment.

Art. 2 1. A Subcommittee on Prevention of Torture and Other Cruel, Inhuman or Degrading Treatment or Punishment of the Committee against Torture (hereinafter referred to as the Subcommittee on Prevention) shall be established and shall carry out the functions laid down in the present Protocol.

2. The Subcommittee on Prevention shall carry out its work within the framework of the Charter of the United Nations and shall be guided by the purposes and principles thereof, as well as the norms of the United Nations concerning the treatment of people deprived of their liberty.

3. Equally, the Subcommittee on Prevention shall be guided by the principles of confidentiality, impartiality, non-selectivity, universality and objectivity.

4. The Subcommittee on Prevention and the States Parties shall cooperate in the implementation of the present Protocol.

Art. 3 Each State Party shall set up, designate or maintain at the domestic level one or several visiting bodies for the prevention of torture and other cruel, inhuman or degrading treatment or punishment (hereinafter referred to as the national preventive mechanism).

Art. 4 1. Each State Party shall allow visits, in accordance with the present Protocol, by the mechanisms referred to in articles 2 and 3 to any place under its jurisdiction and control where persons are or may be deprived of their liberty, either by virtue of an order given by a public authority or at its instigation or with its consent or acquiescence (hereinafter referred to as places of detention). These visits shall be undertaken with a view to strengthening, if necessary, the protection of these persons against torture and other cruel, inhuman or degrading treatment or punishment.

2. For the purposes of the present Protocol, deprivation of liberty means any form of detention or imprisonment or the placement of a person in a public or private custodial setting which that person is not permitted to leave at will by order of any judicial, administrative or other authority.

Part II: Subcommittee on Prevention

Art. 5 1. The Subcommittee on Prevention shall consist of ten members. After the fiftieth ratification of or accession to the present Protocol, the number of the members of the Subcommittee on Prevention shall increase to twenty-five.
2. The members of the Subcommittee on Prevention shall be chosen from among persons of high moral character, having proven professional experience in the field of the administration of justice, in particular criminal law, prison or police administration, or in the various fields relevant to the treatment of persons deprived of their liberty.
3. In the composition of the Subcommittee on Prevention due consideration shall be given to equitable geographic distribution and to the representation of different forms of civilization and legal systems of the States Parties.
4. In this composition consideration shall also be given to balanced gender representation on the basis of the principles of equality and non-discrimination.
5. No two members of the Subcommittee on Prevention may be nationals of the same State.
6. The members of the Subcommittee on Prevention shall serve in their individual capacity, shall be independent and impartial and shall be available to serve the Subcommittee on Prevention efficiently.
Art. 6 1. Each State Party may nominate, in accordance with paragraph 2 of the present article, up to two candidates possessing the qualifications and meeting the requirements set out in article 5, and in doing so shall provide detailed information on the qualifications of the nominees.
2.
(a) The nominees shall have the nationality of a State Party to the present Protocol;
(b) At least one of the two candidates shall have the nationality of the nominating State Party;
(c) No more than two nationals of a State Party shall be nominated;
(d) Before a State Party nominates a national of another State Party, it shall seek and obtain the consent of that State Party.
3. At least five months before the date of the meeting of the States Parties during which the elections will be held, the Secretary-General of the United Nations shall address a letter to the States Parties inviting them to submit their nominations within three months. The Secretary-General shall submit a list, in alphabetical order, of all persons thus nominated, indicating the States Parties that have nominated them.
Art. 7 1. The members of the Subcommittee on Prevention shall be elected in the following manner:

(a) Primary consideration shall be given to the fulfilment of the requirements and criteria of article 5 of the present Protocol;
(b) The initial election shall be held no later than six months after the entry into force of the present Protocol;
(c) The States Parties shall elect the members of the Subcommittee on Prevention by secret ballot;
(d) Elections of the members of the Subcommittee on Prevention shall be held at biennial meetings of the States Parties convened by the Secretary-General of the United Nations. At those meetings, for which two thirds of the States Parties shall constitute a quorum, the persons elected to the Subcommittee on Prevention shall be those who obtain the largest number of votes and an absolute majority of the votes of the representatives of the States Parties present and voting.

2. If during the election process two nationals of a State Party have become eligible to serve as members of the Subcommittee on Prevention, the candidate receiving the higher number of votes shall serve as the member of the Subcommittee on Prevention. Where nationals have received the same number of votes, the following procedure applies:
(a) Where only one has been nominated by the State Party of which he or she is a national, that national shall serve as the member of the Subcommittee on Prevention;
(b) Where both candidates have been nominated by the State Party of which they are nationals, a separate vote by secret ballot shall be held to determine which national shall become the member;
(c) Where neither candidate has been nominated by the State Party of which he or she is a national, a separate vote by secret ballot shall be held to determine which candidate shall be the member.

Art. 8 If a member of the Subcommittee on Prevention dies or resigns, or for any cause can no longer perform his or her duties, the State Party that nominated the member shall nominate another eligible person possessing the qualifications and meeting the requirements set out in article 5, taking into account the need for a proper balance among the various fields of competence, to serve until the next meeting of the States Parties, subject to the approval of the majority of the States Parties. The approval shall be considered given unless half or more of the States Parties respond negatively within six weeks after having been informed by the Secretary-General of the United Nations of the proposed appointment.

Art. 9 The members of the Subcommittee on Prevention shall be elected for a term of four years. They shall be eligible for re-election once if renominated. The term of half the members elected at the first election shall expire at the end of two years; immediately after the first election the names of those members shall be chosen by lot by the Chairman of the meeting referred to in article 7, paragraph 1 (d).

Art. 10 1. The Subcommittee on Prevention shall elect its officers for a term of two years. They may be re-elected.

2. The Subcommittee on Prevention shall establish its own rules of procedure. These rules shall provide, inter alia, that:

(a) Half the members plus one shall constitute a quorum;

(b) Decisions of the Subcommittee on Prevention shall be made by a majority vote of the members present;

(c) The Subcommittee on Prevention shall meet in camera.

3. The Secretary-General of the United Nations shall convene the initial meeting of the Subcommittee on Prevention. After its initial meeting, the Subcommittee on Prevention shall meet at such times as shall be provided by its rules of procedure. The Subcommittee on Prevention and the Committee against Torture shall hold their sessions simultaneously at least once a year.

Part III: Mandate of the Subcommittee on Prevention

Art. 11 The Subcommittee on Prevention shall:

(a) Visit the places referred to in article 4 and make recommendations to States Parties concerning the protection of persons deprived of their liberty against torture and other cruel, inhuman or degrading treatment or punishment;

(b) In regard to the national preventive mechanisms:

   (i) Advise and assist States Parties, when necessary, in their establishment;

   (ii) Maintain direct, and if necessary confidential, contact with the national preventive mechanisms and offer them training and technical assistance with a view to strengthening their capacities;

   (iii) Advise and assist them in the evaluation of the needs and the means necessary to strengthen the protection of persons deprived of their liberty against torture and other cruel, inhuman or degrading treatment or punishment;

   (iv) Make recommendations and observations to the States Parties with a view to strengthening the capacity and the mandate of the national preventive mechanisms for the prevention of torture and other cruel, inhuman or degrading treatment or punishment;

(c) Cooperate, for the prevention of torture in general, with the relevant United Nations organs and mechanisms as well as with the international, regional and national institutions or organizations working towards the strengthening of the protection of all persons against torture and other cruel, inhuman or degrading treatment or punishment.

Art. 12 In order to enable the Subcommittee on Prevention to comply with its mandate as laid down in article 11, the States Parties undertake:

(a) To receive the Subcommittee on Prevention in their territory and grant it access to the places of detention as defined in article 4 of the present Protocol;

(b) To provide all relevant information the Subcommittee on Prevention may request to evaluate the needs and measures that should be adopted to strengthen the protection of persons deprived of their liberty against torture and other cruel, inhuman or degrading treatment or punishment;

(c) To encourage and facilitate contacts between the Subcommittee on Prevention and the national preventive mechanisms;

(d) To examine the recommendations of the Subcommittee on Prevention and enter into dialogue with it on possible implementation measures.

Art. 13 1. The Subcommittee on Prevention shall establish, at first by lot, a programme of regular visits to the States Parties in order to fulfil its mandate as established in article 11.

2. After consultations, the Subcommittee on Prevention shall notify the States Parties of its programme in order that they may, without delay, make the necessary practical arrangements for the visits to be conducted.

3. The visits shall be conducted by at least two members of the Subcommittee on Prevention. These members may be accompanied, if needed, by experts of demonstrated professional experience and knowledge in the fields covered by the present Protocol who shall be selected from a roster of experts prepared on the basis of proposals made by the States Parties, the Office of the United Nations High Commissioner for Human Rights and the United Nations Centre for International Crime Prevention. In preparing the roster, the States Parties concerned shall propose no more than five national experts. The State Party concerned may oppose the inclusion of a specific expert in the visit, whereupon the Subcommittee on Prevention shall propose another expert.

4. If the Subcommittee on Prevention considers it appropriate, it may propose a short follow-up visit after a regular visit.

Art. 14 1. In order to enable the Subcommittee on Prevention to fulfil its mandate, the States Parties to the present Protocol undertake to grant it:

(a) Unrestricted access to all information concerning the number of persons deprived of their liberty in places of detention as defined in article 4, as well as the number of places and their location;

(b) Unrestricted access to all information referring to the treatment of those persons as well as their conditions of detention;

(c) Subject to paragraph 2 below, unrestricted access to all places of detention and their installations and facilities;

(d) The opportunity to have private interviews with the persons deprived of their liberty without witnesses, either personally or with a translator if deemed necessary, as well as with any other person who the Subcommittee on Prevention believes may supply relevant information;

(e) The liberty to choose the places it wants to visit and the persons it wants to interview.

2. Objection to a visit to a particular place of detention may be made only on urgent and compelling grounds of national defence, public safety, natural disaster or serious disorder in the place to be visited that temporarily prevent the carrying out of such a visit. The existence of a declared state of emergency as such shall not be invoked by a State Party as a reason to object to a visit.

Art. 15 No authority or official shall order, apply, permit or tolerate any sanction against any person or organization for having communicated to the Subcommittee on Prevention or to its delegates any information, whether true or false, and no such person or organization shall be otherwise prejudiced in any way.

Art. 16 1. The Subcommittee on Prevention shall communicate its recommendations and observations confidentially to the State Party and, if relevant, to the national preventive mechanism.

2. The Subcommittee on Prevention shall publish its report, together with any comments of the State Party concerned, whenever requested to do so by that State Party. If the State Party makes part of the report public, the Subcommittee on Prevention may publish the report in whole or in part. However, no personal data shall be published without the express consent of the person concerned.

3. The Subcommittee on Prevention shall present a public annual report on its activities to the Committee against Torture.

4. If the State Party refuses to cooperate with the Subcommittee on Prevention according to articles 12 and 14, or to take steps to improve the situation in the light of the recommendations of the Subcommittee on Prevention, the Committee against Torture may, at the request of the Subcommittee on Prevention, decide, by a majority of its members, after the State Party has had

an opportunity to make its views known, to make a public statement on the matter or to publish the report of the Subcommittee on Prevention.

Part IV: National Preventive Mechanisms

Art. 17 Each State Party shall maintain, designate or establish, at the latest one year after the entry into force of the present Protocol or of its ratification or accession, one or several independent national preventive mechanisms for the prevention of torture at the domestic level. Mechanisms established by decentralized units may be designated as national preventive mechanisms for the purposes of the present Protocol if they are in conformity with its provisions.

Art. 18 1. The States Parties shall guarantee the functional independence of the national preventive mechanisms as well as the independence of their personnel.

2. The States Parties shall take the necessary measures to ensure that the experts of the national preventive mechanism have the required capabilities and professional knowledge. They shall strive for a gender balance and the adequate representation of ethnic and minority groups in the country.

3. The States Parties undertake to make available the necessary resources for the functioning of the national preventive mechanisms.

4. When establishing national preventive mechanisms, States Parties shall give due consideration to the Principles relating to the status of national institutions for the promotion and protection of human rights.

Art. 19 The national preventive mechanisms shall be granted at a minimum the power:

(a) To regularly examine the treatment of the persons deprived of their liberty in places of detention as defined in article 4, with a view to strengthening, if necessary, their protection against torture and other cruel, inhuman or degrading treatment or punishment;

(b) To make recommendations to the relevant authorities with the aim of improving the treatment and the conditions of the persons deprived of their liberty and to prevent torture and other cruel, inhuman or degrading treatment or punishment, taking into consideration the relevant norms of the United Nations;

(c) To submit proposals and observations concerning existing or draft legislation.

Art. 20 In order to enable the national preventive mechanisms to fulfil their mandate, the States Parties to the present Protocol undertake to grant them:

(a) Access to all information concerning the number of persons deprived of their liberty in places of detention as defined in article 4, as well as the number of places and their location;
(b) Access to all information referring to the treatment of those persons as well as their conditions of detention;
(c) Access to all places of detention and their installations and facilities;
(d) The opportunity to have private interviews with the persons deprived of their liberty without witnesses, either personally or with a translator if deemed necessary, as well as with any other person who the national preventive mechanism believes may supply relevant information;
(e) The liberty to choose the places they want to visit and the persons they want to interview;
(f) The right to have contacts with the Subcommittee on Prevention, to send it information and to meet with it.

Art. 21 1. No authority or official shall order, apply, permit or tolerate any sanction against any person or organization for having communicated to the national preventive mechanism any information, whether true or false, and no such person or organization shall be otherwise prejudiced in any way.
2. Confidential information collected by the national preventive mechanism shall be privileged. No personal data shall be published without the express consent of the person concerned.

Art. 22 The competent authorities of the State Party concerned shall examine the recommendations of the national preventive mechanism and enter into a dialogue with it on possible implementation measures.

Art. 23 The States Parties to the present Protocol undertake to publish and disseminate the annual reports of the national preventive mechanisms.

Part V: Declaration

Art. 24 1. Upon ratification, States Parties may make a declaration postponing the implementation of their obligations under either part III or part IV of the present Protocol.
2. This postponement shall be valid for a maximum of three years. After due representations made by the State Party and after consultation with the Subcommittee on Prevention, the Committee against Torture may extend that period for an additional two years.

Part VI: Financial Provisions

Art. 25 1. The expenditure incurred by the Subcommittee on Prevention in the implementation of the present Protocol shall be borne by the United Nations.
2. The Secretary-General of the United Nations shall provide the necessary staff and facilities for the effective performance of the functions of the Subcommittee on Prevention under the present Protocol.
Art. 26 1. A Special Fund shall be set up in accordance with the relevant procedures of the General Assembly, to be administered in accordance with the financial regulations and rules of the United Nations, to help finance the implementation of the recommendations made by the Subcommittee on Prevention after a visit to a State Party, as well as education programmes of the national preventive mechanisms.
2. The Special Fund may be financed through voluntary contributions made by Governments, intergovernmental and non-governmental organizations and other private or public entities.

Part VII: Final Provisions

Art. 27 1. The present Protocol is open for signature by any State that has signed the Convention.
2. The present Protocol is subject to ratification by any State that has ratified or acceded to the Convention. Instruments of ratification shall be deposited with the Secretary-General of the United Nations.
3. The present Protocol shall be open to accession by any State that has ratified or acceded to the Convention.
4. Accession shall be effected by the deposit of an instrument of accession with the Secretary-General of the United Nations.
5. The Secretary-General of the United Nations shall inform all States that have signed the present Protocol or acceded to it of the deposit of each instrument of ratification or accession.
Art. 28 1. The present Protocol shall enter into force on the thirtieth day after the date of deposit with the Secretary-General of the United Nations of the twentieth instrument of ratification or accession.
2. For each State ratifying the present Protocol or acceding to it after the deposit with the Secretary-General of the United Nations of the twentieth instrument of ratification or accession, the present Protocol shall enter into force on the thirtieth day after the date of deposit of its own instrument of ratification or accession.

Art. 29 The provisions of the present Protocol shall extend to all parts of federal States without any limitations or exceptions.

Art. 30 No reservations shall be made to the present Protocol.

Art. 31 The provisions of the present Protocol shall not affect the obligations of States Parties under any regional convention instituting a system of visits to places of detention. The Subcommittee on Prevention and the bodies established under such regional conventions are encouraged to consult and cooperate with a view to avoiding duplication and promoting effectively the objectives of the present Protocol.

Art. 32 The provisions of the present Protocol shall not affect the obligations of States Parties to the four Geneva Conventions of 12 August 1949 and the Additional Protocols thereto of 8 June 1977, nor the opportunity available to any State Party to authorize the International Committee of the Red Cross to visit places of detention in situations not covered by international humanitarian law.

Art. 33 1. Any State Party may denounce the present Protocol at any time by written notification addressed to the Secretary-General of the United Nations, who shall thereafter inform the other States Parties to the present Protocol and the Convention. Denunciation shall take effect one year after the date of receipt of the notification by the Secretary-General.

2. Such a denunciation shall not have the effect of releasing the State Party from its obligations under the present Protocol in regard to any act or situation that may occur prior to the date on which the denunciation becomes effective, or to the actions that the Subcommittee on Prevention has decided or may decide to take with respect to the State Party concerned, nor shall denunciation prejudice in any way the continued consideration of any matter already under consideration by the Subcommittee on Prevention prior to the date on which the denunciation becomes effective.

3. Following the date on which the denunciation of the State Party becomes effective, the Subcommittee on Prevention shall not commence consideration of any new matter regarding that State.

Art. 34 Any State Party to the present Protocol may propose an amendment and file it with the Secretary-General of the United Nations. The Secretary-General shall thereupon communicate the proposed amendment to the States Parties to the present Protocol with a request that they notify him whether they favour a conference of States Parties for the purpose of considering and voting upon the proposal. In the event that within four months from the date of such communication at least one third of the States Parties favour such a conference, the Secretary-General shall convene the conference under the auspices of the United Nations. Any amendment adopted by a majority of two thirds of the States Parties present and voting at the conference shall be submitted by the Secretary-General of the United Nations to all States Parties for acceptance.

2. An amendment adopted in accordance with paragraph 1 of the present article shall come into force when it has been accepted by a two -thirds majority of the States Parties to the present Protocol in accordance with their respective constitutional processes.

3. When amendments come into force, they shall be binding on those States Parties that have accepted them, other States Parties still being bound by the provisions of the present Protocol and any earlier amendment that they have accepted.

Art. 35 Members of the Subcommittee on Prevention and of the national preventive mechanisms shall be accorded such privileges and immunities as are necessary for the independent exercise of their functions. Members of the Subcommittee on Prevention shall be accorded the privileges and immunities specified in section 22 of the Convention on the Privileges and Immunities of the United Nations of 13 February 1946, subject to the provisions of section 23 of that Convention.

Art. 36 When visiting a State Party, the members of the Subcommittee on Prevention shall, without prejudice to the provisions and purposes of the present Protocol and such privileges and immunities as they may enjoy:

(a) Respect the laws and regulations of the visited State;

(b) Refrain from any action or activity incompatible with the impartial and international nature of their duties.

Art. 37 1. The present Protocol, of which the Arabic, Chinese, English, French, Russian and Spanish texts are equally authentic, shall be deposited with the Secretary-General of the United Nations.

2. The Secretary-General of the United Nations shall transmit certified copies of the present Protocol to all States.

CHAPTER 10

Convention on the Rights of Persons with Disabilities

Adopted and opened for signature, ratification and accession by General Assembly resolution 61/106 on 13 December 2006
Entry into force 3 May 2008, in accordance with article 45(1)

Preamble

The States Parties to the present Convention,

(a) Recalling the principles proclaimed in the Charter of the United Nations which recognize the inherent dignity and worth and the equal and inalienable rights of all members of the human family as the foundation of freedom, justice and peace in the world,

(b) Recognizing that the United Nations, in the Universal Declaration of Human Rights and in the International Covenants on Human Rights, has proclaimed and agreed that everyone is entitled to all the rights and freedoms set forth therein, without distinction of any kind,

(c) Reaffirming the universality, indivisibility, interdependence and interrelatedness of all human rights and fundamental freedoms and the need for persons with disabilities to be guaranteed their full enjoyment without discrimination,

(d) Recalling the International Covenant on Economic, Social and Cultural Rights, the International Covenant on Civil and Political Rights, the International Convention on the Elimination of All Forms of Racial Discrimination, the Convention on the Elimination of All Forms of Discrimination against Women, the Convention against Torture and Other Cruel, Inhuman or Degrading Treatment or Punishment, the Convention on the Rights of the Child, and the International Convention on the Protection of the Rights of All Migrant Workers and Members of Their Families,

(e) Recognizing that disability is an evolving concept and that disability results from the interaction between persons with. impairments and attitudinal and environmental barriers that hinders their full and effective participation in society on an equal basis with others,

(f) Recognizing the importance of the principles and policy guidelines contained in the World Programme of Action concerning Disabled

Persons and in the Standard Rules on the Equalization of Opportunities for Persons with Disabilities in influencing the promotion, formulation and evaluation of the policies, plans, programmes and actions at the national, regional and international levels to further equalize opportunities for persons with disabilities,

(g) Emphasizing the importance of mainstreaming disability issues as an integral part of relevant strategies of sustainable development,

(h) Recognizing also that discrimination against any person on the basis of disability is a violation of the inherent dignity and worth of the human person,

(i) Recognizing further the diversity of persons with disabilities,

(j) Recognizing the need to promote and protect the human rights of all persons with disabilities, including those who require more intensive support,

(k) Concerned that, despite these various instruments and undertakings, persons with disabilities continue to face barriers in their participation as equal members of society and violations of their human rights in all parts of the world,

(l) Recognizing the importance of international cooperation for improving the living conditions of persons with disabilities in every country, particularly in developing countries,

(m) Recognizing the valued existing and potential contributions made by persons with disabilities to the overall well-being and diversity of their communities, and that the promotion of the full enjoyment by persons with disabilities of their human rights and fundamental freedoms and of full participation by persons with disabilities will result in their enhanced sense of belonging and in significant advances in the human, social and economic development of society and the eradication of poverty,

(n) Recognizing the importance for persons with disabilities of their individual autonomy and independence, including the freedom to make their own choices,

(o) Considering that persons with disabilities should have the opportunity to be actively involved in decision-making processes about policies and programmes, including those directly concerning them,

(p) Concerned about the difficult conditions faced by persons with disabilities who are subject to multiple or aggravated forms of discrimination on the basis of race, colour, sex, language, religion, political or other opinion, national, ethnic, indigenous or social origin, property, birth, age or other status,

(q) Recognizing that women and girls with disabilities are often at greater risk, both within and outside the home, of violence, injury or abuse, neglect or negligent treatment, maltreatment or exploitation,

(r) of all human rights and fundamental freedoms on an equal basis with other children, and recalling obligations to that end undertaken by States Parties to the Convention on the Rights of the Child,

(s) Emphasizing the need to incorporate a gender perspective in all efforts to promote the full enjoyment of human rights and fundamental freedoms by persons with disabilities,

(t) Highlighting the fact that the majority of persons with disabilities live in conditions of poverty, and in this regard recognizing the critical need to address the negative impact of poverty on persons with disabilities,

(u) Bearing in mind that conditions of peace and security based on full respect for the purposes and principles contained in the Charter of the United Nations and observance of applicable human rights instruments are indispensable for the full protection of persons with disabilities, in particular during armed conflicts and foreign occupation,

(v) Recognizing the importance of accessibility to the physical, social, economic and cultural environment, to health and education and to information and communication, in enabling persons with disabilities to fully enjoy all human rights and fundamental freedoms,

(w) Realizing that the individual, having duties to other individuals and to the community to which he or she belongs, is under a responsibility to strive for the promotion and observance of the rights recognized in the International Bill of Human Rights,

(x) Convinced that the family is the natural and fundamental group unit of society and is entitled to protection by society and the State, and that persons with disabilities and their family members should receive the necessary protection and assistance to enable families to. contribute towards the full and equal enjoyment of the rights of persons with disabilities,

(y) Convinced that a comprehensive and integral international convention to promote and protect the rights and dignity of persons with disabilities will make a significant contribution to redressing the profound social disadvantage of persons with disabilities and promote their participation in the civil, political, economic, social and cultural spheres with equal opportunities, in both developing and developed countries,

Have agreed as follows:

Article 1 – Purpose

The purpose of the present Convention is to promote, protect and ensure the full and equal enjoyment of all human rights and fundamental freedoms by all persons with disabilities, and to promote respect for their inherent dignity.

Persons with disabilities include those who have long-term physical, mental, intellectual or sensory impairments which in interaction with various barriers may hinder their full and effective participation in society on an equal basis with others.

Article 2 – Definitions

For the purposes of the present Convention:

"Communication" includes languages, display of text, Braille, tactile communication, large print, accessible multimedia as well as written, audio, plain-language, human-reader and augmentative and alternative modes, means and formats of communication, including accessible information and communication technology;

"Language" includes spoken and signed languages and other forms of non spoken languages;

"Discrimination on the basis of disability" means any distinction, exclusion or restriction on the basis of disability which has the purpose or effect of impairing or nullifying the recognition, enjoyment or exercise, on an equal basis with others, of all human rights and fundamental freedoms in the political, economic, social, cultural, civil or any other field. It includes all forms of discrimination, including denial of reasonable accommodation;

"Reasonable accommodation" means necessary and appropriate modification and adjustments not imposing a disproportionate or undue burden, where needed in a particular case, to ensure to persons with disabilities the enjoyment or exercise on an equal basis with others of all human rights and fundamental freedoms;

"Universal design" means the design of products, environments, programmes and services to be usable by all people, to the greatest extent possible, without the need for adaptation or specialized design. "Universal design" shall not exclude assistive devices for particular groups of persons with disabilities where this is needed.

Article 3 – General Principles

The principles of the present Convention shall be:

(a) Respect for inherent dignity, individual autonomy including the freedom to make one's own choices, and independence of persons;

(b) Non-discrimination;
(c) Full and effective participation and inclusion in society;
(d) Respect for difference and acceptance of persons with disabilities as part of human diversity and humanity;
(e) Equality of opportunity;
(f) Accessibility;
(g) Equality between men and women;
(h) Respect for the evolving capacities of children with disabilities and respect for the right of children with disabilities to preserve their identities.

Article 4 – General Obligations

1. States Parties undertake to ensure and promote the full realization of all human rights and fundamental freedoms for all persons with disabilities without discrimination of any kind on the basis of disability. To this end, States Parties undertake:

(a) To adopt all appropriate legislative, administrative and other measures for the implementation of the rights recognized in the present Convention;
(b) To take all appropriate measures, including legislation, to modify or abolish existing laws, regulations, customs and practices that constitute discrimination against persons with disabilities;
(c) To take into account the protection and promotion of the human rights of persons with disabilities in all policies and programmes;
(d) To refrain from engaging in any act or practice that is inconsistent with the present Convention and to ensure that public authorities and institutions act in conformity with the present Convention;
(e) To take all appropriate measures to eliminate discrimination on the basis of disability by any person, organization or private enterprise;
(f) To undertake or promote research and development of universally designed goods, services, equipment and facilities, as defined in article 2 of the present Convention, which should require the minimum possible adaptation and the least cost to meet the specific needs of a person with disabilities, to promote their availability and use, and to promote universal design in the development of standards and guidelines;
(g) To undertake or promote research and development of, and to promote the availability and use of new technologies, including information and communications technologies, mobility aids, devices and assistive

technologies, suitable for persons with disabilities, giving priority to technologies at an affordable cost;

(h) To provide accessible information to persons with disabilities about mobility aids, devices and assistive technologies, including new technologies, as well as other forms of assistance, support services and facilities;

(i) To promote the training of professionals and staff working with persons with disabilities in the rights recognized in the present Convention so as to better provide the assistance and services guaranteed by those rights.

2. With regard to economic, social and cultural rights, each State Party undertakes to take measures to the maximum of its available resources and, where needed, within the framework of international cooperation, with a view to achieving progressively the full realization of these rights, without prejudice to those obligations contained in the present Convention that are immediately applicable according to international law.

3. In the development and implementation of legislation and policies to implement the present Convention, and in other decision-making processes concerning issues relating to persons with disabilities, States Parties shall closely consult with and actively involve persons with disabilities, including children with disabilities, through their representative organizations.

4. Nothing in the present Convention shall affect any provisions which are more conducive to the realization of the rights of persons with disabilities and which may be contained in the law of a State Party or international law in force for the State. There shall be no restriction upon or derogation from any of the human rights and fundamental freedoms recognized or existing in any State Party to the present Convention pursuant to law, conventions, regulation or custom on the pretext that the present Convention does not recognize such rights or freedoms or that it recognizes them to a lesser extent.

5. The provisions of the present Convention shall extend to all parts of federal States without any limitations or exceptions.

Article 5 – Equality and Non-discrimination

1. States Parties recognize that all persons are equal before and under the law and are entitled without any discrimination to the equal protection and equal benefit of the law.

2. States Parties shall prohibit all discrimination on the basis of disability and guarantee to persons with disabilities equal and effective legal protection against discrimination on all grounds.

3. In order to promote equality and eliminate discrimination, States Parties shall take all appropriate steps to ensure that reasonable accommodation is provided.
4. Specific measures which are necessary to accelerate or achieve de facto equality of persons with disabilities shall not be considered discrimination under the terms of the present Convention.

Article 6 – Women with Disabilities

1. States Parties recognize that women and girls with disabilities are subject to multiple discrimination, and in this regard shall take measures to ensure the full and equal enjoyment by them of all human rights and fundamental freedoms.
2. States Parties shall take all appropriate measures to ensure the full development, advancement and empowerment of women, for the purpose of guaranteeing them the exercise and enjoyment of the human rights and fundamental freedoms set out in the present Convention.

Article 7 – Children with Disabilities

1. States Parties shall take all necessary measures to ensure the full enjoyment. by children with disabilities of all human rights and fundamental freedoms on an equal basis with other children.
2. In all actions concerning children with disabilities, the best interests of the child shall be a primary consideration.
3. States Parties shall ensure that children with disabilities have the right to express their views freely on all matters affecting them, their views being given due weight in accordance with their age and maturity, on an equal basis with other children, and to be provided with disability and age-appropriate assistance to realize that right.

Article 8 – Awareness-Raising

1. States Parties undertake to adopt immediate, effective and appropriate measures:
(a) To raise awareness throughout society, including at the family level, regarding persons with disabilities, and to foster respect for the rights and dignity of persons with disabilities;
(b) To combat stereotypes, prejudices and harmful practices relating to persons with disabilities, including those based on sex and age, in all areas of life;

(c) To promote awareness of the capabilities and contributions of persons with disabilities.

2. Measures to this end include:

(a) Initiating and maintaining effective public awareness campaigns designed:
   (i) To nurture receptiveness to the rights of persons with disabilities;
   (ii) To promote positive perceptions and greater social awareness towards persons with disabilities;
   (iii) To promote recognition of the skills, merits and abilities of persons with disabilities, and of their contributions to the workplace and the labour market;

(b) Fostering at all levels of the education system, including in all children from an early age, an attitude of respect for the rights of persons with disabilities;

(c) Encouraging all organs of the media to portray persons with disabilities in a manner consistent with the purpose of the present Convention;

(d) Promoting awareness-training programmes regarding persons with disabilities and the rights of persons with disabilities.

Article 9 – Accessibility

1. To enable persons with disabilities to live independently and participate fully in all aspects of life, States Parties shall take appropriate measures to ensure to persons with disabilities access, on an equal basis with others, to the physical environment, to transportation, to information and communications, including information and communications technologies and systems, and to other facilities and services open or provided to the public, both in urban and in rural areas. These measures, which shall include the identification and elimination of obstacles and barriers to accessibility, shall apply to, inter alia:

(a) Buildings, roads, transportation and other indoor and outdoor facilities, including schools, housing, medical facilities and workplaces;

(b) Information, communications and other services, including electronic services and emergency services.

2. States Parties shall also take appropriate measures:

(a) To develop, promulgate and monitor the implementation of minimum standards and guidelines for the accessibility of facilities and services open or provided to the public;

(b) To ensure that private entities that offer facilities and services which are open or provided to the public take into account all aspects of accessibility for persons with disabilities;

(c) To provide training for stakeholders on accessibility issues facing persons with disabilities;

(d) To provide in buildings and other facilities open to the public signage in Braille and in easy to read and understand forms;

(e) To provide forms of live assistance and intermediaries, including guides, readers and professional sign language interpreters, to facilitate accessibility to buildings and other facilities open to the public;

(f) To promote other appropriate forms of assistance and support to persons with disabilities to ensure their access to information;

(g) To promote access for persons with disabilities to new information and communications technologies and systems, including the Internet;

(h) To promote the design, development, production and distribution of accessible information and communications technologies and systems at an early stage, so that these technologies and systems become accessible at minimum cost.

Article 10 – Right to Life

States Parties reaffirm that every human being has the inherent right to life and shall take all necessary measures to ensure its effective enjoyment by persons with disabilities on an equal basis with others.

Article 11 – Situations of Risk and Humanitarian Emergencies

States Parties shall take, in accordance with their obligations under international law, including international humanitarian law and international human rights law, all necessary measures to ensure the protection and safety of persons with disabilities in situations of risk, including situations of armed conflict, humanitarian emergencies and the occurrence of natural disasters.

Article 12 – Equal Recognition before the Law

1. States Parties reaffirm that persons with disabilities have the right to recognition everywhere as persons before the law.
2. States Parties shall recognize that persons with disabilities enjoy legal capacity on an equal basis with others in all aspects of life.
3. States Parties shall take appropriate measures to provide access by persons with disabilities to the support they may require in exercising their legal capacity.
4. States Parties shall ensure that all measures that relate to the exercise of legal capacity provide for appropriate and effective safeguards to prevent abuse in accordance with international human rights law. Such safeguards shall ensure that measures relating to the exercise of legal capacity respect the rights, will

and preferences of the person, are free of conflict of interest and undue influence, are proportional and tailored to the person's circumstances, apply for the shortest time possible and are subject to regular review by a competent, independent and impartial authority or judicial body. The safeguards shall be proportional to the degree to which such measures affect the person's rights and interests.
5. Subject to the provisions of this article, States Parties shall take all appropriate and effective measures to ensure the equal right of persons with disabilities to own or inherit property, to control their own financial affairs and to have equal access to bank loans, mortgages and other forms of financial credit, and shall ensure that persons with disabilities are not arbitrarily deprived of their property.

Article 13 – Access to Justice

1. States Parties shall ensure effective access to justice for persons with disabilities on an equal basis with others, including through the provision of procedural and age-appropriate accommodations, in order to facilitate their effective role as direct and indirect participants, including as witnesses, in all legal proceedings, including at investigative and other preliminary stages.
2. In order to help to ensure effective access to justice for persons with disabilities, States Parties shall promote appropriate training for those working in the field of administration of justice, including police and prison staff.

Article 14 – Liberty and Security of Person

1. States Parties shall ensure that persons with disabilities, on an equal basis with others:
(a) Enjoy the right to liberty and security of person;
(b) Are not deprived of their liberty unlawfully or arbitrarily, and that any deprivation of liberty is in conformity with the law, and that the existence of a disability shall in no case justify a deprivation of liberty.
2. States Parties shall ensure that if persons with disabilities are deprived of their liberty through any process, they are, on an equal basis with others, entitled to guarantees in accordance with international human rights law and shall be treated in compliance with the objectives and principles of the present Convention, including by provision of reasonable accommodation.

Article 15 – Freedom from Torture or Cruel, Inhuman or Degrading Treatment or Punishment

1. No one shall be subjected to torture or to cruel, inhuman or degrading treatment or punishment. In particular, no one shall be subjected without his or her free consent to medical or scientific experimentation.
2. States Parties shall take all effective legislative, administrative, judicial or other measures to prevent persons with disabilities, on an equal basis with others, from being subjected to torture or cruel, inhuman or degrading treatment or punishment.

Article 16 – Freedom from Exploitation, Violence and Abuse

1. States Parties shall take all appropriate legislative, administrative, social, educational and other measures to protect persons with disabilities, both within and outside the home, from all forms of exploitation, violence and abuse, including their gender-based aspects.
2. States Parties shall also take all appropriate measures to prevent all forms of exploitation, violence and abuse by ensuring, inter alia, appropriate forms of gender- and age-sensitive assistance and support for persons with disabilities and their families and caregivers, including through the provision of information and education on how to avoid, recognize and report instances of exploitation, violence and abuse. States Parties shall ensure that protection services are age-, gender- and disability-sensitive.
3. In order to prevent the occurrence of all forms of exploitation, violence and abuse, States Parties shall ensure that all facilities and programmes designed to serve persons with disabilities are effectively monitored by independent authorities.
4. States Parties shall take all appropriate measures to promote the physical, cognitive and psychological recovery, rehabilitation and social reintegration of persons with disabilities who become victims of any form of exploitation, violence or abuse, including through the provision of protection services. Such recovery and reintegration shall take place in an environment that fosters the health, welfare, self-respect, dignity and autonomy of the person and takes into account gender- and age-specific needs.
5. States Parties shall put in place effective legislation and policies, including women- and child-focused legislation and policies, to ensure that instances of exploitation, violence and abuse against persons with disabilities are identified, investigated and, where appropriate, prosecuted.

Article 17 – Protecting the Integrity of the Person

Every person with disabilities has a right to respect for his or her physical and mental integrity on an equal basis with others.

Article 18 – Liberty of Movement and Nationality

1. States Parties shall recognize the rights of persons with disabilities to liberty of movement, to freedom to choose their residence and to a nationality, on an equal basis with others, including by ensuring that persons with disabilities:

(a) Have the right to acquire and change a nationality and are not deprived of their nationality arbitrarily or on the basis of disability;

(b) Are not deprived, on the basis of disability, of their ability to obtain, possess and utilize documentation of their nationality or other documentation of identification, or to utilize relevant processes such as immigration proceedings, that may be needed to facilitate exercise of the right to liberty of movement;

(c) Are free to leave any country, including their own;

(d) Are not deprived, arbitrarily or on the basis of disability, of the right to enter their own country.

2. Children with disabilities shall be registered immediately after birth and shall have the right from birth to a name, the right to acquire a nationality and, as far as possible, the right to know and be cared for by their parents.

Article 19 – Living Independently and Being Included in the Community

States Parties to the present Convention recognize the equal right of all persons with disabilities to live in the community, with choices equal to others, and shall take effective and appropriate measures to facilitate full enjoyment by persons with disabilities of this right and their full inclusion and participation in the community, including by ensuring that:

(a) Persons with disabilities have the opportunity to choose their place of residence and where and with whom they live on an equal basis with others and are not obliged to live in a particular living arrangement;

(b) Persons with disabilities have access to a range of in-home, residential and other community support services, including personal assistance necessary to support living and inclusion in the community, and to prevent isolation or segregation from the community;

(c) Community services and facilities for the general population are available on an equal basis to persons with disabilities and are responsive to their needs.

Article 20 – Personal Mobility

States Parties shall take effective measures to ensure personal mobility with the greatest possible independence for persons with disabilities, including by:

(a) Facilitating the personal mobility of persons with disabilities in the manner and at the time of their choice, and at affordable cost;

(b) Facilitating access by persons with disabilities to quality mobility aids, devices, assistive technologies and forms of live assistance and intermediaries, including by making them available at affordable cost;

(c) Providing training in mobility skills to persons with disabilities and to specialist staff working with persons with disabilities;

(d) Encouraging entities that produce mobility aids, devices and assistive technologies to take into account all aspects of mobility for persons with disabilities.

Article 21 – Freedom of Expression and Opinion, and Access to Information

States Parties shall take all appropriate measures to ensure that persons with disabilities can exercise the right to freedom of expression and opinion, including the freedom to seek, receive and impart information and ideas on an equal basis with others and through all forms of communication of their choice, as defined in article 2 of the present Convention, including by:

(a) Providing information intended for the general public to persons with disabilities in accessible formats and technologies appropriate to different kinds of disabilities in a timely manner and without additional cost;

(b) Accepting and facilitating the use of sign languages, Braille, augmentative and alternative communication, and all other accessible means, modes and formats of communication of their choice by persons with disabilities in official interactions;

(c) Urging private entities that provide services to the general public, including through the Internet, to provide information and services in accessible and usable formats for persons with disabilities;

(d) Encouraging the mass media, including providers of information through the Internet, to make their services accessible to persons with disabilities;

(e) Recognizing and promoting the use of sign languages.

Article 22 – Respect for Privacy

1. No person with disabilities, regardless of place of residence or living arrangements, shall be subjected to arbitrary or unlawful interference with his or her privacy, family, home or correspondence or other types of communication or

to unlawful attacks on his or her honour and reputation. Persons with disabilities have the right to the protection of the law against such interference or attacks.
2. States Parties shall protect the privacy of personal, health and rehabilitation information of persons with disabilities on an equal basis with others.

Article 23 – Respect for Home and the Family

1. States Parties shall take effective and appropriate measures to eliminate discrimination against persons with disabilities in all matters relating to marriage, family, parenthood and relationships, on an equal basis with others, so as to ensure that:
(a) The right of all persons with disabilities who are of marriageable age to marry and to found a family on the basis of free and full consent of the intending spouses is recognized;
(b) The rights of persons with disabilities to decide freely and responsibly on the number and spacing of their children and to have access to age appropriate information, reproductive and family planning education are recognized, and the means necessary to enable them to exercise these rights are provided;
(c) Persons with disabilities, including children, retain their fertility on an equal basis with others.
2. States Parties shall ensure the rights and responsibilities of persons with disabilities, with regard to guardianship, wardship, trusteeship, adoption of children or similar institutions, where these concepts exist in national legislation; in all cases the best interests of the child shall be paramount. States Parties shall render appropriate assistance to persons with disabilities in the performance of their child-rearing responsibilities.
3. States Parties shall ensure that children with disabilities have equal rights with respect to family life. With a view to realizing these rights, and to prevent concealment, abandonment, neglect and segregation of children with disabilities, States Parties shall undertake to provide early and comprehensive information, services and support to children with disabilities and their families.
4. States Parties shall ensure that a child shall not be separated from his or her parents against their will, except when competent authorities subject to judicial review determine, in accordance with applicable law and procedures, that such separation is necessary for the best interests of the child. In no case shall a child be separated from parents on the basis of a disability of either the child or one or both of the parents.

5. States Parties shall, where the immediate family is unable to care for a child with disabilities, undertake every effort to provide alternative care within the wider family, and failing that, within the community in a family setting.

Article 24 – Education

1. States Parties recognize the right of persons with disabilities to education. With a view to realizing this right without discrimination and on the basis of equal opportunity, States Parties shall ensure an inclusive education system at all levels and lifelong learning directed to:

(a) The full development of human potential and sense of dignity and self-worth, and the strengthening of respect for human rights, fundamental freedoms and human diversity;

(b) The development by persons with disabilities of their personality, talents and creativity, as well as their mental and physical abilities, to their fullest potential;

(c) Enabling persons with disabilities to participate effectively in a free society.

2. In realizing this right, States Parties shall ensure that:

(a) Persons with disabilities are not excluded from the general education system on the basis of disability, and that children with disabilities are .not excluded from free and compulsory primary education, or from secondary education, on the basis of disability;

(b) Persons with disabilities can access an inclusive, quality and free primary education and secondary education on an equal basis with others in the communities in which they live;

(c) Reasonable accommodation of the individual's requirements is provided;

(d) Persons with disabilities receive the support required, within the general education system, to facilitate their effective education;

(e) Effective individualized support measures are provided in environments that maximize academic and social development, consistent with the goal of full inclusion.

3. States Parties shall enable persons with disabilities to learn life and social development skills to facilitate their full and equal participation in education and as members of the community. To this end, States Parties shall take appropriate measures, including:

(a) Facilitating the learning of Braille, alternative script, augmentative and alternative modes, means and formats of communication and orientation and mobility skills, and facilitating peer support and mentoring;

(b) Facilitating the learning of sign language and the promotion of the linguistic identity of the deaf community;
(c) Ensuring that the education of persons, and in particular children, who are blind, deaf or deafblind, is delivered in the most appropriate languages and modes and means of communication for the individual, and in environments which maximize academic and social development.

4. In order to help ensure the realization of this right, States Parties shall take appropriate measures to employ teachers, including teachers with disabilities, who are qualified in sign language and/or Braille, and to train professionals and staff who work at all levels of education. Such training shall incorporate disability awareness and the use of appropriate augmentative and alternative modes, means and formats of communication, educational techniques and materials to support persons with disabilities.

5. States Parties shall ensure that persons with disabilities are able to access general tertiary education, vocational training, adult education and lifelong learning without discrimination and on an equal basis with others. To this end, States Parties shall ensure that reasonable accommodation is provided to persons with disabilities.

Article 25 – Health

States Parties recognize that persons with disabilities have the right to the enjoyment of the highest attainable standard of health without discrimination on the basis of disability. States Parties shall take all appropriate measures to ensure access for persons with disabilities to health services that are gender-sensitive, including health-related rehabilitation. In particular, States Parties shall:

(a) Provide persons with disabilities with the same range, quality and standard of free or affordable health care and programmes as provided to other persons, including in the area of sexual and reproductive health and population-based public health programmes;
(b) Provide those health services needed by persons with disabilities specifically because of their disabilities, including early identification and intervention as appropriate, and services designed to minimize and prevent further disabilities, including among children and older persons;
(c) Provide these health services as close as possible to people's own communities, including in rural areas;
(d) Require health professionals to provide care of the same quality to persons with disabilities as to others, including on the basis of free and informed consent by, inter alia, raising awareness of the human rights, dignity, autonomy and needs of persons with disabilities through

training and the promulgation of ethical standards for public and private health care;

(e) Prohibit discrimination against persons with disabilities in the provision of health insurance, and life insurance where such insurance is permitted by national law, which shall be provided in a fair and reasonable manner;

(f) Prevent discriminatory denial of health care or health services or food and fluids on the basis of disability.

Article 26 – Habilitation and Rehabilitation

1. States Parties shall take effective and appropriate measures, including through peer support, to enable persons with disabilities to attain and maintain maximum independence, full physical, mental, social and vocational ability, and full inclusion and participation in all aspects of life. To that end, States Parties shall organize, strengthen and extend comprehensive habilitation and rehabilitation services and programmes, particularly in the areas of health, employment, education and social services, in such a way that these services and programmes:

(a) Begin at the earliest possible stage, and are based on the multidisciplinary assessment of individual needs and strengths;

(b) Support participation and inclusion in the community and all aspects of society, are voluntary, and are available to persons with disabilities as close as possible to their own communities, including in rural areas.

2. States Parties shall promote the development of initial and continuing training for professionals and staff working in habilitation and rehabilitation services.

3. States Parties shall promote the availability, knowledge and use of assistive devices and technologies, designed for persons with disabilities, as they relate to habilitation and rehabilitation.

Article 27 – Work and Employment

1. States Parties recognize the right of persons with disabilities to work, on an equal basis with others; this includes the right to the opportunity to gain a living by work freely chosen or accepted in a labour market and work environment that is open, inclusive and accessible to persons with disabilities. States Parties shall safeguard and promote the realization of the right to work, including for those who acquire a disability during the course of employment, by taking appropriate steps, including through legislation, to, inter alia:

(a) Prohibit discrimination on the basis of disability with regard to all matters concerning all forms of employment, including conditions of recruitment, hiring and employment, continuance of employment, career advancement and safe and healthy working conditions;

(b) Protect the rights of persons with disabilities, on an equal basis with others, to just and favourable conditions of work, including equal opportunities and equal remuneration for work of equal value, safe and healthy working conditions, including protection from harassment, and the redress of grievances;

(c) Ensure that persons with disabilities are able to exercise their labour and trade union rights on an equal basis with others;

(d) Enable persons with disabilities to have effective access to general technical and vocational guidance programmes, placement services and vocational and continuing training;

(e) Promote employment opportunities and career advancement for persons with disabilities in the labour market, as well as assistance in finding, obtaining, maintaining and returning to employment;

(f) Promote opportunities for self-employment, entrepreneurship, the development of cooperatives and starting one's own business;

(g) Employ persons with disabilities in the public sector;

(h) Promote the employment of persons with disabilities in the private sector through appropriate policies and measures, which may include affirmative action programmes, incentives and other measures;

(i) Ensure that reasonable accommodation is provided to persons with, disabilities in the workplace;

(j) Promote the acquisition by persons with disabilities of work experience in the open labour market;

(k) Promote vocational and professional rehabilitation, job retention and return-to-work programmes for persons with disabilities.

2. States Parties shall ensure that persons with disabilities are not held in slavery or in servitude, and are protected, on an equal basis with others, from forced or compulsory labour.

Article 28 – Adequate Standard of Living and Social Protection

1. States Parties recognize the right of persons with disabilities to an adequate standard of living for themselves and their families, including adequate food, clothing and housing, and to the continuous improvement of living conditions, and shall take appropriate steps to safeguard and promote the realization of this right without discrimination on the basis of disability.

2. States Parties recognize the right of persons with disabilities to social protection and to the enjoyment of that right without discrimination on the basis

of disability, and shall take appropriate steps to safeguard and promote the realization of this right, including measures:

(a) To ensure equal access by persons with disabilities to clean water services, and to ensure access to appropriate and affordable services, devices and other assistance for disability-related needs;
(b) To ensure access by persons with disabilities, in particular women and girls with disabilities and older persons with disabilities, to social protection programmes and poverty reduction programmes;
(c) To ensure access by persons with disabilities and their families living in situations of poverty to assistance from the State with disability-related expenses, including adequate training, counselling, financial assistance and respite care;
(d) To ensure access by persons with disabilities to public housing programmes;
(e) To ensure equal access by persons with disabilities to retirement benefits and programmes.

Article 29 – Participation in Political and Public Life

States Parties shall guarantee to persons with disabilities political rights and the opportunity to enjoy them on an equal basis with others, and shall undertake:

(a) To ensure that persons with disabilities can effectively and fully participate in political and public life on an equal basis with others, directly or through freely chosen representatives, including the right and opportunity for persons with disabilities to vote and be elected, inter alia, by:
  (i) Ensuring that voting procedures, facilities and materials are appropriate, accessible and easy to understand and use;
  (ii) Protecting the right of persons with disabilities to vote by secret ballot in elections and public referendums without intimidation, and to stand for elections, to effectively hold office and perform all public functions at all levels of government, facilitating the use of assistive and new technologies where appropriate;
  (iii) Guaranteeing the free expression of the will of persons with disabilities as electors and to this end, where necessary, at their request, allowing assistance in voting by a person of their own choice;
(b) To promote actively an environment in which persons with disabilities can effectively and fully participate in the conduct of public affairs, without discrimination and on an equal basis with others, and encourage their participation in public affairs, including:

(i) Participation in non-governmental organizations and associations concerned with the public and political life of the country, and in the activities and administration of political parties;

(ii) Forming and joining organizations of persons with disabilities to represent persons with disabilities at international, national, regional and local levels.

Article 30 – Participation in Cultural Life, Recreation, Leisure and Sport

1. States Parties recognize the right of persons with disabilities to take part on an equal basis with others in cultural life, and shall take all appropriate measures to ensure that persons with disabilities:

(a) Enjoy access to cultural materials in accessible formats;

(b) Enjoy access to television programmes, films, theatre and other cultural activities, in accessible formats;

(c) Enjoy access to places for cultural performances or services, such as theatres, museums, cinemas, libraries and tourism services, and, as far as possible, enjoy access to monuments and sites of national cultural importance.

2. States Parties shall take appropriate measures to enable persons with disabilities to have the opportunity to develop and utilize their creative, artistic and intellectual potential, not only for their own benefit, but also for the enrichment of society.

3. States Parties shall take all appropriate steps, in accordance with international law, to ensure that laws protecting intellectual property rights do not constitute an unreasonable or discriminatory barrier to access by persons with disabilities to cultural materials.

4. Persons with disabilities shall be entitled, on an equal basis with others, to recognition and support of their specific cultural and linguistic identity, including sign languages and deaf culture.

5. With a view to enabling persons with disabilities to participate on an equal basis with others in recreational, leisure and sporting activities, States Parties shall take appropriate measures:

(a) To encourage and promote the participation, to the fullest extent possible, of persons with disabilities in mainstream sporting activities at all levels;

(b) To ensure that persons with disabilities have an opportunity to organize, develop and participate in disability-specific sporting and recreational activities and, to this end, encourage the provision, on an equal basis with others, of appropriate instruction, training and resources;

(c) To ensure that persons with disabilities have access to sporting, recreational and tourism venues;
(d) To ensure that children with disabilities have equal access with other children to participation in play, recreation and leisure and sporting activities, including those activities in the school system;
(e) To ensure that persons with disabilities have access to services from those involved in the organization of recreational, tourism, leisure and sporting activities.

Article 31 – Statistics and Data Collection

1. States Parties undertake to collect appropriate information, including statistical and research data, to enable them to formulate and implement policies to give effect to the present Convention. The process of collecting and maintaining this information shall:
(a) Comply with legally established safeguards, including legislation on data protection, to ensure confidentiality and respect for the privacy of persons with disabilities;
(b) Comply with internationally accepted norms to protect human rights and fundamental freedoms and ethical principles in the collection and use of statistics.
2. The information collected in accordance with this article shall be disaggregated, as appropriate, and used to help assess the implementation of States Parties' obligations under the present Convention and to identify and address the harriers faced by persons with disabilities in exercising their rights.
3. States Parties shall assume responsibility for the dissemination of these statistics and ensure their accessibility to persons with disabilities and others.

Article 32 – International Cooperation

1. States Parties recognize the importance of international cooperation and its promotion, in support of national efforts for the realization of the purpose and objectives of the present Convention, and will undertake appropriate and effective measures in this regard, between and among States and, as appropriate, in partnership with relevant international and regional organizations and civil society, in particular organizations of persons with disabilities. Such measures could include, inter alia:
(a) Ensuring that international cooperation; including international development programmes, is inclusive of and accessible to persons with disabilities;

(b) Facilitating and supporting capacity-building, including through the exchange and sharing of information, experiences, training programmes and best practices;
(c) Facilitating cooperation in research and access to scientific and technical knowledge;
(d) Providing, as appropriate, technical and economic assistance, including by facilitating access to and sharing of accessible and assistive technologies, and through the transfer of technologies.

2. The provisions of this article are without prejudice to the obligations of each. State Party to fulfil its obligations under the present Convention.

Article 33 – National Implementation and Monitoring

1. States Parties, in accordance with their system of organization, shall designate one or more focal points within government for matters relating to the implementation of the present Convention, and shall give due consideration to the establishment or designation of a coordination mechanism within government to facilitate related action in different sectors and at different levels.
2. States Parties shall, in accordance with their legal and administrative systems, maintain, strengthen, designate or establish within the State Party, a framework, including one or more independent mechanisms, as appropriate, to promote, protect and monitor implementation of the present Convention. When designating or establishing such a mechanism, States Parties shall take into account the principles relating to the status and functioning of national institutions for protection and promotion of human rights.
3. Civil society, in particular persons with disabilities and their representative organizations, shall be involved and participate fully in the monitoring process.

Article 34 – Committee on the Rights of Persons with Disabilities

1. There shall be established a Committee on the Rights of Persons with Disabilities (hereafter referred to as "the Committee"), which shall carry out the functions hereinafter provided.
2. The Committee shall consist, at the time of. entry into force of the present Convention, of twelve experts. After an additional sixty ratifications or accessions to the Convention, the membership of the Committee shall increase by six members, attaining a maximum number of eighteen members.
3. The members of the Committee shall serve in their personal capacity and shall be of high moral standing and recognized competence and experience in the field covered by the present Convention. When nominating their candidates, States Parties are invited to give due consideration to the provision set out in article 4, paragraph 3, of the present Convention.

4. The members of the Committee shall be elected by States Parties, consideration being given to equitable geographical distribution, representation of the different forms of civilization and of the principal legal systems, balanced gender representation and participation of experts with disabilities.
5. The members of the Committee shall be elected by secret ballot from a list of persons nominated by the States Parties from among their nationals at meetings of the Conference of States Parties. At those meetings, for which two thirds of States Parties shall constitute a quorum, the persons elected to the Committee shall be those who obtain the largest number of votes and an absolute majority of the votes of the representatives of States Parties present and voting.
6. The initial election shall be held no later than six months after the date of entry into force of the present Convention. At least four months before the date of each election, the Secretary-General of the United Nations shall address a letter to the States Parties inviting them to submit the nominations within two months. The Secretary-General shall subsequently prepare a list in alphabetical order of all persons thus nominated, indicating the State Parties which have nominated them, and shall submit it to the States Parties to the present Convention.
7. The members of the Committee shall be elected for a term of four years. They shall be eligible for re-election once. However, the term of six of the members elected at the first election shall expire at the end of two years; immediately after the first election, the names of these six members shall be chosen by lot by the chairperson of the meeting referred to in paragraph 5 of this article.
8. The election of the six additional members of the Committee shall be held on the occasion of regular elections, in accordance with the relevant provisions of this article.
9. If a member of the Committee dies or resigns or declares that for any other cause she or he can no longer perform her or his duties, the State Party which nominated the member shall appoint another expert possessing the qualifications and meeting the requirements set out in the relevant provisions of this article, to serve for the remainder of the term.
10. The Committee shall establish its own rules of procedure.
11. The Secretary-General of the United Nations shall provide the necessary staff and facilities for the effective performance of the functions of the Committee under the present Convention, and shall convene its initial meeting.
12. With the approval of the General Assembly of the United Nations, the members of the Committee established under the present Convention shall receive emoluments from United Nations resources on such terms and conditions as

the Assembly may decide, having regard to the importance of the Committee's responsibilities.
13. The members of the Committee shall be entitled to the facilities, privileges and immunities of experts on mission for the United Nations as laid down in the relevant sections of the Convention on the Privileges and Immunities of the United Nations.

Article 35 – Reports by States Parties

1. Each State Party shall submit to the Committee, through the Secretary General of the United Nations, a comprehensive report on measures taken to give effect to its obligations under the present Convention and on the progress made in that regard, within two years after the entry into force of the present Convention for the State Party concerned.
2. Thereafter, States Parties shall submit subsequent reports at least every four years and further whenever the Committee so requests.
3. The Committee shall decide any guidelines applicable to the content of the reports.
4. A State Party which has submitted a comprehensive initial report to the Committee need not, in its subsequent reports, repeat information previously provided. When preparing reports to the Committee, States Parties are invited to consider doing so in an open and transparent process and to give due consideration to the provision set out in article 4, paragraph 3, of the present Convention.
5. Reports may indicate factors and difficulties affecting the degree of fulfilment of obligations under the present Convention.

Article 36 – Consideration of Reports

1. Each report shall be considered by the Committee, which shall make such suggestions and general recommendations on the report as it may consider appropriate and shall forward these to the State Party concerned. The State Party may respond with any information it chooses to the Committee. The Committee may request further information from States Parties relevant to the implementation of the present Convention.
2. If a State Party is significantly overdue in the submission of a report, the Committee may notify the State Party concerned of the need to examine the implementation of the present Convention in that State Party, on the basis of reliable information available to the Committee, if the relevant report is not submitted within three months following the notification. The Committee shall invite the State Party concerned to participate in such examination.

Should the State Party respond by submitting the relevant report, the provisions of paragraph 1 of this article will apply.
3. The Secretary-General of the United Nations shall make available the reports to all States Parties.
4. States Parties shall make their reports widely available to the public in their own countries and facilitate access to the suggestions and general recommendations relating to these reports.
5. The Committee shall transmit, as it may consider appropriate, to the specialized agencies, funds and programmes of the United Nations, and other competent bodies, reports from States Parties in order to address a request or indication of a need for technical advice or assistance contained therein, along with the Committee's observations and recommendations, if any, on these requests or indications.

Article 37 – Cooperation between States Parties and the Committee
1. Each State Party shall cooperate with the Committee and assist its members in the fulfilment of their mandate.
2. In its relationship with States Parties, the Committee shall give due consideration to ways and means of enhancing national capacities for the implementation of the present Convention, including through international cooperation.

Article 38 – Relationship of the Committee with Other Bodies
In order to foster the effective implementation of the present Convention and to encourage international cooperation in the field covered by the present Convention:
(a) The specialized agencies and other United Nations organs shall be entitled to be represented at the consideration of the implementation of such provisions of the present Convention as fall within the scope of their mandate. The Committee may invite the specialized agencies and other competent bodies as it may consider appropriate to provide expert advice on the implementation of the Convention in areas falling within the scope of their respective mandates. The Committee may invite specialized agencies and other United Nations organs to submit reports on the implementation of the Convention in areas falling within the scope of their activities;
(b) The Committee, as it discharges its mandate, shall consult, as appropriate, other relevant bodies instituted by international human rights treaties, with a view to ensuring the consistency of their respective reporting guidelines, suggestions and general recommendations, and avoiding duplication and overlap in the performance of their functions.

Article 39 – Report of the Committee

The Committee shall report every two years to the General Assembly and to the Economic and Social Council on its activities, and may make suggestions and general recommendations based on the examination of reports and information received from the States Parties. Such suggestions and general recommendations shall be included in the report of the Committee together with comments, if any, from States Parties.

Article 40 – Conference of States Parties

1. The States Parties shall meet regularly in a Conference of States Parties in order to consider any matter with regard to the implementation of the present Convention.
2. No later than six months after the entry into force of the present Convention, the Conference of States Parties shall be convened by the Secretary-General of the United Nations. The subsequent meetings shall be convened by the Secretary-General biennially or upon the decision of the Conference of States Parties.

Article 41 – Depositary

The Secretary-General of the United Nations shall be the depositary of the present Convention.

Article 42 – Signature

The present Convention shall be open for signature by all States and by regional integration organizations at United Nations Headquarters in New York as of 30 March 2007.

Article 43 – Consent to Be Bound

The present Convention shall be subject to ratification by signatory States and to formal confirmation by signatory regional integration organizations. It shall be open for accession by any State or regional integration organization which has not signed the Convention.

Article 44 – Regional Integration Organizations

1. "Regional integration organization" shall mean an organization constituted by sovereign States of a given region, to which its member States have transferred competence in respect of matters governed by the present Convention. Such organizations shall declare, in their instruments of formal confirmation or accession, the extent of their competence with respect to matters governed

by the present Convention. Subsequently, they shall inform the depositary of any substantial modification in the extent of their competence.
2. References to "States Parties" in the present Convention shall apply to such organizations within the limits of their competence.
3. For the purposes of article 45, paragraph 1, and article 47, paragraphs 2 and 3, of the present Convention, any instrument deposited by a regional integration organization shall not be counted.
4. Regional integration organizations, in matters within their competence, may exercise their right to vote in the Conference of States Parties, with a number of votes equal to the number of their member States that are Parties to the present Convention. Such an organization shall not exercise its right to vote if any of its member States exercises its right, and vice versa.

Article 45 – Entry into Force

1. The present Convention shall enter into force on the thirtieth day after the deposit of the twentieth instrument of ratification or accession.
2. For each State or regional integration organization ratifying, formally confirming or acceding to the present Convention after the deposit of the twentieth such instrument, the Convention shall enter into force on the thirtieth day after the deposit of its own such instrument.

Article 46 – Reservations

1. Reservations incompatible with the object and purpose of the present Convention shall not be permitted.
2. Reservations may be withdrawn at any time.

Article 47 – Amendments

1. Any State Party may propose an amendment to the present Convention and submit it to the Secretary-General of the United Nations. The SecretaryGeneral shall communicate any proposed amendments to States Parties, with a request to be notified whether they favour a conference of States Parties for the purpose of considering and deciding upon the proposals. In the event that, within four months from the date of such communication, at least one third of the States Parties favour such a conference, the Secretary-General shall convene the conference under the auspices of the United Nations. Any amendment adopted by a majority of two thirds of the States Parties present and voting shall be submitted by the Secretary-General to the General Assembly of the United Nations for approval and thereafter to all States Parties for acceptance.
2. An amendment adopted and approved in accordance with paragraph 1 of this article shall enter into force on the thirtieth day after the number of

instruments of acceptance deposited reaches two thirds of the number of States Parties at the date of adoption of the amendment. Thereafter, the amendment shall enter into force for any State Party on the thirtieth day following the deposit of its own instrument of acceptance. An amendment shall be binding only on those States Parties which have accepted it.

3. If so decided by the Conference of States Parties by consensus, an amendment adopted and approved in accordance with paragraph 1 of this article which relates exclusively to articles 34, 38, 39 and 40 shall enter into force for all States Parties on the thirtieth day after the number of instruments of acceptance deposited reaches two thirds of the number of States Parties at the date of adoption of the amendment.

Article 48 – Denunciation

A State Party may denounce the present Convention by written notification to the Secretary-General of the United Nations. The denunciation shall become effective one year after the date of receipt of the notification by the Secretary-General.

Article 49 – Accessible Format

The text of the present Convention shall be made available in accessible formats.

Article 50 – Authentic Texts

The Arabic, Chinese, English, French, Russian and Spanish texts of the present Convention shall be equally authentic.

IN WITNESS THEREOF the undersigned plenipotentiaries, being duly authorized thereto by their respective Governments, have signed the present Convention.

CHAPTER 10.A

Optional Protocol to the Convention on the Rights of Persons with Disabilities

Adopted and opened for signature, ratification and accession by General Assembly resolution 61/106 on 13 December 2006
Entry into force 3 May 2008, in accordance with article 13(1)

The States Parties to the present Protocol have agreed as follows:
Art. 1 1. A State Party to the present Protocol ("State Party") recognizes the competence of the Committee on the Rights of Persons with Disabilities ("the Committee") to receive and consider communications from or on behalf of individuals or groups of individuals subject to its jurisdiction who claim to be victims of a violation by that State Party of the provisions of the Convention.
2. No communication shall be received by the Committee if it concerns a State Party to the Convention that is not a party to the present Protocol.
Art. 2 The Committee shall consider a communication inadmissible when:
(a) The communication is anonymous;
(b) The communication constitutes an abuse of the right of submission of such communications or is incompatible with the provisions of the Convention;
(c) The same matter has already been examined by the Committee or has been or is being examined under another procedure of international investigation or settlement;
(d) All available domestic remedies have not been exhausted. This shall not be the rule where the application of the remedies is unreasonably prolonged or unlikely to bring effective relief;
(e) It is manifestly ill-founded or not sufficiently substantiated; or when
(f) The facts that are the subject of the communication occurred prior to the entry into force of the present Protocol for the State Party concerned unless those facts continued after that date.
Art. 3 Subject to the provisions of article 2 of the present Protocol, the Committee shall bring any communications submitted to it confidentially to the attention of the State Party. Within six months, the receiving State shall submit to the Committee written explanations or statements clarifying the matter and the remedy, if any, that may have been taken by that State.

Art. 4 1. At any time after the receipt of a communication and before a determination on the merits has been reached, the Committee may transmit to the State Party concerned for its urgent consideration a request that the State Party take such interim measures as may be necessary to avoid possible irreparable damage to the victim or victims of the alleged violation.
2. Where the Committee exercises its discretion under paragraph 1 of this article, this does not imply a determination on admissibility or on the merits of the communication.
Art. 5 The Committee shall hold closed meetings when examining communications under the present Protocol. After examining a communication, the Committee shall forward its suggestions and recommendations, if any, to the State Party concerned and to the petitioner.
Art. 6 1. If the Committee receives reliable information indicating grave or systematic violations by a State Party of rights set forth in the Convention, the Committee shall invite that State Party to cooperate in the examination of the information and to this end submit observations with regard to the information concerned.
2. Taking into account any observations that may have been submitted by the State Party concerned as well as any other reliable information available to it, the Committee may designate one or more of its members to conduct an inquiry and to report urgently to the Committee. Where warranted and with the consent of the State Party, the inquiry may include a visit to its territory.
3. After examining the findings of such an inquiry, the Committee, shall transmit these findings to the State Party concerned together with any comments and recommendations.
4. The State Party concerned shall, within six months of receiving the findings, comments and recommendations transmitted by the Committee, submit its observations to the Committee.
5. Such an inquiry shall be conducted confidentially and the cooperation of the State Party shall be sought at all stages of the proceedings.
Art. 7 1. The Committee may invite the State Party concerned to include in its report under article 35 of the Convention details of any measures taken in response to an inquiry conducted under article 6 of the present Protocol.
2. The Committee may, if necessary, after the end of the period of six months referred to in article 6, paragraph 4, invite the State Party concerned to inform it of the measures taken in response to such an inquiry.
Art. 8 Each State Party may, at the time of signature or ratification of the present Protocol or accession thereto, declare that it does not recognize the competence of the Committee provided for in articles 6 and 7.

Art. 9 The Secretary-General of the United Nations shall be the depositary of the present Protocol.
Art. 10 The present Protocol shall be open for signature by signatory States and regional integration organizations of the Convention at United Nations Headquarters in New York as of 30 March 2007.
Art. 11 The present Protocol shall be subject to ratification by signatory States of the present Protocol which have ratified or acceded to the Convention. It shall be subject to formal confirmation by signatory regional integration organizations of the present Protocol which have formally confirmed or acceded to the Convention. It shall be open for accession by any State or regional integration organization which has ratified, formally confirmed or acceded to the Convention and which has not signed the Protocol.
Art. 12 1. "Regional integration organization" shall mean an organization constituted by sovereign States of a given region, to which its member States have transferred competence in respect of matters governed by the Convention and the present Protocol. Such organizations shall declare, in their instruments of formal confirmation or accession the extent of their competence with respect to matters governed by the Convention and the present Protocol. Subsequently, they shall inform the depositary of any substantial modification in the extent of their competence.
2. References to "States Parties" in the present Protocol shall apply to such organizations within the limits of their competence.
3. For the purposes of article 13, paragraph 1, and article 15, paragraph 2, of the present Protocol, any instrument deposited by a regional integration organization shall not be counted.
4. Regional integration organizations, in matters within their competence, may exercise their right to vote in the meeting of States Parties, with a number of votes equal to the number of their member States that are Parties to the present Protocol. Such an organization shall not exercise its right to vote if any of its member States exercises its right, and vice versa.
Art. 13 1. Subject to the entry into force of the Convention, the present Protocol shall enter into force on the thirtieth day after the deposit of the tenth instrument of ratification or accession.
2. For each State or regional integration organization ratifying, formally confirming or acceding to the present Protocol after the deposit of the tenth such instrument, the Protocol shall enter into force on the thirtieth day after the deposit of its own such instrument.
Art. 14 1. Reservations incompatible with the object and purpose of the present Protocol shall not be permitted.
2. Reservations may be withdrawn at any time.

Art. 15 1. Any State Party may propose an amendment to the present Protocol and submit it to the Secretary-General of the United Nations. The Secretary-General shall communicate any proposed amendments to States Parties, with a request to be notified whether they favour a meeting of States Parties for the purpose of considering and deciding upon the proposals. In the event that, within four months from the date of such communication, at least one third of the States Parties favour such a meeting, the Secretary-General shall convene the meeting under the auspices of the United Nations. Any amendment adopted by a majority of two thirds of the States Parties present and voting shall be submitted by the Secretary-General to the General Assembly of the United Nations for approval and thereafter to all States Parties for acceptance.
2. An amendment adopted and approved in accordance with paragraph 1 of this article shall enter into force on the thirtieth day after the number of instruments of acceptance deposited reaches two thirds of the number of States Parties at the date of adoption of the amendment. Thereafter, the amendment shall enter into force for any State Party on the thirtieth day following the deposit of its own instrument of acceptance. An amendment shall be binding only on those States Parties which have accepted it.
Art. 16 A State Party may denounce the present Protocol by written notification to the Secretary-General of the United Nations. The denunciation shall become effective one year after the date of receipt of the notification by the Secretary-General.
Art. 17 The text of the present Protocol shall be made available in accessible formats.
Art. 18 The Arabic, Chinese, English, French, Russian and Spanish texts of the present Protocol shall be equally authentic.
IN WITNESS THEREOF the undersigned plenipotentiaries, being duly authorized thereto by their respective Governments, have signed the present Protocol.

CHAPTER 11

International Convention for the Protection of All Persons from Enforced Disappearance

Adopted and opened for signature, ratification and accession by General Assembly resolution 47/133 of 12 February 1993
Entry into force 23 December 2010, in accordance with article 39(1)

Preamble

The States Parties to this Convention,

Considering the obligation of States under the Charter of the United Nations to promote universal respect for, and observance of, human rights and fundamental freedoms,

Having regard to the Universal Declaration of Human Rights,

Recalling the International Covenant on Economic, Social and Cultural Rights, the International Covenant on Civil and Political Rights and the other relevant international instruments in the fields of human rights, humanitarian law and international criminal law,

Also recalling the Declaration on the Protection of All Persons from Enforced Disappearance adopted by the General Assembly of the United Nations in its resolution 47/133 of 18 December 1992,

Aware of the extreme seriousness of enforced disappearance, which constitutes a crime and, in certain circumstances defined in international law, a crime against humanity,

Determined to prevent enforced disappearances and to combat impunity for the crime of enforced disappearance,

Considering the right of any person not to be subjected to enforced disappearance, the right of victims to justice and to reparation,

Affirming the right of any victim to know the truth about the circumstances of an enforced disappearance and the fate of the disappeared person, and the right to freedom to seek, receive and impart information to this end,

Have agreed on the following articles:

Part I

Art. 1 1. No one shall be subjected to enforced disappearance.

© KARL HANSON ET AL., 2025 | DOI:10.1163/9789004681224_021

2. No exceptional circumstances whatsoever, whether a state of war or a threat of war, internal political instability or any other public emergency, may be invoked as a justification for enforced disappearance.

Art. 2 For the purposes of this Convention, "enforced disappearance" is considered to be the arrest, detention, abduction or any other form of deprivation of liberty by agents of the State or by persons or groups of persons acting with the authorization, support or acquiescence of the State, followed by a refusal to acknowledge the deprivation of liberty or by concealment of the fate or whereabouts of the disappeared person, which place such a person outside the protection of the law.

Art. 3 Each State Party shall take appropriate measures to investigate acts defined in article 2 committed by persons or groups of persons acting without the authorization, support or acquiescence of the State and to bring those responsible to justice.

Art. 4 Each State Party shall take the necessary measures to ensure that enforced disappearance constitutes an offence under its criminal law.

Art. 5 The widespread or systematic practice of enforced disappearance constitutes a crime against humanity as defined in applicable international law and shall attract the consequences provided for under such applicable international law.

Art. 6 1. Each State Party shall take the necessary measures to hold criminally responsible at least:

(a) Any person who commits, orders, solicits or induces the commission of, attempts to commit, is an accomplice to or participates in an enforced disappearance;

(b) A superior who:

- (i) Knew, or consciously disregarded information which clearly indicated, that subordinates under his or her effective authority and control were committing or about to commit a crime of enforced disappearance;
- (ii) Exercised effective responsibility for and control over activities which were concerned with the crime of enforced disappearance; and
- (iii) Failed to take all necessary and reasonable measures within his or her power to prevent or repress the commission of an enforced disappearance or to submit the matter to the competent authorities for investigation and prosecution;

(c) Subparagraph (b) above is without prejudice to the higher standards of responsibility applicable under relevant international law to a military commander or to a person effectively acting as a military commander.

2. No order or instruction from any public authority, civilian, military or other, may be invoked to justify an offence of enforced disappearance.

Art. 7 1. Each State Party shall make the offence of enforced disappearance punishable by appropriate penalties which take into account its extreme seriousness.

2. Each State Party may establish:

(a) Mitigating circumstances, in particular for persons who, having been implicated in the commission of an enforced disappearance, effectively contribute to bringing the disappeared person forward alive or make it possible to clarify cases of enforced disappearance or to identify the perpetrators of an enforced disappearance;

(b) Without prejudice to other criminal procedures, aggravating circumstances, in particular in the event of the death of the disappeared person or the commission of an enforced disappearance in respect of pregnant women, minors, persons with disabilities or other particularly vulnerable persons.

Art. 8 Without prejudice to article 5,

1. A State Party which applies a statute of limitations in respect of enforced disappearance shall take the necessary measures to ensure that the term of limitation for criminal proceedings:

(a) Is of long duration and is proportionate to the extreme seriousness of this offence;

(b) Commences from the moment when the offence of enforced disappearance ceases, taking into account its continuous nature.

2. Each State Party shall guarantee the right of victims of enforced disappearance to an effective remedy during the term of limitation.

Art. 9 1. Each State Party shall take the necessary measures to establish its competence to exercise jurisdiction over the offence of enforced disappearance:

(a) When the offence is committed in any territory under its jurisdiction or on board a ship or aircraft registered in that State;

(b) When the alleged offender is one of its nationals;

(c) When the disappeared person is one of its nationals and the State Party considers it appropriate.

2. Each State Party shall likewise take such measures as may be necessary to establish its competence to exercise jurisdiction over the offence of enforced disappearance when the alleged offender is present in any territory under its jurisdiction, unless it extradites or surrenders him or her to another State in accordance with its international obligations or surrenders him or her to an international criminal tribunal whose jurisdiction it has recognized.

3. This Convention does not exclude any additional criminal jurisdiction exercised in accordance with national law.

Art. 10 1. Upon being satisfied, after an examination of the information available to it, that the circumstances so warrant, any State Party in whose territory a person suspected of having committed an offence of enforced disappearance is present shall take him or her into custody or take such other legal measures as are necessary to ensure his or her presence. The custody and other legal measures shall be as provided for in the law of that State Party but may be maintained only for such time as is necessary to ensure the person's presence at criminal, surrender or extradition proceedings.

2. A State Party which has taken the measures referred to in paragraph 1 of this article shall immediately carry out a preliminary inquiry or investigations to establish the facts. It shall notify the States Parties referred to in article 9, paragraph 1, of the measures it has taken in pursuance of paragraph 1 of this article, including detention and the circumstances warranting detention, and of the findings of its preliminary inquiry or its investigations, indicating whether it intends to exercise its jurisdiction.

3. Any person in custody pursuant to paragraph 1 of this article may communicate immediately with the nearest appropriate representative of the State of which he or she is a national, or, if he or she is a stateless person, with the representative of the State where he or she usually resides.

Art. 11 1. The State Party in the territory under whose jurisdiction a person alleged to have committed an offence of enforced disappearance is found shall, if it does not extradite that person or surrender him or her to another State in accordance with its international obligations or surrender him or her to an international criminal tribunal whose jurisdiction it has recognized, submit the case to its competent authorities for the purpose of prosecution.

2. These authorities shall take their decision in the same manner as in the case of any ordinary offence of a serious nature under the law of that State Party. In the cases referred to in article 9, paragraph 2, the standards of evidence required for prosecution and conviction shall in no way be less stringent than those which apply in the cases referred to in article 9, paragraph 1.

3. Any person against whom proceedings are brought in connection with an offence of enforced disappearance shall be guaranteed fair treatment at all stages of the proceedings. Any person tried for an offence of enforced disappearance shall benefit from a fair trial before a competent, independent and impartial court or tribunal established by law.

Art. 12 1. Each State Party shall ensure that any individual who alleges that a person has been subjected to enforced disappearance has the right to report the facts to the competent authorities, which shall examine the allegation promptly and impartially and, where necessary, undertake without delay a thorough and impartial investigation. Appropriate steps shall be taken, where necessary, to ensure that the complainant, witnesses, relatives of the disappeared person and their defence counsel, as well as persons participating in the investigation, are protected against all ill-treatment or intimidation as a consequence of the complaint or any evidence given.

2. Where there are reasonable grounds for believing that a person has been subjected to enforced disappearance, the authorities referred to in paragraph 1 of this article shall undertake an investigation, even if there has been no formal complaint.

3. Each State Party shall ensure that the authorities referred to in paragraph 1 of this article:

(a) Have the necessary powers and resources to conduct the investigation effectively, including access to the documentation and other information relevant to their investigation;

(b) Have access, if necessary with the prior authorization of a judicial authority, which shall rule promptly on the matter, to any place of detention or any other place where there are reasonable grounds to believe that the disappeared person may be present.

4. Each State Party shall take the necessary measures to prevent and sanction acts that hinder the conduct of an investigation. It shall ensure in particular that persons suspected of having committed an offence of enforced disappearance are not in a position to influence the progress of an investigation by means of pressure or acts of intimidation or reprisal aimed at the complainant, witnesses, relatives of the disappeared person or their defence counsel, or at persons participating in the investigation.

Art. 13 1. For the purposes of extradition between States Parties, the offence of enforced disappearance shall not be regarded as a political offence or as an offence connected with a political offence or as an offence inspired by political motives. Accordingly, a request for extradition based on such an offence may not be refused on these grounds alone.

2. The offence of enforced disappearance shall be deemed to be included as an extraditable offence in any extradition treaty existing between States Parties before the entry into force of this Convention.

3. States Parties undertake to include the offence of enforced disappearance as an extraditable offence in any extradition treaty subsequently to be concluded between them.

4. If a State Party which makes extradition conditional on the existence of a treaty receives a request for extradition from another State Party with which

it has no extradition treaty, it may consider this Convention as the necessary legal basis for extradition in respect of the offence of enforced disappearance.
5. States Parties which do not make extradition conditional on the existence of a treaty shall recognize the offence of enforced disappearance as an extraditable offence between themselves.
6. Extradition shall, in all cases, be subject to the conditions provided for by the law of the requested State Party or by applicable extradition treaties, including, in particular, conditions relating to the minimum penalty requirement for extradition and the grounds upon which the requested State Party may refuse extradition or make it subject to certain conditions.
7. Nothing in this Convention shall be interpreted as imposing an obligation to extradite if the requested State Party has substantial grounds for believing that the request has been made for the purpose of prosecuting or punishing a person on account of that person's sex, race, religion, nationality, ethnic origin, political opinions or membership of a particular social group, or that compliance with the request would cause harm to that person for any one of these reasons.
Art. 14 1. States Parties shall afford one another the greatest measure of mutual legal assistance in connection with criminal proceedings brought in respect of an offence of enforced disappearance, including the supply of all evidence at their disposal that is necessary for the proceedings.
2. Such mutual legal assistance shall be subject to the conditions provided for by the domestic law of the requested State Party or by applicable treaties on mutual legal assistance, including, in particular, the conditions in relation to the grounds upon which the requested State Party may refuse to grant mutual legal assistance or may make it subject to conditions.
Art. 15 States Parties shall cooperate with each other and shall afford one another the greatest measure of mutual assistance with a view to assisting victims of enforced disappearance, and in searching for, locating and releasing disappeared persons and, in the event of death, in exhuming and identifying them and returning their remains.
Art. 16 1. No State Party shall expel, return ("refouler"), surrender or extradite a person to another State where there are substantial grounds for believing that he or she would be in danger of being subjected to enforced disappearance.
2. For the purpose of determining whether there are such grounds, the competent authorities shall take into account all relevant considerations, including, where applicable, the existence in the State concerned of a consistent pattern of gross, flagrant or mass violations of human rights or of serious violations of international humanitarian law.
Art. 17 1. No one shall be held in secret detention.

2. Without prejudice to other international obligations of the State Party with regard to the deprivation of liberty, each State Party shall, in its legislation:

(a) Establish the conditions under which orders of deprivation of liberty may be given;

(b) Indicate those authorities authorized to order the deprivation of liberty;

(c) Guarantee that any person deprived of liberty shall be held solely in officially recognized and supervised places of deprivation of liberty;

(d) Guarantee that any person deprived of liberty shall be authorized to communicate with and be visited by his or her family, counsel or any other person of his or her choice, subject only to the conditions established by law, or, if he or she is a foreigner, to communicate with his or her consular authorities, in accordance with applicable international law;

(e) Guarantee access by the competent and legally authorized authorities and institutions to the places where persons are deprived of liberty, if necessary with prior authorization from a judicial authority;

(f) Guarantee that any person deprived of liberty or, in the case of a suspected enforced disappearance, since the person deprived of liberty is not able to exercise this right, any persons with a legitimate interest, such as relatives of the person deprived of liberty, their representatives or their counsel, shall, in all circumstances, be entitled to take proceedings before a court, in order that the court may decide without delay on the lawfulness of the deprivation of liberty and order the person's release if such deprivation of liberty is not lawful.

3. Each State Party shall assure the compilation and maintenance of one or more up-to-date official registers and/or records of persons deprived of liberty, which shall be made promptly available, upon request, to any judicial or other competent authority or institution authorized for that purpose by the law of the State Party concerned or any relevant international legal instrument to which the State concerned is a party. The information contained therein shall include, as a minimum:

(a) The identity of the person deprived of liberty;

(b) The date, time and place where the person was deprived of liberty and the identity of the authority that deprived the person of liberty;

(c) The authority that ordered the deprivation of liberty and the grounds for the deprivation of liberty;

(d) The authority responsible for supervising the deprivation of liberty;

(e) The place of deprivation of liberty, the date and time of admission to the place of deprivation of liberty and the authority responsible for the place of deprivation of liberty;

(f) Elements relating to the state of health of the person deprived of liberty;
(g) In the event of death during the deprivation of liberty, the circumstances and cause of death and the destination of the remains;
(h) The date and time of release or transfer to another place of detention, the destination and the authority responsible for the transfer.

Art. 18 1. Subject to articles 19 and 20, each State Party shall guarantee to any person with a legitimate interest in this information, such as relatives of the person deprived of liberty, their representatives or their counsel, access to at least the following information:
(a) The authority that ordered the deprivation of liberty;
(b) The date, time and place where the person was deprived of liberty and admitted to the place of deprivation of liberty;
(c) The authority responsible for supervising the deprivation of liberty;
(d) The whereabouts of the person deprived of liberty, including, in the event of a transfer to another place of deprivation of liberty, the destination and the authority responsible for the transfer;
(e) The date, time and place of release;
(f) Elements relating to the state of health of the person deprived of liberty;
(g) In the event of death during the deprivation of liberty, the circumstances and cause of death and the destination of the remains.

2. Appropriate measures shall be taken, where necessary, to protect the persons referred to in paragraph1 of this article, as well as persons participating in the investigation, from any ill-treatment, intimidation or sanction as a result of the search for information concerning a person deprived of liberty.

Art. 19 1. Personal information, including medical and genetic data, which is collected and/or transmitted within the framework of the search for a disappeared person shall not be used or made available for purposes other than the search for the disappeared person. This is without prejudice to the use of such information in criminal proceedings relating to an offence of enforced disappearance or the exercise of the right to obtain reparation.

2. The collection, processing, use and storage of personal information, including medical and genetic data, shall not infringe or have the effect of infringing the human rights, fundamental freedoms or human dignity of an individual.

Art. 20 1. Only where a person is under the protection of the law and the deprivation of liberty is subject to judicial control may the right to information referred to in article 18 be restricted, on an exceptional basis, where strictly necessary and where provided for by law, and if the transmission of the information would adversely affect the privacy or safety of the person, hinder a criminal investigation, or for other equivalent reasons in accordance with the law, and in conformity with applicable international law and with the

objectives of this Convention. In no case shall there be restrictions on the right to information referred to in article 18 that could constitute conduct defined in article 2 or be in violation of article 17, paragraph 1.
2. Without prejudice to consideration of the lawfulness of the deprivation of a person's liberty, States Parties shall guarantee to the persons referred to in article 18, paragraph 1, the right to a prompt and effective judicial remedy as a means of obtaining without delay the information referred to in article 18, paragraph 1. This right to a remedy may not be suspended or restricted in any circumstances.
Art. 21 Each State Party shall take the necessary measures to ensure that persons deprived of liberty are released in a manner permitting reliable verification that they have actually been released. Each State Party shall also take the necessary measures to assure the physical integrity of such persons and their ability to exercise fully their rights at the time of release, without prejudice to any obligations to which such persons may be subject under national law.
Art. 22 Without prejudice to article 6, each State Party shall take the necessary measures to prevent and impose sanctions for the following conduct:
(a) Delaying or obstructing the remedies referred to in article 17, paragraph 2 (f), and article 20, paragraph 2;
(b) Failure to record the deprivation of liberty of any person, or the recording of any information which the official responsible for the official register knew or should have known to be inaccurate;
(c) Refusal to provide information on the deprivation of liberty of a person, or the provision of inaccurate information, even though the legal requirements for providing such information have been met.
Art. 23 1. Each State Party shall ensure that the training of law enforcement personnel, civil or military, medical personnel, public officials and other persons who may be involved in the custody or treatment of any person deprived of liberty includes the necessary education and information regarding the relevant provisions of this Convention, in order to:
(a) Prevent the involvement of such officials in enforced disappearances;
(b) Emphasize the importance of prevention and investigations in relation to enforced disappearances;
(c) Ensure that the urgent need to resolve cases of enforced disappearance is recognized.
2. Each State Party shall ensure that orders or instructions prescribing, authorizing or encouraging enforced disappearance are prohibited. Each State Party shall guarantee that a person who refuses to obey such an order will not be punished.

3. Each State Party shall take the necessary measures to ensure that the persons referred to in paragraph 1 of this article who have reason to believe that an enforced disappearance has occurred or is planned report the matter to their superiors and, where necessary, to the appropriate authorities or bodies vested with powers of review or remedy.

Art. 24 1. For the purposes of this Convention, "victim" means the disappeared person and any individual who has suffered harm as the direct result of an enforced disappearance.

2. Each victim has the right to know the truth regarding the circumstances of the enforced disappearance, the progress and results of the investigation and the fate of the disappeared person. Each State Party shall take appropriate measures in this regard.

3. Each State Party shall take all appropriate measures to search for, locate and release disappeared persons and, in the event of death, to locate, respect and return their remains.

4. Each State Party shall ensure in its legal system that the victims of enforced disappearance have the right to obtain reparation and prompt, fair and adequate compensation.

5. The right to obtain reparation referred to in paragraph 4 of this article covers material and moral damages and, where appropriate, other forms of reparation such as:

(a) Restitution;

(b) Rehabilitation;

(c) Satisfaction, including restoration of dignity and reputation;

(d) Guarantees of non-repetition.

6. Without prejudice to the obligation to continue the investigation until the fate of the disappeared person has been clarified, each State Party shall take the appropriate steps with regard to the legal situation of disappeared persons whose fate has not been clarified and that of their relatives, in fields such as social welfare, financial matters, family law and property rights.

7. Each State Party shall guarantee the right to form and participate freely in organizations and associations concerned with attempting to establish the circumstances of enforced disappearances and the fate of disappeared persons, and to assist victims of enforced disappearance.

Art. 25 1. Each State Party shall take the necessary measures to prevent and punish under its criminal law:

(a) The wrongful removal of children who are subjected to enforced disappearance, children whose father, mother or legal guardian is subjected to enforced disappearance or children born during the captivity of a mother subjected to enforced disappearance;

(b) The falsification, concealment or destruction of documents attesting to the true identity of the children referred to in subparagraph (a) above.

2. Each State Party shall take the necessary measures to search for and identify the children referred to in paragraph 1 (a) of this article and to return them to their families of origin, in accordance with legal procedures and applicable international agreements.

3. States Parties shall assist one another in searching for, identifying and locating the children referred to in paragraph 1 (a) of this article.

4. Given the need to protect the best interests of the children referred to in paragraph 1 (a) of this article and their right to preserve, or to have reestablished, their identity, including their nationality, name and family relations as recognized by law, States Parties which recognize a system of adoption or other form of placement of children shall have legal procedures in place to review the adoption or placement procedure, and, where appropriate, to annul any adoption or placement of children that originated in an enforced disappearance.

5. In all cases, and in particular in all matters relating to this article, the best interests of the child shall be a primary consideration, and a child who is capable of forming his or her own views shall have the right to express those views freely, the views of the child being given due weight in accordance with the age and maturity of the child.

Part II

Art. 26 1. A Committee on Enforced Disappearances (hereinafter referred to as "the Committee") shall be established to carry out the functions provided for under this Convention. The Committee shall consist of ten experts of high moral character and recognized competence in the field of human rights, who shall serve in their personal capacity and be independent and impartial. The members of the Committee shall be elected by the States Parties according to equitable geographical distribution. Due account shall be taken of the usefulness of the participation in the work of the Committee of persons having relevant legal experience and of balanced gender representation.

2. The members of the Committee shall be elected by secret ballot from a list of persons nominated by States Parties from among their nationals, at biennial meetings of the States Parties convened by the Secretary-General of the United Nations for this purpose. At those meetings, for which two thirds of the States Parties shall constitute a quorum, the persons elected to the Committee shall be those who obtain the largest number of votes and an absolute majority of the votes of the representatives of States Parties present and voting.

3. The initial election shall be held no later than six months after the date of entry into force of this Convention. Four months before the date of each election, the Secretary-General of the United Nations shall address a letter to the States Parties inviting them to submit nominations within three months. The Secretary-General shall prepare a list in alphabetical order of all persons thus nominated, indicating the State Party which nominated each candidate, and shall submit this list to all States Parties.
4. The members of the Committee shall be elected for a term of four years. They shall be eligible for re-election once. However, the term of five of the members elected at the first election shall expire at the end of two years; immediately after the first election, the names of these five members shall be chosen by lot by the chairman of the meeting referred to in paragraph 2 of this article.
5. If a member of the Committee dies or resigns or for any other reason can no longer perform his or her Committee duties, the State Party which nominated him or her shall, in accordance with the criteria set out in paragraph 1 of this article, appoint another candidate from among its nationals to serve out his or her term, subject to the approval of the majority of the States Parties. Such approval shall be considered to have been obtained unless half or more of the States Parties respond negatively within six weeks of having been informed by the Secretary-General of the United Nations of the proposed appointment.
6. The Committee shall establish its own rules of procedure.
7. The Secretary-General of the United Nations shall provide the Committee with the necessary means, staff and facilities for the effective performance of its functions. The Secretary-General of the United Nations shall convene the initial meeting of the Committee.
8. The members of the Committee shall be entitled to the facilities, privileges and immunities of experts on mission for the United Nations, as laid down in the relevant sections of the Convention on the Privileges and Immunities of the United Nations.
9. Each State Party shall cooperate with the Committee and assist its members in the fulfilment of their mandate, to the extent of the Committee's functions that the State Party has accepted.

Art. 27 A Conference of the States Parties will take place at the earliest four years and at the latest six years following the entry into force of this Convention to evaluate the functioning of the Committee and to decide, in accordance with the procedure described in article 44, paragraph 2, whether it is appropriate to transfer to another body – without excluding any possibility – the monitoring of this Convention, in accordance with the functions defined in articles 28 to 36.

Art. 28 1. In the framework of the competencies granted by this Convention, the Committee shall cooperate with all relevant organs, offices and specialized agencies and funds of the United Nations, with the treaty bodies instituted by international instruments, with the special procedures of the United Nations and with the relevant regional intergovernmental organizations or bodies, as well as with all relevant State institutions, agencies or offices working towards the protection of all persons against enforced disappearances.
2. As it discharges its mandate, the Committee shall consult other treaty bodies instituted by relevant international human rights instruments, in particular the Human Rights Committee instituted by the International Covenant on Civil and Political Rights, with a view to ensuring the consistency of their respective observations and recommendations.
Art. 29 1. Each State Party shall submit to the Committee, through the Secretary-General of the United Nations, a report on the measures taken to give effect to its obligations under this Convention, within two years after the entry into force of this Convention for the State Party concerned.
2. The Secretary-General of the United Nations shall make this report available to all States Parties.
3. Each report shall be considered by the Committee, which shall issue such comments, observations or recommendations as it may deem appropriate. The comments, observations or recommendations shall be communicated to the State Party concerned, which may respond to them, on its own initiative or at the request of the Committee.
4. The Committee may also request States Parties to provide additional information on the implementation of this Convention.
Art. 30 1. A request that a disappeared person should be sought and found may be submitted to the Committee, as a matter of urgency, by relatives of the disappeared person or their legal representatives, their counsel or any person authorized by them, as well as by any other person having a legitimate interest.
2. If the Committee considers that a request for urgent action submitted in pursuance of paragraph 1 of this article:
(a) Is not manifestly unfounded;
(b) Does not constitute an abuse of the right of submission of such requests;
(c) Has already been duly presented to the competent bodies of the State Party concerned, such as those authorized to undertake investigations, where such a possibility exists;
(d) Is not incompatible with the provisions of this Convention; and
(e) The same matter is not being examined under another procedure of international investigation or settlement of the same nature;

it shall request the State Party concerned to provide it with information on the situation of the persons sought, within a time limit set by the Committee.
3. In the light of the information provided by the State Party concerned in accordance with paragraph 2 of this article, the Committee may transmit recommendations to the State Party, including a request that the State Party should take all the necessary measures, including interim measures, to locate and protect the person concerned in accordance with this Convention and to inform the Committee, within a specified period of time, of measures taken, taking into account the urgency of the situation. The Committee shall inform the person submitting the urgent action request of its recommendations and of the information provided to it by the State as it becomes available.
4. The Committee shall continue its efforts to work with the State Party concerned for as long as the fate of the person sought remains unresolved. The person presenting the request shall be kept informed.
Art. 31 1. A State Party may at the time of ratification of this Convention or at any time afterwards declare that it recognizes the competence of the Committee to receive and consider communications from or on behalf of individuals subject to its jurisdiction claiming to be victims of a violation by this State Party of provisions of this Convention. The Committee shall not admit any communication concerning a State Party which has not made such a declaration.
2. The Committee shall consider a communication inadmissible where:
(a) The communication is anonymous;
(b) The communication constitutes an abuse of the right of submission of such communications or is incompatible with the provisions of this Convention;
(c) The same matter is being examined under another procedure of international investigation or settlement of the same nature; or where
(d) All effective available domestic remedies have not been exhausted. This rule shall not apply where the application of the remedies is unreasonably prolonged.
3. If the Committee considers that the communication meets the requirements set out in paragraph 2 of this article, it shall transmit the communication to the State Party concerned, requesting it to provide observations and comments within a time limit set by the Committee.
4. At any time after the receipt of a communication and before a determination on the merits has been reached, the Committee may transmit to the State Party concerned for its urgent consideration a request that the State Party will take such interim measures as may be necessary to avoid possible irreparable damage to the victims of the alleged violation. Where the Committee exercises

its discretion, this does not imply a determination on admissibility or on the merits of the communication.

5. The Committee shall hold closed meetings when examining communications under the present article. It shall inform the author of a communication of the responses provided by the State Party concerned. When the Committee decides to finalize the procedure, it shall communicate its views to the State Party and to the author of the communication.

Art. 32 A State Party to this Convention may at any time declare that it recognizes the competence of the Committee to receive and consider communications in which a State Party claims that another State Party is not fulfilling its obligations under this Convention. The Committee shall not receive communications concerning a State Party which has not made such a declaration, nor communications from a State Party which has not made such a declaration.

Art. 33 1. If the Committee receives reliable information indicating that a State Party is seriously violating the provisions of this Convention, it may, after consultation with the State Party concerned, request one or more of its members to undertake a visit and report back to it without delay.

2. The Committee shall notify the State Party concerned, in writing, of its intention to organize a visit, indicating the composition of the delegation and the purpose of the visit. The State Party shall answer the Committee within a reasonable time.

3. Upon a substantiated request by the State Party, the Committee may decide to postpone or cancel its visit.

4. If the State Party agrees to the visit, the Committee and the State Party concerned shall work together to define the modalities of the visit and the State Party shall provide the Committee with all the facilities needed for the successful completion of the visit.

5. Following its visit, the Committee shall communicate to the State Party concerned its observations and recommendations.

Art. 34 If the Committee receives information which appears to it to contain well-founded indications that enforced disappearance is being practised on a widespread or systematic basis in the territory under the jurisdiction of a State Party, it may, after seeking from the State Party concerned all relevant information on the situation, urgently bring the matter to the attention of the General Assembly of the United Nations, through the Secretary-General of the United Nations.

Art. 35 1. The Committee shall have competence solely in respect of enforced disappearances which commenced after the entry into force of this Convention.

2. If a State becomes a party to this Convention after its entry into force, the obligations of that State vis-à-vis the Committee shall relate only to enforced

disappearances which commenced after the entry into force of this Convention for the State concerned.

Art. 36 1. The Committee shall submit an annual report on its activities under this Convention to the States Parties and to the General Assembly of the United Nations.

2. Before an observation on a State Party is published in the annual report, the State Party concerned shall be informed in advance and shall be given reasonable time to answer. This State Party may request the publication of its comments or observations in the report.

Part III

Art. 37 Nothing in this Convention shall affect any provisions which are more conducive to the protection of all persons from enforced disappearance and which may be contained in:

(a) The law of a State Party;

(b) International law in force for that State.

Art. 38 1. This Convention is open for signature by all Member States of the United Nations.

2. This Convention is subject to ratification by all Member States of the United Nations. Instruments of ratification shall be deposited with the Secretary-General of the United Nations.

3. This Convention is open to accession by all Member States of the United Nations. Accession shall be effected by the deposit of an instrument of accession with the Secretary-General.

Art. 39 1. This Convention shall enter into force on the thirtieth day after the date of deposit with the Secretary-General of the United Nations of the twentieth instrument of ratification or accession.

2. For each State ratifying or acceding to this Convention after the deposit of the twentieth instrument of ratification or accession, this Convention shall enter into force on the thirtieth day after the date of the deposit of that State's instrument of ratification or accession.

Art. 40 The Secretary-General of the United Nations shall notify all States Members of the United Nations and all States which have signed or acceded to this Convention of the following:

(a) Signatures, ratifications and accessions under article 38;

(b) The date of entry into force of this Convention under article 39.

Art. 41 The provisions of this Convention shall apply to all parts of federal States without any limitations or exceptions.

Art. 42 1. Any dispute between two or more States Parties concerning the interpretation or application of this Convention which cannot be settled through negotiation or by the procedures expressly provided for in this Convention shall, at the request of one of them, be submitted to arbitration. If within six months from the date of the request for arbitration the Parties are unable to agree on the organization of the arbitration, any one of those Parties may refer the dispute to the International Court of Justice by request in conformity with the Statute of the Court.
2. A State may, at the time of signature or ratification of this Convention or accession thereto, declare that it does not consider itself bound by paragraph 1 of this article. The other States Parties shall not be bound by paragraph 1 of this article with respect to any State Party having made such a declaration.
3. Any State Party having made a declaration in accordance with the provisions of paragraph 2 of this article may at any time withdraw this declaration by notification to the Secretary-General of the United Nations.
Art. 43 This Convention is without prejudice to the provisions of international humanitarian law, including the obligations of the High Contracting Parties to the four Geneva Conventions of 12 August 1949 and the two Additional Protocols thereto of 8 June 1977, or to the opportunity available to any State Party to authorize the International Committee of the Red Cross to visit places of detention in situations not covered by international humanitarian law.
Art. 44 1. Any State Party to this Convention may propose an amendment and file it with the Secretary-General of the United Nations. The Secretary-General shall thereupon communicate the proposed amendment to the States Parties to this Convention with a request that they indicate whether they favour a conference of States Parties for the purpose of considering and voting upon the proposal. In the event that within four months from the date of such communication at least one third of the States Parties favour such a conference, the Secretary-General shall convene the conference under the auspices of the United Nations.
2. Any amendment adopted by a majority of two thirds of the States Parties present and voting at the conference shall be submitted by the Secretary-General of the United Nations to all the States Parties for acceptance.
3. An amendment adopted in accordance with paragraph 1 of this article shall enter into force when two thirds of the States Parties to this Convention have accepted it in accordance with their respective constitutional processes.
4. When amendments enter into force, they shall be binding on those States Parties which have accepted them, other States Parties still being bound by the provisions of this Convention and any earlier amendment which they have accepted.

Art. 45 1. This Convention, of which the Arabic, Chinese, English, French, Russian and Spanish texts are equally authentic, shall be deposited with the Secretary-General of the United Nations.
2. The Secretary-General of the United Nations shall transmit certified copies of this Convention to all States referred to in article 38.

CHAPTER 12

African (Banjul) Charter on Human and Peoples' Rights

Adopted by the Organization of African Unity at its 18th Assembly of Heads of State and Government in Nairobi, Kenya on 27 June 1981
Entry into force 21 October 1986

Preamble

The African States members of the Organization of African Unity, parties to the present convention entitled "African Charter on Human and Peoples' Rights",

Recalling Decision 115 (XVI) of the Assembly of Heads of State and Government at its Sixteenth Ordinary Session held in Monrovia, Liberia, from 17 to 20 July 1979 on the preparation of "a preliminary draft on an African Charter on Human and Peoples' Rights providing inter alia for the establishment of bodies to promote and protect human and peoples' rights";

Considering the Charter of the Organization of African Unity, which stipulates that "freedom, equality, justice and dignity are essential objectives for the achievement of the legitimate aspirations of the African peoples";

Reaffirming the pledge they solemnly made in Article 2 of the said Charter to eradicate all forms of colonialism from Africa, to coordinate and intensify their cooperation and efforts to achieve a better life for the peoples of Africa and to promote international cooperation having due regard to the Charter of the United Nations and the Universal Declaration of Human Rights;

Taking into consideration the virtues of their historical tradition and the values of African civilization which should inspire and characterize their reflection on the concept of human and peoples' rights;

Recognizing on the one hand, that fundamental human rights stem from the attributes of human beings, which justifies their international protection and on the other hand that the reality and respect of peoples' rights should necessarily guarantee human rights;

Considering that the enjoyment of rights and freedoms also implies the performance of duties on the part of everyone;

Convinced that it is henceforth essential to pay a particular attention to the right to development and that civil and political rights cannot be dissociated from economic, social and cultural rights in their conception as well as universality and that the satisfaction of economic, social and cultural rights is a guarantee for the enjoyment of civil and political rights;

Conscious of their duty to achieve the total liberation of Africa, the peoples of which are still struggling for their dignity and genuine independence, and undertaking to eliminate colonialism, neo-colonialism, apartheid, zionism and to dismantle aggressive foreign military bases and all forms of discrimination, particularly those based on race, ethnic group, colour, sex, language, religion or political opinions;

Reaffirming their adherence to the principles of human and peoples' rights and freedoms contained in the declarations, conventions and other instruments adopted by the Organization of African Unity, the Movement of Non-Aligned Countries and the United Nations;

Firmly convinced of their duty to promote and protect human and peoples' rights and freedoms and taking into account the importance traditionally attached to these rights and freedoms in Africa;

Have agreed as follows:

Part 1: Rights and Duties

Chapter 1: Human and Peoples' Rights

Art. 1 The Member States of the Organization of African Unity parties to the present Charter shall recognize the rights, duties and freedoms enshrined in this Charter and shall undertake to adopt legislative or other measures to give effect to them.

Art. 2 Every individual shall be entitled to the enjoyment of the rights and freedoms recognized and guaranteed in the present Charter without distinction of any kind such as race, ethnic group, colour, sex, language, religion, political or any other opinion, national and social origin, fortune, birth or other status.

Art. 3 1. Every individual shall be equal before the law.

2. Every individual shall be entitled to equal protection of the law.

Art. 4 Human beings are inviolable. Every human being shall be entitled to respect for his life and the integrity of his person. No one may be arbitrarily deprived of this right.

Art. 5 Every individual shall have the right to the respect of the dignity inherent in a human being and to the recognition of his legal status. All forms of exploitation and degradation of man particularly slavery, slave trade, torture, cruel, inhuman or degrading punishment and treatment shall be prohibited.

Art. 6 Every individual shall have the right to liberty and to the security of his person. No one may be deprived of his freedom except for reasons and conditions previously laid down by law. In particular, no one may be arbitrarily arrested or detained.

Art. 7 1. Every individual shall have the right to have his cause heard. This comprises:

a) the right to an appeal to competent national organs against acts of violating his fundamental rights as recognized and guaranteed by conventions, laws, regulations and customs in force;
b) the right to be presumed innocent until proved guilty by a competent court or tribunal;
c) the right to defense, including the right to be defended by counsel of his choice;
d) the right to be tried within a reasonable time by an impartial court or tribunal.

2. No one may be condemned for an act or omission which did not constitute a legally punishable offence at the time it was committed. No penalty may be inflicted for an offence for which no provision was made at the time it was committed. Punishment is personal and can be imposed only on the offender.

Art. 8 Freedom of conscience, the profession and free practice of religion shall be guaranteed. No one may, subject to law and order, be submitted to measures restricting the exercise of these freedoms.

Art. 9 1. Every individual shall have the right to receive information.

2. Every individual shall have the right to express and disseminate his opinions within the law.

Art. 10 1. Every individual shall have the right to free association provided that he abides by the law.

2. Subject to the obligation of solidarity provided for in Article 29 no one may be compelled to join an association.

Art. 11 Every individual shall have the right to assemble freely with others. The exercise of this right shall be subject only to necessary restrictions provided for by law in particular those enacted in the interest of national security, the safety, health, ethics and rights and freedoms of others.

Art. 12 1. Every individual shall have the right to freedom of movement and residence within the borders of a State provided he abides by the law.

2. Every individual shall have the right to leave any country including his own, and to return to his country. This right may only be subject to restrictions, provided for by law for the protection of national security, law and order, public health or morality.

3. Every individual shall have the right, when persecuted, to seek and obtain asylum in other countries in accordance with the laws of those countries and international conventions.

4. A non-national legally admitted in a territory of a State Party to the present Charter, may only be expelled from it by virtue of a decision taken in accordance with the law.
5. The mass expulsion of non-nationals shall be prohibited. Mass expulsion shall be that which is aimed at national, racial, ethnic or religious groups.
Art. 13 1. Every citizen shall have the right to participate freely in the government of his country, either directly or through freely chosen representatives in accordance with the provisions of the law.
2. Every citizen shall have the right of equal access to the public service of his country.
3. Every individual shall have the right of access to public property and services in strict equality of all persons before the law.
Art. 14 The right to property shall be guaranteed. It may only be encroached upon in the interest of public need or in the general interest of the community and in accordance with the provisions of appropriate laws.
Art. 15 Every individual shall have the right to work under equitable and satisfactory conditions, and shall receive equal pay for equal work.
Art. 16 1. Every individual shall have the right to enjoy the best attainable state of physical and mental health.
2. State Parties to the present Charter shall take the necessary measures to protect the health of their people and to ensure that they receive medical attention when they are sick.
Art. 17 1. Every individual shall have the right to education.
2. Every individual may freely, take part in the cultural life of his community.
3. The promotion and protection of morals and traditional values recognized by the community shall be the duty of the State.
Art. 18 1. The family shall be the natural unit and basis of society. It shall be protected by the State which shall take care of its physical health and moral.
2. The State shall have the duty to assist the family which is the custodian of morals and traditional values recognized by the community.
3. The State shall ensure the elimination of every discrimination against women and also ensure the protection of the rights of women and the child as stipulated in international declarations and conventions.
4. The aged and the disabled shall also have the right to special measures of protection in keeping with their physical or moral needs.
Art. 19 All peoples shall be equal; they shall enjoy the same respect and shall have the same rights. Nothing shall justify the domination of a people by another.
Art. 20 1. All peoples shall have the right to existence. They shall have the unquestionable and inalienable right to self-determination. They shall freely

determine their political status and shall pursue their economic and social development according to the policy they have freely chosen.
2. Colonized or oppressed peoples shall have the right to free themselves from the bonds of domination by resorting to any means recognized by the international community.
3. All peoples shall have the right to the assistance of the State Parties to the present Charter in their liberation struggle against foreign domination, be it political, economic or cultural.
Art. 21 1. All peoples shall freely dispose of their wealth and natural resources. This right shall be exercised in the exclusive interest of the people. In no case shall a people be deprived of it.
2. In case of spoilation the dispossessed people shall have the right to the lawful recovery of its property as well as to an adequate compensation.
3. The free disposal of wealth and natural resources shall be exercised without prejudice to the obligation of promoting international economic cooperation based on mutual respect, equitable exchange and the principles of international law.
4. State Parties to the present Charter shall individually and collectively exercise the right to free disposal of their wealth and natural resources with a view to strengthening African unity and solidarity.
5. State Parties to the present Charter shall undertake to eliminate all forms of foreign economic exploitation particularly that practiced by international monopolies so as to enable their peoples to fully benefit from the advantages derived from their national resources.
Art. 22 1. All peoples shall have the right to their economic, social and cultural development with due regard to their freedom and identity and in the equal enjoyment of the common heritage of mankind.
2. States shall have the duty, individually or collectively, to ensure the exercise of the right to development.
Art. 23 1. All peoples shall have the right to national and international peace and security. The principles of solidarity and friendly relations implicitly affirmed by the Charter of the United Nations and reaffirmed by that of the Organization of African Unity shall govern relations between States.
2. For the purpose of strengthening peace, solidarity and friendly relations, State Parties to the present Charter shall ensure that:
(a) any individual enjoying the right of asylum under Article 12 of the present Charter shall not engage in subversive activities against his country of origin or any other State party to the present Charter;

(b) their territories shall not be used as bases for subversive or terrorist activities against the people of any other State party to the present Charter.

Art. 24 All peoples shall have the right to a general satisfactory environment favorable to their development.

Art. 25 State parties to the present Charter shall have the duty to promote and ensure through teaching, education and publication, the respect of the rights and freedoms contained in the present Charter and to see to it that these freedoms and rights as well as corresponding obligations and duties are understood.

Art. 26 State Parties to the present Charter shall have the duty to guarantee the independence of the Courts and shall allow the establishment and improvement of appropriate national institutions entrusted with the promotion and protection of the rights and freedoms guaranteed by the present Charter.

Chapter II: Duties

Art. 27 1. Every individual shall have duties towards his family and society, the State and other legally recognized communities and the international community.

2. The rights and freedoms of each individual shall be exercised with due regard to the rights of others, collective security, morality and common interest.

Art. 28 Every individual shall have the duty to respect and consider his fellow beings without discrimination, and to maintain relations aimed at promoting, safeguarding and reinforcing mutual respect and tolerance.

Art. 29 The individual shall also have the duty:

1. To preserve the harmonious development of the family and to work for the cohesion and respect of the family; to respect his parents at all times, to maintain them in case of need;
2. To serve his national community by placing his physical and intellectual abilities at its service;
3. Not to compromise the security of the State whose national or resident he is;
4. To preserve and strengthen social and national solidarity, particularly when the latter is threatened;
5. To preserve and strengthen the national independence and the territorial integrity of his country and to contribute to its defense in accordance with the law;
6. To work to the best of his abilities and competence, and to pay taxes imposed by law in the interest of the society;
7. To preserve and strengthen positive African cultural values in his relations with other members of the society, in the spirit of tolerance, dialogue and

consultation and, in general, to contribute to the promotion of the moral well being of society;
8. To contribute to the best of his abilities, at all times and at all levels, to the promotion and achievement of African unity.

Part II: Measures of Safeguard

Chapter 1: Establishment and Organization of the African Commission on Human and Peoples' Rights

Art. 30 An African Commission on Human and Peoples' Rights, hereinafter called "the Commission", shall be established within the Organization of African Unity to promote human and peoples' rights and ensure their protection in Africa.

Art. 31 1. The Commission shall consist of eleven members chosen from amongst African personalities of the highest reputation, known for their high morality, integrity, impartiality and competence in matters of human and peoples' rights; particular consideration being given to persons having legal experience.
2. The members of the Commission shall serve in their personal capacity.

Art. 32 The Commission shall not include more than one national of the same State.

Art. 33 The members of the Commission shall be elected by secret ballot by the Assembly of Heads of State and Government, from a list of persons nominated by the State parties to the present Charter.

Art. 34 Each State party to the present Charter may not nominate more than two candidates. The candidates must have the nationality of one of the State parties to the present Charter. When two candidates are nominated by a State, one of them may not be a national of that State.

Art. 35 1. The Secretary General of the Organization of African Unity shall invite State parties to the present Charter at least four months before the elections to nominate candidates;
2. The Secretary General of the Organization of African Unity shall make an alphabetical list of the persons thus nominated and communicate it to the Heads of State and Government at least one month before the elections.

Art. 36 The members of the Commission shall be elected for a six year period and shall be eligible for re-election. However, the term of office of four of the members elected at the first election shall terminate after two years and the term of office of three others, at the end of four years.

Art. 37 Immediately after the first election, the Chairman of the Assembly of Heads of State and Government of the Organization of African Unity shall draw lots to decide the names of those members referred to in Article 36.
Art. 38 After their election, the members of the Commission shall make a solemn declaration to discharge their duties impartially and faithfully.
Art. 39 1. In case of death or resignation of a member of the Commission, the Chairman of the Commission shall immediately inform the Secretary General of the Organization of African Unity, who shall declare the seat vacant from the date of death or from the date on which the resignation takes effect.
2. If, in the unanimous opinion of other members of the Commission, a member has stopped discharging his duties for any reason other than a temporary absence, the Chairman of the Commission shall inform the Secretary General of the Organization of African Unity, who shall then declare the seat vacant.
3. In each of the cases anticipated above, the Assembly of Heads of State and Government shall replace the member whose seat became vacant for the remaining period of his term unless the period is less than six months.
Art. 40 Every member of the Commission shall be in office until the date his successor assumes office.
Art. 41 The Secretary General of the Organization of African Unity shall appoint the Secretary of the Commission. He shall provide the staff and services necessary for the effective discharge of the duties of the Commission. The Organization of African Unity shall bear the cost of the staff and services.
Art. 42 1. The Commission shall elect its Chairman and Vice Chairman for a two-year period. They shall be eligible for re-election.
2. The Commission shall lay down its rules of procedure.
3. Seven members shall form the quorum.
4. In case of an equality of votes, the Chairman shall have a casting vote.
5. The Secretary-General may attend the meetings of the Commission. He shall neither participate in deliberations nor shall he be entitled to vote. The Chairman of the Commission may, however, invite him to speak.
Art. 43 In discharging their duties, members of the Commission shall enjoy diplomatic privileges and immunities provided for in the General Convention on the Privileges and Immunities of the Organization of African Unity.
Art. 44 Provision shall be made for the emoluments and allowances of the members of the Commission in the Regular Budget of the Organization of African Unity.

Chapter II: Mandate of the Commission

Art. 45 The functions of the Commission shall be:
1. To promote Human and Peoples' Rights and in particular:

a) to collect documents, undertake studies and researches on African problems in the field of human and peoples' rights, organize seminars, symposia and conferences, disseminate information, encourage national and local institutions concerned with human and peoples' rights, and should the case arise, give its views or make recommendations to Governments.
b) to formulae and lay down, principles and rules aimed at solving legal problems relating to human and peoples' rights and fundamental freedoms upon which African Governments may base their legislations.
c) co-operate with other African and international institutions concerned with the promotion and protection of human and peoples' rights.

2. Ensure the protection of human and peoples' rights under conditions laid down by the present Charter.
3. Interpret all the provisions of the present Charter at the request of a State Party, an institution of the OAU or an African organization recognized by the OAU.
4. Perform any other tasks which may be entrusted to it by the Assembly of Heads of State and Government.

Chapter III: Procedure of the Commission

Art. 46 The Commission may resort to any appropriate method of investigation; it may hear from the Secretary-General of the Organization of African Unity or any other person capable of enlightening it.

Communication from States

Art. 47 If a State party to the present Charter has good reasons to believe that another State party to this Charter has violated the provisions of the Charter, it may draw, by written communication, the attention of that State to the matter. This communication shall also be addressed to the Secretary-General of the OAU and to the Chairman of the Commission. Within three months of the receipt of the communication, the State to which the communication is addressed shall give the enquiring State, written explanation or statement elucidating the matter. This should include as much as possible relevant information relating to the laws and rules of procedure applied and applicable and the redress already given or course of action available.
Art. 48 If within three months from the date on which the original communication is received by the State to which it is addressed, the issue is not settled to the satisfaction of the two States involved through bilateral negotiation or by any other peaceful procedure, either State shall have the right to submit the matter to the Commission through the Chairman and shall notify the other States involved.

Art. 49 Notwithstanding the provisions of Article 47, if a State party to the present Charter considers that another State party has violated the provisions of the Charter, it may refer the matter directly to the Commission by addressing a communication to the Chairman, to the Secretary-General of the Organization of African Unity and the State concerned.
Art. 50 The Commission can only deal with a matter submitted to it after making sure that all local remedies, if they exist, have been exhausted, unless it is obvious to the Commission that the procedure of achieving these remedies would be unduly prolonged.
Art. 51 1. The Commission may ask the State concerned to provide it with all relevant information.
2. When the Commission is considering the matter, States concerned may be represented before it and submit written or oral representations.
Art. 52 After having obtained from the States concerned and from other sources all the information it deems necessary and after having tried all appropriate means to reach an amicable solution based on the respect of Human and Peoples' Rights, the Commission shall prepare, within a reasonable period of time from the notification referred to in Article 48, a report stating the facts and its findings. This report shall be sent to the States concerned and communicated to the Assembly of Heads of State and Government.
Art. 53 While transmitting its report, the Commission may make to the Assembly of Heads of State and Government such recommendations as it deems useful.
Art. 54 The Commission shall submit to each Ordinary Session of the Assembly of Heads of State and Government a report on its activities.

Other Communications

Art. 55 1. Before each Session, the Secretary of the Commission shall make a list of the communications other than those of State parties to the present Charter and transmit them to the Members of the Commission, who shall indicate which communications should be considered by the Commission.
2. A communication shall be considered by the Commission if a simple majority of its members so decide.
Art. 56 Communications relating to human and peoples' rights referred to in Article 55 received by the Commission, shall be considered if they:

1. indicate their authors even if the latter requests anonymity,
2. are compatible with the Charter of the Organization of African Unity or with the present Charter,

3. are not written in disparaging or insulting language directed against the State concerned and its institutions or to the Organization of African Unity,
4. are not based exclusively on news disseminated through the mass media,
5. are sent after exhausting local remedies, if any, unless it is obvious that this procedure is unduly prolonged,
6. are submitted within a reasonable period from the time local remedies are exhausted or from the date the Commission is seized with the matter, and
7. do not deal with cases which have been settled by these States involved in accordance with the principles of the Charter of the United Nations, or the Charter of the Organization of African Unity or the provisions of the present Charter.

Art. 57 Prior to any substantive consideration, all communications shall be brought to the knowledge of the State concerned by the Chairman of the Commission.

Art. 58 1. When it appears after deliberations of the Commission that one or more communications apparently relate to special cases which reveal the existence of a series of serious or massive violations of human and peoples' rights, the Commission shall draw the attention of the Assembly of Heads of State and Government to these special cases.

2. The Assembly of Heads of State and Government may then request the Commission to undertake an in-depth study of these cases and make a factual report, accompanied by its finding and recommendations.

3. A case of emergency duly noticed by the Commission shall be submitted by the latter to the Chairman of the Assembly of Heads of State and Government who may request an in-depth study.

Art. 59 1. All measures taken within the provisions of the present Chapter shall remain confidential until such a time as the Assembly of Heads of State and Government shall otherwise decide.

2. However, the report shall be published by the Chairman of the Commission upon the decision of the Assembly of Heads of State and Government.

3. The report on the activities of the Commission shall be published by its Chairman after it has been considered by the Assembly of Heads of State and Government.

Chapter IV: Applicable Principles

Art. 60 The Commission shall draw inspiration from international law on human and peoples' rights, particularly from the provisions of various African instruments on human and peoples' rights, the Charter of the United Nations, the Charter of the Organization of African Unity, the Universal Declaration of Human Rights, other instruments adopted by the United Nations and by African countries in the field of human and peoples' rights as well as from the provisions of various instruments adopted within the Specialized Agencies of the United Nations of which the parties to the present Charter are members.

Art. 61 The Commission shall also take into consideration, as subsidiary measures to determine the principles of law, other general or special international conventions, laying down rules expressly recognized by member states of the Organization of African Unity, African practices consistent with international norms on human and peoples' rights, customs generally accepted as law, general principles of law recognized by African states as well as legal precedents and doctrine.

Art. 62 Each State party shall undertake to submit every two years, from the date the present Charter comes into force, a report on the legislative or other measures taken with a view to giving effects to the rights and freedoms recognized and guaranteed by the present Charter.

Art. 63 1. The present Charter shall be open to signature, ratification or adherence of the member states of the Organization of African Unity.

2. The instruments of ratification or adherence to the present Charter shall be deposited with the Secretary General of the Organization of African Unity.

3. The present Charter shall come into force three months after the reception by the Secretary General of the instruments of ratification or adherence of a simple majority of the member states of the Organization of African Unity.

Part III: General Provisions

Art. 64 1. After the coming into force of the present Charter, members of the Commission shall be elected in accordance with the relevant Articles of the present Charter.

2. The Secretary General of the Organization of African Unity shall convene the first meeting of the Commission at the Headquarters of the Organization within three months of the constitution of the Commission. Thereafter, the Commission shall be convened by its Chairman whenever necessary but at least once a year.

Art. 65 For each of the States that will ratify or adhere to the present Charter after its coming into force, the Charter shall take effect three months after the date of the deposit by that State of the instrument of ratification or adherence.

Art. 66 Special protocols or agreements may, if necessary, supplement the provisions of the present Charter.

Art. 67 The Secretary General of the Organization of African Unity shall inform member states of the Organization of the deposit of each instrument of ratification or adherence.

Art. 68 The present Charter may be amended if a State party makes a written request to that effect to the Secretary General of the Organization of African Unity. The Assembly of Heads of State and Government may only consider the draft amendment after all the States parties have been duly informed of it and the Commission has given its opinion on it at the request of the sponsoring State. The amendment shall be approved by a simple majority of the State parties. It shall come into force for each State which has accepted it in accordance with its constitutional procedure three months after the Secretary General has received notice of the acceptance.

CHAPTER 13

African Charter on the Rights and Welfare of the Child

Adopted by the Organization of African Unity at its 26th Assembly of Heads of State and Government in Addis Ababa, Ethiopia on 11 July 1990
Entry into force 29 November 1999

Preamble

The African Member States of the Organization of African Unity, Parties to the present Charter entitled "African Charter on the Rights and Welfare of the Child",

Considering that the Charter of the Organization of African Unity recognizes the paramountcy of Human Rights and the African Charter on Human and People's Rights proclaimed and agreed that everyone is entitled to all the rights and freedoms recognized and guaranteed therein, without distinction of any kind such as race, ethnic group, colour. sex, language, religion, political or any other opinion, national and social origin, fortune, birth or other status,

Recalling the Declaration on the Rights and Welfare of the African Child (AHG/ST.4 Rev.1) adopted by the Assembly of Heads of State and Government of the Organization of African Unity, at its Sixteenth Ordinary Session in Monrovia, Liberia. from 17 to 20 July, 1979, recognized the need to take all appropriate measures to promote and protect the rights and welfare of the African Child,

Noting with concern that the situation of most African children, remains critical due to the unique factors of their socio-economic, cultural, traditional and developmental circumstances, natural disasters, armed conflicts, exploitation and hunger, and on account of the child's physical and mental immaturity he/she needs special safeguards and care,

Recognizing that the child occupies a unique and privileged position in the African society and that for the full and harmonious development of his personality, the child should grow up in a family environment in an atmosphere of happiness, love and understanding,

Recognizing that the child, due to the needs of his physical and mental development requires particular care with regard to health, physical, mental, moral and social development, and requires legal protection in conditions of freedom, dignity and security,

 | DOI:10.1163/9789004681224_023

Taking into consideration the virtues of their cultural heritage, historical background and the values of the African civilization which should inspire and characterize their reflection on the concept of the rights and welfare of the child,

Considering that the promotion and protection of the rights and welfare of the child also implies the performance of duties on the part of everyone,

Reaffirming adherence to the principles of the rights and welfare of the child contained in the declaration, conventions and other instruments of the Organization of African Unity and in the United Nations and in particular the United Nations Convention on the Rights of the Child; and the OAU Heads of State and Government's Declaration on the Rights and Welfare of the African Child,

Have agreed as follows:

Part 1: Rights and Duties

Chapter 1: Rights and Welfare of the Child

Article 1 – Obligation of States Parties

1. The Member States of the Organization of African Unity Parties to the present Charter shall recognize the rights, freedoms and duties enshrined in this Charter and shall undertake to the necessary steps, in accordance with their Constitutional processes and with the provisions of the present Charter, to adopt such legislative or other measures as may be necessary to give effect to the provisions of this Charter.
2. Nothing in this Charter shall affect any provisions that are more conductive to the realization of the rights and welfare of the child contained in the law of a State Party or in any other international Convention or agreement in force in that State.
3. Any custom, tradition, cultural or religious practice that is inconsistent with the rights, duties and obligations contained in the present Charter shall to the extent of such inconsistency be discouraged.

Article 2 – Definition of a Child

For the purposes of this Charter, a child means every human being below the age of 18 years.

Article 3 – Non-discrimination

Every child shall be entitled to the enjoyment of the rights and freedoms recognized and guaranteed in this Charter irrespective of the child's or his/her parents' or legal guardians' race, ethnic group, colour, sex, language, religion, political or other opinion, national and social origin, fortune, birth or other status.

Article 4 – Best Interests of the Child

1. In all actions concerning the child undertaken by any person or authority the best interests of the child shall be the primary consideration.
2. In all judicial or administrative proceedings affecting a child who is capable of communicating his/her own views, and opportunity shall be provided for the views of the child to be heard either directly or through an impartial representative as a party to the proceedings, and those views shall be taken into consideration by the relevant authority in accordance with the provisions of appropriate law.

Article 5 – Survival and Development

1. Every child has an inherent right to life. This right shall be protected by law.
2. States Parties to the present Charter shall ensure, to the maximum extent possible, the survival, protection and development of the child.
3. Death sentence shall not be pronounced for crimes committed by children.

Article 6 – Name and Nationality

1. Every child shall have the right from his birth to a name.
2. Every child shall be registered immediately after birth.
3. Every child has the right to acquire a nationality.
4. States Parties to the present Charter shall undertake to ensure that their Constitutional legislation recognize the principles according to which a child shall acquire the nationality of the State in the territory of which he has been born if, at the time of the child's birth, he is not granted nationality by any other State in accordance with its laws.

Article 7 – Freedom of Expression

Every child who is capable of communicating his or her own views shall be assured the rights to express his opinions freely in all matters and to disseminate his opinions subject to such restrictions as are prescribed by laws.

Article 8 – Freedom of Association

Every child shall have the right to free association and freedom of peaceful assembly in conformity with the law.

Article 9 – Freedom of Thought, Conscience and Religion

1. Every child shall have the right to freedom of thought, conscience and religion.
2. Parents, and where applicable, legal guardians shall have a duty to provide guidance and direction in the exercise of these rights having regard to the evolving capacities, and best interests of the child.
3. States Parties shall respect the duty of parents and where applicable, legal guardians to provide guidance and direction in the enjoyment of these rights subject to the national laws and policies.

Article 10 – Protection of Privacy

No child shall be subject to arbitrary or unlawful interference with his privacy, family, home or correspondence, or to the attacks upon his honour or reputation, provided that parents or legal guardians shall have the right to exercise reasonable supervision over the conduct of their children. The child has the right to the protection of the law against such interference or attacks.

Article 11 – Education

1. Every child shall have the right to education.
2. The education of the child shall be directed to:
(a) the promotion and development of the child's personality, talents and mental and physical abilities to their fullest potential;
(b) fostering respect for human rights and fundamental freedoms with particular reference to those set out in the provisions of various African instruments on human and peoples' rights and international human rights declarations and conventions;
(c) the preservation and strengthening of positive African morals, traditional values and cultures;
(d) the preparation of the child for responsible life in a free society, in the spirit of understanding tolerance, dialogue, mutual respect and friendship among all peoples ethnic, tribal and religious groups;
(e) the preservation of national independence and territorial integrity;
(f) the promotion and achievements of African Unity and Solidarity;
(g) the development of respect for the environment and natural resources;
(h) the promotion of the child's understanding of primary health care.
3. States Parties to the present Charter shall take all appropriate measures with a view to achieving the full realization of this right and shall in particular:
(a) provide free and compulsory basic education;
(b) encourage the development of secondary education in its different forms and to progressively make it free and accessible to all;

(c) make the higher education accessible to all on the basis of capacity and ability by every appropriate means;
(d) take measures to encourage regular attendance at schools and the reduction of drop-out rate;
(e) take special measures in respect of female, gifted and disadvantaged children, to ensure equal access to education for all sections of the community.

4. States Parties to the present Charter shall respect the rights and duties of parents, and where applicable, of legal guardians to choose for their children schools, other than those established by public authorities, which conform to such minimum standards may be approved by the state, to ensure the religious and moral education of the child in a manner with the evolving capacities of the child.
5. States Parties to the present Charter shall take all appropriate measures to ensure that a child who is subjected to schools or parental discipline shall be treated with humanity and with respect for the inherent dignity of the child and in conformity with the present Charter.
6. States Parties to the present Charter shall take all appropriate measures to ensure that children who become pregnant before completing their education shall have an opportunity to continue with their education on the basis of their individual ability.
7. No part of this Article shall be construed as to interfere with the liberty of individuals and bodies to establish and direct educational institutions subject to the observance of the principles set out in paragraph 1 of this Article and the requirement that the education given in such institutions shall conform to such minimum standards as may be laid down by the states.

Article 12 – Leisure, Recreation and Cultural Activities

1. States Parties recognize the right of the child to rest and leisure, to engage in play and recreational activities appropriate to the age of the child and to participate freely in cultural life and the arts.
2. States Parties shall respect and promote the right of the child to fully participate in cultural and artistic life and shall encourage the provision of appropriate and equal opportunities for cultural, artistic, recreational and leisure activity.

Article 13 – Handicapped Children

1. Every child who is mentally or physically disabled shall have the right to special measures of protection in keeping with his physical and moral needs and

under conditions which ensure his dignity, promote his self-reliance and active participation in the community.
2. States Parties to the present Charter shall ensure, subject to available resources, to a disabled child and to those responsible for his care, of assistance for which application is made and which is appropriate to the child's condition and in particular shall ensure that the disabled child has effective access to training, preparation for employment and recreation opportunities in a manner conducive to the child achieving the fullest possible social integration, individual development and his cultural and moral development.
3. The States Parties to the present Charter shall use their available resources with a view to achieving progressively the full convenience of the mentally and physically disabled person to movement and access to public highway buildings and other places to which the disabled may legitimately want to have access to.

Article 14 – Health and Health Services

1. Every child shall have the right to enjoy the best attainable state of physical, mental and spiritual health.
2. States Parties to the present Charter shall undertake to pursue the full implementation of this right and in particular shall take measures:

(a) to reduce infant and child mortality rate;
(b) to ensure the provision of necessary medical assistance and health care to all children with emphasis on the development of primary health care;
(c) to ensure the provision of adequate nutrition and safe drinking water;
(d) to combat disease and malnutrition within the framework of primary health care through the application of appropriate technology;
(e) to ensure appropriate health care for expectant and nursing mothers;
(f) to develop preventive health care and family life education and provision of service;
(g) to integrate basic health service programmes in national development plans;
(h) to ensure that all sectors of the society, in particular, parents, children, community leaders and community workers are informed and supported in the use of basic knowledge of child health and nutrition, the advantages of breastfeeding, hygiene and environmental sanitation and the prevention of domestic and other accidents;
(i) to ensure the meaningful participation of non-governmental organizations, local communities and the beneficiary population in the planning and management of a basic service programme for children;

(j) to support through technical and financial means, the mobilization of local community resources in the development of primary health care for children.

Article 15 – Child Labour

1. Every child shall be protected from all forms of economic exploitation and from performing any work that is likely to be hazardous or to interfere with the child's physical, mental, spiritual, moral, or social development.

2. States Parties to the present Charter take all appropriate legislative and administrative measures to ensure the full implementation of this Article which covers both the formal and informal sectors of employment and having regard to the relevant provisions of the International Labour Organization's instruments relating to children, States Parties shall in particular:

(a) provide through legislation, minimum wages for admission to every employment;

(b) provide for appropriate regulation of hours and conditions of employment;

(c) provide for appropriate penalties or other sanctions to ensure the effective enforcement of this Article;

(d) promote the dissemination of information on the hazards of child labour to all sectors of the community.

Article 16 – Protection against Child Abuse and Torture

1. States Parties to the present Charter shall take specific legislative, administrative, social and educational measures to protect the child from all forms of torture, inhuman or degrading treatment and especially physical or mental injury or abuse, neglect or maltreatment including sexual abuse, while in the care of a parent, legal guardian or school authority or any other person who has the care of the child.

2. Protective measures under this Article shall include effective procedures for the establishment of special monitoring units to provide necessary support for the child and for those who have the care of the child, as well as other forms of prevention and for identification, reporting referral investigation, treatment, and follow-up of instances of child abuse and neglect.

Article 17 – Administration of Juvenile Justice

1. Every child accused or found guilty of having infringed penal law shall have the right to special treatment in a manner consistent with the child's sense of dignity and worth and which reinforces the child's respect for human rights and fundamental freedoms of others.

2. States Parties to the present Charter shall in particular:
(a) ensure that no child who is detained or imprisoned or otherwise deprived of his/her liberty is subjected to torture, inhuman or degrading treatment or punishment;
(b) ensure that children are separated from adults in their place of detention or imprisonment;
(c) ensure that every child accused of infringing the penal law:
  (i) shall be presumed innocent until duly recognized guilty;
  (ii) shall be informed promptly in a language that he understands and in detail of the charge against him, and shall be entitled to the assistance of an interpreter if he or she cannot understand the language used;
  (iii) shall be afforded legal and other appropriate assistance in the preparation and presentation of his defense;
  (iv) shall have the matter determined as speedily as possible by an impartial tribunal and if found guilty, be entitled to an appeal by a higher tribunal;
  (v) shall not be compelled to give testimony or confess guilt.
(d) prohibit the press and the public from trial.
3. The essential aim of treatment of every child during the trial and also if found guilty of infringing the penal law shall be his or her reformation, re-integration into his or her family and social rehabilitation.
4. There shall be a minimum age below which children shall be presumed not to have the capacity to infringe the penal law.

Article 18 – Protection of the Family

1. The family shall be the natural unit and basis of society. It shall enjoy the protection and support of the State for its establishment and development.
2. States Parties to the present Charter shall take appropriate steps to ensure equality of rights and responsibilities of spouses with regard to children during marriage and in the event of its dissolution. In case the dissolution, provision shall be made for the necessary protection of the child.
3. No child shall be deprived of maintenance by reference to the parents' marital status.

Article 19 – Parent Care and Protection

1. Every child shall be entitled to the enjoyment of parental care and protection and shall, whenever possible, have the right to reside with his or her parents. No child shall be separated from his parents against his will, except when a

judicial authority determines in accordance with the appropriate law, that such separation is in the best interest of the child.
2. Every child who is separated from one or both parents shall have the right to maintain personal relations and direct contact with both parents on a regular basis.
3. Where separation results from the action of a State Party, the State Party shall provide the child, or if appropriate, another member of the family with essential information concerning the whereabouts of the absent member or members of the family. States Parties shall also ensure that the submission of such a request shall not entail any adverse consequences for the person or persons in whose respect it is made.
4. Where a child is apprehended by a State Party, his parents or guardians shall, as soon as possible, be notified of such apprehension by that State Party.

Article 20 – Parental Responsibilities

1. Parents or other persons responsible for the child shall have the primary responsibility for the upbringing and development of the child and shall have the duty:
(a) to ensure that the best interests of the child are their basic concern at all times;
(b) to secure, within their abilities and financial capacities, conditions of living necessary to the child's development; and
(c) to ensure that domestic discipline is administered win humanity and in a manner consistent with the inherent dignity of the child.
2. States Parties to the present Charter shall in accordance with their means and national conditions take all appropriate measures;
(a) to assist parents and other persons responsible for the child and in case of need provide material assistance and support programmes particularly with regard to nutrition, health, education, clothing and housing;
(b) to assist parents and others responsible for the child in the performance of child-rearing and ensure the development of institutions responsible for providing care of children; and
(c) to ensure that the children of working parents are provided with care services and facilities.

Article 21 – Protection against Harmful Social and Cultural Practices

1. States Parties to the present Charter shall take all appropriate measures to eliminate harmful social and cultural practices affecting the welfare, dignity, normal growth and development of the child and in particular:

(a) those customs and practices prejudicial to the health or life of the child; and

(b) those customs and practices discriminatory to the child on the grounds of sex or other status.

2. Child marriage and the betrothal of girls and boys shall be prohibited and effective action, including legislation, shall be taken to specify the minimum age of marriage to be eighteen years and make registration of all marriages in an official registry compulsory.

Article 22 – Armed Conflicts

1. States Parties to this Charter shall undertake to respect and ensure respect for rules of international
humanitarian law applicable in armed conflicts which affect the child.

2. States Parties to the present Charter shall take all necessary measures to ensure that no child shall take a direct part in hostilities and refrain in particular, from recruiting any child.

3. States Parties to the present Charter shall, in accordance with their obligations under international humanitarian law, protect the civilian population in armed conflicts and shall take all feasible measures to ensure the protection and care of children who are affected by armed conflicts. Such rules shall also apply to children in situations of internal armed conflicts, tension and strife.

Article 23 – Refugee Children

1. States Parties to the present Charter shall take all appropriate measures to ensure that a child who is seeking refugee status or who is considered a refugee in accordance with applicable international or domestic law shall, whether unaccompanied or accompanied by parents, legal guardians or close relatives, receive appropriate protection and humanitarian assistance in the enjoyment of the rights set out in this Charter and other international human rights and humanitarian instruments to which the States are parties.

2. States Parties shall undertake to cooperate with existing international organizations which protect and assist refugees in their efforts to protect and assist such a child and to trace the parents or other close relatives or an unaccompanied refugee child in order to obtain information necessary for reunification with the family.

3. Where no parents, legal guardians or close relatives can be found, the child shall be accorded the same protection as any other child permanently or temporarily deprived of his family environment for any reason.

4. The provisions of this Article apply mutatis mutandis to internally displaced children whether through natural disaster, internal armed conflicts, civil strife, breakdown of economic and social order or howsoever caused.

Article 24 – Adoption

States Parties which recognize the system of adoption shall ensure that the best interest of the child shall be the paramount consideration and they shall:

(a) establish competent authorities to determine matters of adoption and ensure that the adoption is carried out in conformity with applicable laws and procedures and on the basis of all relevant and reliable information, that the adoption is permissible in view of the child's status concerning parents, relatives and guardians and that, if necessary, the appropriate persons concerned have given their informed consent to the adoption on the basis of appropriate counselling;

(b) recognize that inter-country adoption in those States who have ratified or adhered to the International Convention on the Rights of the Child or this Charter, may, as the last resort, be considered as an alternative means of a child's care, if the child cannot be placed in a foster or an adoptive family or cannot in any suitable manner be cared for in the child's country of origin;

(c) ensure that the child affected by inter-country adoption enjoys safeguards and standards equivalent to those existing in the case of national adoption;

(d) take all appropriate measures to ensure that, in inter-country adoption, the placement does not result in trafficking or improper financial gain for those who try to adopt a child;

(e) promote, where appropriate, the objectives of this Article by concluding bilateral or multilateral arrangements or agreements, and endeavour, within this framework to ensure that the placement of the child in another country is carried out by competent authorities or organs;

(f) establish a machinery to monitor the well-being of the adopted child.

Article 25 – Separation from Parents

1. Any child who is permanently or temporarily deprived of his family environment for any reason shall be entitled to special protection and assistance;

2. States Parties to the present Charter:

(a) shall ensure that a child who is parentless, or who is temporarily or permanently deprived of his or her family environment, or who in his or her best interest cannot be brought up or allowed to remain in that environment shall be provided with alternative family care, which could include, among others, foster placement, or placement in suitable institutions for the care of children;

(b) shall take all necessary measures to trace and re-unite children with parents or relatives where separation is caused by internal and external displacement arising from armed conflicts or natural disasters.

3. When considering alternative family care of the child and the best interests of the child, due regard shall be paid to the desirability of continuity in a child's up-bringing and to the child's ethnic, religious or linguistic background.

Article 26 – Protection against Apartheid and Discrimination

1. States Parties to the present Charter shall individually and collectively undertake to accord the highest priority to the special needs of children living under Apartheid and in States subject to military destabilization by the Apartheid regime.
2. States Parties to the present Charter shall individually and collectively undertake to accord the highest priority to the special needs of children living under regimes practising racial, ethnic, religious or other forms of discrimination as well as in States subject to military destabilization.
3. States Parties shall undertake to provide whenever possible, material assistance to such children and to direct their efforts towards the elimination of all forms of discrimination and Apartheid on the African Continent.

Article 27 – Sexual Exploitation

1. States Parties to the present Charter shall undertake to protect the child from all forms of sexual exploitation and sexual abuse and shall in particular take measures to prevent:

(a) the inducement, coercion or encouragement of a child to engage in any sexual activity;

(b) the use of children in prostitution or other sexual practices;

(c) the use of children in pornographic activities, performances and materials.

Article 28 – Drug Abuse

States Parties to the present Charter shall take all appropriate measures to protect the child from the use of narcotics and illicit use of psychotropic substances as defined in the relevant international treaties, and to prevent the use of children in the production and trafficking of such substances.

Article 29 – Sale, Trafficking and Abduction

States Parties to the present Charter shall take appropriate measures to prevent:

(a) the abduction, the sale of, or traffic in children for any purpose or in any form, by any person including parents or legal guardians of the child;

(b) the use of children in all forms of begging.

Article 30 – Children of Imprisoned Mothers

1. States Parties to the present Charter shall undertake to provide special treatment to expectant mothers and to mothers of infants and young children who have been accused or found guilty of infringing the penal law and shall in particular:

(a) ensure that a non-custodial sentence will always be first considered when sentencing such mothers;

(b) establish and promote measures alternative to institutional confinement for the treatment of such mothers;

(c) establish special alternative institutions for holding such mothers;

(d) ensure that a mother shall not be imprisoned with her child;

(e) ensure that a death sentence shall not be imposed on such mothers;

(f) the essential aim of the penitentiary system will be the reformation, the integration of the mother to the family and social rehabilitation.

Article 31 – Responsibility of the Child

Every child shall have responsibilities towards his family and society, the State and other legally recognized communities and the international community. The child, subject to his age and ability, and such limitations as may be contained in the present Charter, shall have the duty:

(a) to work for the cohesion of the family, to respect his parents, superiors and elders at all times and to assist them in case of need;

(b) to serve his national community by placing his physical and intellectual abilities at its service;

(c) to preserve and strengthen social and national solidarity;

(d) to preserve and strengthen African cultural values in his relations with other members of the society, in the spirit of tolerance, dialogue and consultation and to contribute to the moral well-being of society;

(e) to preserve and strengthen the independence and the integrity of his country;

(f) to contribute to the best of his abilities, at all times and at all levels, to the promotion and achievement of African Unity.

Part II

Chapter II: Establishment and Organization of the Committee on the Rights and Welfare of the Child

Article 32 – The Committee

An African Committee of Experts on the Rights and Welfare of the Child hereinafter called "the Committee" shall be established within the Organization of African Unity to promote and protect the rights and welfare of the child.

Article 33 – Composition

1. The Committee shall consist of 11 members of high moral standing, integrity, impartiality and competence in matters of the rights and welfare of the child.
2. The members of the Committee shall serve in their personal capacity.
3. The Committee shall not include more than one national of the same State.

Article 34 – Election

As soon as this Charter shall enter into force the members of the Committee shall be elected by secret ballot by the Assembly of Heads of State and Government from a list of persons nominated by the States Parties to the present Charter.

Article 35 – Candidates

Each State Party to the present Charter may nominate not more than two candidates. The candidates must have one of the nationalities of the States Parties to the present Charter. When two candidates are nominated by a State, one of them shall not be a national of that State.

Article 36

1. The Secretary-General of the Organization of African Unity shall invite States Parties to the present Charter to nominate candidates at least six months before the elections.
2. The Secretary-General of the Organization of African Unity shall draw up in alphabetical order, a list of persons nominated and communicate it to the Heads of State and Government at least two months before the elections.

Article 37 – Term of Office

1. The members of the Committee shall be elected for a term of five years and may not be re-elected, however, the term of four of the members elected at the first election shall expire after two years and the term of six others, after four years.

2. Immediately after the first election, the Chairman of the Assembly of Heads of State and Government of the Organization of African Unity shall draw lots to determine the names of those members referred to in sub-paragraph 1 of this Article.
3. The Secretary-General of the Organization of African Unity shall convene the first meeting of Committee at the Headquarters of the Organization within six months of the election of the members of the Committee, and thereafter the Committee shall be convened by its Chairman whenever necessary, at least once a year.

Article 38 – Bureau

1. The Committee shall establish its own Rules of Procedure.
2. The Committee shall elect its officers for a period of two years.
3. Seven Committee members shall form the quorum.
4. In case of an equality of votes, the Chairman shall have a casting vote.
5. The working languages of the Committee shall be the official languages of the OAU.

Article 39 – Vacancy

If a member of the Committee vacates his office for any reason other than the normal expiration of a term, the State which nominated that member shall appoint another member from among its nationals to serve for the remainder of the term – subject to the approval of the Assembly.

Article 40 – Secretariat

The Secretary-General of the Organization of African Unity shall appoint a Secretary for the Committee.

Article 41 – Privileges and Immunities

In discharging their duties, members of the Committee shall enjoy the privileges and immunities provided for in the General Convention on the Privileges and Immunities of the Organization of African Unity.

Chapter III: Mandate and Procedure of the Committee

Article 42 – Mandate

The functions of the Committee shall be:

(a) To promote and protect the rights enshrined in this Charter and in particular to:
  (i) collect and document information, commission interdisciplinary assessment of situations on African problems in

the fields of the rights and welfare of the child, organize meetings, encourage national and local institutions concerned with the rights and welfare of the child, and where necessary give its views and make recommendations to Governments;

(ii) formulate and lay down principles and rules aimed at protecting the rights and welfare of children in Africa;

(iii) cooperate with other African, International and Regional Institutions and Organizations concerned with the promotion and protection of the rights and welfare of the child.

(b) To monitor the implementation and ensure protection of the rights enshrined in this Charter.

(c) To interpret the provisions of the present Charter at the request of a State Party, an Institution of the Organization of African unity or any other person or Institution recognized by the Organization of African Unity, or any State Party.

(d) Perform such other task as may be entrusted to it by the Assembly of Heads of State and Government, Secretary-General of the OAU and any other organs of the OAU, or the United Nations.

Article 43 – Reporting Procedure

1. Every State Party to the present Charter shall undertake to submit to the Committee through the Secretary-General of the Organization of African Unity, reports on the measures they have adopted which give effect to the provisions of this Charter and on the progress made in the enjoyment of these rights:

(a) within two years of the entry into force of the Charter for the State Party concerned; and

(b) and thereafter, every three years.

2. Every report made under this Article shall:

(a) contain sufficient information on the implementation of the present Charter to provide the Committee with comprehensive understanding of the implementation of the Charter in the relevant country; and

(b) shall indicate factors and difficulties, if any, affecting the fulfillment of the obligations contained in the Charter.

3. A State Party which has submitted a comprehensive first report to the Committee need not, in its subsequent reports submitted in accordance with paragraph 1 (a) of this Article, repeat the basic information previously provided.

Article 44 – Communications

1. The Committee may receive communication, from any person, group or non-governmental organization recognized by the Organization of African Unity, by a Member State, or the United Nations relating to any matter covered by this Charter.
2. Every communication to the Committee shall contain the name and address of the author and shall be treated in confidence.

Article 45 – Investigations by the Committee

1. The Committee may, resort to any appropriate method of investigating any matter falling within the ambit of the present Charter, request from the States Parties any information relevant to the implementation of the Charter and may also resort to any appropriate method of investigating the measures the State Party has adopted to implement the Charter.
2. The Committee shall submit to each Ordinary Session of the Assembly of Heads of State and Government every two years, a report on its activities and on any communication made under Article 46 of this Charter.
3. The Committee shall publish its report after it has been considered by the Assembly of Heads of State and Government.
4. States Parties shall make the Committee's reports widely available to the public in their own countries.

Chapter IV: Miscellaneous Provisions

Article 46 – Sources of Inspiration

The Committee shall draw inspiration from International Law on Human Rights, particularly from the provisions of the African Charter on Human and Peoples' Rights, the Charter of the Organization of African Unity, the Universal Declaration on Human Rights, the International Convention on the Rights of the Child, and other instruments adopted by the United Nations and by African countries in the field of human rights, and from African values and traditions.

Article 47 – Signature, Ratification or Adherence

1. The present Charter shall be open to signature by all the Member States of the Organization of African Unity.
2. The present Charter shall be subject to ratification or adherence by Member States of the Organization of African Unity. The instruments of ratification or adherence to the present Charter shall be deposited with the Secretary-General of the Organization of African Unity.
3. The present Charter shall come into force 30 days after the reception by the Secretary-General of the Organization of African Unity of the instruments

of ratification or adherence of 15 Member States of the Organization of African Unity.

Article 48 – Amendment and Revision of the Charter

1. The present Charter may be amended or revised if any State Party makes a written request to that effect to the Secretary-General of the Organization of African Unity, provided that the proposed amendment is not submitted to the Assembly of Heads of State and Government for consideration until all the States Parties have been duly notified of it and the Committee has given its opinion on the amendment.
2. An amendment shall be approved by a simple majority of the States Parties.

CHAPTER 14

American Declaration of the Rights and Duties of Man

Adopted by the 9th International Conference of American States in Bogotá, Colombia, in April 1948

WHEREAS:

The American peoples have acknowledged the dignity of the individual, and their national constitutions recognize that juridical and political institutions, which regulate life in human society, have as their principal aim the protection of the essential rights of man and the creation of circumstances that will permit him to achieve spiritual and material progress and attain happiness;

The American States have on repeated occasions recognized that the essential rights of man are not derived from the fact that he is a national of a certain state, but are based upon attributes of his human personality;

The international protection of the rights of man should be the principal guide of an evolving American law;

The affirmation of essential human rights by the American States together with the guarantees given by the internal regimes of the states establish the initial system of protection considered by the American States as being suited to the present social and juridical conditions, not without a recognition on their part that they should increasingly strengthen that system in the international field as conditions become more favorable,

The Ninth International Conference of American States

AGREES:

To adopt the following

American Declaration of the Rights and Duties of Man

Preamble

All men are born free and equal, in dignity and in rights, and, being endowed by nature with reason and conscience, they should conduct themselves as brothers one to another.

The fulfillment of duty by each individual is a prerequisite to the rights of all. Rights and duties are interrelated in every social and political activity of

 | DOI:10.1163/9789004681224_024

man. While rights exalt individual liberty, duties express the dignity of that liberty.

Duties of a juridical nature presuppose others of a moral nature which support them in principle and constitute their basis.

Inasmuch as spiritual development is the supreme end of human existence and the highest expression thereof, it is the duty of man to serve that end with all his strength and resources.

Since culture is the highest social and historical expression of that spiritual development, it is the duty of man to preserve, practice and foster culture by every means within his power.

And, since moral conduct constitutes the noblest flowering of culture, it is the duty of every man always to hold it in high respect.

Chapter One: Rights

Article I – Right to Life, Liberty and Personal Security

Every human being has the right to life, liberty and the security of his person.

Article II – Right to Equality before Law

All persons are equal before the law and have the rights and duties established in this Declaration, without distinction as to race, sex, language, creed or any other factor.

Article III – Right to Religious Freedom and Worship

Every person has the right freely to profess a religious faith, and to manifest and practice it both in public and in private.

Article IV – Right to Freedom of Investigation, Opinion, Expression and Dissemination

Every person has the right to freedom of investigation, of opinion, and of the expression and dissemination of ideas, by any medium whatsoever.

Article V – Right to Protection of Honor, Personal Reputation, and Private and Family Life

Every person has the right to the protection of the law against abusive attacks upon his honor, his reputation, and his private and family life.

Article VI – Right to a Family and to Protection Thereof

Every person has the right to establish a family, the basic element of society, and to receive protection therefore.

Article VII – Right to Protection for Mothers and Children

All women, during pregnancy and the nursing period, and all children have the right to special protection, care and aid.

Article VIII – Right to Residence and Movement

Every person has the right to fix his residence within the territory of the state of which he is a national, to move about freely within such territory, and not to leave it except by his own will.

Article IX – Right to Inviolability of the Home

Every person has the right to the inviolability of his home.

Article X – Right to the Inviolability and Transmission of Correspondence

Every person has the right to the inviolability and transmission of his correspondence.

Article XI – Right to the Preservation of Health and to Well-Being

Every person has the right to the preservation of his health through sanitary and social measures relating to food, clothing, housing and medical care, to the extent permitted by public and community resources.

Article XII – Right to Education

Every person has the right to an education, which should be based on the principles of liberty, morality and human solidarity.

Likewise every person has the right to an education that will prepare him to attain a decent life, to raise his standard of living, and to be a useful member of society.

The right to an education includes the right to equality of opportunity in every case, in accordance with natural talents, merit and the desire to utilize the resources that the state or the community is in a position to provide.

Every person has the right to receive, free, at least a primary education.

Article XIII – Right to the Benefits of Culture

Every person has the right to take part in the cultural life of the community, to enjoy the arts, and to participate in the benefits that result from intellectual progress, especially scientific discoveries.

He likewise has the right to the protection of his moral and material interests as regards his inventions or any literary, scientific or artistic works of which he is the author.

Article XIV – Right to Work and to Fair Remuneration

Every person has the right to work, under proper conditions, and to follow his vocation freely, insofar as existing conditions of employment permit.

Every person who works has the right to receive such remuneration as will, in proportion to his capacity and skill, assure him a standard of living suitable for himself and for his family.

Article XV – Right to Leisure Time and to the Use Thereof

Every person has the right to leisure time, to wholesome recreation, and to the opportunity for advantageous use of his free time to his spiritual, cultural and physical benefit.

Article XVI – Right to Social Security

Every person has the right to social security which will protect him from the consequences of unemployment, old age, and any disabilities arising from causes beyond his control that make it physically or mentally impossible for him to earn a living.

Article XVII – Right to Recognition of Juridical Personality and Civil Rights

Every person has the right to be recognized everywhere as a person having rights and obligations, and to enjoy the basic civil rights.

Article XVIII – Right to a Fair Trial

Every person may resort to the courts to ensure respect for his legal rights. There should likewise be available to him a simple, brief procedure whereby the courts will protect him from acts of authority that, to his prejudice, violate any fundamental constitutional rights.

Article XIX – Right to Nationality

Every person has the right to the nationality to which he is entitled by law and to change it, if he so wishes, for the nationality of any other country that is willing to grant it to him.

Article XX – Right to Vote and to Participate in Government

Every person having legal capacity is entitled to participate in the government of his country, directly or through his representatives, and to take part in popular elections, which shall be by secret ballot, and shall be honest, periodic and free.

Article XXI – Right of Assembly

Every person has the right to assemble peaceably with others in a formal public meeting or an informal gathering, in connection with matters of common interest of any nature.

Article XXII – Right of Association

Every person has the right to associate with others to promote, exercise and protect his legitimate interests of a political, economic, religious, social, cultural, professional, labor union or other nature.

Article XXIII – Right to Property

Every person has a right to own such private property as meets the essential needs of decent living and helps to maintain the dignity of the individual and of the home.

Article XXIV – Right of Petition

Every person has the right to submit respectful petitions to any competent authority, for reasons of either general or private interest, and the right to obtain a prompt decision thereon.

Article XXV – Right of Protection from Arbitrary Arrest

No person may be deprived of his liberty except in the cases and according to the procedures established by pre-existing law.

No person may be deprived of liberty for nonfulfillment of obligations of a purely civil character.

Every individual who has been deprived of his liberty has the right to have the legality of his detention ascertained without delay by a court, and the right to be tried without undue delay or, otherwise, to be released. He also has the right to humane treatment during the time he is in custody.

Article XXVI – Right to Due Process of Law

Every accused person is presumed to be innocent until proved guilty.

Every person accused of an offense has the right to be given an impartial and public hearing, and to be tried by courts previously established in accordance with pre-existing laws, and not to receive cruel, infamous or unusual punishment.

Article XXVII – Right of Asylum

Every person has the right, in case of pursuit not resulting from ordinary crimes, to seek and receive asylum in foreign territory, in accordance with the laws of each country and with international agreements.

Article XXVIII – Scope of the Rights of Man

The rights of man are limited by the rights of others, by the security of all, and by the just demands of the general welfare and the advancement of democracy.

Chapter two: Duties

Article XXIX – Duties to Society

It is the duty of the individual so to conduct himself in relation to others that each and every one may fully form and develop his personality.

Article XXX – Duties toward Children and Parents

It is the duty of every person to aid, support, educate and protect his minor children, and it is the duty of children to honor their parents always and to aid, support and protect them when they need it.

Article XXXI – Duty to Receive Instruction

It is the duty of every person to acquire at least an elementary education.

Article XXXII – Duty to Vote

It is the duty of every person to vote in the popular elections of the country of which he is a national, when he is legally capable of doing so.

Article XXXIII – Duty to Obey the Law

It is the duty of every person to obey the law and other legitimate commands of the authorities of his country and those of the country in which he may be.

Article XXXIV – Duty to Serve the Community and the Nation

It is the duty of every able-bodied person to render whatever civil and military service his country may require for its defense and preservation, and, in case of public disaster, to render such services as may be in his power.

It is likewise his duty to hold any public office to which he may be elected by popular vote in the state of which he is a national.

Article XXXV – Duties with Respect to Social Security and Welfare

It is the duty of every person to cooperate with the state and the community with respect to social security and welfare, in accordance with his ability and with existing circumstances.

Article XXXVI – Duty to Pay Taxes

It is the duty of every person to pay the taxes established by law for the support of public services.

Article XXXVII – Duty to Work

It is the duty of every person to work, as far as his capacity and possibilities permit, in order to obtain the means of livelihood or to benefit his community.

Article XXXVIII – Duty to Refrain from Political Activities in a Foreign Country

It is the duty of every person to refrain from taking part in political activities that, according to law, are reserved exclusively to the citizens of the state in which he is an alien.

CHAPTER 15

American Convention on Human Rights

Adopted by the Organization of American States at the Inter-American Specialized Conference on Human Rights, San José, Costa Rica, on 22 November 1969
Entry into force 18 July 1978, in accordance with article 74(2)

Preamble

The American states signatory to the present Convention,

Reaffirming their intention to consolidate in this hemisphere, within the framework of democratic institutions, a system of personal liberty and social justice based on respect for the essential rights of man;

Recognizing that the essential rights of man are not derived from one's being a national of a certain state, but are based upon attributes of the human personality, and that they therefore justify international protection in the form of a convention reinforcing or complementing the protection provided by the domestic law of the American states;

Considering that these principles have been set forth in the Charter of the Organization of American States, in the American Declaration of the Rights and Duties of Man, and in the Universal Declaration of Human Rights, and that they have been reaffirmed and refined in other international instruments, worldwide as well as regional in scope;

Reiterating that, in accordance with the Universal Declaration of Human Rights, the ideal of free men enjoying freedom from fear and want can be achieved only if conditions are created whereby everyone may enjoy his economic, social, and cultural rights, as well as his civil and political rights; and

Considering that the Third Special Inter-American Conference (Buenos Aires, 1967) approved the incorporation into the Charter of the Organization itself of broader standards with respect to economic, social, and educational rights and resolved that an inter-American convention on human rights should determine the structure, competence, and procedure of the organs responsible for these matters,

Have agreed upon the following:

DOI:10.1163/9789004681224_025

Part I: State Obligations and Rights Protected

Chapter I: General Obligations

Article 1 – Obligation to Respect Rights

1. The States Parties to this Convention undertake to respect the rights and freedoms recognized herein and to ensure to all persons subject to their jurisdiction the free and full exercise of those rights and freedoms, without any discrimination for reasons of race, color, sex, language, religion, political or other opinion, national or social origin, economic status, birth, or any other social condition.
2. For the purposes of this Convention, "person" means every human being.

Article 2 – Domestic Legal Effects

Where the exercise of any of the rights or freedoms referred to in Article 1 is not already ensured by legislative or other provisions, the States Parties undertake to adopt, in accordance with their constitutional processes and the provisions of this Convention, such legislative or other measures as may be necessary to give effect to those rights or freedoms.

Chapter II: Civil and Political Rights

Article 3 – Right to Juridical Personality

Every person has the right to recognition as a person before the law.

Article 4 – Right to Life

1. Every person has the right to have his life respected. This right shall be protected by law and, in general, from the moment of conception. No one shall be arbitrarily deprived of his life.
2. In countries that have not abolished the death penalty, it may be imposed only for the most serious crimes and pursuant to a final judgment rendered by a competent court and in accordance with a law establishing such punishment, enacted prior to the commission of the crime. The application of such punishment shall not be extended to crimes to which it does not presently apply.
3. The death penalty shall not be reestablished in states that have abolished it.
4. In no case shall capital punishment be inflicted for political offenses or related common crimes.
5. Capital punishment shall not be imposed upon persons who, at the time the crime was committed, were under 18 years of age or over 70 years of age; nor shall it be applied to pregnant women.
6. Every person condemned to death shall have the right to apply for amnesty, pardon, or commutation of sentence, which may be granted in all cases. Capital

punishment shall not be imposed while such a petition is pending decision by the competent authority.

Article 5 – Right to Humane Treatment

1. Every person has the right to have his physical, mental, and moral integrity respected.
2. No one shall be subjected to torture or to cruel, inhuman, or degrading punishment or treatment. All persons deprived of their liberty shall be treated with respect for the inherent dignity of the human person.
3. Punishment shall not be extended to any person other than the criminal.
4. Accused persons shall, save in exceptional circumstances, be segregated from convicted persons, and shall be subject to separate treatment appropriate to their status as unconvicted persons.
5. Minors while subject to criminal proceedings shall be separated from adults and brought before specialized tribunals, as speedily as possible, so that they may be treated in accordance with their status as minors.
6. Punishments consisting of deprivation of liberty shall have as an essential aim the reform and social readaptation of the prisoners.

Article 6 – Freedom from Slavery

1. No one shall be subject to slavery or to involuntary servitude, which are prohibited in all their forms, as are the slave trade and traffic in women.
2. No one shall be required to perform forced or compulsory labor. This provision shall not be interpreted to mean that, in those countries in which the penalty established for certain crimes is deprivation of liberty at forced labor, the carrying out of such a sentence imposed by a competent court is prohibited. Forced labor shall not adversely affect the dignity or the physical or intellectual capacity of the prisoner.
3. For the purposes of this article, the following do not constitute forced or compulsory labor:

a. work or service normally required of a person imprisoned in execution of a sentence or formal decision passed by the competent judicial authority. Such work or service shall be carried out under the supervision and control of public authorities, and any persons performing such work or service shall not be placed at the disposal of any private party, company, or juridical person;

b. military service and, in countries in which conscientious objectors are recognized, national service that the law may provide for in lieu of military service;

c. service exacted in time of danger or calamity that threatens the existence or the well-being of the community; or
d. work or service that forms part of normal civic obligations.

Article 7 – Right to Personal Liberty

1. Every person has the right to personal liberty and security.
2. No one shall be deprived of his physical liberty except for the reasons and under the conditions established beforehand by the constitution of the State Party concerned or by a law established pursuant thereto.
3. No one shall be subject to arbitrary arrest or imprisonment.
4. Anyone who is detained shall be informed of the reasons for his detention and shall be promptly notified of the charge or charges against him.
5. Any person detained shall be brought promptly before a judge or other officer authorized by law to exercise judicial power and shall be entitled to trial within a reasonable time or to be released without prejudice to the continuation of the proceedings. His release may be subject to guarantees to assure his appearance for trial.
6. Anyone who is deprived of his liberty shall be entitled to recourse to a competent court, in order that the court may decide without delay on the lawfulness of his arrest or detention and order his release if the arrest or detention is unlawful. In States Parties whose laws provide that anyone who believes himself to be threatened with deprivation of his liberty is entitled to recourse to a competent court in order that it may decide on the lawfulness of such threat, this remedy may not be restricted or abolished. The interested party or another person in his behalf is entitled to seek these remedies.
7. No one shall be detained for debt. This principle shall not limit the orders of a competent judicial authority issued for nonfulfillment of duties of support.

Article 8 – Right to a Fair Trial

1. Every person has the right to a hearing, with due guarantees and within a reasonable time, by a competent, independent, and impartial tribunal, previously established by law, in the substantiation of any accusation of a criminal nature made against him or for the determination of his rights and obligations of a civil, labor, fiscal, or any other nature.
2. Every person accused of a criminal offense has the right to be presumed innocent so long as his guilt has not been proven according to law. During the proceedings, every person is entitled, with full equality, to the following minimum guarantees:

a. the right of the accused to be assisted without charge by a translator or interpreter, if he does not understand or does not speak the language of the tribunal or court;
b. prior notification in detail to the accused of the charges against him;
c. adequate time and means for the preparation of his defense;
d. the right of the accused to defend himself personally or to be assisted by legal counsel of his own choosing, and to communicate freely and privately with his counsel;
e. the inalienable right to be assisted by counsel provided by the state, paid or not as the domestic law provides, if the accused does not defend himself personally or engage his own counsel within the time period established by law;
f. the right of the defense to examine witnesses present in the court and to obtain the appearance, as witnesses, of experts or other persons who may throw light on the facts;
g. the right not to be compelled to be a witness against himself or to plead guilty; and
h. the right to appeal the judgment to a higher court.

3. A confession of guilt by the accused shall be valid only if it is made without coercion of any kind.
4. An accused person acquitted by a nonappealable judgment shall not be subjected to a new trial for the same cause.
5. Criminal proceedings shall be public, except insofar as may be necessary to protect the interests of justice.

Article 9 – Freedom from Ex Post Facto Laws

No one shall be convicted of any act or omission that did not constitute a criminal offense, under the applicable law, at the time it was committed. A heavier penalty shall not be imposed than the one that was applicable at the time the criminal offense was committed. If subsequent to the commission of the offense the law provides for the imposition of a lighter punishment, the guilty person shall benefit therefrom.

Article 10 – Right to Compensation

Every person has the right to be compensated in accordance with the law in the event he has been sentenced by a final judgment through a miscarriage of justice.

Article 11 – Right to Privacy

1. Everyone has the right to have his honor respected and his dignity recognized.

2. No one may be the object of arbitrary or abusive interference with his private life, his family, his home, or his correspondence, or of unlawful attacks on his honor or reputation.
3. Everyone has the right to the protection of the law against such interference or attacks.

Article 12 – Freedom of Conscience and Religion

1. Everyone has the right to freedom of conscience and of religion. This right includes freedom to maintain or to change one's religion or beliefs, and freedom to profess or disseminate one's religion or beliefs, either individually or together with others, in public or in private.
2. No one shall be subject to restrictions that might impair his freedom to maintain or to change his religion or beliefs.
3. Freedom to manifest one's religion and beliefs may be subject only to the limitations prescribed by law that are necessary to protect public safety, order, health, or morals, or the rights or freedoms of others.
4. Parents or guardians, as the case may be, have the right to provide for the religious and moral education of their children or wards that is in accord with their own convictions.

Article 13 – Freedom of Thought and Expression

1. Everyone has the right to freedom of thought and expression. This right includes freedom to seek, receive, and impart information and ideas of all kinds, regardless of frontiers, either orally, in writing, in print, in the form of art, or through any other medium of one's choice.
2. The exercise of the right provided for in the foregoing paragraph shall not be subject to prior censorship but shall be subject to subsequent imposition of liability, which shall be expressly established by law to the extent necessary to ensure:
   a. respect for the rights or reputations of others; or
   b. the protection of national security, public order, or public health or morals.
3. The right of expression may not be restricted by indirect methods or means, such as the abuse of government or private controls over newsprint, radio broadcasting frequencies, or equipment used in the dissemination of information, or by any other means tending to impede the communication and circulation of ideas and opinions.
4. Notwithstanding the provisions of paragraph 2 above, public entertainments may be subject by law to prior censorship for the sole purpose of regulating access to them for the moral protection of childhood and adolescence.

5. Any propaganda for war and any advocacy of national, racial, or religious hatred that constitute incitements to lawless violence or to any other similar action against any person or group of persons on any grounds including those of race, color, religion, language, or national origin shall be considered as offenses punishable by law.

Article 14 – Right of Reply

1. Anyone injured by inaccurate or offensive statements or ideas disseminated to the public in general by a legally regulated medium of communication has the right to reply or to make a correction using the same communications outlet, under such conditions as the law may establish.
2. The correction or reply shall not in any case remit other legal liabilities that may have been incurred.
3. For the effective protection of honor and reputation, every publisher, and every newspaper, motion picture, radio, and television company, shall have a person responsible who is not protected by immunities or special privileges.

Article 15 – Right of Assembly

The right of peaceful assembly, without arms, is recognized. No restrictions may be placed on the exercise of this right other than those imposed in conformity with the law and necessary in a democratic society in the interest of national security, public safety or public order, or to protect public health or morals or the rights or freedom of others.

Article 16 – Freedom of Association

1. Everyone has the right to associate freely for ideological, religious, political, economic, labor, social, cultural, sports, or other purposes.
2. The exercise of this right shall be subject only to such restrictions established by law as may be necessary in a democratic society, in the interest of national security, public safety or public order, or to protect public health or morals or the rights and freedoms of others.
3. The provisions of this article do not bar the imposition of legal restrictions, including even deprivation of the exercise of the right of association, on members of the armed forces and the police.

Article 17 – Rights of the Family

1. The family is the natural and fundamental group unit of society and is entitled to protection by society and the state.
2. The right of men and women of marriageable age to marry and to raise a family shall be recognized, if they meet the conditions required by domestic

laws, insofar as such conditions do not affect the principle of nondiscrimination established in this Convention.
3. No marriage shall be entered into without the free and full consent of the intending spouses.
4. The States Parties shall take appropriate steps to ensure the equality of rights and the adequate balancing of responsibilities of the spouses as to marriage, during marriage, and in the event of its dissolution. In case of dissolution, provision shall be made for the necessary protection of any children solely on the basis of their own best interests.
5. The law shall recognize equal rights for children born out of wedlock and those born in wedlock.

Article 18 – Right to a Name

Every person has the right to a given name and to the surnames of his parents or that of one of them. The law shall regulate the manner in which this right shall be ensured for all, by the use of assumed names if necessary.

Article 19 – Rights of the Child

Every minor child has the right to the measures of protection required by his condition as a minor on the part of his family, society, and the state.

Article 20 – Right to Nationality

1. Every person has the right to a nationality.
2. Every person has the right to the nationality of the state in whose territory he was born if he does not have the right to any other nationality.
3. No one shall be arbitrarily deprived of his nationality or of the right to change it.

Article 21 – Right to Property

1. Everyone has the right to the use and enjoyment of his property. The law may subordinate such use and enjoyment to the interest of society.
2. No one shall be deprived of his property except upon payment of just compensation, for reasons of public utility or social interest, and in the cases and according to the forms established by law.
3. Usury and any other form of exploitation of man by man shall be prohibited by law.

Article 22 – Freedom of Movement and Residence

1. Every person lawfully in the territory of a State Party has the right to move about in it, and to reside in it subject to the provisions of the law.

2. Every person has the right to leave any country freely, including his own.
3. The exercise of the foregoing rights may be restricted only pursuant to a law to the extent necessary in a democratic society to prevent crime or to protect national security, public safety, public order, public morals, public health, or the rights or freedoms of others.
4. The exercise of the rights recognized in paragraph 1 may also be restricted by law in designated zones for reasons of public interest.
5. No one can be expelled from the territory of the state of which he is a national or be deprived of the right to enter it.
6. An alien lawfully in the territory of a State Party to this Convention may be expelled from it only pursuant to a decision reached in accordance with law.
7. Every person has the right to seek and be granted asylum in a foreign territory, in accordance with the legislation of the state and international conventions, in the event he is being pursued for political offenses or related common crimes.
8. In no case may an alien be deported or returned to a country, regardless of whether or not it is his country of origin, if in that country his right to life or personal freedom is in danger of being violated because of his race, nationality, religion, social status, or political opinions.
9. The collective expulsion of aliens is prohibited.

Article 23 – Right to Participate in Government

1. Every citizen shall enjoy the following rights and opportunities:
   a. to take part in the conduct of public affairs, directly or through freely chosen representatives;
   b. to vote and to be elected in genuine periodic elections, which shall be by universal and equal suffrage and by secret ballot that guarantees the free expression of the will of the voters; and
   c. to have access, under general conditions of equality, to the public service of his country.
2. The law may regulate the exercise of the rights and opportunities referred to in the preceding paragraph only on the basis of age, nationality, residence, language, education, civil and mental capacity, or sentencing by a competent court in criminal proceedings.

Article 24 – Right to Equal Protection

All persons are equal before the law. Consequently, they are entitled, without discrimination, to equal protection of the law.

Article 25 – Right to Judicial Protection

1. Everyone has the right to simple and prompt recourse, or any other effective recourse, to a competent court or tribunal for protection against acts that violate his fundamental rights recognized by the constitution or laws of the state concerned or by this Convention, even though such violation may have been committed by persons acting in the course of their official duties.

2. The States Parties undertake:

a. to ensure that any person claiming such remedy shall have his rights determined by the competent authority provided for by the legal system of the state;
b. to develop the possibilities of judicial remedy; and
c. to ensure that the competent authorities shall enforce such remedies when granted.

Chapter III: Economic, Social, and Cultural Rights

Article 26 – Progressive Development

The States Parties undertake to adopt measures, both internally and through international cooperation, especially those of an economic and technical nature, with a view to achieving progressively, by legislation or other appropriate means, the full realization of the rights implicit in the economic, social, educational, scientific, and cultural standards set forth in the Charter of the Organization of American States as amended by the Protocol of Buenos Aires.

Chapter IV: Suspension of Guarantees, Interpretation, and Application

Article 27 – Suspension of Guarantees

1. In time of war, public danger, or other emergency that threatens the independence or security of a State Party, it may take measures derogating from its obligations under the present Convention to the extent and for the period of time strictly required by the exigencies of the situation, provided that such measures are not inconsistent with its other obligations under international law and do not involve discrimination on the ground of race, color, sex, language, religion, or social origin.

2. The foregoing provision does not authorize any suspension of the following articles: Article 3 (Right to Juridical Personality), Article 4 (Right to Life), Article 5 (Right to Humane Treatment), Article 6 (Freedom from Slavery), Article 9 (Freedom from Ex Post Facto Laws), Article 12 (Freedom of Conscience and Religion), Article 17 (Rights of the Family), Article 18 (Right to a Name), Article 19 (Rights of the Child), Article 20 (Right to Nationality), and Article 23 (Right

to Participate in Government), or of the judicial guarantees essential for the protection of such rights.
3. Any State Party availing itself of the right of suspension shall immediately inform the other States Parties, through the Secretary General of the Organization of American States, of the provisions the application of which it has suspended, the reasons that gave rise to the suspension, and the date set for the termination of such suspension.

Article 28 – Federal Clause

1. Where a State Party is constituted as a federal state, the national government of such State Party shall implement all the provisions of the Convention over whose subject matter it exercises legislative and judicial jurisdiction.
2. With respect to the provisions over whose subject matter the constituent units of the federal state have jurisdiction, the national government shall immediately take suitable measures, in accordance with its constitution and its laws, to the end that the competent authorities of the constituent units may adopt appropriate provisions for the fulfillment of this Convention.
3. Whenever two or more States Parties agree to form a federation or other type of association, they shall take care that the resulting federal or other compact contains the provisions necessary for continuing and rendering effective the standards of this Convention in the new state that is organized.

Article 29 – Restrictions Regarding Interpretation

No provision of this Convention shall be interpreted as:

a. permitting any State Party, group, or person to suppress the enjoyment or exercise of the rights and freedoms recognized in this Convention or to restrict them to a greater extent than is provided for herein;
b. restricting the enjoyment or exercise of any right or freedom recognized by virtue of the laws of any State Party or by virtue of another convention to which one of the said states is a party;
c. precluding other rights or guarantees that are inherent in the human personality or derived from representative democracy as a form of government; or
d. excluding or limiting the effect that the American Declaration of the Rights and Duties of Man and other international acts of the same nature may have.

Article 30 – Scope of Restrictions

The restrictions that, pursuant to this Convention, may be placed on the enjoyment or exercise of the rights or freedoms recognized herein may not be applied except in accordance with laws enacted for reasons of general interest and in accordance with the purpose for which such restrictions have been established.

Article 31 – Recognition of Other Rights

Other rights and freedoms recognized in accordance with the procedures established in Articles 76 and 77 may be included in the system of protection of this Convention.

Chapter V: Personal Responsibilities

Article 32 – Relationship between Duties and Rights

1. Every person has responsibilities to his family, his community, and mankind.
2. The rights of each person are limited by the rights of others, by the security of all, and by the just demands of the general welfare, in a democratic society.

Part II: Means of Protection

Chapter VI: Competent Organs

Art. 33 The following organs shall have competence with respect to matters relating to the fulfillment of the commitments made by the States Parties to this Convention:

a. the Inter-American Commission on Human Rights, referred to as "The Commission;" and
b. the Inter-American Court of Human Rights, referred to as "The Court."

Chapter VII: Inter-American Commission on Human Rights

Section 1: Organization

Art. 34 The Inter-American Commission on Human Rights shall be composed of seven members, who shall be persons of high moral character and recognized competence in the field of human rights.

Art. 35 The Commission shall represent all the member countries of the Organization of American States.

Art. 36 1. The members of the Commission shall be elected in a personal capacity by the General Assembly of the Organization from a list of candidates proposed by the governments of the member states.

2. Each of those governments may propose up to three candidates, who may be nationals of the states proposing them or of any other member state of the Organization of American States. When a slate of three is proposed, at least

one of the candidates shall be a national of a state other than the one proposing the slate.

Art. 37 1. The members of the Commission shall be elected for a term of four years and may be reelected only once, but the terms of three of the members chosen in the first election shall expire at the end of two years. Immediately following that election the General Assembly shall determine the names of those three members by lot.

2. No two nationals of the same state may be members of the Commission.

Art. 38 Vacancies that may occur on the Commission for reasons other than the normal expiration of a term shall be filled by the Permanent Council of the Organization in accordance with the provisions of the Statute of the Commission.

Art. 39 The Commission shall prepare its Statute, which it shall submit to the General Assembly for approval. It shall establish its own Regulations.

Art. 40 Secretariat services for the Commission shall be furnished by the appropriate specialized unit of the General Secretariat of the Organization. This unit shall be provided with the resources required to accomplish the tasks assigned to it by the Commission.

Section 2: Functions

Art. 41 The main function of the Commission shall be to promote respect for and defense of human rights. In the exercise of its mandate, it shall have the following functions and powers:

a. to develop an awareness of human rights among the peoples of America;
b. to make recommendations to the governments of the member states, when it considers such action advisable, for the adoption of progressive measures in favor of human rights within the framework of their domestic law and constitutional provisions as well as appropriate measures to further the observance of those rights;
c. to prepare such studies or reports as it considers advisable in the performance of its duties;
d. to request the governments of the member states to supply it with information on the measures adopted by them in matters of human rights;
e. to respond, through the General Secretariat of the Organization of American States, to inquiries made by the member states on matters related to human rights and, within the limits of its possibilities, to provide those states with the advisory services they request;
f. to take action on petitions and other communications pursuant to its authority under the provisions of Articles 44 through 51 of this Convention; and

g. to submit an annual report to the General Assembly of the Organization of American States.

Art. 42 The States Parties shall transmit to the Commission a copy of each of the reports and studies that they submit annually to the Executive Committees of the Inter-American Economic and Social Council and the Inter- American Council for Education, Science, and Culture, in their respective fields, so that the Commission may watch over the promotion of the rights implicit in the economic, social, educational, scientific, and cultural standards set forth in the Charter of the Organization of American States as amended by the Protocol of Buenos Aires.

Art. 43 The States Parties undertake to provide the Commission with such information as it may request of them as to the manner in which their domestic law ensures the effective application of any provisions of this Convention.

Section 3: Competence

Art. 44 Any person or group of persons, or any nongovernmental entity legally recognized in one or more member states of the Organization, may lodge petitions with the Commission containing denunciations or complaints of violation of this Convention by a State Party.

Art. 45 1. Any State Party may, when it deposits its instrument of ratification of or adherence to this Convention, or at any later time, declare that it recognizes the competence of the Commission to receive and examine communications in which a State Party alleges that another State Party has committed a violation of a human right set forth in this Convention.

2. Communications presented by virtue of this article may be admitted and examined only if they are presented by a State Party that has made a declaration recognizing the aforementioned competence of the Commission. The Commission shall not admit any communication against a State Party that has not made such a declaration.

3. A declaration concerning recognition of competence may be made to be valid for an indefinite time, for a specified period, or for a specific case.

4. Declarations shall be deposited with the General Secretariat of the Organization of American States, which shall transmit copies thereof to the member states of that Organization.

Art. 46 1. Admission by the Commission of a petition or communication lodged in accordance with Articles 44 or 45 shall be subject to the following requirements:

a. that the remedies under domestic law have been pursued and exhausted in accordance with generally recognized principles of international law;

b. that the petition or communication is lodged within a period of six months from the date on which the party alleging violation of his rights was notified of the final judgment;
c. that the subject of the petition or communication is not pending in another international proceeding for settlement; and
d. that, in the case of Article 44, the petition contains the name, nationality, profession, domicile, and signature of the person or persons or of the legal representative of the entity lodging the petition.

2. The provisions of paragraphs 1.a and 1.b of this article shall not be applicable when:

a. the domestic legislation of the state concerned does not afford due process of law for the protection of the right or rights that have allegedly been violated;
b. the party alleging violation of his rights has been denied access to the remedies under domestic law or has been prevented from exhausting them; or
c. there has been unwarranted delay in rendering a final judgment under the aforementioned remedies.

Art. 47 The Commission shall consider inadmissible any petition or communication submitted under Articles 44 or 45 if:

a. any of the requirements indicated in Article 46 has not been met;
b. the petition or communication does not state facts that tend to establish a violation of the rights guaranteed by this Convention;
c. the statements of the petitioner or of the state indicate that the petition or communication is manifestly groundless or obviously out of order; or
d. the petition or communication is substantially the same as one previously studied by the Commission or by another international organization.

Section 4: Procedure

Art. 48 1. When the Commission receives a petition or communication alleging violation of any of the rights protected by this Convention, it shall proceed as follows:

a. If it considers the petition or communication admissible, it shall request information from the government of the state indicated as being responsible for the alleged violations and shall furnish that government a transcript of the pertinent portions of the petition or communication. This information shall be submitted within a reasonable period to be determined by the Commission in accordance with the circumstances of each case.

b. After the information has been received, or after the period established has elapsed and the information has not been received, the Commission shall ascertain whether the grounds for the petition or communication still exist. If they do not, the Commission shall order the record to be closed.
c. The Commission may also declare the petition or communication inadmissible or out of order on the basis of information or evidence subsequently received.
d. If the record has not been closed, the Commission shall, with the knowledge of the parties, examine the matter set forth in the petition or communication in order to verify the facts. If necessary and advisable, the Commission shall carry out an investigation, for the effective conduct of which it shall request, and the states concerned shall furnish to it, all necessary facilities.
e. The Commission may request the states concerned to furnish any pertinent information and, if so requested, shall hear oral statements or receive written statements from the parties concerned.
f. The Commission shall place itself at the disposal of the parties concerned with a view to reaching a friendly settlement of the matter on the basis of respect for the human rights recognized in this Convention.

2. However, in serious and urgent cases, only the presentation of a petition or communication that fulfills all the formal requirements of admissibility shall be necessary in order for the Commission to conduct an investigation with the prior consent of the state in whose territory a violation has allegedly been committed.

Art. 49 If a friendly settlement has been reached in accordance with paragraph 1.f of Article 48, the Commission shall draw up a report, which shall be transmitted to the petitioner and to the States Parties to this Convention, and shall then be communicated to the Secretary General of the Organization of American States for publication. This report shall contain a brief statement of the facts and of the solution reached. If any party in the case so requests, the fullest possible information shall be provided to it.

Art. 50 1. If a settlement is not reached, the Commission shall, within the time limit established by its Statute, draw up a report setting forth the facts and stating its conclusions. If the report, in whole or in part, does not represent the unanimous agreement of the members of the Commission, any member may attach to it a separate opinion. The written and oral statements made by the parties in accordance with paragraph 1.e of Article 48 shall also be attached to the report.

2. The report shall be transmitted to the states concerned, which shall not be at liberty to publish it.
3. In transmitting the report, the Commission may make such proposals and recommendations as it sees fit.
Art. 51 1. If, within a period of three months from the date of the transmittal of the report of the Commission to the states concerned, the matter has not either been settled or submitted by the Commission or by the state concerned to the Court and its jurisdiction accepted, the Commission may, by the vote of an absolute majority of its members, set forth its opinion and conclusions concerning the question submitted for its consideration.
2. Where appropriate, the Commission shall make pertinent recommendations and shall prescribe a period within which the state is to take the measures that are incumbent upon it to remedy the situation examined.
3. When the prescribed period has expired, the Commission shall decide by the vote of an absolute majority of its members whether the state has taken adequate measures and whether to publish its report.

Chapter VIII: Inter-American Court of Human Rights

Section 1: Organization

Art. 52 1. The Court shall consist of seven judges, nationals of the member states of the Organization, elected in an individual capacity from among jurists of the highest moral authority and of recognized competence in the field of human rights, who possess the qualifications required for the exercise of the highest judicial functions in conformity with the law of the state of which they are nationals or of the state that proposes them as candidates.
2. No two judges may be nationals of the same state.
Art. 53 1. The judges of the Court shall be elected by secret ballot by an absolute majority vote of the States Parties to the Convention, in the General Assembly of the Organization, from a panel of candidates proposed by those states.
2. Each of the States Parties may propose up to three candidates, nationals of the state that proposes them or of any other member state of the Organization of American States. When a slate of three is proposed, at least one of the candidates shall be a national of a state other than the one proposing the slate.
Art. 54 1. The judges of the Court shall be elected for a term of six years and may be reelected only once. The term of three of the judges chosen in the first election shall expire at the end of three years. Immediately after the election, the names of the three judges shall be determined by lot in the General Assembly.
2. A judge elected to replace a judge whose term has not expired shall complete the term of the latter.

3. The judges shall continue in office until the expiration of their term. However, they shall continue to serve with regard to cases that they have begun to hear and that are still pending, for which purposes they shall not be replaced by the newly elected judges.

Art. 55 1. If a judge is a national of any of the States Parties to a case submitted to the Court, he shall retain his right to hear that case.

2. If one of the judges called upon to hear a case should be a national of one of the States Parties to the case, any other State Party in the case may appoint a person of its choice to serve on the Court as an ad hoc judge.

3. If among the judges called upon to hear a case none is a national of any of the States Parties to the case, each of the latter may appoint an ad hoc judge.

4. An ad hoc judge shall possess the qualifications indicated in Article 52.

5. If several States Parties to the Convention should have the same interest in a case, they shall be considered as a single party for purposes of the above provisions. In case of doubt, the Court shall decide.

Art. 56 Five judges shall constitute a quorum for the transaction of business by the Court.

Art. 57 The Commission shall appear in all cases before the Court.

Art. 58 1. The Court shall have its seat at the place determined by the States Parties to the Convention in the General Assembly of the Organization; however, it may convene in the territory of any member state of the Organization of American States when a majority of the Court considers it desirable, and with the prior consent of the state concerned. The seat of the Court may be changed by the States Parties to the Convention in the General Assembly by a two-thirds vote.

2. The Court shall appoint its own Secretary.

3. The Secretary shall have his office at the place where the Court has its seat and shall attend the meetings that the Court may hold away from its seat.

Art. 59 The Court shall establish its Secretariat, which shall function under the direction of the Secretary of the Court, in accordance with the administrative standards of the General Secretariat of the Organization in all respects not incompatible with the independence of the Court. The staff of the Court's Secretariat shall be appointed by the Secretary General of the Organization, in consultation with the Secretary of the Court.

Art. 60 The Court shall draw up its Statute which it shall submit to the General Assembly for approval. It shall adopt its own Rules of Procedure.

Section 2: Jurisdiction and Functions

Art. 61 1. Only the States Parties and the Commission shall have the right to submit a case to the Court.

2. In order for the Court to hear a case, it is necessary that the procedures set forth in Articles 48 and 50 shall have been completed.

Art. 62 1. A State Party may, upon depositing its instrument of ratification or adherence to this Convention, or at any subsequent time, declare that it recognizes as binding, ipso facto, and not requiring special agreement, the jurisdiction of the Court on all matters relating to the interpretation or application of this Convention.

2. Such declaration may be made unconditionally, on the condition of reciprocity, for a specified period, or for specific cases. It shall be presented to the Secretary General of the Organization, who shall transmit copies thereof to the other member states of the Organization and to the Secretary of the Court.

3. The jurisdiction of the Court shall comprise all cases concerning the interpretation and application of the provisions of this Convention that are submitted to it, provided that the States Parties to the case recognize or have recognized such jurisdiction, whether by special declaration pursuant to the preceding paragraphs, or by a special agreement.

Art. 63 1. If the Court finds that there has been a violation of a right or freedom protected by this Convention, the Court shall rule that the injured party be ensured the enjoyment of his right or freedom that was violated. It shall also rule, if appropriate, that the consequences of the measure or situation that constituted the breach of such right or freedom be remedied and that fair compensation be paid to the injured party.

2. In cases of extreme gravity and urgency, and when necessary to avoid irreparable damage to persons, the Court shall adopt such provisional measures as it deems pertinent in matters it has under consideration. With respect to a case not yet submitted to the Court, it may act at the request of the Commission.

Art. 64 1. The member states of the Organization may consult the Court regarding the interpretation of this Convention or of other treaties concerning the protection of human rights in the American states. Within their spheres of competence, the organs listed in Chapter X of the Charter of the Organization of American States, as amended by the Protocol of Buenos Aires, may in like manner consult the Court.

2. The Court, at the request of a member state of the Organization, may provide that state with opinions regarding the compatibility of any of its domestic laws with the aforesaid international instruments.

Art. 65 To each regular session of the General Assembly of the Organization of American States the Court shall submit, for the Assembly's consideration, a report on its work during the previous year. It shall specify, in particular, the cases in which a state has not complied with its judgments, making any pertinent recommendations.

Section 3: Procedure

Art. 66 1. Reasons shall be given for the judgment of the Court.
2. If the judgment does not represent in whole or in part the unanimous opinion of the judges, any judge shall be entitled to have his dissenting or separate opinion attached to the judgment.
Art. 67 The judgment of the Court shall be final and not subject to appeal. In case of disagreement as to the meaning or scope of the judgment, the Court shall interpret it at the request of any of the parties, provided the request is made within ninety days from the date of notification of the judgment.
Art. 68 1. The States Parties to the Convention undertake to comply with the judgment of the Court in any case to which they are parties.
2. That part of a judgment that stipulates compensatory damages may be executed in the country concerned in accordance with domestic procedure governing the execution of judgments against the state.
Art. 69 The parties to the case shall be notified of the judgment of the Court and it shall be transmitted to the States Parties to the Convention.

Chapter IX: Common Provisions

Art. 70 1. The judges of the Court and the members of the Commission shall enjoy, from the moment of their election and throughout their term of office, the immunities extended to diplomatic agents in accordance with international law. During the exercise of their official function they shall, in addition, enjoy the diplomatic privileges necessary for the performance of their duties.
2. At no time shall the judges of the Court or the members of the Commission be held liable for any decisions or opinions issued in the exercise of their functions.
Art. 71 The position of judge of the Court or member of the Commission is incompatible with any other activity that might affect the independence or impartiality of such judge or member, as determined in the respective statutes.
Art. 72 The judges of the Court and the members of the Commission shall receive emoluments and travel allowances in the form and under the conditions set forth in their statutes, with due regard for the importance and independence of their office. Such emoluments and travel allowances shall be determined in the budget of the Organization of American States, which shall also include the expenses of the Court and its Secretariat. To this end, the Court shall draw up its own budget and submit it for approval to the General Assembly through the General Secretariat. The latter may not introduce any changes in it.
Art. 73 The General Assembly may, only at the request of the Commission or the Court, as the case may be, determine sanctions to be applied against

members of the Commission or judges of the Court when there are justifiable grounds for such action as set forth in the respective statutes. A vote of a two-thirds majority of the member states of the Organization shall be required for a decision in the case of members of the Commission and, in the case of judges of the Court, a two-thirds majority vote of the States Parties to the Convention shall also be required.

Part III: General and Transitory Provisions

Chapter X: Signature, Ratification, Reservations, Amendments, Protocols, and Denunciation

Art. 74 1. This Convention shall be open for signature and ratification by or adherence of any member state of the Organization of American States.
2. Ratification of or adherence to this Convention shall be made by the deposit of an instrument of ratification or adherence with the General Secretariat of the Organization of American States. As soon as eleven states have deposited their instruments of ratification or adherence, the Convention shall enter into force. With respect to any state that ratifies or adheres thereafter, the Convention shall enter into force on the date of the deposit of its instrument of ratification or adherence.
3. The Secretary General shall inform all member states of the Organization of the entry into force of the Convention.
Art. 75 This Convention shall be subject to reservations only in conformity with the provisions of the Vienna Convention on the Law of Treaties signed on May 23, 1969.
Art. 76 1. Proposals to amend this Convention may be submitted to the General Assembly for the action it deems appropriate by any State Party directly, and by the Commission or the Court through the Secretary General.
2. Amendments shall enter into force for the States ratifying them on the date when two-thirds of the States Parties to this Convention have deposited their respective instruments of ratification. With respect to the other States Parties, the amendments shall enter into force on the dates on which they deposit their respective instruments of ratification.
Art. 77 1. In accordance with Article 31, any State Party and the Commission may submit proposed protocols to this Convention for consideration by the States Parties at the General Assembly with a view to gradually including other rights and freedoms within its system of protection.
2. Each protocol shall determine the manner of its entry into force and shall be applied only among the States Parties to it.

Art. 78 1. The States Parties may denounce this Convention at the expiration of a five-year period from the date of its entry into force and by means of notice given one year in advance. Notice of the denunciation shall be addressed to the Secretary General of the Organization, who shall inform the other States Parties.
2. Such a denunciation shall not have the effect of releasing the State Party concerned from the obligations contained in this Convention with respect to any act that may constitute a violation of those obligations and that has been taken by that state prior to the effective date of denunciation.

Chapter XI: Transitory Provisions

Section 1: Inter-American Commission on Human Rights

Art. 79 Upon the entry into force of this Convention, the Secretary General shall, in writing, request each member state of the Organization to present, within ninety days, its candidates for membership on the Inter-American Commission on Human Rights. The Secretary General shall prepare a list in alphabetical order of the candidates presented, and transmit it to the member states of the Organization at least thirty days prior to the next session of the General Assembly.
Art. 80 The members of the Commission shall be elected by secret ballot of the General Assembly from the list of candidates referred to in Article 79. The candidates who obtain the largest number of votes and an absolute majority of the votes of the representatives of the member states shall be declared elected. Should it become necessary to have several ballots in order to elect all the members of the Commission, the candidates who receive the smallest number of votes shall be eliminated successively, in the manner determined by the General Assembly.

Section 2: Inter-American Court of Human Rights

Art. 81 Upon the entry into force of this Convention, the Secretary General shall, in writing, request each State Party to present, within ninety days, its candidates for membership on the Inter-American Court of Human Rights. The Secretary General shall prepare a list in alphabetical order of the candidates presented and transmit it to the States Parties at least thirty days prior to the next session of the General Assembly.
Art. 82 The judges of the Court shall be elected from the list of candidates referred to in Article 81, by secret ballot of the States Parties to the Convention in the General Assembly. The candidates who obtain the largest number of

votes and an absolute majority of the votes of the representatives of the States Parties shall be declared elected. Should it become necessary to have several ballots in order to elect all the judges of the Court, the candidates who receive the smallest number of votes shall be eliminated successively, in the manner determined by the States Parties.

CHAPTER 15.A

Additional Protocol to the American Convention on Human Rights in the Area of Economic, Social and Cultural Rights

(Protocol of San Salvador)

Adopted by the Eighteenth Regular Session of the General Assembly of the Organization of American States, San Salvador, on 17 November 1988
Entry into force 16 November 1999, in accordance with article 21

Preamble

The States Parties to the American Convention on Human Rights "Pact San José, Costa Rica,"

Reaffirming their intention to consolidate in this hemisphere, within the framework of democratic institutions, a system of personal liberty and social justice based on respect for the essential rights of man;

Recognizing that the essential rights of man are not derived from one's being a national of a certain State, but are based upon attributes of the human person, for which reason they merit international protection in the form of a convention reinforcing or complementing the protection provided by the domestic law of the American States;

Considering the close relationship that exists between economic, social and cultural rights, and civil and political rights, in that the different categories of rights constitute an indivisible whole based on the recognition of the dignity of the human person, for which reason both require permanent protection and promotion if they are to be fully realized, and the violation of some rights in favor of the realization of others can never be justified;

Recognizing the benefits that stem from the promotion and development of cooperation among States and international relations;

Recalling that, in accordance with the Universal Declaration of Human Rights and the American Convention on Human Rights, the ideal of free human beings enjoying freedom from fear and want can only be achieved if conditions are created whereby everyone may enjoy his economic, social and cultural rights as well as his civil and political rights;

Bearing in mind that, although fundamental economic, social and cultural rights have been recognized in earlier international instruments of both world and regional scope, it is essential that those rights be reaffirmed, developed, perfected and protected in order to consolidate in America, on the basis of full respect for the rights of the individual, the democratic representative form of government as well as the right of its peoples to development, self-determination, and the free disposal of their wealth and natural resources; and

Considering that the American Convention on Human Rights provides that draft additional protocols to that Convention may be submitted for consideration to the States Parties, meeting together on the occasion of the General Assembly of the Organization of American States, for the purpose of gradually incorporating other rights and freedoms into the protective system thereof, Have agreed upon the following Additional Protocol to the American Convention on Human Rights "Protocol of San Salvador:"

Article 1 – Obligation to Adopt Measures

The States Parties to this Additional Protocol to the American Convention on Human Rights undertake to adopt the necessary measures, both domestically and through international cooperation, especially economic and technical, to the extent allowed by their available resources, and taking into account their degree of development, for the purpose of achieving progressively and pursuant to their internal legislations, the full observance of the rights recognized in this Protocol.

Article 2 – Obligation to Enact Domestic Legislation

If the exercise of the rights set forth in this Protocol is not already guaranteed by legislative or other provisions, the States Parties undertake to adopt, in accordance with their constitutional processes and the provisions of this Protocol, such legislative or other measures as may be necessary for making those rights a reality.

Article 3 – Obligation of Non-discrimination

The State Parties to this Protocol undertake to guarantee the exercise of the rights set forth herein without discrimination of any kind for reasons related to race, color, sex, language, religion, political or other opinions, national or social origin, economic status, birth or any other social condition.

Article 4 – Inadmissibility of Restrictions

A right which is recognized or in effect in a State by virtue of its internal legislation or international conventions may not be restricted or curtailed on the pretext that this Protocol does not recognize the right or recognizes it to a lesser degree.

Article 5 – Scope of Restrictions and Limitations

The State Parties may establish restrictions and limitations on the enjoyment and exercise of the rights established herein by means of laws promulgated for the purpose of preserving the general welfare in a democratic society only to the extent that they are not incompatible with the purpose and reason underlying those rights.

Article 6 – Right to Work

1. Everyone has the right to work, which includes the opportunity to secure the means for living a dignified and decent existence by performing a freely elected or accepted lawful activity.
2. The State Parties undertake to adopt measures that will make the right to work fully effective, especially with regard to the achievement of full employment, vocational guidance, and the development of technical and vocational training projects, in particular those directed to the disabled. The States Parties also undertake to implement and strengthen programs that help to ensure suitable family care, so that women may enjoy a real opportunity to exercise the right to work.

Article 7 – Just, Equitable, and Satisfactory Conditions of Work

The States Parties to this Protocol recognize that the right to work to which the foregoing article refers presupposes that everyone shall enjoy that right under just, equitable, and satisfactory conditions, which the States Parties undertake to guarantee in their internal legislation, particularly with respect to:

a. Remuneration which guarantees, as a minimum, to all workers dignified and decent living conditions for them and their families and fair and equal wages for equal work, without distinction;
b. The right of every worker to follow his vocation and to devote himself to the activity that best fulfills his expectations and to change employment in accordance with the pertinent national regulations;
c. The right of every worker to promotion or upward mobility in his employment, for which purpose account shall be taken of his qualifications, competence, integrity and seniority;
d. Stability of employment, subject to the nature of each industry and occupation and the causes for just separation. In cases of unjustified

dismissal, the worker shall have the right to indemnity or to reinstatement on the job or any other benefits provided by domestic legislation;

e. Safety and hygiene at work;

f. The prohibition of night work or unhealthy or dangerous working conditions and, in general, of all work which jeopardizes health, safety, or morals, for persons under 18 years of age. As regards minors under the age of 16, the work day shall be subordinated to the provisions regarding compulsory education and in no case shall work constitute an impediment to school attendance or a limitation on benefiting from education received;

g. A reasonable limitation of working hours, both daily and weekly. The days shall be shorter in the case of dangerous or unhealthy work or of night work;

h. Rest, leisure and paid vacations as well as remuneration for national holidays.

Article 8 – Trade Union Rights

1. The States Parties shall ensure:

a. The right of workers to organize trade unions and to join the union of their choice for the purpose of protecting and promoting their interests. As an extension of that right, the States Parties shall permit trade unions to establish national federations or confederations, or to affiliate with those that already exist, as well as to form international trade union organizations and to affiliate with that of their choice. The States Parties shall also permit trade unions, federations and confederations to function freely;

b. The right to strike.

2. The exercise of the rights set forth above may be subject only to restrictions established by law, provided that such restrictions are characteristic of a democratic society and necessary for safeguarding public order or for protecting public health or morals or the rights and freedoms of others. Members of the armed forces and the police and of other essential public services shall be subject to limitations and restrictions established by law.

3. No one may be compelled to belong to a trade union.

Article 9 – Right to Social Security

1. Everyone shall have the right to social security protecting him from the consequences of old age and of disability which prevents him, physically or mentally, from securing the means for a dignified and decent existence. In the

event of the death of a beneficiary, social security benefits shall be applied to his dependents.
2. In the case of persons who are employed, the right to social security shall cover at least medical care and an allowance or retirement benefit in the case of work accidents or occupational disease and, in the case of women, paid maternity leave before and after childbirth.

Article 10 – Right to Health

1. Everyone shall have the right to health, understood to mean the enjoyment of the highest level of physical, mental and social well-being.
2. In order to ensure the exercise of the right to health, the States Parties agree to recognize health as a public good and, particularly, to adopt the following measures to ensure that right:

a. Primary health care, that is, essential health care made available to all individuals and families in the community;
b. Extension of the benefits of health services to all individuals subject to the State's jurisdiction;
c. Universal immunization against the principal infectious diseases;
d. Prevention and treatment of endemic, occupational and other diseases;
e. Education of the population on the prevention and treatment of health problems, and
f. Satisfaction of the health needs of the highest risk groups and of those whose poverty makes them the most vulnerable.

Article 11 – Right to a Healthy Environment

1. Everyone shall have the right to live in a healthy environment and to have access to basic public services.
2. The States Parties shall promote the protection, preservation, and improvement of the environment.

Article 12 – Right to Food

1. Everyone has the right to adequate nutrition which guarantees the possibility of enjoying the highest level of physical, emotional and intellectual development.
2. In order to promote the exercise of this right and eradicate malnutrition, the States Parties undertake to improve methods of production, supply and distribution of food, and to this end, agree to promote greater international cooperation in support of the relevant national policies.

Article 13 – Right to Education

1. Everyone has the right to education.
2. The States Parties to this Protocol agree that education should be directed towards the full development of the human personality and human dignity and should strengthen respect for human rights, ideological pluralism, fundamental freedoms, justice and peace. They further agree that education ought to enable everyone to participate effectively in a democratic and pluralistic society and achieve a decent existence and should foster understanding, tolerance and friendship among all nations and all racial, ethnic or religious groups and promote activities for the maintenance of peace.
3. The States Parties to this Protocol recognize that in order to achieve the full exercise of the right to education:

a. Primary education should be compulsory and accessible to all without cost;

b. Secondary education in its different forms, including technical and vocational secondary education, should be made generally available and accessible to all by every appropriate means, and in particular, by the progressive introduction of free education;

c. Higher education should be made equally accessible to all, on the basis of individual capacity, by every appropriate means, and in particular, by the progressive introduction of free education;

d. Basic education should be encouraged or intensified as far as possible for those persons who have not received or completed the whole cycle of primary instruction;

e. Programs of special education should be established for the handicapped, so as to provide special instruction and training to persons with physical disabilities or mental deficiencies.

4. In conformity with the domestic legislation of the States Parties, parents should have the right to select the type of education to be given to their children, provided that it conforms to the principles set forth above.
5. Nothing in this Protocol shall be interpreted as a restriction of the freedom of individuals and entities to establish and direct educational institutions in accordance with the domestic legislation of the States Parties.

Article 14 – Right to the Benefits of Culture

1. The States Parties to this Protocol recognize the right of everyone:

a. To take part in the cultural and artistic life of the community;

b. To enjoy the benefits of scientific and technological progress;

c. To benefit from the protection of moral and material interests deriving from any scientific, literary or artistic production of which he is the author.

2. The steps to be taken by the States Parties to this Protocol to ensure the full exercise of this right shall include those necessary for the conservation, development and dissemination of science, culture and art.

3. The States Parties to this Protocol undertake to respect the freedom indispensable for scientific research and creative activity.

4. The States Parties to this Protocol recognize the benefits to be derived from the encouragement and development of international cooperation and relations in the fields of science, arts and culture, and accordingly agree to foster greater international cooperation in these fields.

Article 15 – Right to the Formation and the Protection of Families

1. The family is the natural and fundamental element of society and ought to be protected by the State, which should see to the improvement of its spiritual and material conditions.

2. Everyone has the right to form a family, which shall be exercised in accordance with the provisions of the pertinent domestic legislation.

3. The States Parties hereby undertake to accord adequate protection to the family unit and in particular:

a. To provide special care and assistance to mothers during a reasonable period before and after childbirth;

b. To guarantee adequate nutrition for children at the nursing stage and during school attendance years;

c. To adopt special measures for the protection of adolescents in order to ensure the full development of their physical, intellectual and moral capacities;

d. To undertake special programs of family training so as to help create a stable and positive environment in which children will receive and develop the values of understanding, solidarity, respect and responsibility.

Article 16 – Rights of Children

Every child, whatever his parentage, has the right to the protection that his status as a minor requires from his family, society and the State. Every child has the right to grow under the protection and responsibility of his parents; save in exceptional, judicially-recognized circumstances, a child of young age ought not to be separated from his mother. Every child has the right to free and compulsory education, at least in the elementary phase, and to continue his training at higher levels of the educational system.

Article 17 – Protection of the Elderly

Everyone has the right to special protection in old age. With this in view the States Parties agree to take progressively the necessary steps to make this right a reality and, particularly, to:

a. Provide suitable facilities, as well as food and specialized medical care, for elderly individuals who lack them and are unable to provide them for themselves;
b. Undertake work programs specifically designed to give the elderly the opportunity to engage in a productive activity suited to their abilities and consistent with their vocations or desires;
c. Foster the establishment of social organizations aimed at improving the quality of life for the elderly.

Article 18 – Protection of the Handicapped

Everyone affected by a diminution of his physical or mental capacities is entitled to receive special attention designed to help him achieve the greatest possible development of his personality. The States Parties agree to adopt such measures as may be necessary for this purpose and, especially, to:

a. Undertake programs specifically aimed at providing the handicapped with the resources and environment needed for attaining this goal, including work programs consistent with their possibilities and freely accepted by them or their legal representatives, as the case may be;
b. Provide special training to the families of the handicapped in order to help them solve the problems of coexistence and convert them into active agents in the physical, mental and emotional development of the latter;
c. Include the consideration of solutions to specific requirements arising from needs of this group as a priority component of their urban development plans;
d. Encourage the establishment of social groups in which the handicapped can be helped to enjoy a fuller life.

Article 19 – Means of Protection

1. Pursuant to the provisions of this article and the corresponding rules to be formulated for this purpose by the General Assembly of the Organization of American States, the States Parties to this Protocol undertake to submit periodic reports on the progressive measures they have taken to ensure due respect for the rights set forth in this Protocol.
2. All reports shall be submitted to the Secretary General of the OAS, who shall transmit them to the Inter-American Economic and Social Council and the

Inter-American Council for Education, Science and Culture so that they may examine them in accordance with the provisions of this article. The Secretary General shall send a copy of such reports to the Inter-American Commission on Human Rights.

3. The Secretary General of the Organization of American States shall also transmit to the specialized organizations of the inter-American system of which the States Parties to the present Protocol are members, copies or pertinent portions of the reports submitted, insofar as they relate to matters within the purview of those organizations, as established by their constituent instruments.

4. The specialized organizations of the inter-American system may submit reports to the Inter-American Economic and Social Council and the Inter-American Council for Education, Science and Culture relative to compliance with the provisions of the present Protocol in their fields of activity.

5. The annual reports submitted to the General Assembly by the Inter-American Economic and Social Council and the Inter-American Council for Education, Science and Culture shall contain a summary of the information received from the States Parties to the present Protocol and the specialized organizations concerning the progressive measures adopted in order to ensure respect for the rights acknowledged in the Protocol itself and the general recommendations they consider to be appropriate in this respect.

6. Any instance in which the rights established in paragraph a) of Article 8 and in Article 13 are violated by action directly attributable to a State Party to this Protocol may give rise, through participation of the Inter-American Commission on Human Rights and, when applicable, of the Inter-American Court of Human Rights, to application of the system of individual petitions governed by Article 44 through 51 and 61 through 69 of the American Convention on Human Rights.

7. Without prejudice to the provisions of the preceding paragraph, the Inter-American Commission on Human Rights may formulate such observations and recommendations as it deems pertinent concerning the status of the economic, social and cultural rights established in the present Protocol in all or some of the States Parties, which it may include in its Annual Report to the General Assembly or in a special report, whichever it considers more appropriate.

8. The Councils and the Inter-American Commission on Human Rights, in discharging the functions conferred upon them in this article, shall take into account the progressive nature of the observance of the rights subject to protection by this Protocol.

Article 20 – Reservations

The States Parties may, at the time of approval, signature, ratification or accession, make reservations to one or more specific provisions of this Protocol, provided that such reservations are not incompatible with the object and purpose of the Protocol.

Article 21 – Signature, Ratification or Accession Entry into Effect

1. This Protocol shall remain open to signature and ratification or accession by any State Party to the American Convention on Human Rights.
2. Ratification of or accession to this Protocol shall be effected by depositing an instrument of ratification or accession with the General Secretariat of the Organization of American States.
3. The Protocol shall enter into effect when eleven States have deposited their respective instruments of ratification or accession.
4. The Secretary General shall notify all the member states of the Organization of American States of the entry of the Protocol into effect.

Article 22 – Inclusion of other Rights and Expansion of Those Recognized

1. Any State Party and the Inter-American Commission on Human Rights may submit for the consideration of the States Parties meeting on the occasion of the General Assembly proposed amendments to include the recognition of other rights or freedoms or to extend or expand rights or freedoms recognized in this Protocol.
2. Such amendments shall enter into effect for the States that ratify them on the date of deposit of the instrument of ratification corresponding to the number representing two thirds of the States Parties to this Protocol. For all other States Parties they shall enter into effect on the date on which they deposit their respective instrument of ratification.

CHAPTER 16

Convention for the Protection of Human Rights and Fundamental Freedoms

Opened for signature by the member States of the Council of Europe in Rome on 4 November 1950[1]
Amended by Protocol No. 11 and No. 14[2]

The governments signatory hereto, being members of the Council of Europe,

Considering the Universal Declaration of Human Rights proclaimed by the General Assembly of the United Nations on 10th December 1948;

Considering that this Declaration aims at securing the universal and effective recognition and observance of the Rights therein declared;

Considering that the aim of the Council of Europe is the achievement of greater unity between its members and that one of the methods by which that aim is to be pursued is the maintenance and further realisation of human rights and fundamental freedoms;

Reaffirming their profound belief in those fundamental freedoms which are the foundation of justice and peace in the world and are best maintained on the one hand by an effective political democracy and on the other by a common understanding and observance of the human rights upon which they depend;

Being resolved, as the governments of European countries which are like-minded and have a common heritage of political traditions, ideals, freedom

1 European Treaty Series (ETS) No. 5.

2 This page contains the text of the Convention as amended by its Protocol No. 14 (CETS No. 194) as from the date of its entry into force on 1 June 2010. The text of the Convention had been previously amended according to the provisions of Protocol No. 3 (ETS No. 45), which entered into force on 21 September 1970, of Protocol No. 5 (ETS No. 55), which entered into force on 20 December 1971 and of Protocol No. 8 (ETS No. 118), which entered into force on 1 January 1990, and comprised also the text of Protocol No. 2 (ETS No. 44) which, in accordance with Article 5, paragraph 3 thereof, had been an integral part of the Convention since its entry into force on 21 September 1970. All provisions which had been amended or added by these Protocols were replaced by Protocol No. 11 (ETS No. 155), as from the date of its entry into force on 1 November 1998. As from that date, Protocol No. 9 (ETS No. 140), which entered into force on 1 October 1994, was repealed and Protocol No. 10 (ETS no. 146) had lost its purpose.

 | DOI:10.1163/9789004681224_027

and the rule of law, to take the first steps for the collective enforcement of certain of the rights stated in the Universal Declaration,

Have agreed as follows:

Article 1 – Obligation to Respect Human Rights

The High Contracting Parties shall secure to everyone within their jurisdiction the rights and freedoms defined in Section I of this Convention.

Section I: Rights and Freedoms

Article 2 – Right to Life

1. Everyone's right to life shall be protected by law. No one shall be deprived of his life intentionally save in the execution of a sentence of a court following his conviction of a crime for which this penalty is provided by law.
2. Deprivation of life shall not be regarded as inflicted in contravention of this article when it results from the use of force which is no more than absolutely necessary:

a. in defence of any person from unlawful violence;
b. in order to effect a lawful arrest or to prevent the escape of a person lawfully detained;
c. in action lawfully taken for the purpose of quelling a riot or insurrection.

Article 3 – Prohibition of Torture

No one shall be subjected to torture or to inhuman or degrading treatment or punishment.

Article 4 – Prohibition of Slavery and Forced Labour

1. No one shall be held in slavery or servitude.
2. No one shall be required to perform forced or compulsory labour.
3. For the purpose of this article the term "forced or compulsory labour" shall not include:

a. any work required to be done in the ordinary course of detention imposed according to the provisions of Article 5 of this Convention or during conditional release from such detention;
b. any service of a military character or, in case of conscientious objectors in countries where they are recognised, service exacted instead of compulsory military service;

c. any service exacted in case of an emergency or calamity threatening the life or well-being of the community;
d. any work or service which forms part of normal civic obligations.

Article 5 – Right to Liberty and Security

1. Everyone has the right to liberty and security of person. No one shall be deprived of his liberty save in the following cases and in accordance with a procedure prescribed by law:
a. the lawful detention of a person after conviction by a competent court;
b. the lawful arrest or detention of a person for non-compliance with the lawful order of a court or in order to secure the fulfilment of any obligation prescribed by law;
c. the lawful arrest or detention of a person effected for the purpose of bringing him before the competent legal authority on reasonable suspicion of having committed an offence or when it is reasonably considered necessary to prevent his committing an offence or fleeing after having done so;
d. the detention of a minor by lawful order for the purpose of educational supervision or his lawful detention for the purpose of bringing him before the competent legal authority;
e. the lawful detention of persons for the prevention of the spreading of infectious diseases, of persons of unsound mind, alcoholics or drug addicts or vagrants;
f. the lawful arrest or detention of a person to prevent his effecting an unauthorised entry into the country or of a person against whom action is being taken with a view to deportation or extradition.

2. Everyone who is arrested shall be informed promptly, in a language which he understands, of the reasons for his arrest and of any charge against him.

3. Everyone arrested or detained in accordance with the provisions of paragraph 1.c of this Article shall be brought promptly before a judge or other officer authorised by law to exercise judicial power and shall be entitled to trial within a reasonable time or to release pending trial. Release may be conditioned by guarantees to appear for trial.

4. Everyone who is deprived of his liberty by arrest or detention shall be entitled to take proceedings by which the lawfulness of his detention shall be decided speedily by a court and his release ordered if the detention is not lawful.

5. Everyone who has been the victim of arrest or detention in contravention of the provisions of this article shall have an enforceable right to compensation.

Article 6 – Right to a Fair Trial

1. In the determination of his civil rights and obligations or of any criminal charge against him, everyone is entitled to a fair and public hearing within a reasonable time by an independent and impartial tribunal established by law. Judgment shall be pronounced publicly but the press and public may be excluded from all or part of the trial in the interests of morals, public order or national security in a democratic society, where the interests of juveniles or the protection of the private life of the parties so require, or to the extent strictly necessary in the opinion of the court in special circumstances where publicity would prejudice the interests of justice.
2. Everyone charged with a criminal offence shall be presumed innocent until proved guilty according to law.
3. Everyone charged with a criminal offence has the following minimum rights:
a. to be informed promptly, in a language which he understands and in detail, of the nature and cause of the accusation against him;
b. to have adequate time and facilities for the preparation of his defence;
c. to defend himself in person or through legal assistance of his own choosing or, if he has not sufficient means to pay for legal assistance, to be given it free when the interests of justice so require;
d. to examine or have examined witnesses against him and to obtain the attendance and examination of witnesses on his behalf under the same conditions as witnesses against him;
e. to have the free assistance of an interpreter if he cannot understand or speak the language used in court.

Article 7 – No Punishment without Law

1. No one shall be held guilty of any criminal offence on account of any act or omission which did not constitute a criminal offence under national or international law at the time when it was committed. Nor shall a heavier penalty be imposed than the one that was applicable at the time the criminal offence was committed.
2. This article shall not prejudice the trial and punishment of any person for any act or omission which, at the time when it was committed, was criminal according to the general principles of law recognised by civilised nations.

Article 8 – Right to Respect for Private and Family Life

1. Everyone has the right to respect for his private and family life, his home and his correspondence.
2. There shall be no interference by a public authority with the exercise of this right except such as is in accordance with the law and is necessary in a

democratic society in the interests of national security, public safety or the economic well-being of the country, for the prevention of disorder or crime, for the protection of health or morals, or for the protection of the rights and freedoms of others.

Article 9 – Freedom of Thought, Conscience and Religion

1. Everyone has the right to freedom of thought, conscience and religion; this right includes freedom to change his religion or belief and freedom, either alone or in community with others and in public or private, to manifest his religion or belief, in worship, teaching, practice and observance.
2. Freedom to manifest one's religion or beliefs shall be subject only to such limitations as are prescribed by law and are necessary in a democratic society in the interests of public safety, for the protection of public order, health or morals, or for the protection of the rights and freedoms of others.

Article 10 – Freedom of Expression

1. Everyone has the right to freedom of expression. This right shall include freedom to hold opinions and to receive and impart information and ideas without interference by public authority and regardless of frontiers. This article shall not prevent States from requiring the licensing of broadcasting, television or cinema enterprises.
2. The exercise of these freedoms, since it carries with it duties and responsibilities, may be subject to such formalities, conditions, restrictions or penalties as are prescribed by law and are necessary in a democratic society, in the interests of national security, territorial integrity or public safety, for the prevention of disorder or crime, for the protection of health or morals, for the protection of the reputation or rights of others, for preventing the disclosure of information received in confidence, or for maintaining the authority and impartiality of the judiciary.

Article 11 – Freedom of Assembly and Association

1. Everyone has the right to freedom of peaceful assembly and to freedom of association with others, including the right to form and to join trade unions for the protection of his interests.
2. No restrictions shall be placed on the exercise of these rights other than such as are prescribed by law and are necessary in a democratic society in the interests of national security or public safety, for the prevention of disorder or crime, for the protection of health or morals or for the protection of the rights and freedoms of others. This article shall not prevent the imposition of lawful

restrictions on the exercise of these rights by members of the armed forces, of the police or of the administration of the State.

Article 12 – Right to Marry

Men and women of marriageable age have the right to marry and to found a family, according to the national laws governing the exercise of this right.

Article 13 – Right to an Effective Remedy

Everyone whose rights and freedoms as set forth in this Convention are violated shall have an effective remedy before a national authority notwithstanding that the violation has been committed by persons acting in an official capacity.

Article 14 – Prohibition of Discrimination

The enjoyment of the rights and freedoms set forth in this Convention shall be secured without discrimination on any ground such as sex, race, colour, language, religion, political or other opinion, national or social origin, association with a national minority, property, birth or other status.

Article 15 – Derogation in Time of Emergency

1. In time of war or other public emergency threatening the life of the nation any High Contracting Party may take measures derogating from its obligations under this Convention to the extent strictly required by the exigencies of the situation, provided that such measures are not inconsistent with its other obligations under international law.
2. No derogation from Article 2, except in respect of deaths resulting from lawful acts of war, or from Articles 3, 4 (paragraph 1) and 7 shall be made under this provision.
3. Any High Contracting Party availing itself of this right of derogation shall keep the Secretary General of the Council of Europe fully informed of the measures which it has taken and the reasons therefor. It shall also inform the Secretary General of the Council of Europe when such measures have ceased to operate and the provisions of the Convention are again being fully executed.

Article 16 – Restrictions on Political Activity of Aliens

Nothing in Articles 10, 11 and 14 shall be regarded as preventing the High Contracting Parties from imposing restrictions on the political activity of aliens.

Article 17 – Prohibition of Abuse of Rights

Nothing in this Convention may be interpreted as implying for any State, group or person any right to engage in any activity or perform any act aimed at the destruction of any of the rights and freedoms set forth herein or at their limitation to a greater extent than is provided for in the Convention.

Article 18 – Limitation on Use of Restrictions on Rights

The restrictions permitted under this Convention to the said rights and freedoms shall not be applied for any purpose other than those for which they have been prescribed.

Section II: European Court of Human Rights

Article 19 – Establishment of the Court

To ensure the observance of the engagements undertaken by the High Contracting Parties in the Convention and the Protocols thereto, there shall be set up a European Court of Human Rights, hereinafter referred to as "the Court". It shall function on a permanent basis.

Article 20 – Number of Judges

The Court shall consist of a number of judges equal to that of the High Contracting Parties.

Article 21 – Criteria for Office

1. The judges shall be of high moral character and must either possess the qualifications required for appointment to high judicial office or be jurisconsults of recognised competence.
2. The judges shall sit on the Court in their individual capacity.
3. During their term of office the judges shall not engage in any activity which is incompatible with their independence, impartiality or with the demands of a full-time office; all questions arising from the application of this paragraph shall be decided by the Court.

Article 22 – Election of Judges

The judges shall be elected by the Parliamentary Assembly with respect to each High Contracting Party by a majority of votes cast from a list of three candidates nominated by the High Contracting Party.

Article 23 – Terms of Office and Dismissal

1. The judges shall be elected for a period of nine years. They may not be re-elected.

2. The terms of office of judges shall expire when they reach the age of 70.
3. The judges shall hold office until replaced. They shall, however, continue to deal with such cases as they already have under consideration.
4. No judge may be dismissed from office unless the other judges decide by a majority of two-thirds that that judge has ceased to fulfil the required conditions.

Article 24 – Registry and Rapporteurs

1. The Court shall have a registry, the functions and organisation of which shall be laid down in the rules of the Court.
2. When sitting in a single-judge formation, the Court shall be assisted by rapporteurs who shall function under the authority of the President of the Court. They shall form part of the Court's registry.

Article 25 – Plenary Court

The plenary Court shall

(a) elect its President and one or two Vice-Presidents for a period of three years; they may be re-elected;
(b) set up Chambers, constituted for a fixed period of time;
(c) elect the Presidents of the Chambers of the Court; they may be re-elected;
(d) adopt the rules of the Court;
(e) elect the Registrar and one or more Deputy Registrars;
(f) make any request under Article 26, paragraph 2.

Article 26 – Single-Judge Formation, Committees, Chambers and Grand Chamber

1. To consider cases brought before it, the Court shall sit in a single-judge formation, in committees of three judges, in Chambers of seven judges and in a Grand Chamber of seventeen judges. The Court's Chambers shall set up committees for a fixed period of time.
2. At the request of the plenary Court, the Committee of Ministers may, by a unanimous decision and for a fixed period, reduce to five the number of judges of the Chambers.
3. When sitting as a single judge, a judge shall not examine any application against the High Contracting Party in respect of which that judge has been elected.
4. There shall sit as an ex officio member of the Chamber and the Grand Chamber the judge elected in respect of the High Contracting Party concerned. If there is none or if that judge is unable to sit, a person chosen by the

President of the Court from a list submitted in advance by that Party shall sit in the capacity of judge.
5. The Grand Chamber shall also include the President of the Court, the Vice-Presidents, the Presidents of the Chambers and other judges chosen in accordance with the rules of the Court. When a case is referred to the Grand Chamber under Article 43, no judge from the Chamber which rendered the judgment shall sit in the Grand Chamber, with the exception of the President of the Chamber and the judge who sat in respect of the High Contracting Party concerned.

Article 27 – Competence of Single Judges

1. A single judge may declare inadmissible or strike out of the Court's list of cases an application submitted under Article 34, where such a decision can be taken without further examination.
2. The decision shall be final.
3. If the single judge does not declare an application inadmissible or strike it out, that judge shall forward it to a committee or to a Chamber for further examination.

Article 28 – Competence of Committees

1. In respect of an application submitted under Article 34, a committee may, by a unanimous vote,
(a) declare it inadmissible or strike it out of its list of cases, where such decision can be taken without further examination; or
(b) declare it admissible and render at the same time a judgment on the merits, if the underlying question in the case, concerning the interpretation or the application of the Convention or the Protocols thereto, is already the subject of well-established case-law of the Court.
2. Decisions and judgments under paragraph 1 shall be final.
3. If the judge elected in respect of the High Contracting Party concerned is not a member of the committee, the committee may at any stage of the proceedings invite that judge to take the place of one of the members of the committee, having regard to all relevant factors, including whether that Party has contested the application of the procedure under paragraph 1.b.

Article 29 – Decisions by Chambers on Admissibility and Merits

1. If no decision is taken under Article 27 or 28, or no judgment rendered under Article 28, a Chamber shall decide on the admissibility and merits of individual applications submitted under Article 34. The decision on admissibility may be taken separately.

2. A Chamber shall decide on the admissibility and merits of inter-State applications submitted under Article 33. The decision on admissibility shall be taken separately unless the Court, in exceptional cases, decides otherwise.

Article 30 – Relinquishment of Jurisdiction to the Grand Chamber

Where a case pending before a Chamber raises a serious question affecting the interpretation of the Convention or the protocols thereto, or where the resolution of a question before the Chamber might have a result inconsistent with a judgment previously delivered by the Court, the Chamber may, at any time before it has rendered its judgment, relinquish jurisdiction in favour of the Grand Chamber, unless one of the parties to the case objects.

Article 31 – Powers of the Grand Chamber

The Grand Chamber shall

(a) determine applications submitted either under Article 33 or Article 34 when a Chamber has relinquished jurisdiction under Article 30 or when the case has been referred to it under Article 43;

(b) decide on issues referred to the Court by the Committee of Ministers in accordance with Article 46, paragraph 4; and

(c) consider requests for advisory opinions submitted under Article 47.

Article 32 – Jurisdiction of the Court

1. The jurisdiction of the Court shall extend to all matters concerning the interpretation and application of the Convention and the protocols thereto which are referred to it as provided in Articles 33, 34, 46 and 47.

2. In the event of dispute as to whether the Court has jurisdiction, the Court shall decide.

Article 33 – Inter-State Cases

Any High Contracting Party may refer to the Court any alleged breach of the provisions of the Convention and the protocols thereto by another High Contracting Party.

Article 34 – Individual Applications

The Court may receive applications from any person, non-governmental organisation or group of individuals claiming to be the victim of a violation by one of the High Contracting Parties of the rights set forth in the Convention or the protocols thereto. The High Contracting Parties undertake not to hinder in any way the effective exercise of this right.

Article 35 – Admissibility Criteria

1. The Court may only deal with the matter after all domestic remedies have been exhausted, according to the generally recognised rules of international law, and within a period of six months from the date on which the final decision was taken.

2. The Court shall not deal with any application submitted under Article 34 that

(a) is anonymous; or

(b) is substantially the same as a matter that has already been examined by the Court or has already been submitted to another procedure of international investigation or settlement and contains no relevant new information.

3. The Court shall declare inadmissible any individual application submitted under Article 34 if it considers that:

(a) the application is incompatible with the provisions of the Convention or the Protocols thereto, manifestly ill-founded, or an abuse of the right of individual application; or

(b) the applicant has not suffered a significant disadvantage, unless respect for human rights as defined in the Convention and the Protocols thereto requires an examination of the application on the merits and provided that no case may be rejected on this ground which has not been duly considered by a domestic tribunal.

4. The Court shall reject any application which it considers inadmissible under this Article. It may do so at any stage of the proceedings.

Article 36 – Third Party Intervention

1. In all cases before a Chamber or the Grand Chamber, a High Contracting Party one of whose nationals is an applicant shall have the right to submit written comments and to take part in hearings.

2. The President of the Court may, in the interest of the proper administration of justice, invite any High Contracting Party which is not a party to the proceedings or any person concerned who is not the applicant to submit written comments or take part in hearings.

3. In all cases before a Chamber or the Grand Chamber, the Council of Europe Commissioner for Human Rights may submit written comments and take part in hearings.

Article 37 – Striking Out Applications

1. The Court may at any stage of the proceedings decide to strike an application out of its list of cases where the circumstances lead to the conclusion that

(a) the applicant does not intend to pursue his application; or

(b) the matter has been resolved; or
(c) for any other reason established by the Court, it is no longer justified to continue the examination of the application.

However, the Court shall continue the examination of the application if respect for human rights as defined in the Convention and the protocols thereto so requires.

2. The Court may decide to restore an application to its list of cases if it considers that the circumstances justify such a course.

Article 38 – Examination of the Case

The Court shall examine the case together with the representatives of the parties and, if need be, undertake an investigation, for the effective conduct of which the High Contracting Parties concerned shall furnish all necessary facilities.

Article 39 – Friendly Settlements

1. At any stage of the proceedings, the Court may place itself at the disposal of the parties concerned with a view to securing a friendly settlement of the matter on the basis of respect for human rights as defined in the Convention and the Protocols thereto.
2. Proceedings conducted under paragraph 1 shall be confidential.
3. If a friendly settlement is effected, the Court shall strike the case out of its list by means of a decision which shall be confined to a brief statement of the facts and of the solution reached.
4. This decision shall be transmitted to the Committee of Ministers, which shall supervise the execution of the terms of the friendly settlement as set out in the decision.

Article 40 – Public Hearings and Access to Documents

1. Hearings shall be in public unless the Court in exceptional circumstances decides otherwise.
2. Documents deposited with the Registrar shall be accessible to the public unless the President of the Court decides otherwise.

Article 41 – Just Satisfaction

If the Court finds that there has been a violation of the Convention or the protocols thereto, and if the internal law of the High Contracting Party concerned allows only partial reparation to be made, the Court shall, if necessary, afford just satisfaction to the injured party.

Article 42 – Judgments of Chambers

Judgments of Chambers shall become final in accordance with the provisions of Article 44, paragraph 2.

Article 43 – Referral to the Grand Chamber

1. Within a period of three months from the date of the judgment of the Chamber, any party to the case may, in exceptional cases, request that the case be referred to the Grand Chamber.
2. A panel of five judges of the Grand Chamber shall accept the request if the case raises a serious question affecting the interpretation or application of the Convention or the protocols thereto, or a serious issue of general importance.
3. If the panel accepts the request, the Grand Chamber shall decide the case by means of a judgment.

Article 44 – Final Judgments

1. The judgment of the Grand Chamber shall be final.
2. The judgment of a Chamber shall become final
(a) when the parties declare that they will not request that the case be referred to the Grand Chamber; or
(b) three months after the date of the judgment, if reference of the case to the Grand Chamber has not been requested; or
(c) when the panel of the Grand Chamber rejects the request to refer under Article 43.
3. The final judgment shall be published.

Article 45 – Reasons for Judgments and Decisions

1. Reasons shall be given for judgments as well as for decisions declaring applications admissible or inadmissible.
2. If a judgment does not represent, in whole or in part, the unanimous opinion of the judges, any judge shall be entitled to deliver a separate opinion.

Article 46 – Binding Force and Execution of Judgments

1. The High Contracting Parties undertake to abide by the final judgment of the Court in any case to which they are parties.
2. The final judgment of the Court shall be transmitted to the Committee of Ministers, which shall supervise its execution.
3. If the Committee of Ministers considers that the supervision of the execution of a final judgment is hindered by a problem of interpretation of the judgment, it may refer the matter to the Court for a ruling on the question of

interpretation. A referral decision shall require a majority vote of two thirds of the representatives entitled to sit on the Committee.
4. If the Committee of Ministers considers that a High Contracting Party refuses to abide by a final judgment in a case to which it is a party, it may, after serving formal notice on that Party and by decision adopted by a majority vote of two thirds of the representatives entitled to sit on the Committee, refer to the Court the question whether that Party has failed to fulfil its obligation under paragraph 1.
5. If the Court finds a violation of paragraph 1, it shall refer the case to the Committee of Ministers for consideration of the measures to be taken. If the Court finds no violation of paragraph 1, it shall refer the case to the Committee of Ministers, which shall close its examination of the case.

Article 47 – Advisory Opinions

1. The Court may, at the request of the Committee of Ministers, give advisory opinions on legal questions concerning the interpretation of the Convention and the protocols thereto.
2. Such opinions shall not deal with any question relating to the content or scope of the rights or freedoms defined in Section I of the Convention and the protocols thereto, or with any other question which the Court or the Committee of Ministers might have to consider in consequence of any such proceedings as could be instituted in accordance with the Convention.
3. Decisions of the Committee of Ministers to request an advisory opinion of the Court shall require a majority vote of the representatives entitled to sit on the Committee.

Article 48 – Advisory Jurisdiction of the Court

The Court shall decide whether a request for an advisory opinion submitted by the Committee of Ministers is within its competence as defined in Article 47.

Article 49 – Reasons for Advisory Opinions

1. Reasons shall be given for advisory opinions of the Court.
2. If the advisory opinion does not represent, in whole or in part, the unanimous opinion of the judges, any judge shall be entitled to deliver a separate opinion.
3. Advisory opinions of the Court shall be communicated to the Committee of Ministers.

Article 50 – Expenditure on the Court

The expenditure on the Court shall be borne by the Council of Europe.

Article 51 – Privileges and Immunities of Judges

The judges shall be entitled, during the exercise of their functions, to the privileges and immunities provided for in Article 40 of the Statute of the Council of Europe and in the agreements made thereunder.

Section III: Miscellaneous Provisions

Article 52 – Inquiries by the Secretary General

On receipt of a request from the Secretary General of the Council of Europe any High Contracting Party shall furnish an explanation of the manner in which its internal law ensures the effective implementation of any of the provisions of the Convention.

Article 53 – Safeguard for Existing Human Rights

Nothing in this Convention shall be construed as limiting or derogating from any of the human rights and fundamental freedoms which may be ensured under the laws of any High Contracting Party or under any other agreement to which it is a Party.

Article 54 – Powers of the Committee of Ministers

Nothing in this Convention shall prejudice the powers conferred on the Committee of Ministers by the Statute of the Council of Europe.

Article 55 – Exclusion of Other Means of Dispute Settlement

The High Contracting Parties agree that, except by special agreement, they will not avail themselves of treaties, conventions or declarations in force between them for the purpose of submitting, by way of petition, a dispute arising out of the interpretation or application of this Convention to a means of settlement other than those provided for in this Convention.

Article 56 – Territorial Application

1. Any State may at the time of its ratification or at any time thereafter declare by notification addressed to the Secretary General of the Council of Europe that the present Convention shall, subject to paragraph 4 of this Article, extend to all or any of the territories for whose international relations it is responsible.
2. The Convention shall extend to the territory or territories named in the notification as from the thirtieth day after the receipt of this notification by the Secretary General of the Council of Europe.
3. The provisions of this Convention shall be applied in such territories with due regard, however, to local requirements.

4. Any State which has made a declaration in accordance with paragraph 1 of this article may at any time thereafter declare on behalf of one or more of the territories to which the declaration relates that it accepts the competence of the Court to receive applications from individuals, non-governmental organisations or groups of individuals as provided by Article 34 of the Convention.

Article 57 – Reservations

1. Any State may, when signing this Convention or when depositing its instrument of ratification, make a reservation in respect of any particular provision of the Convention to the extent that any law then in force in its territory is not in conformity with the provision. Reservations of a general character shall not be permitted under this article.
2. Any reservation made under this article shall contain a brief statement of the law concerned.

Article 58 – Denunciation

1. A High Contracting Party may denounce the present Convention only after the expiry of five years from the date on which it became a party to it and after six months' notice contained in a notification addressed to the Secretary General of the Council of Europe, who shall inform the other High Contracting Parties.
2. Such a denunciation shall not have the effect of releasing the High Contracting Party concerned from its obligations under this Convention in respect of any act which, being capable of constituting a violation of such obligations, may have been performed by it before the date at which the denunciation became effective.
3. Any High Contracting Party which shall cease to be a member of the Council of Europe shall cease to be a Party to this Convention under the same conditions.
4. The Convention may be denounced in accordance with the provisions of the preceding paragraphs in respect of any territory to which it has been declared to extend under the terms of Article 56.

Article 59 – Signature and Ratification

1. This Convention shall be open to the signature of the members of the Council of Europe. It shall be ratified. Ratifications shall be deposited with the Secretary General of the Council of Europe.
2. The European Union may accede to this Convention.
3. The present Convention shall come into force after the deposit of ten instruments of ratification.

4. As regards any signatory ratifying subsequently, the Convention shall come into force at the date of the deposit of its instrument of ratification.
5. The Secretary General of the Council of Europe shall notify all the members of the Council of Europe of the entry into force of the Convention, the names of the High Contracting Parties who have ratified it, and the deposit of all instruments of ratification which may be effected subsequently.
Done at Rome this 4th day of November 1950, in English and French, both texts being equally authentic, in a single copy which shall remain deposited in the archives of the Council of Europe. The Secretary General shall transmit certified copies to each of the signatories.

CHAPTER 17

European Social Charter (Revised)

Opened for signature by the member States of the Council of Europe in Strasbourg on 3 May 1996[1]
Entry into force 1 July 1999, in accordance with article K

Preamble

The governments signatory hereto, being members of the Council of Europe,

Considering that the aim of the Council of Europe is the achievement of greater unity between its members for the purpose of safeguarding and realising the ideals and principles which are their common heritage and of facilitating their economic and social progress, in particular by the maintenance and further realisation of human rights and fundamental freedoms;

Considering that in the Convention for the Protection of Human Rights and Fundamental Freedoms signed at Rome on 4 November 1950, and the Protocols thereto, the member States of the Council of Europe agreed to secure to their populations the civil and political rights and freedoms therein specified;

Considering that in the European Social Charter opened for signature in Turin on 18 October 1961 and the Protocols thereto, the member States of the Council of Europe agreed to secure to their populations the social rights specified therein in order to improve their standard of living and their social well-being;

Recalling that the Ministerial Conference on Human Rights held in Rome on 5 November 1990 stressed the need, on the one hand, to preserve the indivisible nature of all human rights, be they civil, political, economic, social or cultural and, on the other hand, to give the European Social Charter fresh impetus;

Resolved, as was decided during the Ministerial Conference held in Turin on 21 and 22 October 1991, to update and adapt the substantive contents of the Charter in order to take account in particular of the fundamental social changes which have occurred since the text was adopted;

Recognising the advantage of embodying in a Revised Charter, designed progressively to take the place of the European Social Charter, the rights

1 European Treaty Series (ETS) No. 163.

guaranteed by the Charter as amended, the rights guaranteed by the Additional Protocol of 1988 and to add new rights,

Have agreed as follows:

Part I

The Parties accept as the aim of their policy, to be pursued by all appropriate means both national and international in character, the attainment of conditions in which the following rights and principles may be effectively realised:

1. Everyone shall have the opportunity to earn his living in an occupation freely entered upon.
2. All workers have the right to just conditions of work.
3. All workers have the right to safe and healthy working conditions.
4. All workers have the right to a fair remuneration sufficient for a decent standard of living for themselves and their families.
5. All workers and employers have the right to freedom of association in national or international organisations for the protection of their economic and social interests.
6. All workers and employers have the right to bargain collectively.
7. Children and young persons have the right to a special protection against the physical and moral hazards to which they are exposed.
8. Employed women, in case of maternity, have the right to a special protection.
9. Everyone has the right to appropriate facilities for vocational guidance with a view to helping him choose an occupation suited to his personal aptitude and interests.
10. Everyone has the right to appropriate facilities for vocational training.
11. Everyone has the right to benefit from any measures enabling him to enjoy the highest possible standard of health attainable.
12. All workers and their dependents have the right to social security.
13. Anyone without adequate resources has the right to social and medical assistance.
14. Everyone has the right to benefit from social welfare services.
15. Disabled persons have the right to independence, social integration and participation in the life of the community.
16. The family as a fundamental unit of society has the right to appropriate social, legal and economic protection to ensure its full development.
17. Children and young persons have the right to appropriate social, legal and economic protection.

18. The nationals of any one of the Parties have the right to engage in any gainful occupation in the territory of any one of the others on a footing of equality with the nationals of the latter, subject to restrictions based on cogent economic or social reasons.
19. Migrant workers who are nationals of a Party and their families have the right to protection and assistance in the territory of any other Party.
20. All workers have the right to equal opportunities and equal treatment in matters of employment and occupation without discrimination on the grounds of sex.
21. Workers have the right to be informed and to be consulted within the undertaking.
22. Workers have the right to take part in the determination and improvement of the working conditions and working environment in the undertaking.
23. Every elderly person has the right to social protection.
24. All workers have the right to protection in cases of termination of employment.
25. All workers have the right to protection of their claims in the event of the insolvency of their employer.
26. All workers have the right to dignity at work.
27. All persons with family responsibilities and who are engaged or wish to engage in employment have a right to do so without being subject to discrimination and as far as possible without conflict between their employment and family responsibilities.
28. Workers' representatives in undertakings have the right to protection against acts prejudicial to them and should be afforded appropriate facilities to carry out their functions.
29. All workers have the right to be informed and consulted in collective redundancy procedures.
30. Everyone has the right to protection against poverty and social exclusion.
31. Everyone has the right to housing.

Part II

The Parties undertake, as provided for in Part III, to consider themselves bound by the obligations laid down in the following articles and paragraphs.

Article 1 – The Right to Work

With a view to ensuring the effective exercise of the right to work, the Parties undertake:

1. to accept as one of their primary aims and responsibilities the achievement and maintenance of as high and stable a level of employment as possible, with a view to the attainment of full employment;
2. to protect effectively the right of the worker to earn his living in an occupation freely entered upon;
3. to establish or maintain free employment services for all workers;
4. to provide or promote appropriate vocational guidance, training and rehabilitation.

Article 2 – The Right to Just Conditions of Work

With a view to ensuring the effective exercise of the right to just conditions of work, the Parties undertake:

1. to provide for reasonable daily and weekly working hours, the working week to be progressively reduced to the extent that the increase of productivity and other relevant factors permit;
2. to provide for public holidays with pay;
3. to provide for a minimum of four weeks' annual holiday with pay;
4. to eliminate risks in inherently dangerous or unhealthy occupations, and where it has not yet been possible to eliminate or reduce sufficiently these risks, to provide for either a reduction of working hours or additional paid holidays for workers engaged in such occupations;
5. to ensure a weekly rest period which shall, as far as possible, coincide with the day recognised by tradition or custom in the country or region concerned as a day of rest;
6. to ensure that workers are informed in written form, as soon as possible, and in any event not later than two months after the date of commencing their employment, of the essential aspects of the contract or employment relationship;
7. to ensure that workers performing night work benefit from measures which take account of the special nature of the work.

Article 3 – The Right to Safe and Healthy Working Conditions

With a view to ensuring the effective exercise of the right to safe and healthy working conditions, the Parties undertake, in consultation with employers' and workers' organisations:

1. to formulate, implement and periodically review a coherent national policy on occupational safety, occupational health and the working

environment. The primary aim of this policy shall be to improve occupational safety and health and to prevent accidents and injury to health arising out of, linked with or occurring in the course of work, particularly by minimising the causes of hazards inherent in the working environment;

2. to issue safety and health regulations;
3. to provide for the enforcement of such regulations by measures of supervision;
4. to promote the progressive development of occupational health services for all workers with essentially preventive and advisory functions.

Article 4 – The Right to a Fair Remuneration

With a view to ensuring the effective exercise of the right to a fair remuneration, the Parties undertake:

1. to recognise the right of workers to a remuneration such as will give them and their families a decent standard of living;
2. to recognise the right of workers to an increased rate of remuneration for overtime work, subject to exceptions in particular cases;
3. to recognise the right of men and women workers to equal pay for work of equal value;
4. to recognise the right of all workers to a reasonable period of notice for termination of employment;
5. to permit deductions from wages only under conditions and to the extent prescribed by national laws or regulations or fixed by collective agreements or arbitration awards.

The exercise of these rights shall be achieved by freely concluded collective agreements, by statutory wage-fixing machinery, or by other means appropriate to national conditions.

Article 5 – The Right to Organise

With a view to ensuring or promoting the freedom of workers and employers to form local, national or international organisations for the protection of their economic and social interests and to join those organisations, the Parties undertake that national law shall not be such as to impair, nor shall it be so applied as to impair, this freedom. The extent to which the guarantees provided for in this article shall apply to the police shall be determined by national laws or regulations. The principle governing the application to the members of the armed forces of these guarantees and the extent to which they shall apply to persons in this category shall equally be determined by national laws or regulations.

Article 6 – The Right to Bargain Collectively

With a view to ensuring the effective exercise of the right to bargain collectively, the Parties undertake:

1. to promote joint consultation between workers and employers;
2. to promote, where necessary and appropriate, machinery for voluntary negotiations between employers or employers' organisations and workers' organisations, with a view to the regulation of terms and conditions of employment by means of collective agreements;
3. to promote the establishment and use of appropriate machinery for conciliation and voluntary arbitration for the settlement of labour disputes;

and recognise:

4. the right of workers and employers to collective action in cases of conflicts of interest, including the right to strike, subject to obligations that might arise out of collective agreements previously entered into.

Article 7 – The Right of Children and Young Persons to Protection

With a view to ensuring the effective exercise of the right of children and young persons to protection, the Parties undertake:

1. to provide that the minimum age of admission to employment shall be 15 years, subject to exceptions for children employed in prescribed light work without harm to their health, morals or education;
2. to provide that the minimum age of admission to employment shall be 18 years with respect to prescribed occupations regarded as dangerous or unhealthy;
3. to provide that persons who are still subject to compulsory education shall not be employed in such work as would deprive them of the full benefit of their education;
4. to provide that the working hours of persons under 18 years of age shall be limited in accordance with the needs of their development, and particularly with their need for vocational training;
5. to recognise the right of young workers and apprentices to a fair wage or other appropriate allowances;
6. to provide that the time spent by young persons in vocational training during the normal working hours with the consent of the employer shall be treated as forming part of the working day;
7. to provide that employed persons of under 18 years of age shall be entitled to a minimum of four weeks' annual holiday with pay;
8. to provide that persons under 18 years of age shall not be employed in night work with the exception of certain occupations provided for by national laws or regulations;

9. to provide that persons under 18 years of age employed in occupations prescribed by national laws or regulations shall be subject to regular medical control;
10. to ensure special protection against physical and moral dangers to which children and young persons are exposed, and particularly against those resulting directly or indirectly from their work.

Article 8 – The Right of Employed Women to Protection of Maternity

With a view to ensuring the effective exercise of the right of employed women to the protection of maternity, the Parties undertake:

1. to provide either by paid leave, by adequate social security benefits or by benefits from public funds for employed women to take leave before and after childbirth up to a total of at least fourteen weeks;
2. to consider it as unlawful for an employer to give a woman notice of dismissal during the period from the time she notifies her employer that she is pregnant until the end of her maternity leave, or to give her notice of dismissal at such a time that the notice would expire during such a period;
3. to provide that mothers who are nursing their infants shall be entitled to sufficient time off for this purpose;
4. to regulate the employment in night work of pregnant women, women who have recently given birth and women nursing their infants;
5. to prohibit the employment of pregnant women, women who have recently given birth or who are nursing their infants in underground mining and all other work which is unsuitable by reason of its dangerous, unhealthy or arduous nature and to take appropriate measures to protect the employment rights of these women.

Article 9 – The Right to Vocational Guidance

With a view to ensuring the effective exercise of the right to vocational guidance, the Parties undertake to provide or promote, as necessary, a service which will assist all persons, including the handicapped, to solve problems related to occupational choice and progress, with due regard to the individual's characteristics and their relation to occupational opportunity: this assistance should be available free of charge, both to young persons, including schoolchildren, and to adults.

Article 10 – The Right to Vocational Training

With a view to ensuring the effective exercise of the right to vocational training, the Parties undertake:

1. to provide or promote, as necessary, the technical and vocational training of all persons, including the handicapped, in consultation with employers' and workers' organisations, and to grant facilities for access to higher technical and university education, based solely on individual aptitude;
2. to provide or promote a system of apprenticeship and other systematic arrangements for training young boys and girls in their various employments;
3. to provide or promote, as necessary:
   a. adequate and readily available training facilities for adult workers;
   b. special facilities for the retraining of adult workers needed as a result of technological development or new trends in employment;
4. to provide or promote, as necessary, special measures for the retraining and reintegration of the long-term unemployed;
5. to encourage the full utilisation of the facilities provided by appropriate measures such as:
   a. reducing or abolishing any fees or charges;
   b. granting financial assistance in appropriate cases;
   c. including in the normal working hours time spent on supplementary training taken by the worker, at the request of his employer, during employment;
   d. ensuring, through adequate supervision, in consultation with the employers' and workers' organisations, the efficiency of apprenticeship and other training arrangements for young workers, and the adequate protection of young workers generally.

Article 11 – The Right to Protection of Health

With a view to ensuring the effective exercise of the right to protection of health, the Parties undertake, either directly or in cooperation with public or private organisations, to take appropriate measures designed inter alia:

1. to remove as far as possible the causes of ill-health;
2. to provide advisory and educational facilities for the promotion of health and the encouragement of individual responsibility in matters of health;
3. to prevent as far as possible epidemic, endemic and other diseases, as well as accidents.

Article 12 – The Right to Social Security

With a view to ensuring the effective exercise of the right to social security, the Parties undertake:

1. to establish or maintain a system of social security;

2. to maintain the social security system at a satisfactory level at least equal to that necessary for the ratification of the European Code of Social Security;
3. to endeavour to raise progressively the system of social security to a higher level;
4. to take steps, by the conclusion of appropriate bilateral and multilateral agreements or by other means, and subject to the conditions laid down in such agreements, in order to ensure:
   a. equal treatment with their own nationals of the nationals of other Parties in respect of social security rights, including the retention of benefits arising out of social security legislation, whatever movements the persons protected may undertake between the territories of the Parties;
   b. the granting, maintenance and resumption of social security rights by such means as the accumulation of insurance or employment periods completed under the legislation of each of the Parties.

Article 13 – The Right to Social and Medical Assistance

With a view to ensuring the effective exercise of the right to social and medical assistance, the Parties undertake:

1. to ensure that any person who is without adequate resources and who is unable to secure such resources either by his own efforts or from other sources, in particular by benefits under a social security scheme, be granted adequate assistance, and, in case of sickness, the care necessitated by his condition;
2. to ensure that persons receiving such assistance shall not, for that reason, suffer from a diminution of their political or social rights;
3. to provide that everyone may receive by appropriate public or private services such advice and personal help as may be required to prevent, to remove, or to alleviate personal or family want;
4. to apply the provisions referred to in paragraphs 1, 2 and 3 of this article on an equal footing with their nationals to nationals of other Parties lawfully within their territories, in accordance with their obligations under the European Convention on Social and Medical Assistance, signed at Paris on 11 December 1953.

Article 14 – The Right to Benefit from Social Welfare Services

With a view to ensuring the effective exercise of the right to benefit from social welfare services, the Parties undertake:

1. to promote or provide services which, by using methods of social work, would contribute to the welfare and development of both individuals and groups in the community, and to their adjustment to the social environment;
2. to encourage the participation of individuals and voluntary or other organisations in the establishment and maintenance of such services.

Article 15 – The Right of Persons with Disabilities to Independence, Social Integration and Participation in the Life of the Community

With a view to ensuring to persons with disabilities, irrespective of age and the nature and origin of their disabilities, the effective exercise of the right to independence, social integration and participation in the life of the community, the Parties undertake, in particular:

1. to take the necessary measures to provide persons with disabilities with guidance, education and vocational training in the framework of general schemes wherever possible or, where this is not possible, through specialised bodies, public or private;
2. to promote their access to employment through all measures tending to encourage employers to hire and keep in employment persons with disabilities in the ordinary working environment and to adjust the working conditions to the needs of the disabled or, where this is not possible by reason of the disability, by arranging for or creating sheltered employment according to the level of disability. In certain cases, such measures may require recourse to specialised placement and support services;
3. to promote their full social integration and participation in the life of the community in particular through measures, including technical aids, aiming to overcome barriers to communication and mobility and enabling access to transport, housing, cultural activities and leisure.

Article 16 – The Right of the Family to Social, Legal and Economic Protection

With a view to ensuring the necessary conditions for the full development of the family, which is a fundamental unit of society, the Parties undertake to promote the economic, legal and social protection of family life by such means as social and family benefits, fiscal arrangements, provision of family housing, benefits for the newly married and other appropriate means.

Article 17 – The Right of Children and Young Persons to Social, Legal and Economic Protection

With a view to ensuring the effective exercise of the right of children and young persons to grow up in an environment which encourages the full development of their personality and of their physical and mental capacities, the Parties undertake, either directly or in co-operation with public and private organisations, to take all appropriate and necessary measures designed:

1. a. to ensure that children and young persons, taking account of the rights and duties of their parents, have the care, the assistance, the education and the training they need, in particular by providing for the establishment or maintenance of institutions and services sufficient and adequate for this purpose;
   b. to protect children and young persons against negligence, violence or exploitation;
   c. to provide protection and special aid from the state for children and young persons temporarily or definitively deprived of their family's support;
2. to provide to children and young persons a free primary and secondary education as well as to encourage regular attendance at schools.

Article 18 – The Right to Engage in a Gainful Occupation in the Territory of Other Parties

With a view to ensuring the effective exercise of the right to engage in a gainful occupation in the territory of any other Party, the Parties undertake:

1. to apply existing regulations in a spirit of liberality;
2. to simplify existing formalities and to reduce or abolish chancery dues and other charges payable by foreign workers or their employers;
3. to liberalise, individually or collectively, regulations governing the employment of foreign workers;

and recognise:

4. the right of their nationals to leave the country to engage in a gainful occupation in the territories of the other Parties.

Article 19 – The Right of Migrant Workers and Their Families to Protection and Assistance

With a view to ensuring the effective exercise of the right of migrant workers and their families to protection and assistance in the territory of any other Party, the Parties undertake:

1. to maintain or to satisfy themselves that there are maintained adequate and free services to assist such workers, particularly in obtaining

accurate information, and to take all appropriate steps, so far as national laws and regulations permit, against misleading propaganda relating to emigration and immigration;

2. to adopt appropriate measures within their own jurisdiction to facilitate the departure, journey and reception of such workers and their families, and to provide, within their own jurisdiction, appropriate services for health, medical attention and good hygienic conditions during the journey;
3. to promote co-operation, as appropriate, between social services, public and private, in emigration and immigration countries;
4. to secure for such workers lawfully within their territories, insofar as such matters are regulated by law or regulations or are subject to the control of administrative authorities, treatment not less favourable than that of their own nationals in respect of the following matters:
   a. remuneration and other employment and working conditions;
   b. membership of trade unions and enjoyment of the benefits of collective bargaining;
   c. accommodation;
5. to secure for such workers lawfully within their territories treatment not less favourable than that of their own nationals with regard to employment taxes, dues or contributions payable in respect of employed persons;
6. to facilitate as far as possible the reunion of the family of a foreign worker permitted to establish himself in the territory;
7. to secure for such workers lawfully within their territories treatment not less favourable than that of their own nationals in respect of legal proceedings relating to matters referred to in this article;
8. to secure that such workers lawfully residing within their territories are not expelled unless they endanger national security or offend against public interest or morality;
9. to permit, within legal limits, the transfer of such parts of the earnings and savings of such workers as they may desire;
10. to extend the protection and assistance provided for in this article to self-employed migrants insofar as such measures apply;
11. to promote and facilitate the teaching of the national language of the receiving state or, if there are several, one of these languages, to migrant workers and members of their families;
12. to promote and facilitate, as far as practicable, the teaching of the migrant worker's mother tongue to the children of the migrant worker.

Article 20 – The Right to Equal Opportunities and Equal Treatment in Matters of Employment and Occupation without Discrimination on the Grounds of Sex

With a view to ensuring the effective exercise of the right to equal opportunities and equal treatment in matters of employment and occupation without discrimination on the grounds of sex, the Parties undertake to recognise that right and to take appropriate measures to ensure or promote its application in the following fields:

a. access to employment, protection against dismissal and occupational reintegration;
b. vocational guidance, training, retraining and rehabilitation;
c. terms of employment and working conditions, including remuneration;
d. career development, including promotion.

Article 21 – The Right to Information and Consultation

With a view to ensuring the effective exercise of the right of workers to be informed and consulted within the undertaking, the Parties undertake to adopt or encourage measures enabling workers or their representatives, in accordance with national legislation and practice:

a. to be informed regularly or at the appropriate time and in a comprehensible way about the economic and financial situation of the undertaking employing them, on the understanding that the disclosure of certain information which could be prejudicial to the undertaking may be refused or subject to confidentiality; and
b. to be consulted in good time on proposed decisions which could substantially affect the interests of workers, particularly on those decisions which could have an important impact on the employment situation in the undertaking.

Article 22 – The Right to Take Part in the Determination and Improvement of the Working Conditions and Working Environment

With a view to ensuring the effective exercise of the right of workers to take part in the determination and improvement of the working conditions and working environment in the undertaking, the Parties undertake to adopt or encourage measures enabling workers or their representatives, in accordance with national legislation and practice, to contribute:

a. to the determination and the improvement of the working conditions, work organisation and working environment;
b. to the protection of health and safety within the undertaking;

c. to the organisation of social and socio-cultural services and facilities within the undertaking;
d. to the supervision of the observance of regulations on these matters.

Article 23 – The Right of Elderly Persons to Social Protection

With a view to ensuring the effective exercise of the right of elderly persons to social protection, the Parties undertake to adopt or encourage, either directly or in co-operation with public or private organisations, appropriate measures designed in particular:

- to enable elderly persons to remain full members of society for as long as possible, by means of:
  a. adequate resources enabling them to lead a decent life and play an active part in public, social and cultural life;
  b. provision of information about services and facilities available for elderly persons and their opportunities to make use of them;
- to enable elderly persons to choose their life-style freely and to lead independent lives in their familiar surroundings for as long as they wish and are able, by means of:
  a. provision of housing suited to their needs and their state of health or of adequate support for adapting their housing;
  b. the health care and the services necessitated by their state;
- to guarantee elderly persons living in institutions appropriate support, while respecting their privacy, and participation in decisions concerning living conditions in the institution.

Article 24 – The Right to Protection in Cases of Termination of Employment

With a view to ensuring the effective exercise of the right of workers to protection in cases of termination of employment, the Parties undertake to recognise:

a. the right of all workers not to have their employment terminated without valid reasons for such termination connected with their capacity or conduct or based on the operational requirements of the undertaking, establishment or service;
b. the right of workers whose employment is terminated without a valid reason to adequate compensation or other appropriate relief.

To this end the Parties undertake to ensure that a worker who considers that his employment has been terminated without a valid reason shall have the right to appeal to an impartial body.

Article 25 – The Right of Workers to the Protection of Their Claims in the Event of the Insolvency of Their Employer

With a view to ensuring the effective exercise of the right of workers to the protection of their claims in the event of the insolvency of their employer, the Parties undertake to provide that workers' claims arising from contracts of employment or employment relationships be guaranteed by a guarantee institution or by any other effective form of protection.

Article 26 – The Right to Dignity at Work

With a view to ensuring the effective exercise of the right of all workers to protection of their dignity at work, the Parties undertake, in consultation with employers' and workers' organisations:

1. to promote awareness, information and prevention of sexual harassment in the workplace or in relation to work and to take all appropriate measures to protect workers from such conduct;
2. to promote awareness, information and prevention of recurrent reprehensible or distinctly negative and offensive actions directed against individual workers in the workplace or in relation to work and to take all appropriate measures to protect workers from such conduct.

Article 27 – The Right of Workers with Family Responsibilities to Equal Opportunities and Equal Treatment

With a view to ensuring the exercise of the right to equality of opportunity and treatment for men and women workers with family responsibilities and between such workers and other workers, the Parties undertake:

1. to take appropriate measures:
   a. to enable workers with family responsibilities to enter and remain in employment, as well as to reenter employment after an absence due to those responsibilities, including measures in the field of vocational guidance and training;
   b. to take account of their needs in terms of conditions of employment and social security;
   c. to develop or promote services, public or private, in particular child daycare services and other childcare arrangements;
2. to provide a possibility for either parent to obtain, during a period after maternity leave, parental leave to take care of a child, the duration and conditions of which should be determined by national legislation, collective agreements or practice;
3. to ensure that family responsibilities shall not, as such, constitute a valid reason for termination of employment.

Article 28 – The Right of Workers' Representatives to Protection in the Undertaking and Facilities to Be Accorded to Them

With a view to ensuring the effective exercise of the right of workers' representatives to carry out their functions, the Parties undertake to ensure that in the undertaking:

a. they enjoy effective protection against acts prejudicial to them, including dismissal, based on their status or activities as workers' representatives within the undertaking;
b. they are afforded such facilities as may be appropriate in order to enable them to carry out their functions promptly and efficiently, account being taken of the industrial relations system of the country and the needs, size and capabilities of the undertaking concerned.

Article 29 – The Right to Information and Consultation in Collective Redundancy Procedures

With a view to ensuring the effective exercise of the right of workers to be informed and consulted in situations of collective redundancies, the Parties undertake to ensure that employers shall inform and consult workers' representatives, in good time prior to such collective redundancies, on ways and means of avoiding collective redundancies or limiting their occurrence and mitigating their consequences, for example by recourse to accompanying social measures aimed, in particular, at aid for the redeployment or retraining of the workers concerned.

Article 30 – The Right to Protection against Poverty and Social Exclusion

With a view to ensuring the effective exercise of the right to protection against poverty and social exclusion, the Parties undertake:

a. to take measures within the framework of an overall and co-ordinated approach to promote the effective access of persons who live or risk living in a situation of social exclusion or poverty, as well as their families, to, in particular, employment, housing, training, education, culture and social and medical assistance;
b. to review these measures with a view to their adaptation if necessary.

Article 31 – The Right to Housing

With a view to ensuring the effective exercise of the right to housing, the Parties undertake to take measures designed:

1. to promote access to housing of an adequate standard;
2. to prevent and reduce homelessness with a view to its gradual elimination;

3. to make the price of housing accessible to those without adequate resources.

Part III

Article A – Undertakings

1. Subject to the provisions of Article B below, each of the Parties undertakes:

a. to consider Part I of this Charter as a declaration of the aims which it will pursue by all appropriate means, as stated in the introductory paragraph of that part;

b. to consider itself bound by at least six of the following nine articles of Part II of this Charter: Articles 1, 5, 6, 7, 12, 13, 16, 19 and 20;

c. to consider itself bound by an additional number of articles or numbered paragraphs of Part II of the Charter which it may select, provided that the total number of articles or numbered paragraphs by which it is bound is not less than sixteen articles or sixty-three numbered paragraphs.

2. The articles or paragraphs selected in accordance with sub-paragraphs b and c of paragraph 1 of this article shall be notified to the Secretary General of the Council of Europe at the time when the instrument of ratification, acceptance or approval is deposited.

3. Any Party may, at a later date, declare by notification addressed to the Secretary General that it considers itself bound by any articles or any numbered paragraphs of Part II of the Charter which it has not already accepted under the terms of paragraph 1 of this article. Such undertakings subsequently given shall be deemed to be an integral part of the ratification, acceptance or approval and shall have the same effect as from the first day of the month following the expiration of a period of one month after the date of the notification.

4. Each Party shall maintain a system of labour inspection appropriate to national conditions.

Article B – Links with the European Social Charter and the 1988 Additional Protocol

1. No Contracting Party to the European Social Charter or Party to the Additional Protocol of 5 May 1988 may ratify, accept or approve this Charter without considering itself bound by at least the provisions corresponding to the provisions of the European Social Charter and, where appropriate, of the Additional Protocol, to which it was bound.

2. Acceptance of the obligations of any provision of this Charter shall, from the date of entry into force of those obligations for the Party concerned, result

in the corresponding provision of the European Social Charter and, where appropriate, of its Additional Protocol of 1988 ceasing to apply to the Party concerned in the event of that Party being bound by the first of those instruments or by both instruments.

Part IV

Article C – Supervision of the Implementation of the Undertakings Contained in This Charter

The implementation of the legal obligations contained in this Charter shall be submitted to the same supervision as the European Social Charter.

Article D – Collective Complaints

1. The provisions of the Additional Protocol to the European Social Charter providing for a system of collective complaints shall apply to the undertakings given in this Charter for the States which have ratified the said Protocol.
2. Any State which is not bound by the Additional Protocol to the European Social Charter providing for a system of collective complaints may when depositing its instrument of ratification, acceptance or approval of this Charter or at any time thereafter, declare by notification addressed to the Secretary General of the Council of Europe, that it accepts the supervision of its obligations under this Charter following the procedure provided for in the said Protocol.

Part V

Article E – Non-discrimination

The enjoyment of the rights set forth in this Charter shall be secured without discrimination on any ground such as race, colour, sex, language, religion, political or other opinion, national extraction or social origin, health, association with a national minority, birth or other status.

Article F – Derogations in Time of War or Public Emergency

1. In time of war or other public emergency threatening the life of the nation any Party may take measures derogating from its obligations under this Charter to the extent strictly required by the exigencies of the situation, provided that such measures are not inconsistent with its other obligations under international law.

2. Any Party which has availed itself of this right of derogation shall, within a reasonable lapse of time, keep the Secretary General of the Council of Europe fully informed of the measures taken and of the reasons therefor. It shall likewise inform the Secretary General when such measures have ceased to operate and the provisions of the Charter which it has accepted are again being fully executed.

Article G – Restrictions

1. The rights and principles set forth in Part I when effectively realised, and their effective exercise as provided for in Part II, shall not be subject to any restrictions or limitations not specified in those parts, except such as are prescribed by law and are necessary in a democratic society for the protection of the rights and freedoms of others or for the protection of public interest, national security, public health, or morals.
2. The restrictions permitted under this Charter to the rights and obligations set forth herein shall not be applied for any purpose other than that for which they have been prescribed.

Article H – Relations between the Charter and Domestic Law or International Agreements

The provisions of this Charter shall not prejudice the provisions of domestic law or of any bilateral or multilateral treaties, conventions or agreements which are already in force, or may come into force, under which more favourable treatment would be accorded to the persons protected.

Article I – Implementation of the Undertakings Given

1. Without prejudice to the methods of implementation foreseen in these articles the relevant provisions of Articles 1 to 31 of Part II of this Charter shall be implemented by:

a. laws or regulations;
b. agreements between employers or employers' organisations and workers' organisations;
c. a combination of those two methods;
d. other appropriate means.

2. Compliance with the undertakings deriving from the provisions of paragraphs 1, 2, 3, 4, 5 and 7 of Article 2, paragraphs 4, 6 and 7 of Article 7, paragraphs 1, 2, 3 and 5 of Article 10 and Articles 21 and 22 of Part II of this Charter shall be regarded as effective if the provisions are applied, in accordance with paragraph 1 of this article, to the great majority of the workers concerned.

Article J – Amendments

1. Any amendment to Parts I and II of this Charter with the purpose of extending the rights guaranteed in this Charter as well as any amendment to Parts III to VI, proposed by a Party or by the Governmental Committee, shall be communicated to the Secretary General of the Council of Europe and forwarded by the Secretary General to the Parties to this Charter.
2. Any amendment proposed in accordance with the provisions of the preceding paragraph shall be examined by the Governmental Committee which shall submit the text adopted to the Committee of Ministers for approval after consultation with the Parliamentary Assembly. After its approval by the Committee of Ministers this text shall be forwarded to the Parties for acceptance.
3. Any amendment to Part I and to Part II of this Charter shall enter into force, in respect of those Parties which have accepted it, on the first day of the month following the expiration of a period of one month after the date on which three Parties have informed the Secretary General that they have accepted it.
In respect of any Party which subsequently accepts it, the amendment shall enter into force on the first day of the month following the expiration of a period of one month after the date on which that Party has informed the Secretary General of its acceptance.
4. Any amendment to Parts III to VI of this Charter shall enter into force on the first day of the month following the expiration of a period of one month after the date on which all Parties have informed the Secretary General that they have accepted it.

Part VI

Article K – Signature, Ratification and Entry into Force

1. This Charter shall be open for signature by the member States of the Council of Europe. It shall be subject to ratification, acceptance or approval. Instruments of ratification, acceptance or approval shall be deposited with the Secretary General of the Council of Europe.
2. This Charter shall enter into force on the first day of the month following the expiration of a period of one month after the date on which three member States of the Council of Europe have expressed their consent to be bound by this Charter in accordance with the preceding paragraph.
3. In respect of any member State which subsequently expresses its consent to be bound by this Charter, it shall enter into force on the first day of the month following the expiration of a period of one month after the date of the deposit of the instrument of ratification, acceptance or approval.

Article L – Territorial Application

1. This Charter shall apply to the metropolitan territory of each Party. Each signatory may, at the time of signature or of the deposit of its instrument of ratification, acceptance or approval, specify, by declaration addressed to the Secretary General of the Council of Europe, the territory which shall be considered to be its metropolitan territory for this purpose.

2. Any signatory may, at the time of signature or of the deposit of its instrument of ratification, acceptance or approval, or at any time thereafter, declare by notification addressed to the Secretary General of the Council of Europe, that the Charter shall extend in whole or in part to a non-metropolitan territory or territories specified in the said declaration for whose international relations it is responsible or for which it assumes international responsibility. It shall specify in the declaration the articles or paragraphs of Part II of the Charter which it accepts as binding in respect of the territories named in the declaration.

3. The Charter shall extend its application to the territory or territories named in the aforesaid declaration as from the first day of the month following the expiration of a period of one month after the date of receipt of the notification of such declaration by the Secretary General.

4.Any Party may declare at a later date by notification addressed to the Secretary General of the Council of Europe that, in respect of one or more of the territories to which the Charter has been applied in accordance with paragraph 2 of this article, it accepts as binding any articles or any numbered paragraphs which it has not already accepted in respect of that territory or territories. Such undertakings subsequently given shall be deemed to be an integral part of the original declaration in respect of the territory concerned, and shall have the same effect as from the first day of the month following the expiration of a period of one month after the date of receipt of such notification by the Secretary General.

Article M – Denunciation

1. Any Party may denounce this Charter only at the end of a period of five years from the date on which the Charter entered into force for it, or at the end of any subsequent period of two years, and in either case after giving six months' notice to the Secretary General of the Council of Europe who shall inform the other Parties accordingly.

2. Any Party may, in accordance with the provisions set out in the preceding paragraph, denounce any article or paragraph of Part II of the Charter accepted by it provided that the number of articles or paragraphs by which this Party is bound shall never be less than sixteen in the former case and sixty-three in the

latter and that this number of articles or paragraphs shall continue to include the articles selected by the Party among those to which special reference is made in Article A, paragraph 1, sub-paragraph b.

3. Any Party may denounce the present Charter or any of the articles or paragraphs of Part II of the Charter under the conditions specified in paragraph 1 of this article in respect of any territory to which the said Charter is applicable, by virtue of a declaration made in accordance with paragraph 2 of Article L.

Article N – Appendix

The appendix to this Charter shall form an integral part of it.

Article O – Notifications

The Secretary General of the Council of Europe shall notify the member States of the Council and the Director General of the International Labour Office of:

a. any signature;
b. the deposit of any instrument of ratification, acceptance or approval;
c. any date of entry into force of this Charter in accordance with Article K;
d. any declaration made in application of Articles A, paragraphs 2 and 3, D, paragraphs 1 and 2, F, paragraph 2, L, paragraphs 1, 2, 3 and 4;
e. any amendment in accordance with Article J;
f. any denunciation in accordance with Article M;
g. any other act, notification or communication relating to this Charter.

In witness whereof, the undersigned, being duly authorised thereto, have signed this revised Charter.

Done at Strasbourg, this 3rd day of May 1996, in English and French, both texts being equally authentic, in a single copy which shall be deposited in the archives of the Council of Europe. The Secretary General of the Council of Europe shall transmit certified copies to each member State of the Council of Europe and to the Director General of the International Labour Office.

Appendix to the Revised European Social Charter

Scope of the Revised European Social Charter in terms of persons protected

1. Without prejudice to Article 12, paragraph 4, and Article 13, paragraph 4, the persons covered by Articles 1 to 17 and 20 to 31 include foreigners only in so far as they are nationals of other Parties lawfully resident or working regularly within the territory of the Party concerned, subject to the understanding that these articles are to be interpreted in the light of the provisions of Articles 18 and 19.

   This interpretation would not prejudice the extension of similar facilities to other persons by any of the Parties.

2. Each Party will grant to refugees as defined in the Convention relating to the Status of Refugees, signed in Geneva on 28 July 1951 and in the Protocol of 31 January 1967, and lawfully staying in its territory, treatment as favourable as possible, and in any case not less favourable than under the obligations accepted by the Party under the said convention and under any other existing international instruments applicable to those refugees.
3. Each Party will grant to stateless persons as defined in the Convention on the Status of Stateless Persons done in New York on 28 September 1954 and lawfully staying in its territory, treatment as favourable as possible and in any case not less favourable than under the obligations accepted by the Party under the said instrument and under any other existing international instruments applicable to those stateless persons.

Part I, paragraph 18, and Part II, Article 18, paragraph 1

It is understood that these provisions are not concerned with the question of entry into the territories of the Parties and do not prejudice the provisions of the European Convention on Establishment, signed in Paris on 13 December 1955.

Part II

Art. 1, paragraph 2 This provision shall not be interpreted as prohibiting or authorising any union security clause or practice.

Art. 2, paragraph 6 Parties may provide that this provision shall not apply:

a. to workers having a contract or employment relationship with a total duration not exceeding one month and/or with a working week not exceeding eight hours;
b. where the contract or employment relationship is of a casual and/or specific nature, provided, in these cases, that its non-application is justified by objective considerations.

Art. 3, paragraph 4 It is understood that for the purposes of this provision the functions, organisation and conditions of operation of these services shall be determined by national laws or regulations, collective agreements or other means appropriate to national conditions.

Art. 4, paragraph 4 This provision shall be so understood as not to prohibit immediate dismissal for any serious offence.

Art. 4, paragraph 5 It is understood that a Party may give the undertaking required in this paragraph if the great majority of workers are not permitted to suffer deductions from wages either by law or through collective agreements or arbitration awards, the exceptions being those persons not so covered.

Art. 6, paragraph 4 It is understood that each Party may, insofar as it is concerned, regulate the exercise of the right to strike by law, provided that any further restriction that this might place on the right can be justified under the terms of Article G.

Art. 7, paragraph 2 This provision does not prevent Parties from providing in their legislation that young persons not having reached the minimum age laid down may perform work in so far as it is absolutely necessary for their vocational training where such work is carried out in accordance with conditions prescribed by the competent authority and measures are taken to protect the health and safety of these young persons.

Art. 7, paragraph 8 It is understood that a Party may give the undertaking required in this paragraph if it fulfils the spirit of the undertaking by providing by law that the great majority of persons under eighteen years of age shall not be employed in night work.

Art. 8, paragraph 2 This provision shall not be interpreted as laying down an absolute prohibition. Exceptions could be made, for instance, in the following cases:

a. if an employed woman has been guilty of misconduct which justifies breaking off the employment relationship;
b. if the undertaking concerned ceases to operate;
c. if the period prescribed in the employment contract has expired.

Art. 12, paragraph 4 The words "and subject to the conditions laid down in such agreements" in the introduction to this paragraph are taken to imply inter alia that with regard to benefits which are available independently of any insurance contribution, a Party may require the completion of a prescribed period of residence before granting such benefits to nationals of other Parties.

Art. 13, paragraph 4 Governments not Parties to the European Convention on Social and Medical Assistance may ratify the Charter in respect of this paragraph provided that they grant to nationals of other Parties a treatment which is in conformity with the provisions of the said convention.

Art. 16 It is understood that the protection afforded in this provision covers single-parent families.

Art. 17 It is understood that this provision covers all persons below the age of 18 years, unless under the law applicable to the child majority is attained earlier, without prejudice to the other specific provisions provided by the Charter, particularly Article 7.

This does not imply an obligation to provide compulsory education up to the above-mentioned age.

Art. 19, paragraph 6 For the purpose of applying this provision, the term "family of a foreign worker" is understood to mean at least the worker's spouse and unmarried children, as long as the latter are considered to be minors by the receiving State and are dependent on the migrant worker.

Art. 20 1. It is understood that social security matters, as well as other provisions relating to unemployment benefit, old age benefit and survivor's benefit, may be excluded from the scope of this article.

2. Provisions concerning the protection of women, particularly as regards pregnancy, confinement and the post-natal period, shall not be deemed to be discrimination as referred to in this article.

3. This article shall not prevent the adoption of specific measures aimed at removing de facto inequalities.

4. Occupational activities which, by reason of their nature or the context in which they are carried out, can be entrusted only to persons of a particular sex may be excluded from the scope of this article or some of its provisions. This provision is not to be interpreted as requiring the Parties to embody in laws or regulations a list of occupations which, by reason of their nature or the context in which they are carried out, may be reserved to persons of a particular sex.

Art. 21 and 22 1. For the purpose of the application of these articles, the term "workers' representatives" means persons who are recognised as such under national legislation or practice.

2. The terms "national legislation and practice" embrace as the case may be, in addition to laws and regulations, collective agreements, other agreements between employers and workers' representatives, customs as well as relevant case law.

3. For the purpose of the application of these articles, the term "undertaking" is understood as referring to a set of tangible and intangible components, with or without legal personality, formed to produce goods or provide services for financial gain and with power to determine its own market policy.

4. It is understood that religious communities and their institutions may be excluded from the application of these articles, even if these institutions are "undertakings" within the meaning of paragraph 3. Establishments pursuing activities which are inspired by certain ideals or guided by certain moral concepts, ideals and concepts which are protected by national legislation, may be excluded from the application of these articles to such an extent as is necessary to protect the orientation of the undertaking.

5. It is understood that where in a state the rights set out in these articles are exercised in the various establishments of the undertaking, the Party concerned is to be considered as fulfilling the obligations deriving from these provisions.
6. The Parties may exclude from the field of application of these articles, those undertakings employing less than a certain number of workers, to be determined by national legislation or practice.
Art. 22 1. This provision affects neither the powers and obligations of states as regards the adoption of health and safety regulations for workplaces, nor the powers and responsibilities of the bodies in charge of monitoring their application.
2. The terms "social and socio-cultural services and facilities" are understood as referring to the social and/or cultural facilities for workers provided by some undertakings such as welfare assistance, sports fields, rooms for nursing mothers, libraries, children's holiday camps, etc.
Art. 23, paragraph 1 For the purpose of the application of this paragraph, the term "for as long as possible" refers to the elderly person's physical, psychological and intellectual capacities.
Art. 24 1. It is understood that for the purposes of this article the terms "termination of employment" and "terminated" mean termination of employment at the initiative of the employer.
2. It is understood that this article covers all workers but that a Party may exclude from some or all of its protection the following categories of employed persons:

a. workers engaged under a contract of employment for a specified period of time or a specified task;
b. workers undergoing a period of probation or a qualifying period of employment, provided that this is determined in advance and is of a reasonable duration;
c. workers engaged on a casual basis for a short period.

3. For the purpose of this article the following, in particular, shall not constitute valid reasons for termination of employment:

a. trade union membership or participation in union activities outside working hours, or, with the consent of the employer, within working hours;
b. seeking office as, acting or having acted in the capacity of a workers' representative;
c. the filing of a complaint or the participation in proceedings against an employer involving alleged violation of laws or regulations or recourse to competent administrative authorities;

d. race, colour, sex, marital status, family responsibilities, pregnancy, religion, political opinion, national extraction or social origin;
e. maternity or parental leave;
f. temporary absence from work due to illness or injury.

4. It is understood that compensation or other appropriate relief in case of termination of employment without valid reasons shall be determined by national laws or regulations, collective agreements or other means appropriate to national conditions.

Art. 25 1. It is understood that the competent national authority may, by way of exemption and after consulting organisations of employers and workers, exclude certain categories of workers from the protection provided in this provision by reason of the special nature of their employment relationship.

2. It is understood that the definition of the term "insolvency" must be determined by national law and practice.

3. The workers' claims covered by this provision shall include at least:

a. the workers' claims for wages relating to a prescribed period, which shall not be less than three months under a privilege system and eight weeks under a guarantee system, prior to the insolvency or to the termination of employment;
b. the workers' claims for holiday pay due as a result of work performed during the year in which the insolvency or the termination of employment occurred;
c. the workers' claims for amounts due in respect of other types of paid absence relating to a prescribed period, which shall not be less than three months under a privilege system and eight weeks under a guarantee system, prior to the insolvency or the termination of the employment.

4. National laws or regulations may limit the protection of workers' claims to a prescribed amount, which shall be of a socially acceptable level.

Art. 26 It is understood that this article does not require that legislation be enacted by the Parties. It is understood that paragraph 2 does not cover sexual harassment.

Art. 27 It is understood that this article applies to men and women workers with family responsibilities in relation to their dependent children as well as in relation to other members of their immediate family who clearly need their care or support where such responsibilities restrict their possibilities of preparing for, entering, participating in or advancing in economic activity. The terms "dependent children" and "other members of their immediate family who clearly need their care and support" mean persons defined as such by the national legislation of the Party concerned.

Art. 28 and 29 For the purpose of the application of this article, the term "workers' representatives" means persons who are recognised as such under national legislation or practice.

Part III

It is understood that the Charter contains legal obligations of an international character, the application of which is submitted solely to the supervision provided for in Part IV thereof.

Art. A, paragraph 1 It is understood that the numbered paragraphs may include articles consisting of only one paragraph.

Art. B, paragraph 2 For the purpose of paragraph 2 of Article B, the provisions of the revised Charter correspond to the provisions of the Charter with the same article or paragraph number with the exception of:

a. Article 3, paragraph 2, of the revised Charter which corresponds to Article 3, paragraphs 1 and 3, of the Charter;
b. Article 3, paragraph 3, of the revised Charter which corresponds to Article 3, paragraphs 2 and 3, of the Charter;
c. Article 10, paragraph 5, of the revised Charter which corresponds to Article 10, paragraph 4, of the Charter;
d. Article 17, paragraph 1, of the revised Charter which corresponds to Article 17 of the Charter.

Part V

Art. E A differential treatment based on an objective and reasonable justification shall not be deemed discriminatory.

Art. F The terms "in time of war or other public emergency" shall be so understood as to cover also the threat of war.

Art. I It is understood that workers excluded in accordance with the appendix to Articles 21 and 22 are not taken into account in establishing the number of workers concerned.

Art. J The term "amendment" shall be extended so as to cover also the addition of new articles to the Charter.

CHAPTER 18

European Charter on Fundamental Rights

Proclaimed on 7 December 2000 by the European Parliament, the Council of Ministers and the European Commission
Entry into force 1 December 2009

Preamble

The peoples of Europe, in creating an ever closer union among them, are resolved to share a peaceful future based on common values.

Conscious of its spiritual and moral heritage, the Union is founded on the indivisible, universal values of human dignity, freedom, equality and solidarity; it is based on the principles of democracy and the rule of law. It places the individual at the heart of its activities, by establishing the citizenship of the Union and by creating an area of freedom, security and justice.

The Union contributes to the preservation and to the development of these common values while respecting the diversity of the cultures and traditions of the peoples of Europe as well as the national identities of the Member States and the organisation of their public authorities at national, regional and local levels; it seeks to promote balanced and sustainable development and ensures free movement of persons, services, goods and capital, and the freedom of establishment.

To this end, it is necessary to strengthen the protection of fundamental rights in the light of changes in society, social progress and scientific and technological developments by making those rights more visible in a Charter.

This Charter reaffirms, with due regard for the powers and tasks of the Union and for the principle of subsidiarity, the rights as they result, in particular, from the constitutional traditions and international obligations common to the Member States, the European Convention for the Protection of Human Rights and Fundamental Freedoms, the Social Charters adopted by the Union and by the Council of Europe and the case-law of the Court of Justice of the European Union and of the European Court of Human Rights. In this context the Charter will be interpreted by the courts of the Union and the Member States with due regard to the explanations prepared under the authority of the Praesidium of the Convention which drafted the Charter and updated under the responsibility of the Praesidium of the European Convention.

Enjoyment of these rights entails responsibilities and duties with regard to other persons, to the human community and to future generations.

The Union therefore recognises the rights, freedoms and principles set out hereafter.

Title I: Dignity

Article 1 – Human Dignity

Human dignity is inviolable. It must be respected and protected.

Article 2 – Right to Life

1. Everyone has the right to life.
2. No one shall be condemned to the death penalty, or executed.

Article 3 – Right to the Integrity of the Person

1. Everyone has the right to respect for his or her physical and mental integrity.
2. In the fields of medicine and biology, the following must be respected in particular:

(a) the free and informed consent of the person concerned, according to the procedures laid down by law;

(b) the prohibition of eugenic practices, in particular those aiming at the selection of persons;

(c) the prohibition on making the human body and its parts as such a source of financial gain;

(d) the prohibition of the reproductive cloning of human beings.

Article 4 – Prohibition of Torture and Inhuman or Degrading Treatment or Punishment

No one shall be subjected to torture or to inhuman or degrading treatment or punishment.

Article 5 – Prohibition of Slavery and Forced Labour

1. No one shall be held in slavery or servitude.
2. No one shall be required to perform forced or compulsory labour.
3. Trafficking in human beings is prohibited.

Title II: Freedoms

Article 6 – Right to Liberty and Security

Everyone has the right to liberty and security of person.

Article 7 – Respect for Private and Family Life

Everyone has the right to respect for his or her private and family life, home and communications.

Article 8 – Protection of Personal Data

1. Everyone has the right to the protection of personal data concerning him or her.
2. Such data must be processed fairly for specified purposes and on the basis of the consent of the person concerned or some other legitimate basis laid down by law. Everyone has the right of access to data which has been collected concerning him or her, and the right to have it rectified.
3. Compliance with these rules shall be subject to control by an independent authority.

Article 9 – Right to Marry and Right to Found a Family

The right to marry and the right to found a family shall be guaranteed in accordance with the national laws governing the exercise of these rights.

Article 10 – Freedom of Thought, Conscience and Religion

1. Everyone has the right to freedom of thought, conscience and religion. This right includes freedom to change religion or belief and freedom, either alone or in community with others and in public or in private, to manifest religion or belief, in worship, teaching, practice and observance.
2. The right to conscientious objection is recognised, in accordance with the national laws governing the exercise of this right.

Article 11 – Freedom of Expression and Information

1. Everyone has the right to freedom of expression. This right shall include freedom to hold opinions and to receive and impart information and ideas without interference by public authority and regardless of frontiers.
2. The freedom and pluralism of the media shall be respected.

Article 12 – Freedom of Assembly and of Association

1. Everyone has the right to freedom of peaceful assembly and to freedom of association at all levels, in particular in political, trade union and civic matters, which implies the right of everyone to form and to join trade unions for the protection of his or her interests.
2. Political parties at Union level contribute to expressing the political will of the citizens of the Union.

Article 13 – Freedom of the Arts and Sciences

The arts and scientific research shall be free of constraint. Academic freedom shall be respected.

Article 14 – Right to Education

1. Everyone has the right to education and to have access to vocational and continuing training.
2. This right includes the possibility to receive free compulsory education.
3. The freedom to found educational establishments with due respect for democratic principles and the right of parents to ensure the education and teaching of their children in conformity with their religious, philosophical and pedagogical convictions shall be respected, in accordance with the national laws governing the exercise of such freedom and right.

Article 15 – Freedom to Choose an Occupation and Right to Engage in Work

1. Everyone has the right to engage in work and to pursue a freely chosen or accepted occupation.
2. Every citizen of the Union has the freedom to seek employment, to work, to exercise the right of establishment and to provide services in any Member State.
3. Nationals of third countries who are authorised to work in the territories of the Member States are entitled to working conditions equivalent to those of citizens of the Union.

Article 16 – Freedom to Conduct a Business

The freedom to conduct a business in accordance with Union law and national laws and practices is recognised.

Article 17 – Right to Property

1. Everyone has the right to own, use, dispose of and bequeath his or her lawfully acquired possessions. No one may be deprived of his or her possessions, except in the public interest and in the cases and under the conditions provided for by law, subject to fair compensation being paid in good time for their loss. The use of property may be regulated by law in so far as is necessary for the general interest.
2. Intellectual property shall be protected.

Article 18 – Right to Asylum

The right to asylum shall be guaranteed with due respect for the rules of the Geneva Convention of 28 July 1951 and the Protocol of 31 January 1967 relating to the status of refugees and in accordance with the Treaty on European Union and the Treaty on the Functioning of the European Union (hereinafter referred to as 'the Treaties').

Article 19 – Protection in the Event of Removal, Expulsion or Extradition

1. Collective expulsions are prohibited.
2. No one may be removed, expelled or extradited to a State where there is a serious risk that he or she would be subjected to the death penalty, torture or other inhuman or degrading treatment or punishment.

Title III: Equality

Article 20 – Equality before the Law

Everyone is equal before the law.

Article 21 – Non-discrimination

1. Any discrimination based on any ground such as sex, race, colour, ethnic or social origin, genetic features, language, religion or belief, political or any other opinion, membership of a national minority, property, birth, disability, age or sexual orientation shall be prohibited.
2. Within the scope of application of the Treaties and without prejudice to any of their specific provisions, any discrimination on grounds of nationality shall be prohibited.

Article 22 – Cultural, Religious and Linguistic Diversity

The Union shall respect cultural, religious and linguistic diversity.

Article 23 – Equality between Women and Men

Equality between women and men must be ensured in all areas, including employment, work and pay.

The principle of equality shall not prevent the maintenance or adoption of measures providing for specific advantages in favour of the under-represented sex.

Article 24 – The Rights of the Child

1. Children shall have the right to such protection and care as is necessary for their well-being. They may express their views freely. Such views shall be taken into consideration on matters which concern them in accordance with their age and maturity.

2. In all actions relating to children, whether taken by public authorities or private institutions, the child's best interests must be a primary consideration.
3. Every child shall have the right to maintain on a regular basis a personal relationship and direct contact with both his or her parents, unless that is contrary to his or her interests.

Article 25 – The Rights of the Elderly
The Union recognises and respects the rights of the elderly to lead a life of dignity and independence and to participate in social and cultural life.

Article 26 – Integration of Persons with Disabilities
The Union recognises and respects the right of persons with disabilities to benefit from measures designed to ensure their independence, social and occupational integration and participation in the life of the community.

Title IV: Solidarity
Article 27 – Workers' Right to Information and Consultation within the Undertaking
Workers or their representatives must, at the appropriate levels, be guaranteed information and consultation in good time in the cases and under the conditions provided for by Union law and national laws and practices.

Article 28 – Right of Collective Bargaining and Action
Workers and employers, or their respective organisations, have, in accordance with Union law and national laws and practices, the right to negotiate and conclude collective agreements at the appropriate levels and, in cases of conflicts of interest, to take collective action to defend their interests, including strike action.

Article 29 – Right of Access to Placement Services
Everyone has the right of access to a free placement service.

Article 30 – Protection in the Event of Unjustified Dismissal
Every worker has the right to protection against unjustified dismissal, in accordance with Union law and national laws and practices.

Article 31 – Fair and Just Working Conditions
1. Every worker has the right to working conditions which respect his or her health, safety and dignity.

2. Every worker has the right to limitation of maximum working hours, to daily and weekly rest periods and to an annual period of paid leave.

Article 32 – Prohibition of Child Labour and Protection of Young People at Work

The employment of children is prohibited. The minimum age of admission to employment may not be lower than the minimum school-leaving age, without prejudice to such rules as may be more favourable to young people and except for limited derogations.

Young people admitted to work must have working conditions appropriate to their age and be protected against economic exploitation and any work likely to harm their safety, health or physical, mental, moral or social development or to interfere with their education.

Article 33 – Family and Professional Life

1. The family shall enjoy legal, economic and social protection.
2. To reconcile family and professional life, everyone shall have the right to protection from dismissal for a reason connected with maternity and the right to paid maternity leave and to parental leave following the birth or adoption of a child.

Article 34 – Social Security and Social Assistance

1. The Union recognises and respects the entitlement to social security benefits and social services providing protection in cases such as maternity, illness, industrial accidents, dependency or old age, and in the case of loss of employment, in accordance with the rules laid down by Union law and national laws and practices.
2. Everyone residing and moving legally within the European Union is entitled to social security benefits and social advantages in accordance with Union law and national laws and practices.
3. In order to combat social exclusion and poverty, the Union recognises and respects the right to social and housing assistance so as to ensure a decent existence for all those who lack sufficient resources, in accordance with the rules laid down by Union law and national laws and practices.

Article 35 – Health Care

Everyone has the right of access to preventive health care and the right to benefit from medical treatment under the conditions established by national laws and practices. A high level of human health protection shall be ensured in the definition and implementation of all the Union's policies and activities.

Article 36 – Access to Services of General Economic Interest

The Union recognises and respects access to services of general economic interest as provided for in national laws and practices, in accordance with the Treaties, in order to promote the social and territorial cohesion of the Union.

Article 37 – Environmental Protection

A high level of environmental protection and the improvement of the quality of the environment must be integrated into the policies of the Union and ensured in accordance with the principle of sustainable development.

Article 38 – Consumer Protection

Union policies shall ensure a high level of consumer protection.

Title V: Citizens' Rights

Article 39 – Right to Vote and to Stand as a Candidate at Elections to the European Parliament

1. Every citizen of the Union has the right to vote and to stand as a candidate at elections to the European Parliament in the Member State in which he or she resides, under the same conditions as nationals of that State.
2. Members of the European Parliament shall be elected by direct universal suffrage in a free and secret ballot.

Article 40 – Right to Vote and to Stand as a Candidate at Municipal Elections

Every citizen of the Union has the right to vote and to stand as a candidate at municipal elections in the Member State in which he or she resides under the same conditions as nationals of that State.

Article 41 – Right to Good Administration

1. Every person has the right to have his or her affairs handled impartially, fairly and within a reasonable time by the institutions, bodies, offices and agencies of the Union.

This right includes:

(a) the right of every person to be heard, before any individual measure which would affect him or her adversely is taken;

(b) the right of every person to have access to his or her file, while respecting the legitimate interests of confidentiality and of professional and business secrecy;

(c) the obligation of the administration to give reasons for its decisions.

3. Every person has the right to have the Union make good any damage caused by its institutions by its servants in the performance of their duties, in accordance with the general principles common the laws of the Member States.
4. Every person may write to the institutions of the Union in one of the languages of the Treaties and must have an answer in the same language.

Article 42 – Right of Access to Documents

Any citizen of the Union, and any natural or legal person residing or having its registered office in a Member State, has a right of access to documents of the institutions, bodies, offices and agencies of the Union, whatever their medium.

Article 43 – European Ombudsman

Any citizen of the Union and any natural or legal person residing or having its registered office in a Member State has the right to refer to the European Ombudsman cases of maladministration in the activities of the institutions, bodies, offices or agencies of the Union, with the exception of the Court of Justice of the European Union acting in its judicial role.

Article 44 – Right to Petition

Any citizen of the Union and any natural or legal person residing or having its registered office in a Member State has the right to petition the European Parliament.

Article 45 – Freedom of Movement and of Residence

1. Every citizen of the Union has the right to move and reside freely within the territory of the Member States.
2. Freedom of movement and residence may be granted, in accordance with the Treaties, to nationals of third countries legally resident in the territory of a Member State.

Article 46 – Diplomatic and Consular Protection

Every citizen of the Union shall, in the territory of a third country in which the Member State of which he or she is a national is not represented, be entitled to protection by the diplomatic or consular authorities of any Member State, on the same conditions as the nationals of that Member State.

Title VI: Justice

Article 47 – Right to an Effective Remedy and to a Fair Trial

Everyone whose rights and freedoms guaranteed by the law of the Union are violated has the right to an effective remedy before a tribunal in compliance with the conditions laid down in this Article.

Everyone is entitled to a fair and public hearing within a reasonable time by an independent and impartial tribunal previously established by law. Everyone shall have the possibility of being advised, defended and represented.

Legal aid shall be made available to those who lack sufficient resources in so far as such aid is necessary to ensure effective access to justice.

Article 48 – Presumption of Innocence and Right of Defence

1. Everyone who has been charged shall be presumed innocent until proved guilty according to law.
2. Respect for the rights of the defence of anyone who has been charged shall be guaranteed.

Article 49 – Principles of Legality and Proportionality of Criminal Offences and Penalties

1. No one shall be held guilty of any criminal offence on account of any act or omission which did not constitute a criminal offence under national law or international law at the time when it was committed. Nor shall a heavier penalty be imposed than the one that was applicable at the time the criminal offence was committed. If, subsequent to the commission of a criminal offence, the law provides for a lighter penalty, that penalty shall be applicable.
2. This Article shall not prejudice the trial and punishment of any person for any act or omission which, at the time when it was committed, was criminal according to the general principles recognised by the community of nations.
3. The severity of penalties must not be disproportionate to the criminal offence.

Article 50 – Right Not To Be Tried or Punished Twice in Criminal Proceedings for the Same Criminal Offence

No one shall be liable to be tried or punished again in criminal proceedings for an offence for which he or she has already been finally acquitted or convicted within the Union in accordance with the law.

Title VII: General Provisions Governing the Interpretation and Application of the Charter

Article 51 – Field of Application

1. The provisions of this Charter are addressed to the institutions, bodies, offices and agencies of the Union with due regard for the principle of subsidiarity and to the Member States only when they are implementing Union law. They shall therefore respect the rights, observe the principles and promote the application thereof in accordance with their respective powers and respecting the limits of the powers of the Union as conferred on it in the Treaties.
2. The Charter does not extend the field of application of Union law beyond the powers of the Union or establish any new power or task for the Union, or modify powers and tasks as defined in the Treaties.

Article 52 – Scope and Interpretation of Rights and Principles

1. Any limitation on the exercise of the rights and freedoms recognised by this Charter must be provided for by law and respect the essence of those rights and freedoms. Subject to the principle of proportionality, limitations may be made only if they are necessary and genuinely meet objectives of general interest recognised by the Union or the need to protect the rights and freedoms of others.
2. Rights recognised by this Charter for which provision is made in the Treaties shall be exercised under the conditions and within the limits defined by those Treaties.
3. In so far as this Charter contains rights which correspond to rights guaranteed by the Convention for the Protection of Human Rights and Fundamental Freedoms, the meaning and scope of those rights shall be the same as those laid down by the said Convention. This provision shall not prevent Union law providing more extensive protection.
4. In so far as this Charter recognises fundamental rights as they result from the constitutional traditions common to the Member States, those rights shall be interpreted in harmony with those traditions.
5. The provisions of this Charter which contain principles may be implemented by legislative and executive acts taken by institutions, bodies, offices and agencies of the Union, and by acts of Member States when they are implementing Union law, in the exercise of their respective powers. They shall be judicially cognisable only in the interpretation of such acts and in the ruling on their legality.
6. Full account shall be taken of national laws and practices as specified in this Charter.

7. The explanations drawn up as a way of providing guidance in the interpretation of this Charter shall be given due regard by the courts of the Union and of the Member States.

Article 53 – Level of Protection

Nothing in this Charter shall be interpreted as restricting or adversely affecting human rights and fundamental freedoms as recognised, in their respective fields of application, by Union law and international law and by international agreements to which the Union or all the Member States are party, including the European Convention for the Protection of Human Rights and Fundamental Freedoms, and by the Member States' constitutions.

Article 54 – Prohibition of Abuse of Rights

Nothing in this Charter shall be interpreted as implying any right to engage in any activity or to perform any act aimed at the destruction of any of the rights and freedoms recognised in this Charter or at their limitation to a greater extent than is provided for herein.

CHAPTER 19

Convention for the Protection of Human Rights and Dignity of the Human Being with Regard to the Application of Biology and Medicine: Convention on Human Rights and Biomedicine[1]

(Oviedo Convention)
Adopted by the Committee of Ministers of the Council of Europe on 19 November 1996
Entry into force 1 December 1999, in accordance with article 33

Preamble
The member States of the Council of Europe, the other States and the European Community, signatories hereto,

Bearing in mind the Universal Declaration of Human Rights proclaimed by the General Assembly of the United Nations on 10 December 1948;

Bearing in mind the Convention for the Protection of Human Rights and Fundamental Freedoms of 4 November 1950;

Bearing in mind the European Social Charter of 18 October 1961;

Bearing in mind the International Covenant on Civil and Political Rights and the International Covenant on Economic, Social and Cultural Rights of 16 December 1966;

Bearing in mind the Convention for the Protection of Individuals with regard to Automatic Processing of Personal Data of 28 January 1981;

Bearing also in mind the Convention on the Rights of the Child of 20 November 1989;

Considering that the aim of the Council of Europe is the achievement of a greater unity between its members and that one of the methods by which that aim is to be pursued is the maintenance and further realisation of human rights and fundamental freedoms;

Conscious of the accelerating developments in biology and medicine;

1 The Treaty of Lisbon amending the Treaty on European Union and the Treaty establishing the European Community entered into force on 1 December 2009. As a consequence, as from that date, any reference to the European Economic Community shall be read as the European Union.

Convinced of the need to respect the human being both as an individual and as a member of the human species and recognising the importance of ensuring the dignity of the human being;

Conscious that the misuse of biology and medicine may lead to acts endangering human dignity;

Affirming that progress in biology and medicine should be used for the benefit of present and future generations;

Stressing the need for international co-operation so that all humanity may enjoy the benefits of biology and medicine;

Recognising the importance of promoting a public debate on the questions posed by the application of biology and medicine and the responses to be given thereto;

Wishing to remind all members of society of their rights and responsibilities;

Taking account of the work of the Parliamentary Assembly in this field, including Recommendation 1160 (1991) on the preparation of a convention on bioethics;

Resolving to take such measures as are necessary to safeguard human dignity and the fundamental rights and freedoms of the individual with regard to the application of biology and medicine,

Have agreed as follows:

Chapter 1: General Provisions

Article 1 – Purpose and Object

Parties to this Convention shall protect the dignity and identity of all human beings and guarantee everyone, without discrimination, respect for their integrity and other rights and fundamental freedoms with regard to the application of biology and medicine.

Each Party shall take in its internal law the necessary measures to give effect to the provisions of this Convention.

Article 2 – Primacy of the Human Being

The interests and welfare of the human being shall prevail over the sole interest of society or science.

Article 3 – Equitable Access to Health Care

Parties, taking into account health needs and available resources, shall take appropriate measures with a view to providing, within their jurisdiction, equitable access to health care of appropriate quality.

Article 4 – Professional Standards

Any intervention in the health field, including research, must be carried out in accordance with relevant professional obligations and standards.

Chapter II: Consent

Article 5 – General Rule

An intervention in the health field may only be carried out after the person concerned has given free and informed consent to it.
This person shall beforehand be given appropriate information as to the purpose and nature of the intervention as well as on its consequences and risks.
The person concerned may freely withdraw consent at any time.

Article 6 – Protection of Persons Not Able to Consent

1. Subject to Articles 17 and 20 below, an intervention may only be carried out on a person who does not have the capacity to consent, for his or her direct benefit.
2. Where, according to law, a minor does not have the capacity to consent to an intervention, the intervention may only be carried out with the authorisation of his or her representative or an authority or a person or body provided for by law.
The opinion of the minor shall be taken into consideration as an increasingly determining factor in proportion to his or her age and degree of maturity.
3. Where, according to law, an adult does not have the capacity to consent to an intervention because of a mental disability, a disease or for similar reasons, the intervention may only be carried out with the authorisation of his or her representative or an authority or a person or body provided for by law.
The individual concerned shall as far as possible take part in the authorisation procedure.
4. The representative, the authority, the person or the body mentioned in paragraphs 2 and 3 above shall be given, under the same conditions, the information referred to in Article 5.
5. The authorisation referred to in paragraphs 2 and 3 above may be withdrawn at any time in the best interests of the person concerned.

Article 7 – Protection of Persons Who Have a Mental Disorder

Subject to protective conditions prescribed by law, including supervisory, control and appeal procedures, a person who has a mental disorder of a serious nature may be subjected, without his or her consent, to an intervention aimed at treating his or her mental disorder only where, without such treatment, serious harm is likely to result to his or her health.

Article 8 – Emergency Situation

When because of an emergency situation the appropriate consent cannot be obtained, any medically necessary intervention may be carried out immediately for the benefit of the health of the individual concerned.

Article 9 – Previously Expressed Wishes

The previously expressed wishes relating to a medical intervention by a patient who is not, at the time of the intervention, in a state to express his or her wishes shall be taken into account.

Chapter III: Private Life and Right to Information

Article 10 – Private Life and Right to Information

1. Everyone has the right to respect for private life in relation to information about his or her health.
2. Everyone is entitled to know any information collected about his or her health. However, the wishes of individuals not to be so informed shall be observed.
3. In exceptional cases, restrictions may be placed by law on the exercise of the rights contained in paragraph 2 in the interests of the patient.

Chapter IV: Human Genome

Article 11 – Non-discrimination

Any form of discrimination against a person on grounds of his or her genetic heritage is prohibited.

Article 12 – Predictive Genetic Tests

Tests which are predictive of genetic diseases or which serve either to identify the subject as a carrier of a gene responsible for a disease or to detect a genetic predisposition or susceptibility to a disease may be performed only for health purposes or for scientific research linked to health purposes, and subject to appropriate genetic counselling.

Article 13 – Interventions on the Human Genome

An intervention seeking to modify the human genome may only be undertaken for preventive, diagnostic or therapeutic purposes and only if its aim is not to introduce any modification in the genome of any descendants.

Article 14 – Non-selection of Sex

The use of techniques of medically assisted procreation shall not be allowed for the purpose of choosing a future child's sex, except where serious hereditary sex-related disease is to be avoided.

Chapter V: Scientific Research

Article 15 – General Rule

Scientific research in the field of biology and medicine shall be carried out freely, subject to the provisions of this Convention and the other legal provisions ensuring the protection of the human being.

Article 16 – Protection of Persons Undergoing Research

Research on a person may only be undertaken if all the following conditions are met:

i. there is no alternative of comparable effectiveness to research on humans;
ii. the risks which may be incurred by that person are not disproportionate to the potential benefits of the research;
iii. the research project has been approved by the competent body after independent examination of its scientific merit, including assessment of the importance of the aim of the research, and multidisciplinary review of its ethical acceptability;
iv. the persons undergoing research have been informed of their rights and the safeguards prescribed by law for their protection;
v. the necessary consent as provided for under Article 5 has been given expressly, specifically and is documented. Such consent may be freely withdrawn at any time.

Article 17 – Protection of Persons Not Able to Consent to Research

1. Research on a person without the capacity to consent as stipulated in Article 5 may be undertaken only if all the following conditions are met:

i. the conditions laid down in Article 16, sub-paragraphs i to iv, are fulfilled;
ii. the results of the research have the potential to produce real and direct benefit to his or her health;
iii. research of comparable effectiveness cannot be carried out on individuals capable of giving consent;
iv. the necessary authorisation provided for under Article 6 has been given specifically and in writing; and
v. the person concerned does not object.

2. Exceptionally and under the protective conditions prescribed by law, where the research has not the potential to produce results of direct benefit to the health of the person concerned, such research may be authorised subject to the conditions laid down in paragraph 1, sub-paragraphs i, iii, iv and v above, and to the following additional conditions:

i. the research has the aim of contributing, through significant improvement in the scientific understanding of the individual's condition, disease or disorder, to the ultimate attainment of results capable of conferring benefit to the person concerned or to other persons in the same age category or afflicted with the same disease or disorder or having the same condition;

ii. the research entails only minimal risk and minimal burden for the individual concerned.

Article 18 – Research on Embryos in Vitro

1. Where the law allows research on embryos in vitro, it shall ensure adequate protection of the
embryo.

2. The creation of human embryos for research purposes is prohibited.

Chapter VI: Organ and Tissue Removal from Living Donors for Transplantation Purposes

Article 19 – General Rule

1. Removal of organs or tissue from a living person for transplantation purposes may be carried out solely for the therapeutic benefit of the recipient and where there is no suitable organ or tissue available from a deceased person and no other alternative therapeutic method of comparable effectiveness.

2. The necessary consent as provided for under Article 5 must have been given expressly and specifically either in written form or before an official body.

Article 20 – Protection of Persons Not Able to Consent to Organ Removal

1. No organ or tissue removal may be carried out on a person who does not have the capacity to consent under Article 5.

2. Exceptionally and under the protective conditions prescribed by law, the removal of regenerative tissue from a person who does not have the capacity to consent may be authorised provided the following conditions are met:

i. there is no compatible donor available who has the capacity to consent;

ii. the recipient is a brother or sister of the donor;

iii. the donation must have the potential to be life-saving for the recipient;

iv. the authorisation provided for under paragraphs 2 and 3 of Article 6 has been given specifically and in writing, in accordance with the law and with the approval of the competent body;
v. the potential donor concerned does not object.

Chapter VII: Prohibition of Financial Gain and Disposal of a Part of the Human Body

Article 21 – Prohibition of Financial Gain

The human body and its parts shall not, as such, give rise to financial gain.

Article 22 – Disposal of a Removed Part of the Human Body

When in the course of an intervention any part of a human body is removed, it may be stored and used for a purpose other than that for which it was removed, only if this is done in conformity with appropriate information and consent procedures.

Chapter VIII: Infringements of the Provisions of the Convention

Article 23 – Infringement of the Rights or Principles

The Parties shall provide appropriate judicial protection to prevent or to put a stop to an unlawful infringement of the rights and principles set forth in this Convention at short notice.

Article 24 – Compensation for Undue Damage

The person who has suffered undue damage resulting from an intervention is entitled to fair compensation according to the conditions and procedures prescribed by law.

Article 25 – Sanctions

Parties shall provide for appropriate sanctions to be applied in the event of infringement of the provisions contained in this Convention.

Chapter IX: Relation between This Convention and Other Provisions

Article 26 – Restrictions on the Exercise of the Rights

1. No restrictions shall be placed on the exercise of the rights and protective provisions contained in this Convention other than such as are prescribed by law and are necessary in a democratic society in the interest of public safety, for the prevention of crime, for the protection of public health or for the protection of the rights and freedoms of others.
2. The restrictions contemplated in the preceding paragraph may not be placed on Articles 11, 13, 14, 16, 17, 19, 20 and 21.

Article 27 – Wider Protection

None of the provisions of this Convention shall be interpreted as limiting or otherwise affecting the possibility for a Party to grant a wider measure of protection with regard to the application of biology and medicine than is stipulated in this Convention.

Chapter X: Public Debate

Article 28 – Public Debate

Parties to this Convention shall see to it that the fundamental questions raised by the developments of biology and medicine are the subject of appropriate public discussion in the light, in particular, of relevant medical, social, economic, ethical and legal implications, and that their possible application is made the subject of appropriate consultation.

Chapter XI: Interpretation and Follow-Up of the Convention

Article 29 – Interpretation of the Convention

The European Court of Human Rights may give, without direct reference to any specific proceedings pending in a court, advisory opinions on legal questions concerning the interpretation of the present Convention at the request of:

- the Government of a Party, after having informed the other Parties;
- the Committee set up by Article 32, with membership restricted to the Representatives of the Parties to this Convention, by a decision adopted by a two-thirds majority of votes cast.

Article 30 – Reports on the Application of the Convention

On receipt of a request from the Secretary General of the Council of Europe any Party shall furnish an explanation of the manner in which its internal law ensures the effective implementation of any of the provisions of the Convention.

Chapter XII: Protocols

Article 31 – Protocols

Protocols may be concluded in pursuance of Article 32, with a view to developing, in specific fields, the principles contained in this Convention.

The Protocols shall be open for signature by Signatories of the Convention. They shall be subject to ratification, acceptance or approval. A Signatory may not ratify, accept or approve Protocols without previously or simultaneously ratifying accepting or approving the Convention.

Chapter XIII: Amendments to the Convention

Article 32 – Amendments to the Convention

1. The tasks assigned to "the Committee" in the present article and in Article 29 shall be carried out by the Steering Committee on Bioethics (CDBI), or by any other committee designated to do so by the Committee of Ministers.
2. Without prejudice to the specific provisions of Article 29, each member State of the Council of Europe, as well as each Party to the present Convention which is not a member of the Council of Europe, may be represented and have one vote in the Committee when the Committee carries out the tasks assigned to it by the present Convention.
3. Any State referred to in Article 33 or invited to accede to the Convention in accordance with the provisions of Article 34 which is not Party to this Convention may be represented on the Committee by an observer. If the European Community is not a Party it may be represented on the Committee by an observer.
4. In order to monitor scientific developments, the present Convention shall be examined within the Committee no later than five years from its entry into force and thereafter at such intervals as the Committee may determine.
5. Any proposal for an amendment to this Convention, and any proposal for a Protocol or for an amendment to a Protocol, presented by a Party, the Committee or the Committee of Ministers shall be communicated to the Secretary General of the Council of Europe and forwarded by him to the member States of the Council of Europe, to the European Community, to any Signatory, to any Party, to any State invited to sign this Convention in accordance with the provisions of Article 33 and to any State invited to accede to it in accordance with the provisions of Article 34.
6. The Committee shall examine the proposal not earlier than two months after it has been forwarded by the Secretary General in accordance with paragraph 5. The Committee shall submit the text adopted by a two-thirds majority of the votes cast to the Committee of Ministers for approval. After its approval, this text shall be forwarded to the Parties for ratification, acceptance or approval.
7. Any amendment shall enter into force, in respect of those Parties which have accepted it, on the first day of the month following the expiration of a period of one month after the date on which five Parties, including at least four member States of the Council of Europe, have informed the Secretary General that they have accepted it.

In respect of any Party which subsequently accepts it, the amendment shall enter into force on the first day of the month following the expiration of a period of one month after the date on which that Party has informed the Secretary General of its acceptance.

Chapter XIV: Final Clauses

Article 33 – Signature, Ratification and Entry into Force

1. This Convention shall be open for signature by the member States of the Council of Europe, the non-member States which have participated in its elaboration and by the European Community.
2. This Convention is subject to ratification, acceptance or approval. Instruments of ratification, acceptance or approval shall be deposited with the Secretary General of the Council of Europe.
3. This Convention shall enter into force on the first day of the month following the expiration of a period of three months after the date on which five States, including at least four member States of the Council of Europe, have expressed their consent to be bound by the Convention in accordance with the provisions of paragraph 2 of the present article.
4. In respect of any Signatory which subsequently expresses its consent to be bound by it, the Convention shall enter into force on the first day of the month following the expiration of a period of three months after the date of the deposit of its instrument of ratification, acceptance or approval.

Article 34 – Non-member States

1. After the entry into force of this Convention, the Committee of Ministers of the Council of Europe may, after consultation of the Parties, invite any non-member State of the Council of Europe to accede to this Convention by a decision taken by the majority provided for in Article 20, paragraph d, of the Statute of the Council of Europe, and by the unanimous vote of the representatives of the Contracting States entitled to sit on the Committee of Ministers.
2. In respect of any acceding State, the Convention shall enter into force on the first day of the month following the expiration of a period of three months after the date of deposit of the instrument of accession with the Secretary General of the Council of Europe.

Article 35 – Territories

1. Any Signatory may, at the time of signature or when depositing its instrument of ratification, acceptance or approval, specify the territory or territories to which this Convention shall apply. Any other State may formulate the same declaration when depositing its instrument of accession.
2. Any Party may, at any later date, by a declaration addressed to the Secretary General of the Council of Europe, extend the application of this Convention to any other territory specified in the declaration and for whose international relations it is responsible or on whose behalf it is authorised to give undertakings. In respect of such territory the Convention shall enter into force on the

first day of the month following the expiration of a period of three months after the date of receipt of such declaration by the Secretary General.
3. Any declaration made under the two preceding paragraphs may, in respect of any territory specified in such declaration, be withdrawn by a notification addressed to the Secretary General. The withdrawal shall become effective on the first day of the month following the expiration of a period of three months after the date of receipt of such notification by the Secretary General.

Article 36 – Reservations

1. Any State and the European Community may, when signing this Convention or when depositing the instrument of ratification, acceptance, approval or accession, make a reservation in respect of any particular provision of the Convention to the extent that any law then in force in its territory is not in conformity with the provision. Reservations of a general character shall not be permitted under this article.
2. Any reservation made under this article shall contain a brief statement of the relevant law.
3. Any Party which extends the application of this Convention to a territory mentioned in the declaration referred to in Article 35, paragraph 2, may, in respect of the territory concerned, make a reservation in accordance with the provisions of the preceding paragraphs.
4. Any Party which has made the reservation mentioned in this article may withdraw it by means of a declaration addressed to the Secretary General of the Council of Europe. The withdrawal shall become effective on the first day of the month following the expiration of a period of one month after the date of its receipt by the Secretary General.

Article 37 – Denunciation

1. Any Party may at any time denounce this Convention by means of a notification addressed to the Secretary General of the Council of Europe.
2. Such denunciation shall become effective on the first day of the month following the expiration of a period of three months after the date of receipt of the notification by the Secretary General.

Article 38 – Notifications

The Secretary General of the Council of Europe shall notify the member States of the Council, the European Community, any Signatory, any Party and any other State which has been invited to accede to this Convention of:

a. any signature;

b. the deposit of any instrument of ratification, acceptance, approval or accession;
c. any date of entry into force of this Convention in accordance with Articles 33 or 34;
d. any amendment or Protocol adopted in accordance with Article 32, and the date on which such an amendment or Protocol enters into force;
e. any declaration made under the provisions of Article 35;
f. any reservation and withdrawal of reservation made in pursuance of the provisions of Article 36;
g. any other act, notification or communication relating to this Convention.

In witness whereof the undersigned, being duly authorised thereto, have signed this Convention.

Done at Oviedo (Asturias), this 4th day of April 1997, in English and French, both texts being equally authentic, in a single copy which shall be deposited in the archives of the Council of Europe. The Secretary General of the Council of Europe shall transmit certified copies to each member State of the Council of Europe, to the European Community, to the non-member States which have participated in the elaboration of this Convention, and to any State invited to accede to this Convention.

PART III

Asylum, Migration and Trafficking

CHAPTER 20

Convention Relating to the Status of Refugees

Adopted on 28 July 1951 by the United Nations Conference of Plenipotentiaries on the Status of Refugees and Stateless Persons convened under General Assembly resolution 429 (v) of 14 December 1950
Entry into force 22 April 1954, in accordance with article 43

Preamble

The High Contracting Parties,

Considering that the Charter of the United Nations and the Universal Declaration of Human Rights approved on 10 December 1948 by the General Assembly have affirmed the principle that human beings shall enjoy fundamental rights and freedoms without discrimination,

Considering that the United Nations has, on various occasions, manifested its profound concern for refugees and endeavoured to assure refugees the widest possible exercise of these fundamental rights and freedoms,

Considering that it is desirable to revise and consolidate previous international agreements relating to the status of refugees and to extend the scope of and the protection accorded by such instruments by means of a new agreement,

Considering that the grant of asylum may place unduly heavy burdens on certain countries, and that a satisfactory solution of a problem of which the United Nations has recognized the international scope and nature cannot therefore be achieved without international co-operation,

Expressing the wish that all States, recognizing the social and humanitarian nature of the problem of refugees, will do everything within their power to prevent this problem from becoming a cause of tension between States,

Noting that the United Nations High Commissioner for Refugees is charged with the task of supervising international conventions providing for the protection of refugees, and recognizing that the effective co-ordination of measures taken to deal with this problem will depend upon the co-operation of States with the High Commissioner,

Have agreed as follows:

 | DOI:10.1163/9789004681224_031

Chapter I: General Provisions

Article 1 – Definition of the Term "Refugee"

A. For the purposes of the present Convention, the term "refugee" shall apply to any person who:

(1) Has been considered a refugee under the Arrangements of 12 May 1926 and 30 June 1928 or under the Conventions of 28 October 1933 and 10 February 1938, the Protocol of 14 September 1939 or the Constitution of the International Refugee Organization;

Decisions of non-eligibility taken by the International Refugee Organization during the period of its activities shall not prevent the status of refugee being accorded to persons who fulfil the conditions of paragraph 2 of this section;

(2) As a result of events occurring before 1 January 1951 and owing to well-founded fear of being persecuted for reasons of race, religion, nationality, membership of a particular social group or political opinion, is outside the country of his nationality and is unable or, owing to such fear, is unwilling to avail himself of the protection of that country; or who, not having a nationality and being outside the country of his former habitual residence as a result of such events, is unable or, owing to such fear, is unwilling to return to it.

In the case of a person who has more than one nationality, the term "the country of his nationality" shall mean each of the countries of which he is a national, and a person shall not be deemed to be lacking the protection of the country of his nationality if, without any valid reason based on well-founded fear, he has not availed himself of the protection of one of the countries of which he is a national.

B. (1) For the purposes of this Convention, the words "events occurring before 1 January 1951" in article 1, section A, shall be understood to mean either

(a) "events occurring in Europe before 1 January 1951"; or

(b) "events occurring in Europe or elsewhere before 1 January 1951"; and each Contracting State shall make a declaration at the time of signature, ratification or accession, specifying which of these meanings it applies for the purpose of its obligations under this Convention.

(2) Any Contracting State which has adopted alternative (a) may at any time extend its obligations by adopting alternative (b) by means of a notification addressed to the Secretary-General of the United Nations.

C. This Convention shall cease to apply to any person falling under the terms of section A if:

(1) He has voluntarily re-availed himself of the protection of the country of his nationality; or

(2) Having lost his nationality, he has voluntarily reacquired it; or

(3) He has acquired a new nationality, and enjoys the protection of the country of his new nationality; or
(4) He has voluntarily re-established himself in the country which he left or outside which he remained owing to fear of persecution; or
(5) He can no longer, because the circumstances in connection with which he has been recognized as a refugee have ceased to exist, continue to refuse to avail himself of the protection of the country of his nationality;
Provided that this paragraph shall not apply to a refugee falling under section A (1) of this article who is able to invoke compelling reasons arising out of previous persecution for refusing to avail himself of the protection of the country of nationality;
(6) Being a person who has no nationality he is, because the circumstances in connection with which he has been recognized as a refugee have ceased to exist, able to return to the country of his former habitual residence;
Provided that this paragraph shall not apply to a refugee falling under section A (1) of this article who is able to invoke compelling reasons arising out of previous persecution for refusing to return to the country of his former habitual residence.
D. This Convention shall not apply to persons who are at present receiving from organs or agencies of the United Nations other than the United Nations High Commissioner for Refugees protection or assistance.
When such protection or assistance has ceased for any reason, without the position of such persons being definitively settled in accordance with the relevant resolutions adopted by the General Assembly of the United Nations, these persons shall ipso facto be entitled to the benefits of this Convention.
E. This Convention shall not apply to a person who is recognized by the competent authorities of the country in which he has taken residence as having the rights and obligations which are attached to the possession of the nationality of that country.
F. The provisions of this Convention shall not apply to any person with respect to whom there are serious reasons for considering that:
(a) he has committed a crime against peace, a war crime, or a crime against humanity, as defined in the international instruments drawn up to make provision in respect of such crimes;
(b) he has committed a serious non-political crime outside the country of refuge prior to his admission to that country as a refugee;
(c) he has been guilty of acts contrary to the purposes and principles of the United Nations.

Article 2 – General Obligations

Every refugee has duties to the country in which he finds himself, which require in particular that he conform to its laws and regulations as well as to measures taken for the maintenance of public order.

Article 3 – Non-discrimination

The Contracting States shall apply the provisions of this Convention to refugees without discrimination as to race, religion or country of origin.

Article 4 – Religion

The Contracting States shall accord to refugees within their territories treatment at least as favourable as that accorded to their nationals with respect to freedom to practice their religion and freedom as regards the religious education of their children.

Article 5 – Rights Granted Apart from This Convention

Nothing in this Convention shall be deemed to impair any rights and benefits granted by a Contracting State to refugees apart from this Convention.

Article 6 – The Term "in the Same Circumstances"

For the purposes of this Convention, the term "in the same circumstances" implies that any requirements (including requirements as to length and conditions of sojourn or residence) which the particular individual would have to fulfil for the enjoyment of the right in question, if he were not a refugee, must be fulfilled by him, with the exception of requirements which by their nature a refugee is incapable of fulfilling.

Article 7 – Exemption from Reciprocity

1. Except where this Convention contains more favourable provisions, a Contracting State shall accord to refugees the same treatment as is accorded to aliens generally.
2. After a period of three years' residence, all refugees shall enjoy exemption from legislative reciprocity in the territory of the Contracting States.
3. Each Contracting State shall continue to accord to refugees the rights and benefits to which they were already entitled, in the absence of reciprocity, at the date of entry into force of this Convention for that State.
4. The Contracting States shall consider favourably the possibility of according to refugees, in the absence of reciprocity, rights and benefits beyond those to which they are entitled according to paragraphs 2 and 3, and to extending

exemption from reciprocity to refugees who do not fulfil the conditions provided for in paragraphs 2 and 3.
5. The provisions of paragraphs 2 and 3 apply both to the rights and benefits referred to in articles 13, 18, 19, 21 and 22 of this Convention and to rights and benefits for which this Convention does not provide.

Article 8 – Exemption from Exceptional Measures

With regard to exceptional measures which may be taken against the person, property or interests of nationals of a foreign State, the Contracting States shall not apply such measures to a refugee who is formally a national of the said State solely on account of such nationality. Contracting States which, under their legislation, are prevented from applying the general principle expressed in this article, shall, in appropriate cases, grant exemptions in favour of such refugees.

Article 9 – Provisional Measures

Nothing in this Convention shall prevent a Contracting State, in time of war or other grave and exceptional circumstances, from taking provisionally measures which it considers to be essential to the national security in the case of a particular person, pending a determination by the Contracting State that that person is in fact a refugee and that the continuance of such measures is necessary in his case in the interests of national security.

Article 10 – Continuity of Residence

1. Where a refugee has been forcibly displaced during the Second World War and removed to the territory of a Contracting State, and is resident there, the period of such enforced sojourn shall be considered to have been lawful residence within that territory.
2. Where a refugee has been forcibly displaced during the Second World War from the territory of a Contracting State and has, prior to the date of entry into force of this Convention, returned there for the purpose of taking up residence, the period of residence before and after such enforced displacement shall be regarded as one uninterrupted period for any purposes for which uninterrupted residence is required.

Article 11 – Refugee Seamen

In the case of refugees regularly serving as crew members on board a ship flying the flag of a Contracting State, that State shall give sympathetic consideration to their establishment on its territory and the issue of travel documents to them or their temporary admission to its territory particularly with a view to facilitating their establishment in another country.

Chapter II: Juridical Status

Article 12 – Personal Status

1. The personal status of a refugee shall be governed by the law of the country of his domicile or, if he has no domicile, by the law of the country of his residence.
2. Rights previously acquired by a refugee and dependent on personal status, more particularly rights attaching to marriage, shall be respected by a Contracting State, subject to compliance, if this be necessary, with the formalities required by the law of that State, provided that the right in question is one which would have been recognized by the law of that State had he not become a refugee.

Article 13 – Movable and Immovable Property

The Contracting States shall accord to a refugee treatment as favourable as possible and, in any event, not less favourable than that accorded to aliens generally in the same circumstances, as regards the acquisition of movable and immovable property and other rights pertaining thereto, and to leases and other contracts relating to movable and immovable property.

Article 14 – Artistic Rights and Industrial Property

In respect of the protection of industrial property, such as inventions, designs or models, trade marks, trade names, and of rights in literary, artistic and scientific works, a refugee shall be accorded in the country in which he has his habitual residence the same protection as is accorded to nationals of that country. In the territory of any other Contracting States, he shall be accorded the same protection as is accorded in that territory to nationals of the country in which he has his habitual residence.

Article 15 – Right of Association

As regards non-political and non-profit-making associations and trade unions the Contracting States shall accord to refugees lawfully staying in their territory the most favourable treatment accorded to nationals of a foreign country, in the same circumstances.

Article 16 – Access to Courts

1. A refugee shall have free access to the courts of law on the territory of all Contracting States.
2. A refugee shall enjoy in the Contracting State in which he has his habitual residence the same treatment as a national in matters pertaining to access to the courts, including legal assistance and exemption from cautio judicatum solvi.
3. A refugee shall be accorded in the matters referred to in paragraph 2 in countries other than that in which he has his habitual residence the treatment granted to a national of the country of his habitual residence.

Chapter III: Gainful Employment

Article 17 – Wage-Earning Employment

1. The Contracting States shall accord to refugees lawfully staying in their territory the most favourable treatment accorded to nationals of a foreign country in the same circumstances, as regards the right to engage in wage-earning employment.
2. In any case, restrictive measures imposed on aliens or the employment of aliens for the protection of the national labour market shall not be applied to a refugee who was already exempt from them at the date of entry into force of this Convention for the Contracting State concerned, or who fulfils one of the following conditions:

(a) He has completed three years' residence in the country;
(b) He has a spouse possessing the nationality of the country of residence. A refugee may not invoke the benefit of this provision if he has abandoned his spouse;
(c) He has one or more children possessing the nationality of the country of residence.

3. The Contracting States shall give sympathetic consideration to assimilating the rights of all refugees with regard to wage-earning employment to those of nationals, and in particular of those refugees who have entered their territory pursuant to programmes of labour recruitment or under immigration schemes.

Article 18 – Self-employment

The Contracting States shall accord to a refugee lawfully in their territory treatment as favourable as possible and, in any event, not less favourable than that accorded to aliens generally in the same circumstances, as regards the right to engage on his own account in agriculture, industry, handicrafts and commerce and to establish commercial and industrial companies.

Article 19 – Liberal Professions

1. Each Contracting State shall accord to refugees lawfully staying in their territory who hold diplomas recognized by the competent authorities of that State, and who are desirous of practising a liberal profession, treatment as favourable as possible and, in any event, not less favourable than that accorded to aliens generally in the same circumstances.
2. The Contracting States shall use their best endeavours consistently with their laws and constitutions to secure the settlement of such refugees in the territories, other than the metropolitan territory, for whose international relations they are responsible.

Chapter IV: Welfare

Article 20 – Rationing

Where a rationing system exists, which applies to the population at large and regulates the general distribution of products in short supply, refugees shall be accorded the same treatment as nationals.

Article 21 – Housing

As regards housing, the Contracting States, in so far as the matter is regulated by laws or regulations or is subject to the control of public authorities, shall accord to refugees lawfully staying in their territory treatment as favourable as possible and, in any event, not less favourable than that accorded to aliens generally in the same circumstances.

Article 22 – Public Education

1. The Contracting States shall accord to refugees the same treatment as is accorded to nationals with respect to elementary education.
2. The Contracting States shall accord to refugees treatment as favourable as possible, and, in any event, not less favourable than that accorded to aliens generally in the same circumstances, with respect to education other than elementary education and, in particular, as regards access to studies, the recognition of foreign school certificates, diplomas and degrees, the remission of fees and charges and the award of scholarships.

Article 23 – Public Relief

The Contracting States shall accord to refugees lawfully staying in their territory the same treatment with respect to public relief and assistance as is accorded to their nationals.

Article 24 – Labour Legislation and Social Security

1. The Contracting States shall accord to refugees lawfully staying in their territory the same treatment as is accorded to nationals in respect of the following matters;

(a) In so far as such matters are governed by laws or regulations or are subject to the control of administrative authorities: remuneration, including family allowances where these form part of remuneration, hours of work, overtime arrangements, holidays with pay, restrictions on home work, minimum age of employment, apprenticeship and training, women's work and the work of young persons, and the enjoyment of the benefits of collective bargaining;

(b) Social security (legal provisions in respect of employment injury, occupational diseases, maternity, sickness, disability, old age, death, unemployment, family responsibilities and any other contingency which, according to national laws or regulations, is covered by a social security scheme), subject to the following limitations:

  (i) There may be appropriate arrangements for the maintenance of acquired rights and rights in course of acquisition;

  (ii) National laws or regulations of the country of residence may prescribe special arrangements concerning benefits or portions of benefits which are payable wholly out of public funds, and concerning allowances paid to persons who do not fulfil the contribution conditions prescribed for the award of a normal pension.

2. The right to compensation for the death of a refugee resulting from employment injury or from occupational disease shall not be affected by the fact that the residence of the beneficiary is outside the territory of the Contracting State.
3. The Contracting States shall extend to refugees the benefits of agreements concluded between them, or which may be concluded between them in the future, concerning the maintenance of acquired rights and rights in the process of acquisition in regard to social security, subject only to the conditions which apply to nationals of the States signatory to the agreements in question.
4. The Contracting States will give sympathetic consideration to extending to refugees so far as possible the benefits of similar agreements which may at any time be in force between such Contracting States and non-contracting States.

Chapter v: Administrative Measures

Article 25 – Administrative Assistance

1. When the exercise of a right by a refugee would normally require the assistance of authorities of a foreign country to whom he cannot have recourse, the Contracting States in whose territory he is residing shall arrange that such assistance be afforded to him by their own authorities or by an international authority.
2. The authority or authorities mentioned in paragraph 1 shall deliver or cause to be delivered under their supervision to refugees such documents or certifications as would normally be delivered to aliens by or through their national authorities.
3. Documents or certifications so delivered shall stand in the stead of the official instruments delivered to aliens by or through their national authorities, and shall be given credence in the absence of proof to the contrary.
4. Subject to such exceptional treatment as may be granted to indigent persons, fees may be charged for the services mentioned herein, but such fees shall be moderate and commensurate with those charged to nationals for similar services.
5. The provisions of this article shall be without prejudice to articles 27 and 28.

Article 26 – Freedom of Movement

Each Contracting State shall accord to refugees lawfully in its territory the right to choose their place of residence and to move freely within its territory subject to any regulations applicable to aliens generally in the same circumstances.

Article 27 – Identity Papers

The Contracting States shall issue identity papers to any refugee in their territory who does not possess a valid travel document.

Article 28 – Travel Documents

1. The Contracting States shall issue to refugees lawfully staying in their territory travel documents for the purpose of travel outside their territory, unless compelling reasons of national security or public order otherwise require, and the provisions of the Schedule to this Convention shall apply with respect to such documents. The Contracting States may issue such a travel document to any other refugee in their territory; they shall in particular give sympathetic consideration to the issue of such a travel document to refugees in their territory who are unable to obtain a travel document from the country of their lawful residence.

2. Travel documents issued to refugees under previous international agreements by Parties thereto shall be recognized and treated by the Contracting States in the same way as if they had been issued pursuant to this article.

Article 29 – Fiscal Charges

1. The Contracting States shall not impose upon refugees duties, charges or taxes, of any description whatsoever, other or higher than those which are or may be levied on their nationals in similar situations.
2. Nothing in the above paragraph shall prevent the application to refugees of the laws and regulations concerning charges in respect of the issue to aliens of administrative documents including identity papers.

Article 30 – Transfer of Assets

1. A Contracting State shall, in conformity with its laws and regulations, permit refugees to transfer assets which they have brought into its territory, to another country where they have been admitted for the purposes of resettlement.
2. A Contracting State shall give sympathetic consideration to the application of refugees for permission to transfer assets wherever they may be and which are necessary for their resettlement in another country to which they have been admitted.

Article 31 – Refugees Unlawfully in the Country of Refuge

1. The Contracting States shall not impose penalties, on account of their illegal entry or presence, on refugees who, coming directly from a territory where their life or freedom was threatened in the sense of article 1, enter or are present in their territory without authorization, provided they present themselves without delay to the authorities and show good cause for their illegal entry or presence.
2. The Contracting States shall not apply to the movements of such refugees restrictions other than those which are necessary and such restrictions shall only be applied until their status in the country is regularized or they obtain admission into another country. The Contracting States shall allow such refugees a reasonable period and all the necessary facilities to obtain admission into another country.

Article 32 – Expulsion

1. The Contracting States shall not expel a refugee lawfully in their territory save on grounds of national security or public order.
2. The expulsion of such a refugee shall be only in pursuance of a decision reached in accordance with due process of law. Except where compelling

reasons of national security otherwise require, the refugee shall be allowed to submit evidence to clear himself, and to appeal to and be represented for the purpose before competent authority or a person or persons specially designated by the competent authority.
3. The Contracting States shall allow such a refugee a reasonable period within which to seek legal admission into another country. The Contracting States reserve the right to apply during that period such internal measures as they may deem necessary.

Article 33 – Prohibition of Expulsion or Return ("Refoulement")
1. No Contracting State shall expel or return ("refouler") a refugee in any manner whatsoever to the frontiers of territories where his life or freedom would be threatened on account of his race, religion, nationality, membership of a particular social group or political opinion.
2. The benefit of the present provision may not, however, be claimed by a refugee whom there are reasonable grounds for regarding as a danger to the security of the country in which he is, or who, having been convicted by a final judgement of a particularly serious crime, constitutes a danger to the community of that country.

Article 34 – Naturalization
The Contracting States shall as far as possible facilitate the assimilation and naturalization of refugees. They shall in particular make every effort to expedite naturalization proceedings and to reduce as far as possible the charges and costs of such proceedings.

Chapter VI: Executory and Transitory Provisions

Article 35 – Co-operation of the National Authorities with the United Nations
1. The Contracting States undertake to co-operate with the Office of the United Nations High Commissioner for Refugees, or any other agency of the United Nations which may succeed it, in the exercise of its functions, and shall in particular facilitate its duty of supervising the application of the provisions of this Convention.
2. In order to enable the Office of the High Commissioner or any other agency of the United Nations which may succeed it, to make reports to the competent organs of the United Nations, the Contracting States undertake to provide

them in the appropriate form with information and statistical data requested concerning:

(a) the condition of refugees,
(b) the implementation of this Convention, and
(c) laws, regulations and decrees which are, or may hereafter be, in force relating to refugees.

Article 36 – Information on National Legislation

The Contracting States shall communicate to the Secretary-General of the United Nations the laws and regulations which they may adopt to ensure the application of this Convention.

Article 37 – Relation to Previous Conventions

Without prejudice to article 28, paragraph 2, of this Convention, this Convention replaces, as between Parties to it, the Arrangements of 5 July 1922, 31 May 1924, 12 May 1926, 30 June 1928 and 30 July 1935, the Conventions of 28 October 1933 and 10 February 1938, the Protocol of 14 September 1939 and the Agreement of 15 October 1946.

Chapter VII: Final Clauses

Article 38 – Settlement of Disputes

Any dispute between Parties to this Convention relating to its interpretation or application, which cannot be settled by other means, shall be referred to the International Court of Justice at the request of any one of the parties to the dispute.

Article 39 – Signature, Ratification and Accession

1. This Convention shall be opened for signature at Geneva on 28 July 1951 and shall thereafter be deposited with the Secretary-General of the United Nations. It shall be open for signature at the European Office of the United Nations from 28 July to 31 August 1951 and shall be re-opened for signature at the Headquarters of the United Nations from 17 September 1951 to 31 December 1952.
2. This Convention shall be open for signature on behalf of all States Members of the United Nations, and also on behalf of any other State invited to attend the Conference of Plenipotentiaries on the Status of Refugees and Stateless Persons or to which an invitation to sign will have been addressed by the General Assembly. It shall be ratified and the instruments of ratification shall be deposited with the Secretary-General of the United Nations.

3. This Convention shall be open from 28 July 1951 for accession by the States referred to in paragraph 2 of this article. Accession shall be effected by the deposit of an instrument of accession with the Secretary-General of the United Nations.

Article 40 – Territorial Application Clause

1. Any State may, at the time of signature, ratification or accession, declare that this Convention shall extend to all or any of the territories for the international relations of which it is responsible. Such a declaration shall take effect when the Convention enters into force for the State concerned.
2. At any time thereafter any such extension shall be made by notification addressed to the Secretary-General of the United Nations and shall take effect as from the ninetieth day after the day of receipt by the Secretary-General of the United Nations of this notification, or as from the date of entry into force of the Convention for the State concerned, whichever is the later.
3. With respect to those territories to which this Convention is not extended at the time of signature, ratification or accession, each State concerned shall consider the possibility of taking the necessary steps in order to extend the application of this Convention to such territories, subject, where necessary for constitutional reasons, to the consent of the Governments of such territories.

Article 41 – Federal Clause

In the case of a Federal or non-unitary State, the following provisions shall apply:

(a) With respect to those articles of this Convention that come within the legislative jurisdiction of the federal legislative authority, the obligations of the Federal Government shall to this extent be the same as those of Parties which are not Federal States;

(b) With respect to those articles of this Convention that come within the legislative jurisdiction of constituent States, provinces or cantons which are not, under the constitutional system of the Federation, bound to take legislative action, the Federal Government shall bring such articles with a favourable recommendation to the notice of the appropriate authorities of States, provinces or cantons at the earliest possible moment;

(c) A Federal State Party to this Convention shall, at the request of any other Contracting State transmitted through the Secretary-General of the United Nations, supply a statement of the law and practice of the Federation and its constituent units in regard to any particular provision of the Convention showing the extent to which effect has been given to that provision by legislative or other action.

Article 42 – Reservations

1. At the time of signature, ratification or accession, any State may make reservations to articles of the Convention other than to articles 1, 3, 4, 16 (1), 33, 36–46 inclusive.
2. Any State making a reservation in accordance with paragraph 1 of this article may at any time withdraw the reservation by a communication to that effect addressed to the Secretary-General of the United Nations.

Article 43 – Entry into Force

1. This Convention shall come into force on the ninetieth day following the day of deposit of the sixth instrument of ratification or accession.
2. For each State ratifying or acceding to the Convention after the deposit of the sixth instrument of ratification or accession, the Convention shall enter into force on the ninetieth day following the date of deposit by such State of its instrument of ratification or accession.

Article 44 – Denunciation

1. Any Contracting State may denounce this Convention at any time by a notification addressed to the Secretary-General of the United Nations.
2. Such denunciation shall take effect for the Contracting State concerned one year from the date upon which it is received by the Secretary-General of the United Nations.
3. Any State which has made a declaration or notification under article 40 may, at any time thereafter, by a notification to the Secretary-General of the United Nations, declare that the Convention shall cease to extend to such territory one year after the date of receipt of the notification by the Secretary-General.

Article 45 – Revision

1. Any Contracting State may request revision of this Convention at any time by a notification addressed to the Secretary-General of the United Nations.
2. The General Assembly of the United Nations shall recommend the steps, if any, to be taken in respect of such request.

Article 46 – Notifications by the Secretary-General of the United Nations

The Secretary-General of the United Nations shall inform all Members of the United Nations and nonmember States referred to in article 39:

(a) Of declarations and notifications in accordance with section B of article 1;

(b) Of signatures, ratifications and accessions in accordance with article 39;

(c) Of declarations and notifications in accordance with article 40;
(d) Of reservations and withdrawals in accordance with article 42;
(e) Of the date on which this Convention will come into force in accordance with article 43;
(f) Of denunciations and notifications in accordance with article 44;
(g) Of requests for revision in accordance with article 45.

In faith whereof the undersigned, duly authorized, have signed this Convention on behalf of their respective Governments,

Done at Geneva, this twenty-eighth day of July, one thousand nine hundred and fifty-one, in a single copy, of which the English and French texts are equally authentic and which shall remain deposited in the archives of the United Nations, and certified true copies of which shall be delivered to all Members of the United Nations and to the non-member States referred to in article 39.

CHAPTER 21

International Convention on the Protection of the Rights of All Migrant Workers and Members of Their Families

Adopted and opened for signature, ratification and accession by General Assembly resolution 45/1581 of 18 December 1990
Entry into force 1 July 2003, in accordance with article 87(1)

Preamble

The States Parties to the present Convention,

Taking into account the principles embodied in the basic instruments of the United Nations concerning human rights, in particular the Universal Declaration of Human Rights,[1] the International Covenant on Economic, social and Cultural Rights,[2] the International Covenant on Civil and Political Rights,[3] the International Convention on the Elimination of All Forms of Racial Discrimination,[4] the Convention on the Elimination of All Forms of Discrimination against Women[5] and the Convention on the Rights of the Child,[6]

Taking into account also the principles and standards set forth in the relevant instruments elaborated within the framework of the International Labour Organisation, especially the Convention concerning Migration for Employment (No. 97), the Convention concerning Migrations in Abusive Conditions and the Promotion of Equality of Opportunity and Treatment of Migrant Workers (No. 143), the Recommendation concerning Migration for Employment (No. 86), the Recommendation concerning Migrant workers (No. 151), the Convention concerning Forced or Compulsory Labour (No. 29) and the Convention concerning Abolition of Forced Labour (No. 105),

1 Resolution 217 A (III).
2 Resolution 2200 A (XXI), annex.
3 Resolution 2200 A (XXI), annex.
4 Resolution 2106 A (XX), annex.
5 Resolution 34/180, annex.
6 Resolution 44/25, annex.

 DOI:10.1163/9789004681224_032

Reaffirming the importance of the principles contained in the Convention against Discrimination in Education of the United Nations Educational, Scientific and Cultural Organization,[7]

Recalling the Convention against Torture and Other Cruel, Inhuman or Degrading Treatment or Punishment,[8] the Declaration of the Fourth United Nations Congress on the Prevention of Crime and the Treatment of Offenders,[9] the Code of Conduct for Law Enforcement Officials,[10] and the Slavery conventions,[11]

Recalling that one of the objectives of the International Labour Organisation, as stated in its Constitution, is the protection of the interests of workers when employed in countries other than their own, and bearing in mind the expertise and experience of that organization in matters related to migrant workers and members of their families,

Recognizing the importance of the work done in connection with migrant workers and members of their families in various organs of the United Nations, in particular in the Commission on Human Rights and the Commission for Social Development, and in the Food and Agriculture Organization of the United Nations, the United Nations Educational, Scientific and Cultural Organization and the World Health Organization, as well as in other international organizations,

Recognizing also the progress made by certain States on a regional or bilateral basis towards the protection of the rights of migrant workers and members of their families, as well as the importance and usefulness of bilateral and multilateral agreements in this field,

Realizing the importance and extent of the migration phenomenon, which involves millions of people and affects a large number of States in the international community,

Aware of the impact of the flows of migrant workers on States and people concerned, and desiring to establish norms which may contribute to the harmonization of the attitudes of States through the acceptance of basic

---

7 United Nations, Treaty Series, vol. 429, No. 6193.

8 Resolution 39/46, annex.

9 See Fourth United Nations Congress on the Prevention of Crime and the Treatment of Offenders, Kyoto, Japan, 17–26 August 1970: report prepared by the Secretariat (United Nations publication, Sale No. E. 71.IV.8).

10 Resolution 34/169, annex.

11 See Human Rights: A Compilation of International Instruments (United Nations publication, Sales No. E.88.XIV.1).

principles concerning the treatment of migrant workers and members of their families,

Considering the situation of vulnerability in which migrant workers and members of their families frequently find themselves owing, among other things, to their absence from their State of origin and to the difficulties they may encounter arising from their presence in the State of employment,

Convinced that the rights of migrant workers and members of their families have not been sufficiently recognized everywhere and therefore require appropriate international protection,

Taking into account the fact that migration is often the cause of serious problems for the members of the families of migrant workers as well as for the workers themselves, in particular because of the scattering of the family,

Bearing in mind that the human problems involved in migration are even more serious in the case of irregular migration and convinced therefore that appropriate action should be encouraged in order to prevent and eliminate clandestine movements and trafficking in migrant workers, while at the same time assuring the protection of their fundamental human rights,

Considering that workers who are non-documented or in an irregular situation are frequently employed under less favourable conditions of work than other workers and that certain employers find this an inducement to seek such labour in order to reap the benefits of unfair competition,

Considering also that recourse to the employment of migrant workers who are in an irregular situation will be discouraged if the fundamental human rights of all migrant workers are more widely recognized and, moreover, that granting certain additional rights to migrant workers and members of their families in a regular situation will encourage all migrants and employers to respect and comply with the laws and procedures established by the States concerned,

Convinced, therefore, of the need to bring about the international protection of the rights of all migrant workers and members of their families, reaffirming and establishing basic norms in a comprehensive convention which could be applied universally,

Have agreed as follows:

Part 1: Scope and Definitions

Art. 1 1. The present Convention is applicable, except as otherwise provided hereafter, to all migrant workers and members of their families without distinction of any kind such as sex, race, colour, language, religion or conviction, political or other opinion, national, ethnic or social origin, nationality, age, economic position, property, marital status, birth or other status.

2. The present Convention shall apply during the entire migration process of migrant workers and members of their families, which comprises preparation for migration, departure, transit and the entire period of stay and remunerated activity in the State of employment as well as return to the State of origin or the State of habitual residence.

Art. 2 For the purposes of the present Convention:

1. The term "migrant worker" refers to a person who is to be engaged, is engaged or has been engaged in a remunerated activity in a State of which he or she is not a national.

2.

(a) The term "frontier worker" refers to a migrant worker who retains his or her habitual residence in a neighbouring State to which he or she normally returns every day or at least once a week;

(b) The term "seasonal worker" refers to a migrant worker whose work by its character is dependent on seasonal conditions and is performed only during part of the year;

(c) The term "seafarer", which includes a fisherman, refers to a migrant worker employed on board a vessel registered in a State of which he or she is not a national;

(d) The term "worker on an offshore installation" refers to a migrant worker employed on an offshore installation that is under the jurisdiction of a State of which he or she is not a national;

(e) The term "itinerant worker" refers to a migrant worker who, having his or her habitual residence in one State, has to travel to another State or States for short periods, owing to the nature of his or her occupation;

(f) The term "project-tied worker" refers to a migrant worker admitted to a State of employment for a defined period to work solely on a specific project being carried out in that State by his or her employer;

(g) The term "specified-employment worker" refers to a migrant worker:

  (i) Who has been sent by his or her employer for a restricted and defined period of time to a State of employment to undertake a specific assignment or duty; or

  (ii) Who engages for a restricted and defined period of time in work that requires professional, commercial, technical or other highly specialized skill; or

  (iii) Who, upon the request of his or her employer in the State of employment, engages for a restricted and defined period of time in work whose nature is transitory or brief;

and who is required to depart from the State of employment either at the expiration of his or her authorized period of stay, or earlier if he or she no longer undertakes that specific assignment or duty or engages in that work;

(h) The term "self-employed worker" refers to a migrant worker who is engaged in a remunerated activity otherwise than under a contract of employment and who earns his or her living through this activity normally working alone or together with members of his or her family, and to any other migrant worker recognized as self-employed by applicable legislation of the State of employment or bilateral or multilateral agreements.

Art. 3 The present Convention shall not apply to:

(a) Persons sent or employed by international organizations and agencies or persons sent or employed by a State outside its territory to perform official functions, whose admission and status are regulated by general international law or by specific international agreements or conventions;

(b) Persons sent or employed by a State or on its behalf outside its territory who participate in development programmes and other co-operation programmes, whose admission and status are regulated by agreement with the State of employment and who, in accordance with that agreement, are not considered migrant workers;

(c) Persons taking up residence in a State different from their State of origin as investors;

(d) Refugees and stateless persons, unless such application is provided for in the relevant national legislation of, or international instruments in force for, the State Party concerned;

(e) Students and trainees;

(f) Seafarers and workers on an offshore installation who have not been admitted to take up residence and engage in a remunerated activity in the State of employment.

Art. 4 For the purposes of the present Convention the term "members of the family" refers to persons married to migrant workers or having with them a relationship that, according to applicable law, produces effects equivalent to marriage, as well as their dependent children and other dependent persons who are recognized as members of the family by applicable legislation or applicable bilateral or multilateral agreements between the States concerned.

Art. 5 For the purposes of the present Convention, migrant workers and members of their families:

(a) Are considered as documented or in a regular situation if they are authorized to enter, to stay and to engage in a remunerated activity in the State of employment pursuant to the law of that State and to international agreements to which that State is a party;

(b) Are considered as non-documented or in an irregular situation if they do not comply with the conditions provided for in subparagraph (a) of the present article.

Art. 6 For the purposes of the present Convention:

(a) The term "State of origin" means the State of which the person concerned is a national;

(b) The term "State of employment" means a State where the migrant worker is to be enqaged, is engaged or has been engaged in a remunerated activity, as the case may be;

(c) The term "State of transit" means any State through which the person concerned passes on any journey to the State of employment or from the State of employment to the State of origin or the State of habitual residence.

Part II: Non-discrimination with Respect to Rights

Art. 7 States Parties undertake, in accordance with the international instruments concerning human rights, to respect and to ensure to all migrant workers and members of their families within their territory or subject to their jurisdiction the rights provided for in the present Convention without distinction of any kind such as sex, race, colour, language, religion or conviction, political or other opinion, national, ethnic or social origin, nationality, age, economic position, property, marital status, birth or other status.

Part III: Human Rights of All Migrant Workers and Members of Their Families

Art. 8 1. Migrant workers and members of their families shall be free to leave any State, including their State of origin. This right shall not be subject to any restrictions except those that are provided by law, are necessary to protect national security, public order (ordre public), public health or morals or the rights and freedoms of others and are consistent with the other rights recognized in the present part of the Convention.

2. Migrant workers and members of their families shall have the right at any time to enter and remain in their State of origin.

Art. 9 The right to life of migrant workers and members of their families shall be protected by law.

Art. 10 No migrant worker or member of his or her family shall be subjected to torture or to cruel, inhuman or degrading treatment or punishment.

Art. 11 1. No migrant worker or member of his or her family shall be held in slavery or servitude.

2. No migrant worker or member of his or her family shall be required to perform forced or compulsory labour.

3. Paragraph 2 of the present article shall not be held to preclude, in States where imprisonment with hard labour may be imposed as a punishment for a crime, the performance of hard labour in pursuance of a sentence to such punishment by a competent court.

4. For the purpose of the present article the term "forced or compulsory labour" shall not include:

(a) Any work or service not referred to in paragraph 3 of the present article normally required of a person who is under detention in consequence of a lawful order of a court or of a person during conditional release from such detention;

(b) Any service exacted in cases of emergency or calamity threatening the life or well-being of the community;

(c) Any work or service that forms part of normal civil obligations so far as it is imposed also on citizens of the State concerned.

Art. 12 1. Migrant workers and members of their families shall have the right to freedom of thought, conscience and religion. This right shall include freedom to have or to adopt a religion or belief of their choice and freedom either individually or in community with others and in public or private to manifest their religion or belief in worship, observance, practice and teaching.

2. Migrant workers and members of their families shall not be subject to coercion that would impair their freedom to have or to adopt a religion or belief of their choice.

3. Freedom to manifest one's religion or belief may be subject only to such limitations as are prescribed by law and are necessary to protect public safety, order, health or morals or the fundamental rights and freedoms of others.

4. States Parties to the present Convention undertake to have respect for the liberty of parents, at least one of whom is a migrant worker, and, when applicable, legal guardians to ensure the religious and moral education of their children in conformity with their own convictions.

Art. 13 1. Migrant workers and members of their families shall have the right to hold opinions without interference.

2. Migrant workers and members of their families shall have the right to freedom of expression; this right shall include freedom to seek, receive and impart information and ideas of all kinds, regardless of frontiers, either orally, in writing or in print, in the form of art or through any other media of their choice.
3. The exercise of the right provided for in paragraph 2 of the present article carries with it special duties and responsibilities. It may therefore be subject to certain restrictions, but these shall only be such as are provided by law and are necessary:
(a) For respect of the rights or reputation of others;
(b) For the protection of the national security of the States concerned or of public order (ordre public) or of public health or morals;
(c) For the purpose of preventing any propaganda for war;
(d) For the purpose of preventing any advocacy of national, racial or religious hatred that constitutes incitement to discrimination, hostility or violence.

Art. 14 No migrant worker or member of his or her family shall be subjected to arbitrary or unlawful interference with his or her privacy, family, home, correspondence or other communications, or to unlawful attacks on his or her honour and reputation. Each migrant worker and member of his or her family shall have the right to the protection of the law against such interference or attacks.

Art. 15 No migrant worker or member of his or her family shall be arbitrarily deprived of property, whether owned individually or in association with others. Where, under the legislation in force in the State of employment, the assets of a migrant worker or a member of his or her family are expropriated in whole or in part, the person concerned shall have the right to fair and adequate compensation.

Art. 16 1. Migrant workers and members of their families shall have the right to liberty and security of person.
2. Migrant workers and members of their families shall be entitled to effective protection by the State against violence, physical injury, threats and intimidation, whether by public officials or by private individuals, groups or institutions.
3. Any verification by law enforcement officials of the identity of migrant workers or members of their families shall be carried out in accordance with procedures established by law.
4. Migrant workers and members of their families shall not be subjected individually or collectively to arbitrary arrest or detention; they shall not be deprived of their liberty except on such grounds and in accordance with such procedures as are established by law.
5. Migrant workers and members of their families who are arrested shall be informed at the time of arrest as far as possible in a language they understand

of the reasons for their arrest and they shall be promptly informed in a language they understand of any charges against them.

6. Migrant workers and members of their families who are arrested or detained on a criminal charge shall be brought promptly before a judge or other officer authorized by law to exercise judicial power and shall be entitled to trial within a reasonable time or to release. It shall not be the general rule that while awaiting trial they shall be detained in custody, but release may be subject to guarantees to appear for trial, at any other stage of the judicial proceedings and, should the occasion arise, for the execution of the judgement.

7. When a migrant worker or a member of his or her family is arrested or committed to prison or custody pending trial or is detained in any other manner:

(a) The consular or diplomatic authorities of his or her State of origin or of a State representing the interests of that State shall, if he or she so requests, be informed without delay of his or her arrest or detention and of the reasons therefor;

(b) The person concerned shall have the right to communicate with the said authorities. Any communication by the person concerned to the said authorities shall be forwarded without delay, and he or she shall also have the right to receive communications sent by the said authorities without delay;

(c) The person concerned shall be informed without delay of this right and of rights deriving from relevant treaties, if any, applicable between the States concerned, to correspond and to meet with representatives of the said authorities and to make arrangements with them for his or her legal representation.

8. Migrant workers and members of their families who are deprived of their liberty by arrest or detention shall be entitled to take proceedings before a court, in order that that court may decide without delay on the lawfulness of their detention and order their release if the detention is not lawful. When they attend such proceedings, they shall have the assistance, if necessary without cost to them, of an interpreter, if they cannot understand or speak the language used.

9. Migrant workers and members of their families who have been victims of unlawful arrest or detention shall have an enforceable right to compensation.

Art. 17 1. Migrant workers and members of their families who are deprived of their liberty shall be treated with humanity and with respect for the inherent dignity of the human person and for their cultural identity.

2. Accused migrant workers and members of their families shall, save in exceptional circumstances, be separated from convicted persons and shall be subject to separate treatment appropriate to their status as unconvicted persons.

Accused juvenile persons shall be separated from adults and brought as speedily as possible for adjudication.
3. Any migrant worker or member of his or her family who is detained in a State of transit or in a State of employment for violation of provisions relating to migration, shall be held, in so far as practicable, separately from convicted persons or persons detained pending trial.
4. During any period of imprisonment in pursuance of a sentence imposed by a court of law, the essential aim of the treatment of a migrant worker or a member of his or her family shall be his or her reformation and social rehabilitation. Juvenile offenders shall be separated from adults and be accorded treatment appropriate to their age and legal status.
5. During detention or imprisonment, migrant workers and members of their families shall enjoy the same rights as nationals to visits by members of their families.
6. Whenever a migrant worker is deprived of his or her liberty, the competent authorities of the State concerned shall pay attention to the problems that may be posed for members of his or her family, in particular for spouses and minor children.
7. Migrant workers and members of their families who are subjected to any form of detention or imprisonment in accordance with the law in force in the State of employment or in the State of transit shall enjoy the same rights as nationals of those States who are in the same situation.
8. If a migrant worker or a member of his or her family is detained for the purpose of verifying any infraction of provisions related to migration, he or she shall not bear any costs arising therefrom.
Art. 18 1. Migrant workers and members of their families shall have the right to equality with nationals of the State concerned before the courts and tribunals. In the determination of any criminal charge against them or of their rights and obligations in a suit of law, they shall be entitled to a fair and public hearing by a competent, independent and impartial tribunal established by law.
2. Migrant workers and members of their families who are charged with a criminal offence shall have the right to be presumed innocent until proven guilty according to law.
3. In the determination of any criminal charge against them, migrant workers and members of their families shall be entitled to the following minimum guarantees:
(a) To be informed promptly and in detail in a language they understand of the nature and cause of the charge against them;
(b) To have adequate time and facilities for the preparation of their defence and to communicate with counsel of their own choosing;

(c) To be tried without undue delay;
(d) To be tried in their presence and to defend themselves in person or through legal assistance of their own choosing; to be informed, if they do not have legal assistance, of this right; and to have legal assistance assigned to them, in any case where the interests of justice so require and without payment by them in any such case if they do not have sufficient means to pay;
(e) To examine or have examined the witnesses against them and to obtain the attendance and examination of witnesses on their behalf under the same conditions as witnesses against them;
(f) To have the free assistance of an interpreter if they cannot understand or speak the language used in court;
(g) Not to be compelled to testify against themselves or to confess guilt.

4. In the case of juvenile persons, the procedure shall be such as will take account of their age and the desirability of promoting their rehabilitation.

5. Migrant workers and members of their families convicted of a crime shall have the right to their conviction and sentence being reviewed by a higher tribunal according to law.

6. When a migrant worker or a member of his or her family has, by a final decision, been convicted of a criminal offence and when subsequently his or her conviction has been reversed or he or she has been pardoned on the ground that a new or newly discovered fact shows conclusively that there has been a miscarriage of justice, the person who has suffered punishment as a result of such conviction shall be compensated according to law, unless it is proved that the non-disclosure of the unknown fact in time is wholly or partly attributable to that person.

7. No migrant worker or member of his or her family shall be liable to be tried or punished again for an offence for which he or she has already been finally convicted or acquitted in accordance with the law and penal procedure of the State concerned.

Art. 19 1. No migrant worker or member of his or her family shall be held guilty of any criminal offence on account of any act or omission that did not constitute a criminal offence under national or international law at the time when the criminal offence was committed, nor shall a heavier penalty be imposed than the one that was applicable at the time when it was committed. If, subsequent to the commission of the offence, provision is made by law for the imposition of a lighter penalty, he or she shall benefit thereby.

2. Humanitarian considerations related to the status of a migrant worker, in particular with respect to his or her right of residence or work, should be taken

into account in imposing a sentence for a criminal offence committed by a migrant worker or a member of his or her family.

Art. 20 1. No migrant worker or member of his or her family shall be imprisoned merely on the ground of failure to fulfil a contractual obligation.

2. No migrant worker or member of his or her family shall be deprived of his or her authorization of residence or work permit or expelled merely on the ground of failure to fulfil an obligation arising out of a work contract unless fulfilment of that obligation constitutes a condition for such authorization or permit.

Art. 21 It shall be unlawful for anyone, other than a public official duly authorized by law, to confiscate, destroy or attempt to destroy identity documents, documents authorizing entry to or stay, residence or establishment in the national territory or work permits. No authorized confiscation of such documents shall take place without delivery of a detailed receipt. In no case shall it be permitted to destroy the passport or equivalent document of a migrant worker or a member of his or her family.

Art. 22 1. Migrant workers and members of their families shall not be subject to measures of collective expulsion. Each case of expulsion shall be examined and decided individually.

2. Migrant workers and members of their families may be expelled from the territory of a State Party only in pursuance of a decision taken by the competent authority in accordance with law.

3. The decision shall be communicated to them in a language they understand. Upon their request where not otherwise mandatory, the decision shall be communicated to them in writing and, save in exceptional circumstances on account of national security, the reasons for the decision likewise stated. The persons concerned shall be informed of these rights before or at the latest at the time the decision is rendered.

4. Except where a final decision is pronounced by a judicial authority, the person concerned shall have the right to submit the reason he or she should not be expelled and to have his or her case reviewed by the competent authority, unless compelling reasons of national security require otherwise. Pending such review, the person concerned shall have the right to seek a stay of the decision of expulsion.

5. If a decision of expulsion that has already been executed is subsequently annulled, the person concerned shall have the right to seek compensation according to law and the earlier decision shall not be used to prevent him or her from re-entering the State concerned.

6. In case of expulsion, the person concerned shall have a reasonable opportunity before or after departure to settle any claims for wages and other entitlements due to him or her and any pending liabilities.
7. Without prejudice to the execution of a decision of expulsion, a migrant worker or a member of his or her family who is subject to such a decision may seek entry into a State other than his or her State of origin.
8. In case of expulsion of a migrant worker or a member of his or her family the costs of expulsion shall not be borne by him or her. The person concerned may be required to pay his or her own travel costs.
9. Expulsion from the State of employment shall not in itself prejudice any rights of a migrant worker or a member of his or her family acquired in accordance with the law of that State, including the right to receive wages and other entitlements due to him or her.
Art. 23 Migrant workers and members of their families shall have the right to have recourse to the protection and assistance of the consular or diplomatic authorities of their State of origin or of a state representing the interests of that State whenever the rights recognized in the present Convention are impaired. In particular, in case of expulsion, the person concerned shall be informed of this right without delay and the authorities of the expelling State shall facilitate the exercise of such right.
Art. 24 Every migrant worker and every member of his or her family shall have the right to recognition everywhere as a person before the law.
Art. 25 1. Migrant workers shall enjoy treatment not less favourable than that which applies to nationals of the State of employment in respect of remuneration and:

(a) Other conditions of work, that is to say, overtime, hours of work, weekly rest, holidays with pay, safety, health, termination of the employment relationship and any other conditions of work which, according to national law and practice, are covered by this term;
(b) Other terms of employment, that is to say, minimum age of employment, restriction on home work and any other matters which, according to national law and practice, are considered a term of employment.

2. It shall not be lawful to derogate in private contracts of employment from the principle of equality of treatment referred to in paragraph 1 of the present article.
3. States Parties shall take all appropriate measures to ensure that migrant workers are not deprived of any rights derived from this principle by reason of any irregularity in their stay or employment. In particular, employers shall not be relieved of any legal or contractual obligations, nor shall their obligations be limited in any manner by reason of any such irregularity.

Art. 26 1. States Parties recognize the right of migrant workers and members of their families:

(a) To take part in meetings and activities of trade unions and of any other associations established in accordance with law, with a view to protecting their economic, social, cultural and other interests, subject only to the rules of the organization concerned;

(b) To join freely any trade union and any such association as aforesaid, subject only to the rules of the organization concerned;

(c) To seek the aid and assistance of any trade union and of any such association as aforesaid.

2. No restrictions may be placed on the exercise of these rights other than those that are prescribed by law and which are necessary in a democratic society in the interests of national security, public order (ordre public) or the protection of the rights and freedoms of others.

Art. 27 1. With respect to social security, migrant workers and members of their families shall enjoy in the State of employment the same treatment granted to nationals in so far as they fulfil the requirements provided for by the applicable legislation of that State and the applicable bilateral and multilateral treaties. The competent authorities of the State of origin and the State of employment can at any time establish the necessary arrangements to determine the modalities of application of this norm.

2. Where the applicable legislation does not allow migrant workers and members of their families a benefit, the States concerned shall examine the possibility of reimbursing interested persons the amount of contributions made by them with respect to that benefit on the basis of the treatment granted to nationals who are in similar circumstances.

Art. 28 Migrant workers and members of their families shall have the right to receive any medical care that is urgently required for the preservation of their life or the avoidance of irreparable harm to their health on the basis of equality of treatment with nationals of the State concerned. such emergency medical care shall not be refused them by reason of any irregularity with regard to stay or employment.

Art. 29 Each child of a migrant worker shall have the right to a name, to registration of birth and to a nationality.

Art. 30 Each child of a migrant worker shall have the basic right of access to education on the basis of equality of treatment with nationals of the State concerned. Access to public pre-school educational institutions or schools shall not be refused or limited by reason of the irregular situation with respect to stay or employment of either parent or by reason of the irregularity of the child's stay in the State of employment.

Art. 31 1. States Parties shall ensure respect for the cultural identity of migrant workers and members of their families and shall not prevent them from maintaining their cultural links with their State of origin.
2. States Parties may take appropriate measures to assist and encourage efforts in this respect.
Art. 32 Upon the termination of their stay in the State of employment, migrant workers and members of their families shall have the right to transfer their earnings and savings and, in accordance with the applicable legislation of the States concerned, their personal effects and belongings.
Art. 33 1. Migrant workers and members of their families shall have the right to be informed by the State of origin, the State of employment or the State of transit as the case may be concerning:
(a) Their rights arising out of the present Convention;
(b) The conditions of their admission, their rights and obligations under the law and practice of the State concerned and such other matters as will enable them to comply with administrative or other formalities in that State.
2. States Parties shall take all measures they deem appropriate to disseminate the said information or to ensure that it is provided by employers, trade unions or other appropriate bodies or institutions. As appropriate, they shall co-operate with other States concerned.
3. Such adequate information shall be provided upon request to migrant workers and members of their families, free of charge, and, as far as possible, in a language they are able to understand.
Art. 34 Nothing in the present part of the Convention shall have the effect of relieving migrant workers and the members of their families from either the obligation to comply with the laws and regulations of any State of transit and the State of employment or the obligation to respect the cultural identity of the inhabitants of such States.
Art. 35 Nothing in the present part of the Convention shall be interpreted as implying the regularization of the situation of migrant workers or members of their families who are non-documented or in an irregular situation or any right to such regularization of their situation, nor shall it prejudice the measures intended to ensure sound and equitable conditions for international migration as provided in part VI of the present Convention.

Part IV: Other Rights of Migrant Workers and Members of Their Families Who Are Documented or in a Regular Situation

Art. 36 Migrant workers and members of their families who are documented or in a regular situation in the State of employment shall enjoy the rights set forth in the present part of the Convention in addition to those set forth in part III.

Art. 37 Before their departure, or at the latest at the time of their admission to the state of employment, migrant workers and members of their families shall have the right to be fully informed by the State of origin or the State of employment, as appropriate, of all conditions applicable to their admission and particularly those concerning their stay and the remunerated activities in which they may engage as well as of the requirements they must satisfy in the State of employment and the authority to which they must address themselves for any modification of those conditions.

Art. 38 1. States of employment shall make every effort to authorize migrant workers and members of their families to be temporarily absent without effect upon their authorization to stay or to work, as the case may be. In doing so, States of employment shall take into account the special needs and obligations of migrant workers and members of their families, in particular in their States of origin.

2. Migrant workers and members of their families shall have the right to be fully informed of the terms on which such temporary absences are authorized.

Art. 39 1. Migrant workers and members of their families shall have the right to liberty of movement in the territory of the State of employment and freedom to choose their residence there.

2. The rights mentioned in paragraph 1 of the present article shall not be subject to any restrictions except those that are provided by law, are necessary to protect national security, public order (ordre public), public health or morals, or the rights and freedoms of others and are consistent with the other rights recognized in the present Convention.

Art. 40 1. Migrant workers and members of their families shall have the right to form associations and trade unions in the State of employment for the promotion and protection of their economic, social, cultural and other interests.

2. No restrictions may be placed on the exercise of this right other than these that are prescribed by law and are necessary in a democratic society in the interests of national security, public order (ordre public) or the protection of the rights and freedoms of others.

Art. 41 1. Migrant workers and members of their families shall have the right to participate in public affairs of their State of origin and to vote and to be elected at elections of that State, in accordance with its legislation.
2. The States concerned shall, as appropriate and in accordance with their legislation, facilitate the exercise of these rights.
Art. 42 1. States Parties shall consider the establishment of procedures or institutions through which account may be taken, both in States of origin and in States of employment, of special needs, aspirations and obligations of migrant workers and members of their families and shall envisage, as appropriate, the possibility for migrant workers and members of their families to have their freely chosen representatives in those institutions.
2. States of employment shall facilitate, in accordance with their national legislation, the consultation or participation of migrant workers and members of their families in decisions concerning the life and administration of local communities.
3. Migrant workers may enjoy political rights in the State of employment if that State, in the exercise of its sovereignty, grants them such rights.
Art. 43 1. Migrant workers shall enjoy equality of treatment with nationals of the State of employment in relation to:
(a) Access to educational institutions and services subject to the admission requirements and other regulations of the institutions and services concerned;
(b) Access to vocational guidance and placement services;
(c) Access to vocational training and retraining facilities and institutions;
(d) Access to housing, including social housing schemes, and protection against exploitation in respect of rents;
(e) Access to social and health services, provided that the requirements for participation in the respective schemes are met;
(f) Access to co-operatives and self-managed enterprises, which shall not imply a change of their migration status and shall be subject to the rules and regulations of the bodies concerned;
(g) Access to and participation in cultural life.
2. States Parties shall promote conditions to ensure effective equality of treatment to enable migrant workers to enjoy the rights mentioned in paragraph 1 of the present article whenever the terms of their stay, as authorized by the State of employment, meet the appropriate requirements.
3. States of employment shall not prevent an employer of migrant workers from establishing housing or social or cultural facilities for them. Subject to article 70 of the present Convention, a State of employment may make the

establishment of such facilities subject to the requirements generally applied in that State concerning their installation.

Art. 44 1. States Parties, recognizing that the family is the natural and fundamental group unit of society and is entitled to protection by society and the State, shall take appropriate measures to ensure the protection of the unity of the families of migrant workers.

2. States Parties shall take measures that they deem appropriate and that fall within their competence to facilitate the reunification of migrant workers with their spouses or persons who have with the migrant worker a relationship that, according to applicable law, produces effects equivalent to marriage, as well as with their minor dependent unmarried children.

3. States of employment, on humanitarian grounds, shall favourably consider granting equal treatment, as set forth in paragraph 2 of the present article, to other family members of migrant workers.

Art. 45 1. Members of the families of migrant workers shall, in the State of employment, enjoy equality of treatment with nationals of that State in relation to:

(a) Access to educational institutions and services, subject to the admission requirements and other regulations of the institutions and services concerned;

(b) Access to vocational guidance and training institutions and services, provided that requirements for participation are met;

(c) Access to social and health services, provided that requirements for participation in the respective schemes are met;

(d) Access to and participation in cultural life.

2. States of employment shall pursue a policy, where appropriate in collaboration with the States of origin, aimed at facilitating the integration of children of migrant workers in the local school system, particularly in respect of teaching them the local language.

3. States of employment shall endeavour to facilitate for the children of migrant workers the teaching of their mother tongue and culture and, in this regard, States of origin shall collaborate whenever appropriate.

4. States of employment may provide special schemes of education in the mother tongue of children of migrant workers, if necessary in collaboration with the States of origin.

Art. 46 Migrant workers and members of their families shall, subject to the applicable legislation of the States concerned, as well as relevant international agreements and the obligations of the States concerned arising out of their participation in customs unions, enjoy exemption from import and export duties and taxes in respect of their personal and household effects as well as the equipment necessary to engage in the remunerated activity for which they were admitted to the State of employment:

(a) Upon departure from the State of origin or State of habitual residence;
(b) Upon initial admission to the State of employment;
(c) Upon final departure from the State of employment;
(d) Upon final return to the State of origin or State of habitual residence.

Art. 47 1. Migrant workers shall have the right to transfer their earnings and savings, in particular those funds necessary for the support of their families, from the State of employment to their State of origin or any other State. Such transfers shall be made in conformity with procedures established by applicable legislation of the State concerned and in conformity with applicable international agreements.

2. States concerned shall take appropriate measures to facilitate such transfers.

Art. 48 1. Without prejudice to applicable double taxation agreements, migrant workers and members of their families shall, in the matter of earnings in the State of employment:

(a) Not be liable to taxes, duties or charges of any description higher or more onerous than those imposed on nationals in similar circumstances;
(b) Be entitled to deductions or exemptions from taxes of any description and to any tax allowances applicable to nationals in similar circumstances, including tax allowances for dependent members of their families.

2. States Parties shall endeavour to adopt appropriate measures to avoid double taxation of the earnings and savings of migrant workers and members of their families.

Art. 49 1. Where separate authorizations to reside and to engage in employment are required by national legislation, the States of employment shall issue to migrant workers authorization of residence for at least the same period of time as their authorization to engage in remunerated activity.

2. Migrant workers who in the State of employment are allowed freely to choose their remunerated activity shall neither be regarded as in an irregular situation nor shall they lose their authorization of residence by the mere fact of the termination of their remunerated activity prior to the expiration of their work permits or similar authorizations.

3. In order to allow migrant workers referred to in paragraph 2 of the present article sufficient time to find alternative remunerated activities, the authorization of residence shall not be withdrawn at least for a period corresponding to that during which they may be entitled to unemployment benefits.

Art. 50 1. In the case of death of a migrant worker or dissolution of marriage, the State of employment shall favourably consider granting family members

of that migrant worker residing in that State on the basis of family reunion an authorization to stay; the State of employment shall take into account the length of time they have already resided in that State.
2. Members of the family to whom such authorization is not granted shall be allowed before departure a reasonable period of time in order to enable them to settle their affairs in the State of employment.
3. The provisions of paragraphs 1 and 2 of the present article may not be interpreted as adversely affecting any right to stay and work otherwise granted to such family members by the legislation of the State of employment or by bilateral and multilateral treaties applicable to that State.
Art. 51 Migrant workers who in the State of employment are not permitted freely to choose their remunerated activity shall neither be regarded as in an irregular situation nor shall they lose their authorization of residence by the mere fact of the termination of their remunerated activity prior to the expiration of their work permit, except where the authorization of residence is expressly dependent upon the specific remunerated activity for which they were admitted. Such migrant workers shall have the right to seek alternative employment, participation in public work schemes and retraining during the remaining period of their authorization to work, subject to such conditions and limitations as are specified in the authorization to work.
Art. 52 1. Migrant workers in the State of employment shall have the right freely to choose their remunerated activity, subject to the following restrictions or conditions.
2. For any migrant worker a State of employment may:
(a) Restrict access to limited categories of employment, functions, services or activities where this is necessary in the interests of this State and provided for by national legislation;
(b) Restrict free choice of remunerated activity in accordance with its legislation concerning recognition of occupational qualifications acquired outside its territory. However, States Parties concerned shall endeavour to provide for recognition of such qualifications.
3. For migrant workers whose permission to work is limited in time, a State of employment may also:
(a) Make the right freely to choose their remunerated activities subject to the condition that the migrant worker has resided lawfully in its territory for the purpose of remunerated activity for a period of time prescribed in its national legislation that should not exceed two years;
(b) Limit access by a migrant worker to remunerated activities in pursuance of a policy of granting priority to its nationals or to persons who are assimilated to them for these purposes by virtue of legislation or

bilateral or multilateral agreements. Any such limitation shall cease to apply to a migrant worker who has resided lawfully in its territory for the purpose of remunerated activity for a period of time prescribed in its national legislation that should not exceed five years.

4. States of employment shall prescribe the conditions under which a migrant worker who has been admitted to take up employment may be authorized to engage in work on his or her own account. Account shall be taken of the period during which the worker has already been lawfully in the State of employment.

Art. 53 1. Members of a migrant worker's family who have themselves an authorization of residence or admission that is without limit of time or is automatically renewable shall be permitted freely to choose their remunerated activity under the same conditions as are applicable to the said migrant worker in accordance with article 52 of the present Convention.

2. With respect to members of a migrant worker's family who are not permitted freely to choose their remunerated activity, States Parties shall consider favourably granting them priority in obtaining permission to engage in a remunerated activity over other workers who seek admission to the State of employment, subject to applicable bilateral and multilateral agreements.

Art. 54 1. Without prejudice to the terms of their authorization of residence or their permission to work and the rights provided for in articles 25 and 27 of the present Convention, migrant workers shall enjoy equality of treatment with nationals of the State of employment in respect of:

(a) Protection against dismissal;
(b) Unemployment benefits;
(c) Access to public work schemes intended to combat unemployment;
(d) Access to alternative employment in the event of loss of work or termination of other remunerated activity, subject to article 52 of the present Convention.

2. If a migrant worker claims that the terms of his or her work contract have been violated by his or her employer, he or she shall have the right to address his or her case to the competent authorities of the State of employment, on terms provided for in article 18, paragraph 1, of the present Convention.

Art. 55 Migrant workers who have been granted permission to engage in a remunerated activity, subject to the conditions attached to such permission, shall be entitled to equality of treatment with nationals of the State of employment in the exercise of that remunerated activity.

Art. 56 1. Migrant workers and members of their families referred to in the present part of the Convention may not be expelled from a State of employment, except for reasons defined in the national legislation of that State, and subject to the safeguards established in part III.

2. Expulsion shall not be resorted to for the purpose of depriving a migrant worker or a member of his or her family of the rights arising out of the authorization of residence and the work permit.
3. In considering whether to expel a migrant worker or a member of his or her family, account should be taken of humanitarian considerations and of the length of time that the person concerned has already resided in the State of employment.

Part V: Provisions Applicable to Particular Categories of Migrant Workers and Members of Their Families

Art. 57 The particular categories of migrant workers and members of their families specified in the present part of the Convention who are documented or in a regular situation shall enjoy the rights set forth in part III and, except as modified below, the rights set forth in part IV.
Art. 58 1. Frontier workers, as defined in article 2, paragraph 2 (a), of the present Convention, shall be entitled to the rights provided for in part IV that can be applied to them by reason of their presence and work in the territory of the State of employment, taking into account that they do not have their habitual residence in that State.
2. States of employment shall consider favourably granting frontier workers the right freely to choose their remunerated activity after a specified period of time. The granting of that right shall not affect their status as frontier workers.
Art. 59 1. Seasonal workers, as defined in article 2, paragraph 2 (b), of the present Convention, shall be entitled to the rights provided for in part IV that can be applied to them by reason of their presence and work in the territory of the State of employment and that are compatible with their status in that State as seasonal workers, taking into account the fact that they are present in that State for only part of the year.
2. The State of employment shall, subject to paragraph 1 of the present article, consider granting seasonal workers who have been employed in its territory for a significant period of time the possibility of taking up other remunerated activities and giving them priority over other workers who seek admission to that State, subject to applicable bilateral and multilateral agreements.
Art. 60 Itinerant workers, as defined in article 2, paragraph 2 (e), of the present Convention, shall be entitled to the rights provided for in part IV that can be granted to them by reason of their presence and work in the territory of the State of employment and that are compatible with their status as itinerant workers in that State.

Art. 61 1. Project-tied workers, as defined in article 2, paragraph 2 (f), of the present Convention, and members of their families shall be entitled to the rights provided for in part IV except the provisions of article 43, paragraphs 1 (b) and (c), article 43, paragraph 1 (d), as it pertains to social housing schemes, article 45, paragraph 1 (b), and articles 52 to 55.
2. If a project-tied worker claims that the terms of his or her work contract have been violated by his or her employer, he or she shall have the right to address his or her case to the competent authorities of the State which has jurisdiction over that employer, on terms provided for in article 18, paragraph 1, of the present Convention.
3. Subject to bilateral or multilateral agreements in force for them, the States Parties concerned shall endeavour to enable project-tied workers to remain adequately protected by the social security systems of their States of origin or habitual residence during their engagement in the project. States Parties concerned shall take appropriate measures with the aim of avoiding any denial of rights or duplication of payments in this respect.
4. Without prejudice to the provisions of article 47 of the present Convention and to relevant bilateral or multilateral agreements, States Parties concerned shall permit payment of the earnings of project-tied workers in their State of origin or habitual residence.
Art. 62 1. Specified-employment workers as defined in article 2, paragraph 2 (g), of the present Convention, shall be entitled to the rights provided for in part IV, except the provisions of article 43, paragraphs 1 (b) and (c), article 43, paragraph 1 (d), as it pertains to social housing schemes, article 52, and article 54, paragraph 1 (d).
2. Members of the families of specified-employment workers shall be entitled to the rights relating to family members of migrant workers provided for in part IV of the present Convention, except the provisions of article 53.
Art. 63 1. Self-employed workers, as defined in article 2, paragraph 2 (h), of the present Convention, shall be entitled to the rights provided for in part IV with the exception of those rights which are exclusively applicable to workers having a contract of employment.
2. Without prejudice to articles 52 and 79 of the present Convention, the termination of the economic activity of the self-employed workers shall not in itself imply the withdrawal of the authorization for them or for the members of their families to stay or to engage in a remunerated activity in the State of employment except where the authorization of residence is expressly dependent upon the specific remunerated activity for which they were admitted.

Part VI: Promotion of Sound, Equitable, Humane and Lawful Conditions in Connection with International Migration of Workers and Members of Their Families

Art. 64 1. Without prejudice to article 79 of the present Convention, the States Parties concerned shall as appropriate consult and co-operate with a view to promoting sound, equitable and humane conditions in connection with international migration of workers and members of their families.
2. In this respect, due regard shall be paid not only to labour needs and resources, but also to the social, economic, cultural and other needs of migrant workers and members of their families involved, as well as to the consequences of such migration for the communities concerned.
Art. 65 1. States Parties shall maintain appropriate services to deal with questions concerning international migration of workers and members of their families. Their functions shall include, inter alia:
(a) The formulation and implementation of policies regarding such migration;
(b) An exchange of information, consultation and co-operation with the competent authorities of other States Parties involved in such migration;
(c) The provision of appropriate information, particularly to employers, workers and their organizations on policies, laws and regulations relating to migration and employment, on agreements concluded with other States concerning migration and on other relevant matters;
(d) The provision of information and appropriate assistance to migrant workers and members of their families regarding requisite authorizations and formalities and arrangements for departure, travel, arrival, stay, remunerated activities, exit and return, as well as on conditions of work and life in the State of employment and on customs, currency, tax and other relevant laws and regulations.

2. States Parties shall facilitate as appropriate the provision of adequate consular and other services that are necessary to meet the social, cultural and other needs of migrant workers and members of their families.
Art. 66 1. Subject to paragraph 2 of the present article, the right to undertake operations with a view to the recruitment of workers for employment in another State shall be restricted to:
(a) Public services or bodies of the State in which such operations take place;
(b) Public services or bodies of the State of employment on the basis of agreement between the States concerned;
(c) A body established by virtue of a bilateral or multilateral agreement.

2. Subject to any authorization, approval and supervision by the public authorities of the States Parties concerned as may be established pursuant to the legislation and practice of those States, agencies, prospective employers or persons acting on their behalf may also be permitted to undertake the said operations.

Art. 67 1. States Parties concerned shall co-operate as appropriate in the adoption of measures regarding the orderly return of migrant workers and members of their families to the State of origin when they decide to return or their authorization of residence or employment expires or when they are in the state of employment in an irregular situation.

2. Concerning migrant workers and members of their families in a regular situation, States Parties concerned shall co-operate as appropriate, on terms agreed upon by those States, with a view to promoting adequate economic conditions for their resettlement and to facilitating their durable social and cultural reintegration in the State of origin.

Art. 68 1. States Parties, including States of transit, shall collaborate with a view to preventing and eliminating illegal or clandestine movements and employment of migrant workers in an irregular situation. The measures to be taken to this end within the jurisdiction of each State concerned shall include:

(a) Appropriate measures against the dissemination of misleading information relating to emigration and immigration;

(b) Measures to detect and eradicate illegal or clandestine movements of migrant workers and members of their families and to impose effective sanctions on persons, groups or entities which organize, operate or assist in organizing or operating such movements;

(c) Measures to impose effective sanctions on persons, groups or entities which use violence, threats or intimidation against migrant workers or members of their families in an irregular situation.

2. States of employment shall take all adequate and effective measures to eliminate employment in their territory of migrant workers in an irregular situation, including, whenever appropriate, sanctions on employers of such workers. The rights of migrant workers vis-à-vis their employer arising from employment shall not be impaired by these measures.

Art. 69 1. States Parties shall, when there are migrant workers and members of their families within their territory in an irregular situation, take appropriate measures to ensure that such a situation does not persist.

2. Whenever States Parties concerned consider the possibility of regularizing the situation of such persons in accordance with applicable national legislation and bilateral or multilateral agreements, appropriate account shall be taken of the circumstances of their entry, the duration of their stay in the

States of employment and other relevant considerations, in particular these relating to their family situation.

Art. 70 States Parties shall take measures not less favourable than those applied to nationals to ensure that working and living conditions of migrant workers and members of their families in a regular situation are in keeping with the standards of fitness, safety, health and principles of human dignity.

Art. 71 1. States Parties shall facilitate, whenever necessary, the repatriation to the State of origin of the bodies of deceased migrant workers or members of their families.

2. As regards compensation matters relating to the death of a migrant worker or a member of his or her family, States Parties shall, as appropriate, provide assistance to the persons concerned with a view to the prompt settlement of such matters. Settlement of these matters shall be carried out on the basis of applicable national law in accordance with the provisions of the present Convention and any relevant bilateral or multilateral agreements.

Part VII: Application of the Convention

Art. 72

1.

(a) For the purpose of reviewing the application of the present Convention, there shall be established a Committee on the Protection of the Rights of All Migrant Workers and Members of Their Families (hereinafter referred to as "the Committee");

(b) The Committee shall consist, at the time of entry into force of the present Convention, of ten and, after the entry into force of the Convention for the forty-first State Party, of fourteen experts of high moral standing, impartiality and recognized competence in the field covered by the Convention.

2.

(a) Members of the Committee shall be elected by secret ballot by the States Parties from a list of persons nominated by the States Parties, due consideration being given to equitable geographical distribution, including both States of origin and States of employment, and to the representation of the principal legal systems. Each State Party may nominate one person from among its own nationals;

(b) Members shall be elected and shall serve in their personal capacity.

3. The initial election shall be held no later than six months after the date of the entry into force of the present Convention and subsequent elections

every second year. At least four months before the date of each election, the Secretary-General of the United Nations shall address a letter to all States Parties inviting them to submit their nominations within two months. The Secretary-General shall prepare a list in alphabetical order of all persons thus nominated, indicating the States Parties that have nominated them, and shall submit it to the States Parties not later than one month before the date of the corresponding election, together with the curricula vitae of the persons thus nominated.

4. Elections of members of the Committee shall be held at a meeting of States Parties convened by the Secretary-General at United Nations Headquarters. At that meeting, for which two thirds of the States Parties shall constitute a quorum, the persons elected to the Committee shall be those nominees who obtain the largest number of votes and an absolute majority of the votes of the States Parties present and voting.

5.

(a) The members of the Committee shall serve for a term of four years. However, the terms of five of the members elected in the first election shall expire at the end of two years; immediately after the first election, the names of these five members shall be chosen by lot by the Chairman of the meeting of States Parties;

(b) The election of the four additional members of the Committee shall be held in accordance with the provisions of paragraphs 2, 3 and 4 of the present article, following the entry into force of the Convention for the forty-first State Party. The term of two of the additional members elected on this occasion shall expire at the end of two years; the names of these members shall be chosen by lot by the Chairman of the meeting of States Parties;

(c) The members of the Committee shall be eligible for re-election if renominated.

6. If a member of the Committee dies or resigns or declares that for any other cause he or she can no longer perform the duties of the Committee, the State Party that nominated the expert shall appoint another expert from among its own nationals for the remaining part of the term. The new appointment is subject to the approval of the Committee.

7. The Secretary-General of the United Nations shall provide the necessary staff and facilities for the effective performance of the functions of the Committee.

8. The members of the Committee shall receive emoluments from United Nations resources on such terms and conditions as the General Assembly may decide.

9. The members of the Committee shall be entitled to the facilities, privileges and immunities of experts on mission for the United Nations as laid down in the relevant sections of the Convention on the Privileges and Immunities of the United Nations.[12]

Art. 73 1. States Parties undertake to submit to the Secretary-General of the United Nations for consideration by the Committee a report on the legislative, judicial, administrative and other measures they have taken to give effect to the provisions of the present Convention:

(a) Within one year after the entry into force of the Convention for the State Party concerned;

(b) Thereafter every five years and whenever the Committee so requests.

2. Reports prepared under the present article shall also indicate factors and difficulties, if any, affecting the implementation of the Convention and shall include information on the characteristics of migration flows in which the State Party concerned is involved.

3. The Committee shall decide any further guidelines applicable to the content of the reports.

4. States Parties shall make their reports widely available to the public in their own countries.

Art. 74 1. The Committee shall examine the reports submitted by each State Party and shall transmit such comments as it may consider appropriate to the State Party concerned. This State Party may submit to the Committee observations on any comment made by the Committee in accordance with the present article. The Committee may request supplementary information from States Parties when considering these reports.

2. The Secretary-General of the United Nations shall, in due time before the opening of each regular session of the Committee, transmit to the Director-General of the International Labour Office copies of the reports submitted by States Parties concerned and information relevant to the consideration of these reports, in order to enable the Office to assist the Committee with the expertise the Office may provide regarding those matters dealt with by the present Convention that fall within the sphere of competence of the International Labour Organisation. The Committee shall consider in its deliberations such comments and materials as the Office may provide.

3. The Secretary-General of the United Nations may also, after consultation with the Committee, transmit to other specialized agencies as well as to

12 Resolution 22 A (I).

intergovernmental organizations, copies of such parts of these reports as may fall within their competence.
4. The Committee may invite the specialized agencies and organs of the United Nations, as well as intergovernmental organizations and other concerned bodies to submit, for consideration by the Committee, written information on such matters dealt with in the present Convention as fall within the scope of their activities.
5. The International Labour Office shall be invited by the Committee to appoint representatives to participate, in a consultative capacity, in the meetings of the Committee.
6. The Committee may invite representatives of other specialized agencies and organs of the United Nations, as well as of intergovernmental organizations, to be present and to be heard in its meetings whenever matters falling within their field of competence are considered.
7. The Committee shall present an annual report to the General Assembly of the United Nations on the implementation of the present Convention, containing its own considerations and recommendations, based, in particular, on the examination of the reports and any observations presented by States Parties.
8. The Secretary-General of the United Nations shall transmit the annual reports of the Committee to the States Parties to the present Convention, the Economic and Social Council, the Commission on Human Rights of the United Nations, the Director-General of the International Labour Office and other relevant organizations.
Art. 75 1. The Committee shall adopt its own rules of procedure.
2. The Committee shall elect its officers for a term of two years.
3. The Committee shall normally meet annually.
4. The meetings of the Committee shall normally be held at United Nations Headquarters.
Art. 76 1. A State Party to the present Convention may at any time declare under this article that it recognizes the competence of the Committee to receive and consider communications to the effect that a State Party claims that another State Party is not fulfilling its obligations under the present Convention. Communications under this article may be received and considered only if submitted by a State Party that has made a declaration recognizing in regard to itself the competence of the Committee. No communication shall be received by the Committee if it concerns a State Party which has not made such a declaration. Communications received under this article shall be dealt with in accordance with the following procedure:

(a) If a State Party to the present Convention considers that another State Party is not fulfilling its obligations under the present Convention, it may, by written communication, bring the matter to the attention of that State Party. The State Party may also inform the Committee of the matter. Within three months after the receipt of the communication the receiving State shall afford the State that sent the communication an explanation, or any other statement in writing clarifying the matter which should include, to the extent possible and pertinent, reference to domestic procedures and remedies taken, pending or available in the matter;

(b) If the matter is not adjusted to the satisfaction of both States Parties concerned within six months after the receipt by the receiving State of the initial communication, either State shall have the right to refer the matter to the Committee, by notice given to the Committee and to the other State;

(c) The Committee shall deal with a matter referred to it only after it has ascertained that all available domestic remedies have been invoked and exhausted in the matter, in conformity with the generally recognized principles of international law. This shall not be the rule where, in the view of the Committee, the application of the remedies is unreasonably prolonged;

(d) Subject to the provisions of subparagraph (c) of the present paragraph, the Committee shall make available its good offices to the States Parties concerned with a view to a friendly solution of the matter on the basis of the respect for the obligations set forth in the present Convention;

(e) The Committee shall hold closed meetings when examining communications under the present article;

(f) In any matter referred to it in accordance with subparagraph (b) of the present paragraph, the Committee may call upon the States Parties concerned, referred to in subparagraph (b), to supply any relevant information;

(g) The States Parties concerned, referred to in subparagraph (b) of the present paragraph, shall have the right to be represented when the matter is being considered by the Committee and to make submissions orally and/or in writing;

(h) The Committee shall, within twelve months after the date of receipt of notice under subparagraph (b) of the present paragraph, submit a report, as fellows:

(i) If a solution within the terms of subparagraph (d) of the present paragraph is reached, the Committee shall confine its report to a brief statement of the facts and of the solution reached;

(ii) If a solution within the terms of subparagraph (d) is not reached, the Committee shall, in its report, set forth the relevant facts concerning the issue between the States Parties concerned. The written submissions and record of the oral submissions made by the States Parties concerned shall be attached to the report. The Committee may also communicate only to the States Parties concerned any views that it may consider relevant to the issue between them.

In every matter, the report shall be communicated to the States Parties concerned.

2. The provisions of the present article shall come into force when ten States Parties to the present Convention have made a declaration under paragraph 1 of the present article. Such declarations shall be deposited by the States Parties with the Secretary-General of the United Nations, who shall transmit copies thereof to the other States Parties. A declaration may be withdrawn at any time by notification to the Secretary-General. Such a withdrawal shall not prejudice the consideration of any matter that is the subject of a communication already transmitted under the present article; no further communication by any State Party shall be received under the present article after the notification of withdrawal of the declaration has been received by the Secretary-General, unless the State Party concerned has made a new declaration.

Art. 77 1. A state Party to the present Convention may at any time declare under the present article that it recognizes the competence of the Committee to receive and consider communications from or on behalf of individuals subject to its jurisdiction who claim that their individual rights as established by the present Convention have been violated by that State Party. No communication shall be received by the Committee if it concerns a State Party that has not made such a declaration.

2. The Committee shall consider inadmissible any communication under the present article which is anonymous or which it considers to be an abuse of the right of submission of such communications or to be incompatible with the provisions of the present Convention.

3. The Committee shall not consider any communications from an individual under the present article unless it has ascertained that:

(a) The same matter has not been, and is not being, examined under another procedure of international investigation or settlement;

(b) The individual has exhausted all available domestic remedies; this shall not be the rule where, in the view of the Committee, the application of the remedies is unreasonably prolonged or is unlikely to bring effective relief to that individual.

4. Subject to the provisions of paragraph 2 of the present article, the Committee shall bring any communications submitted to it under this article to the attention of the State Party to the present Convention that has made a declaration under paragraph 1 and is alleged to be violating any provisions of the Convention. Within six months, the receiving State shall submit to the Committee written explanations or statements clarifying the matter and the remedy, if any, that may have been taken by that State.

5. The Committee shall consider communications received under the present article in the light of all information made available to it by or on behalf of the individual and by the State Party concerned.

6. The Committee shall hold closed meetings when examining communications under the present article.

7. The Committee shall forward its views to the State Party concerned and to the individual.

8. The provisions of the present article shall come into force when ten States Parties to the present Convention have made declarations under paragraph 1 of the present article. Such declarations shall be deposited by the States Parties with the Secretary-General of the United Nations, who shall transmit copies thereof to the other States Parties. A declaration may be withdrawn at any time by notification to the Secretary-General. Such a withdrawal shall not prejudice the consideration of any matter that is the subject of a communication already transmitted under the present article; no further communication by or on behalf of an individual shall be received under the present article after the notification of withdrawal of the declaration has been received by the Secretary-General, unless the State Party has made a new declaration.

Art. 78 The provisions of article 76 of the present Convention shall be applied without prejudice to any procedures for settling disputes or complaints in the field covered by the present Convention laid down in the constituent instruments of, or in conventions adopted by, the United Nations and the specialized agencies and shall not prevent the States Parties from having recourse to any procedures for settling a dispute in accordance with international agreements in force between them.

Part VIII: General Provisions

Art. 79 Nothing in the present Convention shall affect the right of each State Party to establish the criteria governing admission of migrant workers and members of their families. Concerning other matters related to their legal situation and treatment as migrant workers and members of their families, States Parties shall be subject to the limitations set forth in the present Convention.
Art. 80 Nothing in the present Convention shall be interpreted as impairing the provisions of the Charter of the United Nations and of the constitutions of the specialized agencies which define the respective responsibilities of the various organs of the United Nations and of the specialized agencies in regard to the matters dealt with in the present Convention.
Art. 81 1. Nothing in the present Convention shall affect more favourable rights or freedoms granted to migrant workers and members of their families by virtue of:
(a) The law or practice of a State Party; or
(b) Any bilateral or multilateral treaty in force for the State Party concerned.
2. Nothing in the present Convention may be interpreted as implying for any State, group or person any right to engage in any activity or perform any act that would impair any of the rights and freedoms as set forth in the present Convention.
Art. 82 The rights of migrant workers and members of their families provided for in the present Convention may not be renounced. It shall not be permissible to exert any form of pressure upon migrant workers and members of their families with a view to their relinquishing or foregoing any of the said rights. It shall not be possible to derogate by contract from rights recognized in the present Convention. States Parties shall take appropriate measures to ensure that these principles are respected.
Art. 83 Each State Party to the present Convention undertakes:
(a) To ensure that any person whose rights or freedoms as herein recognized are violated shall have an effective remedy, notwithstanding that the violation has been committed by persons acting in an official capacity;
(b) To ensure that any persons seeking such a remedy shall have his or her claim reviewed and decided by competent judicial, administrative or legislative authorities, or by any other competent authority provided for by the legal system of the State, and to develop the possibilities of judicial remedy;
(c) To ensure that the competent authorities shall enforce such remedies when granted.

Art. 84 Each State Party undertakes to adopt the legislative and other measures that are necessary to implement the provisions of the present Convention.

Part IX: Final Provisions

Art. 85 The Secretary-General of the United Nations is designated as the depositary of the present Convention.

Art. 86 1. The present Convention shall be open for signature by all States. It is subject to ratification.

2. The present Convention shall be open to accession by any State.

3. Instruments of ratification or accession shall be deposited with the Secretary-General of the United Nations.

Art. 87 1. The present Convention shall enter into force on the first day of the month following a period of three months after the date of the deposit of the twentieth instrument of ratification or accession.

2. For each State ratifying or acceding to the present Convention after its entry into force, the Convention shall enter into force on the first day of the month following a period of three months after the date of the deposit of its own instrument of ratification or accession.

Art. 88 A State ratifying or acceding to the present Convention may not exclude the application of any Part of it, or, without prejudice to article 3, exclude any particular category of migrant workers from its application.

Art. 89 1. Any State Party may denounce the present Convention, not earlier than five years after the Convention has entered into force for the State concerned, by means of a notification in writing addressed to the Secretary-General of the United Nations.

2. Such denunciation shall become effective on the first day of the month following the expiration of a period of twelve months after the date of the receipt of the notification by the Secretary-General of the United Nations.

3. Such a denunciation shall not have the effect of releasing the State Party from its obligations under the present Convention in regard to any act or omission which occurs prior to the date at which the denunciation becomes effective, nor shall denunciation prejudice in any way the continued consideration of any matter which is already under consideration by the Committee prior to the date at which the denunciation becomes effective.

4. Following the date at which the denunciation of a State Party becomes effective, the Committee shall not commence consideration of any new matter regarding that State.

Art. 90 1. After five years from the entry into force of the Convention a request for the revision of the Convention may be made at any time by any State Party by means of a notification in writing addressed to the Secretary-General of the United Nations. The Secretary-General shall thereupon communicate any proposed amendments to the States Parties with a request that they notify him whether they favour a conference of States Parties for the purpose of considering and voting upon the proposals. In the event that within four months from the date of such communication at least one third of the States Parties favours such a conference, the Secretary-General shall convene the conference under the auspices of the United Nations. Any amendment adopted by a majority of the States Parties present and voting shall be submitted to the General Assembly for approval.

2. Amendments shall come into force when they have been approved by the General Assembly of the United Nations and accepted by a two-thirds majority of the States Parties in accordance with their respective constitutional processes.

3. When amendments come into force, they shall be binding on those States Parties that have accepted them, other States Parties still being bound by the provisions of the present Convention and any earlier amendment that they have accepted.

Art. 91 1. The Secretary-General of the United Nations shall receive and circulate to all States the text of reservations made by States at the time of signature, ratification or accession.

2. A reservation incompatible with the object and purpose of the present Convention shall not be permitted.

3. Reservations may be withdrawn at any time by notification to this effect addressed to the Secretary-General of the United Nations, who shall then inform all States thereof. Such notification shall take effect on the date on which it is received.

Art. 92 1. Any dispute between two or more States Parties concerning the interpretation or application of the present Convention that is not settled by negotiation shall, at the request of one of them, be submitted to arbitration. If within six months from the date of the request for arbitration the Parties are unable to agree on the organization of the arbitration, any one of those Parties may refer the dispute to the International Court of Justice by request in conformity with the Statute of the Court.

2. Each State Party may at the time of signature or ratification of the present Convention or accession thereto declare that it does not consider itself bound by paragraph 1 of the present article. The other States Parties shall not be

bound by that paragraph with respect to any State Party that has made such a declaration.

3. Any state Party that has made a declaration in accordance with paragraph 2 of the present article may at any time withdraw that declaration by notification to the Secretary-General of the United Nations.

Art. 93 1. The present Convention, of which the Arabic, Chinese, English, French, Russian and Spanish texts are equally authentic, shall be deposited with the Secretary-General of the United Nations.

2. The Secretary-General of the United Nations shall, transmit certified copies of the present Convention to all States.

IN WITNESS WHEREOF the undersigned plenipotentiaries, being duly authorized thereto by their respective Governments, have signed the present Convention.

CHAPTER 22

Protocol against the Smuggling of Migrants by Land, Sea and Air, Supplementing the United Nations Convention against Transnational Organized Crime

Adopted and adopted for signature, ratification and accession by General Assembly resolution 55/25 of 15 November 2000
Entry into force 28 January 2004, in accordance with article 22

Preamble

The States Parties to this Protocol,

Declaring that effective action to prevent and combat the smuggling of migrants by land, sea and air requires a comprehensive international approach, including cooperation, the exchange of information and other appropriate measures, including socio-economic measures, at the national, regional and international levels,

Recalling General Assembly resolution 54/212 of 22 December 1999, in which the Assembly urged Member States and the United Nations system to strengthen international cooperation in the area of international migration and development in order to address the root causes of migration, especially those related to poverty, and to maximize the benefits of international migration to those concerned, and encouraged, where relevant, interregional, regional and subregional mechanisms to continue to address the question of migration and development,

Convinced of the need to provide migrants with humane treatment and full protection of their rights,

Taking into account the fact that, despite work undertaken in other international forums, there is no universal instrument that addresses all aspects of smuggling of migrants and other related issues,

Concerned at the significant increase in the activities of organized criminal groups in smuggling of migrants and other related criminal activities set forth in this Protocol, which bring great harm to the States concerned,

Also concerned that the smuggling of migrants can endanger the lives or security of the migrants involved,

 DOI:10.1163/9789004681224_033

Recalling General Assembly resolution 53/111 of 9 December 1998, in which the Assembly decided to establish an open-ended intergovernmental ad hoc committee for the purpose of elaborating a comprehensive international convention against transnational organized crime and of discussing the elaboration of, inter alia, an international instrument addressing illegal trafficking in and transporting of migrants, including by sea,

Convinced that supplementing the United Nations Convention against Transnational Organized Crime with an international instrument against the smuggling of migrants by land, sea and air will be useful in preventing and combating that crime,

Have agreed as follows:

I General Provisions

Article 1 – Relation with the United Nations Convention against Transnational Organized Crime

1. This Protocol supplements the United Nations Convention against Transnational Organized Crime. It shall be interpreted together with the Convention.
2. The provisions of the Convention shall apply, mutatis mutandis, to this Protocol unless otherwise provided herein.
3. The offences established in accordance with article 6 of this Protocol shall be regarded as offences established in accordance with the Convention.

Article 2 – Statement of Purpose

The purpose of this Protocol is to prevent and combat the smuggling of migrants, as well as to promote cooperation among States Parties to that end, while protecting the rights of smuggled migrants.

Article 3 – Use of Terms

For the purposes of this Protocol:

(a) "Smuggling of migrants" shall mean the procurement, in order to obtain, directly or indirectly, a financial or other material benefit, of the illegal entry of a person into a State Party of which the person is not a national or a permanent resident;

(b) "Illegal entry" shall mean crossing borders without complying with the necessary requirements for legal entry into the receiving State;

(c) "Fraudulent travel or identity document" shall mean any travel or identity document:

(i) That has been falsely made or altered in some material way by anyone other than a person or agency lawfully authorized to make or issue the travel or identity document on behalf of a State; or

(ii) That has been improperly issued or obtained through misrepresentation, corruption or duress or in any other unlawful manner; or

(iii) That is being used by a person other than the rightful holder;

(d) "Vessel" shall mean any type of water craft, including non-displacement craft and seaplanes, used or capable of being used as a means of transportation on water, except a warship, naval auxiliary or other vessel owned or operated by a Government and used, for the time being, only on government non-commercial service.

Article 4 – Scope of Application

This Protocol shall apply, except as otherwise stated herein, to the prevention, investigation and prosecution of the offences established in accordance with article 6 of this Protocol, where the offences are transnational in nature and involve an organized criminal group, as well as to the protection of the rights of persons who have been the object of such offences.

Article 5 – Criminal Liability of Migrants

Migrants shall not become liable to criminal prosecution under this Protocol for the fact of having been the object of conduct set forth in article 6 of this Protocol.

Article 6 – Criminalization

1. Each State Party shall adopt such legislative and other measures as may be necessary to establish as criminal offences, when committed intentionally and in order to obtain, directly or indirectly, a financial or other material benefit:

(a) The smuggling of migrants;

(b) When committed for the purpose of enabling the smuggling of migrants:

(i) Producing a fraudulent travel or identity document;

(ii) Procuring, providing or possessing such a document;

(c) Enabling a person who is not a national or a permanent resident to remain in the State concerned without complying with the necessary requirements for legally remaining in the State by the means mentioned in subparagraph (b) of this paragraph or any other illegal means.

2. Each State Party shall also adopt such legislative and other measures as may be necessary to establish as criminal offences:

(a) Subject to the basic concepts of its legal system, attempting to commit an offence established in accordance with paragraph 1 of this article;
(b) Participating as an accomplice in an offence established in accordance with paragraph 1 (a), (b) (i) or (c) of this article and, subject to the basic concepts of its legal system, participating as an accomplice in an offence established in accordance with paragraph 1 (b) (ii) of this article;
(c) Organizing or directing other persons to commit an offence established in accordance with paragraph 1 of this article.

3. Each State Party shall adopt such legislative and other measures as may be necessary to establish as aggravating circumstances to the offences established in accordance with paragraph 1 (a), (b) (i) and (c) of this article and, subject to the basic concepts of its legal system, to the offences established in accordance with paragraph 2 (b) and (c) of this article, circumstances:
(a) That endanger, or are likely to endanger, the lives or safety of the migrants concerned; or
(b) That entail inhuman or degrading treatment, including for exploitation, of such migrants.

4. Nothing in this Protocol shall prevent a State Party from taking measures against a person whose conduct constitutes an offence under its domestic law.

II Smuggling of Migrants by Sea

Article 7 – Cooperation

States Parties shall cooperate to the fullest extent possible to prevent and suppress the smuggling of migrants by sea, in accordance with the international law of the sea.

Article 8 – Measures against the Smuggling of Migrants by Sea

1. A State Party that has reasonable grounds to suspect that a vessel that is flying its flag or claiming its registry, that is without nationality or that, though flying a foreign flag or refusing to show a flag, is in reality of the nationality of the State Party concerned is engaged in the smuggling of migrants by sea may request the assistance of other States Parties in suppressing the use of the vessel for that purpose. The States Parties so requested shall render such assistance to the extent possible within their means.

2. A State Party that has reasonable grounds to suspect that a vessel exercising freedom of navigation in accordance with international law and flying the flag or displaying the marks of registry of another State Party is engaged in the

smuggling of migrants by sea may so notify the flag State, request confirmation of registry and, if confirmed, request authorization from the flag State to take appropriate measures with regard to that vessel. The flag State may authorize the requesting State, inter alia:

(a) To board the vessel;
(b) To search the vessel; and
(c) If evidence is found that the vessel is engaged in the smuggling of migrants by sea, to take appropriate measures with respect to the vessel and persons and cargo on board, as authorized by the flag State.

3. A State Party that has taken any measure in accordance with paragraph 2 of this article shall promptly inform the flag State concerned of the results of that measure.

4. A State Party shall respond expeditiously to a request from another State Party to determine whether a vessel that is claiming its registry or flying its flag is entitled to do so and to a request for authorization made in accordance with paragraph 2 of this article.

5. A flag State may, consistent with article 7 of this Protocol, subject its authorization to conditions to be agreed by it and the requesting State, including conditions relating to responsibility and the extent of effective measures to be taken. A State Party shall take no additional measures without the express authorization of the flag State, except those necessary to relieve imminent danger to the lives of persons or those which derive from relevant bilateral or multilateral agreements.

6. Each State Party shall designate an authority or, where necessary, authorities to receive and respond to requests for assistance, for confirmation of registry or of the right of a vessel to fly its flag and for authorization to take appropriate measures. Such designation shall be notified through the Secretary-General to all other States Parties within one month of the designation.

7. A State Party that has reasonable grounds to suspect that a vessel is engaged in the smuggling of migrants by sea and is without nationality or may be assimilated to a vessel without nationality may board and search the vessel. If evidence confirming the suspicion is found, that State Party shall take appropriate measures in accordance with relevant domestic and international law.

Article 9 – Safeguard Clauses

1. Where a State Party takes measures against a vessel in accordance with article 8 of this Protocol, it shall:

(a) Ensure the safety and humane treatment of the persons on board;
(b) Take due account of the need not to endanger the security of the vessel or its cargo;

(c) Take due account of the need not to prejudice the commercial or legal interests of the flag State or any other interested State;

(d) Ensure, within available means, that any measure taken with regard to the vessel is environmentally sound.

2. Where the grounds for measures taken pursuant to article 8 of this Protocol prove to be unfounded, the vessel shall be compensated for any loss or damage that may have been sustained, provided that the vessel has not committed any act justifying the measures taken.

3. Any measure taken, adopted or implemented in accordance with this chapter shall take due account of the need not to interfere with or to affect:

(a) The rights and obligations and the exercise of jurisdiction of coastal States in accordance with the international law of the sea; or

(b) The authority of the flag State to exercise jurisdiction and control in administrative, technical and social matters involving the vessel.

4. Any measure taken at sea pursuant to this chapter shall be carried out only by warships or military aircraft, or by other ships or aircraft clearly marked and identifiable as being on government service and authorized to that effect.

III Prevention, Cooperation and Other Measures

Article 10 – Information

1. Without prejudice to articles 27 and 28 of the Convention, States Parties, in particular those with common borders or located on routes along which migrants are smuggled, shall, for the purpose of achieving the objectives of this Protocol, exchange among themselves, consistent with their respective domestic legal and administrative systems, relevant information on matters such as:

(a) Embarkation and destination points, as well as routes, carriers and means of transportation, known to be or suspected of being used by an organized criminal group engaged in conduct set forth in article 6 of this Protocol;

(b) The identity and methods of organizations or organized criminal groups known to be or suspected of being engaged in conduct set forth in article 6 of this Protocol;

(c) The authenticity and proper form of travel documents issued by a State Party and the theft or related misuse of blank travel or identity documents;

(d) Means and methods of concealment and transportation of persons, the unlawful alteration, reproduction or acquisition or other misuse of travel or identity documents used in conduct set forth in article 6 of this Protocol and ways of detecting them;

(e) Legislative experiences and practices and measures to prevent and combat the conduct set forth in article 6 of this Protocol; and

(f) Scientific and technological information useful to law enforcement, so as to enhance each other's ability to prevent, detect and investigate the conduct set forth in article 6 of this Protocol and to prosecute those involved.

2. A State Party that receives information shall comply with any request by the State Party that transmitted the information that places restrictions on its use.

Article 11 – Border Measures

1. Without prejudice to international commitments in relation to the free movement of people, States Parties shall strengthen, to the extent possible, such border controls as may be necessary to prevent and detect the smuggling of migrants.

2. Each State Party shall adopt legislative or other appropriate measures to prevent, to the extent possible, means of transport operated by commercial carriers from being used in the commission of the offence established in accordance with article 6, paragraph 1 (a), of this Protocol.

3. Where appropriate, and without prejudice to applicable international conventions, such measures shall include establishing the obligation of commercial carriers, including any transportation company or the owner or operator of any means of transport, to ascertain that all passengers are in possession of the travel documents required for entry into the receiving State.

4. Each State Party shall take the necessary measures, in accordance with its domestic law, to provide for sanctions in cases of violation of the obligation set forth in paragraph 3 of this article.

5. Each State Party shall consider taking measures that permit, in accordance with its domestic law, the denial of entry or revocation of visas of persons implicated in the commission of offences established in accordance with this Protocol.

6. Without prejudice to article 27 of the Convention, States Parties shall consider strengthening cooperation among border control agencies by, inter alia, establishing and maintaining direct channels of communication.

Article 12 – Security and Control of Documents

Each State Party shall take such measures as may be necessary, within available means:

(a) To ensure that travel or identity documents issued by it are of such quality that they cannot easily be misused and cannot readily be falsified or unlawfully altered, replicated or issued; and
(b) To ensure the integrity and security of travel or identity documents issued by or on behalf of the State Party and to prevent their unlawful creation, issuance and use.

Article 13 – Legitimacy and Validity of Documents

At the request of another State Party, a State Party shall, in accordance with its domestic law, verify within a reasonable time the legitimacy and validity of travel or identity documents issued or purported to have been issued in its name and suspected of being used for purposes of conduct set forth in article 6 of this Protocol.

Article 14 – Training and Technical Cooperation

1. States Parties shall provide or strengthen specialized training for immigration and other relevant officials in preventing the conduct set forth in article 6 of this Protocol and in the humane treatment of migrants who have been the object of such conduct, while respecting their rights as set forth in this Protocol.

2. States Parties shall cooperate with each other and with competent international organizations, non-governmental organizations, other relevant organizations and other elements of civil society as appropriate to ensure that there is adequate personnel training in their territories to prevent, combat and eradicate the conduct set forth in article 6 of this Protocol and to protect the rights of migrants who have been the object of such conduct. Such training shall include:
(a) Improving the security and quality of travel documents;
(b) Recognizing and detecting fraudulent travel or identity documents;
(c) Gathering criminal intelligence, relating in particular to the identification of organized criminal groups known to be or suspected of being engaged in conduct set forth in article 6 of this Protocol, the methods used to transport smuggled migrants, the misuse of travel or identity documents for purposes of conduct set forth in article 6 and the means of concealment used in the smuggling of migrants;
(d) Improving procedures for detecting smuggled persons at conventional and non-conventional points of entry and exit; and
(e) The humane treatment of migrants and the protection of their rights as set forth in this Protocol.

3. States Parties with relevant expertise shall consider providing technical assistance to States that are frequently countries of origin or transit for persons who have been the object of conduct set forth in article 6 of this Protocol. States Parties shall make every effort to provide the necessary resources, such as vehicles, computer systems and document readers, to combat the conduct set forth in article

Article 15 – Other Prevention Measures

1. Each State Party shall take measures to ensure that it provides or strengthens information programmes to increase public awareness of the fact that the conduct set forth in article 6 of this Protocol is a criminal activity frequently perpetrated by organized criminal groups for profit and that it poses serious risks to the migrants concerned.
2. In accordance with article 31 of the Convention, States Parties shall cooperate in the field of public information for the purpose of preventing potential migrants from falling victim to organized criminal groups.
3. Each State Party shall promote or strengthen, as appropriate, development programmes and cooperation at the national, regional and international levels, taking into account the socio-economic realities of migration and paying special attention to economically and socially depressed areas, in order to combat the root socio-economic causes of the smuggling of migrants, such as poverty and underdevelopment.

Article 16 – Protection and Assistance Measures

1. In implementing this Protocol, each State Party shall take, consistent with its obligations under international law, all appropriate measures, including legislation if necessary, to preserve and protect the rights of persons who have been the object of conduct set forth in article 6 of this Protocol as accorded under applicable international law, in particular the right to life and the right not to be subjected to torture or other cruel, inhuman or degrading treatment or punishment.
2. Each State Party shall take appropriate measures to afford migrants appropriate protection against violence that may be inflicted upon them, whether by individuals or groups, by reason of being the object of conduct set forth in article 6 of this Protocol.
3. Each State Party shall afford appropriate assistance to migrants whose lives or safety are endangered by reason of being the object of conduct set forth in article 6 of this Protocol.
4. In applying the provisions of this article, States Parties shall take into account the special needs of women and children.

5. In the case of the detention of a person who has been the object of conduct set forth in article 6 of this Protocol, each State Party shall comply with its obligations under the Vienna Convention on Consular Relations, where applicable, including that of informing the person concerned without delay about the provisions concerning notification to and communication with consular officers.

Article 17 – Agreements and Arrangements

States Parties shall consider the conclusion of bilateral or regional agreements or operational arrangements or understandings aimed at:

(a) Establishing the most appropriate and effective measures to prevent and combat the conduct set forth in article 6 of this Protocol; or

(b) Enhancing the provisions of this Protocol among themselves.

Article 18 – Return of Smuggled Migrants

1. Each State Party agrees to facilitate and accept, without undue or unreasonable delay, the return of a person who has been the object of conduct set forth in article 6 of this Protocol and who is its national or who has the right of permanent residence in its territory at the time of return.
2. Each State Party shall consider the possibility of facilitating and accepting the return of a person who has been the object of conduct set forth in article 6 of this Protocol and who had the right of permanent residence in its territory at the time of entry into the receiving State in accordance with its domestic law.
3. At the request of the receiving State Party, a requested State Party shall, without undue or unreasonable delay, verify whether a person who has been the object of conduct set forth in article 6 of this Protocol is its national or has the right of permanent residence in its territory.
4. In order to facilitate the return of a person who has been the object of conduct set forth in article 6 of this Protocol and is without proper documentation, the State Party of which that person is a national or in which he or she has the right of permanent residence shall agree to issue, at the request of the receiving State Party, such travel documents or other authorization as may be necessary to enable the person to travel to and re-enter its territory.
5. Each State Party involved with the return of a person who has been the object of conduct set forth in article 6 of this Protocol shall take all appropriate measures to carry out the return in an orderly manner and with due regard for the safety and dignity of the person.
6. States Parties may cooperate with relevant international organizations in the implementation of this article.

7. This article shall be without prejudice to any right afforded to persons who have been the object of conduct set forth in article 6 of this Protocol by any domestic law of the receiving State Party.
8. This article shall not affect the obligations entered into under any other applicable treaty, bilateral or multilateral, or any other applicable operational agreement or arrangement that governs, in whole or in part, the return of persons who have been the object of conduct set forth in article 6 of this Protocol.

IV Final Provisions

Article 19 – Saving Clause

1. Nothing in this Protocol shall affect the other rights, obligations and responsibilities of States and individuals under international law, including international humanitarian law and international human rights law and, in particular, where applicable, the 1951 Convention and the 1967 Protocol relating to the Status of Refugees and the principle of non-refoulement as contained therein.
2. The measures set forth in this Protocol shall be interpreted and applied in a way that is not discriminatory to persons on the ground that they are the object of conduct set forth in article 6 of this Protocol. The interpretation and application of those measures shall be consistent with internationally recognized principles of non-discrimination.

Article 20 – Settlement of Disputes

1. States Parties shall endeavour to settle disputes concerning the interpretation or application of this Protocol through negotiation.
2. Any dispute between two or more States Parties concerning the interpretation or application of this Protocol that cannot be settled through negotiation within a reasonable time shall, at the request of one of those States Parties, be submitted to arbitration. If, six months after the date of the request for arbitration, those States Parties are unable to agree on the organization of the arbitration, any one of those States Parties may refer the dispute to the International Court of Justice by request in accordance with the Statute of the Court.
3. Each State Party may, at the time of signature, ratification, acceptance or approval of or accession to this Protocol, declare that it does not consider itself bound by paragraph 2 of this article. The other States Parties shall not be bound by paragraph 2 of this article with respect to any State Party that has made such a reservation.

4. Any State Party that has made a reservation in accordance with paragraph 3 of this article may at any time withdraw that reservation by notification to the Secretary-General of the United Nations.

Article 21 – Signature, Ratification, Acceptance, Approval and Accession

1. This Protocol shall be open to all States for signature from 12 to 15 December 2000 in Palermo, Italy, and thereafter at United Nations Headquarters in New York until 12 December 2002.
2. This Protocol shall also be open for signature by regional economic integration organizations provided that at least one member State of such organization has signed this Protocol in accordance with paragraph 1 of this article.
3. This Protocol is subject to ratification, acceptance or approval. Instruments of ratification, acceptance or approval shall be deposited with the Secretary-General of the United Nations. A regional economic integration organization may deposit its instrument of ratification, acceptance or approval if at least one of its member States has done likewise. In that instrument of ratification, acceptance or approval, such organization shall declare the extent of its competence with respect to the matters governed by this Protocol. Such organization shall also inform the depositary of any relevant modification in the extent of its competence.
4. This Protocol is open for accession by any State or any regional economic integration organization of which at least one member State is a Party to this Protocol. Instruments of accession shall be deposited with the Secretary-General of the United Nations. At the time of its accession, a regional economic integration organization shall declare the extent of its competence with respect to matters governed by this Protocol. Such organization shall also inform the depositary of any relevant modification in the extent of its competence.

Article 22 – Entry into Force

1. This Protocol shall enter into force on the ninetieth day after the date of deposit of the fortieth instrument of ratification, acceptance, approval or accession, except that it shall not enter into force before the entry into force of the Convention. For the purpose of this paragraph, any instrument deposited by a regional economic integration organization shall not be counted as additional to those deposited by member States of such organization.
2. For each State or regional economic integration organization ratifying, accepting, approving or acceding to this Protocol after the deposit of the fortieth instrument of such action, this Protocol shall enter into force on the

thirtieth day after the date of deposit by such State or organization of the relevant instrument or on the date this Protocol enters into force pursuant to paragraph 1 of this article, whichever is the later.

Article 23 – Amendment

1. After the expiry of five years from the entry into force of this Protocol, a State Party to the Protocol may propose an amendment and file it with the Secretary-General of the United Nations, who shall thereupon communicate the proposed amendment to the States Parties and to the Conference of the Parties to the Convention for the purpose of considering and deciding on the proposal. The States Parties to this Protocol meeting at the Conference of the Parties shall make every effort to achieve consensus on each amendment. If all efforts at consensus have been exhausted and no agreement has been reached, the amendment shall, as a last resort, require for its adoption a two-thirds majority vote of the States Parties to this Protocol present and voting at the meeting of the Conference of the Parties.
2. Regional economic integration organizations, in matters within their competence, shall exercise their right to vote under this article with a number of votes equal to the number of their member States that are Parties to this Protocol. Such organizations shall not exercise their right to vote if their member States exercise theirs and vice versa.
3. An amendment adopted in accordance with paragraph 1 of this article is subject to ratification, acceptance or approval by States Parties.
4. An amendment adopted in accordance with paragraph 1 of this article shall enter into force in respect of a State Party ninety days after the date of the deposit with the Secretary-General of the United Nations of an instrument of ratification, acceptance or approval of such amendment.
5. When an amendment enters into force, it shall be binding on those States Parties which have expressed their consent to be bound by it. Other States Parties shall still be bound by the provisions of this Protocol and any earlier amendments that they have ratified, accepted or approved.

Article 24 – Denunciation

1. A State Party may denounce this Protocol by written notification to the Secretary-General of the United Nations. Such denunciation shall become effective one year after the date of receipt of the notification by the Secretary-General.
2. A regional economic integration organization shall cease to be a Party to this Protocol when all of its member States have denounced it.

Article 25 – Depositary and Languages

1. The Secretary-General of the United Nations is designated depositary of this Protocol.

2. The original of this Protocol, of which the Arabic, Chinese, English, French, Russian and Spanish texts are equally authentic, shall be deposited with the Secretary-General of the United Nations.

IN WITNESS WHEREOF, the undersigned plenipotentiaries, being duly authorized thereto by their respective Governments, have signed this Protocol.

CHAPTER 23

Protocol to Prevent, Suppress and Punish Trafficking in Persons, Especially Women and Children, Supplementing the United Nations Convention against Transnational Organized Crime

Adopted and opened for signature, ratification and accession by General Assembly resolution 55/25 of 15 November 2000
Entry into force 25 December 2003, in accordance with article 17

Preamble

The States Parties to this Protocol,

Declaring that effective action to prevent and combat trafficking in persons, especially women and children, requires a comprehensive international approach in the countries of origin, transit and destination that includes measures to prevent such trafficking, to punish the traffickers and to protect the victims of such trafficking, including by protecting their internationally recognized human rights,

Taking into account the fact that, despite the existence of a variety of international instruments containing rules and practical measures to combat the exploitation of persons, especially women and children, there is no universal instrument that addresses all aspects of trafficking in persons,

Concerned that, in the absence of such an instrument, persons who are vulnerable to trafficking will not be sufficiently protected,

Recalling General Assembly resolution 53/111 of 9 December 1998, in which the Assembly decided to establish an open-ended intergovernmental ad hoc committee for the purpose of elaborating a comprehensive international convention against transnational organized crime and of discussing the elaboration of, inter alia, an international instrument addressing trafficking in women and children,

Convinced that supplementing the United Nations Convention against Transnational Organized Crime with an international instrument for the prevention, suppression and punishment of trafficking in persons, especially women and children, will be useful in preventing and combating that crime,

Have agreed as follows:

I General Provisions

Article 1 – Relation with the United Nations Convention against Transnational Organized Crime

1. This Protocol supplements the United Nations Convention against Transnational Organized Crime. It shall be interpreted together with the Convention.
2. The provisions of the Convention shall apply, mutatis mutandis, to this Protocol unless otherwise provided herein.
3. The offences established in accordance with article 5 of this Protocol shall be regarded as offences established in accordance with the Convention.

Article 2 – Statement of Purpose

The purposes of this Protocol are:

(a) To prevent and combat trafficking in persons, paying particular attention to women and children;

(b) To protect and assist the victims of such trafficking, with full respect for their human rights; and

(c) To promote cooperation among States Parties in order to meet those objectives.

Article 3 – Use of Terms

For the purposes of this Protocol:

(a) "Trafficking in persons" shall mean the recruitment, transportation, transfer, harbouring or receipt of persons, by means of the threat or use of force or other forms of coercion, of abduction, of fraud, of deception, of the abuse of power or of a position of vulnerability or of the giving or receiving of payments or benefits to achieve the consent of a person having control over another person, for the purpose of exploitation. Exploitation shall include, at a minimum, the exploitation of the prostitution of others or other forms of sexual exploitation, forced labour or services, slavery or practices similar to slavery, servitude or the removal of organs;

(b) The consent of a victim of trafficking in persons to the intended exploitation set forth in subparagraph (a) of this article shall be irrelevant where any of the means set forth in subparagraph (a) have been used;

(c) The recruitment, transportation, transfer, harbouring or receipt of a child for the purpose of exploitation shall be considered "trafficking in persons" even if this does not involve any of the means set forth in subparagraph (a) of this article;

(d) "Child" shall mean any person under eighteen years of age.

Article 4 – Scope of Application

This Protocol shall apply, except as otherwise stated herein, to the prevention, investigation and prosecution of the offences established in accordance with article 5 of this Protocol, where those offences are transnational in nature and involve an organized criminal group, as well as to the protection of victims of such offences.

Article 5 – Criminalization

1. Each State Party shall adopt such legislative and other measures as may be necessary to establish as criminal offences the conduct set forth in article 3 of this Protocol, when committed intentionally.

2. Each State Party shall also adopt such legislative and other measures as may be necessary to establish as criminal offences:

(a) Subject to the basic concepts of its legal system, attempting to commit an offence established in accordance with paragraph 1 of this article;

(b) Participating as an accomplice in an offence established in accordance with paragraph 1 of this article; and

(c) Organizing or directing other persons to commit an offence established in accordance with paragraph 1 of this article.

II Protection of Victims of Trafficking in Persons

Article 6 – Assistance to and Protection of Victims of Trafficking in Persons

1. In appropriate cases and to the extent possible under its domestic law, each State Party shall protect the privacy and identity of victims of trafficking in persons, including, inter alia, by making legal proceedings relating to such trafficking confidential.

2. Each State Party shall ensure that its domestic legal or administrative system contains measures that provide to victims of trafficking in persons, in appropriate cases:

(a) Information on relevant court and administrative proceedings;

(b) Assistance to enable their views and concerns to be presented and considered at appropriate stages of criminal proceedings against offenders, in a manner not prejudicial to the rights of the defence.

3. Each State Party shall consider implementing measures to provide for the physical, psychological and social recovery of victims of trafficking in persons, including, in appropriate cases, in cooperation with non-governmental organizations, other relevant organizations and other elements of civil society, and, in particular, the provision of:

(a) Appropriate housing;
(b) Counselling and information, in particular as regards their legal rights, in a language that the victims of trafficking in persons can understand;
(c) Medical, psychological and material assistance; and
(d) Employment, educational and training opportunities.

4. Each State Party shall take into account, in applying the provisions of this article, the age, gender and special needs of victims of trafficking in persons, in particular the special needs of children, including appropriate housing, education and care.

5. Each State Party shall endeavour to provide for the physical safety of victims of trafficking in persons while they are within its territory.

6. Each State Party shall ensure that its domestic legal system contains measures that offer victims of trafficking in persons the possibility of obtaining compensation for damage suffered.

Article 7 – Status of Victims of Trafficking in Persons in Receiving States

1. In addition to taking measures pursuant to article 6 of this Protocol, each State Party shall consider adopting legislative or other appropriate measures that permit victims of trafficking in persons to remain in its territory, temporarily or permanently, in appropriate cases.

2. In implementing the provision contained in paragraph 1 of this article, each State Party shall give appropriate consideration to humanitarian and compassionate factors.

Article 8 – Repatriation of Victims of Trafficking in Persons

1. The State Party of which a victim of trafficking in persons is a national or in which the person had the right of permanent residence at the time of entry into the territory of the receiving State Party shall facilitate and accept, with due regard for the safety of that person, the return of that person without undue or unreasonable delay.

2. When a State Party returns a victim of trafficking in persons to a State Party of which that person is a national or in which he or she had, at the time of entry into the territory of the receiving State Party, the right of permanent residence, such return shall be with due regard for the safety of that person and for

the status of any legal proceedings related to the fact that the person is a victim of trafficking and shall preferably be voluntary.
3. At the request of a receiving State Party, a requested State Party shall, without undue or unreasonable delay, verify whether a person who is a victim of trafficking in persons is its national or had the right of permanent residence in its territory at the time of entry into the territory of the receiving State Party.
4. In order to facilitate the return of a victim of trafficking in persons who is without proper documentation, the State Party of which that person is a national or in which he or she had the right of permanent residence at the time of entry into the territory of the receiving State Party shall agree to issue, at the request of the receiving State Party, such travel documents or other authorization as may be necessary to enable the person to travel to and re-enter its territory.
5. This article shall be without prejudice to any right afforded to victims of trafficking in persons by any domestic law of the receiving State Party.
6. This article shall be without prejudice to any applicable bilateral or multilateral agreement or arrangement that governs, in whole or in part, the return of victims of trafficking in persons.

III Prevention, Cooperation and Other Measures

Article 9 – Prevention of Trafficking in Persons

1. States Parties shall establish comprehensive policies, programmes and other measures:
(a) To prevent and combat trafficking in persons; and
(b) To protect victims of trafficking in persons, especially women and children, from revictimization.
2. States Parties shall endeavour to undertake measures such as research, information and mass media campaigns and social and economic initiatives to prevent and combat trafficking in persons.
3. Policies, programmes and other measures established in accordance with this article shall, as appropriate, include cooperation with non-governmental organizations, other relevant organizations and other elements of civil society.
4. States Parties shall take or strengthen measures, including through bilateral or multilateral cooperation, to alleviate the factors that make persons, especially women and children, vulnerable to trafficking, such as poverty, underdevelopment and lack of equal opportunity.
5. States Parties shall adopt or strengthen legislative or other measures, such as educational, social or cultural measures, including through bilateral and

multilateral cooperation, to discourage the demand that fosters all forms of exploitation of persons, especially women and children, that leads to trafficking.

Article 10 – Information Exchange and Training

1. Law enforcement, immigration or other relevant authorities of States Parties shall, as appropriate, cooperate with one another by exchanging information, in accordance with their domestic law, to enable them to determine:

(a) Whether individuals crossing or attempting to cross an international border with travel documents belonging to other persons or without travel documents are perpetrators or victims of trafficking in persons;

(b) The types of travel document that individuals have used or attempted to use to cross an international border for the purpose of trafficking in persons; and

(c) The means and methods used by organized criminal groups for the purpose of trafficking in persons, including the recruitment and transportation of victims, routes and links between and among individuals and groups engaged in such trafficking, and possible measures for detecting them.

2. States Parties shall provide or strengthen training for law enforcement, immigration and other relevant officials in the prevention of trafficking in persons. The training should focus on methods used in preventing such trafficking, prosecuting the traffickers and protecting the rights of the victims, including protecting the victims from the traffickers. The training should also take into account the need to consider human rights and child- and gender-sensitive issues and it should encourage cooperation with non-governmental organizations, other relevant organizations and other elements of civil society.
3. A State Party that receives information shall comply with any request by the State Party that transmitted the information that places restrictions on its use.

Article 11 – Border Measures

1. Without prejudice to international commitments in relation to the free movement of people, States Parties shall strengthen, to the extent possible, such border controls as may be necessary to prevent and detect trafficking in persons.
2. Each State Party shall adopt legislative or other appropriate measures to prevent, to the extent possible, means of transport operated by commercial carriers from being used in the commission of offences established in accordance with article 5 of this Protocol.

3. Where appropriate, and without prejudice to applicable international conventions, such measures shall include establishing the obligation of commercial carriers, including any transportation company or the owner or operator of any means of transport, to ascertain that all passengers are in possession of the travel documents required for entry into the receiving State.
4. Each State Party shall take the necessary measures, in accordance with its domestic law, to provide for sanctions in cases of violation of the obligation set forth in paragraph 3 of this article.
5. Each State Party shall consider taking measures that permit, in accordance with its domestic law, the denial of entry or revocation of visas of persons implicated in the commission of offences established in accordance with this Protocol.
6. Without prejudice to article 27 of the Convention, States Parties shall consider strengthening cooperation among border control agencies by, inter alia, establishing and maintaining direct channels of communication.

Article 12 – Security and Control of Documents

1. Each State Party shall take such measures as may be necessary, within available means:
(a) To ensure that travel or identity documents issued by it are of such quality that they cannot easily be misused and cannot readily be falsified or unlawfully altered, replicated or issued; and
(b) To ensure the integrity and security of travel or identity documents issued by or on behalf of the State Party and to prevent their unlawful creation, issuance and use.

Article 13 – Legitimacy and Validity of Documents

At the request of another State Party, a State Party shall, in accordance with its domestic law, verify within a reasonable time the legitimacy and validity of travel or identity documents issued or purported to have been issued in its name and suspected of being used for trafficking in persons.

IV Final Provisions

Article 14 – Saving Clause

1. Nothing in this Protocol shall affect the rights, obligations and responsibilities of States and individuals under international law, including international humanitarian law and international human rights law and, in particular, where

applicable, the 1951 Convention and the 1967 Protocol relating to the Status of Refugees and the principle of non-refoulement as contained therein.
2. The measures set forth in this Protocol shall be interpreted and applied in a way that is not discriminatory to persons on the ground that they are victims of trafficking in persons. The interpretation and application of those measures shall be consistent with internationally recognized principles of non-discrimination.

Article 15 – Settlement of Disputes

1. States Parties shall endeavour to settle disputes concerning the interpretation or application of this Protocol through negotiation.
2. Any dispute between two or more States Parties concerning the interpretation or application of this Protocol that cannot be settled through negotiation within a reasonable time shall, at the request of one of those States Parties, be submitted to arbitration. If, six months after the date of the request for arbitration, those States Parties are unable to agree on the organization of the arbitration, any one of those States Parties may refer the dispute to the International Court of Justice by request in accordance with the Statute of the Court.
3. Each State Party may, at the time of signature, ratification, acceptance or approval of or accession to this Protocol, declare that it does not consider itself bound by paragraph 2 of this article. The other States Parties shall not be bound by paragraph 2 of this article with respect to any State Party that has made such a reservation.
4. Any State Party that has made a reservation in accordance with paragraph 3 of this article may at any time withdraw that reservation by notification to the Secretary-General of the United Nations.

Article 16 – Signature, Ratification, Acceptance, Approval and Accession

1. This Protocol shall be open to all States for signature from 12 to 15 December 2000 in Palermo, Italy, and thereafter at United Nations Headquarters in New York until 12 December 2002.
2. This Protocol shall also be open for signature by regional economic integration organizations provided that at least one member State of such organization has signed this Protocol in accordance with paragraph 1 of this article.
3. This Protocol is subject to ratification, acceptance or approval. Instruments of ratification, acceptance or approval shall be deposited with the Secretary-General of the United Nations. A regional economic integration organization may deposit its instrument of ratification, acceptance or approval if at least one of its member States has done likewise. In that instrument of ratification,

acceptance or approval, such organization shall declare the extent of its competence with respect to the matters governed by this Protocol. Such organization shall also inform the depositary of any relevant modification in the extent of its competence.

4. This Protocol is open for accession by any State or any regional economic integration organization of which at least one member State is a Party to this Protocol. Instruments of accession shall be deposited with the Secretary-General of the United Nations. At the time of its accession, a regional economic integration organization shall declare the extent of its competence with respect to matters governed by this Protocol. Such organization shall also inform the depositary of any relevant modification in the extent of its competence.

Article 17 – Entry into Force

1. This Protocol shall enter into force on the ninetieth day after the date of deposit of the fortieth instrument of ratification, acceptance, approval or accession, except that it shall not enter into force before the entry into force of the Convention. For the purpose of this paragraph, any instrument deposited by a regional economic integration organization shall not be counted as additional to those deposited by member States of such organization.

2. For each State or regional economic integration organization ratifying, accepting, approving or acceding to this Protocol after the deposit of the fortieth instrument of such action, this Protocol shall enter into force on the thirtieth day after the date of deposit by such State or organization of the relevant instrument or on the date this Protocol enters into force pursuant to paragraph 1 of this article, whichever is the later.

Article 18 – Amendment

1. After the expiry of five years from the entry into force of this Protocol, a State Party to the Protocol may propose an amendment and file it with the Secretary-General of the United Nations, who shall thereupon communicate the proposed amendment to the States Parties and to the Conference of the Parties to the Convention for the purpose of considering and deciding on the proposal. The States Parties to this Protocol meeting at the Conference of the Parties shall make every effort to achieve consensus on each amendment. If all efforts at consensus have been exhausted and no agreement has been reached, the amendment shall, as a last resort, require for its adoption a two-thirds majority vote of the States Parties to this Protocol present and voting at the meeting of the Conference of the Parties.

2. Regional economic integration organizations, in matters within their competence, shall exercise their right to vote under this article with a number of votes equal to the number of their member States that are Parties to this Protocol. Such organizations shall not exercise their right to vote if their member States exercise theirs and vice versa.
3. An amendment adopted in accordance with paragraph 1 of this article is subject to ratification, acceptance or approval by States Parties.
4. An amendment adopted in accordance with paragraph 1 of this article shall enter into force in respect of a State Party ninety days after the date of the deposit with the Secretary-General of the United Nations of an instrument of ratification, acceptance or approval of such amendment.
5. When an amendment enters into force, it shall be binding on those States Parties which have expressed their consent to be bound by it. Other States Parties shall still be bound by the provisions of this Protocol and any earlier amendments that they have ratified, accepted or approved.

Article 19 – Denunciation

1. A State Party may denounce this Protocol by written notification to the Secretary-General of the United Nations. Such denunciation shall become effective one year after the date of receipt of the notification by the Secretary-General.
2. A regional economic integration organization shall cease to be a Party to this Protocol when all of its member States have denounced it.

Article 20 – Depositary and Languages

1. The Secretary-General of the United Nations is designated depositary of this Protocol.
2. The original of this Protocol, of which the Arabic, Chinese, English, French, Russian and Spanish texts are equally authentic, shall be deposited with the Secretary-General of the United Nations.
IN WITNESS WHEREOF, the undersigned plenipotentiaries, being duly authorized thereto by their respective Governments, have signed this Protocol.

PART IV

Violence and Exploitation

CHAPTER 24

Council of Europe Convention on Protection of Children against Sexual Exploitation and Sexual Abuse[1]

(Lanzarote Convention)

Adopted by the Committee of Ministers of the Council of Europe on 12 July 2007
Entry into force 1 July 2010, in accordance with article 45

Preamble

The member States of the Council of Europe and the other signatories hereto;

Considering that the aim of the Council of Europe is to achieve a greater unity between its members;

Considering that every child has the right to such measures of protection as are required by his or her status as a minor, on the part of his or her family, society and the State;

Observing that the sexual exploitation of children, in particular child pornography and prostitution, and all forms of sexual abuse of children, including acts which are committed abroad, are destructive to children's health and psycho-social development;

Observing that the sexual exploitation and sexual abuse of children have grown to worrying proportions at both national and international level, in particular as regards the increased use by both children and perpetrators of information and communication technologies (ICTs), and that preventing and combating such sexual exploitation and sexual abuse of children require international co-operation;

Considering that the well-being and best interests of children are fundamental values shared by all member States and must be promoted without any discrimination;

Recalling the Action Plan adopted at the 3rd Summit of Heads of State and Governments of the Council of Europe (Warsaw, 16–17 May 2005), calling for the elaboration of measures to stop sexual exploitation of children;

1 The Treaty of Lisbon amending the Treaty on European Union and the Treaty establishing the European Community entered into force on 1 December 2009. As a consequence, as from that date, any reference to the European Economic Community shall be read as the European Union.

 | DOI:10.1163/9789004681224_035

Recalling in particular the Committee of Ministers Recommendation No. R (91) 11 concerning sexual exploitation, pornography and prostitution of, and trafficking in, children and young adults, Recommendation Rec(2001)16 on the protection of children against sexual exploitation, and the Convention on Cybercrime (ETS No. 185), especially Article 9 thereof, as well as the Council of Europe Convention on Action against Trafficking in Human Beings (CETS No. 197);

Bearing in mind the Convention for the Protection of Human Rights and Fundamental Freedoms (1950, ETS No. 5), the revised European Social Charter (1996, ETS No. 163), and the European Convention on the Exercise of Children's Rights (1996, ETS No. 160);

Also bearing in mind the United Nations Convention on the Rights of the Child, especially Article 34 thereof, the Optional Protocol on the sale of children, child prostitution and child pornography, the Protocol to Prevent, Suppress and Punish Trafficking in Persons, Especially Women and Children, supplementing the United Nations Convention against Transnational Organized Crime, as well as the International Labour Organization Convention concerning the Prohibition and Immediate Action for the Elimination of the Worst Forms of Child Labour;

Bearing in mind the Council of the European Union Framework Decision on combating the sexual exploitation of children and child pornography (2004/68/JHA), the Council of the European Union Framework Decision on the standing of victims in criminal proceedings (2001/220/JHA), and the Council of the European Union Framework Decision on combating trafficking in human beings (2002/629/JHA);

Taking due account of other relevant international instruments and programmes in this field, in particular the Stockholm Declaration and Agenda for Action, adopted at the 1st World Congress against Commercial Sexual Exploitation of Children (27–31 August 1996), the Yokohama Global Commitment adopted at the 2nd World Congress against Commercial Sexual Exploitation of Children (17–20 December 2001), the Budapest Commitment and Plan of Action, adopted at the preparatory Conference for the 2nd World Congress against Commercial Sexual Exploitation of Children (20–21 November 2001), the United Nations General Assembly Resolution S-27/2 "A world fit for children" and the three-year programme "Building a Europe for and with children", adopted following the 3rd Summit and launched by the Monaco Conference (4–5 April 2006);

Determined to contribute effectively to the common goal of protecting children against sexual exploitation and sexual abuse, whoever the perpetrator may be, and of providing assistance to victims;

Taking into account the need to prepare a comprehensive international instrument focusing on the preventive, protective and criminal law aspects of the fight against all forms of sexual exploitation and sexual abuse of children and setting up a specific monitoring mechanism,

Have agreed as follows:

Chapter I: Purposes, Non-discrimination Principle and Definitions

Article 1 – Purposes

1. The purposes of this Convention are to:

a. prevent and combat sexual exploitation and sexual abuse of children;

b. protect the rights of child victims of sexual exploitation and sexual abuse;

c. promote national and international co-operation against sexual exploitation and sexual abuse of children.

2. In order to ensure effective implementation of its provisions by the Parties, this Convention sets up a specific monitoring mechanism.

Article 2 – Non-discrimination Principle

The implementation of the provisions of this Convention by the Parties, in particular the enjoyment of measures to protect the rights of victims, shall be secured without discrimination on any ground such as sex, race, colour, language, religion, political or other opinion, national or social origin, association with a national minority, property, birth, sexual orientation, state of health, disability or other status.

Article 3 – Definitions

For the purposes of this Convention:

a. "child" shall mean any person under the age of 18 years;

b. "sexual exploitation and sexual abuse of children" shall include the behaviour as referred to in Articles 18 to 23 of this Convention;

c. "victim" shall mean any child subject to sexual exploitation or sexual abuse.

Chapter II: Preventive Measures

Article 4 – Principles

Each Party shall take the necessary legislative or other measures to prevent all forms of sexual exploitation and sexual abuse of children and to protect children.

Article 5 – Recruitment, Training and Awareness Raising of Persons Working in Contact with Children

1. Each Party shall take the necessary legislative or other measures to encourage awareness of the protection and rights of children among persons who have regular contacts with children in the education, health, social protection, judicial and law-enforcement sectors and in areas relating to sport, culture and leisure activities.
2. Each Party shall take the necessary legislative or other measures to ensure that the persons referred to in paragraph 1 have an adequate knowledge of sexual exploitation and sexual abuse of children, of the means to identify them and of the possibility mentioned in Article 12, paragraph 1.
3. Each Party shall take the necessary legislative or other measures, in conformity with its internal law, to ensure that the conditions to accede to those professions whose exercise implies regular contacts with children ensure that the candidates to these professions have not been convicted of acts of sexual exploitation or sexual abuse of children.

Article 6 – Education for Children

Each Party shall take the necessary legislative or other measures to ensure that children, during primary and secondary education, receive information on the risks of sexual exploitation and sexual abuse, as well as on the means to protect themselves, adapted to their evolving capacity. This information, provided in collaboration with parents, where appropriate, shall be given within a more general context of information on sexuality and shall pay special attention to situations of risk, especially those involving the use of new information and communication technologies.

Article 7 – Preventive Intervention Programmes or Measures

Each Party shall ensure that persons who fear that they might commit any of the offences established in accordance with this Convention may have access, where appropriate, to effective intervention programmes or measures designed to evaluate and prevent the risk of offences being committed.

Article 8 – Measures for the General Public

1. Each Party shall promote or conduct awareness raising campaigns addressed to the general public providing information on the phenomenon of sexual exploitation and sexual abuse of children and on the preventive measures which can be taken.

2. Each Party shall take the necessary legislative or other measures to prevent or prohibit the dissemination of materials advertising the offences established in accordance with this Convention.

Article 9 – Participation of Children, the Private Sector, the Media and Civil Society

1. Each Party shall encourage the participation of children, according to their evolving capacity, in the development and the implementation of state policies, programmes or others initiatives concerning the fight against sexual exploitation and sexual abuse of children.
2. Each Party shall encourage the private sector, in particular the information and communication technology sector, the tourism and travel industry and the banking and finance sectors, as well as civil society, to participate in the elaboration and implementation of policies to prevent sexual exploitation and sexual abuse of children and to implement internal norms through self-regulation or co-regulation.
3. Each Party shall encourage the media to provide appropriate information concerning all aspects of sexual exploitation and sexual abuse of children, with due respect for the independence of the media and freedom of the press.
4. Each Party shall encourage the financing, including, where appropriate, by the creation of funds, of the projects and programmes carried out by civil society aiming at preventing and protecting children from sexual exploitation and sexual abuse.

Chapter III: Specialised Authorities and Co-ordinating Bodies

Article 10 – National Measures of Co-ordination and Collaboration

1. Each Party shall take the necessary measures to ensure the co-ordination on a national or local level between the different agencies in charge of the protection from, the prevention of and the fight against sexual exploitation and sexual abuse of children, notably the education sector, the health sector, the social services and the law-enforcement and judicial authorities.
2. Each Party shall take the necessary legislative or other measures to set up or designate:

a. independent competent national or local institutions for the promotion and protection of the rights of the child, ensuring that they are provided with specific resources and responsibilities;

b. mechanisms for data collection or focal points, at the national or local levels and in collaboration with civil society, for the purpose of observing and evaluating the phenomenon of sexual exploitation and sexual abuse of children, with due respect for the requirements of personal data protection.

3. Each Party shall encourage co-operation between the competent state authorities, civil society and the private sector, in order to better prevent and combat sexual exploitation and sexual abuse of children.

Chapter IV: Protective Measures and Assistance to Victims

Article 11 – Principles

1. Each Party shall establish effective social programmes and set up multidisciplinary structures to provide the necessary support for victims, their close relatives and for any person who is responsible for their care.
2. Each Party shall take the necessary legislative or other measures to ensure that when the age of the victim is uncertain and there are reasons to believe that the victim is a child, the protection and assistance measures provided for children shall be accorded to him or her pending verification of his or her age.

Article 12 – Reporting Suspicion of Sexual Exploitation or Sexual Abuse

1. Each Party shall take the necessary legislative or other measures to ensure that the confidentiality rules imposed by internal law on certain professionals called upon to work in contact with children do not constitute an obstacle to the possibility, for those professionals, of their reporting to the services responsible for child protection any situation where they have reasonable grounds for believing that a child is the victim of sexual exploitation or sexual abuse.
2. Each Party shall take the necessary legislative or other measures to encourage any person who knows about or suspects, in good faith, sexual exploitation or sexual abuse of children to report these facts to the competent services.

Article 13 – Helplines

Each Party shall take the necessary legislative or other measures to encourage and support the setting up of information services, such as telephone or Internet helplines, to provide advice to callers, even confidentially or with due regard for their anonymity.

Article 14 – Assistance to Victims

1. Each Party shall take the necessary legislative or other measures to assist victims, in the short and long term, in their physical and psycho-social recovery. Measures taken pursuant to this paragraph shall take due account of the child's views, needs and concerns.

2. Each Party shall take measures, under the conditions provided for by its internal law, to co- operate with non-governmental organisations, other relevant organisations or other elements of civil society engaged in assistance to victims.
3. When the parents or persons who have care of the child are involved in his or her sexual exploitation or sexual abuse, the intervention procedures taken in application of Article 11, paragraph 1, shall include:
- the possibility of removing the alleged perpetrator;
- the possibility of removing the victim from his or her family environment. The conditions and duration of such removal shall be determined in accordance with the best interests of the child.

4. Each Party shall take the necessary legislative or other measures to ensure that the persons who are close to the victim may benefit, where appropriate, from therapeutic assistance, notably emergency psychological care.

Chapter V: Intervention Programmes or Measures

Article 15 – General Principles

1. Each Party shall ensure or promote, in accordance with its internal law, effective intervention programmes or measures for the persons referred to in Article 16, paragraphs 1 and 2, with a view to preventing and minimising the risks of repeated offences of a sexual nature against children. Such programmes or measures shall be accessible at any time during the proceedings, inside and outside prison, according to the conditions laid down in internal law.
2. Each Party shall ensure or promote, in accordance with its internal law, the development of partnerships or other forms of co-operation between the competent authorities, in particular health-care services and the social services, and the judicial authorities and other bodies responsible for following the persons referred to in Article 16, paragraphs 1 and 2.
3. Each Party shall provide, in accordance with its internal law, for an assessment of the dangerousness and possible risks of repetition of the offences established in accordance with this Convention, by the persons referred to in Article 16, paragraphs 1 and 2, with the aim of identifying appropriate programmes or measures.
4. Each Party shall provide, in accordance with its internal law, for an assessment of the effectiveness of the programmes and measures implemented.

Article 16 – Recipients of Intervention Programmes and Measures

1. Each Party shall ensure, in accordance with its internal law, that persons subject to criminal proceedings for any of the offences established in accordance with this Convention may have access to the programmes or measures

mentioned in Article 15, paragraph 1, under conditions which are neither detrimental nor contrary to the rights of the defence and to the requirements of a fair and impartial trial, and particularly with due respect for the rules governing the principle of the presumption of innocence.
2. Each Party shall ensure, in accordance with its internal law, that persons convicted of any of the offences established in accordance with this Convention may have access to the programmes or measures mentioned in Article 15, paragraph 1.
3. Each Party shall ensure, in accordance with its internal law, that intervention programmes or measures are developed or adapted to meet the developmental needs of children who sexually offend, including those who are below the age of criminal responsibility, with the aim of addressing their sexual behavioural problems.

Article 17 – Information and Consent

1. Each Party shall ensure, in accordance with its internal law, that the persons referred to in Article 16 to whom intervention programmes or measures have been proposed are fully informed of the reasons for the proposal and consent to the programme or measure in full knowledge of the facts.
2. Each Party shall ensure, in accordance with its internal law, that persons to whom intervention programmes or measures have been proposed may refuse them and, in the case of convicted persons, that they are made aware of the possible consequences a refusal might have.

Chapter VI: Substantive Criminal Law

Article 18 – Sexual Abuse

1. Each Party shall take the necessary legislative or other measures to ensure that the following intentional conduct is criminalised:

a. engaging in sexual activities with a child who, according to the relevant provisions of national law, has not reached the legal age for sexual activities;
b. engaging in sexual activities with a child where:
   - use is made of coercion, force or threats; or
   - abuse is made of a recognised position of trust, authority or influence over the child, including within the family; or
   - abuse is made of a particularly vulnerable situation of the child, notably because of a mental or physical disability or a situation of dependence.

2. For the purpose of paragraph 1 above, each Party shall decide the age below which it is prohibited to engage in sexual activities with a child.

3. The provisions of paragraph 1.a are not intended to govern consensual sexual activities between minors.

Article 19 – Offences Concerning Child Prostitution

1. Each Party shall take the necessary legislative or other measures to ensure that the following intentional conduct is criminalised:

a. recruiting a child into prostitution or causing a child to participate in prostitution;
b. coercing a child into prostitution or profiting from or otherwise exploiting a child for such purposes;
c. having recourse to child prostitution.

2. For the purpose of the present article, the term "child prostitution" shall mean the fact of using a child for sexual activities where money or any other form of remuneration or consideration is given or promised as payment, regardless if this payment, promise or consideration is made to the child or to a third person.

Article 20 – Offences Concerning Child Pornography

1. Each Party shall take the necessary legislative or other measures to ensure that the following intentional conduct, when committed without right, is criminalised:

a. producing child pornography;
b. offering or making available child pornography;
c. distributing or transmitting child pornography;
d. procuring child pornography for oneself or for another person;
e. possessing child pornography;
f. knowingly obtaining access, through information and communication technologies, to child pornography.

2. For the purpose of the present article, the term "child pornography" shall mean any material that visually depicts a child engaged in real or simulated sexually explicit conduct or any depiction of a child's sexual organs for primarily sexual purposes.

3. Each Party may reserve the right not to apply, in whole or in part, paragraph 1.a and e to the production and possession of pornographic material:

– consisting exclusively of simulated representations or realistic images of a non-existent child;
– involving children who have reached the age set in application of Article 18, paragraph 2, where these images are produced and possessed by them with their consent and solely for their own private use.

4. Each Party may reserve the right not to apply, in whole or in part, paragraph 1.f.

Article 21 – Offences Concerning the Participation of a Child in Pornographic Performances

1. Each Party shall take the necessary legislative or other measures to ensure that the following intentional conduct is criminalised:

a. recruiting a child into participating in pornographic performances or causing a child to participate in such performances;
b. coercing a child into participating in pornographic performances or profiting from or otherwise exploiting a child for such purposes;
c. knowingly attending pornographic performances involving the participation of children.

2. Each Party may reserve the right to limit the application of paragraph 1.c to cases where children have been recruited or coerced in conformity with paragraph 1.a or b.

Article 22 – Corruption of Children

Each Party shall take the necessary legislative or other measures to criminalise the intentional causing, for sexual purposes, of a child who has not reached the age set in application of Article 18, paragraph 2, to witness sexual abuse or sexual activities, even without having to participate.

Article 23 – Solicitation of Children for Sexual Purposes

Each Party shall take the necessary legislative or other measures to criminalise the intentional proposal, through information and communication technologies, of an adult to meet a child who has not reached the age set in application of Article 18, paragraph 2, for the purpose of committing any of the offences established in accordance with Article 18, paragraph 1.a, or Article 20, paragraph 1.a, against him or her, where this proposal has been followed by material acts leading to such a meeting.

Article 24 – Aiding or Abetting and Attempt

1. Each Party shall take the necessary legislative or other measures to establish as criminal offences, when committed intentionally, aiding or abetting the commission of any of the offences established in accordance with this Convention.

2. Each Party shall take the necessary legislative or other measures to establish as criminal offences, when committed intentionally, attempts to commit the offences established in accordance with this Convention.

3. Each Party may reserve the right not to apply, in whole or in part, paragraph 2 to offences established in accordance with Article 20, paragraph 1.b, d, e and f, Article 21, paragraph 1.c, Article 22 and Article 23.

Article 25 – Jurisdiction

1. Each Party shall take the necessary legislative or other measures to establish jurisdiction over any offence established in accordance with this Convention, when the offence is committed:

a. in its territory; or
b. on board a ship flying the flag of that Party; or
c. on board an aircraft registered under the laws of that Party; or
d. by one of its nationals; or
e. by a person who has his or her habitual residence in its territory.

2. Each Party shall endeavour to take the necessary legislative or other measures to establish jurisdiction over any offence established in accordance with this Convention where the offence is committed against one of its nationals or a person who has his or her habitual residence in its territory.

3. Each Party may, at the time of signature or when depositing its instrument of ratification, acceptance, approval or accession, by a declaration addressed to the Secretary General of the Council of Europe, declare that it reserves the right not to apply or to apply only in specific cases or conditions the jurisdiction rules laid down in paragraph 1.e of this article.

4. For the prosecution of the offences established in accordance with Articles 18, 19, 20, paragraph 1.a, and 21, paragraph 1.a and b, of this Convention, each Party shall take the necessary legislative or other measures to ensure that its jurisdiction as regards paragraph 1.d is not subordinated to the condition that the acts are criminalised at the place where they were performed.

5. Each Party may, at the time of signature or when depositing its instrument of ratification, acceptance, approval or accession, by a declaration addressed to the Secretary General of the Council of Europe, declare that it reserves the right to limit the application of paragraph 4 of this article, with regard to offences established in accordance with Article 18, paragraph 1.b, second and third indents, to cases where its national has his or her habitual residence in its territory.

6. For the prosecution of the offences established in accordance with Articles 18, 19, 20, paragraph 1.a, and 21 of this Convention, each Party shall take the necessary legislative or other measures to ensure that its jurisdiction as regards paragraphs 1.d and e is not subordinated to the condition that the prosecution can only be initiated following a report from the victim or a denunciation from the State of the place where the offence was committed.

7. Each Party shall take the necessary legislative or other measures to establish jurisdiction over the offences established in accordance with this Convention, in cases where an alleged offender is present on its territory and it does not extradite him or her to another Party, solely on the basis of his or her nationality.

8. When more than one Party claims jurisdiction over an alleged offence established in accordance with this Convention, the Parties involved shall, where appropriate, consult with a view to determining the most appropriate jurisdiction for prosecution.
9. Without prejudice to the general rules of international law, this Convention does not exclude any criminal jurisdiction exercised by a Party in accordance with its internal law.

Article 26 – Corporate Liability

1. Each Party shall take the necessary legislative or other measures to ensure that a legal person can be held liable for an offence established in accordance with this Convention, committed for its benefit by any natural person, acting either individually or as part of an organ of the legal person, who has a leading position within the legal person, based on:
a. power of representation of the legal person;
b. an authority to take decisions on behalf of the legal person;
c. can authority to exercise control within the legal person.
2. Apart from the cases already provided for in paragraph 1, each Party shall take the necessary legislative or other measures to ensure that a legal person can be held liable where the lack of supervision or control by a natural person referred to in paragraph 1 has made possible the commission of an offence established in accordance with this Convention for the benefit of that legal person by a natural person acting under its authority.
3. Subject to the legal principles of the Party, the liability of a legal person may be criminal, civil or administrative.
4. Such liability shall be without prejudice to the criminal liability of the natural persons who have committed the offence.

Article 27 – Sanctions and Measures

1. Each Party shall take the necessary legislative or other measures to ensure that the offences established in accordance with this Convention are punishable by effective, proportionate and dissuasive sanctions, taking into account their seriousness. These sanctions shall include penalties involving deprivation of liberty which can give rise to extradition.
2. Each Party shall take the necessary legislative or other measures to ensure that legal persons held liable in accordance with Article 26 shall be subject to effective, proportionate and dissuasive sanctions which shall include monetary criminal or non-criminal fines and may include other measures, in particular:
a. exclusion from entitlement to public benefits or aid;

b. temporary or permanent disqualification from the practice of commercial activities;
c. placing under judicial supervision;
d. judicial winding-up order.

3. Each Party shall take the necessary legislative or other measures to:

a. provide for the seizure and confiscation of:
   - goods, documents and other instrumentalities used to commit the offences, established in accordance with this Convention or to facilitate their commission;
   - proceeds derived from such offences or property the value of which corresponds to such proceeds;
b. enable the temporary or permanent closure of any establishment used to carry out any of the offences established in accordance with this Convention, without prejudice to the rights of bona fide third parties, or to deny the perpetrator, temporarily or permanently, the exercise of the professional or voluntary activity involving contact with children in the course of which the offence was committed.

4. Each Party may adopt other measures in relation to perpetrators, such as withdrawal of parental rights or monitoring or supervision of convicted persons.

5. Each Party may establish that the proceeds of crime or property confiscated in accordance with this article can be allocated to a special fund in order to finance prevention and assistance programmes for victims of any of the offences established in accordance with this Convention.

Article 28 – Aggravating Circumstances

Each Party shall take the necessary legislative or other measures to ensure that the following circumstances, in so far as they do not already form part of the constituent elements of the offence, may, in conformity with the relevant provisions of internal law, be taken into consideration as aggravating circumstances in the determination of the sanctions in relation to the offences established in accordance with this Convention:

c. the offence seriously damaged the physical or mental health of the victim;
d. the offence was preceded or accompanied by acts of torture or serious violence;
e. the offence was committed against a particularly vulnerable victim;
f. the offence was committed by a member of the family, a person cohabiting with the child or a person having abused his or her authority;
g. the offence was committed by several people acting together;

h. the offence was committed within the framework of a criminal organisation;
i. the perpetrator has previously been convicted of offences of the same nature.

Article 29 – Previous Convictions

Each Party shall take the necessary legislative or other measures to provide for the possibility to take into account final sentences passed by another Party in relation to the offences established in accordance with this Convention when determining the sanctions.

Chapter VII: Investigation, Prosecution and Procedural Law

Article 30 – Principles

1. Each Party shall take the necessary legislative or other measures to ensure that investigations and criminal proceedings are carried out in the best interests and respecting the rights of the child.
2. Each Party shall adopt a protective approach towards victims, ensuring that the investigations and criminal proceedings do not aggravate the trauma experienced by the child and that the criminal justice response is followed by assistance, where appropriate.
3. Each Party shall ensure that the investigations and criminal proceedings are treated as priority and carried out without any unjustified delay.
4. Each Party shall ensure that the measures applicable under the current chapter are not prejudicial to the rights of the defence and the requirements of a fair and impartial trial, in conformity with Article 6 of the Convention for the Protection of Human Rights and Fundamental Freedoms.
5. Each Party shall take the necessary legislative or other measures, in conformity with the fundamental principles of its internal law:
- to ensure an effective investigation and prosecution of offences established in accordance with this Convention, allowing, where appropriate, for the possibility of covert operations;
- to enable units or investigative services to identify the victims of the offences established in accordance with Article 20, in particular by analysing child pornography material, such as photographs and audiovisual recordings transmitted or made available through the use of information and communication technologies.

Article 31 – General Measures of Protection

1. Each Party shall take the necessary legislative or other measures to protect the rights and interests of victims, including their special needs as witnesses, at all stages of investigations and criminal proceedings, in particular by:

a. informing them of their rights and the services at their disposal and, unless they do not wish to receive such information, the follow-up given to their complaint, the charges, the general progress of the investigation or proceedings, and their role therein as well as the outcome of their cases;
b. ensuring, at least in cases where the victims and their families might be in danger, that they may be informed, if necessary, when the person prosecuted or convicted is released temporarily or definitively;
c. enabling them, in a manner consistent with the procedural rules of internal law, to be heard, to supply evidence and to choose the means of having their views, needs and concerns presented, directly or through an intermediary, and considered;
d. providing them with appropriate support services so that their rights and interests are duly presented and taken into account;
e. protecting their privacy, their identity and their image and by taking measures in accordance with internal law to prevent the public dissemination of any information that could lead to their identification;
f. providing for their safety, as well as that of their families and witnesses on their behalf, from intimidation, retaliation and repeat victimisation;
g. ensuring that contact between victims and perpetrators within court and law enforcement agency premises is avoided, unless the competent authorities establish otherwise in the best interests of the child or when the investigations or proceedings require such contact.

2. Each Party shall ensure that victims have access, as from their first contact with the competent authorities, to information on relevant judicial and administrative proceedings.

3. Each Party shall ensure that victims have access, provided free of charge where warranted, to legal aid when it is possible for them to have the status of parties to criminal proceedings.

4. Each Party shall provide for the possibility for the judicial authorities to appoint a special representative for the victim when, by internal law, he or she may have the status of a party to the criminal proceedings and where the holders of parental responsibility are precluded from representing the child in such proceedings as a result of a conflict of interest between them and the victim.

5. Each Party shall provide, by means of legislative or other measures, in accordance with the conditions provided for by its internal law, the possibility

for groups, foundations, associations or governmental or non-governmental organisations, to assist and/or support the victims with their consent during criminal proceedings concerning the offences established in accordance with this Convention.
6. Each Party shall ensure that the information given to victims in conformity with the provisions of this article is provided in a manner adapted to their age and maturity and in a language that they can understand.

Article 32 – Initiation of Proceedings

Each Party shall take the necessary legislative or other measures to ensure that investigations or prosecution of offences established in accordance with this Convention shall not be dependent upon the report or accusation made by a victim, and that the proceedings may continue even if the victim has withdrawn his or her statements.

Article 33 – Statute of Limitation

Each Party shall take the necessary legislative or other measures to ensure that the statute of limitation for initiating proceedings with regard to the offences established in accordance with Articles 18, 19, paragraph 1.a and b, and 21, paragraph 1.a and b, shall continue for a period of time sufficient to allow the efficient starting of proceedings after the victim has reached the age of majority and which is commensurate with the gravity of the crime in question.

Article 34 – Investigations

1. Each Party shall adopt such measures as may be necessary to ensure that persons, units or services in charge of investigations are specialised in the field of combating sexual exploitation and sexual abuse of children or that persons are trained for this purpose. Such units or services shall have adequate financial resources.
2. Each Party shall take the necessary legislative or other measures to ensure that uncertainty as to the actual age of the victim shall not prevent the initiation of criminal investigations.

Article 35 – Interviews with the Child

1. Each Party shall take the necessary legislative or other measures to ensure that:
a. interviews with the child take place without unjustified delay after the facts have been reported to the competent authorities;
b. interviews with the child take place, where necessary, in premises designed or adapted for this purpose;

c. interviews with the child are carried out by professionals trained for this purpose;
d. the same persons, if possible and where appropriate, conduct all interviews with the child;
e. the number of interviews is as limited as possible and in so far as strictly necessary for the purpose of criminal proceedings;
f. the child may be accompanied by his or her legal representative or, where appropriate, an adult of his or her choice, unless a reasoned decision has been made to the contrary in respect of that person.

2. Each Party shall take the necessary legislative or other measures to ensure that all interviews with the victim or, where appropriate, those with a child witness, may be videotaped and that these videotaped interviews may be accepted as evidence during the court proceedings, according to the rules provided by its internal law.

3. When the age of the victim is uncertain and there are reasons to believe that the victim is a child, the measures established in paragraphs 1 and 2 shall be applied pending verification of his or her age.

Article 36 – Criminal Court Proceedings

1. Each Party shall take the necessary legislative or other measures, with due respect for the rules governing the autonomy of legal professions, to ensure that training on children's rights and sexual exploitation and sexual abuse of children is available for the benefit of all persons involved in the proceedings, in particular judges, prosecutors and lawyers.

2. Each Party shall take the necessary legislative or other measures to ensure, according to the rules provided by its internal law, that:
a. the judge may order the hearing to take place without the presence of the public;
b. the victim may be heard in the courtroom without being present, notably through the use of appropriate communication technologies.

Chapter VIII: Recording and Storing of Data

Article 37 – Recording and Storing of National Data on Convicted Sexual Offenders

1. For the purposes of prevention and prosecution of the offences established in accordance with this Convention, each Party shall take the necessary legislative or other measures to collect and store, in accordance with the relevant provisions on the protection of personal data and other appropriate rules and guarantees as prescribed by domestic law, data relating to the identity and to

the genetic profile (DNA) of persons convicted of the offences established in accordance with this Convention.
2. Each Party shall, at the time of signature or when depositing its instrument of ratification, acceptance, approval or accession, communicate to the Secretary General of the Council of Europe the name and address of a single national authority in charge for the purposes of paragraph 1.
3. Each Party shall take the necessary legislative or other measures to ensure that the information referred to in paragraph 1 can be transmitted to the competent authority of another Party, in conformity with the conditions established in its internal law and the relevant international instruments.

Chapter IX: International Co-operation

Article 38 – General Principles and Measures for International Co-operation

1. The Parties shall co-operate with each other, in accordance with the provisions of this Convention, and through the application of relevant applicable international and regional instruments, arrangements agreed on the basis of uniform or reciprocal legislation and internal laws, to the widest extent possible, for the purpose of:

a. preventing and combating sexual exploitation and sexual abuse of children;

b. protecting and providing assistance to victims;

c. investigations or proceedings concerning the offences established in accordance with this Convention.

2. Each Party shall take the necessary legislative or other measures to ensure that victims of an offence established in accordance with this Convention in the territory of a Party other than the one where they reside may make a complaint before the competent authorities of their State of residence.
3. If a Party that makes mutual legal assistance in criminal matters or extradition conditional on the existence of a treaty receives a request for legal assistance or extradition from a Party with which it has not concluded such a treaty, it may consider this Convention the legal basis for mutual legal assistance in criminal matters or extradition in respect of the offences established in accordance with this Convention.
4. Each Party shall endeavour to integrate, where appropriate, prevention and the fight against sexual exploitation and sexual abuse of children in assistance programmes for development provided for the benefit of third states.

Chapter X: Monitoring Mechanism

Article 39 – Committee of the Parties

1. The Committee of the Parties shall be composed of representatives of the Parties to the Convention.
2. The Committee of the Parties shall be convened by the Secretary General of the Council of Europe. Its first meeting shall be held within a period of one year following the entry into force of this Convention for the tenth signatory having ratified it. It shall subsequently meet whenever at least one third of the Parties or the Secretary General so requests.
3. The Committee of the Parties shall adopt its own rules of procedure.

Article 40 – Other Representatives

1. The Parliamentary Assembly of the Council of Europe, the Commissioner for Human Rights, the European Committee on Crime Problems (CDPC), as well as other relevant Council of Europe intergovernmental committees, shall each appoint a representative to the Committee of the Parties.
2. The Committee of Ministers may invite other Council of Europe bodies to appoint a representative to the Committee of the Parties after consulting the latter.
3. Representatives of civil society, and in particular non-governmental organisations, may be admitted as observers to the Committee of the Parties following the procedure established by the relevant rules of the Council of Europe.
4. Representatives appointed under paragraphs 1 to 3 above shall participate in meetings of the Committee of the Parties without the right to vote.

Article 41 – Functions of the Committee of the Parties

1. The Committee of the Parties shall monitor the implementation of this Convention. The rules of procedure of the Committee of the Parties shall determine the procedure for evaluating the implementation of this Convention.
2. The Committee of the Parties shall facilitate the collection, analysis and exchange of information, experience and good practice between States to improve their capacity to prevent and combat sexual exploitation and sexual abuse of children.
3. The Committee of the Parties shall also, where appropriate:
   a. facilitate the effective use and implementation of this Convention, including the identification of any problems and the effects of any declaration or reservation made under this Convention;
   b. express an opinion on any question concerning the application of this Convention and facilitate the exchange of information on significant legal, policy or technological developments.

4. The Committee of the Parties shall be assisted by the Secretariat of the Council of Europe in carrying out its functions pursuant to this article.
5. The European Committee on Crime Problems (CDPC) shall be kept periodically informed regarding the activities mentioned in paragraphs 1, 2 and 3 of this article.

Chapter XI: Relationship with Other International Instruments

Article 42 – Relationship with the United Nations Convention on the Rights of the Child and Its Optional Protocol on the Sale of Children, Child Prostitution and Child Pornography

This Convention shall not affect the rights and obligations arising from the provisions of the United Nations Convention on the Rights of the Child and its Optional Protocol on the sale of children, child prostitution and child pornography, and is intended to enhance the protection afforded by them and develop and complement the standards contained therein.

Article 43 – Relationship with Other International Instruments

1. This Convention shall not affect the rights and obligations arising from the provisions of other international instruments to which Parties to the present Convention are Parties or shall become Parties and which contain provisions on matters governed by this Convention and which ensure greater protection and assistance for child victims of sexual exploitation or sexual abuse.
2. The Parties to the Convention may conclude bilateral or multilateral agreements with one another on the matters dealt with in this Convention, for purposes of supplementing or strengthening its provisions or facilitating the application of the principles embodied in it.
3. Parties which are members of the European Union shall, in their mutual relations, apply Community and European Union rules in so far as there are Community or European Union rules governing the particular subject concerned and applicable to the specific case, without prejudice to the object and purpose of the present Convention and without prejudice to its full application with other Parties.

Chapter XII: Amendments to the Convention

Article 44 – Amendments

1. Any proposal for an amendment to this Convention presented by a Party shall be communicated to the Secretary General of the Council of Europe and forwarded by him or her to the member States of the Council of Europe, any signatory, any State Party, the European Community, any State invited to sign this Convention in accordance with the provisions of Article 45, paragraph 1,

and any State invited to accede to this Convention in accordance with the provisions of Article 46, paragraph 1.
2. Any amendment proposed by a Party shall be communicated to the European Committee on Crime Problems (CDPC), which shall submit to the Committee of Ministers its opinion on that proposed amendment.
3. The Committee of Ministers shall consider the proposed amendment and the opinion submitted by the CDPC and, following consultation with the non-member States Parties to this Convention, may adopt the amendment.
4. The text of any amendment adopted by the Committee of Ministers in accordance with paragraph 3 of this article shall be forwarded to the Parties for acceptance.
5. Any amendment adopted in accordance with paragraph 3 of this article shall enter into force on the first day of the month following the expiration of a period of one month after the date on which all Parties have informed the Secretary General that they have accepted it.

Chapter XIII: Final Clauses

Article 45 – Signature and Entry into Force

1. This Convention shall be open for signature by the member States of the Council of Europe, the non-member States which have participated in its elaboration as well as the European Community.
2. This Convention is subject to ratification, acceptance or approval. Instruments of ratification, acceptance or approval shall be deposited with the Secretary General of the Council of Europe.
3. This Convention shall enter into force on the first day of the month following the expiration of a period of three months after the date on which 5 signatories, including at least 3 member States of the Council of Europe, have expressed their consent to be bound by the Convention in accordance with the provisions of the preceding paragraph.
4. In respect of any State referred to in paragraph 1 or the European Community, which subsequently expresses its consent to be bound by it, the Convention shall enter into force on the first day of the month following the expiration of a period of three months after the date of the deposit of its instrument of ratification, acceptance or approval.

Article 46 – Accession to the Convention

1. After the entry into force of this Convention, the Committee of Ministers of the Council of Europe may, after consultation of the Parties to this Convention and obtaining their unanimous consent, invite any non-member State of the Council of Europe, which has not participated in the elaboration of the

Convention, to accede to this Convention by a decision taken by the majority provided for in Article 20.d of the Statute of the Council of Europe, and by unanimous vote of the representatives of the Contracting States entitled to sit on the Committee of Ministers.
2. In respect of any acceding State, the Convention shall enter into force on the first day of the month following the expiration of a period of three months after the date of deposit of the instrument of accession with the Secretary General of the Council of Europe.

Article 47 – Territorial Application

1. Any State or the European Community may, at the time of signature or when depositing its instrument of ratification, acceptance, approval or accession, specify the territory or territories to which this Convention shall apply.
2. Any Party may, at any later date, by a declaration addressed to the Secretary General of the Council of Europe, extend the application of this Convention to any other territory specified in the declaration and for whose international relations it is responsible or on whose behalf it is authorised to give undertakings. In respect of such territory, the Convention shall enter into force on the first day of the month following the expiration of a period of three months after the date of receipt of such declaration by the Secretary General.
3. Any declaration made under the two preceding paragraphs may, in respect of any territory specified in such declaration, be withdrawn by a notification addressed to the Secretary General of the Council of Europe. The withdrawal shall become effective on the first day of the month following the expiration of a period of three months after the date of receipt of such notification by the Secretary General.

Article 48 – Reservations

No reservation may be made in respect of any provision of this Convention, with the exception of the reservations expressly established. Any reservation may be withdrawn at any time.

Article 49 – Denunciation

1. Any Party may, at any time, denounce this Convention by means of a notification addressed to the Secretary General of the Council of Europe.
2. Such denunciation shall become effective on the first day of the month following the expiration of a period of three months after the date of receipt of the notification by the Secretary General.

Article 50 – Notification

The Secretary General of the Council of Europe shall notify the member States of the Council of Europe, any State signatory, any State Party, the European Community, any State invited to sign this Convention in accordance with the provisions of Article 45 and any State invited to accede to this Convention in accordance with the provisions of Article 46 of:

a. any signature;
b. the deposit of any instrument of ratification, acceptance, approval or accession;
c. any date of entry into force of this Convention in accordance with Articles 45 and 46;
d. any amendment adopted in accordance with Article 44 and the date on which such an amendment enters into force;
e. any reservation made under Article 48;
f. any denunciation made in pursuance of the provisions of Article 49;
g. any other act, notification or communication relating to this Convention.

In witness whereof the undersigned, being duly authorised thereto, have signed this Convention.

Done at Lanzarote, this 25th day of October 2007, in English and in French, both texts being equally authentic, in a single copy which shall be deposited in the archives of the Council of Europe. The Secretary General of the Council of Europe shall transmit certified copies to each member State of the Council of Europe, to the non-member States which have participated in the elaboration of this Convention, to the European Community and to any State invited to accede to this Convention.

CHAPTER 25

Council of Europe Convention on Preventing and Combating Violence against Women and Domestic Violence

(Istanbul Convention)
Opened for signature on 11 May 2011

Preamble
The member States of the Council of Europe and the other signatories hereto,

Recalling the Convention for the Protection of Human Rights and Fundamental Freedoms (ETS No. 5, 1950) and its Protocols, the European Social Charter (ETS No. 35, 1961, revised in 1996, ETS No. 163), the Council of Europe Convention on Action against Trafficking in Human Beings (CETS No. 197, 2005) and the Council of Europe Convention on the Protection of Children against Sexual Exploitation and Sexual Abuse (CETS No. 201, 2007);

Recalling the following recommendations of the Committee of Ministers to member States of the Council of Europe: Recommendation Rec(2002)5 on the protection of women against violence, Recommendation CM/Rec(2007)17 on gender equality standards and mechanisms, Recommendation CM/Rec(2010)10 on the role of women and men in conflict prevention and resolution and in peace building, and other relevant recommendations;

Taking account of the growing body of case law of the European Court of Human Rights which sets important standards in the field of violence against women;

Having regard to the International Covenant on Civil and Political Rights (1966), the International Covenant on Economic, Social and Cultural Rights (1966), the United Nations Convention on the Elimination of All Forms of Discrimination Against Women ("CEDAW", 1979) and its Optional Protocol (1999) as well as General Recommendation No. 19 of the CEDAW Committee on violence against women, the United Nations Convention on the Rights of the Child (1989) and its Optional Protocols (2000) and the United Nations Convention on the Rights of Persons with Disabilities (2006);

Having regard to the Rome Statute of the International Criminal Court (2002);

DOI:10.1163/9789004681224_036

Recalling the basic principles of international humanitarian law, and especially the Geneva Convention (IV) relative to the Protection of Civilian Persons in Time of War (1949) and the Additional Protocols I and II (1977) thereto;

Condemning all forms of violence against women and domestic violence;

Recognising that the realisation of de jure and de facto equality between women and men is a key element in the prevention of violence against women;

Recognising that violence against women is a manifestation of historically unequal power relations between women and men, which have led to domination over, and discrimination against, women by men and to the prevention of the full advancement of women;

Recognising the structural nature of violence against women as gender-based violence, and that violence against women is one of the crucial social mechanisms by which women are forced into a subordinate position compared with men;

Recognising, with grave concern, that women and girls are often exposed to serious forms of violence such as domestic violence, sexual harassment, rape, forced marriage, crimes committed in the name of so-called "honour" and genital mutilation, which constitute a serious violation of the human rights of women and girls and a major obstacle to the achievement of equality between women and men;

Recognising the ongoing human rights violations during armed conflicts that affect the civilian population, especially women in the form of widespread or systematic rape and sexual violence and the potential for increased gender-based violence both during and after conflicts;

Recognising that women and girls are exposed to a higher risk of gender-based violence than men;

Recognising that domestic violence affects women disproportionately, and that men may also be victims of domestic violence;

Recognising that children are victims of domestic violence, including as witnesses of violence in the family;

Aspiring to create a Europe free from violence against women and domestic violence,

Have agreed as follows:

Chapter I: Purposes, Definitions, Equality and Non-discrimination, General Obligations

Article 1 – Purposes of the Convention

1. The purposes of this Convention are to:

a. protect women against all forms of violence, and prevent, prosecute and eliminate violence against women and domestic violence;
b. contribute to the elimination of all forms of discrimination against women and promote substantive equality between women and men, including by empowering women;
c. design a comprehensive framework, policies and measures for the protection of and assistance to all victims of violence against women and domestic violence;
d. promote international co-operation with a view to eliminating violence against women and domestic violence;
e. provide support and assistance to organisations and law enforcement agencies to effectively co-operate in order to adopt an integrated approach to eliminating violence against women and domestic violence.

2. In order to ensure effective implementation of its provisions by the Parties, this Convention establishes a specific monitoring mechanism.

Article 2 – Scope of the Convention

1. This Convention shall apply to all forms of violence against women, including domestic violence, which affects women disproportionately.
2. Parties are encouraged to apply this Convention to all victims of domestic violence. Parties shall pay particular attention to women victims of gender-based violence in implementing the provisions of this Convention.
3. This Convention shall apply in times of peace and in situations of armed conflict.

Article 3 – Definitions

For the purpose of this Convention:

a. "violence against women" is understood as a violation of human rights and a form of discrimination against women and shall mean all acts of gender-based violence that result in, or are likely to result in, physical, sexual, psychological or economic harm or suffering to women, including threats of such acts, coercion or arbitrary deprivation of liberty, whether occurring in public or in private life;
b. "domestic violence" shall mean all acts of physical, sexual, psychological or economic violence that occur within the family or domestic unit or between former or current spouses or partners, whether or not the perpetrator shares or has shared the same residence with the victim;
c. "gender" shall mean the socially constructed roles, behaviours, activities and attributes that a given society considers appropriate for women and men;

d. "gender-based violence against women" shall mean violence that is directed against a woman because she is a woman or that affects women disproportionately;
e. "victim" shall mean any natural person who is subject to the conduct specified in points a and b;
f. "women" includes girls under the age of 18.

Article 4 – Fundamental Rights, Equality and Non-discrimination

1. Parties shall take the necessary legislative and other measures to promote and protect the right for everyone, particularly women, to live free from violence in both the public and the private sphere.
2. Parties condemn all forms of discrimination against women and take, without delay, the necessary legislative and other measures to prevent it, in particular by:
- embodying in their national constitutions or other appropriate legislation the principle of equality between women and men and ensuring the practical realisation of this principle;
- prohibiting discrimination against women, including through the use of sanctions, where appropriate;
- abolishing laws and practices which discriminate against women.
3. The implementation of the provisions of this Convention by the Parties, in particular measures to protect the rights of victims, shall be secured without discrimination on any ground such as sex, gender, race, colour, language, religion, political or other opinion, national or social origin, association with a national minority, property, birth, sexual orientation, gender identity, age, state of health, disability, marital status, migrant or refugee status, or other status.
4. Special measures that are necessary to prevent and protect women from gender-based violence shall not be considered discrimination under the terms of this Convention.

Article 5 – State Obligations and Due Diligence

1. Parties shall refrain from engaging in any act of violence against women and ensure that State authorities, officials, agents, institutions and other actors acting on behalf of the State act in conformity with this obligation.
2. Parties shall take the necessary legislative and other measures to exercise due diligence to prevent, investigate, punish and provide reparation for acts of violence covered by the scope of this Convention that are perpetrated by non-State actors.

Article 6 – Gender-Sensitive Policies

Parties shall undertake to include a gender perspective in the implementation and evaluation of the impact of the provisions of this Convention and to promote and effectively implement policies of equality between women and men and the empowerment of women.

Chapter II: Integrated Policies and Data Collection

Article 7 – Comprehensive and Co-ordinated Policies

1. Parties shall take the necessary legislative and other measures to adopt and implement State-wide effective, comprehensive and co-ordinated policies encompassing all relevant measures to prevent and combat all forms of violence covered by the scope of this Convention and offer a holistic response to violence against women.
2. Parties shall ensure that policies referred to in paragraph 1 place the rights of the victim at the centre of all measures and are implemented by way of effective co-operation among all relevant agencies, institutions and organisations.
3. Measures taken pursuant to this article shall involve, where appropriate, all relevant actors, such as government agencies, the national, regional and local parliaments and authorities, national human rights institutions and civil society organisations.

Article 8 – Financial Resources

Parties shall allocate appropriate financial and human resources for the adequate implementation of integrated policies, measures and programmes to prevent and combat all forms of violence covered by the scope of this Convention, including those carried out by non-governmental organisations and civil society.

Article 9 – Non-governmental Organisations and Civil Society

Parties shall recognise, encourage and support, at all levels, the work of relevant non-governmental organisations and of civil society active in combating violence against women and establish effective co-operation with these organisations.

Article 10 – Co-ordinating Body

1. Parties shall designate or establish one or more official bodies responsible for the co-ordination, implementation, monitoring and evaluation of policies and measures to prevent and combat all forms of violence covered by this Convention. These bodies shall co-ordinate the collection of data as referred to in Article 11, analyse and disseminate its results.

2. Parties shall ensure that the bodies designated or established pursuant to this article receive information of a general nature on measures taken pursuant to Chapter VIII.
3. Parties shall ensure that the bodies designated or established pursuant to this article shall have the capacity to communicate directly and foster relations with their counterparts in other Parties.

Article 11 – Data Collection and Research

1. For the purpose of the implementation of this Convention, Parties shall undertake to:

a. collect disaggregated relevant statistical data at regular intervals on cases of all forms of violence covered by the scope of this Convention;
b. support research in the field of all forms of violence covered by the scope of this Convention in order to study its root causes and effects, incidences and conviction rates, as well as the efficacy of measures taken to implement this Convention.

2. Parties shall endeavour to conduct population-based surveys at regular intervals to assess the prevalence of and trends in all forms of violence covered by the scope of this Convention.
3. Parties shall provide the group of experts, as referred to in Article 66 of this Convention, with the information collected pursuant to this article in order to stimulate international co-operation and enable international benchmarking.
4. Parties shall ensure that the information collected pursuant to this article is available to the public.

Chapter III: Prevention

Article 12 – General Obligations

1. Parties shall take the necessary measures to promote changes in the social and cultural patterns of behaviour of women and men with a view to eradicating prejudices, customs, traditions and all other practices which are based on the idea of the inferiority of women or on stereotyped roles for women and men.
2. Parties shall take the necessary legislative and other measures to prevent all forms of violence covered by the scope of this Convention by any natural or legal person.
3. Any measures taken pursuant to this chapter shall take into account and address the specific needs of persons made vulnerable by particular circumstances and shall place the human rights of all victims at their centre.

4. Parties shall take the necessary measures to encourage all members of society, especially men and boys, to contribute actively to preventing all forms of violence covered by the scope of this Convention.
5. Parties shall ensure that culture, custom, religion, tradition or so-called "honour" shall not be considered as justification for any acts of violence covered by the scope of this Convention.
6. Parties shall take the necessary measures to promote programmes and activities for the empowerment of women.

Article 13 – Awareness-Raising

1. Parties shall promote or conduct, on a regular basis and at all levels, awareness-raising campaigns or programmes, including in co-operation with national human rights institutions and equality bodies, civil society and non-governmental organisations, especially women's organisations, where appropriate, to increase awareness and understanding among the general public of the different manifestations of all forms of violence covered by the scope of this Convention, their consequences on children and the need to prevent such violence.
2. Parties shall ensure the wide dissemination among the general public of information on measures available to prevent acts of violence covered by the scope of this Convention.

Article 14 – Education

1. Parties shall take, where appropriate, the necessary steps to include teaching material on issues such as equality between women and men, non-stereotyped gender roles, mutual respect, non-violent conflict resolution in interpersonal relationships, gender-based violence against women and the right to personal integrity, adapted to the evolving capacity of learners, in formal curricula and at all levels of education.
2. Parties shall take the necessary steps to promote the principles referred to in paragraph 1 in informal educational facilities, as well as in sports, cultural and leisure facilities and the media.

Article 15 – Training of Professionals

1. Parties shall provide or strengthen appropriate training for the relevant professionals dealing with victims or perpetrators of all acts of violence covered by the scope of this Convention, on the prevention and detection of such violence, equality between women and men, the needs and rights of victims, as well as on how to prevent secondary victimisation.

2. Parties shall encourage that the training referred to in paragraph 1 includes training on co-ordinated multi-agency co-operation to allow for a comprehensive and appropriate handling of referrals in cases of violence covered by the scope of this Convention.

Article 16 – Preventive Intervention and Treatment Programmes

1. Parties shall take the necessary legislative or other measures to set up or support programmes aimed at teaching perpetrators of domestic violence to adopt non-violent behaviour in interpersonal relationships with a view to preventing further violence and changing violent behavioural patterns.
2. Parties shall take the necessary legislative or other measures to set up or support treatment programmes aimed at preventing perpetrators, in particular sex offenders, from re-offending.
3. In taking the measures referred to in paragraphs 1 and 2, Parties shall ensure that the safety of, support for and the human rights of victims are of primary concern and that, where appropriate, these programmes are set up and implemented in close co-ordination with specialist support services for victims.

Article 17 – Participation of the Private Sector and the Media

1. Parties shall encourage the private sector, the information and communication technology sector and the media, with due respect for freedom of expression and their independence, to participate in the elaboration and implementation of policies and to set guidelines and self-regulatory standards to prevent violence against women and to enhance respect for their dignity.
2. Parties shall develop and promote, in co-operation with private sector actors, skills among children, parents and educators on how to deal with the information and communications environment that provides access to degrading content of a sexual or violent nature which might be harmful.

Chapter IV: Protection and Support

Article 18 – General Obligations

1. Parties shall take the necessary legislative or other measures to protect all victims from any further acts of violence.
2. Parties shall take the necessary legislative or other measures, in accordance with internal law, to ensure that there are appropriate mechanisms to provide for effective co-operation between all relevant state agencies, including the judiciary, public prosecutors, law enforcement agencies, local and regional authorities as well as non-governmental organisations and other relevant organisations and entities, in protecting and supporting victims and witnesses of all forms of violence covered by the scope of this Convention, including by

referring to general and specialist support services as detailed in Articles 20 and 22 of this Convention.

3. Parties shall ensure that measures taken pursuant to this chapter shall:

- be based on a gendered understanding of violence against women and domestic violence and shall focus on the human rights and safety of the victim;
- be based on an integrated approach which takes into account the relationship between victims, perpetrators, children and their wider social environment;
- aim at avoiding secondary victimisation;
- aim at the empowerment and economic independence of women victims of violence;
- allow, where appropriate, for a range of protection and support services to be located on the same premises;
- address the specific needs of vulnerable persons, including child victims, and be made available to them.

4. The provision of services shall not depend on the victim's willingness to press charges or testify against any perpetrator.

5. Parties shall take the appropriate measures to provide consular and other protection and support to their nationals and other victims entitled to such protection in accordance with their obligations under international law.

Article 19 – Information

Parties shall take the necessary legislative or other measures to ensure that victims receive adequate and timely information on available support services and legal measures in a language they understand.

Article 20 – General Support Services

1. Parties shall take the necessary legislative or other measures to ensure that victims have access to services facilitating their recovery from violence. These measures should include, when necessary, services such as legal and psychological counselling, financial assistance, housing, education, training and assistance in finding employment.

2. Parties shall take the necessary legislative or other measures to ensure that victims have access to health care and social services and that services are adequately resourced and professionals are trained to assist victims and refer them to the appropriate services.

Article 21 – Assistance in Individual/Collective Complaints

Parties shall ensure that victims have information on and access to applicable regional and international individual/collective complaints mechanisms. Parties shall promote the provision of sensitive and knowledgeable assistance to victims in presenting any such complaints.

Article 22 – Specialist Support Services

1. Parties shall take the necessary legislative or other measures to provide or arrange for, in an adequate geographical distribution, immediate, short- and long-term specialist support services to any victim subjected to any of the acts of violence covered by the scope of this Convention.
2. Parties shall provide or arrange for specialist women's support services to all women victims of violence and their children.

Article 23 – Shelters

Parties shall take the necessary legislative or other measures to provide for the setting-up of appropriate, easily accessible shelters in sufficient numbers to provide safe accommodation for and to reach out pro-actively to victims, especially women and their children.

Article 24 – Telephone Helplines

Parties shall take the necessary legislative or other measures to set up statewide round-the-clock (24/7) telephone helplines free of charge to provide advice to callers, confidentially or with due regard for their anonymity, in relation to all forms of violence covered by the scope of this Convention.

Article 25 – Support for Victims of Sexual Violence

Parties shall take the necessary legislative or other measures to provide for the setting up of appropriate, easily accessible rape crisis or sexual violence referral centres for victims in sufficient numbers to provide for medical and forensic examination, trauma support and counselling for victims.

Article 26 – Protection and Support for Child Witnesses

1. Parties shall take the necessary legislative or other measures to ensure that in the provision of protection and support services to victims, due account is taken of the rights and needs of child witnesses of all forms of violence covered by the scope of this Convention.
2. Measures taken pursuant to this article shall include age-appropriate psychosocial counselling for child witnesses of all forms of violence covered by

the scope of this Convention and shall give due regard to the best interests of the child.

Article 27 – Reporting

Parties shall take the necessary measures to encourage any person witness to the commission of acts of violence covered by the scope of this Convention or who has reasonable grounds to believe that such an act may be committed, or that further acts of violence are to be expected, to report this to the competent organisations or authorities.

Article 28 – Reporting by Professionals

Parties shall take the necessary measures to ensure that the confidentiality rules imposed by internal law on certain professionals do not constitute an obstacle to the possibility, under appropriate conditions, of their reporting to the competent organisations or authorities if they have reasonable grounds to believe that a serious act of violence covered by the scope of this Convention, has been committed and further serious acts of violence are to be expected.

Chapter V: Substantive Law

Article 29 – Civil Lawsuits and Remedies

1. Parties shall take the necessary legislative or other measures to provide victims with adequate civil remedies against the perpetrator.
2. Parties shall take the necessary legislative or other measures to provide victims, in accordance with the general principles of international law, with adequate civil remedies against State authorities that have failed in their duty to take the necessary preventive or protective measures within the scope of their powers.

Article 30 – Compensation

1. Parties shall take the necessary legislative or other measures to ensure that victims have the right to claim compensation from perpetrators for any of the offences established in accordance with this Convention.
2. Adequate State compensation shall be awarded to those who have sustained serious bodily injury or impairment of health, to the extent that the damage is not covered by other sources such as the perpetrator, insurance or State-funded health and social provisions. This does not preclude Parties from claiming regress for compensation awarded from the perpetrator, as long as due regard is paid to the victim's safety.
3. Measures taken pursuant to paragraph 2 shall ensure the granting of compensation within a reasonable time.

Article 31 – Custody, Visitation Rights and Safety

1. Parties shall take the necessary legislative or other measures to ensure that, in the determination of custody and visitation rights of children, incidents of violence covered by the scope of this Convention are taken into account.
2. Parties shall take the necessary legislative or other measures to ensure that the exercise of any visitation or custody rights does not jeopardise the rights and safety of the victim or children.

Article 32 – Civil Consequences of Forced Marriages

Parties shall take the necessary legislative or other measures to ensure that marriages concluded under force may be voidable, annulled or dissolved without undue financial or administrative burden placed on the victim.

Article 33 – Psychological Violence

Parties shall take the necessary legislative or other measures to ensure that the intentional conduct of seriously impairing a person's psychological integrity through coercion or threats is criminalised.

Article 34 – Stalking

Parties shall take the necessary legislative or other measures to ensure that the intentional conduct of repeatedly engaging in threatening conduct directed at another person, causing her or him to fear for her or his safety, is criminalised.

Article 35 – Physical Violence

Parties shall take the necessary legislative or other measures to ensure that the intentional conduct of committing acts of physical violence against another person is criminalised.

Article 36 – Sexual Violence, Including Rape

1. Parties shall take the necessary legislative or other measures to ensure that the following intentional conducts are criminalised:
   a. engaging in non-consensual vaginal, anal or oral penetration of a sexual nature of the body of another person with any bodily part or object;
   b. engaging in other non-consensual acts of a sexual nature with a person;
   c. causing another person to engage in non-consensual acts of a sexual nature with a third person.
2. Consent must be given voluntarily as the result of the person's free will assessed in the context of the surrounding circumstances.

3. Parties shall take the necessary legislative or other measures to ensure that the provisions of paragraph 1 also apply to acts committed against former or current spouses or partners as recognised by internal law.

Article 37 – Forced Marriage

1. Parties shall take the necessary legislative or other measures to ensure that the intentional conduct of forcing an adult or a child to enter into a marriage is criminalised.
2. Parties shall take the necessary legislative or other measures to ensure that the intentional conduct of luring an adult or a child to the territory of a Party or State other than the one she or he resides in with the purpose of forcing this adult or child to enter into a marriage is criminalised.

Article 38 – Female Genital Mutilation

Parties shall take the necessary legislative or other measures to ensure that the following intentional conducts are criminalised:

a. excising, infibulating or performing any other mutilation to the whole or any part of a woman's labia majora, labia minora or clitoris;
b. coercing or procuring a woman to undergo any of the acts listed in point a;
c. inciting, coercing or procuring a girl to undergo any of the acts listed in point a.

Article 39 – Forced Abortion and Forced Sterilisation

Parties shall take the necessary legislative or other measures to ensure that the following intentional conducts are criminalised:

a. performing an abortion on a woman without her prior and informed consent;
b. performing surgery which has the purpose or effect of terminating a woman's capacity to naturally reproduce without her prior and informed consent or understanding of the procedure.

Article 40 – Sexual Harassment

Parties shall take the necessary legislative or other measures to ensure that any form of unwanted verbal, non-verbal or physical conduct of a sexual nature with the purpose or effect of violating the dignity of a person, in particular when creating an intimidating, hostile, degrading, humiliating or offensive environment, is subject to criminal or other legal sanction.

Article 41 – Aiding or Abetting and Attempt

1. Parties shall take the necessary legislative or other measures to establish as an offence, when committed intentionally, aiding or abetting the commission of the offences established in accordance with Articles 33, 34, 35, 36, 37, 38.a and 39 of this Convention.

2. Parties shall take the necessary legislative or other measures to establish as offences, when committed intentionally, attempts to commit the offences established in accordance with Articles 35, 36, 37, 38.a and 39 of this Convention.

Article 42 – Unacceptable Justifications for Crimes, Including Crimes Committed in the Name of So-called "Honour"

1. Parties shall take the necessary legislative or other measures to ensure that, in criminal proceedings initiated following the commission of any of the acts of violence covered by the scope of this Convention, culture, custom, religion, tradition or so-called "honour" shall not be regarded as justification for such acts. This covers, in particular, claims that the victim has transgressed cultural, religious, social or traditional norms or customs of appropriate behaviour.

2. Parties shall take the necessary legislative or other measures to ensure that incitement by any person of a child to commit any of the acts referred to in paragraph 1 shall not diminish the criminal liability of that person for the acts committed.

Article 43 – Application of Criminal Offences

The offences established in accordance with this Convention shall apply irrespective of the nature of the relationship between victim and perpetrator.

Article 44 – Jurisdiction

1. Parties shall take the necessary legislative or other measures to establish jurisdiction over any offence established in accordance with this Convention, when the offence is committed:

a. in their territory; or
b. on board a ship flying their flag; or
c. on board an aircraft registered under their laws; or
d. by one of their nationals; or
e. by a person who has her or his habitual residence in their territory.

2. Parties shall endeavour to take the necessary legislative or other measures to establish jurisdiction over any offence established in accordance with this Convention where the offence is committed against one of their nationals or a person who has her or his habitual residence in their territory.

3. For the prosecution of the offences established in accordance with Articles 36, 37, 38 and 39 of this Convention, Parties shall take the necessary legislative or other measures to ensure that their jurisdiction is not subordinated to the condition that the acts are criminalised in the territory where they were committed.
4. For the prosecution of the offences established in accordance with Articles 36, 37, 38 and 39 of this Convention, Parties shall take the necessary legislative or other measures to ensure that their jurisdiction as regards points d and e of paragraph 1 is not subordinated to the condition that the prosecution can only be initiated following the reporting by the victim of the offence or the laying of information by the State of the place where the offence was committed.
5. Parties shall take the necessary legislative or other measures to establish jurisdiction over the offences established in accordance with this Convention, in cases where an alleged perpetrator is present on their territory and they do not extradite her or him to another Party, solely on the basis of her or his nationality.
6. When more than one Party claims jurisdiction over an alleged offence established in accordance with this Convention, the Parties involved shall, where appropriate, consult each other with a view to determining the most appropriate jurisdiction for prosecution.
7. Without prejudice to the general rules of international law, this Convention does not exclude any criminal jurisdiction exercised by a Party in accordance with its internal law.

Article 45 – Sanctions and Measures

1. Parties shall take the necessary legislative or other measures to ensure that the offences established in accordance with this Convention are punishable by effective, proportionate and dissuasive sanctions, taking into account their seriousness. These sanctions shall include, where appropriate, sentences involving the deprivation of liberty which can give rise to extradition.
2. Parties may adopt other measures in relation to perpetrators, such as:
- monitoring or supervision of convicted persons;
- withdrawal of parental rights, if the best interests of the child, which may include the safety of the victim, cannot be guaranteed in any other way.

Article 46 – Aggravating Circumstances

Parties shall take the necessary legislative or other measures to ensure that the following circumstances, insofar as they do not already form part of the constituent elements of the offence, may, in conformity with the relevant provisions of internal law, be taken into consideration as aggravating circumstances in the determination of the sentence in relation to the offences established in accordance with this Convention:

a. the offence was committed against a former or current spouse or partner as recognised by internal law, by a member of the family, a person cohabiting with the victim or a person having abused her or his authority;
b. the offence, or related offences, were committed repeatedly;
c. the offence was committed against a person made vulnerable by particular circumstances;
d. the offence was committed against or in the presence of a child;
e. the offence was committed by two or more people acting together;
f. the offence was preceded or accompanied by extreme levels of violence;
g. the offence was committed with the use or threat of a weapon;
h. the offence resulted in severe physical or psychological harm for the victim;
i. the perpetrator had previously been convicted of offences of a similar nature.

Article 47 – Sentences Passed by Another Party

Parties shall take the necessary legislative or other measures to provide for the possibility of taking into account final sentences passed by another Party in relation to the offences established in accordance with this Convention when determining the sentence.

Article 48 – Prohibition of Mandatory Alternative Dispute Resolution Processes or Sentencing

1. Parties shall take the necessary legislative or other measures to prohibit mandatory alternative dispute resolution processes, including mediation and conciliation, in relation to all forms of violence covered by the scope of this Convention.

2. Parties shall take the necessary legislative or other measures to ensure that if the payment of a fine is ordered, due account shall be taken of the ability of the perpetrator to assume his or her financial obligations towards the victim.

Chapter VI: Investigation, Prosecution, Procedural Law and Protective Measures

Article 49 – General Obligations

1. Parties shall take the necessary legislative or other measures to ensure that investigations and judicial proceedings in relation to all forms of violence covered by the scope of this Convention are carried out without undue delay

while taking into consideration the rights of the victim during all stages of the criminal proceedings.
2. Parties shall take the necessary legislative or other measures, in conformity with the fundamental principles of human rights and having regard to the gendered understanding of violence, to ensure the effective investigation and prosecution of offences established in accordance with this Convention.

Article 50 – Immediate Response, Prevention and Protection

1. Parties shall take the necessary legislative or other measures to ensure that the responsible law enforcement agencies respond to all forms of violence covered by the scope of this Convention promptly and appropriately by offering adequate and immediate protection to victims.
2. Parties shall take the necessary legislative or other measures to ensure that the responsible law enforcement agencies engage promptly and appropriately in the prevention and protection against all forms of violence covered by the scope of this Convention, including the employment of preventive operational measures and the collection of evidence.

Article 51 – Risk Assessment and Risk Management

1. Parties shall take the necessary legislative or other measures to ensure that an assessment of the lethality risk, the seriousness of the situation and the risk of repeated violence is carried out by all relevant authorities in order to manage the risk and if necessary to provide co-ordinated safety and support.
2. Parties shall take the necessary legislative or other measures to ensure that the assessment referred to in paragraph 1 duly takes into account, at all stages of the investigation and application of protective measures, the fact that perpetrators of acts of violence covered by the scope of this Convention possess or have access to firearms.

Article 52 – Emergency Barring Orders

Parties shall take the necessary legislative or other measures to ensure that the competent authorities are granted the power to order, in situations of immediate danger, a perpetrator of domestic violence to vacate the residence of the victim or person at risk for a sufficient period of time and to prohibit the perpetrator from entering the residence of or contacting the victim or person at risk. Measures taken pursuant to this article shall give priority to the safety of victims or persons at risk.

Article 53 – Restraining or Protection Orders

1. Parties shall take the necessary legislative or other measures to ensure that appropriate restraining or protection orders are available to victims of all forms of violence covered by the scope of this Convention.

2. Parties shall take the necessary legislative or other measures to ensure that the restraining or protection orders referred to in paragraph 1 are:

- available for immediate protection and without undue financial or administrative burdens placed on the victim;
- issued for a specified period or until modified or discharged;
- where necessary, issued on an ex parte basis which has immediate effect;
- available irrespective of, or in addition to, other legal proceedings;
- allowed to be introduced in subsequent legal proceedings.

3. Parties shall take the necessary legislative or other measures to ensure that breaches of restraining or protection orders issued pursuant to paragraph 1 shall be subject to effective, proportionate and dissuasive criminal or other legal sanctions.

Article 54 – Investigations and Evidence

Parties shall take the necessary legislative or other measures to ensure that, in any civil or criminal proceedings, evidence relating to the sexual history and conduct of the victim shall be permitted only when it is relevant and necessary.

Article 55 – Ex Parte and ex officio Proceedings

1. Parties shall ensure that investigations into or prosecution of offences established in accordance with Articles 35, 36, 37, 38 and 39 of this Convention shall not be wholly dependant upon a report or complaint filed by a victim if the offence was committed in whole or in part on its territory, and that the proceedings may continue even if the victim withdraws her or his statement or complaint.

2. Parties shall take the necessary legislative or other measures to ensure, in accordance with the conditions provided for by their internal law, the possibility for governmental and non-governmental organisations and domestic violence counsellors to assist and/or support victims, at their request, during investigations and judicial proceedings concerning the offences established in accordance with this Convention.

Article 56 – Measures of Protection

1. Parties shall take the necessary legislative or other measures to protect the rights and interests of victims, including their special needs as witnesses, at all stages of investigations and judicial proceedings, in particular by:

a. providing for their protection, as well as that of their families and witnesses, from intimidation, retaliation and repeat victimisation;
b. ensuring that victims are informed, at least in cases where the victims and the family might be in danger, when the perpetrator escapes or is released temporarily or definitively;
c. informing them, under the conditions provided for by internal law, of their rights and the services at their disposal and the follow-up given to their complaint, the charges, the general progress of the investigation or proceedings, and their role therein, as well as the outcome of their case;
d. enabling victims, in a manner consistent with the procedural rules of internal law, to be heard, to supply evidence and have their views, needs and concerns presented, directly or through an intermediary, and considered;
e. providing victims with appropriate support services so that their rights and interests are duly presented and taken into account;
f. ensuring that measures may be adopted to protect the privacy and the image of the victim;
g. ensuring that contact between victims and perpetrators within court and law enforcement agency premises is avoided where possible;
h. providing victims with independent and competent interpreters when victims are parties to proceedings or when they are supplying evidence;
i. enabling victims to testify, according to the rules provided by their internal law, in the courtroom without being present or at least without the presence of the alleged perpetrator, notably through the use of appropriate communication technologies, where available.

2. A child victim and child witness of violence against women and domestic violence shall be afforded, where appropriate, special protection measures taking into account the best interests of the child.

Article 57 – Legal Aid

Parties shall provide for the right to legal assistance and to free legal aid for victims under the conditions provided by their internal law.

Article 58 – Statute of Limitation

Parties shall take the necessary legislative and other measures to ensure that the statute of limitation for initiating any legal proceedings with regard to the offences established in accordance with Articles 36, 37, 38 and 39 of this Convention, shall continue for a period of time that is sufficient and commensurate with the gravity of the offence in question, to allow for the efficient initiation of proceedings after the victim has reached the age of majority.

Chapter VII: Migration and Asylum

Article 59 – Residence Status

1. Parties shall take the necessary legislative or other measures to ensure that victims whose residence status depends on that of the spouse or partner as recognised by internal law, in the event of the dissolution of the marriage or the relationship, are granted in the event of particularly difficult circumstances, upon application, an autonomous residence permit irrespective of the duration of the marriage or the relationship. The conditions relating to the granting and duration of the autonomous residence permit are established by internal law.

2. Parties shall take the necessary legislative or other measures to ensure that victims may obtain the suspension of expulsion proceedings initiated in relation to a residence status dependent on that of the spouse or partner as recognised by internal law to enable them to apply for an autonomous residence permit.

3. Parties shall issue a renewable residence permit to victims in one of the two following situations, or in both:

a. where the competent authority considers that their stay is necessary owing to their personal situation;

b. where the competent authority considers that their stay is necessary for the purpose of their co-operation with the competent authorities in investigation or criminal proceedings.

4. Parties shall take the necessary legislative or other measures to ensure that victims of forced marriage brought into another country for the purpose of the marriage and who, as a result, have lost their residence status in the country where they habitually reside, may regain this status.

Article 60 – Gender-Based Asylum Claims

1. Parties shall take the necessary legislative or other measures to ensure that gender-based violence against women may be recognised as a form of persecution within the meaning of Article 1, A (2), of the 1951 Convention relating to the Status of Refugees and as a form of serious harm giving rise to complementary/subsidiary protection.

2. Parties shall ensure that a gender-sensitive interpretation is given to each of the Convention grounds and that where it is established that the persecution feared is for one or more of these grounds, applicants shall be granted refugee status according to the applicable relevant instruments.

3. Parties shall take the necessary legislative or other measures to develop gender-sensitive reception procedures and support services for asylum-seekers

as well as gender guidelines and gender-sensitive asylum procedures, including refugee status determination and application for international protection.

Article 61 – Non-refoulement

1. Parties shall take the necessary legislative or other measures to respect the principle of non- refoulement in accordance with existing obligations under international law.
2. Parties shall take the necessary legislative or other measures to ensure that victims of violence against women who are in need of protection, regardless of their status or residence, shall not be returned under any circumstances to any country where their life would be at risk or where they might be subjected to torture or inhuman or degrading treatment or punishment.

Chapter VIII: International Co-operation

Article 62 – General Principles

1. Parties shall co-operate with each other, in accordance with the provisions of this Convention, and through the application of relevant international and regional instruments on co-operation in civil and criminal matters, arrangements agreed on the basis of uniform or reciprocal legislation and internal laws, to the widest extent possible, for the purpose of:

a. preventing, combating and prosecuting all forms of violence covered by the scope of this Convention;

b. protecting and providing assistance to victims;

c. investigations or proceedings concerning the offences established in accordance with this Convention;

d. enforcing relevant civil and criminal judgments issued by the judicial authorities of Parties, including protection orders.

2. Parties shall take the necessary legislative or other measures to ensure that victims of an offence established in accordance with this Convention and committed in the territory of a Party other than the one where they reside may make a complaint before the competent authorities of their State of residence.
3. If a Party that makes mutual legal assistance in criminal matters, extradition or enforcement of civil or criminal judgments imposed by another Party to this Convention conditional on the existence of a treaty receives a request for such legal co-operation from a Party with which it has not concluded such a treaty, it may consider this Convention to be the legal basis for mutual legal assistance in criminal matters, extradition or enforcement of civil or criminal judgments imposed by the other Party in respect of the offences established in accordance with this Convention.

4. Parties shall endeavour to integrate, where appropriate, the prevention and the fight against violence against women and domestic violence in assistance programmes for development provided for the benefit of third States, including by entering into bilateral and multilateral agreements with third States with a view to facilitating the protection of victims in accordance with Article 18, paragraph 5.

Article 63 – Measures Relating to Persons at Risk

When a Party, on the basis of the information at its disposal, has reasonable grounds to believe that a person is at immediate risk of being subjected to any of the acts of violence referred to in Articles 36, 37, 38 and 39 of this Convention on the territory of another Party, the Party that has the information is encouraged to transmit it without delay to the latter for the purpose of ensuring that appropriate protection measures are taken. Where applicable, this information shall include details on existing protection provisions for the benefit of the person at risk.

Article 64 – Information

1. The requested Party shall promptly inform the requesting Party of the final result of the action taken under this chapter. The requested Party shall also promptly inform the requesting Party of any circumstances which render impossible the carrying out of the action sought or are likely to delay it significantly.
2. A Party may, within the limits of its internal law, without prior request, forward to another Party information obtained within the framework of its own investigations when it considers that the disclosure of such information might assist the receiving Party in preventing criminal offences established in accordance with this Convention or in initiating or carrying out investigations or proceedings concerning such criminal offences or that it might lead to a request for co-operation by that Party under this chapter.
3. A Party receiving any information in accordance with paragraph 2 shall submit such information to its competent authorities in order that proceedings may be taken if they are considered appropriate, or that this information may be taken into account in relevant civil and criminal proceedings.

Article 65 – Data Protection

Personal data shall be stored and used pursuant to the obligations undertaken by the Parties under the Convention for the Protection of Individuals with regard to Automatic Processing of Personal Data (ETS No. 108).

Chapter IX: Monitoring Mechanism

Article 66 – Group of Experts on Action against Violence against Women and Domestic Violence

1. The Group of experts on action against violence against women and domestic violence (hereinafter referred to as "GREVIO") shall monitor the implementation of this Convention by the Parties.
2. GREVIO shall be composed of a minimum of 10 members and a maximum of 15 members, taking into account a gender and geographical balance, as well as multidisciplinary expertise. Its members shall be elected by the Committee of the Parties from among candidates nominated by the Parties for a term of office of four years, renewable once, and chosen from among nationals of the Parties.
3. The initial election of 10 members shall be held within a period of one year following the entry into force of this Convention. The election of five additional members shall be held following the 25th ratification or accession.
4. The election of the members of GREVIO shall be based on the following principles:

a. they shall be chosen according to a transparent procedure from among persons of high moral character, known for their recognised competence in the fields of human rights, gender equality, violence against women and domestic violence, or assistance to and protection of victims, or having demonstrated professional experience in the areas covered by this Convention;
b. no two members of GREVIO may be nationals of the same State;
c. they should represent the main legal systems;
d. they should represent relevant actors and agencies in the field of violence against women and domestic violence;
e. they shall sit in their individual capacity and shall be independent and impartial in the exercise of their functions, and shall be available to carry out their duties in an effective manner.

5. The election procedure of the members of GREVIO shall be determined by the Committee of Ministers of the Council of Europe, after consulting with and obtaining the unanimous consent of the Parties, within a period of six months following the entry into force of this Convention.
6. GREVIO shall adopt its own rules of procedure.
7. Members of GREVIO, and other members of delegations carrying out the country visits as set forth in Article 68, paragraphs 9 and 14, shall enjoy the privileges and immunities established in the appendix to this Convention.

Article 67 – Committee of the Parties

1. The Committee of the Parties shall be composed of the representatives of the Parties to the Convention.
2. The Committee of the Parties shall be convened by the Secretary General of the Council of Europe. Its first meeting shall be held within a period of one year following the entry into force of this Convention in order to elect the members of GREVIO. It shall subsequently meet whenever one third of the Parties, the President of the Committee of the Parties or the Secretary General so requests.
3. The Committee of the Parties shall adopt its own rules of procedure.

Article 68 – Procedure

1. Parties shall submit to the Secretary General of the Council of Europe, based on a questionnaire prepared by GREVIO, a report on legislative and other measures giving effect to the provisions of this Convention, for consideration by GREVIO.
2. GREVIO shall consider the report submitted in accordance with paragraph 1 with the representatives of the Party concerned.
3. Subsequent evaluation procedures shall be divided into rounds, the length of which is determined by GREVIO. At the beginning of each round GREVIO shall select the specific provisions on which the evaluation procedure shall be based and send out a questionnaire.
4. GREVIO shall define the appropriate means to carry out this monitoring procedure. It may in particular adopt a questionnaire for each evaluation round, which shall serve as a basis for the evaluation procedure of the implementation by the Parties. This questionnaire shall be addressed to all Parties. Parties shall respond to this questionnaire, as well as to any other request of information from GREVIO.
5. GREVIO may receive information on the implementation of the Convention from non-governmental organisations and civil society, as well as from national institutions for the protection of human rights.
6. GREVIO shall take due consideration of the existing information available from other regional and international instruments and bodies in areas falling within the scope of this Convention.
7. When adopting a questionnaire for each evaluation round, GREVIO shall take due consideration of the existing data collection and research in the Parties as referred to in Article 11 of this Convention.
8. GREVIO may receive information on the implementation of the Convention from the Council of Europe Commissioner for Human Rights, the Parliamentary Assembly and relevant specialised bodies of the Council of Europe, as well

as those established under other international instruments. Complaints presented to these bodies and their outcome will be made available to GREVIO.
9. GREVIO may subsidiarily organise, in co-operation with the national authorities and with the assistance of independent national experts, country visits, if the information gained is insufficient or in cases provided for in paragraph 14. During these visits, GREVIO may be assisted by specialists in specific fields.
10. GREVIO shall prepare a draft report containing its analysis concerning the implementation of the provisions on which the evaluation is based, as well as its suggestions and proposals concerning the way in which the Party concerned may deal with the problems which have been identified. The draft report shall be transmitted for comments to the Party which undergoes the evaluation. Its comments shall be taken into account by GREVIO when adopting its report.
11. On the basis of all the information received and the comments by the Parties, GREVIO shall adopt its report and conclusions concerning the measures taken by the Party concerned to implement the provisions of this Convention. This report and the conclusions shall be sent to the Party concerned and to the Committee of the Parties. The report and conclusions of GREVIO shall be made public as from their adoption, together with eventual comments by the Party concerned.
12. Without prejudice to the procedure of paragraphs 1 to 8, the Committee of the Parties may adopt, on the basis of the report and conclusions of GREVIO, recommendations addressed to this Party (a) concerning the measures to be taken to implement the conclusions of GREVIO, if necessary setting a date for submitting information on their implementation, and (b) aiming at promoting co-operation with that Party for the proper implementation of this Convention.
13. If GREVIO receives reliable information indicating a situation where problems require immediate attention to prevent or limit the scale or number of serious violations of the Convention, it may request the urgent submission of a special report concerning measures taken to prevent a serious, massive or persistent pattern of violence against women.
14. Taking into account the information submitted by the Party concerned, as well as any other reliable information available to it, GREVIO may designate one or more of its members to conduct an inquiry and to report urgently to GREVIO. Where warranted and with the consent of the Party, the inquiry may include a visit to its territory.
15. After examining the findings of the inquiry referred to in paragraph 14, GREVIO shall transmit these findings to the Party concerned and, where appropriate, to the Committee of the Parties and the Committee of Ministers of the Council of Europe together with any comments and recommendations.

Article 69 – General Recommendations

GREVIO may adopt, where appropriate, general recommendations on the implementation of this Convention.

Article 70 – Parliamentary Involvement in Monitoring

1. National parliaments shall be invited to participate in the monitoring of the measures taken for the implementation of this Convention.
2. Parties shall submit the reports of GREVIO to their national parliaments.
3. The Parliamentary Assembly of the Council of Europe shall be invited to regularly take stock of the implementation of this Convention.

Chapter X: Relationship with Other International Instruments

Article 71 – Relationship with Other International Instruments

1. This Convention shall not affect obligations arising from other international instruments to which Parties to this Convention are Parties or shall become Parties and which contain provisions on matters governed by this Convention.
2. The Parties to this Convention may conclude bilateral or multilateral agreements with one another on the matters dealt with in this Convention, for purposes of supplementing or strengthening its provisions or facilitating the application of the principles embodied in it.

Chapter XI: Amendments to the Convention

Article 72 – Amendments

1. Any proposal for an amendment to this Convention presented by a Party shall be communicated to the Secretary General of the Council of Europe and forwarded by her or him to the member States of the Council of Europe, any signatory, any Party, the European Union, any State invited to sign this Convention in accordance with the provisions of Article 75, and any State invited to accede to this Convention in accordance with the provisions of Article 76.
2. The Committee of Ministers of the Council of Europe shall consider the proposed amendment and, after having consulted the Parties to this Convention that are not members of the Council of Europe, may adopt the amendment by the majority provided for in Article 20.d of the Statute of the Council of Europe.
3. The text of any amendment adopted by the Committee of Ministers in accordance with paragraph 2 shall be forwarded to the Parties for acceptance.
4. Any amendment adopted in accordance with paragraph 2 shall enter into force on the first day of the month following the expiration of a period of one month after the date on which all Parties have informed the Secretary General of their acceptance.

Chapter XII: Final Clauses

Article 73 – Effects of This Convention

The provisions of this Convention shall not prejudice the provisions of internal law and binding international instruments which are already in force or may come into force, under which more favourable rights are or would be accorded to persons in preventing and combating violence against women and domestic violence.

Article 74 – Dispute Settlement

1. The Parties to any dispute which may arise concerning the application or interpretation of the provisions of this Convention shall first seek to resolve it by means of negotiation, conciliation, arbitration or by any other methods of peaceful settlement accepted by mutual agreement between them.
2. The Committee of Ministers of the Council of Europe may establish procedures of settlement to be available for use by the Parties in dispute if they should so agree.

Article 75 – Signature and Entry into Force

1. This Convention shall be open for signature by the member States of the Council of Europe, the non-member States which have participated in its elaboration and the European Union.
2. This Convention is subject to ratification, acceptance or approval. Instruments of ratification, acceptance or approval shall be deposited with the Secretary General of the Council of Europe.
3. This Convention shall enter into force on the first day of the month following the expiration of a period of three months after the date on which 10 signatories, including at least eight member States of the Council of Europe, have expressed their consent to be bound by the Convention in accordance with the provisions of paragraph 2.
4. In respect of any State referred to in paragraph 1 or the European Union, which subsequently expresses its consent to be bound by it, the Convention shall enter into force on the first day of the month following the expiration of a period of three months after the date of the deposit of its instrument of ratification, acceptance or approval.

Article 76 – Accession to the Convention

1. After the entry into force of this Convention, the Committee of Ministers of the Council of Europe may, after consultation of the Parties to this Convention and obtaining their unanimous consent, invite any non-member State of the Council of Europe, which has not participated in the elaboration of the

Convention, to accede to this Convention by a decision taken by the majority provided for in Article 20.d of the Statute of the Council of Europe, and by unanimous vote of the representatives of the Parties entitled to sit on the Committee of Ministers.
2. In respect of any acceding State, the Convention shall enter into force on the first day of the month following the expiration of a period of three months after the date of deposit of the instrument of accession with the Secretary General of the Council of Europe.

Article 77 – Territorial Application

1. Any State or the European Union may, at the time of signature or when depositing its instrument of ratification, acceptance, approval or accession, specify the territory or territories to which this Convention shall apply.
2. Any Party may, at any later date, by a declaration addressed to the Secretary General of the Council of Europe, extend the application of this Convention to any other territory specified in the declaration and for whose international relations it is responsible or on whose behalf it is authorised to give undertakings. In respect of such territory, the Convention shall enter into force on the first day of the month following the expiration of a period of three months after the date of receipt of such declaration by the Secretary General.
3. Any declaration made under the two preceding paragraphs may, in respect of any territory specified in such declaration, be withdrawn by a notification addressed to the Secretary General of the Council of Europe. The withdrawal shall become effective on the first day of the month following the expiration of a period of three months after the date of receipt of such notification by the Secretary General.

Article 78 – Reservations

1. No reservation may be made in respect of any provision of this Convention, with the exceptions provided for in paragraphs 2 and 3.
2. Any State or the European Union may, at the time of signature or when depositing its instrument of ratification, acceptance, approval or accession, by a declaration addressed to the Secretary General of the Council of Europe, declare that it reserves the right not to apply or to apply only in specific cases or conditions the provisions laid down in:
- Article 30, paragraph 2;
- Article 44, paragraphs 1.e, 3 and 4;
- Article 55, paragraph 1 in respect of Article 35 regarding minor offences;
- Article 58 in respect of Articles 37, 38 and 39;
- Article 59.

3. Any State or the European Union may, at the time of signature or when depositing its instrument of ratification, acceptance, approval or accession, by a declaration addressed to the Secretary General of the Council of Europe, declare that it reserves the right to provide for non-criminal sanctions, instead of criminal sanctions, for the behaviours referred to in Articles 33 and 34.
4. Any Party may wholly or partly withdraw a reservation by means of a declaration addressed to the Secretary General of the Council of Europe. This declaration shall become effective as from its date of receipt by the Secretary General.

Article 79 – Validity and Review of Reservations

1. Reservations referred to in Article 78, paragraphs 2 and 3, shall be valid for a period of five years from the day of the entry into force of this Convention in respect of the Party concerned. However, such reservations may be renewed for periods of the same duration.
2. Eighteen months before the date of expiry of the reservation, the Secretariat General of the Council of Europe shall give notice of that expiry to the Party concerned. No later than three months before the expiry, the Party shall notify the Secretary General that it is upholding, amending or withdrawing its reservation. In the absence of a notification by the Party concerned, the Secretariat General shall inform that Party that its reservation is considered to have been extended automatically for a period of six months. Failure by the Party concerned to notify its intention to uphold or modify its reservation before the expiry of that period shall cause the reservation to lapse.
3. If a Party makes a reservation in conformity with Article 78, paragraphs 2 and 3, it shall provide, before its renewal or upon request, an explanation to GREVIO, on the grounds justifying its continuance.

Article 80 – Denunciation

1. Any Party may, at any time, denounce this Convention by means of a notification addressed to the Secretary General of the Council of Europe.
2. Such denunciation shall become effective on the first day of the month following the expiration of a period of three months after the date of receipt of the notification by the Secretary General.

Article 81 – Notification

The Secretary General of the Council of Europe shall notify the member States of the Council of Europe, the non-member States which have participated in its elaboration, any signatory, any Party, the European Union, and any State invited to accede to this Convention of:

a. any signature;
b. the deposit of any instrument of ratification, acceptance, approval or accession;
c. any date of entry into force of this Convention in accordance with Articles 75 and 76;
d. any amendment adopted in accordance with Article 72 and the date on which such an amendment enters into force;
e. any reservation and withdrawal of reservation made in pursuance of Article 78;
f. any denunciation made in pursuance of the provisions of Article 80;
g. any other act, notification or communication relating to this Convention.

In witness whereof the undersigned, being duly authorised thereto, have signed this Convention.

Done at Istanbul, this 11th day of May 2011, in English and in French, both texts being equally authentic, in a single copy which shall be deposited in the archives of the Council of Europe. The Secretary General of the Council of Europe shall transmit certified copies to each member State of the Council of Europe, to the non-member States which have participated in the elaboration of this Convention, to the European Union and to any State invited to accede to this Convention.

PART V

Child Labour

CHAPTER 26

C138 Minimum Age Convention

(Convention concerning Minimum Age for Admission to Employment)
Adopted on 26 June 1973 by the General Conference of the International Labour Organisation at its 58th session
Entry into force 19 June 1976, in accordance with article 12

The General Conference of the International Labour Organisation,

Having been convened at Geneva by the Governing Body of the International Labour Office, and having met in its Fifty-eighth Session on 6 June 1973, and

Having decided upon the adoption of certain proposals with regard to minimum age for admission to employment, which is the fourth item on the agenda of the session, and

Noting the terms of the Minimum Age (Industry) Convention, 1919, the Minimum Age (Sea) Convention, 1920, the Minimum Age (Agriculture) Convention, 1921, the Minimum Age (Trimmers and Stokers) Convention, 1921, the Minimum Age (Non-Industrial Employment) Convention, 1932, the Minimum Age (Sea) Convention (Revised), 1936, the Minimum Age (Industry) Convention (Revised), 1937, the Minimum Age (Non-Industrial Employment) Convention (Revised), 1937, the Minimum Age (Fishermen) Convention, 1959, and the Minimum Age (Underground Work) Convention, 1965, and

Considering that the time has come to establish a general instrument on the subject, which would gradually replace the existing ones applicable to limited economic sectors, with a view to achieving the total abolition of child labour, and

Having determined that this instrument shall take the form of an international Convention,

adopts this twenty-sixth day of June of the year one thousand nine hundred and seventy-three the following Convention, which may be cited as the Minimum Age Convention, 1973:

Art. 1 Each Member for which this Convention is in force undertakes to pursue a national policy designed to ensure the effective abolition of child labour and to raise progressively the minimum age for admission to employment or work to a level consistent with the fullest physical and mental development of young persons.

Art. 2 1. Each Member which ratifies this Convention shall specify, in a declaration appended to its ratification, a minimum age for admission to employment

or work within its territory and on means of transport registered in its territory; subject to Articles 4 to 8 of this Convention, no one under that age shall be admitted to employment or work in any occupation.
2. Each Member which has ratified this Convention may subsequently notify the Director-General of the International Labour Office, by further declarations, that it specifies a minimum age higher than that previously specified.
3. The minimum age specified in pursuance of paragraph 1 of this Article shall not be less than the age of completion of compulsory schooling and, in any case, shall not be less than 15 years.
4. Notwithstanding the provisions of paragraph 3 of this Article, a Member whose economy and educational facilities are insufficiently developed may, after consultation with the organisations of employers and workers concerned, where such exist, initially specify a minimum age of 14 years.
5. Each Member which has specified a minimum age of 14 years in pursuance of the provisions of the preceding paragraph shall include in its reports on the application of this Convention submitted under article 22 of the Constitution of the International Labour Organisation a statement –
(a) that its reason for doing so subsists; or
(b) that it renounces its right to avail itself of the provisions in question as from a stated date.

Art. 3 1. The minimum age for admission to any type of employment or work which by its nature or the circumstances in which it is carried out is likely to jeopardise the health, safety or morals of young persons shall not be less than 18 years.
2. The types of employment or work to which paragraph 1 of this Article applies shall be determined by national laws or regulations or by the competent authority, after consultation with the organisations of employers and workers concerned, where such exist.
3. Notwithstanding the provisions of paragraph 1 of this Article, national laws or regulations or the competent authority may, after consultation with the organisations of employers and workers concerned, where such exist, authorise employment or work as from the age of 16 years on condition that the health, safety and morals of the young persons concerned are fully protected and that the young persons have received adequate specific instruction or vocational training in the relevant branch of activity.

Art. 4 1. In so far as necessary, the competent authority, after consultation with the organisations of employers and workers concerned, where such exist, may exclude from the application of this Convention limited categories of employment or work in respect of which special and substantial problems of application arise.

2. Each Member which ratifies this Convention shall list in its first report on the application of the Convention submitted under article 22 of the Constitution of the International Labour Organisation any categories which may have been excluded in pursuance of paragraph 1 of this Article, giving the reasons for such exclusion, and shall state in subsequent reports the position of its law and practice in respect of the categories excluded and the extent to which effect has been given or is proposed to be given to the Convention in respect of such categories.
3. Employment or work covered by Article 3 of this Convention shall not be excluded from the application of the Convention in pursuance of this Article.
Art. 5 1. A Member whose economy and administrative facilities are insufficiently developed may, after consultation with the organisations of employers and workers concerned, where such exist, initially limit the scope of application of this Convention.
2. Each Member which avails itself of the provisions of paragraph 1 of this Article shall specify, in a declaration appended to its ratification, the branches of economic activity or types of undertakings to which it will apply the provisions of the Convention.
3. The provisions of the Convention shall be applicable as a minimum to the following: mining and quarrying; manufacturing; construction; electricity, gas and water; sanitary services; transport, storage and communication; and plantations and other agricultural undertakings mainly producing for commercial purposes, but excluding family and small-scale holdings producing for local consumption and not regularly employing hired workers.
4. Any Member which has limited the scope of application of this Convention in pursuance of this Article –

(a) shall indicate in its reports under Article 22 of the Constitution of the International Labour Organisation the general position as regards the employment or work of young persons and children in the branches of activity which are excluded from the scope of application of this Convention and any progress which may have been made towards wider application of the provisions of the Convention;
(b) may at any time formally extend the scope of application by a declaration addressed to the Director-General of the International Labour Office.

Art. 6 This Convention does not apply to work done by children and young persons in schools for general, vocational or technical education or in other training institutions, or to work done by persons at least 14 years of age in undertakings, where such work is carried out in accordance with conditions prescribed by the competent authority, after consultation with the organisations of employers and workers concerned, where such exist, and is an integral part of –

(a) a course of education or training for which a school or training institution is primarily responsible;

(b) a programme of training mainly or entirely in an undertaking, which programme has been approved by the competent authority; or

(c) a programme of guidance or orientation designed to facilitate the choice of an occupation or of a line of training.

Art. 7 1. National laws or regulations may permit the employment or work of persons 13 to 15 years of age on light work which is –

(a) not likely to be harmful to their health or development; and

(b) not such as to prejudice their attendance at school, their participation in vocational orientation or training programmes approved by the competent authority or their capacity to benefit from the instruction received.

2. National laws or regulations may also permit the employment or work of persons who are at least 15 years of age but have not yet completed their compulsory schooling on work which meets the requirements set forth in subparagraphs (a) and (b) of paragraph 1 of this Article.

3. The competent authority shall determine the activities in which employment or work may be permitted under paragraphs 1 and 2 of this Article and shall prescribe the number of hours during which and the conditions in which such employment or work may be undertaken.

4. Notwithstanding the provisions of paragraphs 1 and 2 of this Article, a Member which has availed itself of the provisions of paragraph 4 of Article 2 may, for as long as it continues to do so, substitute the ages 12 and 14 for the ages 13 and 15 in paragraph 1 and the age 14 for the age 15 in paragraph 2 of this Article.

Art. 8 1. After consultation with the organisations of employers and workers concerned, where such exist, the competent authority may, by permits granted in individual cases, allow exceptions to the prohibition of employment or work provided for in Article 2 of this Convention, for such purposes as participation in artistic performances.

2. Permits so granted shall limit the number of hours during which and prescribe the conditions in which employment or work is allowed.

Art. 9 1. All necessary measures, including the provision of appropriate penalties, shall be taken by the competent authority to ensure the effective enforcement of the provisions of this Convention.

2. National laws or regulations or the competent authority shall define the persons responsible for compliance with the provisions giving effect to the Convention.
3. National laws or regulations or the competent authority shall prescribe the registers or other documents which shall be kept and made available by the employer; such registers or documents shall contain the names and ages or dates of birth, duly certified wherever possible, of persons whom he employs or who work for him and who are less than 18 years of age.
Art. 10 1. This Convention revises, on the terms set forth in this Article, the Minimum Age (Industry) Convention, 1919, the Minimum Age (Sea) Convention, 1920, the Minimum Age (Agriculture) Convention, 1921, the Minimum Age (Trimmers and Stokers) Convention, 1921, the Minimum Age (Non-Industrial Employment) Convention, 1932, the Minimum Age (Sea) Convention (Revised), 1936, the Minimum Age (Industry) Convention (Revised), 1937, the Minimum Age (Non-Industrial Employment) Convention (Revised), 1937, the Minimum Age (Fishermen) Convention, 1959, and the Minimum Age (Underground Work) Convention, 1965.
2. The coming into force of this Convention shall not close the Minimum Age (Sea) Convention (Revised), 1936, the Minimum Age (Industry) Convention (Revised), 1937, the Minimum Age (Non-Industrial Employment) Convention (Revised), 1937, the Minimum Age (Fishermen) Convention, 1959, or the Minimum Age (Underground Work) Convention, 1965, to further ratification.
3. The Minimum Age (Industry) Convention, 1919, the Minimum Age (Sea) Convention, 1920, the Minimum Age (Agriculture) Convention, 1921, and the Minimum Age (Trimmers and Stokers) Convention, 1921, shall be closed to further ratification when all the parties thereto have consented to such closing by ratification of this Convention or by a declaration communicated to the Director-General of the International Labour Office.
4. When the obligations of this Convention are accepted –

(a) by a Member which is a party to the Minimum Age (Industry) Convention (Revised), 1937, and a minimum age of not less than 15 years is specified in pursuance of Article 2 of this Convention, this shall ipso jure involve the immediate denunciation of that Convention,
(b) in respect of non-industrial employment as defined in the Minimum Age (Non-Industrial Employment) Convention, 1932, by a Member which is a party to that Convention, this shall ipso jure involve the immediate denunciation of that Convention,
(c) in respect of non-industrial employment as defined in the Minimum Age (Non-Industrial Employment) Convention (Revised), 1937, by a Member which is a party to that Convention, and a minimum age

of not less than 15 years is specified in pursuance of Article 2 of this Convention, this shall ipso jure involve the immediate denunciation of that Convention,

(d) in respect of maritime employment, by a Member which is a party to the Minimum Age (Sea) Convention (Revised), 1936, and a minimum age of not less than 15 years is specified in pursuance of Article 2 of this Convention or the Member specifies that Article 3 of this Convention applies to maritime employment, this shall ipso jure involve the immediate denunciation of that Convention,

(e) in respect of employment in maritime fishing, by a Member which is a party to the Minimum Age (Fishermen) Convention, 1959, and a minimum age of not less than 15 years is specified in pursuance of Article 2 of this Convention or the Member specifies that Article 3 of this Convention applies to employment in maritime fishing, this shall ipso jure involve the immediate denunciation of that Convention,

(f) by a Member which is a party to the Minimum Age (Underground Work) Convention, 1965, and a minimum age of not less than the age specified in pursuance of that Convention is specified in pursuance of Article 2 of this Convention or the Member specifies that such an age applies to employment underground in mines in virtue of Article 3 of this Convention, this shall ipso jure involve the immediate denunciation of that Convention,

if and when this Convention shall have come into force.

5. Acceptance of the obligations of this Convention –

(a) shall involve the denunciation of the Minimum Age (Industry) Convention, 1919, in accordance with Article 12 therof,

(b) in respect of agriculture shall involve the denunciation of the Minimum Age (Agriculture) Convention, 1921, in accordance with Article 9 thereof,

(c) in respect of maritime employment shall involve the denunciation of the Minimum Age (Sea) Convention, 1920, in accordance with Article 10 thereof, and of the Minimum Age (Trimmers and Stokers) Convention, 1921, in accordance with Article 12 thereof,

if and when this Convention shall have come into force.

Art. 11 The formal ratifications of this Convention shall be communicated to the Director-General of the International Labour Office for registration.

Art. 12 1. This Convention shall be binding only upon those Members of the International Labour Organisation whose ratifications have been registered with the Director-General.

2. It shall come into force twelve months after the date on which the ratifications of two Members have been registered with the Director-General.

3. Thereafter, this Convention shall come into force for any Member twelve months after the date on which its ratifications has been registered.

Art. 13 1. A Member which has ratified this Convention may denounce it after the expiration of ten years from the date on which the Convention first comes into force, by an act communicated to the Director-General of the International Labour Office for registration. Such denunciation shall not take effect until one year after the date on which it is registered.

2. Each Member which has ratified this Convention and which does not, within the year following the expiration of the period of ten years mentioned in the preceding paragraph, exercise the right of denunciation provided for in this Article, will be bound for another period of ten years and, thereafter, may denounce this Convention at the expiration of each period of ten years under the terms provided for in this Article.

Art. 14 1. The Director-General of the International Labour Office shall notify all Members of the International Labour Organisation of the registration of all ratifications and denunciations communicated to him by the Members of the Organisation.

2. When notifying the Members of the Organisation of the registration of the second ratification communicated to him, the Director-General shall draw the attention of the Members of the Organisation to the date upon which the Convention will come into force.

Art. 15 The Director-General of the International Labour Office shall communicate to the Secretary-General of the United Nations for registration in accordance with Article 102 of the Charter of the United Nations full particulars of all ratifications and acts of denunciation registered by him in accordance with the provisions of the preceding Articles.

Art. 16 At such times as it may consider necessary the Governing Body of the International Labour Office shall present to the General Conference a report on the working of this Convention and shall examine the desirability of placing on the agenda of the Conference the question of its revision in whole or in part.

Art. 17 1. Should the Conference adopt a new Convention revising this Convention in whole or in part, then, unless the new Convention otherwise provides –

(a) the ratification by a Member of the new revising Convention shall ipso jure involve the immediate denunciation of this Convention, notwithstanding the provisions of Article 13 above, if and when the new revising Convention shall have come into force;

(b) as from the date when the new revising Convention comes into force this Convention shall cease to be open to ratification by the Members.

2. This Convention shall in any case remain in force in its actual form and content for those Members which have ratified it but have not ratified the revising Convention.

Art. 18 The English and French versions of the text of this Convention are equally authoritative.

CHAPTER 26.A

R146 Minimum Age Recommendation

Adopted on 26 June 1973 by the General Conference of the International Labour Organisation at its 58th session

Preamble

The General Conference of the International Labour Organisation,

Having been convened at Geneva by the Governing Body of the International Labour Office, and having met in its Fifty-eighth Session on 6 June 1973, and

Recognising that the effective abolition of child labour and the progressive raising of the minimum age for admission to employment constitute only one aspect of the protection and advancement of children and young persons, and

Noting the concern of the whole United Nations system with such protection and advancement, and

Having adopted the Minimum Age Convention, 1973, and

Desirous to define further certain elements of policy which are the concern of the International Labour Organisation, and

Having decided upon the adoption of certain proposals regarding minimum age for admission to employment, which is the fourth item on the agenda of the session, and

Having determined that these proposals shall take the form of a Recommendation supplementing the Minimum Age Convention, 1973,

adopts this twenty-sixth day of June of the year one thousand nine hundred and seventy-three, the following Recommendation, which may be cited as the Minimum Age Recommendation, 1973:

I National Policy

1. To ensure the success of the national policy provided for in Article 1 of the Minimum Age Convention, 1973, high priority should be given to planning for and meeting the needs of children and youth in national development policies and programmes and to the progressive extension of the inter-related measures necessary to provide the best possible conditions of physical and mental growth for children and young persons.

2. In this connection special attention should be given to such areas of planning and policy as the following:

(a) firm national commitment to full employment, in accordance with the Employment Policy Convention and Recommendation, 1964, and the taking of measures designed to promote employment-oriented development in rural and urban areas;
(b) the progressive extension of other economic and social measures to alleviate poverty wherever it exists and to ensure family living standards and income which are such as to make it unnecessary to have recourse to the economic activity of children;
(c) the development and progressive extension, without any discrimination, of social security and family welfare measures aimed at ensuring child maintenance, including children's allowances;
(d) the development and progressive extension of adequate facilities for education and vocational orientation and training appropriate in form and content to the needs of the children and young persons concerned;
(e) the development and progressive extension of appropriate facilities for the protection and welfare of children and young persons, including employed young persons, and for the promotion of their development.

3. Particular account should as necessary be taken of the needs of children and young persons who do not have families or do not live with their own families and of migrant children and young persons who live and travel with their families. Measures taken to that end should include the provision of fellowships and vocational training.

4. Full-time attendance at school or participation in approved vocational orientation or training programmes should be required and effectively ensured up to an age at least equal to that specified for admission to employment in accordance with Article 2 of the Minimum Age Convention, 1973.

5. (1) Consideration should be given to measures such as preparatory training, not involving hazards, for types of employment or work in respect of which the minimum age prescribed in accordance with Article 3 of the Minimum Age Convention, 1973, is higher than the age of completion of compulsory full-time schooling.

(2) Analogous measures should be envisaged where the professional exigencies of a particular occupation include a minimum age for admission which is higher than the age of completion of compulsory full-time schooling.

II Minimum Age

6. The minimum age should be fixed at the same level for all sectors of economic activity.

7. (1) Members should take as their objective the progressive raising to 16 years of the minimum age for admission to employment or work specified in pursuance of Article 2 of the Minimum Age Convention, 1973.
(2) Where the minimum age for employment or work covered by Article 2 of the Minimum Age Convention, 1973, is still below 15 years, urgent steps should be taken to raise it to that level.
8. Where it is not immediately feasible to fix a minimum age for all employment in agriculture and in related activities in rural areas, a minimum age should be fixed at least for employment on plantations and in the other agricultural undertakings referred to in Article 5, paragraph 3, of the Minimum Age Convention, 1973.

III Hazardous Employment or Work

9. Where the minimum age for admission to types of employment or work which are likely to jeopardise the health, safety or morals of young persons is still below 18 years, immediate steps should be taken to raise it to that level.
10. (1) In determining the types of employment or work to which Article 3 of the Minimum Age Convention, 1973, applies, full account should be taken of relevant international labour standards, such as those concerning dangerous substances, agents or processes (including ionising radiations), the lifting of heavy weights and underground work.
(2) The list of the types of employment or work in question should be re-examined periodically and revised as necessary, particularly in the light of advancing scientific and technological knowledge.
11. Where, by reference to Article 5 of the Minimum Age Convention, 1973, a minimum age is not immediately fixed for certain branches of economic activity or types of undertakings, appropriate minimum age provisions should be made applicable therein to types of employment or work presenting hazards for young persons.

IV Conditions of Employment

12. (1) Measures should be taken to ensure that the conditions in which children and young persons under the age of 18 years are employed or work reach and are maintained at a satisfactory standard. These conditions should be supervised closely.

(2) Measures should likewise be taken to safeguard and supervise the conditions in which children and young persons undergo vocational orientation and training within undertakings, training institutions and schools for vocational or technical education and to formulate standards for their protection and development.

13. (1) In connection with the application of the preceding Paragraph, as well as in giving effect to Article 7, paragraph 3, of the Minimum Age Convention, 1973, special attention should be given to –

(a) the provision of fair remuneration and its protection, bearing in mind the principle of equal pay for equal work;
(b) the strict limitation of the hours spent at work in a day and in a week, and the prohibition of overtime, so as to allow enough time for education and training (including the time needed for homework related thereto), for rest during the day and for leisure activities;
(c) the granting, without possibility of exception save in genuine emergency, of a minimum consecutive period of 12 hours' night rest, and of customary weekly rest days;
(d) the granting of an annual holiday with pay of at least four weeks and, in any case, not shorter than that granted to adults;
(e) coverage by social security schemes, including employment injury, medical care and sickness benefit schemes, whatever the conditions of employment or work may be;
(f) the maintenance of satisfactory standards of safety and health and appropriate instruction and supervision.

(2) Subparagraph (1) of this Paragraph applies to young seafarers in so far as they are not covered in respect of the matters dealt with therein by international labour Conventions or Recommendations specifically concerned with maritime employment.

V Enforcement

14. (1) Measures to ensure the effective application of the Minimum Age Convention, 1973, and of this Recommendation should include –

(a) the strengthening as necessary of labour inspection and related services, for instance by the special training of inspectors to detect abuses in the employment or work of children and young persons and to correct such abuses; and
(b) the strengthening of services for the improvement and inspection of training in undertakings.

(2) Emphasis should be placed on the role which can be played by inspectors in supplying information and advice on effective means of complying with relevant provisions as well as in securing their enforcement.
(3) Labour inspection and inspection of training in undertakings should be closely co-ordinated to provide the greatest economic efficiency and, generally, the labour administration services should work in close co-operation with the services responsible for the education, training, welfare and guidance of children and young persons.
15. Special attention should be paid –
(a) to the enforcement of provisions concerning employment in hazardous types of employment or work; and
(b) in so far as education or training is compulsory, to the prevention of the employment or work of children and young persons during the hours when instruction is available.
16. The following measures should be taken to facilitate the verification of ages:
(a) the public authorities should maintain an effective system of birth registration, which should include the issue of birth certificates;
(b) employers should be required to keep and to make available to the competent authority registers or other documents indicating the names and ages or dates of birth, duly certified wherever possible, not only of children and young persons employed by them but also of those receiving vocational orientation or training in their undertakings;
(c) children and young persons working in the streets, in outside stalls, in public places, in itinerant occupations or in other circumstances which make the checking of employers' records impracticable should be issued licences or other documents indicating their eligibility for such work.

CHAPTER 26.B

R190 Worst Forms of Child Labour Recommendation

Adopted on 17 June 1999 by the General Conference of the International Labour Organisation at its 87th session

Preamble

The General Conference of the International Labour Organization,
Having been convened at Geneva by the Governing Body of the International Labour Office, and having met in its Eighty-seventh Session on 1 June 1999, and
Having adopted the Worst Forms of Child Labour Convention, 1999, and
Having decided upon the adoption of certain proposals with regard to child labour, which is the fourth item on the agenda of the session, and
Having determined that these proposals shall take the form of a Recommendation supplementing the Worst Forms of Child Labour Convention, 1999;
adopts this seventeenth day of June of the year one thousand nine hundred and ninety-nine the following Recommendation, which may be cited as the Worst Forms of Child Labour Recommendation, 1999.

1. The provisions of this Recommendation supplement those of the Worst Forms of Child Labour Convention, 1999 (hereafter referred to as "the Convention"), and should be applied in conjunction with them.

I Programmes of Action

2. The programmes of action referred to in Article 6 of the Convention should be designed and implemented as a matter of urgency, in consultation with relevant government institutions and employers' and workers' organizations, taking into consideration the views of the children directly affected by the worst forms of child labour, their families and, as appropriate, other concerned groups committed to the aims of the Convention and this Recommendation. Such programmes should aim at, inter alia:

(a) identifying and denouncing the worst forms of child labour;

(b) preventing the engagement of children in or removing them from the worst forms of child labour, protecting them from reprisals and

 | DOI:10.1163/9789004681224_039

providing for their rehabilitation and social integration through measures which address their educational, physical and psychological needs;

(c) giving special attention to:

  (i) younger children;

  (ii) the girl child;

  (iii) the problem of hidden work situations, in which girls are at special risk;

  (iv) other groups of children with special vulnerabilities or needs;

(d) identifying, reaching out to and working with communities where children are at special risk;

(e) informing, sensitizing and mobilizing public opinion and concerned groups, including children and their families.

II Hazardous Work

3. In determining the types of work referred to under Article 3(d) of the Convention, and in identifying where they exist, consideration should be given, inter alia, to:

(a) work which exposes children to physical, psychological or sexual abuse;

(b) work underground, under water, at dangerous heights or in confined spaces;

(c) work with dangerous machinery, equipment and tools, or which involves the manual handling or transport of heavy loads;

(d) work in an unhealthy environment which may, for example, expose children to hazardous substances, agents or processes, or to temperatures, noise levels, or vibrations damaging to their health;

(e) work under particularly difficult conditions such as work for long hours or during the night or work where the child is unreasonably confined to the premises of the employer.

4. For the types of work referred to under Article 3(d) of the Convention and Paragraph 3 above, national laws or regulations or the competent authority could, after consultation with the workers' and employers' organizations concerned, authorize employment or work as from the age of 16 on condition that the health, safety and morals of the children concerned are fully protected, and that the children have received adequate specific instruction or vocational training in the relevant branch of activity.

III Implementation

5. (1) Detailed information and statistical data on the nature and extent of child labour should be compiled and kept up to date to serve as a basis for determining priorities for national action for the abolition of child labour, in particular for the prohibition and elimination of its worst forms as a matter of urgency.
(2) As far as possible, such information and statistical data should include data disaggregated by sex, age group, occupation, branch of economic activity, status in employment, school attendance and geographical location. The importance of an effective system of birth registration, including the issuing of birth certificates, should be taken into account.
(3) Relevant data concerning violations of national provisions for the prohibition and elimination of the worst forms of child labour should be compiled and kept up to date.
6. The compilation and processing of the information and data referred to in Paragraph 5 above should be carried out with due regard for the right to privacy.
7. The information compiled under Paragraph 5 above should be communicated to the International Labour Office on a regular basis.
8. Members should establish or designate appropriate national mechanisms to monitor the implementation of national provisions for the prohibition and elimination of the worst forms of child labour, after consultation with employers' and workers' organizations.
9. Members should ensure that the competent authorities which have responsibilities for implementing national provisions for the prohibition and elimination of the worst forms of child labour cooperate with each other and coordinate their activities.
10. National laws or regulations or the competent authority should determine the persons to be held responsible in the event of non-compliance with national provisions for the prohibition and elimination of the worst forms of child labour.
11. Members should, in so far as it is compatible with national law, cooperate with international efforts aimed at the prohibition and elimination of the worst forms of child labour as a matter of urgency by:
(a) gathering and exchanging information concerning criminal offences, including those involving international networks;
(b) detecting and prosecuting those involved in the sale and trafficking of children, or in the use, procuring or offering of children for illicit activities, for prostitution, for the production of pornography or for pornographic performances;
(c) registering perpetrators of such offences.

12. Members should provide that the following worst forms of child labour are criminal offences:
(a) all forms of slavery or practices similar to slavery, such as the sale and trafficking of children, debt bondage and serfdom and forced or compulsory labour, including forced or compulsory recruitment of children for use in armed conflict;
(b) the use, procuring or offering of a child for prostitution, for the production of pornography or for pornographic performances; and
(c) the use, procuring or offering of a child for illicit activities, in particular for the production and trafficking of drugs as defined in the relevant international treaties, or for activities which involve the unlawful carrying or use of firearms or other weapons.

13. Members should ensure that penalties including, where appropriate, criminal penalties are applied for violations of the national provisions for the prohibition and elimination of any type of work referred to in Article 3(d) of the Convention.

14. Members should also provide as a matter of urgency for other criminal, civil or administrative remedies, where appropriate, to ensure the effective enforcement of national provisions for the prohibition and elimination of the worst forms of child labour, such as special supervision of enterprises which have used the worst forms of child labour, and, in cases of persistent violation, consideration of temporary or permanent revoking of permits to operate.

15. Other measures aimed at the prohibition and elimination of the worst forms of child labour might include the following:
(a) informing, sensitizing and mobilizing the general public, including national and local political leaders, parliamentarians and the judiciary;
(b) involving and training employers' and workers' organizations and civic organizations;
(c) providing appropriate training for the government officials concerned, especially inspectors and law enforcement officials, and for other relevant professionals;
(d) providing for the prosecution in their own country of the Member's nationals who commit offences under its national provisions for the prohibition and immediate elimination of the worst forms of child labour even when these offences are committed in another country;
(e) simplifying legal and administrative procedures and ensuring that they are appropriate and prompt;
(f) encouraging the development of policies by undertakings to promote the aims of the Convention;

(g) monitoring and giving publicity to best practices on the elimination of child labour;
(h) giving publicity to legal or other provisions on child labour in the different languages or dialects;
(i) establishing special complaints procedures and making provisions to protect from discrimination and reprisals those who legitimately expose violations of the provisions of the Convention, as well as establishing helplines or points of contact and ombudspersons;
(j) adopting appropriate measures to improve the educational infrastructure and the training of teachers to meet the needs of boys and girls;
(k) as far as possible, taking into account in national programmes of action:
 (i) the need for job creation and vocational training for the parents and adults in the families of children working in the conditions covered by the Convention; and
 (ii) the need for sensitizing parents to the problem of children working in such conditions.

16. Enhanced international cooperation and/or assistance among Members for the prohibition and effective elimination of the worst forms of child labour should complement national efforts and may, as appropriate, be developed and implemented in consultation with employers' and workers' organizations. Such international cooperation and/or assistance should include:
(a) mobilizing resources for national or international programmes;
(b) mutual legal assistance;
(c) technical assistance including the exchange of information;
(d) support for social and economic development, poverty eradication programmes and universal education.

CHAPTER 27

C182 Worst Forms of Child Labour Convention

(Convention concerning the Prohibition and Immediate Action for the Elimination of the Worst Forms of Child Labour Convention)
Adopted on 17 June 1999 by the General Conference of the International Labour Organisation at its 87th session
Entry into force 19 November 2000, in accordance with article 10

The General Conference of the International Labour Organization,

Having been convened at Geneva by the Governing Body of the International Labour Office, and having met in its 87th Session on 1 June 1999, and

Considering the need to adopt new instruments for the prohibition and elimination of the worst forms of child labour, as the main priority for national and international action, including international cooperation and assistance, to complement the Convention and the Recommendation concerning Minimum Age for Admission to Employment, 1973, which remain fundamental instruments on child labour, and

Considering that the effective elimination of the worst forms of child labour requires immediate and comprehensive action, taking into account the importance of free basic education and the need to remove the children concerned from all such work and to provide for their rehabilitation and social integration while addressing the needs of their families, and

Recalling the resolution concerning the elimination of child labour adopted by the International Labour Conference at its 83rd Session in 1996, and

Recognizing that child labour is to a great extent caused by poverty and that the long-term solution lies in sustained economic growth leading to social progress, in particular poverty alleviation and universal education, and

Recalling the Convention on the Rights of the Child adopted by the United Nations General Assembly on 20 November 1989, and

Recalling the ILO Declaration on Fundamental Principles and Rights at Work and its Follow-up, adopted by the International Labour Conference at its 86th Session in 1998, and

Recalling that some of the worst forms of child labour are covered by other international instruments, in particular the Forced Labour Convention, 1930, and the United Nations Supplementary Convention on the Abolition of Slavery, the Slave Trade, and Institutions and Practices Similar to Slavery, 1956, and

DOI:10.1163/9789004681224_040

Having decided upon the adoption of certain proposals with regard to child labour, which is the fourth item on the agenda of the session, and

Having determined that these proposals shall take the form of an international Convention;

adopts this seventeenth day of June of the year one thousand nine hundred and ninety-nine the following Convention, which may be cited as the Worst Forms of Child Labour Convention, 1999.

Art. 1 Each Member which ratifies this Convention shall take immediate and effective measures to secure the prohibition and elimination of the worst forms of child labour as a matter of urgency.

Art. 2 For the purposes of this Convention, the term "child" shall apply to all persons under the age of 18.

Art. 3 For the purposes of this Convention, the term "the worst forms of child labour" comprises:

(a) all forms of slavery or practices similar to slavery, such as the sale and trafficking of children, debt bondage and serfdom and forced or compulsory labour, including forced or compulsory recruitment of children for use in armed conflict;

(b) the use, procuring or offering of a child for prostitution, for the production of pornography or for pornographic performances;

(c) the use, procuring or offering of a child for illicit activities, in particular for the production and trafficking of drugs as defined in the relevant international treaties;

(d) work which, by its nature or the circumstances in which it is carried out, is likely to harm the health, safety or morals of children.

Art. 4 1. The types of work referred to under Article 3(d) shall be determined by national laws or regulations or by the competent authority, after consultation with the organizations of employers and workers concerned, taking into consideration relevant international standards, in particular Paragraphs 3 and 4 of the Worst Forms of Child Labour Recommendation, 1999.

2. The competent authority, after consultation with the organizations of employers and workers concerned, shall identify where the types of work so determined exist.

3. The list of the types of work determined under paragraph 1 of this Article shall be periodically examined and revised as necessary, in consultation with the organizations of employers and workers concerned.

Art. 5 Each Member shall, after consultation with employers' and workers' organizations, establish or designate appropriate mechanisms to monitor the implementation of the provisions giving effect to this Convention.

Art. 6 1. Each Member shall design and implement programmes of action to eliminate as a priority the worst forms of child labour.
2. Such programmes of action shall be designed and implemented in consultation with relevant government institutions and employers' and workers' organizations, taking into consideration the views of other concerned groups as appropriate.
Art. 7 1. Each Member shall take all necessary measures to ensure the effective implementation and enforcement of the provisions giving effect to this Convention including the provision and application of penal sanctions or, as appropriate, other sanctions.
2. Each Member shall, taking into account the importance of education in eliminating child labour, take effective and time-bound measures to:
(a) prevent the engagement of children in the worst forms of child labour;
(b) provide the necessary and appropriate direct assistance for the removal of children from the worst forms of child labour and for their rehabilitation and social integration;
(c) ensure access to free basic education, and, wherever possible and appropriate, vocational training, for all children removed from the worst forms of child labour;
(d) identify and reach out to children at special risk; and
(e) take account of the special situation of girls.
3. Each Member shall designate the competent authority responsible for the implementation of the provisions giving effect to this Convention.
Art. 8 Members shall take appropriate steps to assist one another in giving effect to the provisions of this Convention through enhanced international cooperation and/or assistance including support for social and economic development, poverty eradication programmes and universal education.
Art. 9 The formal ratifications of this Convention shall be communicated to the Director-General of the International Labour Office for registration.
Art. 10 1. This Convention shall be binding only upon those Members of the International Labour Organization whose ratifications have been registered with the Director-General of the International Labour Office.
2. It shall come into force 12 months after the date on which the ratifications of two Members have been registered with the Director-General.
3. Thereafter, this Convention shall come into force for any Member 12 months after the date on which its ratification has been registered.
Art. 11 1. A Member which has ratified this Convention may denounce it after the expiration of ten years from the date on which the Convention first comes into force, by an act communicated to the Director-General of the International

Labour Office for registration. Such denunciation shall not take effect until one year after the date on which it is registered.
2. Each Member which has ratified this Convention and which does not, within the year following the expiration of the period of ten years mentioned in the preceding paragraph, exercise the right of denunciation provided for in this Article, will be bound for another period of ten years and, thereafter, may denounce this Convention at the expiration of each period of ten years under the terms provided for in this Article.
Art. 12 1. The Director-General of the International Labour Office shall notify all Members of the International Labour Organization of the registration of all ratifications and acts of denunciation communicated by the Members of the Organization.
2. When notifying the Members of the Organization of the registration of the second ratification, the Director-General shall draw the attention of the Members of the Organization to the date upon which the Convention shall come into force.
Art. 13 The Director-General of the International Labour Office shall communicate to the Secretary-General of the United Nations, for registration in accordance with article 102 of the Charter of the United Nations, full particulars of all ratifications and acts of denunciation registered by the Director-General in accordance with the provisions of the preceding Articles.
Art. 14 At such times as it may consider necessary, the Governing Body of the International Labour Office shall present to the General Conference a report on the working of this Convention and shall examine the desirability of placing on the agenda of the Conference the question of its revision in whole or in part.
Art. 15 1. Should the Conference adopt a new Convention revising this Convention in whole or in part, then, unless the new Convention otherwise provides –
(a) the ratification by a Member of the new revising Convention shall ipso jure involve the immediate denunciation of this Convention, notwithstanding the provisions of Article 11 above, if and when the new revising Convention shall have come into force;
(b) as from the date when the new revising Convention comes into force, this Convention shall cease to be open to ratification by the Members.
2. This Convention shall in any case remain in force in its actual form and content for those Members which have ratified it but have not ratified the revising Convention.
Art. 16 The English and French versions of the text of this Convention are equally authoritative.

CHAPTER 28

C189 Domestic Workers Convention

(Convention concerning Decent Work for Domestic Workers)
Adopted on 16 June 2011 by the General Conference of the International Labour Organisation at its 100th session
Entry into force 5 September 2013, in accordance with article 21

The General Conference of the International Labour Organization,

Having been convened at Geneva by the Governing Body of the International Labour Office, and having met in its 100th Session on 1 June 2011, and

Mindful of the commitment of the International Labour Organization to promote decent work for all through the achievement of the goals of the ILO Declaration on Fundamental Principles and Rights at Work and the ILO Declaration on Social Justice for a Fair Globalization, and

Recognizing the significant contribution of domestic workers to the global economy, which includes increasing paid job opportunities for women and men workers with family responsibilities, greater scope for caring for ageing populations, children and persons with a disability, and substantial income transfers within and between countries, and

Considering that domestic work continues to be undervalued and invisible and is mainly carried out by women and girls, many of whom are migrants or members of disadvantaged communities and who are particularly vulnerable to discrimination in respect of conditions of employment and of work, and to other abuses of human rights, and

Considering also that in developing countries with historically scarce opportunities for formal employment, domestic workers constitute a significant proportion of the national workforce and remain among the most marginalized, and

Recalling that international labour Conventions and Recommendations apply to all workers, including domestic workers, unless otherwise provided, and

Noting the particular relevance for domestic workers of the Migration for Employment Convention (Revised), 1949 (No. 97), the Migrant Workers (Supplementary Provisions) Convention, 1975 (No. 143), the Workers with Family Responsibilities Convention, 1981 (No. 156), the Private Employment Agencies Convention, 1997 (No. 181), and the Employment Relationship Recommendation, 2006 (No. 198), as well as of the ILO Multilateral Framework

DOI:10.1163/9789004681224_041

on Labour Migration: Non-binding principles and guidelines for a rights-based approach to labour migration (2006), and

Recognizing the special conditions under which domestic work is carried out that make it desirable to supplement the general standards with standards specific to domestic workers so as to enable them to enjoy their rights fully, and

Recalling other relevant international instruments such as the Universal Declaration of Human Rights, the International Covenant on Civil and Political Rights, the International Covenant on Economic, Social and Cultural Rights, the International Convention on the Elimination of All Forms of Racial Discrimination, the Convention on the Elimination of All Forms of Discrimination against Women, the United Nations Convention against Transnational Organized Crime, and in particular its Protocol to Prevent, Suppress and Punish Trafficking in Persons, Especially Women and Children and its Protocol against the Smuggling of Migrants by Land, Sea and Air, the Convention on the Rights of the Child and the International Convention on the Protection of the Rights of All Migrant Workers and Members of Their Families, and

Having decided upon the adoption of certain proposals concerning decent work for domestic workers, which is the fourth item on the agenda of the session, and

Having determined that these proposals shall take the form of an international Convention;

adopts this sixteenth day of June of the year two thousand and eleven the following Convention, which may be cited as the Domestic Workers Convention, 2011.

Art. 1 For the purpose of this Convention:

(a) the term domestic work means work performed in or for a household or households;

(b) the term domestic worker means any person engaged in domestic work within an employment relationship;

(c) a person who performs domestic work only occasionally or sporadically and not on an occupational basis is not a domestic worker.

Art. 2 1. The Convention applies to all domestic workers.

2. A Member which ratifies this Convention may, after consulting with the most representative organizations of employers and workers and, where they exist, with organizations representative of domestic workers and those representative of employers of domestic workers, exclude wholly or partly from its scope:

(a) categories of workers who are otherwise provided with at least equivalent protection;

(b) limited categories of workers in respect of which special problems of a substantial nature arise.

3. Each Member which avails itself of the possibility afforded in the preceding paragraph shall, in its first report on the application of the Convention under article 22 of the Constitution of the International Labour Organisation, indicate any particular category of workers thus excluded and the reasons for such exclusion and, in subsequent reports, specify any measures that may have been taken with a view to extending the application of the Convention to the workers concerned.

Art. 3 1. Each Member shall take measures to ensure the effective promotion and protection of the human rights of all domestic workers, as set out in this Convention.

2. Each Member shall, in relation to domestic workers, take the measures set out in this Convention to respect, promote and realize the fundamental principles and rights at work, namely:

(a) freedom of association and the effective recognition of the right to collective bargaining;
(b) the elimination of all forms of forced or compulsory labour;
(c) the effective abolition of child labour; and
(d) the elimination of discrimination in respect of employment and occupation.

3. In taking measures to ensure that domestic workers and employers of domestic workers enjoy freedom of association and the effective recognition of the right to collective bargaining, Members shall protect the right of domestic workers and employers of domestic workers to establish and, subject to the rules of the organization concerned, to join organizations, federations and confederations of their own choosing.

Art. 4 1. Each Member shall set a minimum age for domestic workers consistent with the provisions of the Minimum Age Convention, 1973 (No. 138), and the Worst Forms of Child Labour Convention, 1999 (No. 182), and not lower than that established by national laws and regulations for workers generally.

2. Each Member shall take measures to ensure that work performed by domestic workers who are under the age of 18 and above the minimum age of employment does not deprive them of compulsory education, or interfere with opportunities to participate in further education or vocational training.

Art. 5 Each Member shall take measures to ensure that domestic workers enjoy effective protection against all forms of abuse, harassment and violence.

Art. 6 Each Member shall take measures to ensure that domestic workers, like workers generally, enjoy fair terms of employment as well as decent working conditions and, if they reside in the household, decent living conditions that respect their privacy.

Art. 7 Each Member shall take measures to ensure that domestic workers are informed of their terms and conditions of employment in an appropriate, verifiable and easily understandable manner and preferably, where possible, through written contracts in accordance with national laws, regulations or collective agreements, in particular:

(a) the name and address of the employer and of the worker;
(b) the address of the usual workplace or workplaces;
(c) the starting date and, where the contract is for a specified period of time, its duration;
(d) the type of work to be performed;
(e) the remuneration, method of calculation and periodicity of payments;
(f) the normal hours of work;
(g) paid annual leave, and daily and weekly rest periods;
(h) the provision of food and accommodation, if applicable;
(i) the period of probation or trial period, if applicable;
(j) the terms of repatriation, if applicable; and
(k) terms and conditions relating to the termination of employment, including any period of notice by either the domestic worker or the employer.

Art. 8 1. National laws and regulations shall require that migrant domestic workers who are recruited in one country for domestic work in another receive a written job offer, or contract of employment that is enforceable in the country in which the work is to be performed, addressing the terms and conditions of employment referred to in Article 7, prior to crossing national borders for the purpose of taking up the domestic work to which the offer or contract applies.

2. The preceding paragraph shall not apply to workers who enjoy freedom of movement for the purpose of employment under bilateral, regional or multilateral agreements, or within the framework of regional economic integration areas.

3. Members shall take measures to cooperate with each other to ensure the effective application of the provisions of this Convention to migrant domestic workers.

4. Each Member shall specify, by means of laws, regulations or other measures, the conditions under which migrant domestic workers are entitled to repatriation on the expiry or termination of the employment contract for which they were recruited.

Art. 9 Each Member shall take measures to ensure that domestic workers:

(a) are free to reach agreement with their employer or potential employer on whether to reside in the household;
(b) who reside in the household are not obliged to remain in the household or with household members during periods of daily and weekly rest or annual leave; and
(c) are entitled to keep in their possession their travel and identity documents.

Art. 10 1. Each Member shall take measures towards ensuring equal treatment between domestic workers and workers generally in relation to normal hours of work, overtime compensation, periods of daily and weekly rest and paid annual leave in accordance with national laws, regulations or collective agreements, taking into account the special characteristics of domestic work.
2. Weekly rest shall be at least 24 consecutive hours.
3. Periods during which domestic workers are not free to dispose of their time as they please and remain at the disposal of the household in order to respond to possible calls shall be regarded as hours of work to the extent determined by national laws, regulations or collective agreements, or any other means consistent with national practice.

Art. 11 Each Member shall take measures to ensure that domestic workers enjoy minimum wage coverage, where such coverage exists, and that remuneration is established without discrimination based on sex.

Art. 12 1. Domestic workers shall be paid directly in cash at regular intervals at least once a month. Unless provided for by national laws, regulations or collective agreements, payment may be made by bank transfer, bank cheque, postal cheque, money order or other lawful means of monetary payment, with the consent of the worker concerned.
2. National laws, regulations, collective agreements or arbitration awards may provide for the payment of a limited proportion of the remuneration of domestic workers in the form of payments in kind that are not less favourable than those generally applicable to other categories of workers, provided that measures are taken to ensure that such payments in kind are agreed to by the worker, are for the personal use and benefit of the worker, and that the monetary value attributed to them is fair and reasonable.

Art. 13 1. Every domestic worker has the right to a safe and healthy working environment. Each Member shall take, in accordance with national laws, regulations and practice, effective measures, with due regard for the specific characteristics of domestic work, to ensure the occupational safety and health of domestic workers.
2. The measures referred to in the preceding paragraph may be applied progressively, in consultation with the most representative organizations of

employers and workers and, where they exist, with organizations representative of domestic workers and those representative of employers of domestic workers.

Art. 14 1. Each Member shall take appropriate measures, in accordance with national laws and regulations and with due regard for the specific characteristics of domestic work, to ensure that domestic workers enjoy conditions that are not less favourable than those applicable to workers generally in respect of social security protection, including with respect to maternity.

2. The measures referred to in the preceding paragraph may be applied progressively, in consultation with the most representative organizations of employers and workers and, where they exist, with organizations representative of domestic workers and those representative of employers of domestic workers.

Art. 15 1. To effectively protect domestic workers, including migrant domestic workers, recruited or placed by private employment agencies, against abusive practices, each Member shall:

(a) determine the conditions governing the operation of private employment agencies recruiting or placing domestic workers, in accordance with national laws, regulations and practice;

(b) ensure that adequate machinery and procedures exist for the investigation of complaints, alleged abuses and fraudulent practices concerning the activities of private employment agencies in relation to domestic workers;

(c) adopt all necessary and appropriate measures, within its jurisdiction and, where appropriate, in collaboration with other Members, to provide adequate protection for and prevent abuses of domestic workers recruited or placed in its territory by private employment agencies. These shall include laws or regulations that specify the respective obligations of the private employment agency and the household towards the domestic worker and provide for penalties, including prohibition of those private employment agencies that engage in fraudulent practices and abuses;

(d) consider, where domestic workers are recruited in one country for work in another, concluding bilateral, regional or multilateral agreements to prevent abuses and fraudulent practices in recruitment, placement and employment; and

(e) take measures to ensure that fees charged by private employment agencies are not deducted from the remuneration of domestic workers.

2. In giving effect to each of the provisions of this Article, each Member shall consult with the most representative organizations of employers and workers

and, where they exist, with organizations representative of domestic workers and those representative of employers of domestic workers.

Art. 16 Each Member shall take measures to ensure, in accordance with national laws, regulations and practice, that all domestic workers, either by themselves or through a representative, have effective access to courts, tribunals or other dispute resolution mechanisms under conditions that are not less favourable than those available to workers generally.

Art. 17 1. Each Member shall establish effective and accessible complaint mechanisms and means of ensuring compliance with national laws and regulations for the protection of domestic workers.

2. Each Member shall develop and implement measures for labour inspection, enforcement and penalties with due regard for the special characteristics of domestic work, in accordance with national laws and regulations.

3. In so far as compatible with national laws and regulations, such measures shall specify the conditions under which access to household premises may be granted, having due respect for privacy.

Art. 18 Each Member shall implement the provisions of this Convention, in consultation with the most representative employers and workers organizations, through laws and regulations, as well as through collective agreements or additional measures consistent with national practice, by extending or adapting existing measures to cover domestic workers or by developing specific measures for them, as appropriate.

Art. 19 This Convention does not affect more favourable provisions applicable to domestic workers under other international labour Conventions.

Art. 20 The formal ratifications of this Convention shall be communicated to the Director-General of the International Labour Office for registration.

Art. 21 1. This Convention shall be binding only upon those Members of the International Labour Organization whose ratifications have been registered with the Director-General of the International Labour Office.

2. It shall come into force twelve months after the date on which the ratifications of two Members have been registered with the Director-General.

3. Thereafter, this Convention shall come into force for any Member twelve months after the date on which its ratification is registered.

Art. 22 1. A Member which has ratified this Convention may denounce it after the expiration of ten years from the date on which the Convention first comes into force, by an act communicated to the Director-General of the International Labour Office for registration. Such denunciation shall not take effect until one year after the date on which it is registered.

2. Each Member which has ratified this Convention and which does not, within the year following the expiration of the period of ten years mentioned in the

preceding paragraph, exercise the right of denunciation provided for in this Article, will be bound for another period of ten years and, thereafter, may denounce this Convention within the first year of each new period of ten years under the terms provided for in this Article.

Art. 23 1. The Director-General of the International Labour Office shall notify all Members of the International Labour Organization of the registration of all ratifications and denunciations that have been communicated by the Members of the Organization.

2. When notifying the Members of the Organization of the registration of the second ratification that has been communicated, the Director-General shall draw the attention of the Members of the Organization to the date upon which the Convention will come into force.

Art. 24 The Director-General of the International Labour Office shall communicate to the Secretary-General of the United Nations for registration in accordance with Article 102 of the Charter of the United Nations full particulars of all ratifications and denunciations that have been registered.

Art. 25 At such times as it may consider necessary, the Governing Body of the International Labour Office shall present to the General Conference a report on the working of this Convention and shall examine the desirability of placing on the agenda of the Conference the question of its revision in whole or in part.

Art. 26 1. Should the Conference adopt a new Convention revising this Convention, then, unless the new Convention otherwise provides:

(a) the ratification by a Member of the new revising Convention shall ipso jure involve the immediate denunciation of this Convention, notwithstanding the provisions of Article 22, if and when the new revising Convention shall have come into force;

(b) as from the date when the new revising Convention comes into force, this Convention shall cease to be open to ratification by the Members.

2. This Convention shall in any case remain in force in its actual form and content for those Members which have ratified it but have not ratified the revising Convention.

Art. 27 The English and French versions of the text of this Convention are equally authoritative.

PART VI

Children in the Justice System

CHAPTER 29

United Nations Standard Minimum Rules for the Administration of Juvenile Justice

(The Beijing Rules)
Adopted by General Assembly resolution 40/33 of 29 November 1985

Part One: General Principles

1 *Fundamental Perspectives*

1.1 Member States shall seek, in conformity with their respective general interests, to further the well-being of the juvenile and her or his family.
1.2 Member States shall endeavour to develop conditions that will ensure for the juvenile a meaningful life in the community, which, during that period in life when she or he is most susceptible to deviant behaviour, will foster a process of personal development and education that is as free from crime and delinquency as possible.
1.3 Sufficient attention shall be given to positive measures that involve the full mobilization of all possible resources, including the family, volunteers and other community groups, as well as schools and other community institutions, for the purpose of promoting the well-being of the juvenile, with a view to reducing the need for intervention under the law, and of effectively, fairly and humanely dealing with the juvenile in conflict with the law.
1.4 Juvenile justice shall be conceived as an integral part of the national development process of each country, within a comprehensive framework of social justice for all juveniles, thus, at the same time, contributing to the protection of the young and the maintenance of a peaceful order in society.
1.5 These Rules shall be implemented in the context of economic, social and cultural conditions prevailing in each Member State.
1.6 Juvenile justice services shall be systematically developed and co-ordinated with a view to improving and sustaining the competence of personnel involved in the services, including their methods, approaches and attitudes.

Commentary

These broad fundamental perspectives refer to comprehensive social policy in general and aim at promoting juvenile welfare to the greatest possible extent,

 | DOI:10.1163/9789004681224_042

which will minimize the necessity of intervention by the juvenile justice system, and in turn, will reduce the harm that may be caused by any intervention. Such care measures for the young, before the onset of delinquency, are basic policy requisites designed to obviate the need for the application of the Rules. Rules 1.1 to 1.3 point to the important role that a constructive social policy for juveniles will play, inter alia, in the prevention of juvenile crime and delinquency. Rule 1.4 defines juvenile justice as an integral part of social justice for juveniles, while rule 1.6 refers to the necessity of constantly improving juvenile justice, without falling behind the development of progressive social policy for juveniles in general and bearing in mind the need for consistent improvement of staff services.

Rule 1.5 seeks to take account of existing conditions in Member States which would cause the manner of implementation of particular rules necessarily to be different from the manner adopted in other States.

2 *Scope of the Rules and Definitions Used*

2.1 The following Standard Minimum Rules shall be applied to juvenile offenders impartially, without distinction of any kind, for example as to race, colour, sex, language, religion, political or other opinions, national or social origin, property, birth or other status.

2.2 For purposes of these Rules, the following definitions shall be applied by Member States in a manner which is compatible with their respective legal systems and concepts:

(a) A juvenile is a child or young person who, under the respective legal systems, may be dealt with for an offence in a manner which is different from an adult;

(b) An offence is any behaviour (act or omission) that is punishable by law under the respective legal systems;

(c) A juvenile offender is a child or young person who is alleged to have committed or who has been found to have committed an offence.

2.3 Efforts shall be made to establish, in each national jurisdiction, a set of laws, rules and provisions specifically applicable to juvenile offenders and institutions and bodies entrusted with the functions of the administration of juvenile justice and designed:

(a) To meet the varying needs of juvenile offencers, while protecting their basic rigths;

(b) To meet the need of society;

(c) To implement the following rules thoroughly and fairly.

Commentary

The Standard Minimum Rules are deliberately formulated so as to be applicable within different legal systems and, at the same time, to set some minimum standards for the handling of juvenile offenders under any definition of a juvenile and under any system of dealing with juvenile offenders. The Rules are always to be applied impartially and without distinction of any kind.

Rule 2.1 therefore stresses the importance of the Rules always being applied impartially and without distinction of any kind. The rule follows the formulation of principle 2 of the Declaration of the Rights of the Child.

Rule 2.2 defines "juvenile" and "offence" as the components of the notion of the "juvenile offender", who is the main subject of these Standard Minimum Rules (see, however, also rules 3 and 4). It should be noted that age limits will depend on, and are explicitly made dependent on, each respective legal system, thus fully respecting the economic, social, political, cultural and legal systems of Member States. This makes for a wide variety of ages coming under the definition of "juvenile", ranging from 7 years to 18 years or above. Such a variety seems inevitable in view of the different national legal systems and does not diminish the impact of these Standard Minimum Rules.

Rule 2.3 is addressed to the necessity of specific national legislation for the optimal implementation of these Standard Minimum Rules, both legally and practically.

3 *Extension of the Rules*

3.1 The relevant provisions of the Rules shall be applied not only to juvenile offenders but also to juveniles who may be proceeded against for any specific behaviour that would not be punishable if committed by an adult.

3.2 Efforts shall be made to extend the principles embodied in the Rules to all juveniles who are dealt with in welfare and care proceedings.

3.3 Efforts shall also be made to extend the principles embodied in the Rules to young adult offenders.

Commentary

Rule 3 extends the protection afforded by the Standard Minimum Rules for the Administration of Juvenile Justice to cover:

(a) The so-called "status offences" prescribed in various national legal systems where the range of behaviour considered to be an offence is wider for juveniles than it is for adults (for example, truancy, school and family disobedience, public drunkenness, etc.) (rule 3.1);

(b) Juvenile welfare and care proceedings (rule 3.2);

(c) Proceedings dealing with young adult offenders, depending of course on each given age limit (rule 3.3).

The extension of the Rules to cover these three areas seems to be justified. Rule 3.1 provides minimum guarantees in those fields, and rule 3.2 is considered a desirable step in the direction of more fair, equitable and humane justice for all juveniles in conflict with the law.

4 *Age of Criminal Responsibility*

4.1 In those legal systems recognizing the concept of the age of criminal responsibility for juveniles, the beginning of that age shall not be fixed at too low an age level, bearing in mind the facts of emotional, mental and intellectual maturity.

Commentary

The minimum age of criminal responsibility differs widely owing to history and culture. The modern approach would be to consider whether a child can live up to the moral and psychological components of criminal responsibility; that is, whether a child, by virtue of her or his individual discernment and understanding, can be held responsible for essentially antisocial behaviour. If the age of criminal responsibility is fixed too low or if there is no lower age limit at all, the notion of responsibility would become meaningless. In general, there is a close relationship between the notion of responsibility for delinquent or criminal behaviour and other social rights and responsibilities (such as marital status, civil majority, etc.).

Efforts should therefore be made to agree on a reasonable lowest age limit that is applicable internationally.

5 *Aims of Juvenile Justice*

5.1 The juvenile justice system shall emphasize the well-being of the juvenile and shall ensure that any reaction to juvenile offenders shall always be in proportion to the circumstances of both the offenders and the offence.

Commentary

Rule 5 refers to two of the most important objectives of juvenile justice. The first objective is the promotion of the well-being of the juvenile. This is the main focus of those legal systems in which juvenile offenders are dealt with by family courts or administrative authorities, but the well-being of the juvenile should also be emphasized in legal systems that follow the criminal court model, thus contributing to the avoidance of merely punitive sanctions. (See also rule 14.)

The second objective is "the principle of proportionality". This principle is well-known as an instrument for curbing punitive sanctions, mostly expressed in terms of just deserts in relation to the gravity of the offence. The response to young offenders should be based on the consideration not only of the gravity of the offence but also of personal circumstances. The individual circumstances of the offender (for example social status, family situation, the harm caused by the offence or other factors affecting personal circumstances) should influence the proportionality of the reactions (for example by having regard to the offender's endeavour to indemnify the victim or to her or his willingness to turn to wholesome and useful life).

By the same token, reactions aiming to ensure the welfare of the young offender may go beyond necessity and therefore infringe upon the fundamental rights of the young individual, as has been observed in some juvenile justice systems. Here, too, the proportionality of the reaction to the circumstances of both the offender and the offence, including the victim, should be safeguarded.

In essence, rule 5 calls for no less and no more than a fair reaction in any given cases of juvenile delinquency and crime. The issues combined in the rule may help to stimulate development in both regards: new and innovative types of reactions are as desirable as precautions against any undue widening of the net of formal social control over juveniles.

6 *Scope of Discretion*

6.1 In view of the varying special needs of juveniles as well as the variety of measures available, appropriate scope for discretion shall be allowed at all stages of proceedings and at the different levels of juvenile justice administration, including investigation, prosecution, adjudication and the follow-up of dispositions.

6.2 Efforts shall be made, however, to ensure sufficient accountability at all stages and levels in the exercise of any such discretion.

6.3 Those who exercise discretion shall be specially qualified or trained to exercise it judiciously and in accordance with their functions and mandates.

Commentary

Rules 6.1, 6.2 and 6.3 combine several important features of effective, fair and humane juvenile justice administration: the need to permit the exercise of discretionary power at all significant levels of processing so that those who make determinations can take the actions deemed to be most appropriate in each individual case; and the need to provide checks and balances in order to curb any abuses of discretionary power and to safeguard the rights of the young offender. Accountability and professionalism are instruments best apt to curb broad discretion. Thus, professional qualifications and expert training are emphasized here as a valuable means of ensuring the judicious exercise of discretion in matters of juvenile offenders. (See also rules 1.6 and 2.2.) The formulation of specific guidelines on the exercise of discretion and the provision of systems of review, appeal and the like in order to permit scrutiny of decisions and accountability are emphasized in this context. Such mechanisms are not specified here, as they do not easily lend themselves to incorporation into international standard minimum rules, which cannot possibly cover all differences in justice systems.

7 *Rights of Juveniles*

7.1 Basic procedural safeguards such as the presumption of innocence, the right to be notified of the charges, the right to remain silent, the right to counsel, the right to the presence of a parent or guardian, the right to confront and cross-examine witnesses and the right to appeal to a higher authority shall be guaranteed at all stages of proceedings.

Commentary

Rule 7.1 emphasizes some important points that represent essential elements for a fair and just trial and that are internationally recognized in existing human rights instruments (See also rule 14.). The presumption of innocence, for instance, is also to be found in article 11 of the Universal Declaration of Human Rights and in article 14, paragraph 2, of the International Covenant on Civil and Political Rights. Rules 14 seq. of these Standard Minimum Rules specify issues that are important for proceedings in juvenile cases, in particular, while rule 7.1 affirms the most basic procedural safeguards in a general way.

8 *Protection of Privacy*

8.1 The juvenile's right to privacy shall be respected at all stages in order to avoid harm being caused to her or him by undue publicity or by the process of labelling.

8.2 In principle, no information that may lead to the identification of a juvenile offender shall be published.

Commentary

Rule 8 stresses the importance of the protection of the juvenile's right to privacy. Young persons are particularly susceptible to stigmatization. Criminological research into labelling processes has provided evidence of the detrimental effects (of different kinds) resulting from the permanent identification of young persons as "delinquent" or "criminal".

Rule 8 stresses the importance of protecting the juvenile from the adverse effects that may result from the publication in the mass media of information about the case (for example the names of young offenders, alleged or convicted). The interest of the individual should be protected and upheld, at least in principle. (The general contents of rule 8 are further specified in rule 2 1.)

9 *Saving Clause*

9.1 Nothing in these Rules shall be interpreted as precluding the application of the Standard Minimum Rules for the Treatment of Prisoners adopted by the United Nations and other human rights instruments and standards recognized by the international community that relate to the care and protection of the young.

Commentary

Rule 9 is meant to avoid any misunderstanding in interpreting and implementing the present Rules in conformity with principles contained in relevant existing or emerging international human rights instruments and standards-such as the Universal Declaration of Human Rights, the International Covenant on Economic, Social and Cultural Rights and the International Covenant on Civil and Political Rights, and the Declaration of the Rights of the Child and the draft convention on the rights of the child. It should be understood that the application of the present Rules is without prejudice to any such international instruments which may contain provisions of wider application (See also rule 27.).

Part Two: Investigation and Prosecution

10 *Initial Contact*

10.1 Upon the apprehension of a juvenile, her or his parents or guardian shall be immediately notified of such apprehension, and, where such immediate notification is not possible, the parents or guardian shall be notified within the shortest possible time thereafter.

10.2 A judge or other competent official or body shall, without delay, consider the issue of release.

10.3 Contacts between the law enforcement agencies and a juvenile offender shall be managed in such a way as to respect the legal status of the juvenile, promote the well-being of the juvenile and avoid harm to her or him, with due regard to the circumstances of the case.

Commentary

Rule 10.1 is in principle contained in rule 92 of the Standard Minimum Rules for the Treatment of Prisoners.

The question of release (rule 10.2) shall be considered without delay by a judge or other competent official. The latter refers to any person or institution in the broadest sense of the term, including community boards or police authorities having power to release an arrested person. (See also the International Covenant on Civil and Political Rights, article 9, paragraph 3.)

Rule 10.3 deals with some fundamental aspects of the procedures and behaviour on the part of the police and other law enforcement officials in cases of juvenile crime. To "avoid harm" admittedly is flexible wording and covers many features of possible interaction (for example the use of harsh language, physical violence or exposure to the environment). Involvement in juvenile justice processes in itself can be "harmful" to juveniles; the term "avoid harm" should be broadly interpreted, therefore, as doing the least harm possible to the juvenile in the first instance, as well as any additional or undue harm. This is especially important in the initial contact with law enforcement agencies, which might profoundly influence the juvenile's attitude towards the State and society. Moreover, the success of any further intervention is largely dependent on such initial contacts. Compassion and kind firmness are important in these situations.

11 *Diversion*

11.1 Consideration shall be given, wherever appropriate, to dealing with juvenile offenders without resorting to formal trial by the competent authority, referred to in rule 14.1 below.

11.2 The police, the prosecution or other agencies dealing with juvenile cases shall be empowered to dispose of such cases, at their discretion, without recourse to formal hearings, in accordance with the criteria laid down for that purpose in the respective legal system and also in accordance with the principles contained in these Rules.

11.3 Any diversion involving referral to appropriate community or other services shall require the consent of the juvenile, or her or his parents or guardian, provided that such decision to refer a case shall be subject to review by a competent authority, upon application.

11.4 In order to facilitate the discretionary disposition of juvenile cases, efforts shall be made to provide for community programmes, such as temporary supervision and guidance, restitution, and compensation of victims.

Commentary

Diversion, involving removal from criminal justice processing and, frequently, redirection to community support services, is commonly practised on a formal and informal basis in many legal systems. This practice serves to hinder the negative effects of subsequent proceedings in juvenile justice administration (for example the stigma of conviction and sentence). In many cases, non-intervention would be the best response. Thus, diversion at the outset and without referral to alternative (social) services may be the optimal response. This is especially the case where the offence is of a non-serious nature and where the family, the school or other informal social control institutions have already reacted, or are likely to react, in an appropriate and constructive manner.

As stated in rule 11.2, diversion may be used at any point of decision-making – by the police, the prosecution or other agencies such as the courts, tribunals, boards or councils. It may be exercised by one authority or several or all authorities, according to the rules and policies of the respective systems and in line with the present Rules. It need not necessarily be limited to petty cases, thus rendering diversion an important instrument.

Rule 11.3 stresses the important requirement of securing the consent of the young offender (or the parent or guardian) to the recommended diversionary measure(s). (Diversion to community service without such consent would contradict the Abolition of Forced Labour Convention.) However, this consent should not be left unchallengeable, since it might sometimes be given out of sheer desperation on the part of the juvenile. The rule underlines that care should be taken to minimize the potential for coercion and intimidation at all levels in the diversion process. Juveniles should not feel pressured (for example in order to avoid court appearance) or be pressured into consenting to diversion programmes. Thus, it is advocated that provision should be made for an objective appraisal of the appropriateness of dispositions involving young offenders by a "competent authority upon application". (The "competent authority" may be different from that referred to in rule 14.)

Rule 11.4 recommends the provision of viable alternatives to juvenile justice processing in the form of community-based diversion. Programmes that involve settlement by victim restitution and those that seek to avoid future conflict with the law through temporary supervision and guidance are especially commended. The merits of individual cases would make diversion appropriate, even when more serious offences have been committed (for example first offence, the act having been committed under peer pressure, etc.).

12 *Specialization within the Police*

12.1 In order to best fulfil their functions, police officers who frequently or exclusively deal with juveniles or who are primarily engaged in the prevention of juvenile crime shall be specially instructed and trained. In large cities, special police units should be established for that purpose.

Commentary

Rule 12 draws attention to the need for specialized training for all law enforcement officials who are involved in the administration of juvenile justice. As police are the first point of contact with the juvenile justice system, it is most important that they act in an informed and appropriate manner.

While the relationship between urbanization and crime is clearly complex, an increase in juvenile crime has been associated with the growth of large cities, particularly with rapid and unplanned growth. Specialized police units would therefore be indispensable, not only in the interest of implementing specific principles contained in the present instrument (such as rule 1.6) but more generally for improving the prevention and control of juvenile crime and the handling of juvenile offenders.

13 *Detention Pending Trial*

13.1 Detention pending trial shall be used only as a measure of last resort and for the shortest possible period of time.

13.2 Whenever possible, detention pending trial shall be replaced by alternative measures, such as close supervision, intensive care or placement with a family or in an educational setting or home.

13.3 Juveniles under detention pending trial shall be entitled to all rights and guarantees of the Standard Minimum Rules for the Treatment of Prisoners adopted by the United Nations.

13.4 Juveniles under detention pending trial shall be kept separate from adults and shall be detained in a separate institution or in a separate part of an institution also holding adults.

13.5 While in custody, juveniles shall receive care, protection and all necessary individual assistance – social, educational, vocational, psychological, medical and physical – that they may require in view of their age, sex and personality.

Commentary

The danger to juveniles of "criminal contamination" while in detention pending trial must not be underestimated. It is therefore important to stress the need for alternative measures. By doing so, rule 13.1 encourages the devising of new and innovative measures to avoid such detention in the interest of the

well-being of the juvenile. Juveniles under detention pending trial are entitled to all the rights and guarantees of the Standard Minimum Rules for the Treatment of Prisoners as well as the International Covenant on Civil and Political Rights, especially article 9 and article 10, paragraphs 2 (b) and 3.
Rule 13.4 does not prevent States from taking other measures against the negative influences of adult offenders which are at least as effective as the measures mentioned in the rule.
Different forms of assistance that may become necessary have been enumerated to draw attention to the broad range of particular needs of young detainees to be addressed (for example females or males, drug addicts, alcoholics, mentally ill juveniles, young persons suffering from the trauma, for example, of arrest, etc.).
Varying physical and psychological characteristics of young detainees may warrant classification measures by which some are kept separate while in detention pending trial, thus contributing to the avoidance of victimization and rendering more appropriate assistance.
The Sixth United Nations Congress on the Prevention of Crime and the Treatment of Offenders, in its resolution 4 on juvenile justice standards, specified that the Rules, inter alia, should reflect the basic principle that pre-trial detention should be used only as a last resort, that no minors should be held in a facility where they are vulnerable to the negative influences of adult detainees and that account should always be taken of the needs particular to their stage of development.

Part Three: Adjudication and Disposition

14 *Competent Authority to Adjudicate*

14.1 Where the case of a juvenile offender has not been diverted (under rule 11), she or he shall be dealt with by the competent authority (court, tribunal, board, council, etc.) according to the principles of a fair and just trial.
14.2 The proceedings shall be conducive to the best interests of the juvenile and shall be conducted in an atmosphere of understanding, which shall allow the juvenile to participate therein and to express herself or himself freely.

Commentary

It is difficult to formulate a definition of the competent body or person that would universally describe an adjudicating authority. "Competent authority" is meant to include those who preside over courts or tribunals (composed of a single judge or of several members), including professional and lay magistrates as well as administrative boards (for example the Scottish and Scandinavian systems) or other more informal community and conflict resolution agencies of an adjudicatory nature.

The procedure for dealing with juvenile offenders shall in any case follow the minimum standards that are applied almost universally for any criminal defendant under the procedure known as "due process of law". In accordance with due process, a "fair and just trial" includes such basic safeguards as the presumption of innocence, the presentation and examination of witnesses, the common legal defences, the right to remain silent, the right to have the last word in a hearing, the right to appeal, etc. (See also rule 7.1.)

15 *Legal Counsel, Parents and Guardians*

15.1 Throughout the proceedings the juvenile shall have the right to be represented by a legal adviser or to apply for free legal aid where there is provision for such aid in the country.

15.2 The parents or the guardian shall be entitled to participate in the proceedings and may be required by the competent authority to attend them in the interest of the juvenile. They may, however, be denied participation by the competent authority if there are reasons to assume that such exclusion is necessary in the interest of the juvenile.

Commentary

Rule 15.1 uses terminology similar to that found in rule 93 of the Standard Minimum Rules for the Treatment of Prisoners. Whereas legal counsel and free legal aid are needed to assure the juvenile legal assistance, the right of the parents or guardian to participate as stated in rule 15.2 should be viewed as general psychological and emotional assistance to the juvenile – a function extending throughout the procedure.

The competent authority's search for an adequate disposition of the case may profit, in particular, from the co-operation of the legal representatives of the juvenile (or, for that matter, some other personal assistant who the juvenile can and does really trust). Such concern can be thwarted if the presence of parents or guardians at the hearings plays a negative role, for instance, if they display a hostile attitude towards the juvenile, hence, the possibility of their exclusion must be provided for.

16. Social Inquiry Reports

16.1 In all cases except those involving minor offences, before the competent authority renders a final disposition prior to sentencing, the background and circumstances in which the juvenile is living or the conditions under which the offence has been committed shall be properly investigated so as to facilitate judicious adjudication of the case by the competent authority.

Commentary

Social inquiry reports (social reports or pre-sentence reports) are an indispensable aid in most legal proceedings involving juveniles. The competent authority should be informed of relevant facts about the juvenile, such as social and family background, school career, educational experiences, etc. For this purpose, some jurisdictions use special social services or personnel attached to the court or board. Other personnel, including probation officers, may serve the same function. The rule therefore requires that adequate social services should be available to deliver social inquiry reports of a qualified nature.

17 *Guiding Principles in Adjudication and Disposition*

17.1 The disposition of the competent authority shall be guided by the following principles:

(a) The reaction taken shall always be in proportion not only to the circumstances and the gravity of the offence but also to the circumstances and the needs of the juvenile as well as to the needs of the society;

(b) Restrictions on the personal liberty of the juvenile shall be imposed only after careful consideration and shall be limited to the possible minimum;

(c) Deprivation of personal liberty shall not be imposed unless the juvenile is adjudicated of a serious act involving violence against another person or of persistence in committing other serious offences and unless there is no other appropriate response;

(d) The well-being of the juvenile shall be the guiding factor in the consideration of her or his case.

17.2 Capital punishment shall not be imposed for any crime committed by juveniles.

17.3 Juveniles shall not be subject to corporal punishment.

17.4 The competent authority shall have the power to discontinue the proceedings at any time.

Commentary

The main difficulty in formulating guidelines for the adjudication of young persons stems from the fact that there are unresolved conflicts of a philosophical nature, such as the following:

(a) Rehabilitation versus just desert;

(b) Assistance versus repression and punishment;

(c) Reaction according to the singular merits of an individual case versus reaction according to the protection of society in general;
(d) General deterrence versus individual incapacitation.

The conflict between these approaches is more pronounced in juvenile cases than in adult cases. With the variety of causes and reactions characterizing juvenile cases, these alternatives become intricately interwoven.

It is not the function of the Standard Minimum Rules for the Administration of Juvenile Justice to prescribe which approach is to be followed but rather to identify one that is most closely in consonance with internationally accepted principles. Therefore the essential elements as laid down in rule 17.1, in particular in subparagraphs (a) and (c), are mainly to be understood as practical guidelines that should ensure a common starting point; if heeded by the concerned authorities (see also rule 5), they could contribute considerably to ensuring that the fundamental rights of juvenile offenders are protected, especially the fundamental rights of personal development and education.

Rule 17.1 (*b*) implies that strictly punitive approaches are not appropriate. Whereas in adult cases, and possibly also in cases of severe offences by juveniles, just desert and retributive sanctions might be considered to have some merit, in juvenile cases such considerations should always be outweighed by the interest of safeguarding the well-being and the future of the young person.

In line with resolution 8 of the Sixth United Nations Congress, rule 17.1 (b) encourages the use of alternatives to institutionalization to the maximum extent possible, bearing in mind the need to respond to the specific requirements of the young. Thus, full use should be made of the range of existing alternative sanctions and new alternative sanctions should be developed, bearing the public safety in mind. Probation should be granted to the greatest possible extent via suspended sentences, conditional sentences, board orders and other dispositions.

Rule 17.1 (c) corresponds to one of the guiding principles in resolution 4 of the Sixth Congress which aims at avoiding incarceration in the case of juveniles unless there is no other appropriate response that will protect the public safety.

The provision prohibiting capital punishment in rule 17.2 is in accordance with article 6, paragraph 5, of the International Covenant on Civil and Political Rights.

The provision against corporal punishment is in line with article 7 of the International Covenant on Civil and Political Rights and the Declaration on the Protection of All Persons from Being Subjected to Torture and Other Cruel, Inhuman or Degrading Treatment or Punishment, as well as the Convention against Torture and Other Cruel, Inhuman or Degrading Treatment or Punishment and the draft convention on the rights of the child.

The power to discontinue the proceedings at any time (rule 17.4) is a characteristic inherent in the handling of juvenile offenders as opposed to adults. At any time, circumstances may become known to the competent authority which would make a complete cessation of the intervention appear to be the best disposition of the case.

18 *Various Disposition Measures*

18.1 A large variety of disposition measures shall be made available to the competent authority, allowing for flexibility so as to avoid institutionalization to the greatest extent possible. Such measures, some of which may be combined, include:

(a) Care, guidance and supervision orders;
(b) Probation;
(c) Community service orders;
(d) Financial penalties, compensation and restitution;
(e) Intermediate treatment and other treatment orders;
(f) Orders to participate in group counselling and similar activities;
(g) Orders concerning foster care, living communities or other educational settings;
(h) Other relevant orders.

18.2 No juvenile shall be removed from parental supervision, whether partly or entirely, unless the circumstances of her or his case make this necessary.

Commentary

Rule 18.1 attempts to enumerate some of the important reactions and sanctions that have been practised and proved successful thus far, in different legal systems. On the whole they represent promising opinions that deserve replication and further development. The rule does not enumerate staffing requirements because of possible shortages of adequate staff in some regions; in those regions measures requiring less staff may be tried or developed.

The examples given in rule 18.1 have in common, above all, a reliance on and an appeal to the community for the effective implementation of alternative dispositions. Community-based correction is a traditional measure that has taken on many aspects. On that basis, relevant authorities should be encouraged to offer community-based services.

Rule 18.2 points to the importance of the family which, according to article 10, paragraph l, of the International Covenant on Economic, Social and Cultural Rights, is "the natural and fundamental group unit of society". Within the family, the parents have not only the right but also the responsibility to care for and supervise their children. Rule 18.2, therefore, requires that the separation of children from their parents is a measure of last resort. It may be resorted to only when the facts of the case clearly warrant this grave step (for example child abuse).

19 ***Least Possible Use of Institutionalization***

19.1 The placement of a juvenile in an institution shall always be a disposition of last resort and for the minimum necessary period.

Commentary

Progressive criminology advocates the use of non-institutional over institutional treatment. Little or no difference has been found in terms of the success of institutionalization as compared to non-institutionalization. The many adverse influences on an individual that seem unavoidable within any institutional setting evidently cannot be outbalanced by treatment efforts. This is especially the case for juveniles, who are vulnerable to negative influences. Moreover, the negative effects, not only of loss of liberty but also of separation from the usual social environment, are certainly more acute for juveniles than for adults because of their early stage of development.

Rule 19 aims at restricting institutionalization in two regards: in quantity ("last resort") and in time ("minimum necessary period"). Rule 19 reflects one of the basic guiding principles of resolution 4 of the Sixth United Nations Congress: a juvenile offender should not be incarcerated unless there is no other appropriate response. The rule, therefore, makes the appeal that if a juvenile must be institutionalized, the loss of liberty should be restricted to the least possible degree, with special institutional arrangements for confinement and bearing in mind the differences in kinds of offenders, offences and institutions. In fact, priority should be given to "open" over "closed" institutions. Furthermore, any facility should be of a correctional or educational rather than of a prison type.

20 ***Avoidance of Unnecessary Delay***

20.1 Each case shall from the outset be handled expeditiously, without any unnecessary delay.

Commentary

The speedy conduct of formal procedures in juvenile cases is a paramount concern. Otherwise whatever good may be achieved by the procedure and the disposition is at risk. As time passes, the juvenile will find it increasingly difficult, if not impossible, to relate the procedure and disposition to the offence, both intellectually and psychologically.

21 ***Records***

21.1 Records of juvenile offenders shall be kept strictly confidential and closed to third parties. Access to such records shall be limited to persons directly concerned with the disposition of the case at hand or other duly authorized persons.

21.2 Records of juvenile offenders shall not be used in adult proceedings in subsequent cases involving the same offender.

Commentary

The rule attempts to achieve a balance between conflicting interests connected with records or files: those of the police, prosecution and other authorities in improving control versus the interests of the juvenile offender. (See also rule 8.) "Other duly authorized persons" would generally include, among others, researchers.

22 ***Need for Professionalism and Training***

22.1 Professional education, in-service training, refresher courses and other appropriate modes of instruction shall be utilized to establish and maintain the necessary professional competence of all personnel dealing with juvenile cases.

22.2 Juvenile justice personnel shall reflect the diversity of juveniles who come into contact with the juvenile justice system. Efforts shall be made to ensure the fair representation of women and minorities in juvenile justice agencies.

Commentary

The authorities competent for disposition may be persons with very different backgrounds (magistrates in the United Kingdom of Great Britain and Northern Ireland and in regions influenced by the common law system; legally trained judges in countries using Roman law and in regions influenced by them; and elsewhere elected or appointed laymen or jurists, members of community-based boards, etc.). For all these authorities, a minimum training in law, sociology, psychology, criminology and behavioural sciences would be required. This is considered as important as the organizational specialization and independence of the competent authority.

For social workers and probation officers, it might not be feasible to require professional specialization as a prerequisite for taking over any function dealing with juvenile offenders. Thus, professional on-the job instruction would be minimum qualifications.

Professional qualifications are an essential element in ensuring the impartial and effective administration of juvenile justice. Accordingly, it is necessary to improve the recruitment, advancement and professional training of personnel and to provide them with the necessary means to enable them to properly fulfil their functions.

All political, social, sexual, racial, religious, cultural or any other kind of discrimination in the selection, appointment and advancement of juvenile justice personnel should be avoided in order to achieve impartiality in the administration of juvenile justice. This was recommended by the Sixth Congress. Furthermore, the Sixth Congress called on Member States to ensure the fair and equal treatment of women as criminal justice personnel and recommended that special measures should be taken to recruit, train and facilitate the advancement of female personnel in juvenile justice administration.

Part Four: Non-institutional Treatment

23 *Effective Implementation of Disposition*

23.1 Appropriate provisions shall be made for the implementation of orders of the competent authority, as referred to in rule 14.1 above, by that authority itself or by some other authority as circumstances may require.

23.2 Such provisions shall include the power to modify the orders as the competent authority may deem necessary from time to time, provided that such modification shall be determined in accordance with the principles contained in these Rules.

Commentary

Disposition in juvenile cases, more so than in adult cases, tends to influence the offender's life for a long period of time. Thus, it is important that the competent authority or an independent body (parole board, probation office, youth welfare institutions or others) with qualifications equal to those of the competent authority that originally disposed of the case should monitor the implementation of the disposition. In some countries, a juge de l'exécution des peines has been installed for this purpose.

The composition, powers and functions of the authority must be flexible; they are described in general terms in rule 23 in order to ensure wide acceptability.

24 *Provision of Needed Assistance*

24.1 Efforts shall be made to provide juveniles, at all stages of the proceedings, with necessary assistance such as lodging, education or vocational training, employment or any other assistance, helpful and practical, in order to facilitate the rehabilitative process.

Commentary

The promotion of the well-being of the juvenile is of paramount consideration. Thus, rule 24 emphasizes the importance of providing requisite facilities, services and other necessary assistance as may further the best interests of the juvenile throughout the rehabilitative process.

25 *Mobilization of Volunteers and Other Community Services*

25.1 Volunteers, voluntary organizations, local institutions and other community resources shall be called upon to contribute effectively to the rehabilitation of the juvenile in a community setting and, as far as possible, within the family unit.

Commentary

This rule reflects the need for a rehabilitative orientation of all work with juvenile offenders. Co-operation with the community is indispensable if the directives of the competent authority are to be carried out effectively. Volunteers and voluntary services, in particular, have proved to be valuable resources but are at present underutilized. In some instances, the co-operation of ex-offenders (including ex-addicts) can be of considerable assistance.

Rule 25 emanates from the principles laid down in rules 1.1 to 1.6 and follows the relevant provisions of the International Covenant on Civil and Political Rights.

Part Five: Institutional Treatment

26 *Objectives of Institutional Treatment*

26.1 The objective of training and treatment of juveniles placed in institutions is to provide care, protection, education and vocational skills, with a view to assisting them to assume socially constructive and productive roles in society.

26.2 Juveniles in institutions shall receive care, protection and all necessary assistance – social, educational, vocational, psychological, medical and physical – that they may require because of their age, sex, and personality and in the interest of their wholesome development.

26.3 Juveniles in institutions shall be kept separate from adults and shall be detained in a separate institution or in a separate part of an institution also holding adults.
26.4 Young female offenders placed in an institution deserve special attention as to their personal needs and problems. They shall by no means receive less care, protection, assistance, treatment and training than young male offenders. Their fair treatment shall be ensured.
26.5 In the interest and well-being of the institutionalized juvenile, the parents or guardians shall have a right of access.
26.6 Inter-ministerial and inter-departmental co-operation shall be fostered for the purpose of providing adequate academic or, as appropriate, vocational training to institutionalized juveniles, with a view to ensuring that they do no leave the institution at an educational disadvantage.

Commentary

The objectives of institutional treatment as stipulated in rules 26.1 and 26.2 would be acceptable to any system and culture. However, they have not yet been attained everywhere, and much more has to be done in this respect.

Medical and psychological assistance, in particular, are extremely important for institutionalized drug addicts, violent and mentally ill young persons.

The avoidance of negative influences through adult offenders and the safeguarding of the well-being of juveniles in an institutional setting, as stipulated in rule 26.3, are in line with one of the basic guiding principles of the Rules, as set out by the Sixth Congress in its resolution 4. The rule does not prevent States from taking other measures against the negative influences of adult offenders, which are at least as effective as the measures mentioned in the rule. (See also rule 13.4.)

Rule 26.4 addresses the fact that female offenders normally receive less attention than their male counterparts. as pointed out by the Sixth Congress. In particular, resolution 9 of the Sixth Congress calls for the fair treatment of female offenders at every stage of criminal justice processes and for special attention to their particular problems and needs while in custody. Moreover, this rule should also be considered in the light of the Caracas Declaration of the Sixth Congress, which, inter alia, calls for equal treatment in criminal justice administration, and against the background of the Declaration on the Elimination of Discrimination against Women and the Convention on the Elimination of All Forms of Discrimination against Women.

The right of access (rule 26.5) follows from the provisions of rules 7.1, 10.1, 15.2 and 18.2. Inter-ministerial and inter-departmental co-operation (rule 26.6) are of particular importance in the interest of generally enhancing the quality of institutional treatment and training.

27 *Application of the Standard Minimum Rules for the Treatment of Prisoners Adopted by the United Nations*

27.1 The Standard Minimum Rules for the Treatment of Prisoners and related recommendations shall be applicable as far as relevant to the treatment of juvenile offenders in institutions, including those in detention pending adjudication.
27.2 Efforts shall be made to implement the relevant principles laid down in the Standard Minimum Rules for the Treatment of Prisoners to the largest possible extent so as to meet the varying needs of juveniles specific to their age, sex and personality.

Commentary

The Standard Minimum Rules for the Treatment of Prisoners were among the first instruments of this kind to be promulgated by the United Nations. It is generally agreed that they have had a world-wide impact. Although there are still countries where implementation is more an aspiration than a fact, those Standard Minimum Rules continue to be an important influence in the humane and equitable administration of correctional institutions.
Some essential protections covering juvenile offenders in institutions are contained in the Standard Minimum Rules for the Treatment of Prisoners (accommodation, architecture, bedding, clothing, complaints and requests, contact with the outside world, food, medical care, religious service, separation of ages, staffing, work, etc.) as are provisions concerning punishment and discipline, and restraint for dangerous offenders. It would not be appropriate to modify those Standard Minimum Rules according to the particular characteristics of institutions for juvenile offenders within the scope of the Standard Minimum Rules for the Administration of Juvenile Justice.
Rule 27 focuses on the necessary requirements for juveniles in institutions (rule 27.1) as well as on the varying needs specific to their age, sex and personality (rule 27.2). Thus, the objectives and content of the rule interrelate to the relevant provisions of the Standard Minimum Rules for the Treatment of Prisoners.

28 *Frequent and Early Recourse to Conditional Release*

28.1 Conditional release from an institution shall be used by the appropriate authority to the greatest possible extent, and shall be granted at the earliest possible time.

28.2 Juveniles released conditionally from an institution shall be assisted and supervised by an appropriate authority and shall receive full support by the community.

Commentary

The power to order conditional release may rest with the competent authority, as mentioned in rule 14.1, or with some other authority. In view of this, it is adequate to refer here to the "appropriate" rather than to the "competent" authority.

Circumstances permitting, conditional release shall be preferred to serving a full sentence. Upon evidence of satisfactory progress towards rehabilitation, even offenders who had been deemed dangerous at the time of their institutionalization can be conditionally released whenever feasible. Like probation, such release may be conditional on the satisfactory fulfilment of the requirements specified by the relevant authorities for a period of time established in the decision, for example relating to "good behaviour" of the offender, attendance in community programmes, residence in half-way houses, etc.

In the case of offenders conditionally released from an institution, assistance and supervision by a probation or other officer (particularly where probation has not yet been adopted) should be provided and community support should be encouraged.

29 *Semi-institutional Arrangements*

29.1 Efforts shall be made to provide semi-institutional arrangements, such as half-way houses, educational homes, day-time training centres and other such appropriate arrangements that may assist juveniles in their proper reintegration into society.

Commentary

The importance of care following a period of institutionalization should not be underestimated. This rule emphasizes the necessity of forming a net of semi-institutional arrangements.

This rule also emphasizes the need for a diverse range of facilities and services designed to meet the different needs of young offenders re-entering the community and to provide guidance and structural support as an important step towards successful reintegration into society.

Part Six: Research, Planning, Policy Formulation and Evaluation

30. Research as a Basis for Planning, Policy Formulation and Evaluation

30.1 Efforts shall be made to organize and promote necessary research as a basis for effective planning and policy formulation.
30.2 Efforts shall be made to review and appraise periodically the trends, problems and causes of juvenile delinquency and crime as well as the varying particular needs of juveniles in custody.
30.3 Efforts shall be made to establish a regular evaluative research mechanism built into the system of juvenile justice administration and to collect and analyse relevant data and information for appropriate assessment and future improvement and reform of the administration.
30.4 The delivery of services in juvenile justice administration shall be systematically planned and implemented as an integral part of national development efforts.

Commentary

The utilization of research as a basis for an informed juvenile justice policy is widely acknowledged as an important mechanism for keeping practices abreast of advances in knowledge and the continuing development and improvement of the juvenile justice system. The mutual feedback between research and policy is especially important in juvenile justice. With rapid and often drastic changes in the life-styles of the young and in the forms and dimensions of juvenile crime, the societal and justice responses to juvenile crime and delinquency quickly become outmoded and inadequate.

Rule 30 thus establishes standards for integrating research into the process of policy formulation and application in juvenile justice administration. The rule draws particular attention to the need for regular review and evaluation of existing programmes and measures and for planning within the broader context of overall development objectives.

A constant appraisal of the needs of juveniles, as well as the trends and problems of delinquency, is a prerequisite for improving the methods of formulating appropriate policies and establishing adequate interventions, at both formal and informal levels. In this context, research by independent persons and bodies should be facilitated by responsible agencies, and it may be valuable to obtain and to take into account the views of juveniles themselves, not only those who come into contact with the system.

The process of planning must particularly emphasize a more effective and equitable system for the delivery of necessary services. Towards that end, there should be a comprehensive and regular assessment of the wide-ranging, particular needs and problems of juveniles and an identification of clear-cut priorities. In that connection, there should also be a co-ordination in the use of existing resources, including alternatives and community support that would be suitable in setting up specific procedures designed to implement and monitor established programmes.

CHAPTER 30

United Nations Guidelines for the Prevention of Juvenile Delinquency

(The Riyadh Guidelines)

Adopted and proclaimed by General Assembly resolution 45/112 of 14 December 1990

I Fundamental Principles

1. The prevention of juvenile delinquency is an essential part of crime prevention in society. By engaging in lawful, socially useful activities and adopting a humanistic orientation towards society and outlook on life, young persons can develop non-criminogenic attitudes.
2. The successful prevention of juvenile delinquency requires efforts on the part of the entire society to ensure the harmonious development of adolescents, with respect for and promotion of their personality from early childhood.
3. For the purposes of the interpretation of the present Guidelines, a child-centred orientation should be pursued. Young persons should have an active role and partnership within society and should not be considered as mere objects of socialization or control.
4. In the implementation of the present Guidelines, in accordance with national legal systems, the well-being of young persons from their early childhood should be the focus of any preventive programme.
5. The need for and importance of progressive delinquency prevention policies and the systematic study and the elaboration of measures should be recognized. These should avoid criminalizing and penalizing a child for behaviour that does not cause serious damage to the development of the child or harm to others. Such policies and measures should involve:

(a) The provision of opportunities, in particular educational opportunities, to meet the varying needs of young persons and to serve as a supportive framework for safeguarding the personal development of all young persons, particularly those who are demonstrably endangered or at social risk and are in need of special care and protection;

(b) Specialized philosophies and approaches for delinquency prevention, on the basis of laws, processes, institutions, facilities and a service

© KARL HANSON ET AL., 2025 | DOI:10.1163/9789004681224_043

delivery network aimed at reducing the motivation, need and opportunity for, or conditions giving rise to, the commission of infractions;

(c) Official intervention to be pursued primarily in the overall interest of the young person and guided by fairness and equity;

(d) Safeguarding the well-being, development, rights and interests of all young persons;

(e) Consideration that youthful behaviour or conduct that does not conform to overall social norms and values is often part of the maturation and growth process and tends to disappear spontaneously in most individuals with the transition to adulthood;

(f) Awareness that, in the predominant opinion of experts, labelling a young person as "deviant", "delinquent" or "pre-delinquent" often contributes to the development of a consistent pattern of undesirable behaviour by young persons.

6. Community-based services and programmes should be developed for the prevention of juvenile delinquency, particularly where no agencies have yet been established. Formal agencies of social control should only be utilized as a means of last resort.

II Scope of the Guidelines

7. The present Guidelines should be interpreted and implemented within the broad framework of the Universal Declaration of Human Rights, the International Covenant on Economic, Social and Cultural Rights, the International Covenant on Civil and Political Rights, the Declaration of the Rights of the Child and the Convention on the Rights of the Child, and in the context of the United Nations Standard Minimum Rules for the Administration of Juvenile Justice (The Beijing Rules), as well as other instruments and norms relating to the rights, interests and well-being of all children and young persons.

8. The present Guidelines should also be implemented in the context of the economic, social and cultural conditions prevailing in each Member State.

III General Prevention

9. Comprehensive prevention plans should be instituted at every level of government and include the following:

(a) In-depth analyses of the problem and inventories of programmes, services, facilities and resources available;

(b) Well-defined responsibilities for the qualified agencies, institutions and personnel involved in preventive efforts;
(c) Mechanisms for the appropriate co-ordination of prevention efforts between governmental and non-governmental agencies;
(d) Policies, programmes and strategies based on prognostic studies to be continuously monitored and carefully evaluated in the course of implementation;
(e) Methods for effectively reducing the opportunity to commit delinquent acts;
(f) Community involvement through a wide range of services and programmes;
(g) Close interdisciplinary co-operation between national, state, provincial and local governments, with the involvement of the private sector, representative citizens of the community to be served, and labour, child-care, health education, social, law enforcement and judicial agencies in taking concerted action to prevent juvenile delinquency and youth crime;
(h) Youth participation in delinquency prevention policies and processes, including recourse to community resources, youth self-help, and victim compensation and assistance programmes;
(i) Specialized personnel at all levels.

IV Socialization Processes

10. Emphasis should be placed on preventive policies facilitating the successful socialization and integration of all children and young persons, in particular through the family, the community, peer groups, schools, vocational training and the world of work, as well as through voluntary organizations. Due respect should be given to the proper personal development of children and young persons, and they should be accepted as full and equal partners in socialization and integration processes.

A *Family*

11. Every society should place a high priority on the needs and well-being of the family and of all its members.

12. Since the family is the central unit responsible for the primary socialization of children, governmental and social efforts to preserve the integrity of the family, including the extended family, should be pursued. The society has a responsibility to assist the family in providing care and protection and in ensuring the physical and mental well-being of children. Adequate arrangements including day-care should be provided.

13. Governments should establish policies that are conducive to the bringing up of children in stable and settled family environments. Families in need of assistance in the resolution of conditions of instability or conflict should be provided with requisite services.

14. Where a stable and settled family environment is lacking and when community efforts to assist parents in this regard have failed and the extended family cannot fulfil this role, alternative placements, including foster care and adoption, should be considered. Such placements should replicate, to the extent possible, a stable and settled family environment, while, at the same time, establishing a sense of permanency for children, thus avoiding problems associated with "foster drift".

15. Special attention should be given to children of families affected by problems brought about by rapid and uneven economic, social and cultural change, in particular the children of indigenous, migrant and refugee families. As such changes may disrupt the social capacity of the family to secure the traditional rearing and nurturing of children, often as a result of role and culture conflict, innovative and socially constructive modalities for the socialization of children have to be designed.

16. Measures should be taken and programmes developed to provide families with the opportunity to learn about parental roles and obligations as regards child development and child care, promoting positive parent-child relationships, sensitizing parents to the problems of children and young persons and encouraging their involvement in family and community-based activities.

17. Governments should take measures to promote family cohesion and harmony and to discourage the separation of children from their parents, unless circumstances affecting the welfare and future of the child leave no viable alternative.

18. It is important to emphasize the socialization function of the family and extended family; it is also equally important to recognize the future role, responsibilities, participation and partnership of young persons in society.

19. In ensuring the right of the child to proper socialization, Governments and other agencies should rely on existing social and legal agencies, but, whenever traditional institutions and customs are no longer effective, they should also provide and allow for innovative measures.

B *Education*

20. Governments are under an obligation to make public education accessible to all young persons.

21. Education systems should, in addition to their academic and vocational training activities, devote particular attention to the following:

(a) Teaching of basic values and developing respect for the child's own cultural identity and patterns, for the social values of the country in which the child is living, for civilizations different from the child's own and for human rights and fundamental freedoms;

(b) Promotion and development of the personality, talents and mental and physical abilities of young people to their fullest potential;

(c) Involvement of young persons as active and effective participants in, rather than mere objects of, the educational process;

(d) Undertaking activities that foster a sense of identity with and of belonging to the school and the community;

(e) Encouragement of young persons to understand and respect diverse views and opinions, as well as cultural and other differences;

(f) Provision of information and guidance regarding vocational training, employment opportunities and career development;

(g) Provision of positive emotional support to young persons and the avoidance of psychological maltreatment;

(h) Avoidance of harsh disciplinary measures, particularly corporal punishment.

22. Educational systems should seek to work together with parents, community organizations and agencies concerned with the activities of young persons.

23. Young persons and their families should be informed about the law and their rights and responsibilities under the law, as well as the universal value system, including United Nations instruments.

24. Educational systems should extend particular care and attention to young persons who are at social risk. Specialized prevention programmes and educational materials, curricula, approaches and tools should be developed and fully utilized.

25. Special attention should be given to comprehensive policies and strategies for the prevention of alcohol, drug and other substance abuse by young persons. Teachers and other professionals should be equipped and trained to prevent and deal with these problems. Information on the use and abuse of drugs, including alcohol, should be made available to the student body.

26. Schools should serve as resource and referral centres for the provision of medical, counselling and other services to young persons, particularly those with special needs and suffering from abuse, neglect, victimization and exploitation.

27. Through a variety of educational programmes, teachers and other adults and the student body should be sensitized to the problems, needs and perceptions of young persons, particularly those belonging to underprivileged, disadvantaged, ethnic or other minority and low-income groups.

28. School systems should attempt to meet and promote the highest professional and educational standards with respect to curricula, teaching and learning methods and approaches, and the recruitment and training of qualified teachers. Regular monitoring and assessment of performance by the appropriate professional organizations and authorities should be ensured.

29. School systems should plan, develop and implement extra-curricular activities of interest to young persons, in co-operation with community groups.

30. Special assistance should be given to children and young persons who find it difficult to comply with attendance codes, and to "drop-outs".

31. Schools should promote policies and rules that are fair and just; students should be represented in bodies formulating school policy, including policy on discipline, and decision-making.

C *Community*

32. Community-based services and programmes which respond to the special needs, problems, interests and concerns of young persons and which offer appropriate counselling and guidance to young persons and their families should be developed, or strengthened where they exist.

33. Communities should provide, or strengthen where they exist, a wide range of community-based support measures for young persons, including community development centres, recreational facilities and services to respond to the special problems of children who are at social risk. In providing these helping measures, respect for individual rights should be ensured.

34. Special facilities should be set up to provide adequate shelter for young persons who are no longer able to live at home or who do not have homes to live in.

35. A range of services and helping measures should be provided to deal with the difficulties experienced by young persons in the transition to adulthood. Such services should include special programmes for young drug abusers which emphasize care, counselling, assistance and therapy-oriented interventions.

36. Voluntary organizations providing services for young persons should be given financial and other support by Governments and other institutions.

37. Youth organizations should be created or strengthened at the local level and given full participatory status in the management of community affairs. These organizations should encourage youth to organize collective and voluntary projects, particularly projects aimed at helping young persons in need of assistance.

38. Government agencies should take special responsibility and provide necessary services for homeless or street children; information about local facilities, accommodation, employment and other forms and sources of help should be made readily available to young persons.
39. A wide range of recreational facilities and services of particular interest to young persons should be established and made easily accessible to them.

D *Mass Media*

40. The mass media should be encouraged to ensure that young persons have access to information and material from a diversity of national and international sources.
41. The mass media should be encouraged to portray the positive contribution of young persons to society.
42. The mass media should be encouraged to disseminate information on the existence of services, facilities and opportunities for young persons in society.
43. The mass media generally, and the television and film media in particular, should be encouraged to minimize the level of pornography, drugs and violence portrayed and to display violence and exploitation disfavourably, as well as to avoid demeaning and degrading presentations, especially of children, women and interpersonal relations, and to promote egalitarian principles and roles.
44. The mass media should be aware of its extensive social role and responsibility, as well as its influence, in communications relating to youthful drug and alcohol abuse. It should use its power for drug abuse prevention by relaying consistent messages through a balanced approach. Effective drug awareness campaigns at all levels should be promoted.

V **Social Policy**

45. Government agencies should give high priority to plans and programmes for young persons and should provide sufficient funds and other resources for the effective delivery of services, facilities and staff for adequate medical and mental health care, nutrition, housing and other relevant services, including drug and alcohol abuse prevention and treatment, ensuring that such resources reach and actually benefit young persons.
46. The institutionalization of young persons should be a measure of last resort and for the minimum necessary period, and the best interests of the young person should be of paramount importance. Criteria authorizing formal intervention of this type should be strictly defined and limited to the following situations: (a) where the child or young person has suffered harm that has

been inflicted by the parents or guardians; (b) where the child or young person has been sexually, physically or emotionally abused by the parents or guardians; (c) where the child or young person has been neglected, abandoned or exploited by the parents or guardians; (d) where the child or young person is threatened by physical or moral danger due to the behaviour of the parents or guardians; and (e) where a serious physical or psychological danger to the child or young person has manifested itself in his or her own behaviour and neither the parents, the guardians, the juvenile himself or herself nor non-residential community services can meet the danger by means other than institutionalization.

47. Government agencies should provide young persons with the opportunity of continuing in full-time education, funded by the State where parents or guardians are unable to support the young persons, and of receiving work experience.

48. Programmes to prevent delinquency should be planned and developed on the basis of reliable, scientific research findings, and periodically monitored, evaluated and adjusted accordingly.

49. Scientific information should be disseminated to the professional community and to the public at large about the sort of behaviour or situation which indicates or may result in physical and psychological victimization, harm and abuse, as well as exploitation, of young persons.

50. Generally, participation in plans and programmes should be voluntary. Young persons themselves should be involved in their formulation, development and implementation.

51. Governments should begin or continue to explore, develop and implement policies, measures and strategies within and outside the criminal justice system to prevent domestic violence against and affecting young persons and to ensure fair treatment to these victims of domestic violence.

VI Legislation and Juvenile Justice Administration

52. Governments should enact and enforce specific laws and procedures to promote and protect the rights and well-being of all young persons.

53. Legislation preventing the victimization, abuse, exploitation and the use for criminal activities of children and young persons should be enacted and enforced.

54. No child or young person should be subjected to harsh or degrading correction or punishment measures at home, in schools or in any other institutions.

55. Legislation and enforcement aimed at restricting and controlling accessibility of weapons of any sort to children and young persons should be pursued.
56. In order to prevent further stigmatization, victimization and criminalization of young persons, legislation should be enacted to ensure that any conduct not considered an offence or not penalized if committed by an adult is not considered an offence and not penalized if committed by a young person.
57. Consideration should be given to the establishment of an office of ombudsman or similar independent organ, which would ensure that the status, rights and interests of young persons are upheld and that proper referral to available services is made. The ombudsman or other organ designated would also supervise the implementation of the Riyadh Guidelines, the Beijing Rules and the Rules for the Protection of Juveniles Deprived of their Liberty. The ombudsman or other organ would, at regular intervals, publish a report on the progress made and on the difficulties encountered in the implementation of the instrument. Child advocacy services should also be established.
58. Law enforcement and other relevant personnel, of both sexes, should be trained to respond to the special needs of young persons and should be familiar with and use, to the maximum extent possible, programmes and referral possibilities for the diversion of young persons from the justice system
59. Legislation should be enacted and strictly enforced to protect children and young persons from drug abuse and drug traffickers.

VII Research, Policy Development and Co-ordination

60. Efforts should be made and appropriate mechanisms established to promote, on both a multidisciplinary and an intradisciplinary basis, interaction and co-ordination between economic, social, educational and health agencies and services, the justice system, youth, community and development agencies and other relevant institutions.
61. The exchange of information, experience and expertise gained through projects, programmes, practices and initiatives relating to youth crime, delinquency prevention and juvenile justice should be intensified at the national, regional and international levels.
62. Regional and international co-operation on matters of youth crime, delinquency prevention and juvenile justice involving practitioners, experts and decision makers should be further developed and strengthened.
63. Technical and scientific co-operation on practical and policy-related matters, particularly in training, pilot and demonstration projects, and on specific issues concerning the prevention of youth crime and juvenile delinquency

should be strongly supported by all Governments, the United Nations system and other concerned organizations.

64. Collaboration should be encouraged in undertaking scientific research with respect to effective modalities for youth crime and juvenile delinquency prevention and the findings of such research should be widely disseminated and evaluated.

65. Appropriate United Nations bodies, institutes, agencies and offices should pursue close collaboration and co-ordination on various questions related to children, juvenile justice and youth crime and juvenile delinquency prevention.

66. On the basis of the present Guidelines, the United Nations Secretariat, in co-operation with interested institutions, should play an active role in the conduct of research, scientific collaboration, the formulation of policy options and the review and monitoring of their implementation, and should serve as a source of reliable information on effective modalities for delinquency prevention.

CHAPTER 31

United Nations Rules for the Protection of Juveniles Deprived of Their Liberty

Adopted by General Assembly resolution 45/113 of 14 December 1990

I Fundamental Perspectives

1. The juvenile justice system should uphold the rights and safety and promote the physical and mental well-being of juveniles. Imprisonment should be used as a last resort.
2. Juveniles should only be deprived of their liberty in accordance with the principles and procedures set forth in these Rules and in the United Nations Standard Minimum Rules for the Administration of Juvenile Justice (The Beijing Rules). Deprivation of the liberty of a juvenile should be a disposition of last resort and for the minimum necessary period and should be limited to exceptional cases. The length of the sanction should be determined by the judicial authority, without precluding the possibility of his or her early release.
3. The Rules are intended to establish minimum standards accepted by the United Nations for the protection of juveniles deprived of their liberty in all forms, consistent with human rights and fundamental freedoms, with a view to counteracting the detrimental effects of all types of detention and to fostering integration in society.
4. The Rules should be applied impartially, without discrimination of any kind as to race, colour, sex, age, language, religion, nationality, political or other opinion, cultural beliefs or practices, property, birth or family status, ethnic or social origin, and disability. The religious and cultural beliefs, practices and moral concepts of the juvenile should be respected.
5. The Rules are designed to serve as convenient standards of reference and to provide encouragement and guidance to professionals involved in the management of the juvenile justice system.
6. The Rules should be made readily available to juvenile justice personnel in their national languages. Juveniles who are not fluent in the language spoken by the personnel of the detention facility should have the right to the services of an interpreter free of charge whenever necessary, in particular during medical examinations and disciplinary proceedings.

 DOI:10.1163/9789004681224_044

7. Where appropriate, States should incorporate the Rules into their legislation or amend it accordingly and provide effective remedies for their breach, including compensation when injuries are inflicted on juveniles. States should also monitor the application of the Rules.

8. The competent authorities should constantly seek to increase the awareness of the public that the care of detained juveniles and preparation for their return to society is a social service of great importance, and to this end active steps should be taken to foster open contacts between the juveniles and the local community.

9. Nothing in the Rules should be interpreted as precluding the application of the relevant United Nations and human rights instruments and standards, recognized by the international community, that are more conducive to ensuring the rights, care and protection of juveniles, children and all young persons.

10. In the event that the practical application of particular Rules contained in sections II to V, inclusive, presents any conflict with the Rules contained in the present section, compliance with the latter shall be regarded as the predominant requirement.

II Scope and Application of the Rules

11. For the purposes of the Rules, the following definitions should apply:

(a) A juvenile is every person under the age of 18. The age limit below which it should not be permitted to deprive a child of his or her liberty should be determined by law;

(b) The deprivation of liberty means any form of detention or imprisonment or the placement of a person in a public or private custodial setting, from which this person is not permitted to leave at will, by order of any judicial, administrative or other public authority.

12. The deprivation of liberty should be effected in conditions and circumstances which ensure respect for the human rights of juveniles. Juveniles detained in facilities should be guaranteed the benefit of meaningful activities and programmes which would serve to promote and sustain their health and selfrespect, to foster their sense of responsibility and encourage those attitudes and skills that will assist them in developing their potential as members of society.

13. Juveniles deprived of their liberty shall not for any reason related to their status be denied the civil, economic, political, social or cultural rights to which they are entitled under national or international law, and which are compatible with the deprivation of liberty.

14. The protection of the individual rights of juveniles with special regard to the legality of the execution of the detention measures shall be ensured by the competent authority, while the objectives of social integration should be secured by regular inspections and other means of control carried out, according to international standards, national laws and regulations, by a duly constituted body authorized to visit the juveniles and not belonging to the detention facility.
15. The Rules apply to all types and forms of detention facilities in which juveniles are deprived of their liberty. Sections I, II, IV and V of the Rules apply to all detention facilities and institutional settings in which juveniles are detained, and section III applies specifically to juveniles under arrest or awaiting trial.
16. The Rules shall be implemented in the context of the economic, social and cultural conditions prevailing in each Member State.

III Juveniles under Arrest or Awaiting Trial

17. Juveniles who are detained under arrest or awaiting trial ("untried") are presumed innocent and shall be treated as such. Detention before trial shall be avoided to the extent possible and limited to exceptional circumstances. Therefore, all efforts shall be made to apply alternative measures. When preventive detention is nevertheless used, juvenile courts and investigative bodies shall give the highest priority to the most expeditious processing of such cases to ensure the shortest possible duration of detention. Untried detainees should be separated from convicted juveniles.
18. The conditions under which an untried juvenile is detained should be consistent with the rules set out below, with additional specific provisions as are necessary and appropriate, given the requirements of the presumption of innocence, the duration of the detention and the legal status and circumstances of the juvenile. These provisions would include, but not necessarily be restricted to, the following:

(a) Juveniles should have the right of legal counsel and be enabled to apply for free legal aid, where such aid is available, and to communicate regularly with their legal advisers. Privacy and confidentiality shall be ensured for such communications;

(b) Juveniles should be provided, where possible, with opportunities to pursue work, with remuneration, and continue education or training, but should not be required to do so. Work, education or training should not cause the continuation of the detention;

(c) Juveniles should receive and retain materials for their leisure and recreation as are compatible with the interests of the administration of justice.

IV The Management of Juvenile Facilities

A *Records*

19. All reports, including legal records, medical records and records of disciplinary proceedings, and all other documents relating to the form, content and details of treatment, should be placed in a confidential individual file, which should be kept up to date, accessible only to authorized persons and classified in such a way as to be easily understood. Where possible, every juvenile should have the right to contest any fact or opinion contained in his or her file so as to permit rectification of inaccurate, unfounded or unfair statements. In order to exercise this right, there should be procedures that allow an appropriate third party to have access to and to consult the file on request. Upon release, the records of juveniles shall be sealed, and, at an appropriate time, expunged.
20. No juvenile should be received in any detention facility without a valid commitment order of a judicial, administrative or other public authority. The details of this order should be immediately entered in the register. No juvenile should be detained in any facility where there is no such register.

B *Admission, Registration, Movement and Transfer*

21. In every place where juveniles are detained, a complete and secure record of the following information should be kept concerning each juvenile received:
(a) Information on the identity of the juvenile;
(b) The fact of and reasons for commitment and the authority therefor;
(c) The day and hour of admission, transfer and release;
(d) Details of the notifications to parents and guardians on every admission, transfer or release of the juvenile in their care at the time of commitment;
(e) Details of known physical and mental health problems, including drug and alcohol abuse.

22. The information on admission, place, transfer and release should be provided without delay to the parents and guardians or closest relative of the juvenile concerned.
23. As soon as possible after reception, full reports and relevant information on the personal situation and circumstances of each juvenile should be drawn up and submitted to the administration.

24. On admission, all juveniles shall be given a copy of the rules governing the detention facility and a written description of their rights and obligations in a language they can understand, together with the address of the authorities competent to receive complaints, as well as the address of public or private agencies and organizations which provide legal assistance. For those juveniles who are illiterate or who cannot understand the language in the written form, the information should be conveyed in a manner enabling full comprehension.
25. All juveniles should be helped to understand the regulations governing the internal organization of the facility, the goals and methodology of the care provided, the disciplinary requirements and procedures, other authorized methods of seeking information and of making complaints and all such other matters as are necessary to enable them to understand fully their rights and obligations during detention.
26. The transport of juveniles should be carried out at the expense of the administration in conveyances with adequate ventilation and light, in conditions that should in no way subject them to hardship or indignity. Juveniles should not be transferred from one facility to another arbitrarily.

C *Classification and Placement*

27. As soon as possible after the moment of admission, each juvenile should be interviewed, and a psychological and social report identifying any factors relevant to the specific type and level of care and programme required by the juvenile should be prepared. This report, together with the report prepared by a medical officer who has examined the juvenile upon admission, should be forwarded to the director for purposes of determining the most appropriate placement for the juvenile within the facility and the specific type and level of care and programme required and to be pursued. When special rehabilitative treatment is required, and the length of stay in the facility permits, trained personnel of the facility should prepare a written, individualized treatment plan specifying treatment objectives and time-frame and the means, stages and delays with which the objectives should be approached.
28. The detention of juveniles should only take place under conditions that take full account of their particular needs, status and special requirements according to their age, personality, sex and type of offence, as well as mental and physical health, and which ensure their protection from harmful influences and risk situations. The principal criterion for the separation of different categories of juveniles deprived of their liberty should be the provision of the type of care best suited to the particular needs of the individuals concerned and the protection of their physical, mental and moral integrity and well-being.

29. In all detention facilities juveniles should be separated from adults, unless they are members of the same family. Under controlled conditions, juveniles may be brought together with carefully selected adults as part of a special programme that has been shown to be beneficial for the juveniles concerned.
30. Open detention facilities for juveniles should be established. Open detention facilities are those with no or minimal security measures. The population in such detention facilities should be as small as possible. The number of juveniles detained in closed facilities should be small enough to enable individualized treatment. Detention facilities for juveniles should be decentralized and of such size as to facilitate access and contact between the juveniles and their families. Small-scale detention facilities should be established and integrated into the social, economic and cultural environment of the community.

D *Physical Environment and Accommodation*

31. Juveniles deprived of their liberty have the right to facilities and services that meet all the requirements of health and human dignity.
32. The design of detention facilities for juveniles and the physical environment should be in keeping with the rehabilitative aim of residential treatment, with due regard to the need of the juvenile for privacy, sensory stimuli, opportunities for association with peers and participation in sports, physical exercise and leisure-time activities. The design and structure of juvenile detention facilities should be such as to minimize the risk of fire and to ensure safe evacuation from the premises. There should be an effective alarm system in case of fire, as well as formal and drilled procedures to ensure the safety of the juveniles. Detention facilities should not be located in areas where there are known health or other hazards or risks.
33. Sleeping accommodation should normally consist of small group dormitories or individual bedrooms, while bearing in mind local standards. During sleeping hours there should be regular, unobtrusive supervision of all sleeping areas, including individual rooms and group dormitories, in order to ensure the protection of each juvenile. Every juvenile should, in accordance with local or national standards, be provided with separate and sufficient bedding, which should be clean when issued, kept in good order and changed often enough to ensure cleanliness.
34. Sanitary installations should be so located and of a sufficient standard to enable every juvenile to comply, as required, with their physical needs in privacy and in a clean and decent manner.
35. The possession of personal effects is a basic element of the right to privacy and essential to the psychological well-being of the juvenile. The right of every juvenile to possess personal effects and to have adequate storage facilities

for them should be fully recognized and respected. Personal effects that the juvenile does not choose to retain or that are confiscated should be placed in safe custody. An inventory thereof should be signed by the juvenile. Steps should be taken to keep them in good condition. All such articles and money should be returned to the juvenile on release, except in so far as he or she has been authorized to spend money or send such property out of the facility. If a juvenile receives or is found in possession of any medicine, the medical officer should decide what use should be made of it.

36. To the extent possible juveniles should have the right to use their own clothing. Detention facilities should ensure that each juvenile has personal clothing suitable for the climate and adequate to ensure good health, and which should in no manner be degrading or humiliating. Juveniles removed from or leaving a facility for any purpose should be allowed to wear their own clothing.

37. Every detention facility shall ensure that every juvenile receives food that is suitably prepared and presented at normal meal times and of a quality and quantity to satisfy the standards of dietetics, hygiene and health and, as far as possible, religious and cultural requirements. Clean drinking water should be available to every juvenile at any time.

E *Education, Vocational Training and Work*

38. Every juvenile of compulsory school age has the right to education suited to his or her needs and abilities and designed to prepare him or her for return to society. Such education should be provided outside the detention facility in community schools wherever possible and, in any case, by qualified teachers through programmes integrated with the education system of the country so that, after release, juveniles may continue their education without difficulty. Special attention should be given by the administration of the detention facilities to the education of juveniles of foreign origin or with particular cultural or ethnic needs. Juveniles who are illiterate or have cognitive or learning difficulties should have the right to special education.

39. Juveniles above compulsory school age who wish to continue their education should be permitted and encouraged to do so, and every effort should be made to provide them with access to appropriate educational programmes.

40. Diplomas or educational certificates awarded to juveniles while in detention should not indicate in any way that the juvenile has been institutionalized.

41. Every detention facility should provide access to a library that is adequately stocked with both instructional and recreational books and periodicals suitable for the juveniles, who should be encouraged and enabled to make full use of it.

42. Every juvenile should have the right to receive vocational training in occupations likely to prepare him or her for future employment.
43. With due regard to proper vocational selection and to the requirements of institutional administration, juveniles should be able to choose the type of work they wish to perform.
44. All protective national and international standards applicable to child labour and young workers should apply to juveniles deprived of their liberty.
45. Wherever possible, juveniles should be provided with the opportunity to perform remunerated labour, if possible within the local community, as a complement to the vocational training provided in order to enhance the possibility of finding suitable employment when they return to their communities. The type of work should be such as to provide appropriate training that will be of benefit to the juveniles following release. The organization and methods of work offered in detention facilities should resemble as closely as possible those of similar work in the community, so as to prepare juveniles for the conditions of normal occupational life.
46. Every juvenile who performs work should have the right to an equitable remuneration. The interests of the juveniles and of their vocational training should not be subordinated to the purpose of making a profit for the detention facility or a third party. Part of the earnings of a juvenile should normally be set aside to constitute a savings fund to be handed over to the juvenile on release. The juvenile should have the right to use the remainder of those earnings to purchase articles for his or her own use or to indemnify the victim injured by his or her offence or to send it to his or her family or other persons outside the detention facility.

F *Recreation*

47. Every juvenile should have the right to a suitable amount of time for daily free exercise, in the open air whenever weather permits, during which time appropriate recreational and physical training should normally be provided. Adequate space, installations and equipment should be provided for these activities. Every juvenile should have additional time for daily leisure activities, part of which should be devoted, if the juvenile so wishes, to arts and crafts skill development. The detention facility should ensure that each juvenile is physically able to participate in the available programmes of physical education. Remedial physical education and therapy should be offered, under medical supervision, to juveniles needing it.

G *Religion*

48. Every juvenile should be allowed to satisfy the needs of his or her religious and spiritual life, in particular by attending the services or meetings provided in the detention facility or by conducting his or her own services and having possession of the necessary books or items of religious observance and instruction of his or her denomination. If a detention facility contains a sufficient number of juveniles of a given religion, one or more qualified representatives of that religion should be appointed or approved and allowed to hold regular services and to pay pastoral visits in private to juveniles at their request. Every juvenile should have the right to receive visits from a qualified representative of any religion of his or her choice, as well as the right not to participate in religious services and freely to decline religious education, counselling or indoctrination.

H *Medical Care*

49. Every juvenile shall receive adequate medical care, both preventive and remedial, including dental, ophthalmological and mental health care, as well as pharmaceutical products and special diets as medically indicated. All such medical care should, where possible, be provided to detained juveniles through the appropriate health facilities and services of the community in which the detention facility is located, in order to prevent stigmatization of the juvenile and promote self-respect and integration into the community.

50. Every juvenile has a right to be examined by a physician immediately upon admission to a detention facility, for the purpose of recording any evidence of prior ill-treatment and identifying any physical or mental condition requiring medical attention.

51. The medical services provided to juveniles should seek to detect and should treat any physical or mental illness, substance abuse or other condition that may hinder the integration of the juvenile into society. Every detention facility for juveniles should have immediate access to adequate medical facilities and equipment appropriate to the number and requirements of its residents and staff trained in preventive health care and the handling of medical emergencies. Every juvenile who is ill, who complains of illness or who demonstrates symptoms of physical or mental difficulties should be examined promptly by a medical officer.

52. Any medical officer who has reason to believe that the physical or mental health of a juvenile has been or will be injuriously affected by continued detention, a hunger strike or any condition of detention should report this fact immediately to the director of the detention facility in question and to

the independent authority responsible for safeguarding the well-being of the juvenile.

53. A juvenile who is suffering from mental illness should be treated in a specialized institution under independent medical management. Steps should be taken, by arrangement with appropriate agencies, to ensure any necessary continuation of mental health care after release.

54. Juvenile detention facilities should adopt specialized drug abuse prevention and rehabilitation programmes administered by qualified personnel. These programmes should be adapted to the age, sex and other requirements of the juveniles concerned, and detoxification facilities and services staffed by trained personnel should be available to drug- or alcohol-dependent juveniles.

55. Medicines should be administered only for necessary treatment on medical grounds and, when possible, after having obtained the informed consent of the juvenile concerned. In particular, they must not be administered with a view to eliciting information or a confession, as a punishment or as a means of restraint. Juveniles shall never be testees in the experimental use of drugs and treatment. The administration of any drug should always be authorized and carried out by qualified medical personnel.

I Notification of Illness, Injury and Death

56. The family or guardian of a juvenile and any other person designated by the juvenile have the right to be informed of the state of health of the juvenile on request and in the event of any important changes in the health of the juvenile. The director of the detention facility should notify immediately the family or guardian of the juvenile concerned, or other designated person, in case of death, illness requiring transfer of the juvenile to an outside medical facility, or a condition requiring clinical care within the detention facility for more than 48 hours. Notification should also be given to the consular authorities of the State of which a foreign juvenile is a citizen.

57. Upon the death of a juvenile during the period of deprivation of liberty, the nearest relative should have the right to inspect the death certificate, see the body and determine the method of disposal of the body. Upon the death of a juvenile in detention, there should be an independent inquiry into the causes of death, the report of which should be made accessible to the nearest relative. This inquiry should also be made when the death of a juvenile occurs within six months from the date of his or her release from the detention facility and there is reason to believe that the death is related to the period of detention.

58. A juvenile should be informed at the earliest possible time of the death, serious illness or injury of any immediate family member and should be

provided with the opportunity to attend the funeral of the deceased or go to the bedside of a critically ill relative.

J *Contacts with the Wider Community*

59. Every means should be provided to ensure that juveniles have adequate communication with the outside world, which is an integral part of the right to fair and humane treatment and is essential to the preparation of juveniles for their return to society. Juveniles should be allowed to communicate with their families, friends and other persons or representatives of reputable outside organizations, to leave detention facilities for a visit to their home and family and to receive special permission to leave the detention facility for educational, vocational or other important reasons. Should the juvenile be serving a sentence, the time spent outside a detention facility should be counted as part of the period of sentence.

60. Every juvenile should have the right to receive regular and frequent visits, in principle once a week and not less than once a month, in circumstances that respect the need of the juvenile for privacy, contact and unrestricted communication with the family and the defence counsel.

61. Every juvenile should have the right to communicate in writing or by telephone at least twice a week with the person of his or her choice, unless legally restricted, and should be assisted as necessary in order effectively to enjoy this right. Every juvenile should have the right to receive correspondence.

62. Juveniles should have the opportunity to keep themselves informed regularly of the news by reading newspapers, periodicals and other publications, through access to radio and television programmes and motion pictures, and through the visits of the representatives of any lawful club or organization in which the juvenile is interested.

K *Limitations of Physical Restraint and the Use of Force*

63. Recourse to instruments of restraint and to force for any purpose should be prohibited, except as set forth in rule 64 below.

64. Instruments of restraint and force can only be used in exceptional cases, where all other control methods have been exhausted and failed, and only as explicitly authorized and specified by law and regulation. They should not cause humiliation or degradation, and should be used restrictively and only for the shortest possible period of time. By order of the director of the administration, such instruments might be resorted to in order to prevent the juvenile from inflicting self-injury, injuries to others or serious destruction of property. In such instances, the director should at once consult medical and other relevant personnel and report to the higher administrative authority.

65. The carrying and use of weapons by personnel should be prohibited in any facility where juveniles are detained.

L *Disciplinary Procedures*

66. Any disciplinary measures and procedures should maintain the interest of safety and an ordered community life and should be consistent with the upholding of the inherent dignity of the juvenile and the fundamental objective of institutional care, namely, instilling a sense of justice, self-respect and respect for the basic rights of every person.

67. All disciplinary measures constituting cruel, inhuman or degrading treatment shall be strictly prohibited, including corporal punishment, placement in a dark cell, closed or solitary confinement or any other punishment that may compromise the physical or mental health of the juvenile concerned. The reduction of diet and the restriction or denial of contact with family members should be prohibited for any purpose. Labour should always be viewed as an educational tool and a means of promoting the self-respect of the juvenile in preparing him or her for return to the community and should not be imposed as a disciplinary sanction. No juvenile should be sanctioned more than once for the same disciplinary infraction. Collective sanctions should be prohibited.

68. Legislation or regulations adopted by the competent administrative authority should establish norms concerning the following, taking full account of the fundamental characteristics, needs and rights of juveniles:

(a) Conduct constituting a disciplinary offence;
(b) Type and duration of disciplinary sanctions that may be inflicted;
(c) The authority competent to impose such sanctions;
(d) The authority competent to consider appeals.

69. A report of misconduct should be presented promptly to the competent authority, which should decide on it without undue delay. The competent authority should conduct a thorough examination of the case.

70. No juvenile should be disciplinarily sanctioned except in strict accordance with the terms of the law and regulations in force. No juvenile should be sanctioned unless he or she has been informed of the alleged infraction in a manner appropriate to the full understanding of the juvenile, and given a proper opportunity of presenting his or her defence, including the right of appeal to a competent impartial authority. Complete records should be kept of all disciplinary proceedings.

71. No juveniles should be responsible for disciplinary functions except in the supervision of specified social, educational or sports activities or in self-government programmes.

M *Inspection and Complaints*

72. Qualified inspectors or an equivalent duly constituted authority not belonging to the administration of the facility should be empowered to conduct inspections on a regular basis and to undertake unannounced inspections on their own initiative, and should enjoy full guarantees of independence in the exercise of this function. Inspectors should have unrestricted access to all persons employed by or working in any facility where juveniles are or may be deprived of their liberty, to all juveniles and to all records of such facilities.

73. Qualified medical officers attached to the inspecting authority or the public health service should participate in the inspections, evaluating compliance with the rules concerning the physical environment, hygiene, accommodation, food, exercise and medical services, as well as any other aspect or conditions of institutional life that affect the physical and mental health of juveniles. Every juvenile should have the right to talk in confidence to any inspecting officer.

74. After completing the inspection, the inspector should be required to submit a report on the findings. The report should include an evaluation of the compliance of the detention facilities with the present rules and relevant provisions of national law, and recommendations regarding any steps considered necessary to ensure compliance with them. Any facts discovered by an inspector that appear to indicate that a violation of legal provisions concerning the rights of juveniles or the operation of a juvenile detention facility has occurred should be communicated to the competent authorities for investigation and prosecution.

75. Every juvenile should have the opportunity of making requests or complaints to the director of the detention facility and to his or her authorized representative.

76. Every juvenile should have the right to make a request or complaint, without censorship as to substance, to the central administration, the judicial authority or other proper authorities through approved channels, and to be informed of the response without delay.

77. Efforts should be made to establish an independent office (ombudsman) to receive and investigate complaints made by juveniles deprived of their liberty and to assist in the achievement of equitable settlements.

78. Every juvenile should have the right to request assistance from family members, legal counsellors, humanitarian groups or others where possible, in order to make a complaint. Illiterate juveniles should be provided with assistance should they need to use the services of public or private agencies and organizations which provide legal counsel or which are competent to receive complaints.

N *Return to the Community*

79. All juveniles should benefit from arrangements designed to assist them in returning to society, family life, education or employment after release. Procedures, including early release, and special courses should be devised to this end.

80. Competent authorities should provide or ensure services to assist juveniles in re-establishing themselves in society and to lessen prejudice against such juveniles. These services should ensure, to the extent possible, that the juvenile is provided with suitable residence, employment, clothing, and sufficient means to maintain himself or herself upon release in order to facilitate successful reintegration. The representatives of agencies providing such services should be consulted and should have access to juveniles while detained, with a view to assisting them in their return to the community.

V Personnel

81. Personnel should be qualified and include a sufficient number of specialists such as educators, vocational instructors, counsellors, social workers, psychiatrists and psychologists. These and other specialist staff should normally be employed on a permanent basis. This should not preclude part-time or volunteer workers when the level of support and training they can provide is appropriate and beneficial. Detention facilities should make use of all remedial, educational, moral, spiritual, and other resources and forms of assistance that are appropriate and available in the community, according to the individual needs and problems of detained juveniles.

82. The administration should provide for the careful selection and recruitment of every grade and type of personnel, since the proper management of detention facilities depends on their integrity, humanity, ability and professional capacity to deal with juveniles, as well as personal suitability for the work.

83. To secure the foregoing ends, personnel should be appointed as professional officers with adequate remuneration to attract and retain suitable women and men. The personnel of juvenile detention facilities should be continually encouraged to fulfil their duties and obligations in a humane, committed, professional, fair and efficient manner, to conduct themselves at all times in such a way as to deserve and gain the respect of the juveniles, and to provide juveniles with a positive role model and perspective.

84. The administration should introduce forms of organization and management that facilitate communications between different categories of staff in each detention facility so as to enhance co-operation between the various services engaged in the care of juveniles, as well as between staff and the administration, with a view to ensuring that staff directly in contact with juveniles are able to function in conditions favourable to the efficient fulfilment of their duties.

85. The personnel should receive such training as will enable them to carry out their responsibilities effectively, in particular training in child psychology, child welfare and international standards and norms of human rights and the rights of the child, including the present Rules. The personnel should maintain and improve their knowledge and professional capacity by attending courses of in-service training, to be organized at suitable intervals throughout their career.

86. The director of a facility should be adequately qualified for his or her task, with administrative ability and suitable training and experience, and should carry out his or her duties on a full-time basis.

87. In the performance of their duties, personnel of detention facilities should respect and protect the human dignity and fundamental human rights of all juveniles, in particular, as follows:

(a) No member of the detention facility or institutional personnel may inflict, instigate or tolerate any act of torture or any form of harsh, cruel, inhuman or degrading treatment, punishment, correction or discipline under any pretext or circumstance whatsoever;

(b) All personnel should rigorously oppose and combat any act of corruption, reporting it without delay to the competent authorities;

(c) All personnel should respect the present Rules. Personnel who have reason to believe that a serious violation of the present Rules has occurred or is about to occur should report the matter to their superior authorities or organs vested with reviewing or remedial power;

(d) All personnel should ensure the full protection of the physical and mental health of juveniles, including protection from physical, sexual and emotional abuse and exploitation, and should take immediate action to secure medical attention whenever required;

(e) All personnel should respect the right of the juvenile to privacy, and in particular should safeguard all confidential matters concerning juveniles or their families learned as a result of their professional capacity;

(f) All personnel should seek to minimize any differences between life inside and outside the detention facility which tend to lessen due respect for the dignity of juveniles as human beings.

CHAPTER 32

United Nations Guidelines on Justice in Matters Involving Child Victims and Witnesses of Crime

Adopted by the Economic and Social Council with resolution 2005/20 on 22 July 2005

I Objectives

1. The present Guidelines on Justice for Child Victims and Witnesses of Crime set forth good practice based on the consensus of contemporary knowledge and relevant international and regional norms, standards and principles.
2. The Guidelines should be implemented in accordance with relevant national legislation and judicial procedures as well as take into consideration legal, social, economic, cultural and geographical conditions. However, States should constantly endeavour to overcome practical difficulties in the application of the Guidelines.
3. The Guidelines provide a practical framework to achieve the following objectives:

(a) To assist in the review of national and domestic laws, procedures and practices so that these ensure full respect for the rights of child victims and witnesses of crime and contribute to the implementation of the Convention on the Rights of the Child,[1] by parties to that Convention;

(b) To assist Governments, international organizations, public agencies, non-governmental and community-based organizations and other interested parties in designing and implementing legislation, policy, programmes and practices that address key issues related to child victims and witnesses of crime;

(c) To guide professionals and, where appropriate, volunteers working with child victims and witnesses of crime in their day-to-day practice in the adult and juvenile justice process at the national, regional and international levels, consistent with the Declaration of Basic Principles of Justice for Victims of Crime and Abuse of Power;[2]

1 General Assembly resolution 44/25, annex.

2 General Assembly resolution 40/34, annex.

(d) To assist and support those caring for children in dealing sensitively with child victims and witnesses of crime.

4. In implementing the Guidelines, each jurisdiction should ensure that adequate training, selection and procedures are put in place to protect and meet the special needs of child victims and witnesses of crime, where the nature of the victimization affects categories of children differently, such as sexual assault of children, especially girls.

5. The Guidelines cover a field in which knowledge and practice are growing and improving. They are neither intended to be exhaustive nor to preclude further development, provided it is in harmony with their underlying objectives and principles.

6. The Guidelines could also be applied to processes in informal and customary systems of justice such as restorative justice and in non- criminal fields of law including, but not limited to, custody, divorce, adoption, child protection, mental health, citizenship, immigration and refugee law.

II Special Considerations

7. The Guidelines were developed:

(a) Cognizant that millions of children throughout the world suffer harm as a result of crime and abuse of power and that the rights of those children have not been adequately recognized and that they may suffer additional hardship when assisting in the justice process;

(b) Recognizing that children are vulnerable and require special protection appropriate to their age, level of maturity and individual special needs;

(c) Recognizing that girls are particularly vulnerable and may face discrimination at all stages of the justice system;

(d) Reaffirming that every effort must be made to prevent victimization of children, including through implementation of the Guidelines for the Prevention of Crime;[3]

(e) Cognizant that children who are victims and witnesses may suffer additional hardship if mistakenly viewed as offenders when they are in fact victims and witnesses;

(f) Recalling that the Convention on the Rights of the Child sets forth requirements and principles to secure effective recognition of the rights of children and that the Declaration of Basic Principles of Justice for Victims of Crime and Abuse of Power sets forth principles to provide

3 Resolution 2002/13, annex.

victims with the right to information, participation, protection, reparation and assistance;

(g) Recalling international and regional initiatives that implement the principles of the Declaration of Basic Principles of Justice for Victims of Crime and Abuse of Power, including the Handbook on Justice for Victims and the Guide for Policy Makers on the Declaration of Basic Principles, both issued by the United Nations Office for Drug Control and Crime Prevention in 1999;

(h) Recognizing the efforts of the International Bureau for Children's Rights in laying the groundwork for the development of guidelines on justice for child victims and witnesses of crime;

(i) Considering that improved responses to child victims and witnesses of crime can make children and their families more willing to disclose instances of victimization and more supportive of the justice process;

(j) Recalling that justice for child victims and witnesses of crime must be assured while safeguarding the rights of accused and convicted offenders;

(k) Bearing in mind the variety of legal systems and traditions, and noting that crime is increasingly transnational in nature and that there is a need to ensure that child victims and witnesses of crime receive equivalent protection in all countries.

III Principles

8. As stated in international instruments and in particular the Convention on the Rights of the Child as reflected in the work of the Committee on the Rights of the Child, and in order to ensure justice for child victims and witnesses of crime, professionals and others responsible for the well-being of those children must respect the following cross-cutting principles:

(a) Dignity. Every child is a unique and valuable human being and as such his or her individual dignity, special needs, interests and privacy should be respected and protected;

(b) Non-discrimination. Every child has the right to be treated fairly and equally, regardless of his or her or the parent's or legal guardian's race, ethnicity, colour, gender, language, religion, political or other opinion, national, ethnic or social origin, property, disability and birth or other status;

(c) Best interests of the child. While the rights of accused and convicted offenders should be safeguarded, every child has the right to have his or her best interests given primary consideration. This includes the right to protection and to a chance for harmonious development:

(i) Protection. Every child has the right to life and survival and to be shielded from any form of hardship, abuse or neglect, including physical, psychological, mental and emotional abuse and neglect;

(ii) Harmonious development. Every child has the right to a chance for harmonious development and to a standard of living adequate for physical, mental, spiritual, moral and social growth. In the case of a child who has been traumatized, every step should be taken to enable the child to enjoy healthy development;

(d) Right to participation. Every child has, subject to national procedural law, the right to express his or her views, opinions and beliefs freely, in his or her own words, and to contribute especially to the decisions affecting his or her life, including those taken in any judicial processes, and to have those views taken into consideration according to his or her abilities, age, intellectual maturity and evolving capacity.

IV Definitions

9. Throughout these Guidelines, the following definitions apply:

(a) "Child victims and witnesses" denotes children and adolescents, under the age of 18, who are victims of crime or witnesses to crime regardless of their role in the offence or in the prosecution of the alleged offender or groups of offenders;

(b) "Professionals" refers to persons who, within the context of their work, are in contact with child victims and witnesses of crime or are responsible for addressing the needs of children in the justice system and for whom these Guidelines are applicable. This includes, but is not limited to, the following: child and victim advocates and support persons; child protection service practitioners; child welfare agency staff; prosecutors and, where appropriate, defence lawyers; diplomatic and consular staff; domestic violence programme staff; judges; court staff; law enforcement officials; medical and mental health professionals; and social workers;

(c) "Justice process" encompasses detection of the crime, making of the complaint, investigation, prosecution and trial and post- trial procedures, regardless of whether the case is handled in a national, international or regional criminal justice system for adults or juveniles, or in a customary or informal system of justice;

(d) "Child-sensitive" denotes an approach that balances the child's right to protection and that takes into account the child's individual needs and views.

V The Right to Be Treated with Dignity and Compassion

10. Child victims and witnesses should be treated in a caring and sensitive manner throughout the justice process, taking into account their personal situation and immediate needs, age, gender, disability and level of maturity and fully respecting their physical, mental and moral integrity.
11. Every child should be treated as an individual with his or her individual needs, wishes and feelings.
12. Interference in the child's private life should be limited to the minimum needed at the same time as high standards of evidence collection are maintained in order to ensure fair and equitable outcomes of the justice process.
13. In order to avoid further hardship to the child, interviews, examinations and other forms of investigation should be conducted by trained professionals who proceed in a sensitive, respectful and thorough manner.
14. All interactions described in these Guidelines should be conducted in a child-sensitive manner in a suitable environment that accommodates the special needs of the child, according to his or her abilities, age, intellectual maturity and evolving capacity. They should also take place in a language that the child uses and understands.

VI The Right to Be Protected from Discrimination

15. Child victims and witnesses should have access to a justice process that protects them from discrimination based on the child's, parent's or legal guardian's race, colour, gender, language, religion, political or other opinion, national, ethnic or social origin, property, disability and birth or other status.
16. The justice process and support services available to child victims and witnesses and their families should be sensitive to the child's age, wishes, understanding, gender, sexual orientation, ethnic, cultural, religious, linguistic and social background, caste, socio-economic condition and immigration or refugee status, as well as to the special needs of the child, including health, abilities and capacities. Professionals should be trained and educated about such differences.

17. In certain cases, special services and protection will need to be instituted to take account of gender and the different nature of specific offences against children, such as sexual assault involving children.
18. Age should not be a barrier to a child's right to participate fully in the justice process. Every child should be treated as a capable witness, subject to examination, and his or her testimony should not be presumed invalid or untrustworthy by reason of the child's age alone as long as his or her age and maturity allow the giving of intelligible and credible testimony, with or without communication aids and other assistance.

VII The Right to Be Informed

19. Child victims and witnesses, their parents or guardians and legal representatives, from their first contact with the justice process and throughout that process, should be promptly and adequately informed, to the extent feasible and appropriate, of, inter alia:
(a) The availability of health, psychological, social and other relevant services as well as the means of accessing such services along with legal or other advice or representation, compensation and emergency financial support, where applicable;
(b) The procedures for the adult and juvenile criminal justice process, including the role of child victims and witnesses, the importance, timing and manner of testimony, and ways in which "questioning" will be conducted during the investigation and trial;
(c) The existing support mechanisms for the child when making a complaint and participating in the investigation and court proceedings;
(d) The specific places and times of hearings and other relevant events;
(e) The availability of protective measures;
(f) The existing mechanisms for review of decisions affecting child victims and witnesses;
(g) The relevant rights for child victims and witnesses pursuant to the Convention on the Rights of the Child and the Declaration of Basic Principles of Justice for Victims of Crime and Abuse of Power.

20. In addition, child victims, their parents or guardians and legal representatives should be promptly and adequately informed, to the extent feasible and appropriate, of:
(a) The progress and disposition of the specific case, including the apprehension, arrest and custodial status of the accused and any pending

changes to that status, the prosecutorial decision and relevant post-trial developments and the outcome of the case;

(b) The existing opportunities to obtain reparation from the offender or from the State through the justice process, through alternative civil proceedings or through other processes.

VIII The Right to Be Heard and to Express Views and Concerns

21. Professionals should make every effort to enable child victims and witnesses to express their views and concerns related to their involvement in the justice process, including by:

(a) Ensuring that child victims and where appropriate witnesses are consulted on the matters set forth in paragraph 19 above;

(b) Ensuring that child victims and witnesses are enabled to express freely and in their own manner their views and concerns regarding their involvement in the justice process, their concerns regarding safety in relation to the accused, the manner in which they prefer to provide testimony and their feelings about the conclusions of the process;

(c) Giving due regard to the child's views and concerns and, if they are unable to accommodate them, explain the reasons to the child.

IX The Right to Effective Assistance

22. Child victims and witnesses and, where appropriate, family members should have access to assistance provided by professionals who have received relevant training as set out in paragraphs 40 to 42 below. This may include assistance and support services such as financial, legal, counselling, health, social and educational services, physical and psychological recovery services and other services necessary for the child's reintegration. All such assistance should address the child's needs and enable him or her to participate effectively at all stages of the justice process.

23. In assisting child victims and witnesses, professionals should make every effort to coordinate support so that the child is not subjected to excessive interventions.

24. Child victims and witnesses should receive assistance from support persons, such as child victim/witness specialists, commencing at the initial report and continuing until such services are no longer required.

25. Professionals should develop and implement measures to make it easier for children to testify or give evidence to improve communication and understanding at the pre-trial and trial stages. These measures may include:

(a) Child victim and witness specialists to address the child's special needs;
(b) Support persons, including specialists and appropriate family members to accompany the child during testimony;
(c) Where appropriate, to appoint guardians to protect the child's legal interests.

X The Right to Privacy

26. Child victims and witnesses should have their privacy protected as a matter of primary importance.
27. Information relating to a child's involvement in the justice process should be protected. This can be achieved through maintaining confidentiality and restricting disclosure of information that may lead to identification of a child who is a victim or witness in the justice process.
28. Measures should be taken to protect children from undue exposure to the public by, for example, excluding the public and the media from the courtroom during the child's testimony, where permitted by national law.

XI The Right to Be Protected from Hardship during the Justice Process

29. Professionals should take measures to prevent hardship during the detection, investigation and prosecution process in order to ensure that the best interests and dignity of child victims and witnesses are respected.
30. Professionals should approach child victims and witnesses with sensitivity, so that they:

(a) Provide support for child victims and witnesses, including accompanying the child throughout his or her involvement in the justice process, when it is in his or her best interests;
(b) Provide certainty about the process, including providing child victims and witnesses with clear expectations as to what to expect in the process, with as much certainty as possible. The child's participation in hearings and trials should be planned ahead of time and every effort should be made to ensure continuity in the relationships between children and the professionals in contact with them throughout the process;

(c) Ensure that trials take place as soon as practical, unless delays are in the child's best interest. Investigation of crimes involving child victims and witnesses should also be expedited and there should be procedures, laws or court rules that provide for cases involving child victims and witnesses to be expedited;
(d) Use child-sensitive procedures, including interview rooms designed for children, interdisciplinary services for child victims integrated in the same location, modified court environments that take child witnesses into consideration, recesses during a child's testimony, hearings scheduled at times of day appropriate to the age and maturity of the child, an appropriate notification system to ensure the child goes to court only when necessary and other appropriate measures to facilitate the child's testimony.

31. Professionals should also implement measures:
(a) To limit the number of interviews: special procedures for collection of evidence from child victims and witnesses should be implemented in order to reduce the number of interviews, statements, hearings and, specifically, unnecessary contact with the justice process, such as through use of video recording;
(b) To ensure that child victims and witnesses are protected, if compatible with the legal system and with due respect for the rights of the defence, from being cross-examined by the alleged perpetrator: as necessary, child victims and witnesses should be interviewed, and examined in court, out of sight of the alleged perpetrator, and separate courthouse waiting rooms and private interview areas should be provided;
(c) To ensure that child victims and witnesses are questioned in a child-sensitive manner and allow for the exercise of supervision by judges, facilitate testimony and reduce potential intimidation, for example by using testimonial aids or appointing psychological experts.

XII The Right to Safety

32. Where the safety of a child victim or witness may be at risk, appropriate measures should be taken to require the reporting of those safety risks to appropriate authorities and to protect the child from such risk before, during and after the justice process.
33. Professionals who come into contact with children should be required to notify appropriate authorities if they suspect that a child victim or witness has been harmed, is being harmed or is likely to be harmed.

34. Professionals should be trained in recognizing and preventing intimidation, threats and harm to child victims and witnesses. Where child victims and witnesses may be the subject of intimidation, threats or harm, appropriate conditions should be put in place to ensure the safety of the child. Such safeguards could include:

(a) Avoiding direct contact between child victims and witnesses and the alleged perpetrators at any point in the justice process;
(b) Using court-ordered restraining orders supported by a registry system;
(c) Ordering pre-trial detention of the accused and setting special "no contact" bail conditions;
(d) Placing the accused under house arrest;
(e) Wherever possible and appropriate, giving child victims and witnesses protection by the police or other relevant agencies and safeguarding their whereabouts from disclosure.

XIII The Right to Reparation

35. Child victims should, wherever possible, receive reparation in order to achieve full redress, reintegration and recovery. Procedures for obtaining and enforcing reparation should be readily accessible and child-sensitive.
36. Provided the proceedings are child-sensitive and respect these Guidelines, combined criminal and reparations proceedings should be encouraged, together with informal and community justice procedures such as restorative justice.
37. Reparation may include restitution from the offender ordered in the criminal court, aid from victim compensation programmes administered by the State and damages ordered to be paid in civil proceedings. Where possible, costs of social and educational reintegration, medical treatment, mental health care and legal services should be addressed. Procedures should be instituted to ensure enforcement of reparation orders and payment of reparation before fines.

XIV The Right to Special Preventive Measures

38. In addition to preventive measures that should be in place for all children, special strategies are required for child victims and witnesses who are particularly vulnerable to recurring victimization or offending.

39. Professionals should develop and implement comprehensive and specially tailored strategies and interventions in cases where there are risks that child victims may be victimized further. These strategies and interventions should take into account the nature of the victimization, including victimization related to abuse in the home, sexual exploitation, abuse in institutional settings and trafficking. The strategies may include those based on government, neighbourhood and citizen initiatives.

XV Implementation

40. Adequate training, education and information should be made available to professionals, working with child victims and witnesses with a view to improving and sustaining specialized methods, approaches and attitudes in order to protect and deal effectively and sensitively with child victims and witnesses.
41. Professionals should be trained to effectively protect and meet the needs of child victims and witnesses, including in specialized units and services.
42. This training should include:
(a) Relevant human rights norms, standards and principles, including the rights of the child;
(b) Principles and ethical duties of their office;
(c) Signs and symptoms that indicate crimes against children;
(d) Crisis assessment skills and techniques, especially for making referrals, with an emphasis placed on the need for confidentiality;
(e) Impact, consequences, including negative physical and psychological effects, and trauma of crimes against children;
(f) Special measures and techniques to assist child victims and witnesses in the justice process;
(g) Cross-cultural and age-related linguistic, religious, social and gender issues;
(h) Appropriate adult-child communication skills;
(i) Interviewing and assessment techniques that minimize any trauma to the child while maximizing the quality of information received from the child;
(j) Skills to deal with child victims and witnesses in a sensitive, understanding, constructive and reassuring manner;
(k) Methods to protect and present evidence and to question child witnesses;
(l) Roles of, and methods used by, professionals working with child victims and witnesses.

43. Professionals should make every effort to adopt an interdisciplinary and cooperative approach in aiding children by familiarizing themselves with the wide array of available services, such as victim support, advocacy, economic assistance, counselling, education, health, legal and social services. This approach may include protocols for the different stages of the justice process to encourage cooperation among entities that provide services to child victims and witnesses, as well as other forms of multidisciplinary work that includes police, prosecutor, medical, social services and psychological personnel working in the same location.
44. International cooperation should be enhanced between States and all sectors of society, both at the national and international levels, including mutual assistance for the purpose of facilitating collection and exchange of information and the detection, investigation and prosecution of transnational crimes involving child victims and witnesses.
45. Professionals should consider utilizing the present Guidelines as a basis for developing laws and written policies, standards and protocols aimed at assisting child victims and witnesses involved in the justice process.
46. Professionals should be enabled to periodically review and evaluate their role, together with other agencies in the justice process, in ensuring the protection of the rights of the child and the effective implementation of the present Guidelines.

CHAPTER 33

Guidelines for the Alternative Care of Children

Adopted by General Assembly resolution 64/142 of 18 December 2009

I Purpose

1. The present Guidelines are intended to enhance the implementation of the Convention on the Rights of the Child and of relevant provisions of other international instruments regarding the protection and well-being of children who are deprived of parental care or who are at risk of being so.
2. Against the background of these international instruments and taking account of the developing body of knowledge and experience in this sphere, the Guidelines set out desirable orientations for policy and practice. They are designed for wide dissemination among all sectors directly or indirectly concerned with issues relating to alternative care, and seek in particular:
(a) To support efforts to keep children in, or return them to, the care of their family or, failing this, to find another appropriate and permanent solution, including adoption and kafala of Islamic law;
(b) To ensure that, while such permanent solutions are being sought, or in cases where they are not possible or are not in the best interests of the child, the most suitable forms of alternative care are identified and provided, under conditions that promote the child's full and harmonious development;
(c) To assist and encourage Governments to better implement their responsibilities and obligations in these respects, bearing in mind the economic, social and cultural conditions prevailing in each State; and
(d) To guide policies, decisions and activities of all concerned with social protection and child welfare in both the public and the private sectors, including civil society.

II General Principles and Perspectives

A *The Child and the Family*

3. The family being the fundamental group of society and the natural environment for the growth, well-being and protection of children, efforts should

primarily be directed to enabling the child to remain in or return to the care of his/her parents, or when appropriate, other close family members. The State should ensure that families have access to forms of support in the caregiving role.

4. Every child and young person should live in a supportive, protective and caring environment that promotes his/her full potential. Children with inadequate or no parental care are at special risk of being denied such a nurturing environment.

5. Where the child's own family is unable, even with appropriate support, to provide adequate care for the child, or abandons or relinquishes the child, the State is responsible for protecting the rights of the child and ensuring appropriate alternative care, with or through competent local authorities and duly authorized civil society organizations. It is the role of the State, through its competent authorities, to ensure the supervision of the safety, well-being and development of any child placed in alternative care and the regular review of the appropriateness of the care arrangement provided.

6. All decisions, initiatives and approaches falling within the scope of the present Guidelines should be made on a case-by-case basis, with a view, notably, to ensuring the child's safety and security, and must be grounded in the best interests and rights of the child concerned, in conformity with the principle of non-discrimination and taking due account of the gender perspective. They should respect fully the child's right to be consulted and to have his/her views duly taken into account in accordance with his/her evolving capacities, and on the basis of his/her access to all necessary information. Every effort should be made to enable such consultation and information provision to be carried out in the child's preferred language.

7. In applying the present Guidelines, determination of the best interests of the child shall be designed to identify courses of action for children deprived of parental care, or at risk of being so, that are best suited to satisfying their needs and rights, taking into account the full and personal development of their rights in their family, social and cultural environment and their status as subjects of rights, both at the time of the determination and in the longer term. The determination process should take account of, inter alia, the right of the child to be heard and to have his/her views taken into account in accordance with his/her age and maturity.

8. States should develop and implement comprehensive child welfare and protection policies within the framework of their overall social and human development policy, with attention to the improvement of existing alternative care provision, reflecting the principles contained in the present Guidelines.

9. As part of efforts to prevent the separation of children from their parents, States should seek to ensure appropriate and culturally sensitive measures:

(a) To support family caregiving environments whose capacities are limited by factors such as disability, drug and alcohol misuse, discrimination against families with indigenous or minority backgrounds, and living in armed conflict regions or under foreign occupation;

(b) To provide appropriate care and protection for vulnerable children, such as child victims of abuse and exploitation, abandoned children, children living on the street, children born out of wedlock, unaccompanied and separated children, internally displaced and refugee children, children of migrant workers, children of asylum-seekers, or children living with or affected by HIV/AIDS and other serious illnesses.

10. Special efforts should be made to tackle discrimination on the basis of any status of the child or parents, including poverty, ethnicity, religion, sex, mental and physical disability, HIV/AIDS or other serious illnesses, whether physical or mental, birth out of wedlock, and socio-economic stigma, and all other statuses and circumstances that can give rise to relinquishment, abandonment and/or removal of a child.

B *Alternative Care*

11. All decisions concerning alternative care should take full account of the desirability, in principle, of maintaining the child as close as possible to his/her habitual place of residence, in order to facilitate contact and potential reintegration with his/her family and to minimize disruption of his/her educational, cultural and social life.

12. Decisions regarding children in alternative care, including those in informal care, should have due regard for the importance of ensuring children a stable home and of meeting their basic need for safe and continuous attachment to their caregivers, with permanency generally being a key goal.

13. Children must be treated with dignity and respect at all times and must benefit from effective protection from abuse, neglect and all forms of exploitation, whether on the part of care providers, peers or third parties, in whatever care setting they may find themselves.

14. Removal of a child from the care of the family should be seen as a measure of last resort and should, whenever possible, be temporary and for the shortest possible duration. Removal decisions should be regularly reviewed and the child's return to parental care, once the original causes of removal have been resolved or have disappeared, should be in the best interests of the child, in keeping with the assessment foreseen in paragraph 49 below.

15. Financial and material poverty, or conditions directly and uniquely imputable to such poverty, should never be the only justification for the removal of a child from parental care, for receiving a child into alternative care, or for preventing his/her reintegration, but should be seen as a signal for the need to provide appropriate support to the family.

16. Attention must be paid to promoting and safeguarding all other rights of special pertinence to the situation of children without parental care, including, but not limited to, access to education, health and other basic services, the right to identity, freedom of religion or belief, language and protection of property and inheritance rights.

17. Siblings with existing bonds should in principle not be separated by placements in alternative care unless there is a clear risk of abuse or other justification in the best interests of the child. In any case, every effort should be made to enable siblings to maintain contact with each other, unless this is against their wishes or interests.

18. Recognizing that, in most countries, the majority of children without parental care are looked after informally by relatives or others, States should seek to devise appropriate means, consistent with the present Guidelines, to ensure their welfare and protection while in such informal care arrangements, with due respect for cultural, economic, gender and religious differences and practices that do not conflict with the rights and best interests of the child.

19. No child should be without the support and protection of a legal guardian or other recognized responsible adult or competent public body at any time.

20. The provision of alternative care should never be undertaken with a prime purpose of furthering the political, religious or economic goals of the providers.

21. The use of residential care should be limited to cases where such a setting is specifically appropriate, necessary and constructive for the individual child concerned and in his/her best interests.

22. In accordance with the predominant opinion of experts, alternative care for young children, especially those under the age of 3 years, should be provided in family-based settings. Exceptions to this principle may be warranted in order to prevent the separation of siblings and in cases where the placement is of an emergency nature or is for a predetermined and very limited duration, with planned family reintegration or other appropriate long-term care solution as its outcome.

23. While recognizing that residential care facilities and family-based care complement each other in meeting the needs of children, where large residential care facilities (institutions) remain, alternatives should be developed in the context of an overall deinstitutionalization strategy, with precise goals and objectives, which will allow for their progressive elimination. To this end,

States should establish care standards to ensure the quality and conditions that are conducive to the child's development, such as individualized and small-group care, and should evaluate existing facilities against these standards. Decisions regarding the establishment of, or permission to establish, new residential care facilities, whether public or private, should take full account of this deinstitutionalization objective and strategy.

Measures to Promote Application

24. States should, to the maximum extent of their available resources and, where appropriate, within the framework of development cooperation, allocate human and financial resources to ensure the optimal and progressive implementation of the present Guidelines throughout their respective territories in a timely manner. States should facilitate active cooperation among all relevant authorities and the mainstreaming of child and family welfare issues within all ministries directly or indirectly concerned.

25. States are responsible for determining any need for, and requesting, international cooperation in implementing the present Guidelines. Such requests should be given due consideration and should receive a favourable response wherever possible and appropriate. The enhanced implementation of the present Guidelines should figure in development cooperation programmes. When providing assistance to a State, foreign entities should abstain from any initiative inconsistent with the Guidelines.

26. Nothing in the present Guidelines should be interpreted as encouraging or condoning lower standards than those that may exist in given States, including in their legislation. Similarly, competent authorities, professional organizations and others are encouraged to develop national or professionally specific guidelines that build upon the letter and spirit of the present Guidelines.

III Scope of the Guidelines

The present Guidelines apply to the appropriate use and conditions of alternative formal care for all persons under the age of 18 years, unless, under the law applicable to the child, majority is attained earlier. Only where indicated do the Guidelines also apply to informal care settings, having due regard for both the important role played by the extended family and the community and the obligations of States for all children not in the care of their parents or legal and customary caregivers, as set out in the Convention on the Rights of the Child.

28. Principles in the present Guidelines are also applicable, as appropriate, to young persons already in alternative care and who need continuing care or

support for a transitional period after reaching the age of majority under applicable law.

29. For the purposes of the present Guidelines, and subject, notably, to the exceptions listed in paragraph 30 below, the following definitions shall apply:

(a) Children without parental care: all children not in the overnight care of at least one of their parents, for whatever reason and under whatever circumstances. Children without parental care who are outside their country of habitual residence or victims of emergency situations may be designated as:
   (i) "Unaccompanied" if they are not cared for by another relative or an adult who by law or custom is responsible for doing so; or
   (ii) "Separated" if they are separated from a previous legal or customary primary caregiver, but who may nevertheless be accompanied by another relative;

(b) Alternative care may take the form of:
   (i) Informal care: any private arrangement provided in a family environment, whereby the child is looked after on an ongoing or indefinite basis by relatives or friends (informal kinship care) or by others in their individual capacity, at the initiative of the child, his/her parents or other person without this arrangement having been ordered by an administrative or judicial authority or a duly accredited body;
   (ii) Formal care: all care provided in a family environment which has been ordered by a competent administrative body or judicial authority, and all care provided in a residential environment, including in private facilities, whether or not as a result of administrative or judicial measures;

(c) With respect to the environment where it is provided, alternative care may be:
   (i) Kinship care: family-based care within the child's extended family or with close friends of the family known to the child, whether formal or informal in nature;
   (ii) Foster care: situations where children are placed by a competent authority for the purpose of alternative care in the domestic environment of a family other than the children's own family that has been selected, qualified, approved and supervised for providing such care;
   (iii) Other forms of family-based or family-like care placements;
   (iv) Residential care: care provided in any non-family-based group setting, such as places of safety for emergency care, transit

centres in emergency situations, and all other short- and long-term residential care facilities, including group homes;

(v) Supervised independent living arrangements for children;

(d) With respect to those responsible for alternative care:

(i) Agencies are the public or private bodies and services that organize alternative care for children;

(ii) Facilities are the individual public or private establishments that provide residential care for children.

30. The scope of alternative care as foreseen in the present Guidelines does not extend, however, to:

(a) Persons under the age of 18 years who are deprived of their liberty by decision of a judicial or administrative authority as a result of being alleged as, accused of or recognized as having infringed the law, and whose situation is covered by the United Nations Standard Minimum Rules for the Administration of Juvenile Justice[1] and the United Nations Rules for the Protection of Juveniles Deprived of Their Liberty;[2]

(b) Care by adoptive parents from the moment the child concerned is effectively placed in their custody pursuant to a final adoption order, as of which moment, for the purposes of the present Guidelines, the child is considered to be in parental care. The Guidelines are, however, applicable to pre-adoption or probationary placement of a child with the prospective adoptive parents, as far as they are compatible with requirements governing such placements as stipulated in other relevant international instruments;

(c) Informal arrangements whereby a child voluntarily stays with relatives or friends for recreational purposes and reasons not connected with the parents' general inability or unwillingness to provide adequate care.

31. Competent authorities and others concerned are also encouraged to make use of the present Guidelines, as applicable, at boarding schools, hospitals, centres for children with mental and physical disabilities or other special needs, camps, the workplace and other places which may be responsible for the care of children.

1 Resolution 40/33, annex.

2 Resolution 45/113, annex.

IV Preventing the Need for Alternative Care

A *Promoting Parental Care*

32. States should pursue policies that ensure support for families in meeting their responsibilities towards the child and promote the right of the child to have a relationship with both parents. These policies should address the root causes of child abandonment, relinquishment and separation of the child from his/her family by ensuring, inter alia, the right to birth registration, and access to adequate housing and to basic health, education and social welfare services, as well as by promoting measures to combat poverty, discrimination, marginalization, stigmatization, violence, child maltreatment and sexual abuse, and substance abuse.

33. States should develop and implement consistent and mutually reinforcing family-oriented policies designed to promote and strengthen parents' ability to care for their children.

34. States should implement effective measures to prevent child abandonment, relinquishment and separation of the child from his/her family. Social policies and programmes should, inter alia, empower families with attitudes, skills, capacities and tools to enable them to provide adequately for the protection, care and development of their children. The complementary capacities of the State and civil society, including non-governmental and community-based organizations, religious leaders and the media should be engaged to this end. These social protection measures should include:

(a) Family strengthening services, such as parenting courses and sessions, the promotion of positive parent-child relationships, conflict resolution skills, opportunities for employment and income generation and, where required, social assistance;

(b) Supportive social services, such as day care, mediation and conciliation services, substance abuse treatment, financial assistance, and services for parents and children with disabilities. Such services, preferably of an integrated and non-intrusive nature, should be directly accessible at the community level and should actively involve the participation of families as partners, combining their resources with those of the community and the carer;

(c) Youth policies aiming at empowering youth to face positively the challenges of everyday life, including when they decide to leave the parental home, and preparing future parents to make informed decisions regarding their sexual and reproductive health and to fulfil their responsibilities in this respect.

35. Various complementary methods and techniques should be used for family support, varying throughout the process of support, such as home visits, group meetings with other families, case conferences and securing commitments by the family concerned. They should be directed towards both facilitating intrafamilial relationships and promoting the family's integration within its community.

36. Special attention should be paid, in accordance with local laws, to the provision and promotion of support and care services for single and adolescent parents and their children, whether or not born out of wedlock. States should ensure that adolescent parents retain all rights inherent to their status both as parents and as children, including access to all appropriate services for their own development, allowances to which parents are entitled, and their inheritance rights. Measures should be adopted to ensure the protection of pregnant adolescents and to guarantee that they do not interrupt their studies. Efforts should also be made to reduce the stigma attached to single and adolescent parenthood.

37. Support and services should be available to siblings who have lost their parents or caregivers and choose to remain together in their household, to the extent that the eldest sibling is both willing and deemed capable of acting as the household head. States should ensure, including through the appointment of a legal guardian, a recognized responsible adult or, where appropriate, a public body legally mandated to act as guardian, as stipulated in paragraph 19 above, that such households benefit from mandatory protection from all forms of exploitation and abuse, and supervision and support on the part of the local community and its competent services, such as social workers, with particular concern for the children's health, housing, education and inheritance rights. Special attention should be given to ensuring that the head of such a household retains all rights inherent to his/her child status, including access to education and leisure, in addition to his/her rights as a household head.

38. States should ensure opportunities for day care, including all-day schooling, and respite care which would enable parents better to cope with their overall responsibilities towards the family, including additional responsibilities inherent in caring for children with special needs.

Preventing Family Separation

39. Proper criteria based on sound professional principles should be developed and consistently applied for assessing the child's and the family's situation, including the family's actual and potential capacity to care for the child, in cases where the competent authority or agency has reasonable grounds to believe that the well-being of the child is at risk.

40. Decisions regarding removal or reintegration should be based on this assessment and should be made by suitably qualified and trained professionals, on behalf of or authorized by a competent authority, in full consultation with all concerned and bearing in mind the need to plan for the child's future.

41. States are encouraged to adopt measures for the integral protection and guarantee of rights during pregnancy, birth and the breastfeeding period, in order to ensure conditions of dignity and equality for the adequate development of the pregnancy and the care of the child. Therefore, support programmes should be provided to future mothers and fathers, particularly adolescent parents, who have difficulty exercising their parental responsibilities. Such programmes should aim at empowering mothers and fathers to exercise their parental responsibilities in conditions of dignity and at avoiding their being induced to surrender their child because of their vulnerability.

42. When a child is relinquished or abandoned, States should ensure that this may take place in conditions of confidentiality and safety for the child, respecting his/her right to access information on his/her origins where appropriate and possible under the law of the State.

43. States should formulate clear policies to address situations where a child has been abandoned anonymously, which indicate whether and how family tracing should be undertaken and reunification or placement within the extended family pursued. Policies should also allow for timely decision-making on the child's eligibility for permanent family placement and for arranging such placements expeditiously.

44. When a public or private agency or facility is approached by a parent or legal guardian wishing to relinquish a child permanently, the State should ensure that the family receives counselling and social support to encourage and enable them to continue to care for the child. If this fails, a social worker or other appropriate professional assessment should be undertaken to determine whether there are other family members who wish to take permanent responsibility for the child, and whether such arrangements would be in the best interests of the child. Where such arrangements are not possible or are not in the best interests of the child, efforts should be made to find a permanent family placement within a reasonable period.

45. When a public or private agency or facility is approached by a parent or caregiver wishing to place a child in care for a short or indefinite period, the State should ensure the availability of counselling and social support to encourage and enable him or her to continue to care for the child. A child should be admitted to alternative care only when such efforts have been exhausted and acceptable and justified reasons for entry into care exist.

46. Specific training should be provided to teachers and others working with children in order to help them to identify situations of abuse, neglect, exploitation or risk of abandonment and to refer such situations to competent bodies.
47. Any decision to remove a child against the will of his/her parents must be made by competent authorities, in accordance with applicable law and procedures and subject to judicial review, the parents being assured the right of appeal and access to appropriate legal representation.
48. When the child's sole or main carer may be the subject of deprivation of liberty as a result of preventive detention or sentencing decisions, non-custodial remand measures and sentences should be taken in appropriate cases wherever possible, the best interests of the child being given due consideration. States should take into account the best interests of the child when deciding whether to remove children born in prison and children living in prison with a parent. The removal of such children should be treated in the same way as other instances where separation is considered. Best efforts should be made to ensure that children remaining in custody with their parent benefit from adequate care and protection, while guaranteeing their own status as free individuals and access to activities in the community.

B *Promoting Family Reintegration*

49. In order to prepare and support the child and the family for his/her possible return to the family, his/her situation should be assessed by a duly designated individual or team with access to multidisciplinary advice, in consultation with the different actors involved (the child, the family, the alternative caregiver), so as to decide whether the reintegration of the child in the family is possible and in the best interests of the child, which steps this would involve and under whose supervision.
50. The aims of the reintegration and the family's and alternative caregiver's principal tasks in this respect should be set out in writing and agreed on by all concerned.
51. Regular and appropriate contact between the child and his/her family specifically for the purpose of reintegration should be developed, supported and monitored by the competent body.
52. Once decided, the reintegration of the child in his/her family should be designed as a gradual and supervised process, accompanied by follow-up and support measures that take account of the child's age, needs and evolving capacities, as well as the cause of the separation.

V Framework of Care Provision

53. In order to meet the specific psychoemotional, social and other needs of each child without parental care, States should take all necessary measures to ensure that the legislative, policy and financial conditions exist to provide for adequate alternative care options, with priority to family- and community-based solutions.
54. States should ensure the availability of a range of alternative care options, consistent with the general principles of the present Guidelines, for emergency, short-term and long-term care.
55. States should ensure that all entities and individuals engaged in the provision of alternative care for children receive due authorization to do so from a competent authority and are subject to regular monitoring and review by the latter in keeping with the present Guidelines. To this end, these authorities should develop appropriate criteria for assessing the professional and ethical fitness of care providers and for their accreditation, monitoring and supervision.
56. With regard to informal care arrangements for the child, whether within the extended family, with friends or with other parties, States should, where appropriate, encourage such carers to notify the competent authorities accordingly so that they and the child may receive any necessary financial and other support that would promote the child's welfare and protection. Where possible and appropriate, States should encourage and enable informal caregivers, with the consent of the child and parents concerned, to formalize the care arrangement after a suitable lapse of time, to the extent that the arrangement has proved to be in the best interests of the child to date and is expected to continue in the foreseeable future.

VI Determination of the Most Appropriate Form of Care

57. Decision-making on alternative care in the best interests of the child should take place through a judicial, administrative or other adequate and recognized procedure, with legal safeguards, including, where appropriate, legal representation on behalf of children in any legal proceedings. It should be based on rigorous assessment, planning and review, through established structures and mechanisms, and should be carried out on a case-by-case basis, by suitably qualified professionals in a multidisciplinary team, wherever possible. It should involve full consultation at all stages with the child, according to his/her evolving capacities, and with his/her parents or legal guardians. To

this end, all concerned should be provided with the necessary information on which to base their opinion. States should make every effort to provide adequate resources and channels for the training and recognition of the professionals responsible for determining the best form of care so as to facilitate compliance with these provisions.

58. Assessment should be carried out expeditiously, thoroughly and carefully. It should take into account the child's immediate safety and well-being, as well as his/her longer-term care and development, and should cover the child's personal and developmental characteristics, ethnic, cultural, linguistic and religious background, family and social environment, medical history and any special needs.

59. The resulting initial and review reports should be used as essential tools for planning decisions from the time of their acceptance by the competent authorities onwards, with a view to, inter alia, avoiding undue disruption and contradictory decisions.

60. Frequent changes in care setting are detrimental to the child's development and ability to form attachments, and should be avoided. Short-term placements should aim at enabling an appropriate permanent solution to be arranged. Permanency for the child should be secured without undue delay through reintegration in his/her nuclear or extended family or, if this is not possible, in an alternative stable family setting or, where paragraph 21 above applies, in stable and appropriate residential care.

61. Planning for care provision and permanency should be carried out from the earliest possible time, ideally before the child enters care, taking into account the immediate and longer-term advantages and disadvantages of each option considered, and should comprise short- and long-term propositions.

62. Planning for care provision and permanency should be based on, notably, the nature and quality of the child's attachment to his/her family, the family's capacity to safeguard the child's well-being and harmonious development, the child's need or desire to feel part of a family, the desirability of the child remaining within his/her community and country, the child's cultural, linguistic and religious background, and the child's relationships with siblings, with a view to avoiding their separation.

63. The plan should clearly state, inter alia, the goals of the placement and the measures to achieve them.

64. The child and his/her parents or legal guardians should be fully informed about the alternative care options available, the implications of each option and their rights and obligations in the matter.

65. The preparation, enforcement and evaluation of a protective measure for a child should be carried out, to the greatest extent possible, with the

participation of his/her parents or legal guardians and potential foster carers and caregivers, with respect to his/her particular needs, convictions and special wishes. At the request of the child, parents or legal guardians, other important persons in the child's life may also be consulted in any decision-making process, at the discretion of the competent authority.

66. States should ensure that any child who has been placed in alternative care by a properly constituted court, tribunal or administrative or other competent body, as well as his/her parents or others with parental responsibility, are given the opportunity to make representations on the placement decision before a court, are informed of their rights to make such representations and are assisted in doing so.

67. States should ensure the right of any child who has been placed in temporary care to regular and thorough review – preferably at least every three months – of the appropriateness of his/her care and treatment, taking into account, notably, his/her personal development and any changing needs, developments in his/her family environment, and the adequacy and necessity of the current placement in these circumstances. The review should be carried out by duly qualified and authorized persons, and should fully involve the child and all relevant persons in the child's life.

68. The child should be prepared for all changes of care settings resulting from the planning and review processes.

VII Provision of Alternative Care

A *Policies*

69. It is a responsibility of the State or appropriate level of government to ensure the development and implementation of coordinated policies regarding formal and informal care for all children who are without parental care. Such policies should be based on sound information and statistical data. They should define a process for determining who has responsibility for a child, taking into account the role of the child's parents or principal caregivers in his/her protection, care and development. Presumptive responsibility, unless shown to be otherwise, is with the child's parents or principal caregivers.

70. All State entities involved in the referral of, and assistance to, children without parental care, in cooperation with civil society, should adopt policies and procedures which favour information-sharing and networking between agencies and individuals in order to ensure effective care, aftercare and protection for these children. The location and/or design of the agency responsible for

the oversight of alternative care should be established so as to maximize its accessibility to those who require the services provided.

71. Special attention should be paid to the quality of alternative care provision, both in residential and in family-based care, in particular with regard to the professional skills, selection, training and supervision of carers. Their role and functions should be clearly defined and clarified with respect to those of the child's parents or legal guardians.

72. In each country, the competent authorities should draw up a document setting out the rights of children in alternative care in keeping with the present Guidelines. Children in alternative care should be enabled to understand fully the rules, regulations and objectives of the care setting and their rights and obligations therein.

73. All alternative care provision should be based on a written statement of the provider's aims and objectives in providing the service and the nature of the provider's responsibilities to the child that reflects the standards set by the Convention on the Rights of the Child, the present Guidelines and applicable law.

All providers should be appropriately qualified or approved in accordance with legal requirements to provide alternative care services.

74. A regulatory framework should be established to ensure a standard process for the referral or admission of a child to an alternative care setting.

75. Cultural and religious practices regarding the provision of alternative care, including those related to gender perspectives, should be respected and promoted to the extent that they can be shown to be consistent with the rights and best interests of the children. The process of considering whether such practices should be promoted should be carried out in a broadly participatory way, involving the cultural and religious leaders concerned, professionals and those caring for children without parental care, parents and other relevant stakeholders, as well as the children themselves.

1 Informal Care

76. With a view to ensuring that appropriate conditions of care are met in informal care provided by individuals or families, States should recognize the role played by this type of care and take adequate measures to support its optimal provision on the basis of an assessment of which particular settings may require special assistance or oversight.

77. Competent authorities should, where appropriate, encourage informal carers to notify the care arrangement and should seek to ensure their access to all available services and benefits likely to assist them in discharging their duty to care for and protect the child.

78. The State should recognize the de facto responsibility of informal carers for the child.
79. States should devise special and appropriate measures designed to protect children in informal care from abuse, neglect, child labour and all other forms of exploitation, with particular attention to informal care provided by non-relatives, or by relatives previously unknown to the children or living far from the children's habitual place of residence.

2 General Conditions Applying to All Forms of Formal Alternative Care Arrangements

80. The transfer of a child into alternative care should be carried out with the utmost sensitivity and in a child-friendly manner, in particular involving specially trained and, in principle, non-uniformed personnel.
81. When a child is placed in alternative care, contact with his/her family, as well as with other persons close to him or her, such as friends, neighbours and previous carers, should be encouraged and facilitated, in keeping with the child's protection and best interests. The child should have access to information on the situation of his/her family members in the absence of contact with them.
82. States should pay special attention to ensuring that children in alternative care because of parental imprisonment or prolonged hospitalization have the opportunity to maintain contact with their parents and receive any necessary counselling and support in that regard.
83. Carers should ensure that children receive adequate amounts of wholesome and nutritious food in accordance with local dietary habits and relevant dietary standards, as well as with the children's religious beliefs. Appropriate nutritional supplementation should also be provided when necessary.
84. Carers should promote the health of the children for whom they are responsible and make arrangements to ensure that medical care, counselling and support are made available as required.
85. Children should have access to formal, non-formal and vocational education in accordance with their rights, to the maximum extent possible in educational facilities in the local community.
86. Carers should ensure that the right of every child, including children with disabilities, living with or affected by HIV/AIDS or having any other special needs, to develop through play and leisure activities is respected and that opportunities for such activities are created within and outside the care setting. Contact with the children and others in the local community should be encouraged and facilitated.
87. The specific safety, health, nutritional, developmental and other needs of babies and young children, including those with special needs, should be

catered for in all care settings, including ensuring their ongoing attachment to a specific carer.

88. Children should be allowed to satisfy the needs of their religious and spiritual life, including by receiving visits from a qualified representative of their religion, and to freely decide whether or not to participate in religious services, religious education or counselling. The child's own religious background should be respected, and no child should be encouraged or persuaded to change his/her religion or belief during a care placement.

89. All adults responsible for children should respect and promote the right to privacy, including appropriate facilities for hygiene and sanitary needs, respecting gender differences and interaction, and adequate, secure and accessible storage space for personal possessions.

90. Carers should understand the importance of their role in developing positive, safe and nurturing relationships with children, and should be able to do so.

91. Accommodation in all alternative care settings should meet the requirements of health and safety.

92. States must ensure through their competent authorities that accommodation provided to children in alternative care, and their supervision in such placements, enable them to be effectively protected against abuse. Particular attention needs to be paid to the age, maturity and degree of vulnerability of each child in determining his/her living arrangements. Measures aimed at protecting children in care should be in conformity with the law and should not involve unreasonable constraints on their liberty and conduct in comparison with children of similar age in their community.

93. All alternative care settings should provide adequate protection to children from abduction, trafficking, sale and all other forms of exploitation. Any consequent constraints on their liberty and conduct should be no more than are strictly necessary to ensure their effective protection from such acts.

94. All carers should promote and encourage children and young people to develop and exercise informed choices, taking account of acceptable risks and the child's age, and according to his/her evolving capacities.

95. States, agencies and facilities, schools and other community services should take appropriate measures to ensure that children in alternative care are not stigmatized during or after their placement. This should include efforts to minimize the identification of children as being looked after in an alternative care setting.

96. All disciplinary measures and behaviour management constituting torture, cruel, inhuman or degrading treatment, including closed or solitary confinement or any other forms of physical or psychological violence that are likely to compromise the physical or mental health of the child, must be strictly

prohibited in conformity with international human rights law. States must take all necessary measures to prevent such practices and ensure that they are punishable by law. Restriction of contact with members of the child's family and other persons of special importance to the child should never be used as a sanction.

97. Use of force and restraints of whatever nature should not be authorized unless strictly necessary for safeguarding the child's or others' physical or psychological integrity, in conformity with the law and in a reasonable and proportionate manner and with respect for the fundamental rights of the child. Restraint by means of drugs and medication should be based on therapeutic needs and should never be employed without evaluation and prescription by a specialist.

98. Children in care should be offered access to a person of trust in whom they may confide in total confidentiality. This person should be designated by the competent authority with the agreement of the child concerned. The child should be informed that legal or ethical standards may require breaching confidentiality under certain circumstances.

99. Children in care should have access to a known, effective and impartial mechanism whereby they can notify complaints or concerns regarding their treatment or conditions of placement. Such mechanisms should include initial consultation, feedback, implementation and further consultation. Young people with previous care experience should be involved in this process, due weight being given to their opinions. This process should be conducted by competent persons trained to work with children and young people.

100. To promote the child's sense of self-identity, a life story book comprising appropriate information, pictures, personal objects and mementoes regarding each step of the child's life should be maintained with the child's participation and made available to the child throughout his/her life.

B *Legal Responsibility for the Child*

101. In situations where the child's parents are absent or are incapable of making day-to-day decisions in the best interests of the child, and the child's placement in alternative care has been ordered or authorized by a competent administrative body or judicial authority, a designated individual or competent entity should be vested with the legal right and responsibility to make such decisions in the place of parents, in full consultation with the child. States should ensure that a mechanism is in place for designating such an individual or entity.

102. Such legal responsibility should be attributed by the competent authorities and be supervised directly by them or through formally accredited entities,

including non-governmental organizations. Accountability for the actions of the individual or entity concerned should lie with the designating body.

103. Persons exercising such legal responsibility should be reputable individuals with relevant knowledge of children's issues, an ability to work directly with children and an understanding of any special and cultural needs of the children to be entrusted to them. They should receive appropriate training and professional support in this regard. They should be in a position to make independent and impartial decisions that are in the best interests of the children concerned and that promote and safeguard each child's welfare.

104. The role and specific responsibilities of the designated person or entity should include:

(a) Ensuring that the rights of the child are protected and, in particular, that the child has appropriate care, accommodation, health-care provision, developmental opportunities, psychosocial support, education and language support;

(b) Ensuring that the child has access to legal and other representation where necessary, consulting with the child so that the child's views are taken into account by decision-making authorities, and advising and keeping the child informed of his/her rights;

(c) Contributing to the identification of a stable solution in the best interests of the child;

(d) Providing a link between the child and various organizations that may provide services to the child;

(e) Assisting the child in family tracing;

(f) Ensuring that, if repatriation or family reunification is carried out, it is done in the best interests of the child;

(g) Helping the child to keep in touch with his/her family, when appropriate.

1 Agencies and Facilities Responsible for Formal Care

105. Legislation should stipulate that all agencies and facilities must be registered and authorized to operate by social welfare services or another competent authority, and that failure to comply with such legislation constitutes an offence punishable by law. Authorization should be granted and be regularly reviewed by the competent authorities on the basis of standard criteria covering, at a minimum, the agency's or facility's objectives, functioning, staff recruitment and qualifications, conditions of care and financial resources and management.

106. All agencies and facilities should have written policy and practice statements, consistent with the present Guidelines, setting out clearly their aims, policies, methods and the standards applied for the recruitment, monitoring,

supervision and evaluation of qualified and suitable carers to ensure that those aims are met.

107. All agencies and facilities should develop a staff code of conduct, consistent with the present Guidelines, that defines the role of each professional and of the carers in particular and includes clear reporting procedures on allegations of misconduct by any team member.

108. The forms of financing care provision should never be such as to encourage a child's unnecessary placement or prolonged stay in care arrangements organized or provided by an agency or facility.

109. Comprehensive and up-to-date records should be maintained regarding the administration of alternative care services, including detailed files on all children in their care, staff employed and financial transactions.

110. The records on children in care should be complete, up to date, confidential and secure, and should include information on their admission and departure and the form, content and details of the care placement of each child, together with any appropriate identity documents and other personal information. Information on the child's family should be included in the child's file as well as in the reports based on regular evaluations. This record should follow the child throughout the alternative care period and be consulted by duly authorized professionals responsible for his/her current care.

111. The above-mentioned records could be made available to the child, as well as to the parents or guardians, within the limits of the child's right to privacy and confidentiality, as appropriate. Appropriate counselling should be provided before, during and after consultation of the record.

112. All alternative care services should have a clear policy on maintaining the confidentiality of information pertaining to each child, which all carers are aware of and adhere to.

113. As a matter of good practice, all agencies and facilities should systematically ensure that, prior to employment, carers and other staff in direct contact with children undergo an appropriate and comprehensive assessment of their suitability to work with children.

114. Conditions of work, including remuneration, for carers employed by agencies and facilities should be such as to maximize motivation, job satisfaction and continuity, and hence their disposition to fulfil their role in the most appropriate and effective manner.

115. Training should be provided to all carers on the rights of children without parental care and on the specific vulnerability of children, in particularly difficult situations, such as emergency placements or placements outside their area of habitual residence. Cultural, social, gender and religious sensitization should also be assured. States should also provide adequate resources

and channels for the recognition of these professionals in order to favour the implementation of these provisions.

116. Training in dealing appropriately with challenging behaviour, including conflict resolution techniques and means to prevent acts of harm or self-harm, should be provided to all care staff employed by agencies and facilities.

117. Agencies and facilities should ensure that, wherever appropriate, carers are prepared to respond to children with special needs, notably those living with HIV/AIDS or other chronic physical or mental illnesses, and children with physical or mental disabilities.

2 Foster Care

118. The competent authority or agency should devise a system, and should train concerned staff accordingly, to assess and match the needs of the child with the abilities and resources of potential foster carers and to prepare all concerned for the placement.

119. A pool of accredited foster carers should be identified in each locality who can provide children with care and protection while maintaining ties to family, community and cultural group.

120. Special preparation, support and counselling services for foster carers should be developed and made available to carers at regular intervals, before, during and after the placement.

121. Carers should have, within fostering agencies and other systems involved with children without parental care, the opportunity to make their voice heard and to influence policy.

122. Encouragement should be given to the establishment of associations of foster carers that can provide important mutual support and contribute to practice and policy development.

C *Residential Care*

123. Facilities providing residential care should be small and be organized around the rights and needs of the child, in a setting as close as possible to a family or small group situation. Their objective should generally be to provide temporary care and to contribute actively to the child's family reintegration or, if this is not possible, to secure his/her stable care in an alternative family setting, including through adoption or kafala of Islamic law, where appropriate.

124. Measures should be taken so that, where necessary and appropriate, a child solely in need of protection and alternative care may be accommodated separately from children who are subject to the criminal justice system.

125. The competent national or local authority should establish rigorous screening procedures to ensure that only appropriate admissions to such facilities are made.
126. States should ensure that there are sufficient carers in residential care settings to allow individualized attention and to give the child, where appropriate, the opportunity to bond with a specific carer. Carers should also be deployed within the care setting in such a way as to implement effectively its aims and objectives and ensure child protection.
127. Laws, policies and regulations should prohibit the recruitment and solicitation of children for placement in residential care by agencies, facilities or individuals.

D *Inspection and Monitoring*

128. Agencies, facilities and professionals involved in care provision should be accountable to a specific public authority, which should ensure, inter alia, frequent inspections comprising both scheduled and unannounced visits, involving discussion with and observation of the staff and the children.
129. To the extent possible and appropriate, inspection functions should include a component of training and capacity-building for care providers.
130. States should be encouraged to ensure that an independent monitoring mechanism is in place, with due consideration for the principles relating to the status of national institutions for the promotion and protection of human rights (the Paris Principles).[3] The monitoring mechanism should be easily accessible to children, parents and those responsible for children without parental care. The functions of the monitoring mechanism should include:
(a) Consulting in conditions of privacy with children in all forms of alternative care, visiting the care settings in which they live and undertaking investigations into any alleged situation of violation of children's rights in those settings, on complaint or on its own initiative;
(b) Recommending relevant policies to appropriate authorities with the aim of improving the treatment of children deprived of parental care and ensuring that it is in keeping with the preponderance of research findings on child protection, health, development and care;
(c) Submitting proposals and observations concerning draft legislation;
(d) Contributing independently to the reporting process under the Convention on the Rights of the Child,2 including to periodic State

3 Resolution 48/134, annex.

party reports to the Committee on the Rights of the Child with regard to the implementation of the present Guidelines.

E *Support for Aftercare*

131. Agencies and facilities should have a clear policy and should carry out agreed procedures relating to the planned and unplanned conclusion of their work with children to ensure appropriate aftercare and/or follow-up. Throughout the period of care, they should systematically aim at preparing children to assume self-reliance and to integrate fully in the community, notably through the acquisition of social and life skills, which are fostered by participation in the life of the local community.

132. The process of transition from care to aftercare should take into consideration children's gender, age, maturity and particular circumstances and include counselling and support, notably to avoid exploitation. Children leaving care should be encouraged to take part in the planning of aftercare life. Children with special needs, such as disabilities, should benefit from an appropriate support system, ensuring, inter alia, avoidance of unnecessary institutionalization. Both the public and the private sectors should be encouraged, including through incentives, to employ children from different care services, particularly children with special needs.

133. Special efforts should be made to allocate to each child, whenever possible, a specialized person who can facilitate his/her independence when leaving care.

134. Aftercare should be prepared as early as possible in the placement and, in any case, well before the child leaves the care setting.

135. Ongoing educational and vocational training opportunities should be imparted as part of life skills education to young people leaving care in order to help them to become financially independent and generate their own income.

136. Access to social, legal and health services, together with appropriate financial support, should also be provided to young people leaving care and during aftercare.

VIII Care Provision for Children Outside Their Country of Habitual Residence

A *Placement of a Child for Care Abroad*

137. The present Guidelines should apply to all public and private entities and all persons involved in arrangements for a child to be sent for care to a country

other than his/her country of habitual residence, whether for medical treatment, temporary hosting, respite care or any other reason.
138. States concerned should ensure that a designated body has responsibility for determining specific standards to be met regarding, in particular, the criteria for selecting carers in the host country and the quality of care and follow-up, as well as for supervising and monitoring the operation of such schemes. To ensure appropriate international cooperation and child protection in such situations, States are encouraged to ratify or accede to the Hague Convention on Jurisdiction, Applicable Law, Recognition, Enforcement and Cooperation in respect of Parental Responsibility and Measures for the Protection of Children, of 19 October 1996.98.

B *Provision of Care for a Child Already Abroad*

140. The present Guidelines, as well as other relevant international provisions, should apply to all public and private entities and all persons involved in arrangements for a child needing care while in a country other than his/her country of habitual residence, for whatever reason.
141. Unaccompanied or separated children already abroad should, in principle, enjoy the same level of protection and care as national children in the country concerned.
142. In determining appropriate care provision, the diversity and disparity of unaccompanied or separated children (such as ethnic and migratory background or cultural and religious diversity) should be taken into consideration on a case-by-case basis.
143. Unaccompanied or separated children, including those who arrive irregularly in a country, should not, in principle, be deprived of their liberty solely for having breached any law governing access to and stay within the territory.
144. Child victims of trafficking should neither be detained in police custody nor subjected to penalties for their involvement under compulsion in unlawful activities.
145. As soon as an unaccompanied child is identified, States are strongly encouraged to appoint a guardian or, where necessary, representation by an organization responsible for his/her care and well-being to accompany the child throughout the status determination and decision-making process.
146. As soon as an unaccompanied or separated child is taken into care, all reasonable efforts should be made to trace his/her family and re-establish family ties, when this is in the best interests of the child and would not endanger those involved.
147. In order to assist in planning the future of an unaccompanied or separated child in a manner that best protects his/her rights, relevant State and social

service authorities should make all reasonable efforts to procure documentation and information in order to conduct an assessment of the child's risk and social and family conditions in his/her country of habitual residence.

148. Unaccompanied or separated children must not be returned to their country of habitual residence:

(a) If, following the risk and security assessment, there are reasons to believe that the child's safety and security are in danger;

(b) Unless, prior to the return, a suitable caregiver, such as a parent, other relative, other adult caretaker, a Government agency or an authorized agency or facility in the country of origin, has agreed and is able to take responsibility for the child and provide him or her with appropriate care and protection;

(c) If, for other reasons, it is not in the best interests of the child, according to the assessment of the competent authorities.

149. With the above aims in mind, cooperation among States, regions, local authorities and civil society associations should be promoted, strengthened and enhanced.

150. The effective involvement of consular services or, failing that, legal representatives of the country of origin should be foreseen, when this is in the best interests of the child and would not endanger the child or his/her family.

151. Those responsible for the welfare of an unaccompanied or separated child should facilitate regular communication between the child and his/her family, except where this is against the child's wishes or is demonstrably not in his/her best interests.

152. Placement with a view to adoption or kafala of Islamic law should not be considered a suitable initial option for an unaccompanied or separated child. States are encouraged to consider this option only after efforts to determine the location of his/her parents, extended family or habitual carers have been exhausted.

IX Care in Emergency Situations

A *Application of the Guidelines*

153. The present Guidelines should continue to apply in situations of emergency arising from natural and man-made disasters, including international and non-international armed conflicts, as well as foreign occupation. Individuals and organizations wishing to work on behalf of children without parental care in emergency situations are strongly encouraged to operate in accordance with the Guidelines.

154. In such circumstances, the State or de facto authorities in the region concerned, the international community and all local, national, foreign and international agencies providing or intending to provide child-focused services should pay special attention:

(a) To ensure that all entities and persons involved in responding to unaccompanied or separated children are sufficiently experienced, trained, resourceful and equipped to do so in an appropriate manner;
(b) To develop, as necessary, temporary and long-term family-based care;
(c) To use residential care only as a temporary measure until family-based care can be developed;
(d) To prohibit the establishment of new residential facilities structured to provide simultaneous care to large groups of children on a permanent or long-term basis;
(e) To prevent the cross-border displacement of children, except under the circumstances described in paragraph 160 below;
(f) To make cooperation with family tracing and reintegration efforts mandatory.

Preventing Separation

155. Organizations and authorities should make every effort to prevent the separation of children from their parents or primary caregivers, unless the best interests of the child so require, and ensure that their actions do not inadvertently encourage family separation by providing services and benefits to children alone rather than to families.

156. Separation initiated by the child's parents or other primary caregivers should be prevented by:

(a) Ensuring that all households have access to basic food and medical supplies and other services, including education;
(b) Limiting the development of residential care options and restricting their use to those situations where it is absolutely necessary.

B *Care Arrangements*

157. Communities should be assisted in playing an active role in monitoring and responding to care and protection issues facing children in their local context.

158. Care within a child's own community, including fostering, should be encouraged, as it provides continuity in socialization and development.

159. As unaccompanied or separated children may be at heightened risk of abuse and exploitation, monitoring and specific support to carers should be foreseen to ensure their protection.

160. Children in emergency situations should not be moved to a country other than that of their habitual residence for alternative care except temporarily for compelling health, medical or safety reasons. In that case, this should be as close as possible to their home, they should be accompanied by a parent or caregiver known to them, and a clear return plan should be established.
161. Should family reintegration prove impossible within an appropriate period or be deemed contrary to the best interests of the child, stable and definitive solutions, such as adoption or kafala of Islamic law, should be envisaged; failing this, other long-term options should be considered, such as foster care or appropriate residential care, including group homes and other supervised living arrangements.

C *Tracing and Family Reintegration*

162. Identifying, registering and documenting unaccompanied or separated children are priorities in any emergency and should be carried out as quickly as possible.
163. Registration activities should be conducted by or under the direct supervision of State authorities and explicitly mandated entities with responsibility for and experience in this task.
164. The confidential nature of the information collected should be respected and systems put in place for safe forwarding and storage of information. Information should only be shared among duly mandated agencies for the purpose of tracing, family reintegration and care.
165. All those engaged in tracing family members or primary legal or customary caregivers should operate within a coordinated system, using standardized forms and mutually compatible procedures, wherever possible. They should ensure that the child and others concerned would not be endangered by their actions.
166. The validity of relationships and the confirmation of the willingness of the child and family members to be reunited must be verified for every child. No action should be taken that may hinder eventual family reintegration, such as adoption, change of name or movement to places far from the family's likely location, until all tracing efforts have been exhausted.
167. Appropriate records of any placement of a child should be made and kept in a safe and secure manner so that reunification can be facilitated in the future.

CHAPTER 34

Guidelines of the Committee of Ministers of the Council of Europe on Child-Friendly Justice

Adopted by the Committee of Ministers of the Council of Europe on 17 November 2010

Preamble

The Committee of Ministers,

Considering that the aim of the Council of Europe is to achieve a greater unity between the member states, in particular by promoting the adoption of common rules in legal matters;

Considering the necessity of ensuring the effective implementation of existing binding universal and European standards protecting and promoting children's rights, including in particular:

- the 1951 United Nations Convention Relating to the Status of Refugees;
- the 1966 International Covenant on Civil and Political Rights;
- the 1966 International Covenant on Economic, Social and Cultural Rights;
- the 1989 United Nations Convention on the Rights of the Child;
- the 2006 United Nations Convention on the Rights of Persons with Disabilities;
- the Convention for the Protection of Human Rights and Fundamental Freedoms (1950, ETS No. 5) (hereafter the "ECHR");
- the European Convention on the Exercise of Children's Rights (1996, ETS No. 160);
- the revised European Social Charter (1996, ETS No. 163);
- the Council of Europe Convention on Contact concerning Children (2003, ETS No. 192);
- the Council of Europe Convention on the Protection of Children against Sexual Exploitation and Sexual Abuse (2007, CETS No. 201);
- the European Convention on the Adoption of Children (Revised) (2008, CETS No. 202);

Considering that, as guaranteed under the ECHR and in line with the case law of the European Court of Human Rights, the right of any person to have access to justice and to a fair trial – in all its components (including in particular the right to be informed, the right to be heard, the right to a legal defence, and the right to be represented) – is necessary in a democratic society and equally applies to children, taking however into account their capacity to form their own views;

Recalling relevant case law of the European Court of Human Rights, decisions, reports or other documents of other Council of Europe institutions and bodies including recommendations of the European Committee for the Prevention of Torture and Inhuman or Degrading Treatment or Punishment (CPT), and statements and opinions of the Council of Europe Commissioner for Human Rights and various recommendations of the Parliamentary Assembly of the Council of Europe;

Noting various recommendations of the Committee of Ministers to member states in the area of children's rights, including Recommendation Rec(2003)5 on measures of detention of asylum seekers, Recommendation Rec(2003)20 concerning new ways of dealing with juvenile delinquency and the role of juvenile justice, Recommendation Rec(2005)5 on the rights of children living in residential institutions, Recommendation Rec(2006)2 on the European Prison Rules, Recommendation CM/Rec(2008)11 on the European Rules for juvenile offenders subject to sanctions or measures and Recommendation CM/Rec(2009)10 on integrated national strategies for the protection of children from violence;

Recalling Resolution No. 2 on child-friendly justice, adopted at the 28th Conference of European Ministers of Justice (Lanzarote, October 2007);

Considering the importance of safeguarding children's rights by United Nations instruments such as:

- the United Nations Standard Minimum Rules for the Administration of Juvenile Justice ("The Beijing Rules", 1985);
- the United Nations Rules for the Protection of Juveniles Deprived of their Liberty ("The Havana Rules", 1990);
- the United Nations Guidelines for the Prevention of Juvenile Delinquency ("The Riyadh Guidelines", 1990);
- the United Nations Guidelines on Justice in Matters involving Child Victims and Witnesses of Crime (ECOSOC Res 2005/20, 2005);
- the Guidance Note of the United Nations Secretary-General: United Nations Approach to Justice for Children (2008);
- the United Nations Guidelines for the Appropriate Use and Conditions of Alternative Care for Children (2009);
- the Principles relating to the Status and Functioning of National Institutions for Protection and Promotion of Human Rights ("The Paris Principles");

Recalling the need to guarantee the effective implementation of existing binding norms concerning children's rights, without preventing member states from introducing or applying higher standards or more favourable measures;

Referring to the Council of Europe Programme "Building a Europe for and with children";

Acknowledging the progress made in member states towards implementing child-friendly justice;

Noting, nonetheless, existing obstacles for children within the justice system such as, among others, the non-existing, partial or conditional legal right to access to justice, the diversity in and complexity of procedures, possible discrimination on various grounds;

Recalling the need to prevent possible secondary victimisation of children by the judicial system in procedures involving or affecting them;

Inviting member states to investigate existing lacunae and problems and identify areas where child-friendly justice principles and practices could be introduced;

Acknowledging the views and opinions of consulted children throughout the member states of the Council of Europe;

Noting that the guidelines aim to contribute to the identification of practical remedies to existing shortcomings in law and in practice;

Adopts the following guidelines to serve as a practical tool for member states in adapting their judicial and non-judicial systems to the specific rights, interests and needs of children and invites member states to ensure that they are widely disseminated among all authorities responsible for or otherwise involved with children's rights in justice.

I Scope and Purpose

1. The guidelines deal with the issue of the place and role, and the views, rights and needs of the child in judicial proceedings and in alternatives to such proceedings.
2. The guidelines should apply to all ways in which children are likely to be, for whatever reason and in whatever capacity, brought into contact with all competent bodies and services involved in implementing criminal, civil or administrative law.
3. The guidelines aim to ensure that, in any such proceedings, all rights of children, among which the right to information, to representation, to participation and to protection, are fully respected with due consideration to the child's level of maturity and understanding and to the circumstances of the case. Respecting children's rights should not jeopardise the rights of other parties involved.

II Definitions

For the purposes of these guidelines on child-friendly justice (here-after "the guidelines"):

a. a "child" means any person under the age of 18 years;

b. a "parent" refers to the person(s) with parental responsibility, according to national law. In case the parent(s) is/are absent or no longer holding parental responsibility, this can be a guardian or an appointed legal representative;

c. "child-friendly justice" refers to justice systems which guarantee the respect and the effective implementation of all children's rights at the highest attainable level, bearing in mind the principles listed below and giving due consideration to the child's level of maturity and understanding and the circumstances of the case. It is, in particular, justice that is accessible, age appropriate, speedy, diligent, adapted to and focused on the needs and rights of the child, respecting the rights of the child including the rights to due process, to participate in and to understand the proceedings, to respect for private and family life and to integrity and dignity.

III Fundamental Principles

1. The guidelines build on the existing principles enshrined in the instruments referred to in the preamble and the case law of the European Court of Human Rights.
2. These principles are further developed in the following sections and should apply to all chapters of these guidelines.

A *Participation*

1. The right of all children to be informed about their rights, to be given appropriate ways to access justice and to be consulted and heard in proceedings involving or affecting them should be respected. This includes giving due weight to the children's views bearing in mind their maturity and any communication difficulties they may have in order to make this participation meaningful.
2. Children should be considered and treated as full bearers of rights and should be entitled to exercise all their rights in a manner that takes into account their capacity to form their own views and the circumstances of the case.

B *Best Interests of the Child*

1. Member states should guarantee the effective implementation of the right of children to have their best interests be a primary consideration in all matters involving or affecting them.

2. In assessing the best interests of the involved or affected children:

a. their views and opinions should be given due weight;

b. all other rights of the child, such as the right to dignity, liberty and equal treatment should be respected at all times;

c. a comprehensive approach should be adopted by all relevant authorities so as to take due account of all interests at stake, including psychological and physical well-being and legal, social and economic interests of the child.

3. The best interests of all children involved in the same procedure or case should be separately assessed and balanced with a view to reconciling possible conflicting interests of the children.

4. While the judicial authorities have the ultimate competence and responsibility for making the final decisions, member states should make, where necessary, concerted efforts to establish multidisciplinary approaches with the objective of assessing the best interests of children in procedures involving them.

C *Dignity*

1. Children should be treated with care, sensitivity, fairness and respect throughout any procedure or case, with special attention for their personal situation, well-being and specific needs, and with full respect for their physical and psychological integrity. This treatment should be given to them, in whichever way they have come into contact with judicial or non-judicial proceedings or other interventions, and regardless of their legal status and capacity in any procedure or case.

2. Children shall not be subjected to torture or inhuman or degrading treatment or punishment.

D *Protection from Discrimination*

1. The rights of children shall be secured without discrimination on any grounds such as sex, race, colour or ethnic background, age, language, religion, political or other opinion, national or social origin, socio-economic background, status of their parent(s), association with a national minority, property, birth, sexual orientation, gender identity or other status.

2. Specific protection and assistance may need to be granted to more vulnerable children, such as migrant children, refugee and asylum-seeking children,

unaccompanied children, children with disabilities, homeless and street children, Roma children, and children in residential institutions.

E *Rule of Law*

1. The rule of law principle should apply fully to children as it does to adults.
2. Elements of due process such as the principles of legality and proportionality, the presumption of innocence, the right to a fair trial, the right to legal advice, the right to access to courts and the right to appeal, should be guaranteed for children as they are for adults and should not be minimised or denied under the pretext of the child's best interests. This applies to all judicial and non-judicial and administrative proceedings.
3. Children should have the right to access appropriate independent and effective complaints mechanisms.

IV Child-Friendly Justice before, during and after Judicial Proceedings

A *General Elements of Child-Friendly Justice*

1 Information and Advice

1. From their first involvement with the justice system or other competent authorities (such as the police, immigration, educational, social or health care services) and throughout that process, children and their parents should be promptly and adequately informed of, inter alia:

a. their rights, in particular the specific rights children have with regard to judicial or non-judicial proceedings in which they are or might be involved, and the instruments available to remedy possible violations of their rights including the opportunity to have recourse to either a judicial or non-judicial proceeding or other interventions. This may include information on the likely duration of proceedings, possible access to appeals and independent complaints mechanisms;

b. the system and procedures involved, taking into consideration the particular place the child will have and the role he or she may play in it and the different procedural steps;

c. the existing support mechanisms for the child when participating in the judicial or non-judicial procedures;

d. the appropriateness and possible consequences of given in-court or out-of-court proceedings;

e. where applicable, the charges or the follow-up given to their complaint;

f. the time and place of court proceedings and other relevant events, such as hearings, if the child is personally affected;
g. the general progress and outcome of the proceedings or intervention;
h. the availability of protective measures;
i. the existing mechanisms for review of decisions affecting the child;
j. the existing opportunities to obtain reparation from the offender or from the state through the justice process, through alternative civil proceedings or through other processes;
k. the availability of the services (health, psychological, social, interpretation and translation, and other) or organisations which can provide support and the means of accessing such services along with emergency financial support, where applicable;
l. any special arrangements available in order to protect as far as possible their best interests if they are resident in another state.

2. The information and advice should be provided to children in a manner adapted to their age and maturity, in a language which they can understand and which is gender and culture sensitive.

3. As a rule, both the child and parents or legal representatives should directly receive the information. Provision of the information to the parents should not be an alternative to communicating the information to the child.

4. Child-friendly materials containing relevant legal information should be made available and widely distributed, and special information services for children such as specialised websites and helplines established.

5. Information on any charges against the child must be given promptly and directly after the charges are brought. This information should be given to both the child and the parents in such a way that they understand the exact charge and the possible consequences.

2 Protection of Private and Family Life

6. The privacy and personal data of children who are or have been involved in judicial or non-judicial proceedings and other interventions should be protected in accordance with national law. This generally implies that no information or personal data may be made available or published, particularly in the media, which could reveal or indirectly enable the disclosure of the child's identity, including images, detailed descriptions of the child or the child's family, names or addresses, audio and video records, etc.

7. Member states should prevent violations of the privacy rights as mentioned under guideline 6 above by the media through legislative measures or monitoring self-regulation by the media.

8. Member states should stipulate limited access to all records or documents containing personal and sensitive data of children, in particular in proceedings involving them. If the transfer of personal and sensitive data is necessary, while taking into account the best interests of the child, member states should regulate this transfer in line with relevant data protection legislation.
9. Whenever children are being heard or giving evidence in judicial or non-judicial proceedings or other interventions, where appropriate, this should preferably take place in camera. As a rule, only those directly involved should be present, provided that they do not obstruct children in giving evidence.
10. Professionals working with and for children should abide by the strict rules of confidentiality, except where there is a risk of harm to the child.

3 Safety (Special Preventive Measures)

11. In all judicial and non-judicial proceedings or other interventions, children should be protected from harm, including intimidation, reprisals and secondary victimisation.
12. Professionals working with and for children should, where necessary, be subject to regular vetting, according to national law and without prejudice to the independence of the judiciary, to ensure their suitability to work with children.
13. Special precautionary measures should apply to children when the alleged perpetrator is a parent, a member of the family or a primary caregiver.

4 Training of Professionals

14. All professionals working with and for children should receive necessary interdisciplinary training on the rights and needs of children of different age groups, and on proceedings that are adapted to them.
15. Professionals having direct contact with children should also be trained in communicating with them at all ages and stages of development, and with children in situations of particular vulnerability.

5 Multidisciplinary Approach

16. With full respect of the child's right to private and family life, close co-operation between different professionals should be encouraged in order to obtain a comprehensive understanding of the child, and an assessment of his or her legal, psychological, social, emotional, physical and cognitive situation.
17. A common assessment framework should be established for professionals working with or for children (such as lawyers, psychologists, physicians, police, immigration officials, social workers and mediators) in proceedings or interventions that involve or affect children to provide any necessary support to

those taking decisions, enabling them to best serve children's interests in a given case.

18. While implementing a multidisciplinary approach, professional rules on confidentiality should be respected.

6 Deprivation of Liberty

19. Any form of deprivation of liberty of children should be a measure of last resort and be for the shortest appropriate period of time.

20. When deprivation of liberty is imposed, children should, as a rule, be held separately from adults. When children are detained with adults, this should be for exceptional reasons and based solely on the best interests of the child. In all circumstances, children should be detained in premises suited to their needs.

21. Given the vulnerability of children deprived of liberty, the importance of family ties and promoting the reintegration into society, competent authorities should ensure respect and actively support the fulfilment of the rights of the child as set out in universal and European instruments. In addition to other rights, children in particular should have the right to:

a. maintain regular and meaningful contact with parents, family and friends through visits and correspondence, except when restrictions are required in the interests of justice and the interests of the child. Restrictions on this right should never be used as a punishment;

b. receive appropriate education, vocational guidance and training, medical care, and enjoy freedom of thought, conscience and religion and access to leisure, including physical education and sport;

c. access programmes that prepare children in advance for their return to their communities, with full attention given to them in respect of their emotional and physical needs, their family relationships, housing, schooling and employment possibilities and socio-economic status.

22. The deprivation of liberty of unaccompanied minors, including those seeking asylum, and separated children should never be motivated or based solely on the absence of residence status.

B *Child-Friendly Justice before Judicial Proceedings*

23. The minimum age of criminal responsibility should not be too low and should be determined by law.

24. Alternatives to judicial proceedings such as mediation, diversion (of judicial mechanisms) and alternative dispute resolution should be encouraged whenever these may best serve the child's best interests. The preliminary use of such alternatives should not be used as an obstacle to the child's access to justice.

25. Children should be thoroughly informed and consulted on the opportunity to have recourse to either a court proceeding or alternatives outside court settings. This information should also explain the possible consequences of each option. Based on adequate information, both legal and otherwise, a choice should be available to use either court procedures or alternatives for these proceedings whenever they exist. Children should be given the opportunity to obtain legal advice and other assistance in determining the appropriateness and desirability of the proposed alternatives. In making this decision, the views of the child should be taken into account.

26. Alternatives to court proceedings should guarantee an equivalent level of legal safeguards. Respect for children's rights as described in these guidelines and in all relevant legal instruments on the rights of the child should be guaranteed to the same extent in both in-court and out-of-court proceedings.

C *Children and the Police*

27. Police should respect the personal rights and dignity of all children and have regard to their vulnerability, that is, take account of their age and maturity and any special needs of those who may be under a physical or mental disability or have communication difficulties.

28. Whenever a child is apprehended by the police, the child should be informed in a manner and in language that is appropriate to his or her age and level of understanding of the reason for which he or she has been taken into custody. Children should be provided with access to a lawyer and be given the opportunity to contact their parents or a person whom they trust.

29. Save in exceptional circumstances, the parent(s) should be informed of the child's presence in the police station, given details of the reason why the child has been taken into custody and be asked to come to the station.

30. A child who has been taken into custody should not be questioned in respect of criminal behaviour, or asked to make or sign a statement concerning such involvement, except in the presence of a lawyer or one of the child's parents or, if no parent is available, another person whom the child trusts. The parent or this person may be excluded if suspected of involvement in the criminal behaviour or if engaging in conduct which amounts to an obstruction of justice.

31. Police should ensure that, as far as possible, no child in their custody is detained together with adults.

32. Authorities should ensure that children in police custody are kept in conditions that are safe and appropriate to their needs.

33. In member states where this falls under their mandate, prosecutors should ensure that child-friendly approaches are used throughout the investigation process.

D *Child-Friendly Justice during Judicial Proceedings*

1 Access to Court and to the Judicial Process

34. As bearers of rights, children should have recourse to remedies to effectively exercise their rights or act upon violations of their rights. The domestic law should facilitate where appropriate the possibility of access to court for children who have sufficient understanding of their rights and of the use of remedies to protect these rights, based on adequately given legal advice.
35. Any obstacles to access to court, such as the cost of the proceedings or the lack of legal counsel, should be removed.
36. In cases of certain specific crimes committed against children, or certain aspects of civil or family law, access to court should be granted for a period of time after the child has reached the age of majority where necessary. Member states are encouraged to review their statutes of limitations.

2 Legal Counsel and Representation

37. Children should have the right to their own legal counsel and representation, in their own name, in proceedings where there is, or could be, a conflict of interest between the child and the parents or other involved parties.
38. Children should have access to free legal aid, under the same or more lenient conditions as adults.
39. Lawyers representing children should be trained in and knowledgeable on children's rights and related issues, receive ongoing and indepth training and be capable of communicating with children at their level of understanding.
40. Children should be considered as fully fledged clients with their own rights and lawyers representing children should bring forward the opinion of the child.
41. Lawyers should provide the child with all necessary information and explanations concerning the possible consequences of the child's views and/or opinions.
42. In cases where there are conflicting interests between parents and children, the competent authority should appoint either a guardian ad litem or another independent representative to represent the views and interests of the child.
43. Adequate representation and the right to be represented independently from the parents should be guaranteed, especially in proceedings where the parents, members of the family or caregivers are the alleged offenders.

3 Right to Be Heard and to Express Views

44. Judges should respect the right of children to be heard in all matters that affect them or at least to be heard when they are deemed to have a sufficient understanding of the matters in question. Means used for this purpose should be adapted to the child's level of understanding and ability to communicate and take into account the circumstances of the case. Children should be consulted on the manner in which they wish to be heard.
45. Due weight should be given to the child's views and opinion in accordance with his or her age and maturity.
46. The right to be heard is a right of the child, not a duty of the child.
47. A child should not be precluded from being heard solely on the basis of age. Whenever a child takes the initiative to be heard in a case that affects him or her, the judge should not, unless it is in the child's best interests, refuse to hear the child and should listen to his or her views and opinion on matters concerning him or her in the case.
48. Children should be provided with all necessary information on how effectively to use the right to be heard. However, it should be explained to them that their right to be heard and to have their views taken into consideration may not necessarily determine the final decision.
49. Judgments and court rulings affecting children should be duly reasoned and explained to them in language that children can understand, particularly those decisions in which the child's views and opinions have not been followed.

4 Avoiding Undue Delay

50. In all proceedings involving children, the urgency principle should be applied to provide a speedy response and protect the best interests of the child, while respecting the rule of law.
51. In family law cases (for example parentage, custody, parental abduction), courts should exercise exceptional diligence to avoid any risk of adverse consequences on the family relations.
52. When necessary, judicial authorities should consider the possibility of taking provisional decisions or making preliminary judgments to be monitored for a certain period of time in order to be reviewed later.
53. In accordance with the law, judicial authorities should have the possibility to take decisions which are immediately enforceable in cases where this would be in the best interests of the child.

5 Organisation of the Proceedings, Child-Friendly Environment and Child-Friendly Language

54. In all proceedings, children should be treated with respect for their age, their special needs, their maturity and level of understanding, and bearing in mind any communication difficulties they may have. Cases involving children should be dealt with in non-intimidating and child-sensitive settings.
55. Before proceedings begin, children should be familiarised with the layout of the court or other facilities and the roles and identities of the officials involved.
56. Language appropriate to children's age and level of understanding should be used.
57. When children are heard or interviewed in judicial and non-judicial proceedings and during other interventions, judges and other professionals should interact with them with respect and sensitivity.
58. Children should be allowed to be accompanied by their parents or, where appropriate, an adult of their choice, unless a reasoned decision has been made to the contrary in respect of that person.
59. Interview methods, such as video or audio-recording or pre-trial hearings in camera, should be used and considered as admissible evidence.
60. Children should be protected, as far as possible, against images or information that could be harmful to their welfare. In deciding on disclosure of possibly harmful images or information to the child, the judge should seek advice from other professionals, such as psychologists and social workers.
61. Court sessions involving children should be adapted to the child's pace and attention span: regular breaks should be planned and hearings should not last too long. To facilitate the participation of children to their full cognitive capacity and to support their emotional stability, disruption and distractions during court sessions should be kept to a minimum.
62. As far as appropriate and possible, interviewing and waiting rooms should be arranged for children in a child-friendly environment.
63. As far as possible, specialist courts (or court chambers), procedures and institutions should be established for children in conflict with the law. This could include the establishment of specialised units within the police, the judiciary, the court system and the prosecutor's office.

6 Evidence/Statements by Children

64. Interviews of and the gathering of statements from children should, as far as possible, be carried out by trained professionals. Every effort should be made for children to give evidence in the most favourable settings and under the most suitable conditions, having regard to their age, maturity and level of understanding and any communication difficulties they may have.

65. Audiovisual statements from children who are victims or witnesses should be encouraged, while respecting the right of other parties to contest the content of such statements.
66. When more than one interview is necessary, they should preferably be carried out by the same person, in order to ensure coherence of approach in the best interests of the child.
67. The number of interviews should be as limited as possible and their length should be adapted to the child's age and attention span.
68. Direct contact, confrontation or interaction between a child victim or witness with alleged perpetrators should, as far as possible, be avoided unless at the request of the child victim.
69. Children should have the opportunity to give evidence in criminal cases without the presence of the alleged perpetrator.
70. The existence of less strict rules on giving evidence such as absence of the requirement for oath or other similar declarations, or other child-friendly procedural measures, should not in itself diminish the value given to a child's testimony or evidence.
71. Interview protocols that take into account different stages of the child's development should be designed and implemented to underpin the validity of children's evidence. These should avoid leading questions and thereby enhance reliability.
72. With regard to the best interests and well-being of children, it should be possible for a judge to allow a child not to testify.
73. A child's statements and evidence should never be presumed invalid or untrustworthy by reason only of the child's age.
74. The possibility of taking statements of child victims and witnesses in specially designed child-friendly facilities and a child-friendly environment should be examined.

E *Child-Friendly Justice after Judicial Proceedings*

75. The child's lawyer, guardian ad litem or legal representative should communicate and explain the given decision or judgment to the child in a language adapted to the child's level of understanding and should give the necessary information on possible measures that could be taken, such as appeal or independent complaint mechanisms.
76. National authorities should take all necessary steps to facilitate the execution of judicial decisions/rulings involving and affecting children without delay.

77. When a decision has not been enforced, children should be informed, possibly through their lawyer, guardian ad litem or legal representative, of available remedies either through non-judicial mechanisms or access to justice.
78. Implementation of judgments by force should be a measure of last resort in family cases when children are involved.
79. After judgments in highly conflictual proceedings, guidance and support should be offered, ideally free of charge, to children and their families by specialised services.
80. Particular health care and appropriate social and therapeutic intervention programmes or measures for victims of neglect, violence, abuse or other crimes should be provided, ideally free of charge, and children and their caregivers should be promptly and adequately informed of the availability of such services.
81. The child's lawyer, guardian or legal representative should have a mandate to take all necessary steps to claim for damages during or after criminal proceedings in which the child was a victim. Where appropriate, the costs could be covered by the state and recovered from the perpetrator.
82. Measures and sanctions for children in conflict with the law should always be constructive and individualised responses to the committed acts, bearing in mind the principle of proportionality, the child's age, physical and mental well-being and development and the circumstances of the case. The right to education, vocational training, employment, rehabilitation and reintegration should be guaranteed.
83. In order to promote the reintegration within society, and in accordance with the national law, criminal records of children should be non-disclosable outside the justice system on reaching the age of majority. Exceptions for the disclosure of such information can be permitted in cases of serious offences, inter alia for reasons of public safety or when employment with children is concerned.

V Promoting Other Child-Friendly Actions

Member states are encouraged to:

a. promote research into all aspects of child-friendly justice, including child-sensitive interviewing techniques and dissemination of information and training on such techniques;
b. exchange practice and promote co-operation in the field of child-friendly justice internationally;

c. promote the publication and widest possible dissemination of child-friendly versions of relevant legal instruments;
d. set up, or maintain and reinforce where necessary, information offices for children's rights, possibly linked to bar associations, welfare services, (children's) ombudsmen, Non-governmental Organisations (NGOs), etc.;
e. facilitate children's access to courts and complaint mechanisms and further recognise and facilitate the role of NGOs and other independent bodies or institutions such as children's ombudsmen in supporting children's effective access to courts and independent complaint mechanisms, both on a national and international level;
f. consider the establishment of a system of specialised judges and lawyers for children and further develop courts in which both legal and social measures can be taken in favour of children and their families;
g. develop and facilitate the use by children and others acting on their behalf of universal and European human and children's rights protection mechanisms for the pursuit of justice and protection of rights when domestic remedies do not exist or have been exhausted;
h. make human rights, including children's rights, a mandatory component in the school curricula and for professionals working with children;
i. develop and support systems aimed at raising the awareness of parents on children's rights;
j. set up child-friendly, multi-agency and interdisciplinary centres for child victims and witnesses where children could be interviewed and medically examined for forensic purposes, comprehensively assessed and receive all relevant therapeutic services from appropriate professionals;
k. set up specialised and accessible support and information services, such as online consultation, help lines and local community services free of charge;
l. ensure that all concerned professionals working in contact with children in justice systems receive appropriate support and training, and practical guidance in order to guarantee and implement adequately the rights of children, in particular while assessing children's best interests in all types of procedures involving or affecting them.

VI Monitoring and Assessment

Member states are also encouraged to:
a. review domestic legislation, policies and practices to ensure the necessary reforms to implement these guidelines;

b. to speedily ratify, if not yet done so, relevant Council of Europe conventions concerning children's rights;

c. periodically review and evaluate their working methods within the child-friendly justice setting;

d. maintain or establish a framework, including one or more independent mechanisms, as appropriate, to promote and monitor implementation of the present guidelines, in accordance with their judicial and administrative systems;

e. ensure that civil society, in particular organisations, institutions and bodies which aim to promote and to protect the rights of the child, participate fully in the monitoring process.

PART VII

Private International Law

CHAPTER 35

Convention on the Civil Aspects of International Child Abduction

Concluded at The Hague on 25 October 1980
Entry into force 1 December 1983, in accordance with article 38

The States signatory to the present Convention,

Firmly convinced that the interests of children are of paramount importance in matters relating to their custody,

Desiring to protect children internationally from the harmful effects of their wrongful removal or retention and to establish procedures to ensure their prompt return to the State of their habitual residence, as well as to secure protection for rights of access,

Have resolved to conclude a Convention to this effect, and have agreed upon the following provisions –

Chapter I: Scope of the Convention

Art. 1 The objects of the present Convention are –

a) to secure the prompt return of children wrongfully removed to or retained in any Contracting State; and

b) to ensure that rights of custody and of access under the law of one Contracting State are effectively respected in the other Contracting States.

Art. 2 Contracting States shall take all appropriate measures to secure within their territories the implementation of the objects of the Convention. For this purpose they shall use the most expeditious procedures available.

Art. 3 The removal or the retention of a child is to be considered wrongful where –

a) it is in breach of rights of custody attributed to a person, an institution or any other body, either jointly or alone, under the law of the State in which the child was habitually resident immediately before the removal or retention; and

b) at the time of removal or retention those rights were actually exercised, either jointly or alone, or would have been so exercised but for the removal or retention.

The rights of custody mentioned in sub-paragraph a) above, may arise in particular by operation of law or by reason of a judicial or administrative decision, or by reason of an agreement having legal effect under the law of that State.

Art. 4 The Convention shall apply to any child who was habitually resident in a Contracting State immediately before any breach of custody or access rights. The Convention shall cease to apply when the child attains the age of 16 years.

Art. 5 For the purposes of this Convention –

a) "rights of custody" shall include rights relating to the care of the person of the child and, in particular, the right to determine the child's place of residence;

b) "rights of access" shall include the right to take a child for a limited period of time to a place other than the child's habitual residence.

Chapter II: Central Authorities

Art. 6 A Contracting State shall designate a Central Authority to discharge the duties which are imposed by the Convention upon such authorities.

Federal States, States with more than one system of law or States having autonomous territorial organisations shall be free to appoint more than one Central Authority and to specify the territorial extent of their powers. Where a State has appointed more than one Central Authority, it shall designate the Central Authority to which applications may be addressed for transmission to the appropriate Central Authority within that State.

Art. 7 Central Authorities shall co-operate with each other and promote cooperation amongst the competent authorities in their respective States to secure the prompt return of children and to achieve the other objects of this Convention.

In particular, either directly or through any intermediary, they shall take all appropriate measures –

a) to discover the whereabouts of a child who has been wrongfully removed or retained;

b) to prevent further harm to the child or prejudice to interested parties by taking or causing to be taken provisional measures;

c) to secure the voluntary return of the child or to bring about an amicable resolution of the issues;

d) to exchange, where desirable, information relating to the social background of the child;

e) to provide information of a general character as to the law of their State in connection with the application of the Convention;
f) to initiate or facilitate the institution of judicial or administrative proceedings with a view to obtaining the return of the child and, in a proper case, to make arrangements for organising or securing the effective exercise of rights of access;
g) where the circumstances so require, to provide or facilitate the provision of legal aid and advice, including the participation of legal counsel and advisers;
h) to provide such administrative arrangements as may be necessary and appropriate to secure the safe return of the child;
i) to keep each other informed with respect to the operation of this Convention and, as far as possible, to eliminate any obstacles to its application.

Chapter III: Return of Children

Art. 8 Any person, institution or other body claiming that a child has been removed or retained in breach of custody rights may apply either to the Central Authority of the child's habitual residence or to the Central Authority of any other Contracting State for assistance in securing the return of the child.
The application shall contain –
a) information concerning the identity of the applicant, of the child and of the person alleged to have removed or retained the child;
b) where available, the date of birth of the child;
c) the grounds on which the applicant's claim for return of the child is based;
d) all available information relating to the whereabouts of the child and the identity of the person with whom the child is presumed to be.

The application may be accompanied or supplemented by –
e) an authenticated copy of any relevant decision or agreement;
f) a certificate or an affidavit emanating from a Central Authority, or other competent authority of the State of the child's habitual residence, or from a qualified person, concerning the relevant law of that State;
g) any other relevant document.

Art. 9 If the Central Authority which receives an application referred to in Article 8 has reason to believe that the child is in another Contracting State, it shall directly and without delay transmit the application to the Central Authority of that Contracting State and inform the requesting Central Authority, or the applicant, as the case may be.

Art. 10 The Central Authority of the State where the child is shall take or cause to be taken all appropriate measures in order to obtain the voluntary return of the child.

Art. 11 The judicial or administrative authorities of Contracting States shall act expeditiously in proceedings for the return of children.

If the judicial or administrative authority concerned has not reached a decision within six weeks from the date of commencement of the proceedings, the applicant or the Central Authority of the requested State, on its own initiative or if asked by the Central Authority of the requesting State, shall have the right to request a statement of the reasons for the delay. If a reply is received by the Central Authority of the requested State, that Authority shall transmit the reply to the Central Authority of the requesting State, or to the applicant, as the case may be.

Art. 12 Where a child has been wrongfully removed or retained in terms of Article 3 and, at the date of the commencement of the proceedings before the judicial or administrative authority of the Contracting State where the child is, a period of less than one year has elapsed from the date of the wrongful removal or retention, the authority concerned shall order the return of the child forthwith.

The judicial or administrative authority, even where the proceedings have been commenced after the expiration of the period of one year referred to in the preceding paragraph, shall also order the return of the child, unless it is demonstrated that the child is now settled in its new environment.

Where the judicial or administrative authority in the requested State has reason to believe that the child has been taken to another State, it may stay the proceedings or dismiss the application for the return of the child.

Art. 13 Notwithstanding the provisions of the preceding Article, the judicial or administrative authority of the requested State is not bound to order the return of the child if the person, institution or other body which opposes its return establishes that –

a) the person, institution or other body having the care of the person of the child was not actually exercising the custody rights at the time of removal or retention, or had consented to or subsequently acquiesced in the removal or retention; or

b) there is a grave risk that his or her return would expose the child to physical or psychological harm or otherwise place the child in an intolerable situation.

The judicial or administrative authority may also refuse to order the return of the child if it finds that the child objects to being returned and has attained an age and degree of maturity at which it is appropriate to take account of its views.

In considering the circumstances referred to in this Article, the judicial and administrative authorities shall take into account the information relating to the social background of the child provided by the Central Authority or other competent authority of the child's habitual residence.

Art. 14 In ascertaining whether there has been a wrongful removal or retention within the meaning of Article 3, the judicial or administrative authorities of the requested State may take notice directly of the law of, and of judicial or administrative decisions, formally recognised or not in the State of the habitual residence of the child, without recourse to the specific procedures for the proof of that law or for the recognition of foreign decisions which would otherwise be applicable.

Art. 15 The judicial or administrative authorities of a Contracting State may, prior to the making of an order for the return of the child, request that the applicant obtain from the authorities of the State of the habitual residence of the child a decision or other determination that the removal or retention was wrongful within the meaning of Article 3 of the Convention, where such a decision or determination may be obtained in that State. The Central Authorities of the Contracting States shall so far as practicable assist applicants to obtain such a decision or determination.

Art. 16 After receiving notice of a wrongful removal or retention of a child in the sense of Article 3, the judicial or administrative authorities of the Contracting State to which the child has been removed or in which it has been retained shall not decide on the merits of rights of custody until it has been determined that the child is not to be returned under this Convention or unless an application under this Convention is not lodged within a reasonable time following receipt of the notice.

Art. 17 The sole fact that a decision relating to custody has been given in or is entitled to recognition in the requested State shall not be a ground for refusing to return a child under this Convention, but the judicial or administrative authorities of the requested State may take account of the reasons for that decision in applying this Convention.

Art. 18 The provisions of this Chapter do not limit the power of a judicial or administrative authority to order the return of the child at any time.

Art. 19 A decision under this Convention concerning the return of the child shall not be taken to be a determination on the merits of any custody issue.

Art. 20 The return of the child under the provisions of Article 12 may be refused if this would not be permitted by the fundamental principles of the requested State relating to the protection of human rights and fundamental freedoms.

Chapter IV: Rights of Access

Art. 21 An application to make arrangements for organising or securing the effective exercise of rights of access may be presented to the Central Authorities of the Contracting States in the same way as an application for the return of a child.

The Central Authorities are bound by the obligations of co-operation which are set forth in Article 7 to promote the peaceful enjoyment of access rights and the fulfilment of any conditions to which the exercise of those rights may be subject. The Central Authorities shall take steps to remove, as far as possible, all obstacles to the exercise of such rights.

The Central Authorities, either directly or through intermediaries, may initiate or assist in the institution of proceedings with a view to organising or protecting these rights and securing respect for the conditions to which the exercise of these rights may be subject.

Chapter V: General Provisions

Art. 22 No security, bond or deposit, however described, shall be required to guarantee the payment of costs and expenses in the judicial or administrative proceedings falling within the scope of this Convention.

Art. 23 No legalisation or similar formality may be required in the context of this Convention.

Art. 24 Any application, communication or other document sent to the Central Authority of the requested State shall be in the original language, and shall be accompanied by a translation into the official language or one of the official languages of the requested State or, where that is not feasible, a translation into French or English.

However, a Contracting State may, by making a reservation in accordance with Article 42, object to the use of either French or English, but not both, in any application, communication or other document sent to its Central Authority.

Art. 25 Nationals of the Contracting States and persons who are habitually resident within those States shall be entitled in matters concerned with the application of this Convention to legal aid and advice in any other Contracting State on the same conditions as if they themselves were nationals of and habitually resident in that State.

Art. 26 Each Central Authority shall bear its own costs in applying this Convention.

Central Authorities and other public services of Contracting States shall not impose any charges in relation to applications submitted under this Convention. In particular, they may not require any payment from the applicant towards the costs and expenses of the proceedings or, where applicable, those arising from the participation of legal counsel or advisers. However, they may require the payment of the expenses incurred or to be incurred in implementing the return of the child.

However, a Contracting State may, by making a reservation in accordance with Article 42, declare that it shall not be bound to assume any costs referred to in the preceding paragraph resulting from the participation of legal counsel or advisers or from court proceedings, except insofar as those costs may be covered by its system of legal aid and advice.

Upon ordering the return of a child or issuing an order concerning rights of access under this Convention, the judicial or administrative authorities may, where appropriate, direct the person who removed or retained the child, or who prevented the exercise of rights of access, to pay necessary expenses incurred by or on behalf of the applicant, including travel expenses, any costs incurred or payments made for locating the child, the costs of legal representation of the applicant, and those of returning the child.

Art. 27 When it is manifest that the requirements of this Convention are not fulfilled or that the application is otherwise not well founded, a Central Authority is not bound to accept the application. In that case, the Central Authority shall forthwith inform the applicant or the Central Authority through which the application was submitted, as the case may be, of its reasons.

Art. 28 A Central Authority may require that the application be accompanied by a written authorisation empowering it to act on behalf of the applicant, or to designate a representative so to act.

Art. 29 This Convention shall not preclude any person, institution or body who claims that there has been a breach of custody or access rights within the meaning of Article 3 or 21 from applying directly to the judicial or administrative authorities of a Contracting State, whether or not under the provisions of this Convention.

Art. 30 Any application submitted to the Central Authorities or directly to the judicial or administrative authorities of a Contracting State in accordance with the terms of this Convention, together with documents and any other information appended thereto or provided by a Central Authority, shall be admissible in the courts or administrative authorities of the Contracting States.

Art. 31 In relation to a State which in matters of custody of children has two or more systems of law applicable in different territorial units –

a) any reference to habitual residence in that State shall be construed as referring to habitual residence in a territorial unit of that State;

b) any reference to the law of the State of habitual residence shall be construed as referring to the law of the territorial unit in that State where the child habitually resides.

Art. 32 In relation to a State which in matters of custody of children has two or more systems of law applicable to different categories of persons, any reference to the law of that State shall be construed as referring to the legal system specified by the law of that State.

Art. 33 A State within which different territorial units have their own rules of law in respect of custody of children shall not be bound to apply this Convention where a State with a unified system of law would not be bound to do so.

Art. 34 This Convention shall take priority in matters within its scope over the Convention of 5 October 1961 concerning the powers of authorities and the law applicable in respect of the protection of minors, as between Parties to both Conventions. Otherwise the present Convention shall not restrict the application of an international instrument in force between the State of origin and the State addressed or other law of the State addressed for the purposes of obtaining the return of a child who has been wrongfully removed or retained or of organising access rights.

Art. 35 This Convention shall apply as between Contracting States only to wrongful removals or retentions occurring after its entry into force in those States.

Where a declaration has been made under Article 39 or 40, the reference in the preceding paragraph to a Contracting State shall be taken to refer to the territorial unit or units in relation to which this Convention applies.

Art. 36 Nothing in this Convention shall prevent two or more Contracting States, in order to limit the restrictions to which the return of the child may be subject, from agreeing among themselves to derogate from any provisions of this Convention which may imply such a restriction.

Chapter VI: Final Clauses

Art. 37 The Convention shall be open for signature by the States which were Members of the Hague Conference on Private International Law at the time of its Fourteenth Session.

It shall be ratified, accepted or approved and the instruments of ratification, acceptance or approval shall be deposited with the Ministry of Foreign Affairs of the Kingdom of the Netherlands.

Art. 38 Any other State may accede to the Convention.

The instrument of accession shall be deposited with the Ministry of Foreign Affairs of the Kingdom of the Netherlands.

The Convention shall enter into force for a State acceding to it on the first day of the third calendar month after the deposit of its instrument of accession.

The accession will have effect only as regards the relations between the acceding State and such Contracting States as will have declared their acceptance of the accession. Such a declaration will also have to be made by any Member State ratifying, accepting or approving the Convention after an accession. Such declaration shall be deposited at the Ministry of Foreign Affairs of the Kingdom of the Netherlands; this Ministry shall forward, through diplomatic channels, a certified copy to each of the Contracting States.
The Convention will enter into force as between the acceding State and the State that has declared its acceptance of the accession on the first day of the third calendar month after the deposit of the declaration of acceptance.
Art. 39 Any State may, at the time of signature, ratification, acceptance, approval or accession, declare that the Convention shall extend to all the territories for the international relations of which it is responsible, or to one or more of them. Such a declaration shall take effect at the time the Convention enters into force for that State.
Such declaration, as well as any subsequent extension, shall be notified to the Ministry of Foreign Affairs of the Kingdom of the Netherlands.
Art. 40 If a Contracting State has two or more territorial units in which different systems of law are applicable in relation to matters dealt with in this Convention, it may at the time of signature, ratification, acceptance, approval or accession declare that this Convention shall extend to all its territorial units or only to one or more of them and may modify this declaration by submitting another declaration at any time.
Any such declaration shall be notified to the Ministry of Foreign Affairs of the Kingdom of the Netherlands and shall state expressly the territorial units to which the Convention applies.
Art. 41 Where a Contracting State has a system of government under which executive, judicial and legislative powers are distributed between central and other authorities within that State, its signature or ratification, acceptance or approval of, or accession to this Convention, or its making of any declaration in terms of Article 40 shall carry no implication as to the internal distribution of powers within that State.
Art. 42 Any State may, not later than the time of ratification, acceptance, approval or accession, or at the time of making a declaration in terms of Article 39 or 40, make one or both of the reservations provided for in Article 24 and Article 26, third paragraph. No other reservation shall be permitted.
Any State may at any time withdraw a reservation it has made. The withdrawal shall be notified to the Ministry of Foreign Affairs of the Kingdom of the Netherlands.

The reservation shall cease to have effect on the first day of the third calendar month after the notification referred to in the preceding paragraph.

Art. 43 The Convention shall enter into force on the first day of the third calendar month after the deposit of the third instrument of ratification, acceptance, approval or accession referred to in Articles 37 and 38.

Thereafter the Convention shall enter into force –

(1) for each State ratifying, accepting, approving or acceding to it subsequently, on the first day of the third calendar month after the deposit of its instrument of ratification, acceptance, approval or accession;

(2) for any territory or territorial unit to which the Convention has been extended in conformity with Article 39 or 40, on the first day of the third calendar month after the notification referred to in that Article.

Art. 44 The Convention shall remain in force for five years from the date of its entry into force in accordance with the first paragraph of Article 43 even for States which subsequently have ratified, accepted, approved it or acceded to it.

If there has been no denunciation, it shall be renewed tacitly every five years.

Any denunciation shall be notified to the Ministry of Foreign Affairs of the Kingdom of the Netherlands at least six months before the expiry of the five year period. It may be limited to certain of the territories or territorial units to which the Convention applies.

The denunciation shall have effect only as regards the State which has notified it. The Convention shall remain in force for the other Contracting States.

Art. 45 The Ministry of Foreign Affairs of the Kingdom of the Netherlands shall notify the States Members of the Conference, and the States which have acceded in accordance with Article 38, of the following –

(1) the signatures and ratifications, acceptances and approvals referred to in Article 37;

(2) the accessions referred to in Article 38;

(3) the date on which the Convention enters into force in accordance with Article 43;

(4) the extensions referred to in Article 39;

(5) the declarations referred to in Articles 38 and 40;

(6) the reservations referred to in Article 24 and Article 26, third paragraph, and the withdrawals referred to in Article 42;

(7) the denunciations referred to in Article 44.

In witness whereof the undersigned, being duly authorised thereto, have signed this Convention.

Done at The Hague, on the 25th day of October, 1980, in the English and French languages, both texts being equally authentic, in a single copy which shall be deposited in the archives of the Government of the Kingdom of the Netherlands, and of which a certified copy shall be sent, through diplomatic channels, to each of the States Members of the Hague Conference on Private International Law at the date of its Fourteenth Session.

CHAPTER 36

Convention on Protection of Children and Co-operation in Respect of Intercountry Adoption

Concluded at The Hague on 29 May 1993
Entry into force 1 May 1995, in accordance with article 46

The States signatory to the present Convention,

Recognising that the child, for the full and harmonious development of his or her personality, should grow up in a family environment, in an atmosphere of happiness, love and understanding,

Recalling that each State should take, as a matter of priority, appropriate measures to enable the child to remain in the care of his or her family of origin,

Recognising that intercountry adoption may offer the advantage of a permanent family to a child for whom a suitable family cannot be found in his or her State of origin,

Convinced of the necessity to take measures to ensure that intercountry adoptions are made in the best interests of the child and with respect for his or her fundamental rights, and to prevent the abduction, the sale of, or traffic in children,

Desiring to establish common provisions to this effect, taking into account the principles set forth in international instruments, in particular the United Nations Convention on the Rights of the Child, of 20 November 1989, and the United Nations Declaration on Social and Legal Principles relating to the Protection and Welfare of Children, with Special Reference to Foster Placement and Adoption Nationally and Internationally (General Assembly Resolution 41/85, of 3 December 1986),

Have agreed upon the following provisions –

Chapter I: Scope of the Convention

Art. 1 The objects of the present Convention are –

a) to establish safeguards to ensure that intercountry adoptions take place in the best interests of the child and with respect for his or her fundamental rights as recognised in international law;

 | DOI:10.1163/9789004681224_049

b) to establish a system of co-operation amongst Contracting States to ensure that those safeguards are respected and thereby prevent the abduction, the sale of, or traffic in children;
c) to secure the recognition in Contracting States of adoptions made in accordance with the Convention.

Art. 2 (1) The Convention shall apply where a child habitually resident in one Contracting State ("the State of origin") has been, is being, or is to be moved to another Contracting State ("the receiving State") either after his or her adoption in the State of origin by spouses or a person habitually resident in the receiving State, or for the purposes of such an adoption in the receiving State or in the State of origin.
(2) The Convention covers only adoptions which create a permanent parent-child relationship.

Art. 3 The Convention ceases to apply if the agreements mentioned in Article 17, sub-paragraph c, have not been given before the child attains the age of eighteen years.

Chapter II: Requirements for Intercountry Adoptions

Art. 4 An adoption within the scope of the Convention shall take place only if the competent authorities of the State of origin –
a) have established that the child is adoptable;
b) have determined, after possibilities for placement of the child within the State of origin have been given due consideration, that an intercountry adoption is in the child's best interests;
c) have ensured that
   (1) the persons, institutions and authorities whose consent is necessary for adoption, have been counselled as may be necessary and duly informed of the effects of their consent, in particular whether or not an adoption will result in the termination of the legal relationship between the child and his or her family of origin,
   (2) such persons, institutions and authorities have given their consent freely, in the required legal form, and expressed or evidenced in writing,
   (3) the consents have not been induced by payment or compensation of any kind and have not been withdrawn, and
   (4) the consent of the mother, where required, has been given only after the birth of the child; and
d) have ensured, having regard to the age and degree of maturity of the child, that

(1) he or she has been counselled and duly informed of the effects of the adoption and of his or her consent to the adoption, where such consent is required,
(2) consideration has been given to the child's wishes and opinions,
(3) the child's consent to the adoption, where such consent is required, has been given freely, in the required legal form, and expressed or evidenced in writing, and
(4) such consent has not been induced by payment or compensation of any kind.

Art. 5 An adoption within the scope of the Convention shall take place only if the competent authorities of the receiving State –
a) have determined that the prospective adoptive parents are eligible and suited to adopt;
b) have ensured that the prospective adoptive parents have been counselled as may be necessary; and
c) have determined that the child is or will be authorised to enter and reside permanently in that State.

Chapter III: Central Authorities and Accredited Bodies

Art. 6 (1) A Contracting State shall designate a Central Authority to discharge the duties which are imposed by the Convention upon such authorities.
(2) Federal States, States with more than one system of law or States having autonomous territorial units shall be free to appoint more than one Central Authority and to specify the territorial or personal extent of their functions. Where a State has appointed more than one Central Authority, it shall designate the Central Authority to which any communication may be addressed for transmission to the appropriate Central Authority within that State.
Art. 7 (1) Central Authorities shall co-operate with each other and promote co-operation amongst the competent authorities in their States to protect children and to achieve the other objects of the Convention.
(2) They shall take directly all appropriate measures to –
a) provide information as to the laws of their States concerning adoption and other general information, such as statistics and standard forms;
b) keep one another informed about the operation of the Convention and, as far as possible, eliminate any obstacles to its application.

Art. 8 Central Authorities shall take, directly or through public authorities, all appropriate measures to prevent improper financial or other gain in connection with an adoption and to deter all practices contrary to the objects of the Convention.

Art. 9 Central Authorities shall take, directly or through public authorities or other bodies duly accredited in their State, all appropriate measures, in particular to –

a) collect, preserve and exchange information about the situation of the child and the prospective adoptive parents, so far as is necessary to complete the adoption;

b) facilitate, follow and expedite proceedings with a view to obtaining the adoption;

c) promote the development of adoption counselling and post-adoption services in their States;

d) provide each other with general evaluation reports about experience with intercountry adoption;

e) reply, in so far as is permitted by the law of their State, to justified requests from other Central Authorities or public authorities for information about a particular adoption situation.

Art. 10 Accreditation shall only be granted to and maintained by bodies demonstrating their competence to carry out properly the tasks with which they may be entrusted.

Art. 11 An accredited body shall –

a) pursue only non-profit objectives according to such conditions and within such limits as may be established by the competent authorities of the State of accreditation;

b) be directed and staffed by persons qualified by their ethical standards and by training or experience to work in the field of intercountry adoption; and

c) be subject to supervision by competent authorities of that State as to its composition, operation and financial situation.

Art. 12 A body accredited in one Contracting State may act in another Contracting State only if the competent authorities of both States have authorised it to do so.

Art. 13 The designation of the Central Authorities and, where appropriate, the extent of their functions, as well as the names and addresses of the accredited bodies shall be communicated by each Contracting State to the Permanent Bureau of the Hague Conference on Private International Law.

Chapter IV: Procedural Requirements in Intercountry Adoption

Art. 14 Persons habitually resident in a Contracting State, who wish to adopt a child habitually resident in another Contracting State, shall apply to the Central Authority in the State of their habitual residence.

Art. 15 (1) If the Central Authority of the receiving State is satisfied that the applicants are eligible and suited to adopt, it shall prepare a report including information about their identity, eligibility and suitability to adopt, background, family and medical history, social environment, reasons for adoption, ability to undertake an intercountry adoption, as well as the characteristics of the children for whom they would be qualified to care.
(2) It shall transmit the report to the Central Authority of the State of origin.
Art. 16 (1) If the Central Authority of the State of origin is satisfied that the child is adoptable, it shall –

a) prepare a report including information about his or her identity, adoptability, background, social environment, family history, medical history including that of the child's family, and any special needs of the child;
b) give due consideration to the child's upbringing and to his or her ethnic, religious and cultural background;
c) ensure that consents have been obtained in accordance with Article 4; and
d) determine, on the basis in particular of the reports relating to the child and the prospective adoptive parents, whether the envisaged placement is in the best interests of the child.

(2) It shall transmit to the Central Authority of the receiving State its report on the child, proof that the necessary consents have been obtained and the reasons for its determination on the placement, taking care not to reveal the identity of the mother and the father if, in the State of origin, these identities may not be disclosed.
Art. 17 Any decision in the State of origin that a child should be entrusted to prospective adoptive parents may only be made if –

a) the Central Authority of that State has ensured that the prospective adoptive parents agree;
b) the Central Authority of the receiving State has approved such decision, where such approval is required by the law of that State or by the Central Authority of the State of origin;
c) the Central Authorities of both States have agreed that the adoption may proceed; and
d) it has been determined, in accordance with Article 5, that the prospective adoptive parents are eligible and suited to adopt and that the child is or will be authorised to enter and reside permanently in the receiving State.

Art. 18 The Central Authorities of both States shall take all necessary steps to obtain permission for the child to leave the State of origin and to enter and reside permanently in the receiving State.

Art. 19 (1) The transfer of the child to the receiving State may only be carried out if the requirements of Article 17 have been satisfied.
(2) The Central Authorities of both States shall ensure that this transfer takes place in secure and appropriate circumstances and, if possible, in the company of the adoptive or prospective adoptive parents.
(3) If the transfer of the child does not take place, the reports referred to in Articles 15 and 16 are to be sent back to the authorities who forwarded them.
Art. 20 The Central Authorities shall keep each other informed about the adoption process and the measures taken to complete it, as well as about the progress of the placement if a probationary period is required.
Art. 21 (1) Where the adoption is to take place after the transfer of the child to the receiving State and it appears to the Central Authority of that State that the continued placement of the child with the prospective adoptive parents is not in the child's best interests, such Central Authority shall take the measures necessary to protect the child, in particular –

a) to cause the child to be withdrawn from the prospective adoptive parents and to arrange temporary care;
b) in consultation with the Central Authority of the State of origin, to arrange without delay a new placement of the child with a view to adoption or, if this is not appropriate, to arrange alternative long-term care; an adoption shall not take place until the Central Authority of the State of origin has been duly informed concerning the new prospective adoptive parents;
c) as a last resort, to arrange the return of the child, if his or her interests so require.

(2) Having regard in particular to the age and degree of maturity of the child, he or she shall be consulted and, where appropriate, his or her consent obtained in relation to measures to be taken under this Article.
Art. 22 (1) The functions of a Central Authority under this Chapter may be performed by public authorities or by bodies accredited under Chapter III, to the extent permitted by the law of its State.
(2) Any Contracting State may declare to the depositary of the Convention that the functions of the Central Authority under Articles 15 to 21 may be performed in that State, to the extent permitted by the law and subject to the supervision of the competent authorities of that State, also by bodies or persons who –

a) meet the requirements of integrity, professional competence, experience and accountability of that State; and
b) are qualified by their ethical standards and by training or experience to work in the field of intercountry adoption.

(3) A Contracting State which makes the declaration provided for in paragraph 2 shall keep the Permanent Bureau of the Hague Conference on Private International Law informed of the names and addresses of these bodies and persons.
(4) Any Contracting State may declare to the depositary of the Convention that adoptions of children habitually resident in its territory may only take place if the functions of the Central Authorities are performed in accordance with paragraph 1.
(5) Notwithstanding any declaration made under paragraph 2, the reports provided for in Articles 15 and 16 shall, in every case, be prepared under the responsibility of the Central Authority or other authorities or bodies in accordance with paragraph 1.

Chapter V: Recognition and Effects of the Adoption

Art. 23 (1) An adoption certified by the competent authority of the State of the adoption as having been made in accordance with the Convention shall be recognised by operation of law in the other Contracting States. The certificate shall specify when and by whom the agreements under Article 17, sub-paragraph c), were given.
(2) Each Contracting State shall, at the time of signature, ratification, acceptance, approval or accession, notify the depositary of the Convention of the identity and the functions of the authority or the authorities which, in that State, are competent to make the certification. It shall also notify the depositary of any modification in the designation of these authorities.
Art. 24 The recognition of an adoption may be refused in a Contracting State only if the adoption is manifestly contrary to its public policy, taking into account the best interests of the child.
Art. 25 Any Contracting State may declare to the depositary of the Convention that it will not be bound under this Convention to recognise adoptions made in accordance with an agreement concluded by application of Article 39, paragraph 2.
Art. 26 (1) The recognition of an adoption includes recognition of
a) the legal parent-child relationship between the child and his or her adoptive parents;
b) parental responsibility of the adoptive parents for the child;
c) the termination of a pre-existing legal relationship between the child and his or her mother and father, if the adoption has this effect in the Contracting State where it was made.

(2) In the case of an adoption having the effect of terminating a pre-existing legal parent-child relationship, the child shall enjoy in the receiving State, and

in any other Contracting State where the adoption is recognised, rights equivalent to those resulting from adoptions having this effect in each such State.
(3) The preceding paragraphs shall not prejudice the application of any provision more favourable for the child, in force in the Contracting State which recognises the adoption.
Art. 27 (1) Where an adoption granted in the State of origin does not have the effect of terminating a pre-existing legal parent-child relationship, it may, in the receiving State which recognises the adoption under the Convention, be converted into an adoption having such an effect –
a) if the law of the receiving State so permits; and
b) if the consents referred to in Article 4, sub-paragraphs c and d, have been or are given for the purpose of such an adoption.
(2) Article 23 applies to the decision converting the adoption.

Chapter VI: General Provisions

Art. 28 The Convention does not affect any law of a State of origin which requires that the adoption of a child habitually resident within that State take place in that State or which prohibits the child's placement in, or transfer to, the receiving State prior to adoption.
Art. 29 There shall be no contact between the prospective adoptive parents and the child's parents or any other person who has care of the child until the requirements of Article 4, sub-paragraphs a) to c), and Article 5, sub-paragraph a), have been met, unless the adoption takes place within a family or unless the contact is in compliance with the conditions established by the competent authority of the State of origin.
Art. 30 (1) The competent authorities of a Contracting State shall ensure that information held by them concerning the child's origin, in particular information concerning the identity of his or her parents, as well as the medical history, is preserved.
(2) They shall ensure that the child or his or her representative has access to such information, under appropriate guidance, in so far as is permitted by the law of that State.
Art. 31 Without prejudice to Article 30, personal data gathered or transmitted under the Convention, especially data referred to in Articles 15 and 16, shall be used only for the purposes for which they were gathered or transmitted.
Art. 32 (1) No one shall derive improper financial or other gain from an activity related to an intercountry adoption.
(2) Only costs and expenses, including reasonable professional fees of persons involved in the adoption, may be charged or paid.

(3) The directors, administrators and employees of bodies involved in an adoption shall not receive remuneration which is unreasonably high in relation to services rendered.

Art. 33 A competent authority which finds that any provision of the Convention has not been respected or that there is a serious risk that it may not be respected, shall immediately inform the Central Authority of its State. This Central Authority shall be responsible for ensuring that appropriate measures are taken.

Art. 34 If the competent authority of the State of destination of a document so requests, a translation certified as being in conformity with the original must be furnished. Unless otherwise provided, the costs of such translation are to be borne by the prospective adoptive parents.

Art. 35 The competent authorities of the Contracting States shall act expeditiously in the process of adoption.

Art. 36 In relation to a State which has two or more systems of law with regard to adoption applicable in different territorial units –

a) any reference to habitual residence in that State shall be construed as referring to habitual residence in a territorial unit of that State;
b) any reference to the law of that State shall be construed as referring to the law in force in the relevant territorial unit;
c) any reference to the competent authorities or to the public authorities of that State shall be construed as referring to those authorised to act in the relevant territorial unit;
d) any reference to the accredited bodies of that State shall be construed as referring to bodies accredited in the relevant territorial unit.

Art. 37 In relation to a State which with regard to adoption has two or more systems of law applicable to different categories of persons, any reference to the law of that State shall be construed as referring to the legal system specified by the law of that State.

Art. 38 A State within which different territorial units have their own rules of law in respect of adoption shall not be bound to apply the Convention where a State with a unified system of law would not be bound to do so.

Art. 39 (1) The Convention does not affect any international instrument to which Contracting States are Parties and which contains provisions on matters governed by the Convention, unless a contrary declaration is made by the States Parties to such instrument.

(2) Any Contracting State may enter into agreements with one or more other Contracting States, with a view to improving the application of the Convention in their mutual relations. These agreements may derogate only from the

provisions of Articles 14 to 16 and 18 to 21. The States which have concluded such an agreement shall transmit a copy to the depositary of the Convention.
Art. 40 No reservation to the Convention shall be permitted.
Art. 41 The Convention shall apply in every case where an application pursuant to Article 14 has been received after the Convention has entered into force in the receiving State and the State of origin.
Art. 42 The Secretary General of the Hague Conference on Private International Law shall at regular intervals convene a Special Commission in order to review the practical operation of the Convention.

Chapter VII: Final Clauses

Art. 43 (1) The Convention shall be open for signature by the States which were Members of the Hague Conference on Private International Law at the time of its Seventeenth Session and by the other States which participated in that Session.
(2) It shall be ratified, accepted or approved and the instruments of ratification, acceptance or approval shall be deposited with the Ministry of Foreign Affairs of the Kingdom of the Netherlands, depositary of the Convention.
Art. 44 (1) Any other State may accede to the Convention after it has entered into force in accordance with Article 46, paragraph 1.
(2) The instrument of accession shall be deposited with the depositary.
(3) Such accession shall have effect only as regards the relations between the acceding State and those Contracting States which have not raised an objection to its accession in the six months after the receipt of the notification referred to in sub-paragraph b) of Article 48. Such an objection may also be raised by States at the time when they ratify, accept or approve the Convention after an accession. Any such objection shall be notified to the depositary.
Art. 45 (1) If a State has two or more territorial units in which different systems of law are applicable in relation to matters dealt with in the Convention, it may at the time of signature, ratification, acceptance, approval or accession declare that this Convention shall extend to all its territorial units or only to one or more of them and may modify this declaration by submitting another declaration at any time.
(2) Any such declaration shall be notified to the depositary and shall state expressly the territorial units to which the Convention applies.
(3) If a State makes no declaration under this Article, the Convention is to extend to all territorial units of that State.
Art. 46 (1) The Convention shall enter into force on the first day of the month following the expiration of three months after the deposit of the third instrument of ratification, acceptance or approval referred to in Article 43.

(2) Thereafter the Convention shall enter into force –

a) for each State ratifying, accepting or approving it subsequently, or acceding to it, on the first day of the month following the expiration of three months after the deposit of its instrument of ratification, acceptance, approval or accession;

b) for a territorial unit to which the Convention has been extended in conformity with Article 45, on the first day of the month following the expiration of three months after the notification referred to in that Article.

Art. 47 (1) A State Party to the Convention may denounce it by a notification in writing addressed to the depositary.

(2) The denunciation takes effect on the first day of the month following the expiration of twelve months after the notification is received by the depositary. Where a longer period for the denunciation to take effect is specified in the notification, the denunciation takes effect upon the expiration of such longer period after the notification is received by the depositary.

Art. 48 The depositary shall notify the States Members of the Hague Conference on Private International Law, the other States which participated in the Seventeenth Session and the States which have acceded in accordance with Article 44, of the following –

a) the signatures, ratifications, acceptances and approvals referred to in Article 43;

b) the accessions and objections raised to accessions referred to in Article 44;

c) the date on which the Convention enters into force in accordance with Article 46;

d) the declarations and designations referred to in Articles 22, 23, 25 and 45;

e) the agreements referred to in Article 39;

f) the denunciations referred to in Article 47.

In witness whereof the undersigned, being duly authorised thereto, have signed this Convention.

Done at The Hague, on the 29th day of May 1993, in the English and French languages, both texts being equally authentic, in a single copy which shall be deposited in the archives of the Government of the Kingdom of the Netherlands, and of which a certified copy shall be sent, through diplomatic channels, to each of the States Members of the Hague Conference on Private International Law at the date of its Seventeenth Session and to each of the other States which participated in that Session.

CHAPTER 37

Convention on Jurisdiction, Applicable Law, Recognition, Enforcement and Co-operation in Respect of Parental Responsibility and Measures for the Protection of Children

Concluded at The Hague on 19 October 1996
Entry into force 1 January 2002, in accordance with article 61

The States signatory to the present Convention,

Considering the need to improve the protection of children in international situations,

Wishing to avoid conflicts between their legal systems in respect of jurisdiction, applicable law, recognition and enforcement of measures for the protection of children,

Recalling the importance of international co-operation for the protection of children,

Confirming that the best interests of the child are to be a primary consideration,

Noting that the Convention of 5 October 1961 concerning the powers of authorities and the law applicable in respect of the protection of minors is in need of revision,

Desiring to establish common provisions to this effect, taking into account the United Nations Convention on the Rights of the Child of 20 November 1989,

Have agreed on the following provisions –

Chapter 1: Scope of the Convention

Art. 1 (1) The objects of the present Convention are –

a) to determine the State whose authorities have jurisdiction to take measures directed to the protection of the person or property of the child;
b) to determine which law is to be applied by such authorities in exercising their jurisdiction;
c) to determine the law applicable to parental responsibility;

 | DOI:10.1163/9789004681224_050

d) to provide for the recognition and enforcement of such measures of protection in all Contracting States;

e) to establish such co-operation between the authorities of the Contracting States as may be necessary in order to achieve the purposes of this Convention.

(2) For the purposes of this Convention, the term 'parental responsibility' includes parental authority, or any analogous relationship of authority determining the rights, powers and responsibilities of parents, guardians or other legal representatives in relation to the person or the property of the child.

Art. 2 The Convention applies to children from the moment of their birth until they reach the age of 18 years.

Art. 3 The measures referred to in Article 1 may deal in particular with –

a) the attribution, exercise, termination or restriction of parental responsibility, as well as its delegation;

b) rights of custody, including rights relating to the care of the person of the child and, in particular, the right to determine the child's place of residence, as well as rights of access including the right to take a child for a limited period of time to a place other than the child's habitual residence;

c) guardianship, curatorship and analogous institutions;

d) the designation and functions of any person or body having charge of the child's person or property, representing or assisting the child;

e) the placement of the child in a foster family or in institutional care, or the provision of care by kafala or an analogous institution;

f) the supervision by a public authority of the care of a child by any person having charge of the child;

g) the administration, conservation or disposal of the child's property.

Art. 4 The Convention does not apply to –

a) the establishment or contesting of a parent-child relationship;

b) decisions on adoption, measures preparatory to adoption, or the annulment or revocation of adoption;

c) the name and forenames of the child;

d) emancipation;

e) maintenance obligations;

f) trusts or succession;

g) social security;

h) public measures of a general nature in matters of education or health;

i) measures taken as a result of penal offences committed by children;

j) decisions on the right of asylum and on immigration.

Chapter II: Jurisdiction

Art. 5 (1) The judicial or administrative authorities of the Contracting State of the habitual residence of the child have jurisdiction to take measures directed to the protection of the child's person or property.
(2) Subject to Article 7, in case of a change of the child's habitual residence to another Contracting State, the authorities of the State of the new habitual residence have jurisdiction.

Art. 6 (1) For refugee children and children who, due to disturbances occurring in their country, are internationally displaced, the authorities of the Contracting State on the territory of which these children are present as a result of their displacement have the jurisdiction provided for in paragraph 1 of Article 5.
(2) The provisions of the preceding paragraph also apply to children whose habitual residence cannot be established.

Art. 7 (1) In case of wrongful removal or retention of the child, the authorities of the Contracting State in which the child was habitually resident immediately before the removal or retention keep their jurisdiction until the child has acquired a habitual residence in another State, and

a) each person, institution or other body having rights of custody has acquiesced in the removal or retention; or
b) the child has resided in that other State for a period of at least one year after the person, institution or other body having rights of custody has or should have had knowledge of the whereabouts of the child, no request for return lodged within that period is still pending, and the child is settled in his or her new environment.

(2) The removal or the retention of a child is to be considered wrongful where –

a) it is in breach of rights of custody attributed to a person, an institution or any other body, either jointly or alone, under the law of the State in which the child was habitually resident immediately before the removal or retention; and
b) at the time of removal or retention those rights were actually exercised, either jointly or alone, or would have been so exercised but for the removal or retention.

The rights of custody mentioned in sub-paragraph a above, may arise in particular by operation of law or by reason of a judicial or administrative decision, or by reason of an agreement having legal effect under the law of that State.
(3) So long as the authorities first mentioned in paragraph 1 keep their jurisdiction, the authorities of the Contracting State to which the child has been removed or in which he or she has been retained can take only such urgent

measures under Article 11 as are necessary for the protection of the person or property of the child.

Art. 8 (1) By way of exception, the authority of a Contracting State having jurisdiction under Article 5 or 6, if it considers that the authority of another Contracting State would be better placed in the particular case to assess the best interests of the child, may either

- request that other authority, directly or with the assistance of the Central Authority of its State, to assume jurisdiction to take such measures of protection as it considers to be necessary, or
- suspend consideration of the case and invite the parties to introduce such a request before the authority of that other State.

(2) The Contracting States whose authorities may be addressed as provided in the preceding paragraph are

a) a State of which the child is a national,
b) a State in which property of the child is located,
c) a State whose authorities are seised of an application for divorce or legal separation of the child's parents, or for annulment of their marriage,
d) a State with which the child has a substantial connection.

(3) The authorities concerned may proceed to an exchange of views.

(4) The authority addressed as provided in paragraph 1 may assume jurisdiction, in place of the authority having jurisdiction under Article 5 or 6, if it considers that this is in the child's best interests.

Art. 9 (1) If the authorities of a Contracting State referred to in Article 8, paragraph 2, consider that they are better placed in the particular case to assess the child's best interests, they may either

- request the competent authority of the Contracting State of the habitual residence of the child, directly or with the assistance of the Central Authority of that State, that they be authorised to exercise jurisdiction to take the measures of protection which they consider to be necessary, or
- invite the parties to introduce such a request before the authority of the Contracting State of the habitual residence of the child.

(2) The authorities concerned may proceed to an exchange of views.

(3) The authority initiating the request may exercise jurisdiction in place of the authority of the Contracting State of the habitual residence of the child only if the latter authority has accepted the request.

Art. 10 (1) Without prejudice to Articles 5 to 9, the authorities of a Contracting State exercising jurisdiction to decide upon an application for divorce or legal separation of the parents of a child habitually resident in another Contracting State, or for annulment of their marriage, may, if the law of their State so provides, take measures directed to the protection of the person or property of such child if

a) at the time of commencement of the proceedings, one of his or her parents habitually resides in that State and one of them has parental responsibility in relation to the child, and
b) the jurisdiction of these authorities to take such measures has been accepted by the parents, as well as by any other person who has parental responsibility in relation to the child, and is in the best interests of the child.

(2) The jurisdiction provided for by paragraph 1 to take measures for the protection of the child ceases as soon as the decision allowing or refusing the application for divorce, legal separation or annulment of the marriage has become final, or the proceedings have come to an end for another reason.

Art. 11 (1) In all cases of urgency, the authorities of any Contracting State in whose territory the child or property belonging to the child is present have jurisdiction to take any necessary measures of protection.

(2) The measures taken under the preceding paragraph with regard to a child habitually resident in a Contracting State shall lapse as soon as the authorities which have jurisdiction under Articles 5 to 10 have taken the measures required by the situation.

(3) The measures taken under paragraph 1 with regard to a child who is habitually resident in a non-Contracting State shall lapse in each Contracting State as soon as measures required by the situation and taken by the authorities of another State are recognised in the Contracting State in question.

Art. 12 (1) Subject to Article 7, the authorities of a Contracting State in whose territory the child or property belonging to the child is present have jurisdiction to take measures of a provisional character for the protection of the person or property of the child which have a territorial effect limited to the State in question, in so far as such measures are not incompatible with measures already taken by authorities which have jurisdiction under Articles 5 to 10.

(2) The measures taken under the preceding paragraph with regard to a child habitually resident in a Contracting State shall lapse as soon as the authorities which have jurisdiction under Articles 5 to 10 have taken a decision in respect of the measures of protection which may be required by the situation.

(3) The measures taken under paragraph 1 with regard to a child who is habitually resident in a non-Contracting State shall lapse in the Contracting State where the measures were taken as soon as measures required by the situation and taken by the authorities of another State are recognised in the Contracting State in question.

Art. 13 (1) The authorities of a Contracting State which have jurisdiction under Articles 5 to 10 to take measures for the protection of the person or property of the child must abstain from exercising this jurisdiction if, at the time of the commencement of the proceedings, corresponding measures have been requested from the authorities of another Contracting State having jurisdiction under Articles 5 to 10 at the time of the request and are still under consideration.
(2) The provisions of the preceding paragraph shall not apply if the authorities before whom the request for measures was initially introduced have declined jurisdiction.
Art. 14 The measures taken in application of Articles 5 to 10 remain in force according to their terms, even if a change of circumstances has eliminated the basis upon which jurisdiction was founded, so long as the authorities which have jurisdiction under the Convention have not modified, replaced or terminated such measures.

Chapter III: Applicable Law

Art. 15 (1) In exercising their jurisdiction under the provisions of Chapter II, the authorities of the Contracting States shall apply their own law.
(2) However, in so far as the protection of the person or the property of the child requires, they may exceptionally apply or take into consideration the law of another State with which the situation has a substantial connection.
(3) If the child's habitual residence changes to another Contracting State, the law of that other State governs, from the time of the change, the conditions of application of the measures taken in the State of the former habitual residence.
Art. 16 (1) The attribution or extinction of parental responsibility by operation of law, without the intervention of a judicial or administrative authority, is governed by the law of the State of the habitual residence of the child.
(2) The attribution or extinction of parental responsibility by an agreement or a unilateral act, without intervention of a judicial or administrative authority, is governed by the law of the State of the child's habitual residence at the time when the agreement or unilateral act takes effect.
(3) Parental responsibility which exists under the law of the State of the child's habitual residence subsists after a change of that habitual residence to another State.
(4) If the child's habitual residence changes, the attribution of parental responsibility by operation of law to a person who does not already have such responsibility is governed by the law of the State of the new habitual residence.

Art. 17 The exercise of parental responsibility is governed by the law of the State of the child's habitual residence. If the child's habitual residence changes, it is governed by the law of the State of the new habitual residence.
Art. 18 The parental responsibility referred to in Article 16 may be terminated, or the conditions of its exercise modified, by measures taken under this Convention.
Art. 19 (1) The validity of a transaction entered into between a third party and another person who would be entitled to act as the child's legal representative under the law of the State where the transaction was concluded cannot be contested, and the third party cannot be held liable, on the sole ground that the other person was not entitled to act as the child's legal representative under the law designated by the provisions of this Chapter, unless the third party knew or should have known that the parental responsibility was governed by the latter law.
(2) The preceding paragraph applies only if the transaction was entered into between persons present on the territory of the same State.
Art. 20 The provisions of this Chapter apply even if the law designated by them is the law of a non-Contracting State.
Art. 21 (1) In this Chapter the term "law" means the law in force in a State other than its choice of law rules.
(2) However, if the law applicable according to Article 16 is that of a non-Contracting State and if the choice of law rules of that State designate the law of another non-Contracting State which would apply its own law, the law of the latter State applies. If that other non-Contracting State would not apply its own law, the applicable law is that designated by Article 16.
Art. 22 The application of the law designated by the provisions of this Chapter can be refused only if this application would be manifestly contrary to public policy, taking into account the best interests of the child.

Chapter IV: Recognition and Enforcement

Art. 23 (1) The measures taken by the authorities of a Contracting State shall be recognised by operation of law in all other Contracting States.
(2) Recognition may however be refused –
a) if the measure was taken by an authority whose jurisdiction was not based on one of the grounds provided for in Chapter II;
b) if the measure was taken, except in a case of urgency, in the context of a judicial or administrative proceeding, without the child having been provided the opportunity to be heard, in violation of fundamental principles of procedure of the requested State;

c) on the request of any person claiming that the measure infringes his or her parental responsibility, if such measure was taken, except in a case of urgency, without such person having been given an opportunity to be heard;
d) if such recognition is manifestly contrary to public policy of the requested State, taking into account the best interests of the child;
e) if the measure is incompatible with a later measure taken in the non-Contracting State of the habitual residence of the child, where this later measure fulfils the requirements for recognition in the requested State;
f) if the procedure provided in Article 33 has not been complied with.

Art. 24 Without prejudice to Article 23, paragraph 1, any interested person may request from the competent authorities of a Contracting State that they decide on the recognition or non-recognition of a measure taken in another Contracting State. The procedure is governed by the law of the requested State.

Art. 25 The authority of the requested State is bound by the findings of fact on which the authority of the State where the measure was taken based its jurisdiction.

Art. 26 (1) If measures taken in one Contracting State and enforceable there require enforcement in another Contracting State, they shall, upon request by an interested party, be declared enforceable or registered for the purpose of enforcement in that other State according to the procedure provided in the law of the latter State.

(2) Each Contracting State shall apply to the declaration of enforceability or registration a simple and rapid procedure.

(3) The declaration of enforceability or registration may be refused only for one of the reasons set out in Article 23, paragraph 2.

Art. 27 Without prejudice to such review as is necessary in the application of the preceding Articles, there shall be no review of the merits of the measure taken.

Art. 28 Measures taken in one Contracting State and declared enforceable, or registered for the purpose of enforcement, in another Contracting State shall be enforced in the latter State as if they had been taken by the authorities of that State. Enforcement takes place in accordance with the law of the requested State to the extent provided by such law, taking into consideration the best interests of the child.

Chapter V: Co-operation

Art. 29 (1) A Contracting State shall designate a Central Authority to discharge the duties which are imposed by the Convention on such authorities.

(2) Federal States, States with more than one system of law or States having autonomous territorial units shall be free to appoint more than one Central Authority and to specify the territorial or personal extent of their functions. Where a State has appointed more than one Central Authority, it shall designate the Central Authority to which any communication may be addressed for transmission to the appropriate Central Authority within that State.

Art. 30 (1) Central Authorities shall co-operate with each other and promote co-operation amongst the competent authorities in their States to achieve the purposes of the Convention.

(2) They shall, in connection with the application of the Convention, take appropriate steps to provide information as to the laws of, and services available in, their States relating to the protection of children.

Art. 31 The Central Authority of a Contracting State, either directly or through public authorities or other bodies, shall take all appropriate steps to –

a) facilitate the communications and offer the assistance provided for in Articles 8 and 9 and in this Chapter;
b) facilitate, by mediation, conciliation or similar means, agreed solutions for the protection of the person or property of the child in situations to which the Convention applies;
c) provide, on the request of a competent authority of another Contracting State, assistance in discovering the whereabouts of a child where it appears that the child may be present and in need of protection within the territory of the requested State.

Art. 32 On a request made with supporting reasons by the Central Authority or other competent authority of any Contracting State with which the child has a substantial connection, the Central Authority of the Contracting State in which the child is habitually resident and present may, directly or through public authorities or other bodies,

a) provide a report on the situation of the child;
b) request the competent authority of its State to consider the need to take measures for the protection of the person or property of the child.

Art. 33 (1) If an authority having jurisdiction under Articles 5 to 10 contemplates the placement of the child in a foster family or institutional care, or the provision of care by kafala or an analogous institution, and if such placement or such provision of care is to take place in another Contracting State, it shall first consult with the Central Authority or other competent authority of the latter State. To that effect it shall transmit a report on the child together with the reasons for the proposed placement or provision of care.

(2) The decision on the placement or provision of care may be made in the requesting State only if the Central Authority or other competent authority of

the requested State has consented to the placement or provision of care, taking into account the child's best interests.

Art. 34 (1) Where a measure of protection is contemplated, the competent authorities under the Convention, if the situation of the child so requires, may request any authority of another Contracting State which has information relevant to the protection of the child to communicate such information.

(2) A Contracting State may declare that requests under paragraph 1 shall be communicated to its authorities only through its Central Authority.

Art. 35 (1) The competent authorities of a Contracting State may request the authorities of another Contracting State to assist in the implementation of measures of protection taken under this Convention, especially in securing the effective exercise of rights of access as well as of the right to maintain direct contacts on a regular basis.

(2) The authorities of a Contracting State in which the child does not habitually reside may, on the request of a parent residing in that State who is seeking to obtain or to maintain access to the child, gather information or evidence and may make a finding on the suitability of that parent to exercise access and on the conditions under which access is to be exercised. An authority exercising jurisdiction under Articles 5 to 10 to determine an application concerning access to the child, shall admit and consider such information, evidence and finding before reaching its decision.

(3) An authority having jurisdiction under Articles 5 to 10 to decide on access may adjourn a proceeding pending the outcome of a request made under paragraph 2, in particular, when it is considering an application to restrict or terminate access rights granted in the State of the child's former habitual residence.

(4) Nothing in this Article shall prevent an authority having jurisdiction under Articles 5 to 10 from taking provisional measures pending the outcome of the request made under paragraph 2.

Art. 36 In any case where the child is exposed to a serious danger, the competent authorities of the Contracting State where measures for the protection of the child have been taken or are under consideration, if they are informed that the child's residence has changed to, or that the child is present in another State, shall inform the authorities of that other State about the danger involved and the measures taken or under consideration.

Art. 37 An authority shall not request or transmit any information under this Chapter if to do so would, in its opinion, be likely to place the child's person or property in danger, or constitute a serious threat to the liberty or life of a member of the child's family.

Art. 38 (1) Without prejudice to the possibility of imposing reasonable charges for the provision of services, Central Authorities and other public authorities

of Contracting States shall bear their own costs in applying the provisions of this Chapter.
(2) Any Contracting State may enter into agreements with one or more other Contracting States concerning the allocation of charges.
Art. 39 Any Contracting State may enter into agreements with one or more other Contracting States with a view to improving the application of this Chapter in their mutual relations. The States which have concluded such an agreement shall transmit a copy to the depositary of the Convention.

Chapter VI: General Provisions

Art. 40 (1) The authorities of the Contracting State of the child's habitual residence, or of the Contracting State where a measure of protection has been taken, may deliver to the person having parental responsibility or to the person entrusted with protection of the child's person or property, at his or her request, a certificate indicating the capacity in which that person is entitled to act and the powers conferred upon him or her.
(2) The capacity and powers indicated in the certificate are presumed to be vested in that person, in the absence of proof to the contrary.
(3) Each Contracting State shall designate the authorities competent to draw up the certificate.
Art. 41 Personal data gathered or transmitted under the Convention shall be used only for the purposes for which they were gathered or transmitted.
Art. 42 The authorities to whom information is transmitted shall ensure its confidentiality, in accordance with the law of their State.
Art. 43 All documents forwarded or delivered under this Convention shall be exempt from legalisation or any analogous formality.
Art. 44 Each Contracting State may designate the authorities to which requests under Articles 8, 9 and 33 are to be addressed.
Art. 45 (1) The designations referred to in Articles 29 and 44 shall be communicated to the Permanent Bureau of the Hague Conference on Private International Law.
(2) The declaration referred to in Article 34, paragraph 2, shall be made to the depositary of the Convention.
Art. 46 A Contracting State in which different systems of law or sets of rules of law apply to the protection of the child and his or her property shall not be bound to apply the rules of the Convention to conflicts solely between such different systems or sets of rules of law.
Art. 47 In relation to a State in which two or more systems of law or sets of rules of law with regard to any matter dealt with in this Convention apply in different territorial units –

(1) any reference to habitual residence in that State shall be construed as referring to habitual residence in a territorial unit;
(2) any reference to the presence of the child in that State shall be construed as referring to presence in a territorial unit;
(3) any reference to the location of property of the child in that State shall be construed as referring to location of property of the child in a territorial unit;
(4) any reference to the State of which the child is a national shall be construed as referring to the territorial unit designated by the law of that State or, in the absence of relevant rules, to the territorial unit with which the child has the closest connection;
(5) any reference to the State whose authorities are seised of an application for divorce or legal separation of the child's parents, or for annulment of their marriage, shall be construed as referring to the territorial unit whose authorities are seised of such application;
(6) any reference to the State with which the child has a substantial connection shall be construed as referring to the territorial unit with which the child has such connection;
(7) any reference to the State to which the child has been removed or in which he or she has been retained shall be construed as referring to the relevant territorial unit to which the child has been removed or in which he or she has been retained;
(8) any reference to bodies or authorities of that State, other than Central Authorities, shall be construed as referring to those authorised to act in the relevant territorial unit;
(9) any reference to the law or procedure or authority of the State in which a measure has been taken shall be construed as referring to the law or procedure or authority of the territorial unit in which such measure was taken;
(10) any reference to the law or procedure or authority of the requested State shall be construed as referring to the law or procedure or authority of the territorial unit in which recognition or enforcement is sought.

Art. 48 For the purpose of identifying the applicable law under Chapter III, in relation to a State which comprises two or more territorial units each of which has its own system of law or set of rules of law in respect of matters covered by this Convention, the following rules apply –

a) if there are rules in force in such a State identifying which territorial unit's law is applicable, the law of that unit applies;
b) in the absence of such rules, the law of the relevant territorial unit as defined in Article 47 applies.

Art. 49 For the purpose of identifying the applicable law under Chapter III, in relation to a State which has two or more systems of law or sets of rules of law applicable to different categories of persons in respect of matters covered by this Convention, the following rules apply –

a) if there are rules in force in such a State identifying which among such laws applies, that law applies;

b) in the absence of such rules, the law of the system or the set of rules of law with which the child has the closest connection applies.

Art. 50 This Convention shall not affect the application of the Convention of 25 October 1980 on the Civil Aspects of International Child Abduction, as between Parties to both Conventions. Nothing, however, precludes provisions of this Convention from being invoked for the purposes of obtaining the return of a child who has been wrongfully removed or retained or of organising access rights.

Art. 51 In relations between the Contracting States this Convention replaces the Convention of 5 October 1961 concerning the powers of authorities and the law applicable in respect of the protection of minors, and the Convention governing the guardianship of minors, signed at The Hague 12 June 1902, without prejudice to the recognition of measures taken under the Convention of 5 October 1961 mentioned above.

Art. 52 (1) This Convention does not affect any international instrument to which Contracting States are Parties and which contains provisions on matters governed by the Convention, unless a contrary declaration is made by the States Parties to such instrument.

(2) This Convention does not affect the possibility for one or more Contracting States to conclude agreements which contain, in respect of children habitually resident in any of the States Parties to such agreements, provisions on matters governed by this Convention.

(3) Agreements to be concluded by one or more Contracting States on matters within the scope of this Convention do not affect, in the relationship of such States with other Contracting States, the application of the provisions of this Convention.

(4) The preceding paragraphs also apply to uniform laws based on special ties of a regional or other nature between the States concerned.

Art. 53 (1) The Convention shall apply to measures only if they are taken in a State after the Convention has entered into force for that State.

(2) The Convention shall apply to the recognition and enforcement of measures taken after its entry into force as between the State where the measures have been taken and the requested State.

Art. 54 (1) Any communication sent to the Central Authority or to another authority of a Contracting State shall be in the original language, and shall be accompanied by a translation into the official language or one of the official

languages of the other State or, where that is not feasible, a translation into French or English.
(2) However, a Contracting State may, by making a reservation in accordance with Article 60, object to the use of either French or English, but not both.
Art. 55 (1) A Contracting State may, in accordance with Article 60,
a) reserve the jurisdiction of its authorities to take measures directed to the protection of property of a child situated on its territory;
b) reserve the right not to recognise any parental responsibility or measure in so far as it is incompatible with any measure taken by its authorities in relation to that property.
(2) The reservation may be restricted to certain categories of property.
Art. 56 The Secretary General of the Hague Conference on Private International Law shall at regular intervals convoke a Special Commission in order to review the practical operation of the Convention.

Chapter VII: Final Clauses

Art. 57 (1) The Convention shall be open for signature by the States which were Members of the Hague Conference on Private International Law at the time of its Eighteenth Session.
(2) It shall be ratified, accepted or approved and the instruments of ratification, acceptance or approval shall be deposited with the Ministry of Foreign Affairs of the Kingdom of the Netherlands, depositary of the Convention.
Art. 58 (1) Any other State may accede to the Convention after it has entered into force in accordance with Article 61, paragraph 1.
(2) The instrument of accession shall be deposited with the depositary.
(3) Such accession shall have effect only as regards the relations between the acceding State and those Contracting States which have not raised an objection to its accession in the six months after the receipt of the notification referred to in sub-paragraph b of Article 63. Such an objection may also be raised by States at the time when they ratify, accept or approve the Convention after an accession. Any such objection shall be notified to the depositary.
Art. 59 (1) If a State has two or more territorial units in which different systems of law are applicable in relation to matters dealt with in this Convention, it may at the time of signature, ratification, acceptance, approval or accession declare that the Convention shall extend to all its territorial units or only to one or more of them and may modify this declaration by submitting another declaration at any time.
(2) Any such declaration shall be notified to the depositary and shall state expressly the territorial units to which the Convention applies.

(3) If a State makes no declaration under this Article, the Convention is to extend to all territorial units of that State.

Art. 60 (1) Any State may, not later than the time of ratification, acceptance, approval or accession, or at the time of making a declaration in terms of Article 59, make one or both of the reservations provided for in Articles 54, paragraph 2, and 55. No other reservation shall be permitted.

(2) Any State may at any time withdraw a reservation it has made. The withdrawal shall be notified to the depositary.

(3) The reservation shall cease to have effect on the first day of the third calendar month after the notification referred to in the preceding paragraph.

Art. 61 (1) The Convention shall enter into force on the first day of the month following the expiration of three months after the deposit of the third instrument of ratification, acceptance or approval referred to in Article 57.

(2) Thereafter the Convention shall enter into force –

a) for each State ratifying, accepting or approving it subsequently, on the first day of the month following the expiration of three months after the deposit of its instrument of ratification, acceptance, approval or accession;
b) for each State acceding, on the first day of the month following the expiration of three months after the expiration of the period of six months provided in Article 58, paragraph 3;
c) for a territorial unit to which the Convention has been extended in conformity with Article 59, on the first day of the month following the expiration of three months after the notification referred to in that Article.

Art. 62 (1) A State Party to the Convention may denounce it by a notification in writing addressed to the depositary. The denunciation may be limited to certain territorial units to which the Convention applies.

(2) The denunciation takes effect on the first day of the month following the expiration of twelve months after the notification is received by the depositary. Where a longer period for the denunciation to take effect is specified in the notification, the denunciation takes effect upon the expiration of such longer period.

Art. 63 The depositary shall notify the States Members of the Hague Conference on Private International Law and the States which have acceded in accordance with Article 58 of the following –

a) the signatures, ratifications, acceptances and approvals referred to in Article 57;
b) the accessions and objections raised to accessions referred to in Article 58;

c) the date on which the Convention enters into force in accordance with Article 61;
d) the declarations referred to in Articles 34, paragraph 2, and 59;
e) the agreements referred to in Article 39;
f) the reservations referred to in Articles 54, paragraph 2, and 55 and the withdrawals referred to in Article 60, paragraph 2;
g) the denunciations referred to in Article 62.

In witness whereof the undersigned, being duly authorised thereto, have signed this Convention.

Done at The Hague, on the 19th day of October 1996, in the English and French languages, both texts being equally authentic, in a single copy which shall be deposited in the archives of the Government of the Kingdom of the Netherlands, and of which a certified copy shall be sent, through diplomatic channels, to each of the States Members of the Hague Conference on Private International Law at the date of its Eighteenth Session.

CHAPTER 38

Convention on the International Recovery of Child Support and Other Forms of Family Maintenance

Concluded 23 November 2007
Entry into force 1 January 2013, in accordance with article 60

The States signatory to the present Convention,

Desiring to improve co-operation among States for the international recovery of child support and other forms of family maintenance,

Aware of the need for procedures which produce results and are accessible, prompt, efficient, cost-effective, responsive and fair,

Wishing to build upon the best features of existing Hague Conventions and other international instruments, in particular the United Nations Convention on the Recovery Abroad of Maintenance of 20 June 1956,

Seeking to take advantage of advances in technologies and to create a flexible system which can continue to evolve as needs change and further advances in technology create new opportunities,

Recalling that, in accordance with Articles 3 and 27 of the United Nations Convention on the Rights of the Child of 20 November 1989,

- in all actions concerning children the best interests of the child shall be a primary consideration,
- every child has a right to a standard of living adequate for the child's physical, mental, spiritual, moral and social development,
- the parent(s) or others responsible for the child have the primary responsibility to secure, within their abilities and financial capacities, the conditions of living necessary for the child's development, and
- States Parties should take all appropriate measures, including the conclusion of international agreements, to secure the recovery of maintenance for the child from the parent(s) or other responsible persons, in particular where such persons live in a State different from that of the child,

Have resolved to conclude this Convention and have agreed upon the following provisions –

Chapter 1: Object, Scope and Definitions

Article 1 – Object

The object of the present Convention is to ensure the effective international recovery of child support and other forms of family maintenance, in particular by –

a) establishing a comprehensive system of co-operation between the authorities of the Contracting States;
b) making available applications for the establishment of maintenance decisions;
c) providing for the recognition and enforcement of maintenance decisions; and
d) requiring effective measures for the prompt enforcement of maintenance decisions.

Article 2 – Scope

(1) This Convention shall apply –

a) to maintenance obligations arising from a parent-child relationship towards a person under the age of 21 years;
b) to recognition and enforcement or enforcement of a decision for spousal support when the application is made with a claim within the scope of sub-paragraph a); and
c) with the exception of Chapters II and III, to spousal support.

(2) Any Contracting State may reserve, in accordance with Article 62, the right to limit the application of the Convention under sub-paragraph 1 a), to persons who have not attained the age of 18 years. A Contracting State which makes this reservation shall not be entitled to claim the application of the Convention to persons of the age excluded by its reservation.

(3) Any Contracting State may declare in accordance with Article 63 that it will extend the application of the whole or any part of the Convention to any maintenance obligation arising from a family relationship, parentage, marriage or affinity, including in particular obligations in respect of vulnerable persons. Any such declaration shall give rise to obligations between two Contracting States only in so far as their declarations cover the same maintenance obligations and parts of the Convention.

(4) The provisions of this Convention shall apply to children regardless of the marital status of the parents.

Article 3 – Definitions

For the purposes of this Convention –

a) "creditor" means an individual to whom maintenance is owed or is alleged to be owed;
b) "debtor" means an individual who owes or who is alleged to owe maintenance;
c) "legal assistance" means the assistance necessary to enable applicants to know and assert their rights and to ensure that applications are fully and effectively dealt with in the requested State. The means of providing such assistance may include as necessary legal advice, assistance in bringing a case before an authority, legal representation and exemption from costs of proceedings;
d) "agreement in writing" means an agreement recorded in any medium, the information contained in which is accessible so as to be usable for subsequent reference;
e) "maintenance arrangement" means an agreement in writing relating to the payment of maintenance which -
    i) has been formally drawn up or registered as an authentic instrument by a competent authority; or
    ii) has been authenticated by, or concluded, registered or filed with a competent authority, and may be the subject of review and modification by a competent authority;
f) "vulnerable person" means a person who, by reason of an impairment or insufficiency of his or her personal faculties, is not able to support him or herself.

Chapter II: Administrative Co-operation

Article 4 – Designation of Central Authorities

(1) A Contracting State shall designate a Central Authority to discharge the duties that are imposed by the Convention on such an authority.
(2) Federal States, States with more than one system of law or States having autonomous territorial units shall be free to appoint more than one Central Authority and shall specify the territorial or personal extent of their functions. Where a State has appointed more than one Central Authority, it shall designate the Central Authority to which any communication may be addressed for transmission to the appropriate Central Authority within that State.
(3) The designation of the Central Authority or Central Authorities, their contact details, and where appropriate the extent of their functions as specified in paragraph 2, shall be communicated by a Contracting State to the Permanent Bureau of the Hague Conference on Private International Law at the time when the instrument of ratification or accession is deposited or when a declaration

is submitted in accordance with Article 61. Contracting States shall promptly inform the Permanent Bureau of any changes.

Article 5 – General Functions of Central Authorities

Central Authorities shall –

a) co-operate with each other and promote co-operation amongst the competent authorities in their States to achieve the purposes of the Convention;
b) seek as far as possible solutions to difficulties which arise in the application of the Convention.

Article 6 – Specific Functions of Central Authorities

(1) Central Authorities shall provide assistance in relation to applications under Chapter III. In particular they shall –

a) transmit and receive such applications;
b) initiate or facilitate the institution of proceedings in respect of such applications.

(2) In relation to such applications they shall take all appropriate measures –

a) where the circumstances require, to provide or facilitate the provision of legal assistance;
b) to help locate the debtor or the creditor;
c) to help obtain relevant information concerning the income and, if necessary, other financial circumstances of the debtor or creditor, including the location of assets;
d) to encourage amicable solutions with a view to obtaining voluntary payment of maintenance, where suitable by use of mediation, conciliation or similar processes;
e) to facilitate the ongoing enforcement of maintenance decisions, including any arrears;
f) to facilitate the collection and expeditious transfer of maintenance payments;
g) to facilitate the obtaining of documentary or other evidence;
h) to provide assistance in establishing parentage where necessary for the recovery of maintenance;
i) to initiate or facilitate the institution of proceedings to obtain any necessary provisional measures that are territorial in nature and the purpose of which is to secure the outcome of a pending maintenance application;
j) to facilitate service of documents.

(3) The functions of the Central Authority under this Article may, to the extent permitted under the law of its State, be performed by public bodies, or other

bodies subject to the supervision of the competent authorities of that State. The designation of any such public bodies or other bodies, as well as their contact details and the extent of their functions, shall be communicated by a Contracting State to the Permanent Bureau of the Hague Conference on Private International Law. Contracting States shall promptly inform the Permanent Bureau of any changes.
(4) Nothing in this Article or Article 7 shall be interpreted as imposing an obligation on a Central Authority to exercise powers that can be exercised only by judicial authorities under the law of the requested State.

Article 7 – Requests for Specific Measures

(1) A Central Authority may make a request, supported by reasons, to another Central Authority to take appropriate specific measures under Article 6(2) b), c), g), h), i) and j) when no application under Article 10 is pending. The requested Central Authority shall take such measures as are appropriate if satisfied that they are necessary to assist a potential applicant in making an application under Article 10 or in determining whether such an application should be initiated.
(2) A Central Authority may also take specific measures on the request of another Central Authority in relation to a case having an international element concerning the recovery of maintenance pending in the requesting State.

Article 8 – Central Authority Costs

(1) Each Central Authority shall bear its own costs in applying this Convention.
(2) Central Authorities may not impose any charge on an applicant for the provision of their services under the Convention save for exceptional costs arising from a request for a specific measure under Article 7.
(3) The requested Central Authority may not recover the costs of the services referred to in paragraph 2 without the prior consent of the applicant to the provision of those services at such cost.

Chapter III: Applications through Central Authorities

Article 9 – Application through Central Authorities

An application under this Chapter shall be made through the Central Authority of the Contracting State in which the applicant resides to the Central Authority of the requested State. For the purpose of this provision, residence excludes mere presence.

Article 10 – Available Applications

(1) The following categories of application shall be available to a creditor in a requesting State seeking to recover maintenance under this Convention –

a) recognition or recognition and enforcement of a decision;
b) enforcement of a decision made or recognised in the requested State;
c) establishment of a decision in the requested State where there is no existing decision, including where necessary the establishment of parentage;
d) establishment of a decision in the requested State where recognition and enforcement of a decision is not possible, or is refused, because of the lack of a basis for recognition and enforcement under Article 20, or on the grounds specified in Article 22 b) or e);
e) modification of a decision made in the requested State;
f) modification of a decision made in a State other than the requested State.

(2) The following categories of application shall be available to a debtor in a requesting State against whom there is an existing maintenance decision –

a) recognition of a decision, or an equivalent procedure leading to the suspension, or limiting the enforcement, of a previous decision in the requested State;
b) modification of a decision made in the requested State;
c) modification of a decision made in a State other than the requested State.

(3) Save as otherwise provided in this Convention, the applications in paragraphs 1 and 2 shall be determined under the law of the requested State, and applications in paragraphs 1 c) to f) and 2 b) and c) shall be subject to the jurisdictional rules applicable in the requested State.

Article 11 – Application Contents

(1) All applications under Article 10 shall as a minimum include –

a) a statement of the nature of the application or applications;
b) the name and contact details, including the address and date of birth of the applicant;
c) the name and, if known, address and date of birth of the respondent;
d) the name and date of birth of any person for whom maintenance is sought;
e) the grounds upon which the application is based;
f) in an application by a creditor, information concerning where the maintenance payment should be sent or electronically transmitted;
g) save in an application under Article 10(1) a) and (2) a), any information or document specified by declaration in accordance with Article 63 by the requested State;

h) the name and contact details of the person or unit from the Central Authority of the requesting State responsible for processing the application.

(2) As appropriate, and to the extent known, the application shall in addition in particular include –

a) the financial circumstances of the creditor;

b) the financial circumstances of the debtor, including the name and address of the employer of the debtor and the nature and location of the assets of the debtor;

c) any other information that may assist with the location of the respondent.

(3) The application shall be accompanied by any necessary supporting information or documentation including documentation concerning the entitlement of the applicant to free legal assistance. In the case of applications under Article 10(1) a) and (2) a), the application shall be accompanied only by the documents listed in Article 25.

(4) An application under Article 10 may be made in the form recommended and published by the Hague Conference on Private International Law.

Article 12 – Transmission, Receipt and Processing of Applications and Cases through Central Authorities

(1) The Central Authority of the requesting State shall assist the applicant in ensuring that the application is accompanied by all the information and documents known by it to be necessary for consideration of the application.

(2) The Central Authority of the requesting State shall, when satisfied that the application complies with the requirements of the Convention, transmit the application on behalf of and with the consent of the applicant to the Central Authority of the requested State. The application shall be accompanied by the transmittal form set out in Annex 1. The Central Authority of the requesting State shall, when requested by the Central Authority of the requested State, provide a complete copy certified by the competent authority in the State of origin of any document specified under Articles 16(3), 25(1) a), b) and d) and (3) b) and 30(3).

(3) The requested Central Authority shall, within six weeks from the date of receipt of the application, acknowledge receipt in the form set out in Annex 2, and inform the Central Authority of the requesting State what initial steps have been or will be taken to deal with the application, and may request any further necessary documents and information. Within the same six-week period, the requested Central Authority shall provide to the requesting Central Authority the name and contact details of the person or unit responsible for responding to inquiries regarding the progress of the application.

(4) Within three months after the acknowledgement, the requested Central Authority shall inform the requesting Central Authority of the status of the application.
(5) Requesting and requested Central Authorities shall keep each other informed of –
a) the person or unit responsible for a particular case;
b) the progress of the case,
and shall provide timely responses to enquiries.
(6) Central Authorities shall process a case as quickly as a proper consideration of the issues will allow.
(7) Central Authorities shall employ the most rapid and efficient means of communication at their disposal.
(8) A requested Central Authority may refuse to process an application only if it is manifest that the requirements of the Convention are not fulfilled. In such case, that Central Authority shall promptly inform the requesting Central Authority of its reasons for refusal.
(9) The requested Central Authority may not reject an application solely on the basis that additional documents or information are needed. However, the requested Central Authority may ask the requesting Central Authority to provide these additional documents or information. If the requesting Central Authority does not do so within three months or a longer period specified by the requested Central Authority, the requested Central Authority may decide that it will no longer process the application. In this case, it shall inform the requesting Central Authority of this decision.

Article 13 – Means of Communication

Any application made through Central Authorities of the Contracting States in accordance with this Chapter, and any document or information appended thereto or provided by a Central Authority, may not be challenged by the respondent by reason only of the medium or means of communication employed between the Central Authorities concerned.

Article 14 – Effective Access to Procedures

(1) The requested State shall provide applicants with effective access to procedures, including enforcement and appeal procedures, arising from applications under this Chapter.
(2) To provide such effective access, the requested State shall provide free legal assistance in accordance with Articles 14 to 17 unless paragraph 3 applies.
(3) The requested State shall not be obliged to provide such free legal assistance if and to the extent that the procedures of that State enable the applicant to

make the case without the need for such assistance, and the Central Authority provides such services as are necessary free of charge.
(4) Entitlements to free legal assistance shall not be less than those available in equivalent domestic cases.
(5) No security, bond or deposit, however described, shall be required to guarantee the payment of costs and expenses in proceedings under the Convention.

Article 15 – Free Legal Assistance for Child Support Applications

(1) The requested State shall provide free legal assistance in respect of all applications by a creditor under this Chapter concerning maintenance obligations arising from a parent-child relationship towards a person under the age of 21 years.
(2) Notwithstanding paragraph 1, the requested State may, in relation to applications other than those under Article 10(1) a) and b) and the cases covered by Article 20(4), refuse free legal assistance if it considers that, on the merits, the application or any appeal is manifestly unfounded.

Article 16 – Declaration to Permit Use of Child-Centred Means Test

(1) Notwithstanding Article 15(1), a State may declare, in accordance with Article 63, that it will provide free legal assistance in respect of applications other than under Article 10(1) a) and b) and the cases covered by Article 20(4), subject to a test based on an assessment of the means of the child.
(2) A State shall, at the time of making such a declaration, provide information to the Permanent Bureau of the Hague Conference on Private International Law concerning the manner in which the assessment of the child's means will be carried out, including the financial criteria which would need to be met to satisfy the test.
(3) An application referred to in paragraph 1, addressed to a State which has made the declaration referred to in that paragraph, shall include a formal attestation by the applicant stating that the child's means meet the criteria referred to in paragraph 2. The requested State may only request further evidence of the child's means if it has reasonable grounds to believe that the information provided by the applicant is inaccurate.
(4) If the most favourable legal assistance provided for by the law of the requested State in respect of applications under this Chapter concerning maintenance obligations arising from a parent-child relationship towards a child is more favourable than that provided for under paragraphs 1 to 3, the most favourable legal assistance shall be provided.

Article 17 – Applications Not Qualifying under Article 15 or Article 16

In the case of all applications under this Convention other than those under Article 15 or Article 16 –

a) the provision of free legal assistance may be made subject to a means or a merits test;

b) an applicant, who in the State of origin has benefited from free legal assistance, shall be entitled, in any proceedings for recognition or enforcement, to benefit, at least to the same extent, from free legal assistance as provided for by the law of the State addressed under the same circumstances.

Chapter IV: Restrictions on Bringing Proceedings

Article 18 – Limit on Proceedings

(1) Where a decision is made in a Contracting State where the creditor is habitually resident, proceedings to modify the decision or to make a new decision cannot be brought by the debtor in any other Contracting State as long as the creditor remains habitually resident in the State where the decision was made.

(2) Paragraph 1 shall not apply –

a) where, except in disputes relating to maintenance obligations in respect of children, there is agreement in writing between the parties to the jurisdiction of that other Contracting State;

b) where the creditor submits to the jurisdiction of that other Contracting State either expressly or by defending on the merits of the case without objecting to the jurisdiction at the first available opportunity;

c) where the competent authority in the State of origin cannot, or refuses to, exercise jurisdiction to modify the decision or make a new decision; or

d) where the decision made in the State of origin cannot be recognised or declared enforceable in the Contracting State where proceedings to modify the decision or make a new decision are contemplated.

Chapter V: Recognition and Enforcement

Article 19 – Scope of the Chapter

(1) This Chapter shall apply to a decision rendered by a judicial or administrative authority in respect of a maintenance obligation. The term "decision" also includes a settlement or agreement concluded before or approved by such an authority. A decision may include automatic adjustment by indexation and a requirement to pay arrears, retroactive maintenance or interest and a determination of costs or expenses.

(2) If a decision does not relate solely to a maintenance obligation, the effect of this Chapter is limited to the parts of the decision which concern maintenance obligations.
(3) For the purpose of paragraph 1, "administrative authority" means a public body whose decisions, under the law of the State where it is established –
a) may be made the subject of an appeal to or review by a judicial authority; and
b) have a similar force and effect to a decision of a judicial authority on the same matter.
(4) This Chapter also applies to maintenance arrangements in accordance with Article 30.
(5) The provisions of this Chapter shall apply to a request for recognition and enforcement made directly to a competent authority of the State addressed in accordance with Article 37.

Article 20 – Bases for Recognition and Enforcement

(1) A decision made in one Contracting State ("the State of origin") shall be recognised and enforced in other Contracting States if –
a) the respondent was habitually resident in the State of origin at the time proceedings were instituted;
b) the respondent has submitted to the jurisdiction either expressly or by defending on the merits of the case without objecting to the jurisdiction at the first available opportunity;
c) the creditor was habitually resident in the State of origin at the time proceedings were instituted;
d) the child for whom maintenance was ordered was habitually resident in the State of origin at the time proceedings were instituted, provided that the respondent has lived with the child in that State or has resided in that State and provided support for the child there;
e) except in disputes relating to maintenance obligations in respect of children, there has been agreement to the jurisdiction in writing by the parties; or
f) the decision was made by an authority exercising jurisdiction on a matter of personal status or parental responsibility, unless that jurisdiction was based solely on the nationality of one of the parties.
(2) A Contracting State may make a reservation, in accordance with Article 62, in respect of paragraph 1 c), e) or f).
(3) A Contracting State making a reservation under paragraph 2 shall recognise and enforce a decision if its law would in similar factual circumstances confer or would have conferred jurisdiction on its authorities to make such a decision.

(4) A Contracting State shall, if recognition of a decision is not possible as a result of a reservation under paragraph 2, and if the debtor is habitually resident in that State, take all appropriate measures to establish a decision for the benefit of the creditor. The preceding sentence shall not apply to direct requests for recognition and enforcement under Article 19(5) or to claims for support referred to in Article 2(1) b).
(5) A decision in favour of a child under the age of 18 years which cannot be recognised by virtue only of a reservation in respect of paragraph 1 c), e) or f) shall be accepted as establishing the eligibility of that child for maintenance in the State addressed.
(6) A decision shall be recognised only if it has effect in the State of origin, and shall be enforced only if it is enforceable in the State of origin.

Article 21 – Severability and Partial Recognition and Enforcement

(1) If the State addressed is unable to recognise or enforce the whole of the decision, it shall recognise or enforce any severable part of the decision which can be so recognised or enforced.
(2) Partial recognition or enforcement of a decision can always be applied for.

Article 22 – Grounds for Refusing Recognition and Enforcement

Recognition and enforcement of a decision may be refused if –

a) recognition and enforcement of the decision is manifestly incompatible with the public policy ("ordre public") of the State addressed;
b) the decision was obtained by fraud in connection with a matter of procedure;
c) proceedings between the same parties and having the same purpose are pending before an authority of the State addressed and those proceedings were the first to be instituted;
d) the decision is incompatible with a decision rendered between the same parties and having the same purpose, either in the State addressed or in another State, provided that this latter decision fulfils the conditions necessary for its recognition and enforcement in the State addressed;
e) in a case where the respondent has neither appeared nor was represented in proceedings in the State of origin –
    i) when the law of the State of origin provides for notice of proceedings, the respondent did not have proper notice of the proceedings and an opportunity to be heard; or
    ii) when the law of the State of origin does not provide for notice of the proceedings, the respondent did not have proper notice of the

decision and an opportunity to challenge or appeal it on fact and law; or

f) the decision was made in violation of Article 18.

Article 23 – Procedure on an Application for Recognition and Enforcement

(1) Subject to the provisions of the Convention, the procedures for recognition and enforcement shall be governed by the law of the State addressed.

(2) Where an application for recognition and enforcement of a decision has been made through Central Authorities in accordance with Chapter III, the requested Central Authority shall promptly either –

a) refer the application to the competent authority which shall without delay declare the decision enforceable or register the decision for enforcement; or

b) if it is the competent authority take such steps itself.

(3) Where the request is made directly to a competent authority in the State addressed in accordance with Article 19(5), that authority shall without delay declare the decision enforceable or register the decision for enforcement.

(4) A declaration or registration may be refused only on the ground set out in Article 22 a). At this stage neither the applicant nor the respondent is entitled to make any submissions.

(5) The applicant and the respondent shall be promptly notified of the declaration or registration, made under paragraphs 2 and 3, or the refusal thereof in accordance with paragraph 4, and may bring a challenge or appeal on fact and on a point of law.

(6) A challenge or an appeal is to be lodged within 30 days of notification under paragraph 5. If the contesting party is not resident in the Contracting State in which the declaration or registration was made or refused, the challenge or appeal shall be lodged within 60 days of notification.

(7) A challenge or appeal may be founded only on the following –

a) the grounds for refusing recognition and enforcement set out in Article 22;

b) the bases for recognition and enforcement under Article 20;

c) the authenticity or integrity of any document transmitted in accordance with Article 25(1) a), b) or d) or (3) b).

(8) A challenge or an appeal by a respondent may also be founded on the fulfilment of the debt to the extent that the recognition and enforcement relates to payments that fell due in the past.

(9) The applicant and the respondent shall be promptly notified of the decision following the challenge or the appeal.

(10) A further appeal, if permitted by the law of the State addressed, shall not have the effect of staying the enforcement of the decision unless there are exceptional circumstances.
(11) In taking any decision on recognition and enforcement, including any appeal, the competent authority shall act expeditiously.

Article 24 – Alternative Procedure on an Application for Recognition and Enforcement

(1) Notwithstanding Article 23(2) to (11), a State may declare, in accordance with Article 63, that it will apply the procedure for recognition and enforcement set out in this Article.
(2) Where an application for recognition and enforcement of a decision has been made through Central Authorities in accordance with Chapter III, the requested Central Authority shall promptly either –
a) refer the application to the competent authority which shall decide on the application for recognition and enforcement; or
b) if it is the competent authority, take such a decision itself.
(3) A decision on recognition and enforcement shall be given by the competent authority after the respondent has been duly and promptly notified of the proceedings and both parties have been given an adequate opportunity to be heard.
(4) The competent authority may review the grounds for refusing recognition and enforcement set out in Article 22 a), c) and d) of its own motion. It may review any grounds listed in Articles 20, 22 and 23(7) c) if raised by the respondent or if concerns relating to those grounds arise from the face of the documents submitted in accordance with Article 25.
(5) A refusal of recognition and enforcement may also be founded on the fulfilment of the debt to the extent that the recognition and enforcement relates to payments that fell due in the past.
(6) Any appeal, if permitted by the law of the State addressed, shall not have the effect of staying the enforcement of the decision unless there are exceptional circumstances.
(7) In taking any decision on recognition and enforcement, including any appeal, the competent authority shall act expeditiously.

Article 25 – Documents

(1) An application for recognition and enforcement under Article 23 or Article 24 shall be accompanied by the following –
a) a complete text of the decision;

b) a document stating that the decision is enforceable in the State of origin and, in the case of a decision by an administrative authority, a document stating that the requirements of Article 19(3) are met unless that State has specified in accordance with Article 57 that decisions of its administrative authorities always meet those requirements;
c) if the respondent did not appear and was not represented in the proceedings in the State of origin, a document or documents attesting, as appropriate, either that the respondent had proper notice of the proceedings and an opportunity to be heard, or that the respondent had proper notice of the decision and the opportunity to challenge or appeal it on fact and law;
d) where necessary, a document showing the amount of any arrears and the date such amount was calculated;
e) where necessary, in the case of a decision providing for automatic adjustment by indexation, a document providing the information necessary to make the appropriate calculations;
f) where necessary, documentation showing the extent to which the applicant received free legal assistance in the State of origin.

(2) Upon a challenge or appeal under Article 23(7) c) or upon request by the competent authority in the State addressed, a complete copy of the document concerned, certified by the competent authority in the State of origin, shall be provided promptly –
a) by the Central Authority of the requesting State, where the application has been made in accordance with Chapter III;
b) by the applicant, where the request has been made directly to a competent authority of the State addressed.

(3) A Contracting State may specify in accordance with Article 57 –
a) that a complete copy of the decision certified by the competent authority in the State of origin must accompany the application;
b) circumstances in which it will accept, in lieu of a complete text of the decision, an abstract or extract of the decision drawn up by the competent authority of the State of origin, which may be made in the form recommended and published by the Hague Conference on Private International Law; or
c) that it does not require a document stating that the requirements of Article 19(3) are met.

Article 26 – Procedure on an Application for Recognition

This Chapter shall apply mutatis mutandis to an application for recognition of a decision, save that the requirement of enforceability is replaced by the requirement that the decision has effect in the State of origin.

Article 27 – Findings of Fact

Any competent authority of the State addressed shall be bound by the findings of fact on which the authority of the State of origin based its jurisdiction.

Article 28 – No Review of the Merits

There shall be no review by any competent authority of the State addressed of the merits of a decision.

Article 29 – Physical Presence of the Child or the Applicant Not Required

The physical presence of the child or the applicant shall not be required in any proceedings in the State addressed under this Chapter.

Article 30 – Maintenance Arrangements

(1) A maintenance arrangement made in a Contracting State shall be entitled to recognition and enforcement as a decision under this Chapter provided that it is enforceable as a decision in the State of origin.

(2) For the purpose of Article 10(1) a) and b) and (2) a), the term "decision" includes a maintenance arrangement.

(3) An application for recognition and enforcement of a maintenance arrangement shall be accompanied by the following –

a) a complete text of the maintenance arrangement; and
b) a document stating that the particular maintenance arrangement is enforceable as a decision in the State of origin.

(4) Recognition and enforcement of a maintenance arrangement may be refused if -

a) the recognition and enforcement is manifestly incompatible with the public policy of the State addressed;
b) the maintenance arrangement was obtained by fraud or falsification;
c) the maintenance arrangement is incompatible with a decision rendered between the same parties and having the same purpose, either in the State addressed or in another State, provided that this latter decision fulfils the conditions necessary for its recognition and enforcement in the State addressed.

(5) The provisions of this Chapter, with the exception of Articles 20, 22, 23(7) and 25(1) and (3), shall apply mutatis mutandis to the recognition and enforcement of a maintenance arrangement save that –

a) a declaration or registration in accordance with Article 23(2) and (3) may be refused only on the ground set out in paragraph 4 a);
b) a challenge or appeal as referred to in Article 23(6) may be founded only on the following –
   i) the grounds for refusing recognition and enforcement set out in paragraph 4;
   ii) the authenticity or integrity of any document transmitted in accordance with paragraph 3;
c) as regards the procedure under Article 24(4), the competent authority may review of its own motion the ground for refusing recognition and enforcement set out in paragraph 4 a) of this Article. It may review all grounds listed in paragraph 4 of this Article and the authenticity or integrity of any document transmitted in accordance with paragraph 3 if raised by the respondent or if concerns relating to those grounds arise from the face of those documents.

(6) Proceedings for recognition and enforcement of a maintenance arrangement shall be suspended if a challenge concerning the arrangement is pending before a competent authority of a Contracting State.
(7) A State may declare, in accordance with Article 63, that applications for recognition and enforcement of a maintenance arrangement shall only be made through Central Authorities.
(8) A Contracting State may, in accordance with Article 62, reserve the right not to recognise and enforce a maintenance arrangement.

Article 31 – Decisions Produced by the Combined Effect of Provisional and Confirmation Orders

Where a decision is produced by the combined effect of a provisional order made in one State and an order by an authority in another State ("the confirming State") confirming the provisional order –

a) each of those States shall be deemed for the purposes of this Chapter to be a State of origin;
b) the requirements of Article 22 e) shall be met if the respondent had proper notice of the proceedings in the confirming State and an opportunity to oppose the confirmation of the provisional order;
c) the requirement of Article 20(6) that a decision be enforceable in the State of origin shall be met if the decision is enforceable in the confirming State; and

d) Article 18 shall not prevent proceedings for the modification of the decision being commenced in either State.

Chapter VI: Enforcement by the State Addressed

Article 32 – Enforcement under Internal Law

(1) Subject to the provisions of this Chapter, enforcement shall take place in accordance with the law of the State addressed.
(2) Enforcement shall be prompt.
(3) In the case of applications through Central Authorities, where a decision has been declared enforceable or registered for enforcement under Chapter V, enforcement shall proceed without the need for further action by the applicant.
(4) Effect shall be given to any rules applicable in the State of origin of the decision relating to the duration of the maintenance obligation.
(5) Any limitation on the period for which arrears may be enforced shall be determined either by the law of the State of origin of the decision or by the law of the State addressed, whichever provides for the longer limitation period.

Article 33 – Non-discrimination

The State addressed shall provide at least the same range of enforcement methods for cases under the Convention as are available in domestic cases.

Article 34 – Enforcement Measures

(1) Contracting States shall make available in internal law effective measures to enforce decisions under this Convention.
(2) Such measures may include –
a) wage withholding;
b) garnishment from bank accounts and other sources;
c) deductions from social security payments;
d) lien on or forced sale of property;
e) tax refund withholding;
f) withholding or attachment of pension benefits;
g) credit bureau reporting;
h) denial, suspension or revocation of various licenses (for example, driving licenses);
i) the use of mediation, conciliation or similar processes to bring about voluntary compliance.

Article 35 – Transfer of Funds

(1) Contracting States are encouraged to promote, including by means of international agreements, the use of the most cost-effective and efficient methods available to transfer funds payable as maintenance.
(2) A Contracting State, under whose law the transfer of funds is restricted, shall accord the highest priority to the transfer of funds payable under this Convention.

Chapter VII: Public Bodies

Article 36 – Public Bodies as Applicants

(1) For the purposes of applications for recognition and enforcement under Article 10(1) a) and b) and cases covered by Article 20(4), "creditor" includes a public body acting in place of an individual to whom maintenance is owed or one to which reimbursement is owed for benefits provided in place of maintenance.
(2) The right of a public body to act in place of an individual to whom maintenance is owed or to seek reimbursement of benefits provided to the creditor in place of maintenance shall be governed by the law to which the body is subject.
(3) A public body may seek recognition or claim enforcement of –

a) a decision rendered against a debtor on the application of a public body which claims payment of benefits provided in place of maintenance;
b) a decision rendered between a creditor and debtor to the extent of the benefits provided to the creditor in place of maintenance.

(4) The public body seeking recognition or claiming enforcement of a decision shall upon request furnish any document necessary to establish its right under paragraph 2 and that benefits have been provided to the creditor.

Chapter VIII: General Provisions

Article 37 – Direct Requests to Competent Authorities

(1) The Convention shall not exclude the possibility of recourse to such procedures as may be available under the internal law of a Contracting State allowing a person (an applicant) to seise directly a competent authority of that State in a matter governed by the Convention including, subject to Article 18, for the purpose of having a maintenance decision established or modified.
(2) Articles 14(5) and 17 b) and the provisions of Chapters V, VI, VII and this Chapter, with the exception of Articles 40(2), 42, 43(3), 44(3), 45 and 55, shall apply in relation to a request for recognition and enforcement made directly to a competent authority in a Contracting State.

(3) For the purpose of paragraph 2, Article 2(1) a) shall apply to a decision granting maintenance to a vulnerable person over the age specified in that sub-paragraph where such decision was rendered before the person reached that age and provided for maintenance beyond that age by reason of the impairment.

Article 38 – Protection of Personal Data

Personal data gathered or transmitted under the Convention shall be used only for the purposes for which they were gathered or transmitted.

Article 39 – Confidentiality

Any authority processing information shall ensure its confidentiality in accordance with the law of its State.

Article 40 – Non-disclosure of Information

(1) An authority shall not disclose or confirm information gathered or transmitted in application of this Convention if it determines that to do so could jeopardise the health, safety or liberty of a person.
(2) A determination to this effect made by one Central Authority shall be taken into account by another Central Authority, in particular in cases of family violence.
(3) Nothing in this Article shall impede the gathering and transmitting of information by and between authorities in so far as necessary to carry out the obligations under the Convention.

Article 41 – No Legalisation

No legalisation or similar formality may be required in the context of this Convention.

Article 42 – Power of Attorney

The Central Authority of the requested State may require a power of attorney from the applicant only if it acts on his or her behalf in judicial proceedings or before other authorities, or in order to designate a representative so to act.

Article 43 – Recovery of Costs

(1) Recovery of any costs incurred in the application of this Convention shall not take precedence over the recovery of maintenance.
(2) A State may recover costs from an unsuccessful party.

(3) For the purposes of an application under Article 10(1) b) to recover costs from an unsuccessful party in accordance with paragraph 2, the term "creditor" in Article 10(1) shall include a State.
(4) This Article shall be without prejudice to Article 8.

Article 44 – Language Requirements

(1) Any application and related documents shall be in the original language, and shall be accompanied by a translation into an official language of the requested State or another language which the requested State has indicated, by way of declaration in accordance with Article 63, it will accept, unless the competent authority of that State dispenses with translation.
(2) A Contracting State which has more than one official language and cannot, for reasons of internal law, accept for the whole of its territory documents in one of those languages shall, by declaration in accordance with Article 63, specify the language in which such documents or translations thereof shall be drawn up for submission in the specified parts of its territory.
(3) Unless otherwise agreed by the Central Authorities, any other communications between such Authorities shall be in an official language of the requested State or in either English or French. However, a Contracting State may, by making a reservation in accordance with Article 62, object to the use of either English or French.

Article 45 – Means and Costs of Translation

(1) In the case of applications under Chapter III, the Central Authorities may agree in an individual case or generally that the translation into an official language of the requested State may be made in the requested State from the original language or from any other agreed language. If there is no agreement and it is not possible for the requesting Central Authority to comply with the requirements of Article 44(1) and (2), then the application and related documents may be transmitted with translation into English or French for further translation into an official language of the requested State.
(2) The cost of translation arising from the application of paragraph 1 shall be borne by the requesting State unless otherwise agreed by Central Authorities of the States concerned.
(3) Notwithstanding Article 8, the requesting Central Authority may charge an applicant for the costs of translation of an application and related documents, except in so far as those costs may be covered by its system of legal assistance.

Article 46 – Non-unified Legal Systems – Interpretation

(1) In relation to a State in which two or more systems of law or sets of rules of law with regard to any matter dealt with in this Convention apply in different territorial units –

a) any reference to the law or procedure of a State shall be construed as referring, where appropriate, to the law or procedure in force in the relevant territorial unit;
b) any reference to a decision established, recognised, recognised and enforced, enforced or modified in that State shall be construed as referring, where appropriate, to a decision established, recognised, recognised and enforced, enforced or modified in the relevant territorial unit;
c) any reference to a judicial or administrative authority in that State shall be construed as referring, where appropriate, to a judicial or administrative authority in the relevant territorial unit;
d) any reference to competent authorities, public bodies, and other bodies of that State, other than Central Authorities, shall be construed as referring, where appropriate, to those authorised to act in the relevant territorial unit;
e) any reference to residence or habitual residence in that State shall be construed as referring, where appropriate, to residence or habitual residence in the relevant territorial unit;
f) any reference to location of assets in that State shall be construed as referring, where appropriate, to the location of assets in the relevant territorial unit;
g) any reference to a reciprocity arrangement in force in a State shall be construed as referring, where appropriate, to a reciprocity arrangement in force in the relevant territorial unit;
h) any reference to free legal assistance in that State shall be construed as referring, where appropriate, to free legal assistance in the relevant territorial unit;
i) any reference to a maintenance arrangement made in a State shall be construed as referring, where appropriate, to a maintenance arrangement made in the relevant territorial unit;
j) any reference to recovery of costs by a State shall be construed as referring, where appropriate, to the recovery of costs by the relevant territorial unit.

(2) This Article shall not apply to a Regional Economic Integration Organisation.

Article 47 – Non-unified Legal Systems – Substantive Rules

(1) A Contracting State with two or more territorial units in which different systems of law apply shall not be bound to apply this Convention to situations which involve solely such different territorial units.
(2) A competent authority in a territorial unit of a Contracting State with two or more territorial units in which different systems of law apply shall not be bound to recognise or enforce a decision from another Contracting State solely because the decision has been recognised or enforced in another territorial unit of the same Contracting State under this Convention.
(3) This Article shall not apply to a Regional Economic Integration Organisation.

Article 48 – Co-ordination with Prior Hague Maintenance Conventions

In relations between the Contracting States, this Convention replaces, subject to Article 56(2), the Hague Convention of 2 October 1973 on the Recognition and Enforcement of Decisions Relating to Maintenance Obligations and the Hague Convention of 15 April 1958 concerning the recognition and enforcement of decisions relating to maintenance obligations towards children in so far as their scope of application as between such States coincides with the scope of application of this Convention.

Article 49 – Co-ordination with the 1956 New York Convention

In relations between the Contracting States, this Convention replaces the United Nations Convention on the Recovery Abroad of Maintenance of 20 June 1956, in so far as its scope of application as between such States coincides with the scope of application of this Convention.

Article 50 – Relationship with Prior Hague Conventions on Service of Documents and Taking of Evidence

This Convention does not affect the Hague Convention of 1 March 1954 on civil procedure, the Hague Convention of 15 November 1965 on the Service Abroad of Judicial and Extrajudicial Documents in Civil or Commercial Matters and the Hague Convention of 18 March 1970 on the Taking of Evidence Abroad in Civil or Commercial Matters.

Article 51 – Co-ordination of Instruments and Supplementary Agreements

(1) This Convention does not affect any international instrument concluded before this Convention to which Contracting States are Parties and which contains provisions on matters governed by this Convention.

(2) Any Contracting State may conclude with one or more Contracting States agreements, which contain provisions on matters governed by the Convention, with a view to improving the application of the Convention between or among themselves, provided that such agreements are consistent with the objects and purpose of the Convention and do not affect, in the relationship of such States with other Contracting States, the application of the provisions of the Convention. The States which have concluded such an agreement shall transmit a copy to the depositary of the Convention.
(3) Paragraphs 1 and 2 shall also apply to reciprocity arrangements and to uniform laws based on special ties between the States concerned.
(4) This Convention shall not affect the application of instruments of a Regional Economic Integration Organisation that is a Party to this Convention, adopted after the conclusion of the Convention, on matters governed by the Convention provided that such instruments do not affect, in the relationship of Member States of the Regional Economic Integration Organisation with other Contracting States, the application of the provisions of the Convention. As concerns the recognition or enforcement of decisions as between Member States of the Regional Economic Integration Organisation, the Convention shall not affect the rules of the Regional Economic Integration Organisation, whether adopted before or after the conclusion of the Convention.

Article 52 – Most Effective Rule

(1) This Convention shall not prevent the application of an agreement, arrangement or international instrument in force between the requesting State and the requested State, or a reciprocity arrangement in force in the requested State that provides for –

a) broader bases for recognition of maintenance decisions, without prejudice to Article 22 f) of the Convention;
b) simplified, more expeditious procedures on an application for recognition or recognition and enforcement of maintenance decisions;
c) more beneficial legal assistance than that provided for under Articles 14 to 17; or
d) procedures permitting an applicant from a requesting State to make a request directly to the Central Authority of the requested State.

(2) This Convention shall not prevent the application of a law in force in the requested State that provides for more effective rules as referred to in paragraph 1 a) to c). However, as regards simplified, more expeditious procedures referred to in paragraph 1 b), they must be compatible with the protection offered to the parties under Articles 23 and 24, in particular as regards the rights of the

parties to be duly notified of the proceedings and be given adequate opportunity to be heard and as regards the effects of any challenge or appeal.

Article 53 – Uniform Interpretation

In the interpretation of this Convention, regard shall be had to its international character and to the need to promote uniformity in its application.

Article 54 – Review of Practical Operation of the Convention

(1) The Secretary General of the Hague Conference on Private International Law shall at regular intervals convene a Special Commission in order to review the practical operation of the Convention and to encourage the development of good practices under the Convention.
(2) For the purpose of such review, Contracting States shall co-operate with the Permanent Bureau of the Hague Conference on Private International Law in the gathering of information, including statistics and case law, concerning the practical operation of the Convention.

Article 55 – Amendment of Forms

(1) The forms annexed to this Convention may be amended by a decision of a Special Commission convened by the Secretary General of the Hague Conference on Private International Law to which all Contracting States and all Members shall be invited. Notice of the proposal to amend the forms shall be included in the agenda for the meeting.
(2) Amendments adopted by the Contracting States present at the Special Commission shall come into force for all Contracting States on the first day of the seventh calendar month after the date of their communication by the depositary to all Contracting States.
(3) During the period provided for in paragraph 2 any Contracting State may by notification in writing to the depositary make a reservation, in accordance with Article 62, with respect to the amendment. The State making such reservation shall, until the reservation is withdrawn, be treated as a State not Party to the present Convention with respect to that amendment.

Article 56 – Transitional Provisions

(1) The Convention shall apply in every case where –

a) a request pursuant to Article 7 or an application pursuant to Chapter III has been received by the Central Authority of the requested State after the Convention has entered into force between the requesting State and the requested State;

b) a direct request for recognition and enforcement has been received by the competent authority of the State addressed after the Convention has entered into force between the State of origin and the State addressed.

(2) With regard to the recognition and enforcement of decisions between Contracting States to this Convention that are also Parties to either of the Hague Maintenance Conventions mentioned in Article 48, if the conditions for the recognition and enforcement under this Convention prevent the recognition and enforcement of a decision given in the State of origin before the entry into force of this Convention for that State, that would otherwise have been recognised and enforced under the terms of the Convention that was in effect at the time the decision was rendered, the conditions of that Convention shall apply.

(3) The State addressed shall not be bound under this Convention to enforce a decision or a maintenance arrangement, in respect of payments falling due prior to the entry into force of the Convention between the State of origin and the State addressed, except for maintenance obligations arising from a parent-child relationship towards a person under the age of 21 years.

Article 57 – Provision of Information Concerning Laws, Procedures and Services

(1) A Contracting State, by the time its instrument of ratification or accession is deposited or a declaration is submitted in accordance with Article 61 of the Convention, shall provide the Permanent Bureau of the Hague Conference on Private International Law with –

a) a description of its laws and procedures concerning maintenance obligations;
b) a description of the measures it will take to meet the obligations under Article 6;
c) a description of how it will provide applicants with effective access to procedures, as required under Article 14;
d) a description of its enforcement rules and procedures, including any limitations on enforcement, in particular debtor protection rules and limitation periods;
e) any specification referred to in Article 25(1) b) and (3).

(2) Contracting States may, in fulfilling their obligations under paragraph 1, utilise a country profile form recommended and published by the Hague Conference on Private International Law.

(3) Information shall be kept up to date by the Contracting States.

Chapter IX: Final Provisions

Article 58 – Signature, Ratification and Accession

(1) The Convention shall be open for signature by the States which were Members of the Hague Conference on Private International Law at the time of its Twenty-First Session and by the other States which participated in that Session.
(2) It shall be ratified, accepted or approved and the instruments of ratification, acceptance or approval shall be deposited with the Ministry of Foreign Affairs of the Kingdom of the Netherlands, depositary of the Convention.
(3) Any other State or Regional Economic Integration Organisation may accede to the Convention after it has entered into force in accordance with Article 60(1).
(4) The instrument of accession shall be deposited with the depositary.
(5) Such accession shall have effect only as regards the relations between the acceding State and those Contracting States which have not raised an objection to its accession in the 12 months after the date of the notification referred to in Article 65. Such an objection may also be raised by States at the time when they ratify, accept or approve the Convention after an accession. Any such objection shall be notified to the depositary.

Article 59 – Regional Economic Integration Organisations

(1) A Regional Economic Integration Organisation which is constituted solely by sovereign States and has competence over some or all of the matters governed by this Convention may similarly sign, accept, approve or accede to this Convention. The Regional Economic Integration Organisation shall in that case have the rights and obligations of a Contracting State, to the extent that the Organisation has competence over matters governed by the Convention.
(2) The Regional Economic Integration Organisation shall, at the time of signature, acceptance, approval or accession, notify the depositary in writing of the matters governed by this Convention in respect of which competence has been transferred to that Organisation by its Member States. The Organisation shall promptly notify the depositary in writing of any changes to its competence as specified in the most recent notice given under this paragraph.
(3) At the time of signature, acceptance, approval or accession, a Regional Economic Integration Organisation may declare in accordance with Article 63 that it exercises competence over all the matters governed by this Convention and that the Member States which have transferred competence to the Regional Economic Integration Organisation in respect of the matter in question shall be bound by this Convention by virtue of the signature, acceptance, approval or accession of the Organisation.

(4) For the purposes of the entry into force of this Convention, any instrument deposited by a Regional Economic Integration Organisation shall not be counted unless the Regional Economic Integration Organisation makes a declaration in accordance with paragraph 3.
(5) Any reference to a "Contracting State" or "State" in this Convention shall apply equally to a Regional Economic Integration Organisation that is a Party to it, where appropriate. In the event that a declaration is made by a Regional Economic Integration Organisation in accordance with paragraph 3, any reference to a "Contracting State" or "State" in this Convention shall apply equally to the relevant Member States of the Organisation, where appropriate.

Article 60 – Entry into Force

(1) The Convention shall enter into force on the first day of the month following the expiration of three months after the deposit of the second instrument of ratification, acceptance or approval referred to in Article 58.
(2) Thereafter the Convention shall enter into force –

a) for each State or Regional Economic Integration Organisation referred to in Article 59(1) subsequently ratifying, accepting or approving it, on the first day of the month following the expiration of three months after the deposit of its instrument of ratification, acceptance or approval;
b) for each State or Regional Economic Integration Organisation referred to in Article 58(3) on the day after the end of the period during which objections may be raised in accordance with Article 58(5);
c) for a territorial unit to which the Convention has been extended in accordance with Article 61, on the first day of the month following the expiration of three months after the notification referred to in that Article.

Article 61 – Declarations with Respect to Non-unified Legal Systems

(1) If a State has two or more territorial units in which different systems of law are applicable in relation to matters dealt with in the Convention, it may at the time of signature, ratification, acceptance, approval or accession declare in accordance with Article 63 that this Convention shall extend to all its territorial units or only to one or more of them and may modify this declaration by submitting another declaration at any time.
(2) Any such declaration shall be notified to the depositary and shall state expressly the territorial units to which the Convention applies.
(3) If a State makes no declaration under this Article, the Convention shall extend to all territorial units of that State.
(4) This Article shall not apply to a Regional Economic Integration Organisation.

Article 62 – Reservations

(1) Any Contracting State may, not later than the time of ratification, acceptance, approval or accession, or at the time of making a declaration in terms of Article 61, make one or more of the reservations provided for in Articles 2(2), 20(2), 30(8), 44(3) and 55(3). No other reservation shall be permitted.
(2) Any State may at any time withdraw a reservation it has made. The withdrawal shall be notified to the depositary.
(3) The reservation shall cease to have effect on the first day of the third calendar month after the notification referred to in paragraph 2.
(4) Reservations under this Article shall have no reciprocal effect with the exception of the reservation provided for in Article 2(2).

Article 63 – Declarations

(1) Declarations referred to in Articles 2(3), 11(1) g), 16(1), 24(1), 30(7), 44(1) and (2), 59(3) and 61(1), may be made upon signature, ratification, acceptance, approval or accession or at any time thereafter, and may be modified or withdrawn at any time.
(2) Declarations, modifications and withdrawals shall be notified to the depositary.
(3) A declaration made at the time of signature, ratification, acceptance, approval or accession shall take effect simultaneously with the entry into force of this Convention for the State concerned.
(4) A declaration made at a subsequent time, and any modification or withdrawal of a declaration, shall take effect on the first day of the month following the expiration of three months after the date on which the notification is received by the depositary.

Article 64 – Denunciation

(1) A Contracting State to the Convention may denounce it by a notification in writing addressed to the depositary. The denunciation may be limited to certain territorial units of a multi-unit State to which the Convention applies.
(2) The denunciation shall take effect on the first day of the month following the expiration of 12 months after the date on which the notification is received by the depositary. Where a longer period for the denunciation to take effect is specified in the notification, the denunciation shall take effect upon the expiration of such longer period after the date on which the notification is received by the depositary.

Article 65 – Notification

The depositary shall notify the Members of the Hague Conference on Private International Law, and other States and Regional Economic Integration Organisations which have signed, ratified, accepted, approved or acceded in accordance with Articles 58 and 59 of the following –

a) the signatures, ratifications, acceptances and approvals referred to in Articles 58 and 59;
b) the accessions and objections raised to accessions referred to in Articles 58(3) and (5) and 59;
c) the date on which the Convention enters into force in accordance with Article 60;
d) the declarations referred to in Articles 2(3), 11(1) g), 16(1), 24(1), 30(7), 44(1) and (2), 59(3) and 61(1);
e) the agreements referred to in Article 51(2);
f) the reservations referred to in Articles 2(2), 20(2), 30(8), 44(3) and 55(3), and the withdrawals referred to in Article 62(2);
g) the denunciations referred to in Article 64.

In witness whereof the undersigned, being duly authorised thereto, have signed this Convention.

Done at The Hague, on the 23rd day of November 2007, in the English and French languages, both texts being equally authentic, in a single copy which shall be deposited in the archives of the Government of the Kingdom of the Netherlands, and of which a certified copy shall be sent, through diplomatic channels, to each of the Members of the Hague Conference on Private International Law at the date of its Twenty-First Session and to each of the other States which have participated in that Session.

CHAPTER 38.A

Protocol on the Law Applicable to Maintenance Obligations

Concluded 23 November 2007
Entry into force 1 August 2013, in accordance with article 25

The States signatory to this Protocol,

Desiring to establish common provisions concerning the law applicable to maintenance obligations,

Wishing to modernise the Hague Convention of 24 October 1956 on the law applicable to maintenance obligations towards children and the Hague Convention of 2 October 1973 on the Law Applicable to Maintenance Obligations,

Wishing to develop general rules on applicable law that may supplement the Hague Convention of 23 November 2007 on the International Recovery of Child Support and Other Forms of Family Maintenance,

Have resolved to conclude a Protocol for this purpose and have agreed upon the following provisions –

Article 1 – Scope

(1) This Protocol shall determine the law applicable to maintenance obligations arising from a family relationship, parentage, marriage or affinity, including a maintenance obligation in respect of a child regardless of the marital status of the parents.
(2) Decisions rendered in application of this Protocol shall be without prejudice to the existence of any of the relationships referred to in paragraph 1.

Article 2 – Universal Application

This Protocol applies even if the applicable law is that of a non-Contracting State.

Article 3 – General Rule on Applicable Law

(1) Maintenance obligations shall be governed by the law of the State of the habitual residence of the creditor, save where this Protocol provides otherwise.

(2) In the case of a change in the habitual residence of the creditor, the law of the State of the new habitual residence shall apply as from the moment when the change occurs.

Article 4 – Special Rules Favouring Certain Creditors

(1) The following provisions shall apply in the case of maintenance obligations of –

a) parents towards their children;
b) persons, other than parents, towards persons who have not attained the age of 21 years, except for obligations arising out of the relationships referred to in Article 5; and
c) children towards their parents.

(2) If the creditor is unable, by virtue of the law referred to in Article 3, to obtain maintenance from the debtor, the law of the forum shall apply.

(3) Notwithstanding Article 3, if the creditor has seised the competent authority of the State where the debtor has his habitual residence, the law of the forum shall apply. However, if the creditor is unable, by virtue of this law, to obtain maintenance from the debtor, the law of the State of the habitual residence of the creditor shall apply.

(4) If the creditor is unable, by virtue of the laws referred to in Article 3 and paragraphs 2 and 3 of this Article, to obtain maintenance from the debtor, the law of the State of their common nationality, if there is one, shall apply.

Article 5 – Special Rule with Respect to Spouses and Ex-spouses

In the case of a maintenance obligation between spouses, ex-spouses or parties to a marriage which has been annulled, Article 3 shall not apply if one of the parties objects and the law of another State, in particular the State of their last common habitual residence, has a closer connection with the marriage. In such a case the law of that other State shall apply.

Article 6 – Special Rule on Defence

In the case of maintenance obligations other than those arising from a parent-child relationship towards a child and those referred to in Article 5, the debtor may contest a claim from the creditor on the ground that there is no such obligation under both the law of the State of the habitual residence of the debtor and the law of the State of the common nationality of the parties, if there is one.

Article 7 – Designation of the Law Applicable for the Purpose of a Particular Proceeding

(1) Notwithstanding Articles 3 to 6, the maintenance creditor and debtor for the purpose only of a particular proceeding in a given State may expressly designate the law of that State as applicable to a maintenance obligation.
(2) A designation made before the institution of such proceedings shall be in an agreement, signed by both parties, in writing or recorded in any medium, the information contained in which is accessible so as to be usable for subsequent reference.

Article 8 – Designation of the Applicable Law

(1) Notwithstanding Articles 3 to 6, the maintenance creditor and debtor may at any time designate one of the following laws as applicable to a maintenance obligation –

a) the law of any State of which either party is a national at the time of the designation;
b) the law of the State of the habitual residence of either party at the time of designation;
c) the law designated by the parties as applicable, or the law in fact applied, to their property regime;
d) the law designated by the parties as applicable, or the law in fact applied, to their divorce or legal separation.

(2) Such agreement shall be in writing or recorded in any medium, the information contained in which is accessible so as to be usable for subsequent reference, and shall be signed by both parties.
(3) Paragraph 1 shall not apply to maintenance obligations in respect of a person under the age of 18 years or of an adult who, by reason of an impairment or insufficiency of his or her personal faculties, is not in a position to protect his or her interest.
(4) Notwithstanding the law designated by the parties in accordance with paragraph 1, the question of whether the creditor can renounce his or her right to maintenance shall be determined by the law of the State of the habitual residence of the creditor at the time of the designation.
(5) Unless at the time of the designation the parties were fully informed and aware of the consequences of their designation, the law designated by the parties shall not apply where the application of that law would lead to manifestly unfair or unreasonable consequences for any of the parties.

Article 9 – "Domicile" Instead of "Nationality"

A State which has the concept of "domicile" as a connecting factor in family matters may inform the Permanent Bureau of the Hague Conference on Private International Law that, for the purpose of cases which come before its authorities, the word "nationality" in Articles 4 and 6 is replaced by "domicile" as defined in that State.

Article 10 – Public Bodies

The right of a public body to seek reimbursement of a benefit provided to the creditor in place of maintenance shall be governed by the law to which that body is subject.

Article 11 – Scope of the Applicable Law

The law applicable to the maintenance obligation shall determine inter alia –

a) whether, to what extent and from whom the creditor may claim maintenance;
b) the extent to which the creditor may claim retroactive maintenance;
c) the basis for calculation of the amount of maintenance, and indexation;
d) who is entitled to institute maintenance proceedings, except for issues relating to procedural capacity and representation in the proceedings;
e) prescription or limitation periods;
f) the extent of the obligation of a maintenance debtor, where a public body seeks reimbursement of benefits provided for a creditor in place of maintenance.

Article 12 – Exclusion of Renvoi

In the Protocol, the term "law" means the law in force in a State other than its choice of law rules.

Article 13 – Public Policy

The application of the law determined under the Protocol may be refused only to the extent that its effects would be manifestly contrary to the public policy of the forum.

Article 14 – Determining the Amount of Maintenance

Even if the applicable law provides otherwise, the needs of the creditor and the resources of the debtor as well as any compensation which the creditor was awarded in place of periodical maintenance payments shall be taken into account in determining the amount of maintenance.

Article 15 – Non-application of the Protocol to Internal Conflicts

(1) A Contracting State in which different systems of law or sets of rules of law apply to maintenance obligations shall not be bound to apply the rules of the Protocol to conflicts solely between such different systems or sets of rules of law.

(2) This Article shall not apply to a Regional Economic Integration Organisation.

Article 16 – Non-unified Legal Systems – Territorial

(1) In relation to a State in which two or more systems of law or sets of rules of law with regard to any matter dealt with in this Protocol apply in different territorial units –

a) any reference to the law of a State shall be construed as referring, where appropriate, to the law in force in the relevant territorial unit;
b) any reference to competent authorities or public bodies of that State shall be construed as referring, where appropriate, to those authorised to act in the relevant territorial unit;
c) any reference to habitual residence in that State shall be construed as referring, where appropriate, to habitual residence in the relevant territorial unit;
d) any reference to the State of which two persons have a common nationality shall be construed as referring to the territorial unit designated by the law of that State or, in the absence of relevant rules, to the territorial unit with which the maintenance obligation is most closely connected;
e) any reference to the State of which a person is a national shall be construed as referring to the territorial unit designated by the law of that State or, in the absence of relevant rules, to the territorial unit with which the person has the closest connection.

(2) For the purpose of identifying the applicable law under the Protocol in relation to a State which comprises two or more territorial units each of which has its own system of law or set of rules of law in respect of matters covered by this Protocol, the following rules apply –

a) if there are rules in force in such a State identifying which territorial unit's law is applicable, the law of that unit applies;
b) in the absence of such rules, the law of the relevant territorial unit as defined in paragraph 1 applies.

(3) This Article shall not apply to a Regional Economic Integration Organisation.

Article 17 – Non-unified Legal Systems – Inter-personal Conflicts

For the purpose of identifying the applicable law under the Protocol in relation to a State which has two or more systems of law or sets of rules of law applicable to different categories of persons in respect of matters covered by this Protocol, any reference to the law of such State shall be construed as referring to the legal system determined by the rules in force in that State.

Article 18 – Co-ordination with Prior Hague Maintenance Conventions

As between the Contracting States, this Protocol replaces the Hague Convention of 2 October 1973 on the Law Applicable to Maintenance Obligations and the Hague Convention of 24 October 1956 on the law applicable to maintenance obligations towards children.

Article 19 Co-ordination with Other Instruments

(1) This Protocol does not affect any other international instrument to which Contracting States are or become Parties and which contains provisions on matters governed by the Protocol, unless a contrary declaration is made by the States Parties to such instrument.
(2) Paragraph 1 also applies to uniform laws based on special ties of a regional or other nature between the States concerned.

Article 20 – Uniform Interpretation

In the interpretation of this Protocol, regard shall be had to its international character and to the need to promote uniformity in its application.

Article 21 – Review of the Practical Operation of the Protocol

(1) The Secretary General of the Hague Conference on Private International Law shall as necessary convene a Special Commission in order to review the practical operation of the Protocol.
(2) For the purpose of such review Contracting States shall co-operate with the Permanent Bureau of the Hague Conference on Private International Law in the gathering of case law concerning the application of the Protocol.

Article 22 – Transitional Provisions

This Protocol shall not apply to maintenance claimed in a Contracting State relating to a period prior to its entry into force in that State.

Article 23 – Signature, Ratification and Accession

(1) This Protocol is open for signature by all States.
(2) This Protocol is subject to ratification, acceptance or approval by the signatory States.
(3) This Protocol is open for accession by all States.

(4) Instruments of ratification, acceptance, approval or accession shall be deposited with the Ministry of Foreign Affairs of the Kingdom of the Netherlands, depositary of the Protocol.

Article 24 – Regional Economic Integration Organisations

(1) A Regional Economic Integration Organisation which is constituted solely by sovereign States and has competence over some or all of the matters governed by the Protocol may equally sign, accept, approve or accede to the Protocol. The Regional Economic Integration Organisation shall in that case have the rights and obligations of a Contracting State, to the extent that the Organisation has competence over matters governed by the Protocol.
(2) The Regional Economic Integration Organisation shall, at the time of signature, acceptance, approval or accession, notify the depositary in writing of the matters governed by the Protocol in respect of which competence has been transferred to that Organisation by its Member States. The Organisation shall promptly notify the depositary in writing of any changes to its competence as specified in the most recent notice given under this paragraph.
(3) At the time of signature, acceptance, approval or accession, a Regional Economic Integration Organisation may declare, in accordance with Article 28, that it exercises competence over all the matters governed by the Protocol and that the Member States which have transferred competence to the Regional Economic Integration Organisation in respect of the matter in question shall be bound by the Protocol by virtue of the signature, acceptance, approval or accession of the Organisation.
(4) For the purposes of the entry into force of the Protocol, any instrument deposited by a Regional Economic Integration Organisation shall not be counted unless the Regional Economic Integration Organisation makes a declaration under paragraph 3.
(5) Any reference to a "Contracting State" or "State" in the Protocol applies equally to a Regional Economic Integration Organisation that is a Party to it, where appropriate. In the event that a declaration is made by a Regional Economic Integration Organisation under paragraph 3, any reference to a "Contracting State" or "State" in the Protocol applies equally to the relevant Member States of the Organisation, where appropriate.

Article 25 – Entry into Force

(1) The Protocol shall enter into force on the first day of the month following the expiration of three months after the deposit of the second instrument of ratification, acceptance, approval or accession referred to in Article 23.
(2) Thereafter the Protocol shall enter into force –

a) for each State or each Regional Economic Integration Organisation referred to in Article 24 subsequently ratifying, accepting or approving the Protocol or acceding to it, on the first day of the month following the expiration of three months after the deposit of its instrument of ratification, acceptance, approval or accession;
b) for a territorial unit to which the Protocol has been extended in accordance with Article 26, on the first day of the month following the expiration of three months after notification of the declaration referred to in that Article.

Article 26 – Declarations with Respect to Non-unified Legal Systems

(1) If a State has two or more territorial units in which different systems of law are applicable in relation to matters dealt with in this Protocol, it may at the time of signature, ratification, acceptance, approval or accession declare in accordance with Article 28 that the Protocol shall extend to all its territorial units or only to one or more of them and may modify this declaration by submitting another declaration at any time.
(2) Any such declaration shall be notified to the depositary and shall state expressly the territorial units to which the Protocol applies.
(3) If a State makes no declaration under this Article, the Protocol is to extend to all territorial units of that State.
(4) This Article shall not apply to a Regional Economic Integration Organisation.

Article 27 – Reservations

No reservations may be made to this Protocol.

Article 28 – Declarations

(1) Declarations referred to in Articles 24(3) and 26(1) may be made upon signature, ratification, acceptance, approval or accession or at any time thereafter, and may be modified or withdrawn at any time.
(2) Declarations, modifications and withdrawals shall be notified to the depositary.
(3) A declaration made at the time of signature, ratification, acceptance, approval or accession shall take effect simultaneously with the entry into force of this Protocol for the State concerned.
(4) A declaration made at a subsequent time, and any modification or withdrawal of a declaration, shall take effect on the first day of the month following the expiration of three months after the date on which the notification is received by the depositary.

Article 29 – Denunciation

(1) A Contracting State to this Protocol may denounce it by a notification in writing addressed to the depositary. The denunciation may be limited to certain territorial units of a State with a non-unified legal system to which the Protocol applies.
(2) The denunciation shall take effect on the first day of the month following the expiration of 12 months after the date on which the notification is received by the depositary. Where a longer period for the denunciation to take effect is specified in the notification, the denunciation shall take effect upon the expiration of such longer period after the date on which the notification is received by the depositary.

Article 30 – Notification

The depositary shall notify the Members of the Hague Conference on Private International Law, and other States and Regional Economic Integration Organisations which have signed, ratified, accepted, approved or acceded in accordance with Articles 23 and 24 of the following –

a) the signatures and ratifications, acceptances, approvals and accessions referred to in Articles 23 and 24;
b) the date on which this Protocol enters into force in accordance with Article 25;
c) the declarations referred to in Articles 24(3) and 26(1);
d) the denunciations referred to in Article 29.

In witness whereof the undersigned, being duly authorised thereto, have signed this Protocol.
Done at The Hague, on the 23rd day of November 2007, in the English and French languages, both texts being equally authentic, in a single copy which shall be deposited in the archives of the Government of the Kingdom of the Netherlands, and of which a certified copy shall be sent, through diplomatic channels, to each of the Members of the Hague Conference on Private International Law at the date of its Twenty-First Session and to each of the other States which have participated in that Session.

www.ingramcontent.com/pod-product-compliance
Lightning Source LLC
Chambersburg PA
CBHW071329230926
51849CB00002B/345
* 9 7 8 9 0 0 4 6 8 1 2 1 7 *